FOREIGN LAW AND COMPARATIVE METHODOLOGY

Foreign Law and Comparative Methodology: a Subject and a Thesis

BASIL S. MARKESINIS

·HART·
PUBLISHING
OXFORD
1997

Hart Publishing
Oxford
UK

Hart Publishing is a specialist legal publisher based in Oxford, England.
To order further copies of this book or to request a list of other
publications please write to:

Hart Publishing, 19 Whitehouse Road, Oxford, OX1 4PA
Telephone: +44 (0)1865 434459 or Fax: (0)1865 794882
e-mail: hartpub@janep.demon.co.uk

Payment may be made by cheque payable to 'Hart Publishing' or by
credit card.

British Library Cataloguing in Publication Data
Data Available
ISBN 1–901362–03–5

Typeset in 10pt Sabon
by SetAll, Abingdon
Printed in Great Britain on acid-free paper
by Biddles Ltd, Guildford and King's Lynn

To:
ROY GOODE, WERNER LORENZ, and DAVID WILLIAMS

Mentors and friends in good times and bad
With grateful thanks

Foreword

It is a singular privilege to be invited to provide this foreword because this book is written by a remarkable man, Basil Markesinis. Basil Markesinis is an academic lawyer with a *cause*. A *cause* for which he has campaigned with a persistence, intelligence, dedication, energy and vigour which I do not believe any one else could match.

The *cause* involves persuading English lawyers, be they academics, practitioners or judges as to the benefits which are to be derived from comparative legal studies. Basil Markesinis is already having some success. This is no mean achievement since the instinctive attitude of most English lawyers was that comparative law has little to offer. This was particularly true of their attitude to the civil jurisdictions across the channel.

As part of his campaign, Basil Markesinis established two institutes, the Leiden Institute of Anglo American Law in Holland, and in this country the Oxford Centre of European Law. Their respective titles and the places where they are situated illustrate Basil Markesinis' strategy. They are intended to encourage the study of common law on the continent and civil law here. The importance of their foundation is underlined by the sum approaching £6 million which has already been raised by Basil Markesinis for his two institutions.

This year Basil Markesinis has been a law don for 30 years. It is understandable that he would wish to celebrate both this event and the establishment of the Institute and the Centre by publishing a compilation of 20 articles selected from his prolific writings which support the *cause* and demonstrate just how important it is.

The first article, subtitled *A Subject and a Thesis*, explains the Markesinis technique of presenting his subject through the examination of cases decided in the different jurisdictions. This method is a method of learning and understanding law which has an instinctive appeal to the common law lawyers, who I suspect are the primary audience at which this book is directed. It demonstrates that given the same problem the different systems regularly provide in practice the same answer. Even when the systems differ the policy is still similar and so the courts in each jurisdiction tend to produce the same answer to the same or similar factual situations.

It compliments another strategy which is also spelt out in the same article. This is to educate the judiciary as to the value of a comparative approach in the belief that if they demonstrate in their judgments that they are influenced by comparable decisions in other jurisdictions, this will encourage practitioners to respond and, if the practitioners respond, the academics would be forced to do the same. This approach, as the article points out, may involve turning the traditional approach on its head, but I accept that recent history suggests it is working so far as the senior judiciary and the practitioners are concerned. (I am not qualified to speak as to the academics but I am confident that they will not wish to lag behind).

The Appellate Committee of the Lords are already increasingly demanding comparative material from practitioners in cases where an appeal before them could involve the development of the law. While in the past the assistance would be expected to be limited to that available from other common law jurisdictions, this is no longer the situation. Lord Goff leads but is not alone in being interested in German and French decisions. The same is true, but to a lesser extent, of the Court of Appeal (because of the nature of its case load). The interest in what is happening in foreign jurisdictions is confirmed and encouraged by the increasing number of forums with other jurisdictions in which the British judiciary are now involved. I have myself attended discussions with my American, Canadian, Australian, New Zealand, South African, Indian, Hong Kong, Chinese, Mauritian, French and Israeli colleagues. I am looking forward to adding Germany and Japan to my list in the next 12 months. I set out this list not to illustrate the success I have had in indulging my taste for foreign travel but as evidence that judicial isolationism is now a thing of the past. The judiciary appreciates that a proper performance of their responsibilities involves a knowledge of what is happening in other jurisdictions. Indeed, one reason why I am confident that the judicial assistant (the Anglo version of law clerks) will soon be a permanent feature of the English system is that the practitioners alone can no longer be expected to satisfy the English judiciary's hunger to be kept abreast of what is happening in other parts of the world.

You do not however need to share Basil Markesinis' ambitions to enjoy the articles in this book. If you read the book you will probably end up a supporter, if you are not already, of his conviction as to the benefits of a comparative approach. You will almost certainly end up infected by his enthusiasm for this approach. You will find the selection of subjects on which the articles focus of great topical interest and the book seductive of your attention until finished. In other words the contents are the best possible confirmation of my initial comments about the exceptional qualities of the author.

9 May, 1997

The Rt. Hon. the Lord Woolf,
Master of the Rolls.
Royal Courts of Justice
London

Preface and Acknowledgements

Thirty years of academic life is a long enough time to amass intellectual debts and also to realise that the time is running out for repaying them. All I can thus do is to mention the names (in alphabetical order) of those colleagues who, over the years, inspired my work, encouraged me to bring out (and then stand by) my own ideas, and lent a helpful hand in promoting my academic career. They are: Guido Alpa (Rome), David Anderson (Austin, Texas), Laurent Aynès (Paris I), Christian von Bar (Osnabrück), Frank Berman (London), Tom Bingham (London), Peter Birks (Oxford), the late Ernst von Caemmerer (Freiburg), Kevin Clermont (Cornell), Paul Davies (Oxford), the late Stanley de Smith (Cambridge), the late Patrick Devlin (London), Georges Durry (Paris II), John Fleming (Berkeley), Francesco Francioni (Siena), Andreas Gasis (Athens), Walter van Gerven (Leuven), Robert Goff (London), Roy Goode (Oxford), the late Gino Gorla (Rome), Giovanni Grotanelli dei Santi (Siena), Arthur Hartkamp (Utrecht), Jeffrey Jowell (University College London), the late Jack Hamson (Cambridge), the late Robert Heuston (Dublin), Tony Honoré (Oxford), the late Otto Kahn-Freund (Oxford), Page Keeton (Austin, Texas), Tim Koopmans (the Hague), Hein Kötz (Hamburg), the late Harry Lawson (Oxford), Noelle Lenoir (Paris), Werner Lorenz (Munich), Marcus Lutter (Bonn), Peter Martin (Cornell), George Michaelides-Nouaros (Athens), the late Christian Mouly (Montpelier), Michael Mustill (London), Barry Nicholas (Oxford), Dawn Oliver (University College London), Etienne Picard (Paris I), the late Eustace Roskill (London), Bernard Rudden (Oxford), Hein Schermers (Leiden), John Spencer (Cambridge), Johan Steyn (London), Marcel Storme (Ghent), John Triantaphillopoulos (Athens), André Tunc (Paris I), Genevieve Viney (Paris I), Bill Wade (Cambridge), Tony Weir (Cambridge), David Williams (Cambridge), Rt. Hon. the Lord Woolf, Master of the Rolls (London) and Mark Yudof (Austin, Texas).

Ideas are not enough. One must find the raw material to flesh them out and give them a modicum of plausibility. The following law librarians have been of invaluable assistance: David Gunn and Jon Pratter (Tarlton Law Library, University of Texas at Austin), Jules Winterton, (Institute of Advanced Legal Studies, London), Mr Riss, (Institute of Comparative Law of the University of Munich), and Keith MacVeigh and Peter Zawada (Squire Law Library, Cambridge).

This book marks thirty years in academic life in tenured positions in the Universities of Athens, Cambridge, London, Leiden and Oxford as well as visiting lectures in twenty other Universities. As far as I am concerned, it is a most happy coincidence that the produce of these years of research and teaching is now appearing in book form published by *Hart Publishing* since to Richard Hart, in his previous incarnation, I owe an awful lot for producing five of my most widely used books.

Last but not least I record a huge debt of gratitude to my wife Eugenie, my daughter Julietta, and my son Spyros-George, for allowing me (without a murmur of complaint) to be such a neglectful husband and father over so many weekends, Christmas days, and Easter days which I should have spent with them rather than working in various libraries. My family life has, in fact, been the most rewarding thing that has ever happened to me in my fifty-three years, and that is saying a great deal, since I have been fortunate enough to receive much more recognition from friends than I really deserve.

Acknowledgements

The essays which are reprinted in this volume first appeared in the following journals or books and are reproduced here with grateful thanks.

"The Comparatist: Or a Plea for a Broader Legal Education" in *Pressing Problems in the Law*, vol 2, (ed. by P.B.H. Birks, 1996), pp. 107–18; "The Destructive and Constructive Role of the Comparative Lawyer", 57 *Rabels Zeitschrift für ausländisches und internationales Privatrecht* (1993), pp. 438–48; "Cause and Consideration: A Study in Parallel", (1978) *Cambridge Law Journal*, pp. 53–75; "The Legacy of History on German Contract Law" (co-authored with Dr. Gerhard Dannemann) in *Essays for Roy Goode* (ed. by Ross Cranston, 1997), pp. 1–28; "Il Ruolo della Giurisprudenza nella Comparazione Giuridica" in 1992 *Contrato e Impressa*, pp. 1350–86; "A Matter of Style" in (1994) 110 *Law Quarterly Review*, pp. 607–28; "Learning from Europe and Learning in Europe" in *The Gradual Convergence. Foreign Ideas, Foreign Influences, and English Law on the Eve of the 21st Century* (ed. by B. S. Markesinis, 1994), pp. 1–32; "Bridging Legal Cultures" in (1993) 27 *Israel Law Review*, pp. 363–83; "Conceptualism, Pragmatism, and Courage. A Common Lawyer Looks at Some Judgments of the German Federal Court" in (1986) 34 *The American Journal of Comparative Law*, pp. 349–67; "Policy Factors and the Law of Tort" in *The Cambridge Lectures* (ed. D. Mendes da Costa, 1981), pp. 199–227; "An Expanding Tort Law—The Price of a Rigid Contract Law" in (1987) 103 *Law Quarterly Review*, pp. 354–97; "The Random Element of their Lordships Infallible Judgment: An Economic and Comparative Analysis of the Tort of Negligence from *Anns* to *Murphy*" (co-authored with Dr. Simon Deakin) in (1992) 55 *The Modern Law Review*, pp. 619–46; "Five Days in the House of Lords: Some Comparative Reflections on *White* v. *Jones*" in (1995) 3 *Torts Law Journal*, pp. 169–201; "La Perversion de Notions de Responsabilité Civile Delictuelle par la Pratique de l'Assurance" in 1983 *Revue Internationale de Droit Comparé*, pp. 301–17; "The Right to be Let Alone Versus Freedom of Speech" (1986) *Public Law*, pp. 67–82; "Subtle Ways of Legal Borrowing. Some Comparative Reflections on the Report of the Calcutt Committee 'On Privacy and related matters' " in *Festschrift für Werner Lorenz zum sibzigsten Geburstag* (ed. by B. Pfister and M. R. Will, 1991), pp. 717–37; "Some Comparative Reflections on the Right of Privacy of Public Figures in Public Places" in *Privacy and Loyalty* (ed. by P. B. H. Birks, 1997), pp. 113–31; "Litigation Mania in England, Germany, and the United States: Are we so Very Different?" in (1990) *Cambridge Law Journal*, pp. 233–76.

Grateful thanks are also due to Mr Dietmar Schluter for his invaluable assistance with the proof-reading and the preparation of the table of cases.

Contents

Table of Cases

Common law cases

French cases (in chronological order)

German cases (in chronological order)

Bundesverfassungsgericht

Reichsgericht

Bundesgerichtshof

1

Foreign Law and Comparative Methodology: A Subject and a Thesis

When I was sixteen and more interested in art than anything else, my father gave me a book entitled *Bild und Abbild*. It was an attractive coffee table book, the photos and text of which went further than the title suggested. For they showed how paintings or their themes had been copied, imitated, and adapted through the ages, providing many artists with a way of learning and perfecting their art by relying on the works of their predecessors.

This book made a great impression on me. It also made me conscious of the fact that in the world of art one could find endless repetitions and variations on themes. More emerged from the mere perusal of the names of those who had copied and imitated. For what, in a way, this book also showed was that some themes have held a constant fascination for artists; that most things that had to be said had, in some form or another, already been expressed by someone; and that often the only way one could stamp one's individuality on a subject or a theme was through the way one chose to express it, the basic idea itself being already common property. Total originality, in short, was and is very rare; and when it is achieved, its creators tend to return to it in different forms and guises, often for the very legitimate reason of perfecting the original idea.

In later life I discovered that the same could be said of music, literature, philosophy and when, because of family tradition, I was finally sucked into law, I also found that this was also true of my professional subject. Inevitably, therefore in a book which contains a collection of essays published over twenty years one must start by admitting the influence others have had upon one's work. In my case the list is long, since I have been fortunate enough to have met, and in varying degrees worked with, all but one of those who influenced my legal thought. Ernst Rabel (the one exception), Max Rheinstein, Otto Kahn-Freund, Harry Lawson, Gino Gorla and Robert Heuston belong to the group of "greats" who are no longer with us; André Tunc, Werner Lorenz, Tony Honoré, John Fleming, and Hein Kötz to the generation which, at a pinch, one could almost call contempories. Jack Hamson belongs to a category all of his own. For in addition to having been a close and loyal friend, he exercised his influence on me through his character and comportment rather than through his publications which, unfortunately given his great gift for elegant writing, remained slender throughout his life.

With mentors such as these I was, inevitably, destined to develop a European outlook (and have remained proud of it ever since). However, having worked with them and read their works repeatedly, I also became conscious of the difficulty of saying something new which they had not already said or foreshadowed. From the outset of my academic career I thus sought to find and develop ideas which, if not entirely my own, I might, one day, claim to bear the signs of my particular brand of comparative law and my own philosophy about how my subject should be taught.

If thinking up new ideas and approaches for comparative methodology was not easy, teaching foreign law in a descriptive manner was, in the beginning at least, not so difficult. For when I started my career in Cambridge in the early 1970s there was, in England, a remarkable dearth of comparative law teachers, books and articles. Cohn's *Manual of German Law*—a book now seriously out of date and yet still rewarding to read (especially if one tries to understand its author's very acute mind)—and Amos and Walton's *French Law*—which provided more information than ideas about French law—were the only books available to those who could not read French or German. (At that time Zweigert's and Kötz's magnificent *Einführung in die Rechtsvergleichung aus dem Gebiete des Privatrechts* had not been completed even in the original, German version; the first *English* edition had to wait until 1977.) To these I would add Buckland and MacNair, *Roman Law and Common Law*, since I was fascinated by their ability to show that classical Roman law (in which I was originally trained, especially in its Byzantine phase) and the common law, were really closer to each other than I had been led to believe in my years as a law student in the Continent of Europe.

I find it amazing (and gratifying to note) that in the intervening twenty-five years or so there has been a veritable explosion in writing in the area of foreign and comparative law. Though I would not for a moment claim that my work played a part in bringing about this hyper-activity I can, I think truthfully, state that I swam with this current and, to continue with this metaphor, was one of the first to jump into the sea. What still remains to be done is to convince my colleagues that comparative law and methodology are not the exclusive domain of the select few, but can and should be used by all of them when teaching their own topics of national law. This belief is strengthened by the impact that European (in the sense of Community) law is having on numerous branches of English law and the parallel need which exists to take it, too, into account when teaching almost all of our core subjects.

But what were the themes or ideas which have come to dominate my thought and work during these last twenty-five years? Though much of my time was spent writing two English text books—on Torts and Agency—both of which have seen three editions so far (and now are heading for a fourth)—as well as a two-volume comparative monograph with the late Harry Lawson, my real work was in the themes which I tried to develop in my articles, twenty of which are now reproduced in this book, substantially in an un-altered form.

Looking at them again I think they have, in the main, withstood the passage of time and also reveal the main co-ordinates or themes of my work, present in an unconscious manner in the beginning, consciously, even aggressively asserted in later years. Since they run through all the essays included in this book, it might help the reader if I were to alert him to them myself. It is for him to judge how successfully I have pursued them; but, at the very least, this collection of essays shows that to varying degrees they have been with me for all my working life and I, in turn, have remained loyal to them. They are five.

First is the need to create an audience for my subject; and in later years I expressed this in Pirandelian terms. (My Shimizu Lecture was entitled "Comparative Law: A Subject in Search of an Audience". Here I have reproduced the Italian version, partly because it is slightly more polished than the original, and partly because it later became the topic of wider discussion in that country than it did in my own.)

The need alluded to above was felt not only because classes were always small, the subject apparently holding out no attraction to students who increasingly viewed (and view) a law degree as a professional qualification, but also because somehow one always seemed to have to justify one's chosen discipline in a way that those who taught mainstream subjects did not have to do. (In Germany to this day, young jurists who wish to specialise in the subject, will always offer it as the third arrow in a quiver which, invariably, includes civil law and private international law.) This need to "re-package" the subject became even more pronounced when, from the early 1980s, I began teaching in the United States and discovered that one really had to "sell" one's course if one were to avoid lecturing to an empty room. Obviously it worked, since I have been teaching in the United States ever since (and on one occasion was even offered the chair which had once been held by a most distinguished German *émigré*.)

One way of achieving this aim was by merging the common and civil law teaching techniques and presenting my subject through cases. This may sound almost self-evident now; but apart from Professor von Mehren's pioneering comparative law case book (first published in 1957 and now in its second edition, written in partnership with Professor Gordley), it was not so in the late 1960s when some of the gurus of comparative law in my country, for instance Professor Kurt Lipstein, even proclaimed that comparative *torts* could not be taught through cases.[1] I was determined to prove this view wrong, and set about doing so on every occasion I was given to give a lecture to a mixed audience. In doing so, I increasingly became convinced that the method, though difficult to employ in practice since it required looking up numerous court decisions before finding the "right" parallels, not only "created" an audience but was also intellectually fully justified. A number of essays included in this book attempt to substantiate this claim; and I think it has

---

[1] "Protected Interests in the Law of Torts", (1963) 22 *Camb. L. Journ.* 25 *et seq.*

proved its worth in my *German Law of Torts* which reached its third edition a mere ten years after it first saw the light of day and will soon appear as part of a two-volume treatise entitled *The German Law of Obligations*.

My belief in the utility of teaching foreign law through cases was strengthened by experience which demonstrated that foreign students feel comfortable in a factual environment they recognise. Their "reserve" or scepticism towards foreign law also decreased as one was able to show them that results were, as often as not, similar; and that even the reasoning was, on occasion, transplantable if subject to some modifications. The first fully-blown piece to attempt this approach was my "The Not so Dissimilar Tort and Delict" which was, on the initiative of Professor Glanville Williams, offered to and accepted for publication by the *Law Quarterly Review* in 1977[2] but which, for reasons of space, I had to omit from this collection.

Teaching foreign law through cases provided me with further advantages. For, first I could, temporarily at least, put the foreign concepts aside and, instead, try to discover the real but unexpressed policy issues that lie behind these factual situations. A functional rather than conceptual approach was attempted in my "Cause and Consideration: A Study in Parallel"[3] where, instead of attempting to argue (as some authors had tried to do before me) that the notions are really variations on the same theme, or trying to defend their existence (as the late Jack Dawson once thought I had done), I endeavoured to show that English law uses a wide range of concepts to perform the functions which in French law are achieved through the medium of *cause*. The reverse is true of the German term *Geschäftsgrundlage* which often, in comparative literature, is treated as the rough equivalent to our notion of frustration. The problem is that it is not only that. For under their term, the Germans include four very distinct situations namely: (a) inability, due to unforseen events, to fulfil the primary purpose of the contract; (b) cases where the contractual performance has become strictly and literally impossible; (c) cases where because of some unforeseen contingency, performance has become "impracticable" and (d) common mistakes as to present facts, in American law often called mistake in basic assumptions.

This approach was taken further as one tried to discover the policy reasons that lay, unexpressed, behind judicial decisions and accounted for the same results. Whether these were unconscious echoes of the ideas propagated by the German Free School or the American Realists, I cannot say. But I went down that path because I felt, and feel, that it helps bridge the gap between common law and civil law which is otherwise left yawning if the systems are examined only from the point of view of their concepts. My "Policy in the Law of Torts"[4] was one result; and the methodology adopted there was to prove very helpful when, in the late 1970s and early 1980s, I collaborated with

[2] 93 *LQR* 78 *et seq.*
[3] Below, Ch. 4.

the late Harry Lawson and persuaded him to produce a radically modernised version of his old classic *Negligence in the Civil Law* under the new heading *Tortious Liability for Unintentional Harm in the Common Law and the Civil Law.*[5]

The search for the policy reasons strengthened my functional rather than conceptual approach, and here much of John Fleming's work—including a marvellous piece he wrote for the *Canadian Bar Review* in the early 1950s[6]— was to prove of enduring value. I thus tried to make the French and German cases the starting point of my discussion, often down-playing the vigorous theoretical debates that had taken place in the Universities of those countries, in favour of exegesis, comparison, and historical excursus which I always tried to weave into my lectures. If this meant sacrificing something of the dogmatic side of the foreign system, I felt it was a price well worth paying; and I repeatedly quoted one of Harry Lawson's aphorisms that "A good lecture consists of a studied measure of inaccuracy". For by leaving these doctrinal debates out of my classes, I was gaining the interest of my students; and without this first step, there could be no developing interest in foreign and comparative law at all. Indeed, as time went by, I wondered whether it really mattered if I said little about, say, the German disputes as to whether "illegality" is determined by the act or the result or how it might differ in § 823 I BGB and 831 BGB. Anyway, with hindsight one notes that some of these debates have even subsided in the country where they originated. And others—what for instance is the real difference in practice between a contract with protective effects and *Drittschadensliquidation*—failed, in practice, to elicit a clear and convincing difference even from my German colleagues. All one got was references to structural deficiencies in the Code and the like; but all these could be ignored with impunity for the purposes of teaching German law to English students. For why should an American student care that the Germans got their vicarious liability rule wrong? I could give many more examples but one more, this time from contract, will suffice. It is the notion of "factual contract", which in Germany provoked much writing in the 1950s, but which has now been totally abandoned by the German courts. So I stuck with my hunch and have not regretted my obstinacy.

This process is taken further in my piece "The Legacy of History on German Contract Law"[7] which outlined in many respects the method which Professor Werner Lorenz, Dr.Gerhard Dannemann, and I employed in writing the companion volume to my *German Law of Torts*, entitled, *The German Law of Contract and Restitution.*[8] For here we were faced with a Pandectist

---

[4] Below, Ch. 12.

[5] Published by the Cambridge University Press in 1982 and translated into Japanese in 1997.

[6] "Remoteness and Duty: The Control Devices in Liability for Negligence", (1953) 31 *Can. Bar Rev.* 471.

[7] Below, Ch. 5.

[8] Which forms part of the aforementioned *The German Law of Obligations* (1997).

structure which was much more rigid and, arguably, oppressive (at least to a foreign lawyer working with this material) than the one encountered in the German law of delict. One was thus forced to "deconstruct" and then "reconstruct" German law in order to make it more palatable to an Anglo-American audience without, however, sacrificing its accuracy and, if I may continue with a different metaphor, its flavour.[9] Once again the readers of this volume must, in the end, decide how this thesis has worked in practice; and how it remains to be improved (by us in future editions of our book or by others who find some merit in it, and decide to employ it in their own work). Yet one consequence of this approach was that it enabled us to bring the two systems closer together than has hitherto been believed to be the case and, once again, emphasize similarities and transplantability rather than stand behind impenetrable walls. This brings me to the second theme of my work.

This is my willingness to stress my ideological belief in Europe. Having settled on (a) an "aim" (I must persuade more Anglo-American students to become interested in foreign law, thus broadening their legal education) and (b) the "method" (teaching functionally the law through cases), I felt the need to emphasize similarities rather than harp on about differences between the common law and the modern civil law (which, of course, did not mean that I was not aware of their existence). This gave me a "purpose" which was really part of my wider philosophy about Europe as well as being an instinctive reaction to numerous Continental lawyers who, in my early years, had tried to drill into my mind (and not without scorn) how different the civil law tradition was from that of "les pays anglo-saxon".[10]

But long ago I decided to go a step further and admit my attachment to things European. I was, after all, "European", as I tried to show in my inaugural lecture at the University of Oxford and I saw no reason why I should not only proclaim my rich cultural heritage but also defend it from other "cultures" which are insidiously trying to dilute it. I accept that such admissions

---

[9] When in my youth I had to translate one of Gotthold Ephraim Lessing's *Fabeln*—in those days one tried to learn a foreign langauge through its literature and not with the help of specially concocted texts on political correctness—I was advised to deconstruct the text grammatically—find the *Hauptsatz*, the *Nebensatz*, the prepositions which went with each verb—and then to try to re-construct the text in plausible English. Many decades later, the grammatical lesson was no longer boring the student but inspiring the law teacher. By the way, the text in question was: "*Als der Löwe mit dem Esel, der ihm durch seine fürchterliche Stimme die Tiere sollte jagen helfen, nach dem Walde ging, rief ihm eine naseweise Krähe von dem Baume zu: Ein schöner Gesellschafter! Schämst du dich nicht, mit einem Esel zu gehen?—Wen ich brauchen kann, versetzte der Löwe, dem kann ich ja wohl Seite gönnen.*" i.e. "When the lion went into the woods with the donkey, expecting that the latter's dreadful voice would help him hunt animals, from high above the trees a cheeky crow cried out to the lion: 'What a partner you have chosen! Aren't you ashamed to be going at your task with a donkey?' 'If I need it', retorted the lion, 'I can please myself'."

[10] The counterpart, which I have heard from many a learned English jurist (and judge) is, of course, how "*Europe*" (sic) is governed by the Napoleonic Code". For a recent illustration of this tendency see: Professor Jack Beatson, "Has the Common Law a Future" Inaugural lecture delivered at the University of Cambridge on 29 April 1996, p.10. Let any of my readers try that on any German jurist and see how he will react!

bring one perilously close to politics and an area of acute contemporary controversy over the future of the political and economic shape of Europe in the twenty-first century which has generated valid and honestly held diametrically-opposed views. Yet, I have chosen not only to mention my predilection but also to defend it openly since I agree with the view expressed by a distinguished contemporary Oxford historian who wrote[11]—and I paraphrase here slightly—that "the craft of [law] is not practised, and should not be studied, in a vacuum". My writings thus saw the light of day at a time when much of the contemporary agonizing over the future of Europe has been taking place. I made no secret of my belief in an ever-closer European cooperation. European unity (whatever shape it might take) does not, however, require uniformity. Yet, if it is to come about, it does assume mutual understanding and respect as well as an awareness that we have more things that unite us than we have that divide us. Those who are aware of contemporary German legal/historical writings on this wider topic will, again, note the "elective affinity". My problem was thus how could I help bring about this increased awareness of a common heritage? And whose minds should I attempt to win over to my cause?

Ruminations of this kind increasingly led me to develop my third and related theme namely, the belief that the best way I could promote my subject (and my theme) was by attracting the attention of our judges and proving to them their potential utility in their work. If they became interested in foreign law, so ran my reasoning, they might encourage practitioners to make greater use of it in their pleadings; and if this happened, academics working on the products of the courts, would then be forced to take the subject seriously and also try to make it "judge-friendly". In starting with the courts and not the Universities, I confess I was standing the creature on its head![12] But I felt compelled to try this approach since by the early 1980s I had become convinced that my subject was stagnating, especially in my old University— Cambridge; or, which seemed to me just as unhealthy, was being swallowed up by another subject.[13]

This climate and this thesis also convinced me that in law as well as politics the personality and background of the legal actors was an important part in understanding the courts, their work and their decisions.[14] This line

---

[11] Professor J.H. Elliott, *Richelieu and Olivares*, Canto (ed.) (CUP, 1991) 159.

[12] Though in another sense, of course, I was merely following the English and not Continental legal tradition by treating the judges and not the academics as the senior partners of the law-making process.

[13] In the past it was international law that had swallowed up comparative law; in the 1980s Community law had become the usurper instead, as I believe is right, the natural partner of comparative law along with legal history.

[14] Echoes here, of course, of Max Rheinstein's *Rechtshonoratioren*—the key legal figures who have, throughout the centuries, been the motors of progress and reform. Rheinstein's theory can be found in his "Die Rechtshonoratioren und ihr Einfluss auf Charakter und Funktionen der Rechtsordnungen, (1970) 34 *RabelsZ*, 1 *et seq*.

of reasoning spawned different articles: one emphasizing *The Gradual Convergence* of the European systems—the title of a book born out of a conference which I helped organise in London mainly for judges and legal practitioners.[15] Another work, entitled *The Comparatist*,[16] returned to the need to look at the personalities of the jurists in order to understand what they were doing, while a third—*Five Days in the House of Lords*[17]—extended this idea to our judges.

In reality this point is only touched upon in this last article, which contains my experience of spending five days in the House of Lords as a "junior junior". Though in this piece I focused on (and criticised) the judgment of Lord Mustill—because I (somewhat presumptuously) felt that I had enough material to "disagree with him"—my "concerns" apply also to the work of other distinguished judges, as well. The question, at its simplest, was and is what happens when you are arguing a case before a judge who, like Lord Goff (on matters of restitution) and Lord Wolfe (on matters of public law) to give but two examples, have clear, carefully-thought out, *philosophical* views about the underlying problem? As I have said, the same Carlislian approach— the hero as a judge—could be tried one day on other judges; and I think I have enough material to give it a comparative dimension as well even though French and German judges are shielded by their unanimous, anonymous (civil) decisions.[18] For, to return to England, nowadays, we have jurists on the English Bench who have written extensively on some subjects and, in any event, given clear signs in their writings (and sometimes in their judgments) of strongly-held philosophical views about the law and its limits *vis-à-vis* the powers of elected politicians. So in my works I laid down a marker; and, secretly perhaps, hope that one day someone like Lord Mustill, who many years ago was—all-too-briefly—my pupil master, will take up the challenge and respond!

White v. Jones[19] in fact gave me the long-awaited chance to try out my theory about the way one could and should use foreign law before our courts. I say long awaited, for already in the mid-1970s I was corresponding with Lord Denning about the nature of the harm suffered by the plaintiff in *Dutton v. Bognor Regis Urban District Council*.[20] The equivalent German cases[21] said—I think rightly—that this was not material, physical harm but economic

---

[15] And published by the Oxford University Press in 1994.

[16] Below, Ch. 2.

[17] Below, Ch. 15.

[18] Yet think, for instance, of Josserand, of his views on extra-marital cohabitations expressed while he was a law Professor, and then, finally, look at what trouble he brought to the French law of torts by introducing them into the grammatically neutral text of art. 1382 CC; and could not the same be said of German law and jurists such as Professor Nipperdey who had combined the academic with the judicial office? This kind of study has, of course, been undertaken more fully in the case of American judges.

[19] [1993] 3 WLR 730.

[20] [1972] 1 QB 373.

[21] BGH 27 May 1963, BGHZ 39, 358; BGH 30 May 1963, BGHZ 39, 366.

loss; and I had the temerity to write this to Lord Denning only to discover that he found the time to write back, talk to me, charm me in a number of private encounters (as he did almost everyone whom he met) and, at one stage, even try to entice me to the British Institute of International and Comparative Law. Yet Denning, not infrequently overruled in those days was, on this occasion, approved by the House of Lords in *Anns* v. *Merton London Borough Council*[22], a result that galled me since by then my brilliant colleague from Trinity College, Cambridge—Tony Weir—had produced one of his inimitable translations of the German texts and had made sure (through a friend) that they had been placed before their Lordships when *Anns* was being heard. Yet the foreign experience was neither used nor cited; and it was ignored again when their Lordships were hearing *Murphy*[23] even though by then I had had personally the opportunity to hand over copies of this material to Lord Oliver who happened to be visiting my Institute in Leiden where he gave a lecture[24] foreshadowing his opinion in *Murphy*. In retrospect, of course, I realise that I was day-dreaming by thinking that conversations of this kind between a senior judge and a junior don could have any impact at all on the former, Lord Denning being, of course, an exception in having a voracious appetite for new ideas and being willing to rely on his own research of the law. I clearly had to wait; and *White* v. *Jones* seemed to be the opportunity I had been waiting for during all my academic life.

In the end *White* v. *Jones* was something of a disappointment—and I say this even though my side won the case (largely due to the calm but rigorous advocacy skills of John Mitting QC) and much use was made by at least two of their Lordships of the foreign material which I had prepared for the respondents. Yet I refer to the litigation as (something) of a disappointment for a number of reasons.

In my view it is a shame that neither we nor the judges made full use of this foreign material. Thus, despite the valiant efforts of Mr James Quirk (the first "junior" for the respondents), we failed to exploit the fact that a liability rule in almost all other jurisdictions had no perceptible insurance consequences even though insurance points took up, at the behest of the Law Society which had supported the appeal, one full morning of the hearings.[25] We also refused, I think correctly in tactical (but not intellectual) terms, to draw their Lordships into the contractual aspects of the case. Yet, this is not simply a disagreement over what the academic and the practitioner hopes to get out of a litigated dispute. In my view, the consequences of us arguing the case purely as a tort case will be felt in years to come. Thus, despite the Law Commission's recent re-assertion of the need to modernise the privity

[22] [1978] AC 728.
[23] *Murphy* v. *Brentwood DC* [1991] 1 AC 398.
[24] Entitled "Judicial Legislation" and subsequently re-published in *The Clifford Chance Lectures, vol I, Bridging the Channel* (1996) pp. 11–30.
[25] For further details on this see my "Five Days in the House of Lords".

doctrine, this particular factual configuration is left in limbo; an unsatisfactory result given that the decision has no clear *ratio decidendi*; and stands ill at ease with other recent pronouncements of the House of Lords. Strangely, therefore, one might even assert that, indirectly, the comparative material had its greatest impact on Lord Mustill who gave the most powerful opinion against my side and this simply because it clearly made him think and re-think the troublesome topic of the proper boundaries of contract and tort. No citation reveals this incontrovertibly; yet I submit this suggests itself to anyone who reads Lord Mustill's brilliant dissent carefully and does so in conjunction with his earlier, thought-provoking "Kuala Lumpur Lecture"[26]. Overall, therefore, the experience made me conscious of the amount of further work that we, the so-called full-time comparatists, still have to do before we can convince our judges to use foreign material. Like all crusades, this was proving hardest on the crusader!

My insistence on the insurance aspects of the litigation (and the lessons one could draw from foreign practices) brings me to the fourth major theme of my work; the need to look at law in a broader context. Here, perhaps, one can find a bridge between my functional and focused approach on the one hand and the cultural aims of the French school exemplified by the work of René David on the other. Once again, however, I declare my own preference for the historical/comparative approach initiated in Germany by such great figures as Koschaker, Wieacker, and Coing (and now brilliantly continued by Professors Zimmermann, Schulze and others) and the contemporary, comparative approach found in the works of such German scholars as Zweigert, Lorenz, Drobnig, Grossfeld, Kötz, Schlectriem and von Bar to mention but a few.

By broader context, however, I mean all sorts of topics, not all of which are covered in the normal teaching of most branches of the law. I have thus favoured the use of empirical data in the teaching of the law and, in appropriate cases, in real life situations, but also warned about legal transplants or imitations which did not make proper allowances for the background differences which exist between legal systems.[27]

My "Atkin"[28] and "Cohen"[29] lectures (delivered respectively at the Reform Club in London and the Hebrew University of Jerusalem) took up some of these points; and as a teacher I have found that this extra dimension in the presentation of the topics always attracts the attention and interest of my classes. I think, however, that this empirical dimension can have useful practical applications as well; and this certainly proved to be the case when I had

---

[26] Entitled "Negligence in the World of Finance" (1992) 5 *The Supreme Court Journal*, 1.

[27] See my "Bridging Legal Cultures", below Ch. 11, echoing here some brilliant pieces by Kahn-Freund enriched, however, by an interest in empirical data which I picked up during my years in the United States and, especially, from the work of John Fleming.

[28] Below, Ch. 20.

[29] Below, Ch. 11.

the chance to serve on a panel of five experts who were asked by a Federal Court of Cincinnati to determine levels of compensation in the first world-wide class action sanctioned by an American court. Our work and the legal problems we encountered in this complex litigation, have been well described by Professor Harold Luntz, one of our team, in his "Heart Valves, Class Actions and Remedies: Lessons for Australia?"[30] so I need say no more about this at this stage.

Studying the law in action also revealed a reality that did not often coincide with what the books said about a foreign system and set me on course for the fifth and last theme in my work.

Once again, my intellectual unrest started in the 1980s. The Pearson Committee for instance, had, earlier on, recommended the introduction, in some cases, of the annuity system of paying damages and, among the comparative material it included in its survey, was German law. Yet, despite a Codal provision to this effect, the legal system of that country has, in divers situations, developed in practice a method of lump sum payments, not least because this makes it easier for its lawyers to collect their fees in one fell swoop! In fact, the reverse of what Pearson implied in places actually happens in Germany. This is because the law in the books does not coincide with the law in action.

Another line of interest was, thus, clearly emerging both in my research and, even more in my teaching, as I increasingly developed a keenness to challenge or at least question widely-held assumptions. Who had more statutory law in the area of torts? Professor von Bar's research showed it was the English not the Germans. Who was more generous in tort awards; judge or jury? The Henderson/ Clermont/ Eisenberg studies in the United States injected some serious doubts about jury generosity.[31] (Though, like others, I have maintained in my work[32] that a major problem with jury awards is their unpredictability and the adverse effect this has on settlements.) Was it preferable to litigate in the United States than in England (or Scotland)? Enormous variations in State awards, coupled with differing (and fluctuating attitudes) over the doctrine of *forum non conveniens*, suggested that a much more nuanced view had to be taken of the matter. How did the abandonment of contributory fault as a defence in driving accident cases affect the moral content of tort law and, just as importantly, the cost of insurance? Comparisons between France and Germany proved illuminating; and, again, I felt added a new dimension to the teaching of my subject which, I believed and still do so, was drily described in the traditional text books.

---

[30] In Nicholas Mullany, (ed.) *Torts in the Nineties* 1996.

[31] Eisenberg and Henderson, "Inside the Quiet Revolution in Products Liability", 39 *UCLA* 731 ff (1992); Clermont and Eisenberg, "Trial by Jury or Judge: Transcending Empiricism", 77 *Cornell L. Rev.* (1992), both seminal empirical studies on American tort law in action.

[32] For instance in my "Litigation Mania in England, Germany and the United States", below, Ch. 20.

My curiosity and work in all these matters were greatly helped by spending more and more time abroad, talking with academics and practitioners, and discovering which were the topics which really interested the "real" world. With the passage of time, I discovered that other colleagues of my generation (such as Professor John Bell) were also deriving visible benefits from prolonged stays abroad.[33] This increased exposure to the foreign, real world; and also made me realise how foreign employers or legal multinational firms valued students with double qualifications. For in the last twenty-five years, during which I have been in academic teaching, the number of multinational firms which have followed their multinational clients has increased dramatically; and our joining the European Community—now the European Union— led to the proliferation of British legal firms doing business in Europe. These firms increasingly asked me for a new "product", a multi-lingual, flexibly-minded, lawyer who could move both physically and mentally with some ease in different legal environments. The appearance of the Erasmus programme, of which I have expressed doubts because of its desire to accommodate too many Universities and the huge paper work which it carries in its wake[34] was, nevertheless, a further incentive to legal mobility which was now the new "buzz-word".

On the academic front these changes led me to attempt two innovations, by now in my capacity as Director of the newly-founded Oxford Centre for the Advanced Study of European and Comparative Law. They deserve some extra space since, in my view, they give a hint of things to come.

The first was the joint funding of posts at my Centre to be held by academic lawyers of the sponsoring country. Some of these posts are meant to be held by foreign colleagues for a prolonged period of time; others are visiting fellowships, meant to bring a constant stream of foreign talent to Oxford and, we hope, provoke a cross-fertilisation of ideas.

Oxford was not the first to introduce four-year degrees with a year or more of study abroad; indeed, in my opinion, the four-year course organised by King's College, London, and the University of Paris I, still remains the best on offer. But, I think, Oxford has been the first to make such extensive use of foreign talent in its teaching. For our foreign visitors not only teach their law in the original language to those of our students who are taking part in our four-year degrees;[35] but are also participating in seminars and tutorials given to the bulk of our (mainly British) students and, in this way, constantly making them aware of the foreign possibility, the foreign dimension to each of the problems they examine. The amount of information these exercises impart is considerable; but the psychological effect on our insular mentality—often

---

[33] See his "English Law and French Law—Not so Different?", (1995) 48 *Current Legal Problems* 63.

[34] A point I criticised in "Learning from Europe and Learning in Europe", included in *The Gradual Convergence* (1994), 1 *et seq.*

[35] At present some 30 students who go to France, Germany, and the Netherlands.

found in teachers as well as students—is the most long-lasting and beneficial effect of this type of cooperation. Indeed, our partnerships with leading foreign Universities are now leading them to invite members of the Oxford Law Faculty to teach at regular intervals their own students; and I am convinced that this, again, offers another way towards the revival (some would say), the creation I would prefer to argue, of a new *ius commune Europaeum*. Incidentally, I find this a much more satisfactory way for promoting the awareness of our common legal heritage and dispelling the myth which has persuaded my English colleagues that we are the "odd men out" in the world of European legal ideas and thus also discourages them from studying foreign law. Quite the contrary; on a whole host of issues English law is closer to French law than it is to German law (e.g. breach of contract, vicarious liability, transfer of property in corporeal movables) while on others (e.g. the need to balance free speech versus human privacy) English and German law may have much more in common in terms of shared values than English law has with the law in the United States. Clearly, more work has to be done; but there are enough surprises there to tantalise us all into further, joint research if only to prove whether our hunches about foreign systems are correct or not.

This has, indeed, already started to happen at my Centre. Two of the pieces included here—the one with Dr. Gerhard Dannemann and the other with Dr. Nico Nolte—are products of this kind of research. The collaboration with Dr. Nolte, for instance, was in order to produce a paper for one of Professor Birk's seminars, held bi-annually at All Souls College; and it soon led us both to the belief that what was needed was not further abstract discussions about a possible definition of privacy, but something more concrete, more capable of dispelling English fears about the possible introduction of a privacy right than the horror stories peddled by our Press. I suppose the fate of what we produced will be determined by politics and, in particular, the stranglehold that the Press nowadays has over our politicians. Our study, however, continuing the work I started in my *German Law of Torts* and, drawing on Dr Nolte's own detailed research of the subject, offers the first concrete step for anyone who wishes to take the matter further in a serious way.

In any event, the way we got together and worked in this case, brings me back to some of the earlier themes which I have stressed in my work over the years. For my entrepreneurial activities in the mid-1990s are linking up nicely with my earlier aspirations about my subject. The circle seems to be complete; and, perhaps, this is another reason for wishing to bring these pieces together in one volume.

Yet I cannot finish this introduction without saying something about the difficulties involved in this, arguably, the most important phase of my life's work.

The first difficulty need not be laboured but only mentioned; it involves an inordinate amount of time spent on administration and fund-raising, with the inevitable high price of forcing one to set aside one's avowed aim in life: teaching and the doing of research. At some stage in the near future Universities, including my own, will have to re-evaluate the role of professors, at any rate those to whom they entrust administrative duties which increasingly bear some resemblance to the duties of deans of American Law Schools. But the second obstacle needs stressing for, in my view, here lies the key to the future of my subject.

The difficulty to which I am alluding is none other than the mentality block that stops many lawyers from even developing a passing interest in what happens abroad. Alas, in the Anglo-American world we find this also with languages under the pretext that most people speak ours so why should we bother to learn theirs. This block makes us introverted and insular—and I use the word advisedly, and pejoratively precisely because so many Englishmen regard their insularity as an asset. Among the reasons or rather the excuses for such lack of interest, one finds some which are more plausible than others. Of these, the lack of reliable information in English about the foreign systems, is the one which I have tried to address in my life's work but I admit it is only slowly being resolved. Time, alone, will show whether the work which was started by my generation of comparative lawyers in the late 1970s and later will bear better fruits than that of the immediate past generation in this country; but at least we tried, with an open mind, un-encumbered by the prejudices left from the dark years of the Second World War and with the kind of optimism which the European ideal gave to many of us during the post-War years.

2

The Comparatist¹ (or a Plea for a Broader Legal Education)

"Probe everything and retain the best"
(St Paul, I, Thessalonians, 21)

Oscar Wilde's views about those who lose not one but both parents are well known.² How he would have reacted to someone who is about to deliver his fourth inaugural lecture is a matter of speculation. For my part, however, I feel that this record³ allows me some latitude to avoid delivering a lecture on a narrow and purely legal point. This may not be a bad thing since an inaugural lecture is, in essence, a public lecture and thus should be addressed to the entire university community and not only to one's own faculty. This must be particulary apposite in this case since our University, under the umbrella structure of the *Europaeum*, is attempting to bring together not only lawyers from different systems but also scholars from different disciplines. I have thus chosen to highlight some of the attributes which those involved in my subject should possess. I am reinforced in my view that this is a fitting topic for discussion since up to now much has been written about comparative law—not least by Oxford Scholars⁴—but little about its thespians. This lecture could be seen as a first, if idiosyncratic, attempt to fill the gap.⁵

---

¹ An inaugural lecture delivered in the University of Oxford on 23 February 1996. The piece is reprinted from *The Yearbook of European Law*, 1996.

² "To lose one parent, . . . may be regarded as a misfortune; to lose both looks like carelessness" Lady Bracknell, *The Importance of Being Earnest*, Act One.

³ My first inaugural lecture (in Leiden) dealt with *The Aliakmon*. It was published in (1987) 103 *LQR* 354 *et seq*. The second lecture (at QMW) was concerned with *Smith* v. *Littlewoods*; and it appeared in (1989) 105 *LQR* 104 *et seq*. The third (University College London), dealt with the wider topic of judicial styles, and it was included in (1994) 110 *LQR* 607 *et seq*.

⁴ Notably by F.H. Lawson, "The Field of Comparative Law" (1949) 61 *Juridical Review* 1 *et seq*., and Sir Otto Kahn-Freund in his "Comparative Law as an Academic Subject" (1966) 82 *LQR* 40 *et seq*., and "On Uses and Abuses of Comparative Law" (1974) 37 *MLR* 1 *et seq*. To these, I might be allowed to add my own piece: "Comparative Law—A Subject in search of an Audience" (1990) 53 *MLR* 1 *et seq*.

⁵ In *Studi in Memoriam di Tullio Ascarelli* (Casa Editrice Dott. A. Giuffrè, 1969), vol. III, 1409–15, Dr. Kurt Nadelmann described various attempts made some thirty-five years ago to compile a volume of essays on the great comparative lawyers of the last two centuries. The attempt failed, partly perhaps because it degenerated into an effort "to give many nations representation and even to balance the number of representatives" (p.1411). Overall, however, the aim of the project was to produce a "biographical historical work". In this paper my aim is to discover some of the traits which the great comparatists shared with great historical figures and to suggest that we should continue to encourage their acquisition in the future. The need to study

Being an historian *manqué* myself, I have always been attracted by the study of the lives of great men and women; and the relationship of history and law to this day holds for me a great fascination. If there were some kind of historical equivalent to the "Desert Island Discs" series I think I would be eager to explain why I would be intrigued to find myself in the company of Disraeli, Erasmus, Luther, Montaigne, Aristotle and the Roman God Janus. It may be a coincidence that this list contains one figure from each of the countries with which I have been fortunate enough to have enjoyed a very close association (though I am sorry that lack of space limits me to only one). More interesting, however, may be the fact that all of the above seem to have had attributes which, I believe, should be found in the true comparatist. In any event, it is not, I think, a coincidence that many of these qualities or attributes were also possessed in abundance by the great figures of my subject such as Kelsen, Rabel, Rheinstein, Ehrenzweig, Wolf and others and, indeed, those who have held (and hold) the chair of comparative law in Oxford. In that sense, therefore, this lecture could be seen as a personal tribute to the Oxford School.

I mentioned Disraeli first, and since he represents England on my list I feel I ought to start with him. I say England but not the English for, as Lord Blake[6] and others who have written eloquently about him clearly suggest, though he tried to be more English than the English, his Jewishness was never far below the surface. To this I largely attribute his perceptiveness, his wiliness,[7] his perseverance,[8] and his sense of enduring gratitude to those who helped him in difficult times. Lord Blake, in fact, gives us in his book[9] an extraordinary example of how Disraeli re-paid his debts of honour, even though apparently his tradesmen had to take their chance! These are features that seem to me to keep cropping up in Disraeli's life and in his relations with others. They are the features that make his complex personality so fascinating. Perhaps, they are also the kind of features that give away the fact that in some respects at least he remained an 'outsider' to the end.[10] Yet it was the outsider's quality

the backgrounds of academic lawyers was recently stressed by Lord Rodger of Earlsferry in his John Maurice Kelly Memorial Lecture entitled "Savigny in the Strand" (Dublin, 1995).

[6] *Disraeli* (London, Eyre and Spottiswoode, 1967). See, also, The Centenary Romanes Lecture, delivered in Oxford on 10 November 1992 under the title "Gladstone, Disraeli, and Queen Victoria" (Oxford, Clarendon Press, 1993).

[7] So obvious in his letters to the Queen, a selection of which has been published by W.F. Monypenny and G.E. Buckle under the title *The Life of Benjamin Disraeli*, 6 vols (London, 1910–20) and A.C. Benson and Viscount Esher *Letters of Queen Victoria*, 3 vols (London, 1907).

[8] Gladstone was aware of this attribute and phrased it thus: "Disraeli is a man who is *never beaten* . . . Every reverse, every defeat is to him only an admonition to wait and catch his opportunity of retrieving and more than retrieving his position". Blake, The Centenary Romanes Lecture, delivered in Oxford on 10 November 1992 under the title "Gladstone, Disraeli, and Queen Victoria" (1993), 3.

[9] *Disraeli,* above n. 6, 705–6.

[10] "To the end of his days he remained an alien figure, never truly merged in the social and political order which after a lifetime of vicissitudes he had so strangely come to dominate at last." Blake, above n. 6, 17

which must also have contributed to the insights he acquired[11] on the psyche of the nation he governed, and nourished, from the early school days, the desire to dominate through wit, cunning, or sheer force of personality.

To a greater or lesser degree these are features shared by most of the exiled comparatists of the post-Second World War years; and in my view, they were a source of strength. For the comparatist who shares this double identity is, I believe, able to bring insights to his subject which the national lawyer will rarely have. He is the observer of a chess game who sees a move that the players, themselves, often miss. He can stress weaknesses in his adopted system (as Kahn-Freund did[12]) because he has not lived with them to the point where they have become second nature and thus acceptable. For him the argument "we have always done things in this way" holds no water;[13] and if his views cannot prevail, he must treat the set-back as "an admonition to wait and catch his opportunity" later.

Yet the comparatist, like most converts, is not only a questioning observer but often also a ferocious defender of his new environment. Francis Mann was such a one. Like Disraeli, he fought for the honour and grandeur of things English though unlike him, he was never accused of "alien patriotism".[14] Still, his non-English background was, I think, evident to those who knew what to look out for; and it was also suggested by the doggedness of his perseverance. He simply would not let go where others, more English than he, having made their point, would have paused or, even modestly, expressed some doubts about its validity.

If there is a contradiction in the features which I have just stressed (critical and admiring approach towards the host country), it is a conscious one. The "outsider" is forced by circumstances of life to look both ways; and even when the focus is set in one direction the other side is never entirely out of sight. We shall come to Janus later; but this is a Janus type of characteristic which a comparatist must possess. Rheinstein, Rabel, Kelsen, Ehrenzweig, Kahn-Freund, John Fleming possessed it to the nth degree; and those who were not born with it, like Harry Lawson or Jack Dawson, acquired it with the passage of time. Lawson, to give but one instance, is obviously attracted by what he found on the Continent. His books and many articles do not conceal this

---

[11] These are often found in his famous trilogy of *romans à thèse* (as, for instance, his comment about "two nations" made in *Sybil*, Bk II, Ch. 5.) which, though written between 1844–7, give invaluable clues about his views on many political, social, religious, and racial issues which occupied his later years in politics.

[12] Especially in the areas of labour and family law.

[13] For him the question is "what would it be right to do this time" and not "what did we do last time?" Such an approach, of course, is typical of the civilian and not the common law mind which adheres to precedent. However, let us not forget that adherence to precedent is weaker in the United States (and other common law jurisdictions) than it is in England; and that even with us it may be showing signs of some weakening. The two ways of thinking may thus be converging!

[14] As Gladstone accused Disraeli. See Robert Blake, "Disraeli and Gladstone", The Leslie Stephen Lecture (Cambridge University Press, 1969), 8.

fascination; and, I think, he had a particularly soft spot for France. Yet in what, conceivably, was his best work he chose to defend the "Rational Strength of English Law",[15] and not to extol the virtues of the foreign law. The man who has fully understood and admired the internal logic and consistency of the German Civil Code, as Maitland had done before him, now feels almost compelled to demonstrate that his system, as well, has an unnoticed internal logic and rational strength. The double intellectual loyalty is a feature of the true comparatist for while appreciating the "new" he never ceases to miss the "old". When the double allegiance is lost, the scholar is no longer a comparatist but an expert on foreign law. He has become a thoroughbred and is no longer a mongrel.[16]

But in Disraeli's life we also see all the signs of the struggle for survival and the perseverance that goes with it and marshals in its aid many attractive (and less attractive) qualities. Our comparatists—and now I am again including those from the United States—were, in their vast majority *émigrés* of some sort or another;[17] and one of the observations often made, I think with some measure of accuracy, is the decline suffered by my subject as the *émigré* stream dried out.[18] More about this later. Here, however, suffice it to stress the hardship which the outsiders had to face in surviving in a different environment and also managing to make their mark on it. We get a glimpse of these difficulties when reading a recent excellent study of the German Jewish *émigrés* in the United States;[19] and I hope one day a comparable study could be done of the United Kingdom.[20]

Desiderius Erasmus of Rotterdam personifies for me wide and tireless literary productivity, citizenship of the world, tolerance, and a belief in evolutionary reform which he advocated with telling satire and, even, sparkling wit.

---

[15] The title of his Hamlyn Lectures.

[16] Though, as we have seen from the common law world, the thoroughbreds can also through their deep understanding of foreign law, achieve similar heights of penetrating scholarship. Thus, to give but one illustration, the current generation of German comparatists—Lorenz, Stoll, Drobnig, Lutter, Großveld, Kötz, von Bar—have wrested back the comparative law crown which the War years had allowed to pass to the United States.

[17] And for Oxford this is not a new phenomenon. We find it, for instance, in the generation of Italians of the 16th century (which includes such luminaries as Alberico Gentili) as much as in the generation of central European, Jewish *émigrés* of the mid-War years.

[18] In his obituary of Francis Mann in *The Guardian* of 20 September 1991 Sir Leonard Hoffmann (as he then was) rightly attributed the enrichment of the English academic scene to the years of the Hitler terror.

[19] M. Lutter, E.C. Stiefel and M. Hoeflich (eds.), *Der Einfluß deutscher Emigranten auf die Rechtsentwicklung in den USA und in Deutschland. Vorträge und Referate des Bonner Symposium im September 1991* (Tübingen, J.C.B.Mohr (Paul Siebeck), 1994). For further information see E.C. Stiefel and F. Mecklenburg, *Deutsche Juristen im amerikanischen Exil (1933–1955)* (Tübingen, J.C.B.Mohr (Paul Siebeck), 1991).

[20] Though Professor Lipstein wrote an elegant piece about the Jewish immigrants in England in J.Carlebach, G.Hirschfeld, A.Newman, A. Paucker and P. Pulzer (eds.), *Second Chance. Two Centuries of German-speaking Jews in the United Kingdom* (Tübingen, J.C.B.Mohr (Paul Siebeck), 1991), 221–9.

If, as modern scholarship asserts,[21] he additionally invented the charisma of the absent professor he was, again, a pioneer in realising the importance of the new medium—the printed book—during the years of its infancy.

These are qualities which a comparatist must also strive to acquire and perfect. He must broaden the range of tools used for the study of law even if he is criticised as Erasmus was by the great and powerful of the two Universities which never fell under his charm: Paris and Leuven. Like Erasmus he must hold fast to the conviction that true learning is the source of all good and virtuous action. And, again like Erasmus, starting with the status quo, he must be willing to question its rules and their rationale. When doing this he must also learn to be patient and see his reforming ideas receive wider acceptance with the passage of time. No lesser a judge than Lord Devlin used to maintain that the common law is quick to resist new ideas but, in the end, succumbs to them and absorbs them.[22] Lord Diplock agreed; though, for good measure, he added that "he who sets out to alter the habits and mind of judges must be possessed of stamina and . . . blessed with longevity".[23] Most of my comparatist heroes had these attributes, as well!

The Calcutt Reports[24] embody, in my view, an Erasmian approach to reforming our patchy and defective law of privacy. They were modest in their scope, moderate in tone, gradual in their technique.[25] If they failed it is not, I think, because they were defective but because weak politicians these days are so dominated by the wishes of powerful press barons.

But when sensible reform is stone-walled, one must move from Erasmus to Luther. For Erasmus was a man "all for tolerance but who would not fight for it."[26] The attributes of patience and resignation must thus, on occasion, give way to the obstinate pursuit of one's most sacred beliefs. If blood is to be spilt—metaphorically speaking—so be it. Luther now becomes our model.

Erasmus and Luther started off as mutual admirers. A deferential letter of Luther's dated 28 March 1519 shows the Reformer admitting his intellectual indebtedness to the Humanist; it also shows him with a certain inferiority complex when writing to a stylist more accomplished than himself.[27] But it was not long before relations became highly strained. The immoderate

---

[21] See Lisa Jardine's immensely scholarly work *Erasmus, Man of Letters. The Construction of Charisma in Print* (1993).

[22] "The Judge as Lawmaker", 4th Chorley Lecture, re-published in *The Judge* (1979), 1.

[23] Tribute to Professor Sir Arthur Goodhart published in (1975) 91 *LQR* 457–8 and 461.

[24] *Report of the Committee on Privacy and related Matters*, Cmnd. 1102 (HMSO, 1990); *Review of Press Self-Regulation*, Cmnd. 2135 (HMSO, 1993).

[25] On which see Markesinis "Subtle ways of Legal Borrowing: Some Reflections on the Report of the Calcutt Committee On Privacy and Related Matters" in B. Pfister and M. Will (eds.), *Festschrift für Werner Lorenz zum Siebzigsten Geburtstag* (Tübingen, J.C.B.Mohr (Paul Siebeck), 1991), 717–37.

[26] Hendrik Willem van Loon, Introduction to *The Praise of Folly* (1942), 7.

[27] P. Smith, *The Life and Letters of Martin Luther* (Boston, Houghton Mifflin Co., 1911), 200–1.

language of the great German undoubtedly played its part.[28] Here, as on so many other occasions, his fervent beliefs made him quarrelsome, even with some of his closest associates. The Diet of Augsburg for instance in 1530 saw him clash with his most learned but moderate disciple, Philip Melanchthon. From the correspondence which survives, Melanchthon comes out of this quarrel as the more reasonable and likeable of the two. But it is the teacher's stubbornness that made him the "leader" and his friend the disciple. It was the stubborn refusal to compromise which won the day. Luther may not have left us a pleasant image. The Papal bull, *Exurge Domine* of 15 June 1520, published a year later in Regensburg, summons the Lord to "arise and protect the vineyard Thou gavest Peter from the wild beast who is devouring it". Its language is colourful;[29] it also captures the Reformer's temperament. But if Luther left his mark on history—and Thomas Mann for one considers him one of the three makers of modern Germany[30]—it is precisely because his greatness was so uncompromising. I often see Kahn-Freund in similar terms; and the same goes for such distinguished *émigré* historians as Geoffrey Elton[31] and Walter Ullmann, both of whom I have had the privilege of knowing in my Cambridge days.

If I can move again to law, the comparatist must, in a few selected matters which are of fundamental importance to him, be ready to make his stand, too. He must not move; and if he is right, time if not God will help him. To return to privacy: I hope the battle is not lost. If Parliament and government are paralysed, I ask our judges to act. Let them look at other systems—the German for instance—where the press prevented reform. And let them look carefully and see how their German counterparts assumed the reforming task themselves and carried it out with caution and pragmatism. Let them finally look at how the change has worked in practice in all the countries where it has taken hold. The free world has not come to an end; the press has not become less free. Just as the success of Lutheranism did not destroy the

---

[28] At the end, the venom was such that when Erasmus died Luther claimed that he had died "without light, without the cross, and without God". Prior to that he had called him an "atheist a blasphemer, an Arian, and, worst of all, one who makes jokes of serious things and serious business of jokes". See P. Smith, above n. 27, 211.

[29] *Bulla Contra Erores Martini Luther et Sequatium: Cum mandato Reuerendissimi domini Episcopi Ratisponen(sis)*, published in Regensburg in 1521. One author has described this language as "a fatuous attempt to be relevant since at the moment of issue he [i.e. the Pope Leo X] was at his hunting lodge hunting wild boar". James Atkinson, *The Trial of Luther* (New York, Stein and Day, 1971), 83–4. This, however, seems to ignore the fact that Papal Bulls invariably used colourful language in both their titles and the preludes precisely because of the effect this had on ordinary people. In any event, the metaphor seems also to be apt.

[30] In a little known, at least among the non-specialists, essay entitled "Goethe, das deutsche Wunder" (reprinted in *Dichter und Herrscher, Europäischer Geist in Fünf Jahrhunderten*, Essays selected by Rudolf Hochhutch, (Grütersloh, Bertelsmann Lesering, 1964). Mann's other two figures are Goethe (as the title of the essay suggests) and Bismarck.

[31] Interestingly enough his grandfather Siegfried Sommer was Kaiser William II's best friend at the Gymnasium in Kassel and later, with a little help from the Emperor, rose to become a judge. On Williams rabid anti-semitism in later life see John G.Rohl, *The Kaiser and His Court. William II and the Government of Germany* (Cambridge University Press, 1994), Ch. 8.

Christian faith but, on the contrary, brought about a spiritual and organisational revival of the Catholic church, so will our press emerge with greater credibility if through judicial restraint and not only ineffectual self-regulation, it is forced to put its house in order. The same could be said of the doctrine of privity of contract, repeatedly condemned by judges and academics alike and yet left untouched by all who make law. This is a judicial deference to the legislator which does not become the common law.

Luther holds out other examples to the comparatist. His linguistic abilities, though not as elegant as Erasmus', show, nevertheless, what can be done if one can move freely from one language to another. It was, after all, the use of the Greek texts which helped Luther overcome the poverty of the latin word *penitentia* which, in English, can mean both penitence and penance.[32] It was the first meaning which was to be so crucial to Lutheranism.

In a world of international conventions and contractual transaction, where use is made of many official languages, the same could be true for the modern lawyer as well. And like Luther, he too, must not hesitate to amplify the language of the translation if this amplification helps reveal the true meaning of the original text. Take one famous example: Luther's rendering of Romans iii, 28. The Greek text is usually rendered in English as "Therefore we conclude that a man is justified by faith without the deeds of the law". Luther was not content with a literal translation. Faith alone—*sola fide*—was the key to his belief; so he added the word "*sola*". When attacked for this (admittedly bold) textual interference with the original, he defended himself by writing a text which deserves to be quoted in full:

> "This is my testament and my translation and if I have made any mistakes (though I never falsified intentionally) I will not let the papists judge me . . . As to Romans iii,28, if the word 'alone' is not found in the Latin or Greek texts, yet the passage has that meaning and must be rendered so in order to make it clear and strong in German."[33]

Could we not do the same these days when translating the word *sonstiges Recht* of paragraph 823, I BGB? Would it be wrong contextually to interject the word "absolute" between the two words of the verbatim rendering of the text? Examples of this kind abound in my *German Law of Torts* for anyone who bothers to compare the translations with the originals; but "insertions" of this type must be attempted with great caution.

Michel de Montaigne could not be more different from Luther. Reclusive for most of his life after his thirty-eighth birthday, refined, a firm believer in the value of friendships, a great proponent of persuasion through moderate and civilised conversation, a man of supreme tolerance. What else could he

---

[32] Christ's words in the Vulgate appear as "Penitentiam agite!" which could be taken as "Repent ye" or "Do penance". Most priests of the time understood the text in the latter form but Erasmus, in his *Paraphrases to the New Testament*, read the words as meaning "repent". This influenced Luther in the formulation of the text of the first of his famous *Wurttenberg Theses*.

[33] P. Smith, above n. 27, 267.

be, being the son of a Spanish-Jewish mother—Disraeli always referred to the Sephardic Jews as the "most aristocratic of races" whatever that may actually mean—a Catholic father (whose faith he shared) but with one brother and one sister who were fervent Protestants? In all things the opposite, to the Papal "bull"; a Harry Lawson, not a Kahn-Freund.

His *Essays* were written during periodic withdrawals from worldly affairs[34]—a lesson here for us all namely, that we no longer devote enough time to reflection, consumed as we are by teaching (which is what we are paid to do), research (which is what we should be encouraged to do more), and shifting paper work for constant and rather useless evaluations, which the decade of the 1980s bequeathed to academe with such devastating long-term effects (and here speaks someone who was once a fervent admirer of the brave new world). I suspect Professor Rudden's elegant contribution to European scholarship may well come to be seen in a similar light.

Montaigne's essay on friendship is not only a moving piece; it has a symbolic significance for the comparatist.[35] For this is, par excellence, the branch of the law where progress is made through contacts, partnerships, and the discovery of kindred spirits in foreign lands (though, admittedly, Montaigne's essay did not approach his topic from this angle).[36] To put it differently, the *rapprochement* between legal systems cannot be achieved in the ivory tower. One must travel abroad, work abroad, talk to colleagues from abroad, in an attempt to understand whether the foreign law one finds in the books is really as different from one's own when it comes to being applied in practice.[37] I have devoted most of my work to showing how the study of foreign law through cases diminishes apparent differences; and if I had more time, and could actually put into practice what I am advocating here, I would look at the law in action and show that the differences which separate us are smaller than they seem; and a recent article by Professor John Bell has done the same in another area of the law.

Bell's work confirms the validity of the above advice.[38] For he apparently

---

[34] Mainly between 1571 and 1588. Montaigne died in 1592 at the age of fifty-nine.

[35] And the lawyer, in general, since (following Aristotle, *The Nichomachean Ethics*, VIII.1.4) he states that "good legislators have given more thought to friendship than to justice": *De l' Amitié*, Ch. 28, book One of *Essays*.(English translation by George Ives, pp. 245–7 of the Hermitage edition (1925) with an introduction by André Gide.)

[36] The point is made in a somewhat different form by Tony Weir in his elegant piece "Friendships in the Law" published in (1988) 4 *The Tulane Civil Law Forum* 61–93. But, apart from one exception (Holmes-Laski), Weir writes about lawyers who came from the same country and were friends, rather than friendships that cut across national borders. Rabel and Llewellyn, Holmes and Pollock, Holmes and Laski, Gierke and Maitland, Hamson, René Cassin and René David, Schlesinger and Lorenz—those are the friendships that lead to the cross-fertilisation of ideas and much more besides.

[37] For an interesting illustration see Markesinis, *The German Law of Torts*, 3rd edn. (Oxford, Clarendon Press, 1994), 917–20.

[38] "English Law and French Law—Not So Different?", (1995) 48 *Current Legal Problems* 63 *et seq.*, esp.86 *et seq.* Recently, Professor Treitel told the author that his treatise on the law of frustration "could not have been written in the Bodleian".

spent over six months sitting in deliberations of the Conseil d'Etat, reading the files, and listening to many hours of argument. His conclusions coincide with those of a member of the Cour de cassation who recently gave us his own remarkable account of what happens behind the scenes in France's highest civil court.[39] Both of these jurists agree that all the types of argument found in the common law are also present in the French setting: "formalist grammar, legal adaptation, equity, institutional competence, and personification of the author". Arguments from precedent, consequentialist and policy arguments are also commonly utilised at these private encounters with the result that Professor Bell concludes "that supposed differences in the *structure* of legal reasoning . . . turn in reality into differences in *presentation* of legal argumentation by judges in the way the legal sources are set out in academic texts".[40] These are important and useful observations even though it can be argued that Professor Bell may still be under-estimating the importance that a different "appearance" or "presentation" may have on the law. For a different "appearance" or "surface" can affect the information imparted to students learning law through the study of cases. It also means that the real reasons for a decision remain concealed to subsequent generations of judges and, more importantly, practitioners who are thus forced to present their case in a more legalistic manner and without the opportunity to address the real (but unexpressed) concerns of the judge. Yet, notwithstanding this reservation about part of Professor Bell's conclusions, there is no denying that his research has opened new vistas in the understanding of foreign law; and this became possible only because he was able and willing to spend some time working in the foreign environment and not merely studying it from books. Work of this kind must thus continue; and it must be combined with the study of law in action. Our Socio-Legal Studies Centre can, I think, help promote such understanding even further.

This knowledge and understanding also requires calm, open-minded, tolerant social intercourse with the foreign lawyer. Montaigne's essay "On the Art of Conversation" must be one of the most elegant pieces written on the subject (Pascal certainly thought so); and its lessons could, if properly digested, help broaden the minds of all younger lawyers whether they are of the comparative kind or not. And Montaigne does all this eloquently with words though he, himself, asserts[41] that words "must serve and follow". Here is a beautiful extract from the famous text.

"Je veux que les choses surmontent, et qu'elles remplissent de façon l'imagination de celui qui écoute, qu'il n'ait aucune souvenance des mots."

---

[39] Michel Lasser, "Judicial (Self) Portraits: Judicial Discourse in the French Legal System", (1995) 104 *Yale L.J.* 1325 *et seq*.
[40] Bell, above n. 38, 87–9.
[41] In the essay entitled *De l'institution des enfants*, Ch 26 of Book One of the *Essays*.

And he concludes:

"Le parler que j'aime, c'est un parler simple et naif, tel sur le papier qu'à la bouche; un parler succulent et nerveux, court et serré, non tant délicat et peigné comme véhément et brusque."

Not bad advice for writing an essay or, come to that, a legal opinion or a judicial decision.

On reflection there is one thing that all of the above personages had in common and which is found in an even more pronounced form in my other idol: Aristotle.

Aristotle must be many people's choice. For teachers he is the luckiest of them all, for he could claim Alexander the Great as his pupil. To the jurisprude, he is the author of the *Nichomachean Ethics*; to the political scientist, the author of *Politics*. Comparatists could claim him as the father of their subject for his work on the Constitution of Athens and on other ancient Greek city states, though alas this has been lost to posterity.[42] And, like many of the contemporary breed of comparatists, he suffered the threat of state prosecution (by the Athenians of the fourth century) as well as unjust treatment by his own teacher Plato who refused to appoint him as his successor to the Academy, choosing his own nephew instead.[43] Apparently Aristotle, too, wrote a book on "Friendship"; though it has been disputed whether it was a separate treatise or formed part (book VIII) of the *Nichomachean Ethics*.[44] But here I have included him for his polymathy. For Aristotle tried, successfully within the limitations of his time, to match depth of knowledge with breadth.[45] The comparatist must take stock of his example; and learn at least two lessons bearing in mind that he is very unlikely to be an Aristotle!

First is the need to keep our curriculum wide and our education broad.[46] The pursuit of excellence these days clashes with market forces which seem to dictate quick and cheap results. We must buck the market and stick to the tradition that made this the finest law faculty in the land. At the same time, we must take note of what the real world is telling us: that what the student of tomorrow needs is skills, ability to think and to apply his knowledge to new areas, and more languages. I have always advocated this last point most strongly; and even felt that it might not be a bad thing to make some language credits an essential part of the modern law degree. But only one of my

---

[42] Though Plato's *Laws* may be a good rival.

[43] Arguably, because of Aristotle's "marked lack of homosexuality". Thus, G.E.M. Anscombe and P.T. Geach, *Three Philosophers* (Oxford, B. Blackwell, 1961), Introduction.

[44] In that sense see Sir Alexander Grant's, *The Ethics of Aristotle*, 2nd edn. (London, Longmans, Green, 1866) vol II, 249. Modern scholarship, however, has its doubts.

[45] Diogenes Laertius *Lives of Eminent Philosophers*, vol I, V, 22 (trans. by R.D. Hicks) (London, W. Heinemann Ltd., 1925), 464–74 gives a full list of the works he (apparently) wrote.

[46] For an excellent collection of essays on this point see *The Frontiers of Liability*, a collection of essays edited by Professor Peter Birks (Butterworths, 1994).

colleagues—Professor Roy Goode—has, so far, shared strongly the same belief; but then he has always seen ahead of his time.[47]

That, then, is the first lesson from Aristotle: rounded knowledge. In later life I was intrigued to read that this was, essentially, the message of Sir Frederick Pollock in a public lecture he delivered in this University on 22 May 1886, entitled "Oxford Law Studies". For he there urged his law students to read Homer, Virgil, Dante, Rabelais and Goethe in the original![48] But it is a sign of how the culture of our times has been impoverished that this suggestion can no longer be credibly made even in a place of learning such as this. To put it differently: it would be comforting to think that this tradition of polymathy has not come to an end with the retirement of colleagues like Professor Honoré or Professor Treitel (who must also be included in this University's list of eminent comparatists). Comforting but not, I think, correct.

The second lesson is an indirect one and only partially contradicts the first. Not every one can even aspire to such breadth of achievements. Beyond a certain point, narrowing one's focus is essential in order to sharpen it. Comparative law does not exist; but the comparative method is best taught if one tries to employ it within manageable parameters which are fixed by the scholar's own interests and predilections. I have tried my best with torts; Professor Kevin Gray (in this country) and Professor Mary Ann Glendon (in the United States) have done it in family law;[49] other colleagues are now following in labour law, criminal law and procedure.[50] It would be good fortune, indeed, if the new Oxford Centre which has been entrusted to my care could create the conditions that would enable other members of the law faculty to employ the method in their own fields and reap the rich harvests.

So finally to Janus—an essentially Italic or, more precisely, Roman God (for he appears in no other mythology). We possess no statue or bust of him; but it is his bi-frontal depiction, on some (but not all) coins, which has left us with his enduring image. He ranked second only to Jupiter; and as the God

---

[47] My suggestion, however, is not novel. In 1854 the Faculty of Advocates in Edinburgh required that prospective entrants should be subject to a compulsory examination of two modern languages "one of them being German". See Lord Rodger of Earlsferry "Scottish Advocates in the Nineteenth Century; The German Connection" (1994) 110 *LQR* 563, 571.

[48] *Oxford Lectures and Other Discourses* (London, Macmillan and Co., 1890), 108.

[49] See, for instance, Gray's *Re-allocation of Property on Divorce* (Abingdon, Professional Books, 1977). Glendon's work is, in this respect, even more prolific. Thus, see *The New Family and the New Property* (Harvard University Press, 1981); *Abortion and Divorce in Western Law. American Failures, European Challenges* (Harvard University Press, 1987).

[50] Such as Professor John Spencer ("French and English Criminal Procedure: A Brief Comparison" in B.S. Markesinis (ed.), *The Gradual Convergence: Foreign Ideas, Foreign Influences and English Law on the Eve of the 21st century* (Oxford, Clarendon Press, 1994) pp.33–45; see, also, "Court Experts and Expert Witnesses: Have we a Lesson to Learn from the French?" (1993) *Current Legal Problems*, 213–36, and Dr Roderick Munday ("Jury Trial, Continental Style" (1993) 13 *Legal Studies* 204) of the University of Cambridge. For labour law, the works of Professor Hepple, Dr. Mark Freedland and Mr Paul Davies provide excellent illustrations but this is no place to be giving bibliographical lists.

of departure and return he was, by extension, the God of all means of communication. He was also the God of all beginnings and ends and thus, also,
considered as the promoter of all initiatives. One of his symbols was the key:
it opened all doors and, metaphorically speaking, the door to all knowledge.
A kind of male Pandora or an Eve, but without sin and without punishment.
With such attributes, he is bound to be of interest to the lawyer; the comparative lawyer in particular.[51]

It is the double vision, to which I have already referred however, that
intrigues me most; and looking in two directions is not enough. The comparative lawyer must also have a different, double look: backwards and forwards.
To put it in another way: legal history in my view goes hand in hand with
comparative law. For the past often explains what may otherwise be obscure
in the present.

Take, for instance, the legal rule which, until recently, was part of English
tort law and which required that half of the amount of social security contributions received by a victim of a tort be deducted from his tort award. Why
half? No tort text book did other than mention the rule; but Simon Deakin
and I felt that in the book which we have co-authored[52] some mention had to
be made of the reason. If nothing else this showed that, in its inception at
least, the rule was not as strange as it now seems to be.

Legal history, of course, is even more important to comparative law since
often it explains why different systems have gone down different routes while
solving a particular problem. Comparative lawyers thus do not feel threatened
by legal historians as some Romanists feel endangered[53] by the inevitable
growth of comparative studies but, on the contrary, welcome the combination
of talents and disciplines. For many of the "peculiarities" of, say, the German
Civil Code can easily be explained to a common lawyer by having recourse
to history; and a combined historical and comparative approach may even
come to convince the German lawyer, himself, that the origin of some of his
rules may no longer be a good enough reason for retaining them. The fragmented way the German Code deals with the notion of breach of contract or,
more accurately for them, "irregularities of performance", which it inherited
largely from the writings of Mommsen,[54] offers such an example; and current
proposals to alter the status quo, by introducing a unitary notion of breach
(*Pflichtverletzung*) in a way that would be more recognisable to a common

---

[51] *New Larousse Encyclopedia of Mythology* (with an Introduction by Robert Graves)
(London, New York, Sydney and Toronto, Hamlyn, 1959), under "Roman Mythology". The reliable information we possess about the God, his name, his origin and his cult is scanty and contradictory. See L. A. MacKay "Janus" in *University of California Publications in Classical
Philology*, vol. XV, no 4 (University of California Press, 1961), 157–82.

[52] *Tort Law*, 3rd edn. (1994), 698.

[53] See, for instance, the comments of Lord Rodger of Earlsferry in his John Maurice Kelly
Memorial Lecture, "Savigny in the Strand" (Dublin, 1995), 23–4.

[54] "Die Unmöglichkeit der Leistung in ihrem Einfluss auf obligatorische Verhältnisse', I
Beiträge zum Obligationenrecht" (Braunschweig, G.U. Schwetschke und Sohn (M.Bruhn), 1853).

lawyer, illustrate the point I am making.[55] The Roman tendency to think in terms of unilateral obligations and not bilateral contracts is also the ultimate cause of the late appearance of "recission" into the German scheme of things as well as a protracted debate over the issue of quantification of damages in cases of "breach".[56]

Yet I would go further and argue knowledge of political and social history is often necessary for the teaching of foreign law. The German law of privacy or informed consent cannot be fully understood without some understanding of the excesses of the Nazi era. Neither can the ingenious introduction of the strict liability rules in France be fully understood if the social effects of the growing industrialisation of that country, coupled with the legislative paralysis that prevailed in France in the 1880s, are not fully explained to the reader. On the contrary, Emile Zola's *Germinal* or Thomas Hardy's *Tess of the Durbervilles* may give some idea of the social conditions which prevailed at the time which made life for the ordinary workers unbearable and nourished the growth of the socialist movement. The genius of Bismarck also becomes evident in the passing of the first worker-protection laws in Europe in the early 1980s, even if his motives were cynical; and the narrow-mindedness and arrogance of the young Kaiser, who dismissed him during the first year of his reign, is patently obvious in the anti-socialist laws he tried to pass a decade later. History clarifies the legal rules; and in my twenty-five-year teaching experience, it certainly has convinced me that it makes the teaching of the law more fun.[57]

The knowledge of the past can be used to explain the present; it can also help inspire its improvement. In his Butterworth lecture[58] Professor Birks showed us how the punitive element in the Roman law of delict could profitably be used to smooth away some of the doctrinal anomalies which the

---

[55] See *Abschlussbericht der Kommission zur Überarbeitung des Schuldrechts* (ed. Bundesminister der Justiz, 1992, Bundesanzeiger). It is no coincidence, of course, that the Committee that made these proposals contained eminent legal historians (such as Professor Medicus) *and* comparatists (such as Professors Kötz and Schlechtriem). For a recent discussion of these proposals see W. Rolland, *Vorschläge für ein neues Schuldrecht in Deutschland* (Centro di Studi e ricerche di diritto comparato e straniero, University of Rome, 1990). W. Ernst, "Kernfragen der Schuldrechtsreform" 1994 *JZ* 801; D. Medicus, "Vorschläge zur Überarbeitung des Schuldrechts: Das allgemeine Recht der Leistungsstörungen" 1992 *NJW* 2384; J. Schapp, "Probleme der Reform des Leistungsstörungsrechts" 1993 *JZ* 637 and, most recently, H. Kötz, "Referat" in *Verhandlungen des 60. Deutschen Juristentages* (Beck Verlag, 1994) K 9. Another example of an unfortunate legacy of history can be found in § 831 BGB, to a large extent the product of misapprehension of Roman texts.

[56] For further details see H. G. Leser, *Der Rücktritt vom Vertrag. Abwicklungsverhältnis und Gestaltungsbefugnisse bei Leistungsstörungen* (Tübingen, J.C.B. Mohr (Paul Siebeck), 1975), 10 *et seq.*, 122 *et seq.*

[57] The famous "Mephisto" decision of the German Constitutional Court (BVerfGE 30,173, reproduced in English with historical notes in Markesinis *The German Law of Torts*, 3rd edn. (1994) 358–70) really comes to life when its legal peculiarities are set against the political and cultural life of Germany during the Nazi era and the years that followed the collapse of the dreadful regime.

[58] "Civil Wrongs: A New World". *Butterworth Lectures 1990–1* (1992).

English law of obligations still experiences as a result of the formulary system of its past. Though, personally, I feel uncomfortable with punitive damages in tort actions,[59] I think Professor Birks' example shows very clearly how the past can be put to the service of modern lawyers.

Birks is, of course, not advocating a return to the past but skilfully seeking inspiration from it. The lawyer like the politician, may admire the past; but he must also know that he cannot revive it. The Byzantine Emperor Julian, known as the Apostate, was warned about this in one of the most elegant and, as it turned out, the last of the Delphic prophecies.[60] He did not heed it. Those who are worried by the amplitude of modern tort law must also take heed. "Resignation rather than litigation" is no longer an acceptable solution to modern accidents and modern suffering—especially as the Welfare State seems to be rolling back its frontiers; nor, it seems to me, is it an answer to the excess of modern tort law. A mixed bag of reforms may provide a better solution; but this is not the place to discuss this complex issue.

Seeing ahead is a gift; seeing too much ahead, bears no fruits but, on the contrary, courts danger. History offers support for this proposition, as well. Take Machiavelli for instance. He was ignored and under-used by his contemporaries, guilty of being too much ahead of his time. Nowadays, even educated people know him only for his famous book—*Il Principe;* and have hardly heard of his other great work—*Discorsi sopra la prima Deca di Tito Livio*—which puts him along side Guicciardini as one of Italy's earliest and most astute historians, or his comedy—*Mandragora*—which one of the greatest scholars[61] of our times described as "the comedy of a society of which the 'Prince' is the tragedy".

In law, too, we find many similar examples. Windscheid felt strongly that some theory was needed when altered circumstances affected contractual performance; but his views, modified and improved (by, among others, his son-in-law Oertmann) had to wait for fifty years before changed socio-economic circumstances brought them back to the fore.[62] No lesser a scholar than Sir Percy Winfield wrote in 1952 a small book about *Quasi Contract*; but it marked the cadence of a distinguished career. It was brief; it took no notice

---

[59] See my *Tort Law* (with Simon Deakin) 3rd edn. (Oxford, Clarendon Press, 1994), 687–61.

[60] εἴπατε τῷ βασιλῆϊ. χαμαὶ πέσε δαίδαλος αὐλά.

ούκέτι Φοῖβος ἔχει καλύβαν, οὐ μάντιδα δάφνην.

οὐ παγὰν λαλέουσαν, ἀπέσβετο καὶ λάλον ὕδωρ.

"Tell the King, the fairwrought hall has fallen to the ground. No longer has Phoebus a hut, nor a prophetic laurel, nor a spring that speaks. The water of speech even is quenched" H.W. Parke and D.E.W. Wormell, *The Delphic Oracle* (Basil Blackwell, Oxford, 1956) vol. I, 290; vol.II, 194.

[61] Professor Pasquale Villari, *The Life and Times of Nicolo Machiavelli*, vol II (London, T. Fisher Unwin, 1891), 372.

[62] For a brief but very readable summary in English see Werner Lorenz, "Contract Modification as a Result of Change of Circumstances" in Jack Beatson and Daniel Friedmann (eds.), *Good Faith and Fault in Contract Law* (Oxford, Clarendon Press, 1995), 357, esp. 361 *et seq.*

of transatlantic writings; it drew its inspiration mainly from English history; it was even uneasy with its title. Fourteen more years were to pass before younger authors, willing to be inspired by what was happening in the United States, and with fresh ideas, were able to put the subject on the map. So ripe was the time for Goff and Jones, that thirty years later not only has their *magnum opus* reached its fourth edition; it has also spawned new books and a growing number of articles. The lawyer, like the politician, must get his timing right; and this is particularly true of the comparatist.

The Oxford comparatists possessed this sense of timing. Though it is rarely remembered, Harry Lawson was one of the first to start in the late 1950s the whole debate about the Ombudsman.[63] Like Professor David Mitrany, who almost contemporaneously was making a similar appeal,[64] Lawson drew his inspiration from Sweden; but being the true comparatist that he was, he also recommended a series of modifications which would ensure that the transplanted institution was not rejected by its new environment. As is well known, the Parliamentary Commissioner Act came into force precisely ten years later.

In the 1970s Professor Nicholas wrote a long piece about the case law of the Conseil Constitutionnel in the area of human rights.[65] It was a learned piece; but it also showed confidence in the growing assertiveness of the young court that many, even in France, might have hesitated to commit to writing. Time proved Nicholas right; and the Conseil Constituionnel has come of age. We cannot all claim such prophetic powers; but, like T.S. Eliot, we must remember that time past and time present makes time future.[66] And Janus must have got the balance about right, for he was never ungratefully cast aside nor ignored, but worshipped for approximately nine centuries![67] Professor Nicholas' work has thus proved what a gift it is to be able to look both sideways (i.e. towards the common law and the civil law) and backwards and forwards (into the past and into the future).

Breadth of knowledge, wider culture, adaptability, perseverance if not determination (often fostered by great personal suffering), an ability to look at the law—in Roscoe Pound's words "from without" as well as "from within"[68]— all great comparatists had these attributes to a lesser or greater extent. That is true of those who worked in England as well as of those who operated in

---

[63] "An Inspector-General of Administration", (1957) *Public Law* (Summer edn.).

[64] In two articles entitled "Protecting the Citizen" published in the *Manchester Guardian* of 6 and 7 August 1957.

[65] "Fundamental Rights and Judicial Review in France" (1978) *Public Law*, 82,155.

[66] "Time present and time past
Are both perhaps present in time future
And time future contained in time past"
Four Quartets; Burnt Norton

[67] His cult was, apparently, established by Romulus or Numa; and his temple in the Forum was still in existence during the reigns of Commodus, Gordius II and, possibly, during the 4th century.

[68] *The Spirit of the Common Law* (Boston, Marshall Jones Co., 1921), 212.

the United States; and it is also true of the autochthonous giants like Harry Lawson and Jack Dawson. But are we likely to find such features in the next generation? Natural optimism apart, I must admit, that prima facie the signs are not propitious.

Culture, tolerance, and universalism certainly seem to be, if not in decline, under serious threat. If not the market, then certainly the government, seems to have been pressing for larger numbers of students; but it remains unprepared to cover the cost of a proper education. The market, we are told, also seems to demand a shorter legal education, leading increasingly to more and more people with only the rudiments of a legal training. We have grown accustomed these days to speaking of the core; but, who wishes to be left with the core and not enjoy the whole apple as well if one may stay with this metaphor for a moment? I am firmly in Professor Birks' camp on this point;[69] and if he burns in hell for his ideas I shall be there with him (though, happily I note, there is also some precedent to suggest that Regius Professors in this University can also end up being beatified).[70] I take this view not merely because of my belief in a liberal education, but also because, in my view, these modern trends will, in the long run, leave our young lawyers at a disadvantage *vis-à-vis* some of their best European counterparts. Roman law, Jurisprudence, comparative law, are thus tottering on the brink—the first perhaps more so than the others. If they survive it is, more often than not, because somehow some law schools have managed to make them compulsory subjects and/or because they happen to have among their staff one of the dwindling number of talented specialists.[71] Only in legal history, but then again mainly in Germany, do we see an interesting revival brought about by the "Europeanisation" of the subject which was inspired during the post-War period by the great figures of Paul Koschaker,[72] Franz Wieacker,[73] and Helmut Coing.[74]

Personally, I regret just as much the lack of interest in history in general as well as the neglect of modern languages; and yet even the modernisers of the law curriculum acknowledge their importance since they are often heard to say that a linguist turned lawyer often makes for a better practitioner. Why

[69] "Adjudication and Interpretation in the Common Law: a Century of Change" (1994) 14 *Legal Studies*, 156 *et seq*. See, also, Professor Dawn Oliver's elegant essay "Teaching and Learning Law: The Pressures on the Liberal Law Degree" in P. Birks (ed.), *Reviewing Legal Education* (Oxford, 1994), 77 *et seq*.

[70] This happened to John Storey, the first holder of the Regius Chair who was sent to the gallows in 1571 for treason but was beatified by Pope Leo XIII in 1886.

[71] Professors Reinhard Zimmermann and Peter Birks offer shining examples of what can be achieved; but the question as to whether they can reverse the tide cannot be ignored.

[72] *Europa und das römische Recht* (C. H. Beck, München, Berlin, 1st edn. 1947, 4th edn. 1966).

[73] *Privatrechtsgeschichte der Neuzeit*, 2nd edn., (1st edn 1952, Göttingen, Vandenhoeck and Ruprecht, 1967), now available in an English translation by Tony Weir (Oxford, Clarendon Press, 1995).

[74] *Europäisches Privatrecht*, 2 vols (München, C. H. Beck, 1985/89). See, also, by the same author "Das Recht als Element der europäischen Kultur", (1984) *HZ* 238, 1 and "Europäisierung der Rechtswissenschaft", 1990 *NJW* 937.

cannot we aim to broaden the range of equipment that we give to our students rather than trying to let them loose in the world after one and a half or two or at maximum three years of University education? I find Pollock's plea for a legal education which combines the discipline of analyzing legal texts with the study of humanities and liberal arts as inspiring now as I suspect his audience did one hundred and ten years ago; and lest my approach be thought romantically out of touch with modern realities and "unbusinesslike", let me remind them of the depth and breadth of the training that a good French or German law student will receive after a period of University training that can be almost twice as long as ours. To be sure, ours may be cheaper; but then poor is the state that sees education in terms of price rather than value and protests such a dislike for the Aristotelian concept of "aristocracy".

The narrowing of the curriculum has, certainly in the post- War years, been combined with reduced academic travel.[75] Recruitment to academic posts is still done at the end of a successful year doing the BCL or some comparable degree. Experience at the Bar or as a solicitor is not demanded; and it is found comparatively rarely. Active research for, say, the Ph.D degree is, in this country, still the exception; and if it has started before recruitment, it will be delayed if not killed off by the unconscionable teaching load that we place on the shoulders of our younger and under-paid colleagues. Travel, work experience, and research in a foreign University are thus a positive rarity. Yet, the further I go back and look at some of our great legal luminaries, the more I am struck by the extent of their travels and the breadth of their reading.

One does not have to go as far back as the era of Alberico Gentili—an Italian welcomed by Oxford and, indeed, the Sovereign with open arms—to be struck by the shining cosmopolitanism of that generation of dons; just look at the writings of jurists of the turn of the century—Lord Macmillan, Pollock, Dicey, Anson, Bryce, Lawson, Cardozo, Llewellyn, Oliver Wendell Holmes, Brandeis—and note how effortlessly they weave into their texts foreign authors and not only legal ones at that! Lord Rodger's learned piece, referred to above,[76] gives more examples which cover the Scottish scene.

I recently had occasion to look at a list of books read by Mr. Justice Holmes. A photocopy is to be found in the Tarlton Law Library of the University of Texas.[77] He kept it copiously to the end of his life. It mentions the books he read every year, sometimes accompanied by notes on their contents. In some cases, he tells us which of them he read aloud to himself; and towards the end of his life, he even tells us which ones he left unfinished!

---

[75] How much this enriched the Scottish legal education can be seen from Lord Rodger's article entitled "Scottish Advocates in the Nineteenth Century: The German Connection", (1994) 110 *LQR* 563.

[76] See the previous note.

[77] On "loan of indefinite duration" to its Director Professor Roy Mersky who generously allowed me to consult it. The original forms part of the Holmes collection held at the Harvard Law School Library. A second copy of this note book—known as "the black book"—can be found in the library of the United States Supreme Court.

Browsing at this list one is left speechless by its breadth. The authors range from Dante to Mistral (hardly known these days outside France); Marx to Bergson; Aristotle to Benjamin Constant (read both as a constitutional theorist and as a novelist); Voltaire to Auguste Renan and, of course, Herbert Spencer who, some years later appeared with such effect in the *Lochner*[78] decision. Clearly, he read their works in the original; and he combined this extra-legal reading with a keen interest in the debates of the Pandektists in the Germany of his time.[79] Roman law and legal history are particularly well represented in his list;[80] and a reference in 1883 to Ludwig von Bar's *Die Lehre vom Causalzusamenhange*, which was published in Leipzig in 1871, shows how remarkably up to date he was with the European legal literature of his times. But that, of course, was Holmes; and today's emphasis on the "core" will not, as a rule at least, produce such jurists!

The decline of these two factors becomes more frightening when seen against the recent trend, especially in this country, towards a popular kind of nationalism. I do not know if it is more dangerous when it appears in the pages of the popular press—which to my dying days I shall maintain is one of the most cynically destructive forces of this century—than when it comes from intelligent politicians of the new right. Either way, it strengthens the individual at the expense of the universal; it narrows rather than broadens the mind; it keeps stereotypical and divisive prejudices alive. The interest to learn from others cannot flourish in such a climate; and tolerance for, let alone interest in, different ideas is also weakened, even if lip service is often paid to the virtues of an open mind. And tolerance is further strained these days as new waves of militant immigrants understandably fuel national fears; but that takes me far beyond my subject so I shall stop!

Yet, perversely perhaps, I remain optimistic; and in the European idea and ideal I see—I wish to see—a source of optimism. Let me elaborate somewhat this thought.

[78] *Lochner v. New York* 198 U.S. 45,75, described by Judge Posner as "the greatest judicial opinion of the last hundred years": *Law and Literature. A Misunderstood Relation* (1988), 285.

[79] For instance, he has copious notes on C.G. Bruns' *Das Recht des Besitzes im Mittelalter und in der Gegenwart* (Tübingen, Laupp, 1848); Carl Friedrich von Savigny, *Das Recht des Besitzes* (Wien, Carl Gerold Sohn, 1803, 7th edn. 1865, though he is mainly using the English tranlation by Sir Erskine Perry) and sections of his *Traité de droit Romain* (which were read in 1886); Rudolf von Jhering's *Geist des römischen Rechts auf den verschiedenen Stufen seiner Entwicklung* (1875); an article by Puchta on "Besitz", (published in Weiske's *Rechtslexikon*, vol 2, Leipzig, 1844) and B. Windscheid *Lehrbuch des Pandektenrechts* (Franfurt am Main, Literarische Anstalt Rutten und Roening, 1875) etc. But as Holmes' most recent biographer is at pains to show—*Justice Oliver Wendell Holmes: Law and the Inner Self* (New York, Oxford University Press, 1993), 134 *et seq.*—the learned Justice was critical of the German tendency to subordinate all too often the Roman texts to the rigours of the logic of the *Pandektenwissenschaft*.

[80] In addition to the German works on Roman law cited above one also finds extensive notes on Michelet's *Origines du droit Français*, Sohm's *La procedure de la Lex Salica*, and Laferrière's *Essai sur l'histoire du droit Francais*. The list given here is by no means exhaustive of the judge's reading.

The itinerant academic of the sixteenth and seventeenth centuries may have disappeared for good, but the institutional substitute is with us. Erasmus the man has gone; Erasmus the Community programme is here! I was once critical[81] of these programmes which aim to increase student mobility. I still have serious doubts about the depth of learning that can be acquired from the short type of visits that they facilitate; and I also dislike their bureaucratic structures which, along with other excesses, give "Europe" a bad name. Yet mobility has been achieved; and I have, myself, been surprised to find out how broadening an effect it has on the mind of students, especially those who come from less privileged Universities than ours and thus have even less of a chance to be exposed to different ideas and different cultures. This is the second year that Oxford students have spent some time in Leiden; and it is the fifth year for those students whom I helped move from the East end of London to the Netherlands. All of them, of course, missed the unique richness and individuality of the tutorial system; but all of them equally felt that they benefited from being exposed to different subjects, perhaps not available in their home institution, or being taught from a distinctly different angle. Above all they experienced—I have done so for years myself while teaching mixed audiences—that in the intellectual environment of the classroom, national and ethnic differences melt into the background; prejudices are suppressed or disappear; learning from each other is encouraged; life-long friendships are formed. These are beliefs forged by experience; and a teacher is just as much entitled to convey them to his pupils as he must try to transmit to them his knowledge of his subject. To paraphrase Montaigne: "I have shaped my subject and my subject has shaped me."[82] I, for one, admit it freely.

These transnational programmes the Centre for the Advanced Study of European and Comparative Law will try to encourage and improve further by trying to make the stay abroad longer and by increasing the level of preparedness of the students whom we shall send to foreign countries. This task will undoubtedly be helped by the presence of the foreign colleagues whom my Centre has as Deputy Directors and who are here thanks to the generosity of their respective governments. As I said, they will assist us in preparing our "export" students, each instructing them in their *own* language and their *own* system; and they will assist our own faculty to broaden its horizons by taking part in our regular lectures and seminars and giving us the perspective of their own system. I hope this Oxford innovation will find imitators in other Universities; and if it does, I am confident that support from abroad will also be forthcoming.

I find the logic behind this endeavour irresistible, for ever since modern, eminent scientists demonstrated the relativity of laws which their ancestors

---

[81] See my comments in my introductory chapter to the series of essays which I edited under the general title *The Gradual Convergence etc.* (1994).

[82] "Je n' ai pas plus fait mon livre que mon livre m'a fait". *De Démentir*, Ch. 18 of book II of the *Essays*.

regarded as absolute, all the rest of us have been forced to become less super-
cilious in the assertion of our dogmas. Even lawyers have not escaped this
trend as increased contact with Europe has made them feel less sure of their
creed and slowly, slowly but surely, open up to outside influences.[83] This is a
position which I find attractive; and I shall promote it like Erasmus and
defend it like Luther.

But what about the so-called market forces which, apparently, demand the
quick results and non-legal law degrees? Can they shatter my creed? I am confident that here, too, the position is changing, at least for the more ambitious
type of student who comes from the strongest law faculties and is going to
the leading law firms. The support my Centre has received from leading firms
of City solicitors, confirms this belief of mine. For the leading City firms are,
themselves, increasingly asked to provide "packages" for their international
clients who do not wish to know whether X or Y can be done in England or
in France but who ask for advice that cuts across borders. The firms I have
been talking to need the human product we intend to produce. They need
lawyers who can speak foreign languages; they need lawyers who know something about foreign law; and they need young lawyers with an ability to move
both physically and mentally from one country to another without moaning
about how things are better at home! I have great confidence in the emerging
partnership between leading City firms and the Oxford Law Faculty, for they
are both striving for the same goal, even if in matters of relative detail their
specific aims are different. The universal will thus once again triumph over
the particular, even if the way this is achieved takes a different form than it
did in the past. To put it differently, in the 1940s and 1950s, charismatic *émigrés* gave a boost to comparative studies at a time when there was still relatively little practical demand. As we approach the end of this millennium,
practical needs will take over from where the giants of the past left my subject. In the 1990s knowledge of foreign law is coming into its own as
Community law did in the decade of the 1980s.

So, am I being realistic or am I just a dreamer? I do not think I am the latter, if for no other reason than that I have no time to indulge in idle dreams.
For I am busy fund-raising; and mine must be one of the few chairs that was
expressly advertised as having as one of its aims fund-raising for the building
of the Oxford Centre and the Oxford Institute. And this is a novelty that cannot pass unnoticed. For here is another attribute that seems to have been
added to the endless list of desired qualities that teachers in my area of the
law must nowadays possess. Demanding though this may be, it is neither
illogical nor un-scholarly, since it is up to the specialists of foreign law to
spear-head the kind of contacts I have alluded to and which modern univer-

---

[83] I have paraphrased here Lord Macmillan's view from his "Two Ways of Thinking"
(reprinted in *Law and Other Things* (Cambridge University Press, 1938), 76, 101)—a true gem in
the literature of comparative law and the product of a man who had Janus's ability to see clearly
and impassionedly in two directions.

sites need. This will, of course, deny me the pleasures of living in "ornamental seclusion from the follies and fusses of the world",[84] which is another way of saying that I shall miss the splendours of College life! But it will at least offer the satisfaction of metaphorically-speaking putting me back into the world of medieval Italy where my ancestors excelled in business and trade; and taking me forward into the City of London where Clifford Chance has its headquarters and dispenses the kind of legal services modern businessmen require. The kind of partnership established in Oxford between academe and the legal profession must not fail. I shall do my best to see that it does not.

[84] Max Beerbohm, *Zuleika Dobson*, Ch. IX.

3

The Destructive and Constructive Role of the Comparative Lawyer

1. INTRODUCTORY REMARKS

It is, I am told, customary for a new Academician to address briefly this august body and today I do so with a sense of humility that is only exceeded by that of gratitude for an honour which is no less welcome for being undeserved.

It is a truism to assert that we live in transitional times when the security that accompanies established practices gives way to the challenges posed by an uncertain future. Law is not immune from such changes even though its rules can and often do survive the disappearance of the socio-economic conditions that first gave them birth. Comparative law, which is my chosen vocation, has also been affected by this phenomenon. For as I have repeatedly argued,[1] its conceptual apparatus, developed roughly at the turn of this century, has focused on a type of legal science that studied rules, classified idealised private bourgeois law, underplayed the significance of public law, and gave pride of place to case law in the Anglo-American legal systems, and to civil codes in the Romano-Germanic systems. The tools, classifications, and teaching techniques that came out of this movement have served their purpose. They are, however, increasingly proving inadequate for the analysis of modern legal problems. To paraphrase Maitland,[2] we have buried the representatives of that school of thought and we must not allow them to rule us from their graves. As my title suggests, today's comparative lawyer must first destroy some myths and then proceed to construct the new foundations of his subject.

---

[1] Most recently B. S. Markesinis, "Comparative Law, A Subject in Search of an Audience" (1990) 53 *Mod. L. Rev.* 1–21; see also Mary Ann Glendon, *Abortion and Divorce in Western Law, American Failures, European Challenges* (1987) Introduction (reviewed by Eike von Hippel, 53 [1989] *RabelsZ* 795–8).

[2] "The forms of action we have buried, but they still rule us from the grave"; F. W. Maitland, *The Forms of Action at Common Law, A Course of Lectures*, A. H. Chaytor/W. J. Whittaker (1936; repr. 1963) 2.

2. THE DESTRUCTION OF MYTHS

Having been educated on both sides of the Channel, I grew up with myths about the "other" system which were, sooner rather than later, destroyed as I lived and worked in different countries. Here are four of the most persistent; and others could be mentioned.

I. A codification *"can provide [an] accessible and complete formulation of the law"* and can *"enable the development of the law in a planned manner"*. Neither the French nor the German lawyer will recognise their systems in this statement, yet it came from Lord Scarman,[3] one of England's most respected judges, ironically when he was serving as Chairman of the Law Commission in the mid-1960s which was empowered to look at foreign law for inspiration.[4] For can one find the French law of delict in the five meagre articles of the Code Civil? Or is the French law of unjust enrichment to be found anywhere in that Code? Or did articles 1119 and 1165 provide the basis of a planned development of the French notion of "stipulation pour autrui"?[5] And is not the same true of the German Code which saw its section on contractual remedies reshaped before the printing ink had a chance to dry? Or saw a mundanely-phrased provision—§242 BGB—acquire a unique significance as it provided the springboard for unprecedented judicial activism? Or was the judicial creation of a general right of personality planned or even permitted by the draughtsmen of the German Code?

II. *Codal regimes are rigid and not adaptable*. That is what most English lawyers think. One example will suffice. Quite recently, no lesser a person than Lord Denning stated on the BBC World Service programme "that once a law is codified it is very difficult to change it . . .". Yet is this statement borne out by what I have already said? And if you wish for another example, the amelioration of the legal position of victims of traffic accidents in France will provide it. Examples such as these—and many more could be advanced both from Germany and France—not only disprove the English conviction that the law contained in Codes is immutable, but also give the lie to another widely-held view among common lawyers, namely that Continental judges are timid rather than bold, interpreters rather than creators, subservient to academic doctrine rather than its leaders. Look at what German judges did to their family law in the 1950s, or how they have been expanding their law of contract, for example in the area of liability for negligent certifications, and ask

---

[3] Scarman, "Codification and Judge-made Law, A Problem of Co-existence", Lecture delivered in the University of Birmingham in 1966, 19.

[4] Law Commissions Act 1965, s. 3(1)(f).

[5] Cf. the wise observation of F. H. Lawson: "The French courts have so *disturbed* the balance between articles 1119 and 1120 of the Code as to make the recognition of third party rights in contract normal instead of exceptional, as was assuredly the intention of the compilers"; Frederick H. Lawson, *A Common Lawyer Looks at the Civil Law, Five Lectures* (1953; repr. 1977) 56 (emphasis added) (The Thomas M. Cooley Lectures, Ser. 5).

yourself whether you can still describe them as timid, mechanically applying the law, and following the dictates of academics!

III.   *The common law's emphasis on case law techniques makes it admirably adaptable to new circumstances.* This is the reverse of the previous myth and one commonly held by Continental jurists who, in most cases, have a very vague idea of the enormous volume of our statutory law. Yet test the validity of this view against the modernisation of the law of tort in England (but not America)[6] during the last fifty years or so and it will soon be proved false. Thus, the survival of actions was allowed in 1934 after the Law Reform (Miscellaneous Provisions) Act was passed. Contribution among tortfeasors was made possible the next year with the Law Reform (Married Women and Tortfeasors) Act. Two years later, Crown Immunity was removed by the Crown Proceedings Act. Greater protection of various types of unlawful entrants on another person's property was only achieved after two legislative interventions in the form of the Occupiers' Liability Acts of 1957 and 1982. Users of highways are nowadays largely protected by the Highways (Miscellaneous Provisions) Act of 1961. Marital immunities were removed after the Law Reform (Husband and Wife) Act of 1962 came into force. A stricter form of liability for defective products was officially confirmed (with prompting by the European Community in the form of the Consumer Protection Act 1987). My list can be expanded further. Instead, however, I would like to draw your attention to the fact that this surrender of law reform to Parliament has also come about in even (relatively) lesser matters. In *Pirelli General Cable Works Ltd.* v. *Oscar Faber and Partners*[7] the House of Lords was unhappy with a certain aspect of the complicated law of limitation; but they refused to do anything themselves and, instead, prompted Parliament to intervene in the form of the Latent Damages Act 1986. In *Gammell* v. *Wilson*[8] the House of Lords was, again, unhappy about a technical rule concerning damages for "lost years" which were allowed to survive for the benefit of the estate; but the change had to come through statute—the Administration of Justice Act 1982. *The Aliakmon*[9] revealed weakness in the law concerning

---

[6] The reasons why American law in general, tort law in particular, have been largely modernised by the courts are complex. Among them, however, one would mention the paralysis of legislatures, as a result of pressures from competing lobbies, and the absence of an effective welfare state to take care of the basic needs of tort victims. In the face of the above, it is hardly surprising that elected (State) judges have found it easier to implement a popularly-inspired "program for reform". That this has resulted, in Professor Fleming's felicitous phrase, in a "programme without a budget" is, of course, another and very troublesome matter; see John G. Fleming, *The American Tort Process* (1988) 13.

[7] [1983] 2 AC 1.

[8] [1982] AC 27.

[9] *Leigh and Sillivan Ltd.* v. *The Aliakmon Shipping Co. Ltd.* [1986] 1 AC 875 considered in a comparative context by Hein Kötz, "The Doctrine of Privity of Contract in the Context of Contracts Protecting the Interests of Third Parties" (1990) 10 *Tel Aviv University Studies in Law* 195–212; B. S. Markesinis, "An Expanding Tort Law—The Price of a Rigid Contract Law" 103 (1987) *L. Q. Rev.* 354–97.

carriage of goods by sea. Legislation, again, has been proposed to correct this problem.

Yet Parliament does not always oblige and the law remains unchanged even though the courts have expressed their disapproval of it. In *Morgans* v. *Launchbury*[10] a sensible change was proposed in the context of vicarious liability; but the House of Lords felt that it should be left to the legislator to give effect to this and he has not done so. In the *Gordon Kaye*[11] litigation our Court of Appeal found our law of privacy defective, but again left it to Parliament to reform. Our law of privity has attracted repeated criticism by the House of Lords, but no change has been made since Parliament has not found this a pressing social problem crying out for reform.[12]

The most recent example of judicial reluctance to expand the law, especially in the context of consumer protection which the current House of Lords strongly believes should be left to Parliament, can be seen in the recent judgment of Lord Bridge in the *D. & F. Estates* case.[13] For there, after referring to the decision of the New Zealand Court of Appeal in *Mount Albert Borough Council* v. *Johnson*[14] where the Court held that a development company which had employed independent contractors to build a block of flats owed a duty of care towards one of the purchasers whose flat was damaged by subsidence, his Lordship went on to say:

> "As a matter of social policy this conclusion may be entirely admirable . . . As a matter of legal principle, however, I can discover no basis on which it is open to the court to embody this policy in the law without the assistance of the legislature and it is again, in my opinion, a dangerous course for the Common law to embark upon the adoption of novel policies which it sees as an instrument of social justice but to which, unlike the legislature, it is unable to set carefully defined limitations."[15]

Apart from the fact that the very last words of the statement itself are disproved by the carefully crafted rule laid down in *D. & F. Estates*, the proposition that our courts should abdicate to the legislator their creative role is hardly compatible with either past reality or foreign conception of what English courts can do.

---

[10] [1971] 2 QB 245, CA; reversed in [1973] AC 127.

[11] Discussed by B. S. Markesinis, "Subtle Ways of Legal Borrowing, Some Comparative Reflections on the Report of *the Calcutt* Committee 'On Privacy and Related Matters' ", in *FS Werner Lorenz* (Tübingen, 1991) 717–37.

[12] For a good discussion of the current law and its shortcomings see The Law Commission, Consultation Paper No. 121 "Privity of Contract: Contracts for the Benefit of Third Parties" (Her Majesty's Stationery Office, 1991).

[13] *D. & F. Estates Ltd. and others* v. *Church Commissioners for England and others* [1989] AC 177.

[14] [1979] 2 NZLR 234.

[15] *D. & F. Estates Ltd. and 0thers* v. *Church Commissioners for England and others* (above n. 13) 210.

IV.   One of my favourite myths is that *a foreign system has nothing to offer us*. In a rather schizophrenic way this can often become the complete reverse: *the foreign solution can protect us against all ills*. The first part of this myth is so obvious in the modern context of exaggerated declarations of sovereignty and chauvinistic introvertedness that it needs no illustration. But let me give an example of the reverse side of the myth.

In England we have, in recent times, experienced some spectacular examples of miscarriages of criminal justice. Personally, I feel that the mistakes of the system have been allowed to cloud its strengths. Nevertheless, if our media are anything to go by, none of those evils would have arisen if we had introduced in our system the institution of "juge d'instruction". Thus, in its leading article of 8 March 1991, *The Times* claimed that "the accusatorial system, which ought in theory to protect the innocent, can become a steam-roller which crushes him" and then, for good measure, concluded that "an inquisitorial system where the court pursues its own inquiry could be better than our present system of criminal justice".

What these admirers of the French institution have never told their audiences is that the institution of "juge d'instruction", copied from the French by the Germans, was abolished by them in 1974; that the institution disappeared from the Italian scene when the new Code of Criminal Procedure came into force; and that twice since the last War it was seriously attacked in its own country. Nor has the wider public been told that in 92 per cent of French criminal cases no "instruction" takes place; that in the 8 per cent of cases where it does, the intervention of the judge adds, on average, 9 months to the delay of the criminal process (compared to the one month it took when it was first instituted in 1808 by the Code d'instruction criminelle); and that it is conducted by young, often very inexperienced judges, fresh out of the École nationale de la magistrature. Where would we find such judges to do this work for us if we were to follow the French example?

Now, all this is not to say that our system is perfect;[16] that we should not take the prosecution out of the hands of the police; that we do not have to devise (as we have recently done) better methods to safeguard the accused against false or uncorroborated confessions; or, indeed, that we do not need to alter our rose-tinted image of our police. But the defects in our system will not disappear by the importation of foreign institutions, lock, stock and barrel, especially if our understanding of how they really work in their own habitat is so inadequate.[17] There is, therefore, plenty of room here for proper, empirical, comparative study which I am happy to say is slowly gaining acceptance in England.

---

[16] For thoughtful criticism see Lord Justice Bingham's account in "The English Criminal Trial, The Credits and the Debits", Lecture delivered at the Leiden Institute of Anglo-American Law (Leiden University, 1992).

[17] For a useful collection of essays see Mireille Delmoas-Marty (ed.), *Procès pénal et droits de l'homme*, (1992).

3. CONSTRUCTING BRIDGES BETWEEN SYSTEMS AND LAWYERS

This list of myths that have to be destroyed is large but we must now allow it to dominate this paper. Destruction is never good for its own sake. In my opinion, it is justifiable only when something better can be put in the place of what is being demolished. Broadly speaking, I would bring my constructive suggestions under three headings: making foreign law more intelligible to our own lawyers; making foreign law more digestible to our own lawyers; and, finally, making foreign lawyers more available to our own lawyers. Let me look at these points in turn.

I. *Making foreign law more intelligible to our own lawyers.* By this I mean that we must try to overcome obstacles of terminology and classification in order to show that foreign law is not very different from ours but only appears to be so. In law familiarity often breeds interest, not contempt.

Many years ago, as a beginner in the teaching profession, I recall trying to explain the tort of "nuisance" to some French lawyers who were barely younger than myself. They and I were stuck! We could not even find our subject in the tort books. Even the term was untranslatable, though its connection with "*nuire*" and "*noceo*" is, once you are told of this, as obvious as it is direct. Then I read Professor Lawson's marvellous *Cooley Lectures* and the mist started to lift.[18] History could explain everything; and in my opinion, history and comparative law often go together. For as the Roman forms of action were progressively stripped of the procedural content, they came to be classified in those parts of the substantive law with which they had the greatest affinity. Not surprisingly, therefore, the *rei vindicatio*, the *actio negatoria* and the *actio-quasi-negatoria* found their niche in the law of property since they regulated, as the French put it so felicitously, the "*troubles de voisinage*". And this not only made sense; it also tied in so well with the continental emphasis on rights which contrast so sharply with the English focus on wrongs and remedies. When you manage to make the foreign law intelligible to your own colleagues, you are more than halfway towards getting them interested in its solutions and idea. You leave it in its original apparel, and you perpetuate the idea that it is different, strange, and even unattractive.

We find another example of this in an area of the law which is currently causing much concern in my country. Quite simply put, it deals with whether negligently inflicted pure economic loss should be compensated through the law of torts. Can accountants, for example, be held liable towards third parties for loss of this kind? Not according to English law;[19] and the German Code, in its tort section[20] and in its specialised status,[21] basically takes the

---

[18] *Lawson* (above n. 5) 142–5.
[19] *Caparo Industries plc v Dickman and others*, [1990] 2 AC 605.
[20] §823 I BGB.
[21] §323 HGB

same approach. And yet look at what the German courts have done where the statute has not tied their hands completely. Look how they have stretched their law of contract.[22] Look how they have overcome the strictures of a very carefully drafted Code. Ask yourselves whether, as the Bundesgerichtshof (BGH) once put it, they are not "unhinging" the law of contract.[23] And even ponder the way they, the German courts, normally so dependent on a close dialogue with academics, have chosen to ignore them in this context.[24]

Once again, the methodological differences must first be explained to the student; and history and accident often give you the starting points. But once these differences are cleared out of the way, and the foreign system is made intelligible to the outside observer, you can start noticing the similarities and even questioning the rationale of the rules—yours and theirs. In the area we have been talking about, the Germans, *mirabile dictu*, come much closer to the English; and the gap that now appears is not between the common law and the civil law, but between the Germanic and Romanistic version of the civil law.

Let us pursue for a moment this question of accountants' liability; and let us compare the Anglo-German solution on the one hand with Dutch law on the other.[25] In theory, where "mandatory" audits are concerned the differences are unbridgeable: Anglo-German law denies liability in principle, but Dutch law allows it. Yet, despite such a liberal rule, the Dutch law reports contain few cases. Such differences may lead to some creative research of the *practice* of the law and not its *theory*; *and here may lie the answer*. For, I am told, in The Netherlands it is fairly common to refer a dispute first to the accountants' Disciplinary Board (composed of accountants and lawyers) to determine in a procedure which is, apparently, both informal and quick whether the accountant has violated the rules of his profession (but not the issue of civil or criminal liability). If the accountant is absolved, that is the

---

[22] For example BGH 19.3.1986, JZ 1986, 1111; 26.11.1986, NJW 1987, 1758 (1759). The extension through the notion of contracts with protective effects *vis-à-vis* third parties can be seen in, inter alia, BGH 28.2.1977, BGHZ 69, 82 (86); 2.11.1983, NJW 1984, 355; 26.11.1986 (this note) 1759.

[23] In the context of expanding tort actions to cover damages caused *to* products see BGH 18.1.1983, BGHZ 86, 256 (translated in B. S. Markesinis, *A Comparative Introduction to the German Law of Torts*[2] 1990 384).

[24] For a discussion of the case law dealing with products see Günter Hager, "Zum Schutzbereich der Produzentenhaftung" 184 (1984) *AcP* 413–38; Erich Steffen, "Die Bedeutung der 'Stoffgleichheit' mit dem 'Mangelunwert' für die Herstellerhaftung aus Weiterfresserschäden" 1988 *VersR* 977–80; Hans Josef Kullmann, "Die Rechtsprechung des BGH zum Produkthaftpflichtrecht in den Jahren 1989/90" 1991 *NJW* 675–83. The rich case law concerning negligent certifications is considered critically by, among others, Arno Lang, "Die Rechtsprechung des Bundesgerichtshofes zur Dritthaftung der Wirtschaftsprüfer und anderer Sachverständiger" 1988 *WM* 1001–8; Werner F. Ebke/Hansjörg Scheel, "Die Haftung des Wirtschaftsprüfers für fahrlässig verusachte Vermögensschäden Dritter" 1991 *WM* 389–98.

[25] For a brief account see "De beropepsaansprakelijkheid van de accountant, Caparo Industries plc. v. Dickman and Others" 1990 *Ned. Jbl.* 1682; Jansen, "Enkele Aspecten van beroepsaansprakelijkheid Recht op een scheme schaats", in F. H. A. Arisz (ed.) *Essays* (1991).

end of the story. But if he is found to be in breach of the professional rules, a compromise is usually worked out. If this does not happen and litigation ensues it will not, necessarily, lead to a judgment for the plaintiff, since the few reported cases that exist suggest that the courts can use against him causation and contributory negligence and thus deprive him of a final or complete victory. Liability in the theory thus does not mean liability in practice; though the Dutch accounting profession is increasingly weary of the increasing size of the claims.

II. *Making foreign law digestible to our own lawyers.* Having explained differences in methodology and conceptualism, and having decided that the foreign law may contain an interesting idea, what do you do next? Law can learn from medicine: pure transplants rarely work. The grafting of the new organ on a different body must be done carefully, the rejection mechanism must be suppressed. In law, I think, this means, at times, reshaping the foreign idea in a way that can come into your system with a minimum of resistance and dislocation. Briefly, here are two examples.

The Ombudsman, as we all know, is a Scandinavian idea, but it came to England and, indeed, we have seen a proliferation of Ombudsmen in recent times. A cardinal step in ensuring the success of the institution (in my opinion not as great as is sometimes thought, but that is another matter) was the adaptation of the institution in a way that made it palatable to English Parliamentary techniques.[26] For in England, the citizen, traditionally, has complained about maladministration through his Member of Parliament. Direct access to a new organ would have undermined this link and so it was avoided. Complaints have to be channelled to the Ombudsman through the intervention of a Member of Parliament. The institution underwent a change as it crossed the North Sea; but this alteration made the immigrant acceptable.

More recent and closer to my own interests is the current debate about the lack of a general right of privacy and whether English law needs one or not. As you would expect, the Press has violently opposed the creation of such a right. But our Press behaves badly; and less than two years ago a sensational case involving a television actor who was photographed while seriously ill in his hospital bed excited the public and, more importantly, the "Calcutt" Committee which was, at the time, investigating the deficiencies of the English law. I have discussed this interesting case elsewhere,[27] so I shall not bore you with a repetition of its facts and of the various arguments put forward by both sides. Suffice it to say here that the "Calcutt" Committee correctly felt that cases like these should not be allowed to arise again in the future.[28] But

---

[26] On this see R. Gregory/P. Hutchesson, *The Parliamentary Ombudsman, A Study in the Control of Administrative Action* (1975).

[27] Markesinis (above, n. 9).

[28] Its Report—Report of the Committee on Privacy and Related Matters, Chairman David Calcutt, Cmnd. 1102 (1990)—makes good reading; and, interestingly enough, makes excellent use of foreign materials.

instead of recommending a general right of privacy which would have been opposed by the Press, would have been described as indefinable by academics and would have caused a political uproar, the Committee shrewdly chose to recommend a series of specific measures which, if enacted, would bring English law closer to the laws of France and Germany. It would thus appear that the greater respect accorded to human privacy in Continental legal systems can only penetrate our law in the form of specific, mostly criminal rules, rather than in the form of manifestos about the sanctity of "*l'intimité de la vie privée*".

III. *Making the foreign lawyer more available to our own.* In a sense this is the most unusual and original of my points, and the one that places on the modern comparatist the heavy mantle of the diplomat, the mediator, even the fixer. For whether he is operating as a teacher, sifting the unending paperwork that comes with modern schemes like the Erasmus programme, or organising conferences, joint ventures, or, even, setting up institutes in foreign lands (as I have been allowed to do in Leiden), the comparatist must constantly find ways to get the lawyers from the different countries working closer together. It is to me a mystery that modern lawyers are not already studying and working closer together at a time when modern business and increased travel makes this so necessary; a mystery that can only be explained by the conservatism of the legal profession which makes it so fearful of innovations of any kind.

4. CONCLUDING REMARKS

How, then, should we set about achieving some of the things that I have suggested? We need, of course, to keep an open mind and to co-operate more than we have done in the past. But we also need two more things: time to be idle and courage.

The methodology of comparative law I have advocated in my published work needs much hard work so it may come as a surprise to hear me advocate idleness. But the term is used provocatively to illustrate the need to get further away from the unending administrative duties that burden modern academics. In reality, of course, the term I have in mind is leisure in the sense of opportunity afforded by unoccupied time. And the opportunity I miss most is the opportunity to think, the occasion to reflect, the chance to discuss. All these are simply not there as a result of our administrative burdens, and also the demands made on our time to collect and collate the ever-growing primary material of our discipline. It seems to me that time for reflection is needed for every lawyer but for none more so than the comparatist. And you can only do that if you have unoccupied time. As Johnson put it more elegantly, "[a]ll intellectual improvement arises from leisure";[29] and I await the appearance of a man of Erasmus' stature who will praise leisure not folly.

[29] Boswell, *Life of Johnson*, ed. by R. W. Chapham, rev. by J. O. Fleeman, introd. by P. Rogers (Oxford University Press, 1980) 514.

He who is interested in other people's law must have a gregarious and extrovert disposition and yet he must also be prepared to see his interest condemn him to an unusual kind of loneliness. For the comparatist becomes more lonely as he realises that he has to learn more than he can ever possibly understand. This leads to an intense, omnivorous erudition; but it also comes with a sense of desperation as he realises early on in his career what Socrates proclaimed towards the end of his: the more one reads the less one really knows. Yet the quest for understanding others as much as learning about them, must and will continue in our shrinking world. And often, by accident rather than by design, it leads to some unique insights into the law and its rules, as well as underscoring the commonness of human suffering and the universality of the basic notions of justice which one's nationalistic schooling has done so much to blur.

The comparatist must, however, also have courage—courage that goes beyond that which is needed to fight the loneliness of true scholarship. His is a courage different in kind and not just in intensity. It is the courage to tolerate accusations of disloyalty levied against him by his fellow countrymen as his criticisms of their law strike closer to the bone; and it is the courage to ignore the criticisms of his foreign colleagues who may treat him—often but not always rightly—as a superficial outside observer of their systems. But a comparatist must persevere and remain true to his vocation as an international and not national lawyer. For all the true comparatists that I have ever met seem to me to be de facto if not de iure citizens of many countries, lovers of many cultures, unbound by the exigencies of modern nationalism, perhaps even nostalgic for the days of a ius commune.

The comparatist must withstand the attacks on his work—worse still the neglect of his work—by recalling how Lord Devlin once described "[t]he law [as] the gatekeeper of the status quo". And the learned judge continued: "There is always a host of new ideas galloping around the outskirts of society's thought. All of them seek admission but each must first win its spurs; the law at first resists, but will submit to a conqueror and become his servant".[30] This is the challenge that confronts the comparative methodology I am advocating, and that will be its destiny if it is properly pursued.

But at the end of the day, the determination to persevere will come not from belief in the *intellectual value of the comparatist's work*, but from his conviction of the *intrinsic value of his aims*: to increase mutual understanding, to destroy artificial barriers; to promote reconsideration of sacred doctrines; to encourage the bringing together of lawyers with common interests. That, at least, is my personal creed. Let me contribute, even in a small way to bringing about this better understanding, and I shall gladly leave to others the fame that many believe may come (but rarely last) from academic publications. To

---

[30] Patrick Devlin, "The Judge as Lawmaker", The Fourth Chorley Lecture at the London School of Economics, delivered on 25 June 1975, in *idem, The Judge* (1979) 1.

make such a claim in the halls of a learned Academy may strike you as odd; but seeing our work in a proper perspective is also something that one learns from the study and comparison of different legal ideas. To tell "immortals" that they are transient is not an accusation, but a compliment; for it is another way of reminding them that they are human!

4

Cause and Consideration: a Study in Parallel

1. INTRODUCTION

Students interested in the concept of *cause* and consideration must, surely, have been struck by two things. The first is the extraordinary tenacity which has enabled these concepts to survive the attacks of eloquent critics who have doubled their utility.[1] The second is their equally remarkable ability to accommodate the most divergent comparative theories. For the study of the two notions has led some to argue they are, in reality, the same[2];others to insist that they are totally different[3]; while yet another school of thought could be

---

[1] See, in particular, the *6th Interim Report of the Law Revision Committee*, Cmnd. 5449 (1937) and the literature it gave rise to notably, Hamson, 54 *L.Q.R.* 233; Mason, 41 *Col. L. Rev.* 825; Chloros, 17 *I.C.L.Q.* 137. For a more recent discussion of the concept see, Atiyah, *Consideration in Contracts: A Fundamental Restatement* (Canberra, 1971). For literature in the U.S. see, inter alia, Lorenzen, 28 *Yale L.J.* 621 (1919); Shiller, *The Counterpart of Consideration in Foreign Legal Systems*,N.Y. Law Revision Commission, 2nd Ann.Rep. 103 (1936); Glaser, 46 *Dickinson L.R.* 12–25 (1941).

In the francophone countries the attack against *cause* began in 1826 when the Belgian jurist Ernest published his pamphlet *La cause est-elle une condition essentielle pour la validité des conventions*? His view was subsequently developed by Laurent, in his *Principes de droit civil français*, Vol.16 No.111 and others then followed. But it was not until Planiol took on the attack in his *Traité élémentaire de droit civil*, Vol.11. No. 1037 that the concept looked as if it were to be abandoned. The counter-attack came with H. Capitant's *De la cause des obligations* (1927) and though many of his views have been subsequently questioned, the utility of the concept has, on the whole, been accepted. Thus, see the *Travaux of the Commission pour la revision du Code Civil, 1947–48*, 277. The extensive francophone literature can be found in the *Dalloz, Encyclopédie Juridique*, Vol.1 (1951 and supplements) under the word *cause*.

[2] See, for example, the older case law of the Supreme Court of the former colony of Cape of Good Hope: *Alexander* v. *Perry* (1874) 4 Buch. 59; *Tradesmen's Benefit Society* v. *Du Preez* (1887) 5 Sup. Ct. 269; *Mtembu* v. *Webster* (1904) 23 Sup. Ct. 323. Earlier law, however, had gone the other way. See, *Jacobson* v. *Norton* (1841) 2 Menzies 221.

[3] The case law quoted above, note 2, and the views of Lord de Villiers which had inspired these decisions came under severe attack by another South African judge, Sir John Kotzé in his *Causa and Consideration in the Roman and Roman Dutch law of contract* (1922). The view that *cause* and consideration are really different concepts has been accepted by most cases decided in former British possessions in which the Roman-Dutch law played an important part. See, for example, *Rood* v. *Wallach* (1904) T.S. 187 (Transvaal); *Lipton* v. *Buchanan* (1904) 8 New L.R. 49 (Ceylon); *Jayawickreme* v. *Amarasuriya* (1918) P.C. 119 L.T. 499. In Quebec, article 984 of the Civil Code, reproducing article 1108 of the French CC, states *in finem* that a valid contract requires "A lawful *cause or consideration*" but it is generally accepted that consideration here is not used in the technical sense understood by common lawyers but as a mere alternative to the word *cause*. See, for example, H. Newman, "The Doctrine of Cause or Consideration in the Civil

taken to doubt whether there is "any point in comparing *cause* and consideration, even to contrast the two".[4]

The study of the legal system of many countries—notably of the systems of West Germany,[5] and Switzerland[6]—reveals that there can be built a theory of contract which ignores the concepts of *cause* (as the French understand it) or consideration (as the common lawyers have come to apply it over the years). But, surely, this is not the proper way to demonstrate that they are useless, since it can be shown that their abolition would require the invention of some other concept to perform their functions.[7] What matters, therefore, is to discover if the German family of legal systems has adopted other notions or devices which carry out for them the functions that *cause* and consideration perform for French and English law respectively.[8] Equally interesting is the comparison of French and English law on this point and, it is submitted, this can best be done by taking *cause* and consideration, analysing them, and discovering the specific purposes that each of them fulfils. Only then can a meaningful comparison be made.

This has been attempted in this article and two of the most interesting conclusions to emerge from this study can be stated from the outset. First, it will be seen that most (though not all) of the solutions reached by the French law through the medium of *cause* are perfectly acceptable to English law too, though in this country they would be achieved by having recourse to a multitude of concepts such as illegality, public policy, unjust enrichment, frustration and, of course, consideration itself. Secondly, it is arguable that similarities can be found not only in the area of practical results but also in the reasoning that lies behind them. And where this is not so, the French approach is, invariably, neater and more convincing; and it can also be transposed into our system and save it from a process of reasoning which at best can be regarded as elliptical. Even though the pursuit of elegance and consistency is not an end in itself, it may lead to doctrinal coherence which holds out attractions to teacher and practitioner alike.

Law" in (1932) 30 *Canadian Bar Review* 662, 664. For Louisiana see J.H. Drake in 4 *Michigan L.R.* 19–41 (1905) but cf. Glaser in 46 *Dickinson L.R.* 12–25 (1941).

[4] See F.H. Lawson, *A Common Lawyer looks at the Civil Law* (1953), p. 160. Yet it is doubtful whether too much should be read into this statement since the learned author has, himself, made some thought-provoking comparative observations in the 2nd edition of Buckland and McNair's *Roman Law and Common Law: A Comparative Outline* (1965), pp. 228–36. Equally important to the comparative lawyer are Professor R. David's remarks in "Cause et Consideration", *Mélanges Maury*, pp. 111 *et seq*.

[5] Para. 145 BGB. Both concepts are also unknown to the Scandinavian legal systems.

[6] Article 17, Federal Code of Obligations.

[7] Was it not Voltaire who said: "*Si Dieu n'existait pas il faudrait l'inventer*"?

[8] That this is so can be seen in Professor von Mehren's work "Civil-Law Analogues to Consideration: An Exercise in Comparative Analysis", 72 *Harv.L.Rev.* 1009 et seq (1959). In this article we shall concentrate only on comparative aspects of the two doctrines which have not been discussed in Professor von Mehren's learned article.

It has already been intimated that *cause* is by far the wider of the two concepts under comparison; it is, therefore, convenient to use it as the starting point of this study of the two systems in parallel.

2. ABSENCE OF CAUSE[9]

A. Synallagmatic or Bilateral Contracts

There is little doubt that *cause* and consideration represent a kind of form—a check, one could say, on the unrestricted application of the philosophical doctrine of the autonomy of the will which is prepared to ascribe legally binding effects to the mere coincidence of the wills of the contracting parties. But for these two concepts, both English and French law would have moved from one extreme to another: from an era of extreme formalism to one dominated by the theory of consensualism. Neither system saw wisdom in such a *volte face* and in the concepts of *cause* and consideration they found the means to avoid it. But though the reasons which led to the introduction of these concepts were broadly analogous, the process of their emergence was quite different. In France the theory of *cause* was really the product of a prolonged moral and philosophical pre-occupation with the human will which, in law, was allowed to produce effects only if it was externalised for an ascertainable and specific purpose. In bilateral contracts this could only be the *prestation* (undertaking) of the other party. Consideration, on the other hand, was devised by commercially-minded lawyers at a time when they were anxious to escape from their formalistic mediaeval laws and expand their law of contracts. *Assumpsit* provided the means for expansion while consideration ensured that it remained under control. As Mr Fifoot has put it: "The 'mystery of consideration' which the Victorian lawyers found so fascinating" is little "more than the practical answer to an urgent problem".[10] Through different routes *cause* and consideration thus came to underline the interdependence of obligations of the contracting parties. (The Greek word "synallagma" = exchange, indicates this).

The similarities go further. Though both systems were anxious to establish a *quid pro quo* before enforcing a promise, they were not prepared to allow their judges to inquire into the motives or intentions of the contracting parties; hence both concepts were understood in the most abstract terms possible. "Motive is not the same thing with consideration", said Patteson J. in

---

[9] Article 1131 CC "*L'obligation sans cause, ou sur une fausse cause, ou sur une cause illicite, ne peut avoir aucun effet*". In this section we shall discuss the absence of *cause* and in the next we shall focus on illicit *cause*. *Fausse cause* can be omitted for it is either a *cause erronée* which is tantamount to no cause; or it is a *cause simulée* which is valid if the underlying, real *cause* is licit. See Paris, 16 octobre 1956, D. 1957, Somm. 17 and cf. Req. 9 novembre 1891, D.P. 92, 1, 151.

[10] *History and Sources of the Common Law, Tort and Contract* (1949), p.399.

Thomas v. *Thomas*[11] and the distinction was clearly drawn by the draftsmen and early commentators of the Code Civil. More important, neither of the systems under comparison was prepared to investigate the approximate equivalence of the obligations.[12] The idea of an underlying bargain meant that it was for the parties to protect their interests as best they could; a result which was also reached in France via a more philosophical route, *viz.*, through the concept of autonomy of the will. "*Qui dit contractuel dit juste*", Fouillée's well-known aphorism echoed the spirit of his age.

True, one finds in the French law the concept of *lésion*. Equally noticeable, however, is the degree to which it is ignored by the Code.[13] English law, too, has its peculiarity. Though the courts will not investigate the "adequacy" of consideration they will inquire whether it is real or "valuable" (as it is sometimes confusingly called) and will strike down a contract if they are convinced that the plaintiff has procured the defendant's promise by doing or promising to do something which he is already bound to do.[14] This is no place to examine the logic of such a rule though one might observe that it is somewhat peculiar that such a limitation should be adopted by a system which based its notion of contract so firmly on the idea of a freely concluded bargain. If the parties choose to contract on such terms why should the law upset their arrangements? Not surprisingly, one could add, this part of the law of consideration has come under attack from many quarters and it is well-known that in 1937 the Law Revision Committee recommended some fairly drastic amendments.

French law appears to have been spared the harshness of such a rule. Indeed, it is only Pothier who raises the issue somewhat indirectly when he states that, "*la promesse que je fais à mon debiteur de lui donner quelque chose*

---

[11] (1842) 2 QB 851, 859.

[12] In England this was firmly established by the end of the sixteenth century. Thus, it was said in *Sturlyn* v. *Albany*, Croke, Eliz. 67 that "When a thing is to be done by the plaintiff, be it never so small, this is a sufficient consideration to ground an action" and in *Knight* v. *Rushworth*, Croke, Eliz. 469 Anderson C.J. agreed that "the smallness of a consideration is not material". By contrast the old French law, influenced by the canonist ideas of a *iustum contrapassum*, had adopted a generalised theory of *lesio enormis* which was progressively eroded and finally reduced to relative insignificance.

[13] Apart from articlse 1118 CC and 1674 CC the other cases of *lésion* recognised by the Code are of a secondary importance. See, for example, articles 887, 2 CC; 1854 CC. By contrast the legislator has not been inactive and, during periods of monetary instability, has intervened in a number of specific instances.

[14] Lord Denning MR has consistently refused to accept such a rule. In *Ward* v. *Byham* (1956) 1 WLR 496 at 498, he said that "a promise to perform an existing duty, or the performance of it, should be regarded as good consideration, because it is a benefit to the person to whom it is given". And in *Williams* v. *Williams* (1957) 1 WLR 148, 151 he qualified this by adding: "so long as there is nothing in the transaction which is contrary to the public interest". Attractive as this idea is, however, it is not easy to reconcile it with some of the authorities. That "an agreement to do an act which the promisor is under an existing obligation to a third party to do, may. . .amount to a valid consideration" is no longer seriously in dispute. See *N.Z. Shipping Co.* v. *Satterthwaite* (1975) AC 154, at 168.

pour qu'il fasse ce qu'il était obligé de faire, est une promesse nulle" on the grounds that it has an illicit *cause*.[15]

Now it is submitted that Pothier's statement is ambiguous on a number of crucial points which hinder any further comparative discussion. To begin with, Pothier does not make it clear whether the debtor's obligation is imposed upon him by law (e.g., *Collins* v. *Godefroy*[16]) or whether it exists as a result of an agreement with the creditor (e.g., *Stilk* v. *Myrick*[17]) or, finally, whether it is the result of an agreement with a third party. A further difficulty arises from the fact that Pothier makes the result depend upon whether the debtor demanded (*a exigée*)[18] the promise from the creditor (in exchange for performing his own, existing, obligation)—in which case the contract is null for "illicit *cause*"—or the creditor voluntarily made it—in which case it is regarded as a valid gift. It is difficult however, to see why the *cause* in the first case is illicit unless one understands Pothier's rather colourless term *a exigée* as implying the use of unlawful means or some other legally reprehensible behaviour. Nor is it correct to say (at any rate under the régime of the Code) that if the creditor made the promise of his own free will the contract is a valid gift; for it does not comply with the formalities prescribed by the law (i.e. it is not in notarial form).

To overcome these difficulties a Canadian commentator has justified Pothier's pronouncement of the contract as void on the grounds of complete *absence* of *cause*.[19] If this is correct it would appear that the promise of the debtor to discharge an existing duty (whether imposed by agreement with the creditor or other person) would not constitute a valid *cause* and English and French law would, once again, achieve converging solutions. It is doubtful, however, whether this interpretation can be supported by the text of the Code, and the lack of any judicial authority on the point would seem to suggest that the problem does not really exist or, if it does, that it has not occupied the time of the French courts. On this interpretation, therefore, French law differs from the English.

Subject to the point just made, it is probably correct to assert that in bilateral contracts *cause* is the equivalent of executory consideration.[20] Both seem to tie together the two undertakings and, it could be said, they represent the price paid by the creditor (promisee) in exchange for the *prestation* of the debtor (promisor). From this inter-dependence of promises a number of important consequences will flow and to these we must now turn our attention.

---

[15] *Oeuvres de Pothier* (ed. Bugnet) Vol.11. No. 46.

[16] (1831) 1 B & Ad 950 See, also, *Glasbrook Brothers Ltd*. v. *Glamorgan County Council* [1925] AC 270.

[17] (1809) 2 Camp. 317.

[18] "Exacted" is the word used by W.D. Evans in his translation of Pothier's "Treatise" published in London in 1806.

[19] H.Newman, above no. 3, p.670.

[20] As Domat seems to suggest. See F.H. Lawson's comments in *Roman Law and Common Law*, 233.

I.   *Absence of* cause *or consideration at the time of conclusion of the contract.* Given the inter-dependence of *prestations* in bilateral contracts French law has consistently held that if the *objet* (subject matter) of the sale has ceased to exist at the time of the sale the contract is void (art. 1601 CC). More precisely, the obligation of the seller is void for lack of subject matter (*objet*) while the obligation of the buyer is void for lack of consideration (*cause*). Similar reasoning has also been applied in order to hold void a contract of insurance of a car when it was proved that, unknown to both parties, the car had been destroyed at the time when the insurance contract was made.[21] *Couturier* v. *Hastie*[22] can offer an English example though the actual justification of the result has been the subject of fierce controversy.[23] Whatever view one takes, however, it is indisputable that the absence of the contemplated subject matter decisively influenced the outcome of this case. Section 6 of the Sale of Goods Act 1979 supports this conclusion though it has been argued that this section applies only to cases of goods which have perished but not necessarily to goods which have never existed in the first place.

Similar results may also be achieved by both systems where the parties have contracted on the common but erroneous assumption that there exists a certain state of affairs which forms the foundation of their contract. In *Strickland* v. *Turner*,[24] for example, the plaintiff bought and paid for an annuity upon the life of a person who, unknown to both him and the seller of the annuity, had already died. It was held that, as at the time of the purchase of the annuity it had ceased to exist, the plaintiff was entitled to recover back the whole of the purchase money from the defendant (seller) on the grounds that the money had been paid without consideration.

In French law, too, a commonly held but erroneous assumption can nullify a contract. French courts have often invalidated *contrats de rente viagère* on such grounds and have attributed the result to lack of *cause*. A *contrat de rente viagère* is an agreement, usually bilateral, between two persons whereby one (the *débitrentier)* undertakes to pay another (the *créditrentier)* an annuity for an *uncertain* period of time. This could be for as long as the *créditrentier* lives or, occasionally, for as long as a third party remains alive.[25] If, therefore, the parties make such an agreement for so long as X, a third person, is alive and it turns out that, unknown to both of them, X was already dead at the time of the contract, the transaction is void. The explanation is that it has been

---

[21]   See, also, Civ. 22 novembre 1909 D.P. 1910. 1. 407.

[22]   (1852) 8 Exch. 40; reversed (1853) 9 Exch. 102; reversal affirmed (1856) 5 HL Cas 673.

[23]   See, in particular, Professor Atiyah's views in 73 *L.Q.R.* 340; 24 *M.L.R.* 421 and 2 *Ottawa L.R.* 337.

[24]   (1852) 7 Exch. 208, *Scott* v. *Coulson* [1903] 2 Ch. 249.

[25]   Article 1971 CC *"La rente viagère peut être constituée, soit la tête de celui qui en fournit le prix, soit sur la tête d'un tiers, qui n'a aucun droit d'en jouir".*

deprived of its *alea*, the uncertainty which is essential in this type of contract which constitutes the common *cause* of the transaction.[26]

Galloway v. *Galloway*[27] offers another parallel. In that case, as is well known, a separation deed between a man and a woman was declared to be a nullity because the parties had signed it on the common but erroneous belief that they were married which, in actual fact, they were not. The agreement was based on the common assumption that the marriage was valid and hence, when that turned out not to be the case, the contract was void. An amusing counterpart can also be found in French law in the so-called *contrat de remplacement*. This peculiar type of contract enabled A, who was about to be drafted into the army, to agree with B that in consideration of A paying B a certain sum of money B would offer himself as a substitute and serve in A's place. Throughout the nineteenth century such contracts were not regarded as contrary to public policy and were thus held valid to the profit, no doubt, of many tender young men of the wealthier classes. But where A contracted with B on the common but erroneous assumption that A was under a duty to serve in the Army whereas in fact he was not, the contract was held to be void; there was nothing for B to perform and A's obligation to pay B was thus without *cause*.[28] Once again, therefore, the result was achieved by having recourse to the doctrine of *cause* and the inter-dependence of the obligations of the parties.

II.   *Failure of cause or consideration after the contract has been concluded.*

(a)   *Total failure of consideration or absence of cause. Cause* and consideration do not exhaust their usefulness once the contract has been formed. On the contrary, they ensure that the balance struck by the parties themselves in the first place is not disturbed during the subsequent life of the contract. Partial or total failure of one of the *prestations* will thus, inevitably, affect the other also. In France, this extension of the doctrine of *cause* well into the post-formation period of the contract is the result of judicial activism[29] and cannot be found in the older theories on *cause*. The following formula has been repeated time and again by the Court of Cassation: ". . . *dans un contrat synallagmatique, l'obligation de l'une des parties a pour cause l'obligation de l'autra et réciproquement, en sort que, si l'obligation de l'une n'est pas remplie, quel qu'en soit le motif, l'obligation de l'autre devient sans cause*".[30]

The position in England is not dissimilar though it has not always received

---

[26] Article 1974 CC "*Tout contrat de rente viagère créé sur la tête d'une personne qui était morte au jour du contrat, ne produit aucun effet.*" Art. 1975 C.C. "*Il en est de même du contrat par lequel la rente a été créé sur la tête d'une personne atteinte de la maladie dont elle est décédée dans les vingt jours de la date du contrat*". On these see Capitant, above n. 1, pp. 215 *et seq.*

[27] (1914) 30 TLR 531

[28] *Michel c. Ronet*, Req. 30 juillet 1873 D.P. 1873. 1. 330

[29] Not always welcomed by academics. See, for example, H.L. and J. Mazeaud, *Leçons de droit civil*, Vol.11, A, No. 266.

[30] *Conjoints Ceccaldi c. Albertini*, Civ. 14 avril 1891, D.P. 1891. 1. 329.

the theoretical attention it has been given in France.[31] The interdependence of the *prestations* requires that if one party does not fulfil his part of the bargain, the other be given certain remedies to redress the balance. What these remedies are will depend in both systems upon whether the defaulting party has been prevented from performing his part of the contract by reasons outside his control or not. In England, in cases of excusable non-performance, the concept of failure of consideration (far less technical than the doctrine of consideration proper) has an important part to play. This, at any rate, is true in some of the so-called frustration cases though it has not always been made clear by the courts. In *Taylor* v. *Caldwell*[32] one can find an excellent illustration.

It will be remembered that that case firmly laid down the rule that if it is proved that the continued availability of a certain person or thing is essential to the attainment of the fundamental object which the parties had in mind, then the *contract* is discharged and *both* parties are released from their obligations if, due to some extraneous reason, the person or thing in question has ceased to exist. The rule, though well-established, is not beyond question and can produce awkward results.[33] One could well ask, for example, why should the *contract* be discharged, and not merely the "innocent" party *from his obligation* to perform *his* part of the bargain? More relevant to our theme, however, is another question: *why* is the innocent party discharged? Blackburn J's judgment clearly implies that *both* parties are discharged for the *same reason* once the subject matter of the contract has ceased to exist. Yet this is not so since different explanations exist for each party. Mr Caldwell need not pay damages for he has broken no promise. His was an *obligation de diligence*, to use the French but most appropriate terminology, not an *obligation de résultat*. His duty was to take care of the hall and to deliver it to Mr Taylor on the appointed day and this obligation he did not breach. Mr Taylor, on the other hand, is released not because of subsequent impossibility; his obligation is to pay money and, bankruptcy apart, there can be no *legal* impossibility in such cases. The reason why *he* is released is clear; because he did not get what he bargained for, or, to put it in more technical language, because there has been failure of consideration (or, in the case of *Taylor* v. *Caldwell*,[34] substantial failure of consideration). That this is so is demonstrated, inter alia, by the law of sales of goods. Clearly, the position of

---

[31] A recent attempt (by Francis Dawson, 91 *L.Q.R.* 380) to utilise the concepts of dependent and independent promises to explain the operation of exception clauses has been convincingly criticised (by Brian Coote, 40 *M.L.R.* 31 at 41), but it has, nevertheless, helped to re-emphasize their usefulness in understanding discharge for breach. It is submitted that the French approach illustrates this point most clearly.

[32] (1863) 3 B & S 826.

[33] For example, *Harbutt's "Plasticine" Ltd.* v. *Wayne Tank & Pump Co. Ltd.* [1970] 1 QB 447. On this unfortunate case see J.A. Weir's pithy remarks in [1970] *C.L.J.* 189 and, for a more detailed critique, Brian Coote in [1970] *C.L.J.* 221.

[34] (1863) 3 B & S 826.

the seller, where goods have perished after the contract has been concluded, depends on whether the goods were specific within the meaning of section 7 of the Sale of Goods Act 1893,[35] and specific in this sense does not necessarily mean specific as understood in the rules dealing with the passing of property. The buyer on the other hand is discharged for failure of consideration which, in this case, depends upon the passing of property. If the property has not passed to him before the goods perish he is freed for failure of consideration. But if he had acquired the property in the goods then he remains liable for the price even though the seller is freed as a result of his own obligation having become impossible (section 20 of the Sale of Goods Act),[36] which clearly illustrates that in a situation like *Taylor* v. *Caldwell*[37] one party only may be discharged.

This clear reasoning can be found in French law. Article 1722 of the Code expressly states that "*si pendant la durée du bail, la chose louée est détruite en totalité par cas fortuit, le bail est résilié de plein droit. . . .*" while article 1741 CC provides a similar rule for the event of loss of the *chose louée*. From these and other specific articles of the Code,[38] French lawyers have developed the so-called *théorie des risques* which is squarely based on the concept of *cause* and the interdependence of the *prestations* of the parties. It has been succinctly summarised in the following way in Professor Weill's masterly textbook[39]:

> "*Quand un cas de force majeure empêche l'un des contractants d'accomplir sa prestation, non seulement celui ci est exonéré, mais l'autre contractant est également libéré. Cette solution est commandée par la notion de cause: les obligations réciproques des parties dans les contrats synallagmatiques se servant mutuellment de cause, quand l'une disparaît par impossibilité fortuite d'éxécution, l'autre s'éteint également, faute de cause.*"

[35] Section 7. "Where there is an agreement to sell specific goods, and subsequently the goods, without any fault on the part of the seller or buyer, perish before the risk passes to the buyer, the agreement is thereby avoided." For the doubts as to the meaning of the word "specific" see Chalmers, *Sale of Goods*, 17th edn., by M. Mark, p.100.

[36] Section 20. "Unless otherwise agreed, the goods remain at the seller's risk until the property therein is transferred to the buyer, but when the property therein is transferred to the buyer, the goods are at the buyer's risk whether delivery has been made or not."

[37] (1863) 3 B & S 826.

[38] For example, art. 1788 CC "*Si, dans le cas où l'ouvrier fournit la matière, la chose vient à périr, de quelque manière que ce soit, avant d'être livrée, la perte en est pour l'ouvrier, à moins que le maître ne fût en demeure de recevoir la chose*". See, also, arts. 1790 CC and 1867 CC.

Para. 323 BGB states "If the performance due from one party under a mutual contract becomes impossible because of a circumstance for which neither he nor the other party is responsible, he loses the claim to counter performance"; in case of partial impossibility the counter-performance is diminished in accordance with paras. 472, 473 BGB. It will be noticed that this solution is analogous to though more rigid than that accepted by French law.

[39] *Droit Civil. Les obligations* (1975), No 498.

And the similarity is extended further since article 1138 CC[40] in effect reproduces the rule of section 20 of the Sale of Goods Act 1893,[41] by stating that the aforementioned general principle does not apply in the case of a sale in which the property in the goods (though not the goods themselves) has passed to the buyer. In such a case if the goods are destroyed the risk lies with the buyer, not, however, as a result of the rule *res perit creditori* but solely as a result of the quite different rule *res perit domino*.

(b)   *Partial failure of consideration or absence of cause.* So far we have been talking of total or complete impossibility in the performance of one of the obigations and its effect on the counter-prestation. Similar rules, however, apply where there is partial impossibility in one of the *prestations*. This general statement has to be amplified in a number of ways.

Thus, first of all it must be made clear that even partial destruction or deterioration of the subject matter may bring into operation the above-mentioned rules and, to use the English terminology, frustrate the contract. *Taylor* v. *Caldwell*[42] shows that the same is true of English law since, it will be remembered, the contract in that case referred to "the Surrey Gardens and music hall" and it was discharged even though it was only the hall that had ceased to exist. *Asfar* v. *Blundell*[43] could also be given as an illustration of severe damage which the law regards as being tantamount to a total loss. The crucial consideration in such cases is, clearly, the magnitude of the effects of the frustrating event even though this may not be always clear from the phrasing of the judgments. Thus cases like *Herne Bay Steamboat Co.* v. *Hutton*[44] can be justified on the grounds that they involved partial though not substantial failure of consideration.[45] We shall see that similar considerations determine the solutions adopted by the French law.

The starting point in French law is, as every civilian knows, the Code. But, as so often is the case, the Code does not contain a general provision but simply particular rules which are treated by academics and the courts as instances of an existing but unexpressed general principle. In this present case the crucial provision can be found in article 1722 CC which unequivocally states that if the thing hired is partially destroyed the "lessor"[46] is under no obligation to pay damages to the "lessee" and the "lessee" can either demand a reduc-

---

[40] Article 1138. "*L'obligation de livre la chose est parfait par le seul consentement des parties contractantes.*

Elle rend le créancier propriétaire et met la chose à ses risques dès l'instant où elle a dû être livrée, encore que la tradition n'en ait point été faite, à moins que le débiteur ne soit en demeure de la livrer; auquel cas la chose reste aux risques de ce dernier."

[41] Quoted in n. 35, above.

[42] (1863) 3 B & S 826.

[43] [1896] 1 QB 123.

[44] [1903] 2 KB 683.

[45] R.G. McElroy and G. Williams, "The Coronation Cases" (1941) 4 *M.L.R.* 241; (1941) 5 *M.L.R.* 1.

[46] Article 1722 CC "*Si, pendant la durée du bail, la chose louée est détruite en totalité par cas fortuit, le bail est résilié de plein droit; si elle n'est détruite qu'en partie, le preneur peut, suivant les*

tion of his obligation *or* apply to the courts for resolution of the contract. At this juncture we are only concerned with the latter option given to the "lessee" and it is necessary to make two observations. First, that article 1722 CC is, as already stated, considered to be a particular application of a more general rule, and therefore, the solution it offers to the problem of partial performance is accepted for all cases of partial but excusable performance of the obligation of one of the parties to a contract and it is not restricted to "leases". Secondly, that though article 1722 CC talks of partial *destruction* it has, in fact, been widely interpreted by the courts to apply to all cases where, in the opinion of the judge *"le bail n'offre plus* d'utilité *pour le preneur"* for in such cases his (the "lessee's") *"obligation se trouve . . . dépourvue de cause".*[47] If, therefore, a building is let to the plaintiff for the purpose of being used as a music hall and, subsequently, the military authorities decide that the operation of music halls shall be suspended, the "lessee" (plaintiff) will not have to pay the rent even though the building is still in existence and available to her to use for any other purpose.[48] As the court at first instance put it:

> *"Attendue, en droit, qui le prix du loyer payé au bailleur n'étant que la représentation de la jouissance paisible assurée au locataire dans les terms de l'art.* 1719 C.Civ., *le locataire est fondé à reéclamer l'exonération complète du prix de ce loyer, lorsqu'il fait la preuve qu'à raison d'événements fortuits auxquels il est demeuré absolument étranger et constituant des cas de force majeure incontestable, il s'est trouvé, malgré lui, dans l'impossibilité de jouir de la location et d'en retirer aucun des avantages en vue desquels il avait contracté."*[49]

The explanation of this judgment can be found by asking the question: "What did the 'lessee' pay for?" The facts, as given in the judgment, make the answer

---

circonstances, demander ou une diminution du prix, ou la résiliation même du bail. Dans l'un et l'autre cas, il n'ya lieu à aucun dédommagement."
  In the discussion that follows in the text the term bail is, *faute de mieux*, translated as lease. Technically speaking, however, the word lease is in this context misleading since in English law (and unlike French law) a lease is more than a mere contract: it creates an interest in land. Hence the view that whatever happens to the premises "the lease would remain. The estate in the land would still be vested in the tenant". *Cricklewood Property and Investment Trust Ltd.* v. *Leighton's Investment Trust Ltd.* [1945] AC 221, 234. This is not true in French law. The term "hire" should also be avoided since, strictly speaking, it refers to a type of bailment in which the bailee receives the possession of a *chattel* and the right to use it in consideration for a price that has to be paid to the bailor, and here we are dealing with immovables. It would also necessitate the use of the words "hirer" and "letter" which, to the present writer, sound rather awkward, particularly the latter. So, "lessor" and "lessee" have been used and, in order to stress that they are not used in their technical sense, they are printed in inverted commas.
  [47] A number of cases decided during the Franco-Prussian War of 1870 decided this and the litigation that followed the two Great Wars has confirmed the solution stated in the text beyond doubt. See, for example, Paris, 23 décembre 1871, S. 1873. 2. 36; D. 71. 2. 225; Poitiers, 12 juillet 1915, G.P. 1916, 172; Nancy, 22 juin 1916, G.P. 1916, 160; Paris, 21 janvier 1916, G.P. 1916, 254; Paris, 3 mars 1917, Gaz. Trib., 6 juin 1918, etc. etc.
  [48] But the plaintiff is obliged to pay rent for the part of the building which she uses as her residence.
  [49] G.P. 1916, 255.

clear: "a building *to be used* as a music hall"[50] and since this had become impossible, her obligation, too, was brought to an end for lack of *cause*. Before leaving this section one might, perhaps, add that a similar method of reasoning could be used to explain cases like *Krell* v. *Henry*[51] and, indeed, it has been argued that *Krell* v. *Henry*[52] should be regarded as a case of total (or, at the very least, substantial) failure of consideration rather than a case of impossibility of performance. Intellectual neatness apart, this, *inter alia* means that the contract is *not* discharged at the option of *either* party (as the Court of Appeal seems to suggest in *Krell* v. *Henry*[53] but *only* at the option of the hirer. That this is obviously right can be tested by asking the question: "What would have happened if the hirer insisted upon using the flat on the appointed day even though there was no procession?" The answer must, surely, be that the letter could not have prevented him from so doing. In French law this solution could never be in doubt and comparison with English law demonstrates the intellectual neatness and consistency of the French approach.

If, however, the partial impossibility or destruction is not serious enough to discharge the contract in the above sense, *quid iuris?* The problem can be really split into two: (a) does the promiser (debtor), who through no fault of his own is unable to perform part of his obligation, have to pay damages for the part which he has failed to perform? (b) What is he entitled to claim in exchange for his part performance: the entire counter-*prestation?* a proportional part of it? or, indeed, nothing at all?

For present purposes, question (a) above, can be answered very briefly. Both systems provide the same answer in principle by accepting that impossibility falling short of frustration may provide an excuse to the promisor.[54] A sick employee, for example, who does not go to his work, will not be in breach of his contract of employment even though his illness may not be serious enough to frustrate the contract.[55] Equally, a farmer who agrees to sell 500 tons of wheat grown (i.e., to be grown) on his land but who through no fault of his own only produces 300 tons will not be liable in damages for the 200 tons

---

[50] From the terms of the "lease" quoted in the judgment at first instance it is clear that the plaintiff and the defendant had clearly negotiated the hiring of a music hall which was to be used as a music hall (at 255). The Court of Appeal, confirming in part the award made by the lower court, laconically asserted that the defendant "*avait loué à la dame Rasimi* (the plaintiff) *un établissement à usage de théâtre*" and that "*les prescriptions administratives n'ont affecté que les modalités de l'exploitation théâtrale, sans atteindre tout ou partie de la chose louée*". It was otherwise, however, from the moment when the interference of the authorities became less stringent even though the exploitation of the theatre continued to be financially very onerous for the plaintiff.

[51] [1903] 2 KB 740.

[52] *Ibid*. On this see McElroy and Williams, "The Coronation Cases 1" (1941) 4 *M.L.R.* 241, 254.

[53] *Ibid*. See, also, R.G. McElroy and G. Williams *Impossibility of Performance* (1941), pp. 88 *et seq.*

[54] For a brief discussion see Treitel, *The Law of Contract* (1975), pp. 573 *et seq.*

[55] Treitel, n. 54 above, pp. 549, 589–90.

which he failed to produce.[56] The solution is similar in French law. Article 1722 CC states this expressly as far as "leases" are concerned and, as we have seen, both courts and academics are prepared to give it a very wide area of application.

The answer to question (b) above, however, is more difficult and it reveals both a difference between the systems as well as a considerable degree of disorder in the English approach. It is best if we examine the topic following a distinction which both systems appear to adopt *viz.,* the distinction between entire and divisible contracts.

In severable or divisible contracts complete performance is not required to found an action. A seaman, for example, who has agreed to be paid per month will be entitled to claim remuneration for each completed month even if he fails to work throughout the entire voyage[57]; but it will be otherwise if his obligation is to serve until the vessel reaches the port of destination.[58] Similarly, if in a building contract the builder has agreed to be paid specified sums as the work progresses, he will be entitled to claim an appropriate sum whereas he will not be entitled to claim a penny if the agreement is for him to be paid only on completion of the work.[59] Instalment contracts offer, of course, the clearest examples and in these payment keeps pace with performance. Consequently, no money can be claimed while one party is not performing his part of the contract. Needless to say, cases dealing with the above-mentioned type of situations can be found in both systems and the French attitude has been well summarised by Capitant who has said[60] that in such cases, "*les tribunaux décident sans hesiter que le contrat est suspendu, en tant que l'exécution de l'une des obligations est rendu impossible, l'autre contractant se trouve dispensé d'executer la sienne*".

But in the case of entire contracts the common law has adopted a different and, it is submitted, unnecessarily harsh solution by adopting the principle that partial performance gives no right to payment at all. This is no place to discuss the case law which has been examined in some detail by Professor Glanville Williams.[61] Suffice it to say that the common law approach is markedly different from that of the French law (and, indeed, the other civilian systems) which allow the injured party to demand a diminution of his own *prestation* but also oblige him to pay something towards the part performance of the counter-obligation. On the other hand it is easy to over-state this undoubted difference, for the common law rule is subject to a number of important exceptions, notably the doctrine of substantial performance and the

---

[56] *Howell* v. *Coupland* (1876)1 QBD 258. Re-confirmed in *H. R. and S.Sainsbury Ltd.* v. *Street* (1972) 1 WLR 834. But, in the absence of any contrary agreement, the seller remains liable for the part of the crop he has in fact produced.
[57] *Taylor* v. *Laird* (1856) 25 LJEx 329.
[58] *Cutter* v. *Powell* (1795) 6 TR 320.
[59] *Sumpter* v. *Hedges* [1898] 1 QB 673.
[60] See above n. 1, p.319 quoting the relevant case-law.
[61] "Partial Performance of Entire Contracts" (1941) 57 *L.Q.R.* 373, 490.

tendency of the courts to construe, where possible, contracts as divisible rather than as entire[62] and thus allow a claim for partial performance. It is submitted, therefore, that, once again, the differences tend to be attenuated in practice.

B. Unilateral Contracts[63]

Cause is an essential ingredient of bilateral as well as unilateral contracts but whereas in the former type it performs, as we have seen, important functions, in the latter its utility is seriously restricted. According to the classical theory of *cause* a distinction is made between the so-called *contrats réelles* (the Roman contracts *in re*)—which include the *prêt, dépôt* and *gage*—and the unilateral promise to pay a sum of money. In both situations there is a unilateral obligation to pay the loan (*prêt*) return the object that had been deposited (*dépôt*) or pawned (*gage*) or pay the sum agreed *once* the object in question was delivered to the promisor (in the case of contracts *in re*) or there is a valid and lawful obligation pre-existent in the case of the unilateral promise to pay a sum of money. In these cases, *cause* helps justify the rule that the obligation in unilateral contracts by one of the parties does not come into existence until the other party has done all that is required of him. In English law, too, though we do not speak of contracts *in re*, similar rules can be found. Thus, in the case of a deposit the obligation of the bailee to keep the chattel and return it to the bailor upon demand "arises only upon actual delivery of the chattel to him and his acceptance of the deposit".[64] And in the case of a pledge "delivery, either actual or constructive, of the articles pledged in consideration of the debt or advance is essential"[65] for the validity of the transaction. However, apart from justifying such results, *cause* has little else to do. This at any rate, was the position according to the classical theory of *cause* for, we shall see, more modern theories are prepared to see *cause* in a different light and utilise it to control the legality and morality of some transactions. Thus, a loan to a woman in exchange for her sexual favours has been struck down on the grounds of *cause immorale*.[66] More about this, however, in the next section.

Unilateral promises to pay a sum of money require a further word. They are, as we have seen, valid and enforceable if they are supported by a *cause préexistante*. In English law such promises would be unenforceable unless they were under seal, since they deal with situations which in our system would be

---

[62] "Contracts may be so made; but they require plain words to shew that such a bargain (*i.e.*, an entire contract) was really intended", *Button v. Thompson* (1869) LR 4 CP 330, 342.

[63] The role of *cause* in the case of gifts is not discussed in this article, partly because gifts are not considered as contracts by the common law (though they are by the civil law) but largely because the significance of *cause* in the case of gifts is minimal.

[64] *Chitty on Contracts*, 24th edn. Vol 11, No. 2213.

[65] *Ibid.*, No. 2279.

[66] Req. 17 avril 1923, D.P. 1923. 1. 172.

regarded as examples of past consideration. But a note of warning should be sounded. A number of cases discussed under this heading, notably the cases of *obligations naturelles* (unenforceable contracts),[67] show that in practical terms the difference between English and French law is, yet again, attenuated.[68] Thus payments of gambling debts (which are not, normally, enforceable in a court of law) or the discharge of a debt which is statute-barred[69] at the time of payment will be valid in both systems.

3. ILLICIT CAUSE

Article 1131 CC states that an obligation with an illicit *cause* cannot have any legal effect whilst article 1133 CC defines illicit *cause* as one which is "prohibited by law or is contrary to good morals or (the notion of) *ordre public*".[70] The questions that have to be answered are first, which contracts are tainted by illegality and, secondly, what are the consequences of such illegality?

When deciding which contracts are tainted by illegality one cannot help but notice the shift of emphasis that has been brought about by French case law. Originally, as already stated, *cause* was clearly distinguished from motives, this approach being the result of a considerable degree of suspicion which prevailed against the judiciary when the Code was drafted. Consequently, the early jurists were anxious to deprive judges of any opportunity they might have had to control the motives or ultimate intentions of the parties to a contract. The result was that only transactions which were *ex facie* unlawful could be declared invalid. The sale of a gambling house or a brothel, for example, has traditionally been held to be void on the grounds of immoral *cause*.[71] More precisely, the vendor's obligation failed because of an *objet illicite* whereas the purchaser's obligation failed on the grounds of *cause illicite*. Not surprisingly, therefore, most judgments were based on both *objet* and *cause* being illicit. But suppose, for example, the sale of a house which the parties are selling and buying respectively *in order to use* it as a brothel. Here neither subject matter (*objet*) nor *cause* (as understood by the classical

---

[67] Weill, above n. 39, No. 257.
[68] See, generally, M.J.P. Walton's remarks in (1919) *Rev. Trim dr. Civ.* 469 *et seq.*
[69] Cheshire and Fifoot, below n. 90, 625.
[70] Cf. para. 138 BGB. "(1) A legal transaction which is against public policy is void. (2) A legal transaction is also void whereby a person exploiting the need, carelessness or inexperience of another, causes to be promised or granted to himself or to a third party in exchange for a performance, pecuniary advantages which exceed the value of the performance to such an extent that under the circumstances, the pecuniary advantages are in obvious disproportion to the performance."
[71] For example: Civ. 15 décembre 1873, D.P. 1874. 1. 222; S. 1874.1.241; Req. 17 juillet 1905, D.P. 1906. 1. 72; 1 octobre 1940, G.P. 1940, 2. 146; Trib. Seine, 25 novembre 1936, D.H. 1937. 142, etc.

theory) are illicit and the courts would be unable to interfere.[72] What is immoral are the motives of the parties and with the traditional and rigid demarcation between *cause* and motives the courts found themselves unable to intervene. Such a position is arguable and defensible when the parties have different motives or they are prompted into concluding the contract in question as a result of many and varied motives only one of which is illicit or immoral. But what if a *motif determinant* can be found, shared by both parties, which could be described as the main purpose of the contract? Does not motive then enter into the contractual field and approximate the more abstract concept of *cause*? The English courts have for many decades now taken such a view and have been prepared to consider as illegal a contract which though *ex facie* lawful, both parties intend to exploit for an illegal purpose. The case of *Pearce* v. *Brooks*[73] is a colourful illustration. After some hesitation the French courts, too, have come to distinguish between contracts which are illegal in their inception (to use the Cheshire and Fifoot terminology) and contracts which though lawful in their inception are to be exploited for an illegal or immoral purpose by one of the parties without the knowledge of the other and in this they have been aided by the new understanding of *cause*. Thus, in the words of Capitant they are prepared to annul not only "*les obligations qui ont à proprement parler une cause illicite ou immorale, mais . . . également . . . tous les contrats synallagmatiques, qui, bien qu'ayant pour objet des prestations licites, poursuivent cependant, dans l'intention commune des parties, une fin contraire à l'ordre public ou aux bonnes moeurs*".[74]

Thus, in *Conte* v. *Fould*, the court took the view that a contract between a publican and the electoral agent of a parliamentary candidate (Fould) to deliver goods (drinks) gratuitously to the publican's customers in exchange for their vote at the forthcoming elections was void for immoral *cause* and hence no payment could be claimed by the plaintiff (the publican). Its reasoning was as follows:

"*Attendu que vainement le demandeur voudrait distinguer entre la "cause" de la dette,. . .qui, d'après lui, résiderait dans la livraison de marchandises et la destination desdites marchandises, qui serait seulement le 'motif' de l'obligation; Attendu, en effet, que la Jurisprudence repousse avec raison cette distinction, quand il est certain, comme en l'espèce, que l'objet du contrat doit, dans l'intention des parties au moment*

---

[72] Thus in *Comp. d'assurance Le Monde c. Havard*, S. 1904. 1. 509, the court refused to avoid a contract of insurance of a brothel on the grounds that "*les prestations (réciproques des parties) étaient licites en elle-mêmes; qu'elles ne différaient en rien des prestations stipulées dans tous les contrats de cette nature, et qu'elles n'ont pu devenir illicites, par cela seul que les risques assurés dépendaient d'une maison de tolérance; qu'elles ne sauraient être considérées comment ayant eu en vue la création, le maintien ou l'exploitation d'un établissement de cette nature; qu'elles n'impliquent par suite aucune immoralité susceptible d'entrainer l'annulation de la convention*". A summary of this case can also be found in D.P. 1906, 5, 33. There are other cases which also adopt this marked distinction between *cause* proper and ulterior motives but in the view of what is said in the text, above, they do not represent the current view on the matter.

[73] (1866) LR Exch 213.

[74] See above n. 1, 240.

de la convention, servir à un usage prohibé, car alors le motif est en connexion si étroite avec la cause que le caractère illégal ou immoral de l'un affecte l'autre nécessairement."[75]

As Capitant has argued, in such cases "*Le but économique poursuivi s'est trouvé ainsi rattaché à l'opération juridique. Séparer l'une de l'autre serait donc tronquer la volonté des contractants*". However, for this to happen the illegal or immoral intention of one of the parties must be known to[76] if not actually agreed (*convenu*) by the other and, following an *arrêt de principe* of the Court of Cassation in 1956[77] the latter is now the prevailing view. Thus a contract which is illegal in its inception will be void and the cases examined under this heading have exact equivalents in the common law. By way of illustration suffice it to mention contracts relating to brothels,[78] or gaming houses[79] (where they are not expressly allowed); contracts intended to bring about an extra marital cohabitation[80]; contracts to defraud the revenue[81], contracts corrupting officials and, more generally, public life[82]; contracts prohibiting an individual from exercising his basic freedoms such as his right to marry[83] etc., etc.

---

[75] Trib. civ. Tarbes, 14 mars 1899. D.P. 1904.2.201; S. 1900. 2. 219.

[76] Paris, 12 mai 1949, G.P. 1949, 2, 48.

[77] Civ. 4 décembre 1956, Sem. Jur. 1957, 10008 and obs. J. Mazeaud, G.P. 1957, 1, 183; Rev. trim. dr. civ. 1957, 329.

[78] *Leases of buildings to be used as brothels*: Paris 30 novembre 1839, S.40.2. 121; Lyons 11 juillet 1862, S. 63. 2. 165; Paris 26 décembre 1899, G.P.1. 132; Civ.27 décembre 1945, G.P. 1946. 1. 88. *Sales of buildings to be used as brothels*: Civ. 15 décembre 1873, D.P. 1874. 1. 222; Req. 17 juillet 1905, D.P.1906. 1. 72; Trib. Seine, 25 novembre 1936, D.H. 1937. 142. *Loans to purchase brothels*: Paris 26 janvier 1894 and Req. 1 avril 1895, S. 96.1.289, D.P. 95.1. 263, Trib. civ. Bruxelles 5 déc 1894, Pas belge, 95. *Supplies to brothels:* Trib. Comm. Seine, 1 mai 1888, G.P., 1 mai 1888, G.P. 1888.1. 797; Trib Liège, 14 novembre 1896, Pas. belge, 97.3.75, Trib. civ. Nice 18 novembre 1909, Rec.G.Trib. 1910.1.119.

[79] Civ. 17 janvier 1944. D. 1945, somm p.2.

[80] Civ. 26 mars 1860, D.P. 1860, 1, 255; Civ. 8 octobre 1957, D. 1958, 317 (and note Esmein). But it is otherwise if the money is paid or the gift is made to mark the end of the extra-marital connection. Civ. 11 mars 1918, S. 1, 170; Civ. 6 octobre 1959, D. 1960, 515 and note Malaurie, Sem.Jur. 1959, 11, 11305 (note Esmein); Civ. 16 octobre 1967, Sem.Jur. 1967, 11, 15287, Rev.trim.dr.civ. 1968, 178 obs. Savatier. See, also, R Rodière, "Le menage de fait devant la loi" in *Travaux de l'Association Henri Capitant*, 1957. A Distinction between a *concubinage simple* and *adultérin* has also been taken, the law taking a harsher view in the case of the latter. See, Amiens, 30 novembre 1961, D. 1962, Somm. 61; Civ. 16 octobre 1956, G.P. 14–16, Rev. trim. dr. civ. 1957, obs. Savatier; Paris 14 juin 1955, D. 1956, Somm. 38; J.C.P. 1956, 11, 9303. For English law see, *Benyon* v. *Nettlefold* (1850) 3 Mac & G 94; *Ayerst* v. *Jenkins* (1873) LR 16 Exch 275 though it is said that these cases lay down the rule only with regard to *future cohabitation*. Payment made to recompense past cohabitation or to mark the end of cohabitation would not be enforceable in this country since it would be treated as a case of past consideration. It is otherwise, however, if it is made under seal: *Nye* v. *Moseley* (1826) 6 B & C 133.

[81] Pau 16 octobre 1956, D. 1957, 17 Cf. *Miller* v. *Karlinski* (1945) 62 TLR 85; *Napier* v. *National Business Agency Ltd* [1951] 2 All ER 264.

[82] Req. 15 mars 1911, D. 1911, 1. 382; Civ. 3 avril 1912, 1, 382; Civ. 23 avril 1898, D. 1898, 1, 415. Cf. *Garforth* v. *Fearon* (1787) 1 Hy. Bl. 328; *Parkinson* v. *College of Ambulance Ltd., and Harrison* [1925] 2 KB 1 and now Honours (Prevention of Abuses) Act 1925, etc.

[83] Paris 30 avril 1963, Rec. G.P. 1963. 1. 405 (contract of employment prohibiting air hostess from marrying).

Let us now turn briefly to the consequences of illegality. We have already noted that in French law a contract illegal or immoral in its inception will be void, absolutely void. This would, normally, mean four things[84]: first, that if the contract were still executory both parties would be relieved from performing their respective obligations; secondly, that there would be no liability to pay damages for not performing such obligations; thirdly, that any money paid or any chattels delivered under such an illegal contract would be recoverable and, finally, property in any goods transferred would remain in the *tradens*. But in the case of immoral or illegal contracts the third and fourth rules, above, are subject to a number of important modifications.

Thus: (a)   Where the contract has an immoral or illicit *cause* which is shared by both parties (in the sense described above) neither party will be allowed to recover what he has given to the other under the illegal contract. The result is similar to that accepted in English law and in both countries it is invariably justified by the Latin maxim *nemo auditur suam turpitudinem allegans* or *in pari delicto potior est conditio defendentis* with the consequence that "gains and losses remain where they have accrued or fallen". In France this solution can trace its origin directly to the Roman law and is beyond dispute even though the Code, by remaining silent on this point, has encouraged some theoretical doubts.[85] This, at any rate, is the traditional view, for the courts have for some one hundred years now been adopting a slightly different position and have been applying the *nemo auditur* rule to *immoral* transactions but have, on the whole, been avoiding it in cases of *illicit* transactions.[86] Here then lies a difference with English law.

(b) The rule that property in the case of a void contract does not pass is also modified. As between the parties to the illicit transaction the rule is theoretical since neither can establish against the other a cause of action. But what about third parties who are innocent and have given, to use the English term, valuable consideration? In England since *Singh* v. *Ali*[87] and *Belvoir Finance Co. Ltd.* v. *Stapleton*[88] it looks as if the buyer under an illegal contract of sale can acquire ownership in the goods even though he is in *pari delicto*. The reason, according to Lord Denning, is "because the transferor, having fully achieved his unworthy end, cannot be allowed to turn round and repudiate the means by which he did it—he cannot throw over the

---

[84] In French law the various types of nullities and their effects are, invariably, discussed under a separate heading or chapter in a manner which a common lawyer can only describe as admirable as it is systematic. For a discussion, at times critical, of the common law approach, see Honoré, 75 *S.A.L.J.* 32 *et seq.*; Turpin, 72 *S.A.L.J.* 58 *et seq.*

[85] See Carbonnier, *Droit civil* (1975), Vol I. No. 29 and Vol IV, p. 164.

[86] In this sense, Colin—la Morandière, No. 105; Ripert—Boulanger, *Traité de droit civil* (1957), Vol II, Nos. 762, 763. Aix, 28 mars 1945, J.C.P. 46, 2, 3063 and *cf.* Civ. 20 juillet 1844, S. 1844, 1, 582; Civ. 13 juillet 1885, S. 1886, 1. 205;Req. 24 octobre 1928, G.P. 1928 s. 747. Older case law can be found in Capitant's work. For a new monograph see P. Le Tourneau, *La règle* "*Nemo auditur . . .*" Paris, 1970.

[87] [1960] AC 167.

[88] [1971] 1 QB 210.

transfer".[89] The inescapable consequence of this is that an innocent third party obtaining the goods from the transferee will acquire property in them, a result which can be described as equitable even though it was achieved in a circuitous manner which has not escaped powerful criticism.[90]

The solution in French law is similar though it has avoided the weakness of the above-mentioned English decisions. As between transferor and transferee property in the goods is *not* transferred.[91] But innocent third parties may be able to rely on the provision of article 2279 CC according to which *"En fait de meubles, la possession vaut titre"* and thus escape the harshness of the general principle which would otherwise deprive them of the property in goods which they had innocently acquired.

4. CONCLUSIONS

What then are the conclusions of this brief comparative sketch? That the practical results achieved by the system under comparison would be broadly analogous no one could really have doubted. The similarities in the socio-economic background are such that they made this an almost inevitable outcome. As Professor Esmein wisely remarked some eighty years ago,[92]

> *"souvent le résultat practique, la satisfaction donnée aux besoins économiques et sociaux, sont devenus sensiblement les mêmes en Angleterre et en France, comme il est naturel chez deux grandes nations voisines et également civilisées"* and he continued, *"Mais le but a été atteint par des moyens divers, par l'application de règles techniques fort différentes"*.

With great respect to the eminent French jurist one must qualify his last statement by asserting that not only the results achieved through different technical rules are analogous but that the reasoning that lies behind them is more similar than students of comparative law are often led to believe.

In the law of obligations *growing* similarity in *reasoning* is gradually emerging. For example, it is clearly evident in some areas of the law of torts.[93] The German and English cases that deal with negligently inflicted economic loss reveal this[94] and even systems such as the Dutch, which are avowedly based

---

[89] [1960] AC 167 at p. 176.

[90] See, for example, Cheshire and Fifoot, *Law of Contract*, 9th edn. by M.P. Furmston, at pp. 348–9.

[91] Though subject to what has been said above, this does not mean that the things transferred can be recovered. The *nemo auditur* rule, which Lord Denning appeared to quote in *Singh* v. *Ali* [1960] AC 167, 176, ensures this.

[92] (1893) Nouv. Rev. Hist. 555.

[93] See, for example, B.S. Markesinis, "The not so dissimilar tort and delict" (1977) 93 L.Q.R. 78–123.

[94] BGHZ 41, 123; NJW 1964, 720; OLG Karlsruhe, NJW 1975, 221; BGH, NJW 1976, 1740 and cf. *S.C.M. (U.K.) Ltd* v. *W.J.Whittall and Son, Ltd.* [1971] 1 QB 337; *Spartan Steel and Alloys, Ltd.* v. *Martin and Co (Contractors) Ltd.* [1973] 1 QB 27.

on the French Code Civil, are moving in the same direction. Equally notice-able must be the introduction into the German law of torts of the concept of duty of care. And students of Professor Nipperdey's theory,[95] that *negligent* conduct that causes damage to one of the interests mentioned in paragraph 823, I BGB is "unlawful" (*widerrechtlich*) only if it is in breach of the general duty imposed upon persons to take care not to injure others (the *Allgemeine Sorgfalpflicht*) will see in it reasoning quite analogous to that prevailing in our law of negligence. The comparative study of *cause* and consideration appears to suggest that similarity in reasoning can also be found in the law of con-tract.

This, of course, is not to suggest a lack of differences. Differences are many and obvious and many of them have been noted in the preceding pages. But one deserves most attention since it has helped conceal the equally important similarities that exist between the two systems. It can be found in the consid-erable theoretical attention that has been paid to the concept of *cause*. This is partly the result of the civilian mind which is interested in theory as it is concerned with practical solutions; but it is, primarily, the result of the many and eloquent attacks that have been launched against the concept. For, unlike consideration, every time *cause* came under attack it emerged more convinc-ing and more coherently conceived. Academics and the courts alike were forced to work out the practical implications and from their endeavours there emerged a concept which runs through the entire law of contract performing a number of important and different functions. It is an ingredient necessary for the formation of a valid contract; it will be used to invalidate unlawful or immoral transactions; and it will also justify the consequences that flow from an excusable failure to perform one of the obligations of a bilateral contract. *Cause* thus follows contract from birth to death, from formation to discharge. By contrast, consideration has been overburdened by technical rules, and its importance has, in most cases, been restricted to the stage of formation of the contract. For the post-information stage other concepts have been called upon to perform in England what *cause* has achieved in France. Illegality, mistake, impossibility, frustration proper, are some, and the result is inevitable frag-mentation and, at times, reasoning which is elliptical and intellectually unsat-isfying. *Taylor* v. *Caldwell*[96] (and the cases that have relied on it like *Harbutt's Plasticine*) have been used to illustrate the point. They also show that the French reasoning finds a counterpart in the doctrine of failure (total or partial) of consideration which could and should be used more often to jus-tify results which are currently explained by a strained extension of the notion of impossibility.

---

[95] *Rechtswidrigkeit, Sozialadäquanz, Fahrlässigkeit und Schuld im Zivilrecht*, in 1957 NWJ 1777. See, also, von Caemmerer, "Wandlungen des Deliktsrecht" in (1960) II *100 Jahre Deutches Rechtsleben* 49 et seq.
[96] (1863) 3 B & S 826.

One or two further points can be mentioned in passing. This brief study provides yet further evidence (if any is still required) of the fact that French law can be as case-orientated as English law (though it has avoided much of the rigour of the doctrine of *stare decisis*). It also demonstrates that the view advanced by many in this country, namely, that codification encourages the "planned" development of the law or that it can provide "a compact, accessible and complete formulation of the law",[97] is often unsubstantiated by civilian experience. Anyone who studies articles 1131–1133 or 1384 CC can see that the above statements are apt to mislead. Indeed, it is tempting to paraphrase Professor David and say that in these areas "the overall appearance of [French Law] resembles an impressionist painting; the legal rules, considered individually, are but points. One must step back in order to detect the general patterns of the composition".[98]

The careful examination of the cases also shows that their outcome is often determined by consideration of policy. Nowhere is this more clearly demonstrated[99] than in the case of gifts to mistresses and in the way the courts have used *cause* (in theory a most abstract concept) in order to invalidate them when they are given "in exchange" for sexual favours but uphold their validity whenever they mark the termination of the extra-marital connection! Here, as indeed elsewhere in the law of obligations, policy and law cannot and, arguably, should not be dissociated. This is true of French law as it is of English law though, admittedly, it is more difficult to discern the policy arguments in the French judicial decisions which are notorious for their rigorous brevity.[100]

In view of the above, it is submitted that further comparative study of this topic would be greatly facilitated if attention was focused on the functional problems which *cause* and consideration try to resolve; and when this is done, it will become clear that the similarities in the results as well as in the reasoning are greater than they are often suspected to be.

---

[97] These are two of the five benefits which codification, apparently, entails according to Lord Scarman. *Codification and Judge-made Law*—off-print of a lecture delivered on 20 October 1966 to the Law Faculty of the University of Birmingham, p.19.

[98] *French Law. Its Structure, Sources, and Methodology.* English translation by M. Kindred (1972), p. 77.

[99] But, of course, examples from other parts of the law of contract can be quoted. Thus, in the area of offer and acceptance, see Req. 21 mars 1932, D. 1933. 1. 65 and Professor Carbonnier's comments, above n. 85, Vol.1, p.68.

[100] As Dr Bernard Rudden has pertinently remarked ("Courts and Codes in England, France and Soviet Russia", 48 *Tulane Law Rev.*, 1010 at 1022): "The very act of decision implies a choice; but the French grammatical technique enables the judge to conceal it".

5

The Legacy of History on German Contract Law*

1. PRELIMINARY OBSERVATIONS

In his famous Hamlyn lectures, delivered precisely forty years ago, the late Lord Devlin argued that "it is impossible to understand any English institution of any antiquity unless you know something of its history".[1] His comment is as valid of German law as it is of English law; and in this paper we would like to offer some examples which substantiate this assertion. More importantly, however, we hope that our comments will show how history shaped not only the form and substance of German private law in general, the law of obligations in particular but, just as importantly, how it affected the method of legal reasoning and the teaching of law. It is these differences which make German law so "different" from the common law and often discourage their meaningful comparison. One of the points that emerges from this paper—but which will not be pursued here in any detail—is that once one has mastered the art of re-packaging German law in order to make it attractive

---

* The best accounts of the topics discussed in this paper can be found in the classic works of W. Flume, *Allgemeiner Teil des bürgerlichen Rechts*, Bd 2, 3rd edn. (1979); K. Larenz,*Allgemeiner Teil des deutschen Bürgerlichen Rechts*, 7th edn. (1989) and *Lehrbuch des Schuldrechts*, vol. I, *Allgemeiner Teil*, 14th edn. (1987), and D. Medicus, *Allgemeiner Teil des BGB*, 6th edn. (1994) and *Schuldrecht*, vol. I *Allgemeiner Teil*, 6th edn. (1992) and vol. II *Besonderer Teil*, 5th edn. (1992). From the smaller books one should, perhaps, mention Hans Brox's *Allgemeiner Teil des Bürgerlichen Gesetzbuchs*, 18th edn. (1994) since it is short, clear, and will appear more readable to a foreign student. Short but compact (and full of ideas) is also D.Medicus' *Bürgerliches Recht*, 16th edn. (1994). The literature on German legal history is vast. Heinrich Mitteis' *Deutsche Rechtsgeschichte* (1949), 18th edn. (with Heinz Lieberich) (1988) and *Deutsches Privatrecht* (1950), 10th edn., again with Lieberich (1988), are classics of a sort, though they approach their subject in purely germanic terms. On the other hand Paul Koschaker's *Europa und das römische Recht* (1947), 2nd edn. (1966) and Franz Wieacker's *Privatrechtsgeschichte der Neuzeit* (1952), 2nd edn. (1967), place German legal history firmly within the wider context of the development of modern European culture. This is also emphasised by Coing inter alia in his "Das Recht als Element der europaischen Kultur" 1984 238 *HZ* 1.

Excellent English accounts can be found in Reinhard Zimmermann's works, notably in his *The Law of Obligations: Roman Foundations of the Civilian Tradition* (1990). For a more recen contribution see "Savigny's Legacy. Legal History, Comparative Law, and the Emergence of a European Legal Science" (1966) 112 *LQR* 576. Interesting insights into the state of German legal science during the 19th century can also be found in a collection of essays edited by Professor Mathias Reimann entitled *The Reception of Continental Ideas in the Common Law World 1820–1920* (1993).

[1] *Trial by Jury* (1966 reprint), 4.

to an English audience, one can then discover the similarities that exist between these two systems and investigate where, precisely, the one system may be able to assist the improvement of the other.

For obvious reasons, this paper will be divided into five sections. The second, which will follow these introductory observations, will sketch the historical development of German law so as to put the sections which follow into their proper context. How this history affected the structure of the Code will be discussed in section three. Section four will then examine how it affected legal reasoning. A final section (five) will put forward some tentative points, suggesting how this research can be taken further in the interests of further meaningful comparison of the two systems.

2. AN HISTORICAL SKETCH

A. *The Tortured Path to Unity*

When the German Civil Code (*Bürgerliches Gesetzbuch* or BGB for short) came into force on 1 January 1900 it not only coincided with the beginning of a new century but also marked the end of the long process of the unification of the German state. Legal historians would probably treat the enactment in 1495 of the *Reichskammergerichtsordnung*—the statute which regulated the establishment and organization of the Imperial Court—as the first step towards this process. The fact that this enactment chronologically also more or less coincides with the consolidation of Hapsburg hegemony, may also speak in its favour. But if, indeed, it really is the first stepping-point of the unification process, it is a tenuous one at best. The superiority of this court among the multiple courts that existed in the lands populated by Germanic people was nominal rather than real, since the Emperor's own effective power over his Empire was feeble. And the "unity" of the Reich in those days was, in cultural terms, very different from that which came three and a half centuries later; for at the close of the Middle Ages it was a union centred in the Catholic South (Austria) and not, as was later to be the case, one dominated by the Protestant North (Prussia). Still, despite these and other reservations, the enactment of 1495 had a symbolic value if for no other reason that it gave the court a fixed abode (Frankfurt) and marked the official recognition of Roman law trained judges. Later, this "innovation" became fashionable even in local courts. This, along with a trend-setting statute—*The Carolina* (largely influenced by the work of that remarkable man Baron von Schwartzenberg)— which was enacted in 1532, put the coping stone on the powers of the old, lay German judges (the *Schöffen*) and marked the beginning of the "Reception" of Roman law. In the sixteenth and seventeenth centuries Roman law thus became known as the common law (*gemeines Recht*) of the German nation; and on the eve of the nineteenth century codification, it was still the main legal system in much of the geographic area which in post-Second World War times was known as Western Germany i.e. roughly Bavaria, Hannover, Hessen, Holstein and Württemberg.

The phenomenon of the Reception has captivated legal historians for in Germany (more so than in France) it was so massive and wholehearted that it succeeded in marginalising considerable Germanic achievements in the legal field. These are all the more remarkable since they were accomplished in an otherwise fragmented and war-torn country which had suffered successive disasters (physical and man-made) since the demise of the Hohenstaufen rule in the early part of the thirteenth century.

The (first) German Reich thus remained legally and politically fragmented despite the claim of its Emperors and its people to represent the natural heirs to the Roman empire (*Heiliges Römisches Reich Deutscher Nation*); and this fragmentation (coupled with constant wars both on his eastern and western fronts) explain both the Emperor's vain attempts to repress the spreading in the sixteenth century of the Reformation in the Northern and Eastern provinces of his Empire, as well as the ease with which Roman law came to be seen as the natural as well as neutral legal system that could fill the political vacuum of the time. This political chaos, reinforced by religious wars which reached new peaks in the seventeenth century giving Europe its first flavour of a "World War"—the Thirty Years War—ensured that legal disunity remained a feature of German political as well as legal history until the formal demise of the First Reich in 1806 at the hands of Napoleon. For by this time, as contemporary legal maps of Germany clearly show, even Roman law had lost some ground, the northern and eastern provinces having come under the domination of the Prussian Land Law of 1794 (*Allgemeines Landrecht für die preußischen Staaten*)—a monstrously long enactment which covered both public and private law and represented the closest Germany ever came towards falling under the spell of the School of Natural Law. At the same time, the Rhine countries, had moved legally closer to the fashionable French Civil Code. During this period Bavaria continued to assert its legal and cultural independence by being governed by its own *Codex Maximilianus Bavaricus Civilis* of 1756 which had codified the Roman-based law of the previous century but also displayed visible signs of the legislator's belief in the tenets of the era of Enlightenment. Indeed Bavaria has jealously guarded its "separateness" ever since, constantly playing in Germany the kind of role that Texas enjoys in the United States, and even threatening political cessation during the early life of the Second Reich (1871) the creation of which its indebted King Ludwig had supported in exchange for the Prussian bankers servicing his debts.[2] Finally, the Habsburg territories of Austria and Bohemia were by now governed by the *Allgemeines Bürgerliches Gesetzbuch* of 1811.

---

[2] Even as recently as the mid-1940s Bavaria threatened not to sign what became known as the Constitution of Bonn of 1949 unless it was given separate citizenship. But, in the end, the demand was dropped as a result of pressure from the victorious "allies".

The nineteenth century thus became the true turning point in the process for German unity. Yet the century began inauspiciously in so far as the Germany which emerged from the Napoleonic era had now opted for the form of a Confederation (*Deutscher Bund* not a *Reich*) of forty-one "German" states, and a loose confederation at that. These, then, were highly complex political times, where northerners were increasingly trying to dominate suspicious southerners, and politicians, men of letters, and dreamers of all kinds, urged their audiences to think of "Germany above all"[3]—a call that was later to acquire sinister overtones—but seeing the process that would lead to this result in very different terms.

It is in this context that the next legal battle was destined to be fought. For barely had the post-Napoleonic settlement been agreed upon, when Thibaut and Savigny began their great intellectual duel. Thibaut was to fire the first shot—in 1814—with his pamphlet entitled *Über die Notwendigkeit eines allgemeinen bürgerlichen Rechts für Deutschland* (On the Necessity of a General Civil Code for Germany), in which he proposed that Germany follow France's example and adopt a unifying Civil Code. This would have the advantage of rendering the disparate law more accessible; and, arguably more importantly, it would facilitate the unification of the German nation. It provoked Savigny's thunder in the equally forcefully expressed tract *Vom Beruf unserer Zeit für Gesetzgebung und Rechtswissenschaft* (On the Vocation of our Age for Legislation and Legal Science) where he argued in favour of the study of the law within its historical context[4] and eventual adaptation and rejuvenation, instead of a hurried attempt to emulate the French Code for which he had little regard. That Savigny's claim that the time was not ripe for a unifying code was bound to win the day seems, at any rate with hindsight, inevitable. But it is still something of a paradox that his search for the roots of German legal culture was to take him back to Roman law and ignore the indigenous products. The fact that this fits in with the reality that Roman law, as we have seen, had been adopted in the bulk of Germany in the sixteenth and seventeenth centuries, moderates only slightly the unusual direction of this cultural trend, for Savigny and his followers were not interested in Roman law as it had been applied in Germany during the sixteenth and seventeenth centuries, but turned their attention to the original sources (*Zurück zu den Quellen*). A more likely explanation must be found in the fact that this movement was really part of the wider trend which during the nineteenth century, pushed much of Germany (and the rest of Europe) to re-adopt the aesthetic ideas and

---

[3] That, at least, is what the first (and subsequently maligned) verse of Hoffman von Fallersleben's poem "*Das Lied der Deutschen*" suggests. But it is the French-inspired third verse which has survived (since 1952) as Germany's National Anthem. The music, of course, was composed by Hayden for the Austrian Emperor Franz Josef on 12 February 1797, though it is better known as the theme in the second movement of the *Streichquartett* in C major, Opus 76. 3.

[4] This need to study the past to understand and shape the present is a central theme in Savigny's work. He thus refers to it in his classic work *System des heutigen Römischen Rechts*, vol. I (1840), XV as "der lebendige Zusammenhang"—the vital connection.

ideals of classicism. But this move also had the unfortunate consequence of discarding the not inconsiderable advances made on classical Roman law by the *opinio communis doctorum* and the *usus fori* (the practices of the high courts of France, Germany, Italy and Spain, which were often quoted outside their respective geographical borders) during the sixteenth and seventeenth centuries. Additionally, it also had the side effect of marginalising the work which the germanists—such as Eichhorn, Beseler, the Grimm brothers, and Otto von Gierke—were doing in order to show how important the purely Germanic elements were in the development of the cultural identity of the new country.

Yet, surprising or not, what matters is the effect that this school had on German legal science[5] and, in some instances, the final contents of the Code. Three consequences in particular must be mentioned from the very outset, even if briefly, since they affected the entire material discussed in this piece.

First, as already stated, the historical school undoubtedly stimulated an extensive study of ancient texts and shaped the minds of the legal scholars—the Pandektists—who, in one form or another, dominated Germany throughout the nineteenth century and left their imprint on subsequent generations of lawyers. This intellectual re-orientation left a strong mark on the content of the Code as a whole, but in particular on the General Part and the law of contract since solutions were often adopted on the basis that they had been espoused (or, which was worse, were thought to have been espoused) nearly two thousand years earlier by Roman law.

Examples of this phenomenon abound in the Code; and they are exceptionally numerous in the law of contract. We see this clearly in the approach taken towards the problem of irregularities of performance where the Code, following Mommsen's teachings[6], chose to regulate two types of such irregularity—delay (*Verzug*) and impossibility (*Unmöglichkeit*, understood in a narrow, physical sense)—but deliberately excluded what is, arguably, the most common and difficult type of "breach"—i.e. bad performance. The model here was largely Roman—the regime which applied to obligations *certam rem dare*—an odd choice for two reasons. First, it made German law diverge radically from the general model adopted both by English and French law; and, secondly, because such a diversion (with all the problems which it brought in its wake) could have easily been avoided if the Code had stuck here, as it did in so many other instances, to the other Roman model—that of consensual contracts. Likewise, a mis-understanding of Roman texts, coupled with the

---

[5] And the United States as well. Thus see Stefan Riesenfeld "The Impact of German Legal Ideas and Institutions on Legal Thought and Institutions in the United States"; Mathias Reimann, "A Career in Itself. The German Professorate as a Model for American Legal Academica"; James E. Herget, "The Influence of German Thought on American Jurisprudence, 1880–1918", all printed in M. Reimann (ed.), *The Reception of Continental Ideas in the Common Law World 1820–1920* (1993) at pp. 89 *et seq.*, 165 *et seq.*, and 203 *et seq.*, respecptively.

[6] "Die Unmöglichkeit der Leistung in ihrem Einfluß auf obligatorische Verhältnisse" (1853), I *Beiträge zum Obligationenrecht*.

desire (which back-fired) to protect small industrial concerns at a time of nascent industrialisation, led the draftsmen of the Code to adopt the unfortunate tort law rule contained in § 831 BGB which makes masters only liable for their own faults (in selecting and/or supervising their employees) but not for the faults committed by these employees in the course of their employment.

There were other areas of the law where adherence to Roman doctrine gave rise to difficulties. Two more instances will be given to illustrate how oppressive the influence of the past could be on the present.

The first example comes from the Roman tendency to see even bilateral contracts as consisting of unilateral obligations which were merely brought together by occasional rules which underlined their inter-dependence. This gave rise to difficulties where, for instance, damages had to be quantified as a result of the purchaser's inability or refusal to pay the purchase price. In such cases was the vendor obliged to perform his obligation to the full and then proceed against the purchaser (the so-called *Austauschtheorie*)? Alternatively, should the Roman way of looking at contractual obligations be jettisoned in favour of an approach which looked at the entire contractual transaction? This second approach, which, with some modifications eventually (but not without much intellectual agonising) came to be adopted by the Code[7] and the courts[8], meant that the contract should be seen as a whole and the innocent party would be absolved from performing his obligation and, instead, allowed to claim only the difference between the situation that had resulted from the breach and the situation as it would have been had the contract been performed in the envisaged way (*Differenztheorie*).

Another, and for present purposes final example, relevant both to contract and to tort, can be found in the Pandektist understanding of a text from Gaius' Institutes[9] which led them to the conclusion that Roman law was unwilling to protect through the law of obligations personal and incorporeal interests—a view which led to the adoption of the unfortunate provision found in § 253 BGB. This led to substantial difficulties in awarding damages for violation of personality rights, which received wider recognition in the 1950s, while also impeding the award of damages for pain and suffering whenever the cause of action was contractual rather than delictual.[10]

Secondly, the return to the original Roman sources meant that all material that had not attracted the attention of the Roman lawyers, but had been developed by the learned doctors of the *ius commune*, was ignored by the

---

[7] e.g. § 326 BGB.

[8] See, for instance, RG 13. 3. 1902, RGZ 50, 255, 262 *et seq.*; BGH 9. 5. 1956, BGHZ 20, 338, 343.

[9] IV, 48.

[10] For further details in English see Markesinis, *The German Law of Torts*, 3rd edn. (1994) pp. 25 and 689–90.

nineteenth Pandektists and left outside the Code.[11] This meant that important parts of commercial law, such as bills of exchange, insurance contracts, the regulations of corporations, patents and copyrights (as well as strict liability in the area of tort law) were very largely ignored by the new Civil Code as was, essentially, the regulation of labour relations. All these matters the *Pandektenwissenschaft* considered almost below its dignity and left to the representatives of the *Deutsches Privatrecht* to deal with, often with the result that they had to be regulated by separate enactments and outside the framework of the BGB. This tendency was strongly condemned by Otto von Gierke, probably the harshest critic of the new Code, and a crucial extract from his critique deserves to be quoted in full since it impinges on the kind of education young lawyers received for a long time. He thus wrote[12]:

> "[I]t is a fatal error—an error committed by the draft of the German Civil Code—to think the social work can be left to special legislation so that the general private law can be shaped, without regard to the task that has thus been shifted, in a purely individualistic manner. There thus exist two systems ruled by completely different spirits: a system of the general civil law that contains the 'pure' private law, and a mass of special laws in which a private law, tarnished by and blended with public law, governs. On the one side a living, popular, socially coloured law full of inner stimulus, on the other an abstract mould, romanistic, individualistic, ossified in dead dogmatics. The real and true private law can now develop in all its logical splendour oblivious of the heretical special laws . . . *But the general law, is the native soil out of which the special laws also grow. By contact with the general law our youth learn legal thinking. The judges take their nourishment from it. What a fatal abyss opens before us! What a schism between the spirit of the normal administration of justice and the administrative jurisdiction that is being extended further and further! What a . . . danger of stagnation and degeneration of jurisprudence . . .*"

The last few lines from this marvellous statement have been italicised since the criticism they contain may still be valid; and it may be valid even to the way common lawyers (both in England and the United States) teach their law of contract, often ignoring commercial, labour, or social accretions[13] to their subject leaving them to be discussed by other colleagues in more specialised courses offered in advanced years but, invariably, only taken by a few students.

Thirdly, as will be explained more fully in the next sub-section, this movement introduced a new methodological approach to law, spending untold effort in schematizing, ordering, and integrating the concepts of Roman law and building a "system". As Zweigert and Kötz have put it:[14]

---

[11] Only exceptionally did institutions borrowed from the commercial law manage to penetrate the Civil Code, arguably the most notable instance being the remedy of rescission. For a fuller account see Leser, *Der Rücktritt vom Vertrag* (1975) 10 *et seq.*

[12] *Die soziale Aufgabe des Privatrechts* (1889), 16.

[13] Not to mention the growing impact which constitutional law is having on most parts of private law.

[14] *An Introduction to Comparative Law*, 2nd edn. (1992), 146.

"Their method of treatment was once again marked by that exaggerated dogmatism which we noted in the period of the law of Reason, [i.e 17th and 18th century] save that it was directed to rules of Roman law rather than particular postulates supposedly grounded in reason."

The first book of the Code which, in its entirety, took twenty years to produce, exemplifies these ideas and their intellectual fruits. This influenced the style of the enactment as much as the style of legal reasoning and of legal education that resulted from it.

Finally, as already hinted, many of the developments /achievements of the period of the *Ius Commune* were generally discarded by the Pandektists and, in some cases, excluded by the Code. For instance, the synthesis of the Roman approach in the area of torts, which had led to the kind of wider formulations of tort liability found in the Codes of France and the Low Countries, was abandoned in favour of a more detailed (and in some cases ludicrously narrow) regulation of the subject.[15]

The same was true of the transformation of the Roman *actio de in rem verso* into a general action to recover losses flowing from the unjust enrichment of another person which was one of the most interesting achievements of the Natural School of law (though the BGB eventually reached a similar breadth by adopting Savigny's approach[16] of "merging" the Roman law *condictiones* into the general approach now found in § 812 BGB). It must, however, also be noted that other achievements of the period of *ius commune*, such as the gradual development of the notion of contracts in favour of third parties, the liberalisation of the law of assignment, and the development of the law of agency (or, more accurately, representation), were retained by the new school. Two concluding remarks will suffice to complete our sketch of the unification process.

First one must note that the political union, achieved as a result of the wars, first against Austria (which effectively ensured the triumph of the idea of the "smaller Germany" i.e., one without the Austrian Empire within its bounds) and then against France, followed and did not precede a considerable degree of economic union which took shape from the 1830s onwards.[17] In the beginning, this too, took the confrontational form of a customs union of the northern states competing with a custom union of southern states. In the end, however, the north triumphed in the financial arena as it did later in the political one, the Austrians being almost constantly outfoxed in their manoeuvres by Bismarck, arguably the greatest German statesman of all times.

Secondly, legal unification did not, in all respects, have to wait for political union though it undoubtedly received a great impetus from it. Thus, the "Law of Negotiable Instruments" (*Wechselordnung*) was unified in 1848; and in

---

[15] See, for instance, §§ 824 and 825 BGB.

[16] *System des heutigen Römischen Rechts*, Beilage XIV, 5, pp. 503 *et seq*., and 525.

[17] The first landmark was the creation of the Deutscher Zollverein (Customs Union) of 1833.

1861 the much more important "Commercial Code" (*Allgemeines Handels-gesetzbuch*) was agreed upon—though like the 1848 enactment, it was left to the members of the Confederation to turn it into municipal law. A year later an attempt was even made to draft a Civil Code—the so called *Dresdner Entwurf*—but this came to nothing. But after the establishment of the Second Reich, Imperial statutes (i.e. statutes applying to the whole of the Empire) started coming fast out of the legislature. Thus, within a short period of time, important statutes imposing strict liability for carriage by rail, (*Reich-shaftpflichtgesetz* of 1871), the "Law Regulating the Organisation of the Imperial Courts" (*Gerichtsverfassungsgesetz*), the law on Insolvency (*Konkursordnung*), and the law on "Civil Procedure" (*Zivilprozeßordnung*) came into existence. The last to receive the Royal Assent (in 1896) and come into force on 1 January 1900 was, as already mentioned, the Civil Code (*Bürgerliches Gestzbuch*). The legal unification was, at last, complete; and as we shall note below, the document that completed this process has left a deep mark on the kind of legal education that young Germans receive to this day. Otto von Gierke's views on this point have already been quoted.

B. The Triumph of the Learned Man

The expression belongs to the late Jack Dawson, one of the greatest comparatists of our times; and he used it in his Cooley Lectures[18] to describe the growing influence which German academics acquired in sixteenth and seventeenth centuries in the making and not just the teaching of the law. This accounted for the Reception of Roman law, already alluded to above; but it accounted for much more besides.

First, besides importing Roman law into the country, it progressively gave Universities a unique role in German legal culture. For they not only influenced the development of the law but, for a while, actually shaped it themselves by literally drafting the opinions of the courts through the machinery of "dispatching of the record" (*Aktenversendung*) to the nearest law school to opine on the matter in hand. Though this usurpation of judicial power did not prevail in quite the whole of the Empire and, in any event, subsided with the passage of time, it left a strong tradition of a judicial dialogue with academics which German judges to this day conduct with their academic brethren. To this day this is clearly evident in the judgments of the German courts which are replete with academic citations.[19]

Secondly and relatedly, this environment encouraged the appearance in Germany of jurists with philosophical and jurisprudential leanings, something which stands in stark contrast to the kind of pragmatic lawyers to which

---

[18] *The Oracles of the Law*, 1955.
[19] On this see Kötz, "Scholarship and the Courts: A Comparative Survey" in D.S. Clark (ed.), *Comparative and Private International Law; Essays in Honour of J.H. Merryman on his Seventieth birthday* (1990), 183–95.

Napoleon was happy and, indeed, eager to entrust the future of legal education and, indeed, the English legal tradition which lasted well into the nineteenth century, if not longer. The result was the flowering in Germany of
jurisprudential theories which dominated the nineteenth century and spilt well
into the twentieth, affecting not only countries of the Germanic world but also
France and the United States, especially during the turn of the twentieth century. Three of these schools of thought influenced German law, its teaching,
and interpretation to such a great extent that they must be mentioned here
briefly. (The fourth, the so-called "Free School" of thought, born as a reaction to the first school, had no effect on practising lawyers so it will be omitted from this brief account[20]).

The so-called school of the *Begriffsjurisprudenz* followed the Historical
school from about the 1850s onwards and included among its proponents such
eminent Pandektists as Puchta and Ihering. Its followers believed that each
legal concept should be rigorously analysed and then "fitted" into the framework of a particular legal institution (*Rechtsinstitut*) such as marriage, family, real property, inheritance, and the like. All institutions, in turn formed
part of the "legal system". The ultimate purpose was to create a complete and
closed system of legal concepts that would then be capable of embracing all
situations of life and provide them, almost mechanically, with a legal solution. In this world, academics were assigned pride of place since they were the
system builders. Practising lawyers—including judges—would merely have to
subsume facts under the appropriate concept and thus find the answer to the
questions put to them. This way of thinking, so different from that found in
common law systems, had a profound effect on the style of the Code, the
interpretation of legal rules, the filling of legal gaps, and the development of
a legal science. As we shall stress below, this approach to law also still dictates certain thinking patterns of German lawyers.

It was not much before the enactment of the Code, however, that the
excesses of this school led many jurists to feel that, in the words of Oliver
Wendell Holmes, the life of the law is not merely logic but experience.
Certainly, the legal judgment as a mere exercise in deductive logic taking place
within a closed system soon came to be seriously questioned; and a greater
desire for the search of the policy reasons behind the judicial opinion started
to emerge. So, the *Interessenjurisprudenz* emerged as a sensible reaction to this
first school arguing that life did not exist for the sake of concepts but, on the
contrary, that the concepts were there to serve life's needs. This school scored
a triumph of sorts when it converted Ihering to its cause who then argued its
tenets eloquently in his famous book *Der Zweck im Recht* (The Purpose in

---

[20] Much of the efforts of the *Freirechtler* focused on pointing out the weaknesses of the
Begriffsjurisprudenz and its use of formal logic. But the Free School also encouraged judges to be
open as to how they reach their conclusions while also encouraging a well-rounded education in
the humanities and the social sciences. Much of this found greater response in the United States
than it did in Germany.

the Law) which first appeared in 1877–1883.[21] Philipp Heck, another of this school's later proponents, put its views clearly when he argued[22] that behind all legal regulations lie certain values which lawgivers wish to assert, promote, or balance against one another. It was thus wrong to pretend that the judge's role was merely an expert exercise in deductive logic. This school thus aspired to discover these values and to encourage lawyers not to hide their real reasoning behind concepts.[23] The result was a considerable liberalisation from the strictures of the first school of thought even though by now it had left its indelible marks on German legal culture and, just as importantly, on the image it has with foreign lawyers.

This move towards a search for values continued and even strengthened after the collapse of the Nazi regime and the end of the Second World War and led to the newest variant of the school—the jurisprudence of values or the *Wertungsjurisprudenz*. In turn this led to a search for higher and even more abstractly expressed values in the Constitution and the entire legal order which were then "concretised" in the realms of private law such as contract, labour, family, and tort law and given the form of legal rules. The creation of the so-called general right of personality (*allgemeines Persönlichkeitsrecht*), discussed in great detail elsewhere,[24] exemplifies this process. Indeed, the Constitutional Court expressly adopted this approach when it sanctioned the creation of the new "protected interest" (under § 823 I BGB) when it said:

> "Occasionally, the law can be found outside the positive legal rules erected by the state; this is law which emanates from the entire constitutional order and which has as its purpose the 'correction' of written law. It is for the judge to 'discover' this law and through his opinions give it concrete effect. The Constitution does not restrict judges to apply statutes in their literary sense when deciding cases put before them. Such an approach assumes a basic completeness of statutory rules which is not attainable in practice . . . The insight of the judge may bring to light certain values of society . . . which are implicitly accepted by the constitutional order but which have received an insufficient expression in statutory texts. The judge's decision can help realize such ideas and give effect to such values."[25]

It would serve no real purpose to continue here this inevitably simplistic presentation of complicated German theories. Professor Larenz's

---

[21] Two years later appeared another of Ihering's works—*Scherz und Ernst in der Jurisprudenz* (Levity and Ernestness in Jurisprudence)—which confirmed him not only as an able but also humorous critic of the School to which he once belonged. Years later, Roscoe Pound would refer to Ihering as "a jurist by the grace of God".

[22] *Das Problem der Rechtsgewinnung* (1912), *Gesetzesauslegung und Interessenjurisprudenz* (1914) and in what was, arguably, his most famous work, *Begriffsbildung und Interessenjurisprudenz* (1932).

[23] See RG 3.2.1914, RGZ 84, 125, where the new school scores a clear victory over the old legal reasoning.

[24] Markesinis, *The German Law of Torts*, pp. 352–447.

[25] BVerfG 14. 2. 1973, BVerfGE 34, 269, 287.

Methodenlehre der Rechtswissenschaft[26] is generally regarded as containing the best account of these movements. But the common law reader may be allowed to enquire whether the end result may not reveal ideas and theories which were explored just as much by common lawyers (for instance the American realists) as they were by the German counterparts. If he is historically minded he may even assume, often with just cause, that Germanic ideas served as starting points for American theorising. One might even go further and argue that the policy-oriented approach, found in both the German and American systems, may bring them closer together than common rumour may have us believe. Yet the style of writing, be it judicial or academic, and the reasoning processes still remain very different, as is in many respects the pedagogical purpose ascribed to the law schools of the respective countries. Contrasts thus exist and they remain sharp. The remaining part of this paper will thus try to show how they have affected the organisation of legal material, especially as it affects the law of contracts and how German lawyers are taught to approach their Code. The comparative lawyer is thus still forced to "deconstruct" German law in order to make it acceptable to his common law readers; and this is one of the other theses put forward in this essay.

3. THE STRUCTURE OF THE CIVIL CODE

Anyone who decides to codify a subject as vast as civil law must first decide what he wishes to include in his code and then develop a notion of how the different component parts of this area of law relate to each other. If nothing else, the need to number provisions in the code entails the necessity of an internal order. This is certainly how the German jurists felt during the last century when they spent over twenty years drafting their Code. Their meticulous approach contrasts sharply with the more "hurried" enactment of the equally famous French Civil Code. Before going into the substance of the German law of contract every lawyer, be he a student or a practioner, is, therefore, well advised to a take a careful look at the structure of the Civil Code and acquire some notion at least of how the various parts relate to each other.

Thus, the Civil Code (*Bürgerliches Gesetzbuch*—henceforth BGB for short) consists of five parts, which are called *Bücher* (books). Book 1 contains the so-called general part, replete with rules that are relevant to the entire civil law and, indeed, the science of law as a whole. But it also contains important rules concerning the law of contracts such as the rules that determine the formation of contract as well as general rules about the ability of one person to act for another (representation). Book 2 (§§ 241–853 BGB) covers in greater detail the law of obligations (*Schuldrecht*), which includes contracts, unjust

---

[26] 6th edn., 1991.

enrichment, and torts. Book 3 (§§ 854–1296 BGB) regulates the law of property (*Sachenrecht*), while the law of domestic relations (*Familienrecht*) is treated in Book 4 (§§ 1297–1921). Finally, the fifth book (§§ 1922–2385) covers inheritance law *(Erbrecht)*. People are born, acquire legal rights, enter into legal relationships, purchase goods and land, marry, have children, sometimes divorce, and, eventually, die, invariably leaving a number of loose ends which need tying up. The Code follows this natural rhythm in its arrangement of its material.

As hinted already, the Civil Code does not cover all of private law within its bounds. Even important parts of the law of contract—such as the rules concerning formation of contracts, capacity, illegality, agency etc.—have, for reasons of logical classification, been excluded from the second book of the Code and are, instead, found in Book One. By contrast, this material receives special attention in all the standard Anglo-American text books on the subject, so the Anglo-American reader must always be mentally prepared to overcome artificial hurdles of classification in order to discover his material. Moreover, recent times have seen the enactment of important contract law statutes which, for practical or doctrinal considerations, have not been incorporated into the BGB . Among them we note the *Gesetz zur Regelung des Rechts der Allgemeinen Geschäftsbedingungen* ("Standard Contract Terms Act"), the *Verbraucherkreditgesetz,*("Consumer Credit Act."), the *Versicherungsvertragsgesetz* ("Insurance Contracts Act") and the *Gesetz über den Widerruf von Haustürgeschäften und ähnlichen Geschäften* ("Act on Avoidance of Contracts Negotiated Away From Business Premises"). In addition, and for the historical reasons already alluded to, specific rules which apply to commercial businesses only, have been left to a different Code, i.e. the *Handelsgesetzbuch* ("Commercial Code"). This Code regulates the activities of commercial entities, contains rules about the commercial registry and commercial agents, covers various commercial partnerships, provides rules for book-keeping by commercial businesses, regulates specific commercial contracts (e.g., shipping) and adapts some of the rules of the BGB to a commercial background, e.g. by requiring the buyer of goods under a commercial contract to inspect the goods immediately after delivery (§ 377 HGB).[27] Company law is also largely regulated by specific statutes, which lie outside the Civil Code, such as the *Aktiengesetz* ("Stock Corporation Act") and the *Gesetz betreffend die Gesellschaften mit beschränkter Haftung* ("Limited Liability Company Act"). The German lawyer thus has to spend much of his training learning how to inter-relate this rich and diverse material. This contrasts sharply with the method found in most American law schools where little attempt seems to be made to relate the various parts of even the law of obligations.

---

[27] For an overview on the Commercial Code and commercial law, see Dannemann, *An Introduction to German Civil and Commercial Law*, pp. 67–88.

More interestingly, the Civil Code contains only rudimentary rules on labour law (§§ 611–30 BGB); and history and the individualistic spirit which influenced the drafting of the Code, can explain this omission. Most of employment law and the law of industrial relations are covered by a variety of different statutes, with much gap-filling provided by the jurisprudence of the labour courts, their creative activity having started in depression years of the post-First World War period and having been greatly expanded in the 1960s and 1970s. Much of this case law has also been inspired by the consitutional background giving evidence of the modern phenomenon of the constitutionalisation of private law.

The same can be said for other parts of private law. Thus, separate statutes regulate civil procedure in general *(Zivilprozeßordnung*—"Code of Civil Procedure"), a topic which figures much more prominently in the German academic curriculum than it does in the Anglo-American university scene, and insolvency *(Konkursordnung, Vergleichsordnung*—soon to be replaced by a unified *Insolvenzordnung,* Insolvency Act). Private International Law is mainly covered by the *Einführungsgesetz zum BGB* ("Introductory Act to the Civil Code"). The overall picture is one thus one of considerable complexity.

4. THE STYLE OF THE CODE AND THE REASONING PROCESS IT ENCOURAGES

If one takes a look at the style in which the BGB was drafted, one feels inclined to agree with Zweigert and Kötz[28] when they state that:

"The BGB is not addressed to the citizen at all, but rather to the professional lawyer; it deliberately eschews easy comprehensibility and waives all claims to educate its reader; instead of dealing with particular cases in a clear and concrete manner it adopts throughout an abstract conceptual language which the layman, and often enough the foreign lawyer as well, finds largely incomprehensible, but which the trained expert, after many years of familiarity, cannot help admiring for its precision and rigour of thought."

The abstraction of rules, the use of concepts, and a combination of general clauses with specific regulations, are particularly characteristic of the way in which the BGB has been drafted. For reasons of convenience, the discussion that follows has been divided into six sub-headings.

A. Abstraction of Legal Rules

All legal rules involve an element of abstraction. Rules are meant to be general and thus to apply not just to one but to a variety of similar situations. In the process of law-making the reasons why a certain situation should be

---

[28] *An Introduction to Comparative Law,* 150.

treated in a certain way are abstracted from the specific facts of this situation and generalized so that they apply to different, albeit similar situations as well. Thus, abstraction occurs when the requirements are defined which must be met in order for a rule to be applied. If, for example, rules on the passing of risk are to apply to all sales of goods, these rules must apply to the sale of an ocean cruiser which is worth £100 million, but also to the sale of a light bulb which costs £1.

The law of contract (the subject of this piece) is a further abstraction of all those rules which are common to sales, tenancy, works, employment, guarantee and other contracts. For example, the discovery that all these contracts come into being when one party makes an offer which the other party accepts, enables the formulation of general rules on formation of contracts, rather than specific rules which apply only to the formation of sales contracts, tenancy contracts, etc.

But abstraction can be exaggerated and produce unintended casualties. This occurs if the scope of a rule is stretched beyond the scope of its underlying rationale. For example, the rule that contractual ties require an agreement between the parties serves to protect freedom of contract. Yet this rule can be unsatisfactory when applied to the following situation. A offers a reward of £100 to anyone who returns A's beloved lost poodle "Daisy". B, without knowledge of this offer, finds "Daisy" and spends time and money in tracing A, its owner. If B learns about the reward only after having returned the poodle, can he claim the money from A? The answer is "no" in English law[29] but "yes" in German law because it was felt that justice required a deviation from the normal rule (and, indeed, was introduced by § 657 BGB).

Similarly, the doctrine of consideration can be overly generalised if applied to alterations of an existing contract rather than to the formation of a new contract. We can use the following example to illustrate the point just made. C has, for twenty years, worked diligently and faithfully as an accountant for company D. D offers and C accepts additional pension benefits as an expression of D's gratitude. When C retires, should the new management be allowed to evade the company's earlier promise for want of consideration? Probably not. But achieving this desired result may require some ingenuity if the effect of the general rule is to be avoided.

These examples demonstrate that too much abstraction or generalization can be a problem even under English law, which shows a low level of abstraction in comparison with German law. They also demonstrate that a high level of abstraction in legal rules can be counterbalanced by the creation of exceptions, e.g., by not applying the doctrine of consideration to alterations of an existing contract.

If there was an award for the highest level of abstraction in any code, the *Bürgerliches Gesetzbuch* would be a clear favourite to win it. This, however,

---

[29] See Treitel, *The Law of Contract*, 8th edn. (1993).

should not frighten the student of German law. German civil law can, without excessive ingenuity, be presented in a less rigorously abstracted form. This, in fact, has been one of our main aims in a book on German law which we are in the process of writing with Professor Werner Lorenz in which we have, time and again, eschewed the pandektist structure of the BGB in favour of an approach which will make it more user-friendly towards a common law readership. Notwithstanding our avowed aim, however, we also feel that it is useful to understand the structure of the BGB, even if one does not follow it in the detail. For this reason, the remarks which follow aim to demonstrate the different ways in which the German Civil Code has acquired its structure by the abstraction of rules. Future articles of German private law can, perhaps, be read against these general observatons.

B. *Concentric Circles of Rules: The General Part of the BGB*

Abstraction typically occurs in concentric circles within the German Civil Code. If we take again the example of a sales contract, we can distinguish at least seven circles of rules which can govern such a contract.[30] Let us demonstrate this by returning to our earlier example.

The seventh and innermost circle is formed by specific rules on sales contracts, e.g. on when the risk passes to the buyer (usually when the seller hands over the goods to the buyer, §§ 446–7 BGB).

If we ask for the buyer's remedies when the seller delays delivery, we must move to the sixth circle, i.e. contracts where one party performs his part of the bargain for the sake of the other's performance (*gegenseitige Verträge*), which will equally apply to delay by e.g. landlords, employees, or shippers. For parties to these contracts, § 326 BGB provides the right to set a period of grace and, after it has lapsed, to claim damages for non-performance, or to avoid the contract. This is similar to the English rules on "making the time of the essence".

When we discuss the sale of *non-existing* goods, we reach the fifth concentric circle, i.e. general rules on contracts. These rules apply to all contracts, including gratuitous contracts such as donation.[31] In our example, § 305 BGB will provide the answer, since this provision makes a contract void the performance of which is impossible *ab initio*.

We leave the law of contract and move on to the fourth circle if we want to know how the buyer's damages for breach of warranty are to be calculated, or whether the seller can plead a set-off with another claim. The applicable rules are common to the entire law of obligations. Paragraphs 249–54 BGB

---

[30] If this reminds the common law reader of Dante's "Hell", to the German theoretician it is pure Paradise. Indeed, it was an eminent Pandektist—Rudolf von Ihering—who wrote a book about the *Paradise of Legal Concepts*.

[31] Another paradox here for the common lawyer who is not accustomed to treating gift as a contract.

govern damages, regardless of whether they are authorised by the law of contracts or torts. Similarly, the right to declare a set-off (§§ 387–96 BGB) does not depend on whether claim or counterclaim are based in contract, *negotiorum gestio*, restitution, or torts. Other rules, common to the entire law of obligations, include those on performance in general; on assignment; interest; place and time of performance; and on plurality of debtors or of creditors; but also general provisions on delay and on impossibility of performance.

Even the law of obligations becomes too narrow when we turn to questions of illegality, e.g. whether a contract for the supply of arms is void for violation of a statutory prohibition. By now, we have to leave Book 2 of the BGB (the law of obligations) and take a closer look at Book 1, the General Part, and in particular at § 134 BGB. This provision on illegality applies to any *Rechtsgeschäft* or legal transaction, including contracts, but also to transactions in property or family law as well as to wills, to name a few. The General Part of the BGB, it should be remembered, applies to all other areas of the Civil Code and indeed of private law. The law which is common to legal transactions is therefore the third concentric circle, which also comprises the rules on immorality (§ 138) and form requirements (§§ 125–9).

If we want to know whether a sales contract is affected by mistake, we arrive at the second concentric circle, the so-called *Willenserklärung* or declaration of intention. This heading encompasses all those rules which are common to one-sided legal transactions (wills, acts of rescission or avoidance, notices to quit, the granting of consent, etc.) and to those declarations which make up a contract, i.e., to both offer and acceptance. The same circle also includes the rules on deceit, duress and representation, and those on capacity to enter into legal transactions.

The first and widest circle is reached when we wish to know whom the seller should sue for the purchase price if the goods were sold e.g. to a football fan club. (Of course, if the football club is "registered", different rules will apply.) The answer is provided by § 54 BGB: not the club, since it has no legal capacity, but the person who acted, or the individual members on behalf of whom the president of this club ordered the goods. This concerns *Rechtsfähigkeit*, i.e. the capacity to be the subject of rights in private law; and it forms part of the first title of the first book of the Code which also tells us whether a baby which dies within hours after birth can acquire claims in tort (e.g., for medical malpractice) or a share in the estate. (The answer is positive in both cases.) This also shows that persons who have no contractual capacity of their own (the baby) will still have legal capacity so that they can acquire claims and rights. The same first circle also includes rules in paras. 90–103 BGB on what can be the object of a right.

The first book of the BGB, the so-called *Allgemeiner Teil* or General Part, therefore consists largely of rules which English law would consider in a contract course, but which German law, it is submitted with a greater degree of logic, has placed on a higher level of abstraction and has generalised in such a way as to apply throughout the law of contract, restitution, tort, property, family, inheritance, company and intellectual property law, as well as the other areas of private law. In particular, (and as already stated) the General Part sets out the rules for formation of contract and policing of contract. The General Part is, therefore, mainly a product of the technique of abstraction in concentric circles.

By describing the technique of abstraction as one of concentric circles, we have resorted to a geometrical metaphor. German textbooks will frequently borrow a similar metaphor from algebra and explain this technique as "placing common rules of private law outside the brackets", whereby Book 1 of the BGB is outside and Books 2–5 are inside the brackets. Like most metaphors, however, this one is simplified. We have seen above that there are many more brackets within these brackets, and a more accurate algebraical representation of the BGB's technique would look so complicated that it would create more confusion than illumination, so no such attempt shall be made here. Indeed, we have already gone too far down the path that German lawyers like to take but common lawyers find confusing. A few words, however, must be said about the BGB's fervent desire to resort to such refined techniques and excess generalisation. For it would be idle to deny that these techniques do not also offer some advantages to the draftsman of a code.

First among them is the fact that they save space and avoid repetition. Admittedly, this is a goal which is hardly ever pursued by those who draft English statutes and therefore, perhaps, difficult to explain to lawyers who are not unduly concerned by the fact that, for instance, the English Consumer Credit Act 1974 consists of 193 sections which, together with numerous annexes, fill 212 printed pages. If we compare this to the 19 sections (or eight pages in the statute-book) taken up by the German equivalent statute—the *Verbraucherkreditgesetz*—we note a genuine difference in drafting techniques. This, of course, is a topic on its own so here we are content merely to bring it to the attention of our readers.

Secondly, these techniques of abstraction help to treat like situations alike and, therefore, promote consistency within the private law. For the same reason, they facilitate the development of more remote areas of the law with the help of more widely-used provisions.

Thirdly, refined levels of abstraction allow for refined solutions. Let us return to the example of the person who found the lost poodle "Daisy" and the question whether he can claim the reward of £100 offered by the distressed owner even if the finder was not aware of the reward when returning the poodle. This, as we saw, is a no problem area for German law. This situation is not considered as a contract which failed to come into existence for want of an acceptance. Rather, it amounts to a one-sided legal transaction, consisting of an offer of reward (*Auslobung*, §§ 657–61 BGB), a declaration of intention which, by statutory exception, need not to be communicated to the party which qualifies for the award. This example may help us to appreciate the versatility of the German Civil Code's regulatory mechanisms.

Notwithstanding the above comments, the virtues of this approach are much diminished by its inherent vices. So what are these vices?

First, a high level of generalisation which necessitates many exceptions. A regulation of mistake which is common to contracts, marriages, and wills alike, bears the hallmarks of a grand design. But hardly any marriage would be safe if either spouse could rescind wedlock under English rules on misrepresentation or under German rules about "essential characteristics of a person" in § 119(2) BGB. Modifications are therefore necessary; and, inevitably, they tarnish the elegance of the general rule.

Secondly, by allocating rules to so many different circles, legal problems are artificially dissected and therefore become more complicated. This can be illustrated with the following example. A agrees to restore an old ceiling painting for B and sets about doing the work. After A has restored half of the painting, the entire ceiling suddenly collapses overnight. Is A required to do anything more under the contract? And can A require B to pay the agreed price? We first have to go to circle five (contracts in general) to find out that the contract remains valid because performance only became impossible *after* its conclusion (§ 306). We then have to move to circle four (general law of obligations) to learn that A is discharged of any liability under the contract because A is not to blame for the impossibility (§ 275). In order to find out whether A can require B to pay, we must at this stage move to circle six (*gegenseitige Verträge*) to find out that, since B did not act negligently, A cannot claim the contract price. But if we then go to circle seven (specific contracts: contracts for works), we learn that A is nevertheless entitled to such a proportion of the contract price as corresponds to the work already undertaken (i.e., half the price) plus any expenses not covered by this. (This is because section 645 BGB makes the client strictly liable for any deterioration of the client's own materials which the contractor uses for the work.) This distribution of one problem over four different areas of the BGB will often create unnecessary confusion. All this may remind one of Dante's complex vision of hell. Nevertheless, however admirable it may be in one respect it is utterly unsuitable for the purposes of teaching German law to common lawyers. One must, in other words, try to follow the method adopted by one of us when writing *The German Law of Torts* and try to anglicise the German law of Contracts.

These doubts, however, should not lead to the opposite extreme of discrediting all general rules. In this context one must therefore note the example of the Dutch Civil Code which has modified the BGB's approach by formulating rules of similar generality in Book 3 (which applies throughout the law of obligations, property, and inheritance but excludes family law) while setting out in Book 6 those rules which apply to the entire law of obligations. It would, therefore, appear to be the case that the Dutch Code—the most recent, major enactment in this branch of the law—has opted for the advantages of a general approach but avoided some at least of the excesses of the BGB. (A similar approach has, incidentally, been adopted in the recently re-drafted Czech and Slovak Code.)

C. *Overlapping Circles of Rules: The "Principle of Abstraction"*

So far we have been talking about concentric circles, and have generously overlooked the fact that the fourth of the circles mentioned above is not really concentric to circles three and two: with torts and restitution, the law of obligations (the fourth circle) comprises two areas of law where obligations arise without the use of legal transactions (the third circle) or declarations of legal intention (the second circle). This can serve to illustrate the second mode of abstraction, i.e. by partially overlapping rather than by concentric circles.

We can illustrate this by returning to the example of a sales contract. The rules on transfer of property (passing of title) are not to be found within sales law, but rather in property law. Paragraphs 929–35 BGB govern the intentional transfer of property in chattels, regardless of the nature of the underlying obligation. If one person transfers property to another, it does not matter for the purposes of §§ 929–35 whether this is done under a contract of sale, donation or barter, as a security for a loan, or because a shareholder pays up a contribution in kind e.g. by transferring his or her car to the company. In all these situations, it is not the rules on these specific contracts, but rather the property law rules in §§ 929–35 which will decide whether and when property has passed from one party onto another.

This is related to another typical feature of the German Civil Code, the so-called principle of abstraction (*Abstraktionsprinzip*). Since so much in the BGB is about abstraction, this term is not fully indicative of the meaning which it carries: the BGB distinguishes between the creation of an obligation (*Verpflichtung*), e.g. by contract, and the actual disposition of a right (*Verfügung*) and perceives these as two separate acts, whereby the second is "abstracted" from the first. For example, a sales contract creates the obligations to pay the price and to transfer title in the goods. However, the sales contract itself does nothing to transfer property in the goods. This actual transfer is a separate legal transaction, the *Verfügung*, which again requires offer and acceptance plus, usually, the transfer of physical power over the goods (§§ 929 *et seq.* BGB). As a consequence, if a sales contract is rescinded on the grounds of mistake, this does not necessarily mean that the transfer of property in the goods has been (or could be) terminated as well. Therefore, the seller cannot rely on proprietary remedies, but only on restitution to claim back the goods.

This principle is not limited to the transfer of property. Similarly, the assignment of a claim is a disposition, to be distinguished from a contract by which one party promises to assign a claim to the other party. Of course, all this is largely a category of the mind rather than a category of reality. When buying milk at a store, Germans will not exchange three separate verbal agreements with the cashier according to which (a) they will enter into an obligation to pay the purchase price and take delivery of the milk, (b) they transfer to the shop owner the property in the cash which they hand over and (c) property in the milk passes to the customer. Nevertheless, according to the Civil Code, there are these three separate contracts, of which (a) creates obligations, and (b) and (c) are dispositions. Things might look different, however, when a new car is sold. Both seller and buyer will be conscious of the fact that they are bound by a contract weeks before delivery occurs, and the seller will do everything to make sure that title does not pass to the buyer before the buyer has paid the full purchase price. It is reasonable to assume that in such a case, even the "little guy in the street"—the German equivalent to the English "man on the Clapham omnibus"—will perceive that signing a contract and becoming the owner of a car are two different events.

The practical importance of this principle of abstraction is somewhat limited and frequently overestimated. The most important consequence is arguably that deficiencies in the contract which creates the obligations (such as illegality, immorality, mistake, deceit, duress, lack of contractual intention) do not automatically affect the validity of transfer of title under this contract. Consequently, third parties can subsequently acquire title from a buyer of goods which were sold under a contract which was affected by mistake etc. This is exactly what English law aims to achieve by the rule in *White* v. *Garden*[32], according to which a person who was fraudulently induced to sell goods cannot rescind once an innocent third party has subsequently purchased these goods[33]. German law has no need for such a rule precisely because of the principle of abstraction (and also because it allows the *bona fide* acquisition of title under §§ 932 *et seq*. BGB). The principle of abstraction thus makes it unnecessary that interests of third parties interfere with the validity of a contract.

Another benefit of the principle of abstraction is that it facilitates the analysis of the international sales of goods, in particular if, at the time of the transfer of property, the goods are not located in the country whose law governs the sale. Since the principle of abstraction considers the sale contract and the transfer of property as two different agreements, no particular problems arise from the fact that these two are governed by two different municipal laws.

Once again, however, one must stress that it is not entirely evident that these benefits are worth the conceptual complications which the principle of abstraction entails. It is also fair to mention that the principle has been subjected to so many exceptions that one sometimes wonders whether it is honoured more in the breach than in its observance.[34]

---

[32] (1851) 10 CB 919.
[33] See Treitel, above n. 29, at p. 331.
[34] For a full discussion see Zweigert and Kötz, 1st edn. vol. I, pp. 177–89.

D. *General Clauses and Specific Regulations*

Continental codifications, especially those inspired by the German Code, make widespread use of so-called general clauses (*Generalklauseln*). These are legal provisions which use wide and often vague formulations to sum up the general rule for what sometimes constitutes entire areas of law. Perhaps the best example can be found in the French Code Civil which, in Article 1382, sums up the law of torts with breathtaking generality and (apparent) simplicity:

> "Any human conduct which causes damage to another, obliges the person whose fault caused the damage to make amends."

If we are to remain within the geometrical analogy which we used above, general clauses are employed for the abstraction of rules within one given circle of rules. Usually, general clauses will be supplemented by more specific regulations which can state exceptions to which the general clause should not apply, modifications, or other additional rules. The provisions on contracts in favour of third parties can serve as an example for the way in which the BGB has made use of general clauses.

In German law and unlike English law, a third party can acquire rights under a contract made between other parties, provided that this was the intention of the parties to the contract. This is precisely what § 328 BGB states in general terms. Paragraph 330 BGB makes a presumption in favour of such a contract for one particularly frequent category, namely life insurance contracts, while §§ 331–2 BGB set out additional rules for contracts whereby the third party acquires the right upon the death of one of the parties to the contract (which again relates to life insurance). By this, the BGB provides precise solutions for frequent types of contracts in favour of third parties, and at the same time leaves the door open for all other situations in which it might be useful that a third party be allowed to claim under a contract to which it is not a party, situations which often were unforeseeable at the time when the BGB was drafted. Thus, new cases need not be squeezed into a strait-jacket of existing detailed regulations, while at the same time such detailed regulations exist where a need for them could be perceived at the time of the drafting of the statute.

The obvious disadvantage of general clauses is that they can leave too much open, and in particular that they are too wide and thus cover more ground than they should. For example, the above-mentioned provision of Article 1382 of the French Code Civil essentially creates liability for any negligent infliction of pure economic loss, a result which both English and German law are keen to avoid. This is why those who drafted the German Civil Code did not adopt in their tort law a proposition as broad as Article 1382 CC and opted, instead, for a combination of general and more specific clauses which, however, in their turn create problems of their own.[35]

---

[35] See Markesinis, *The German Law of Torts*, Ch. 2.

Notwithstanding the above, the BGB counts amongst its paragraphs some very wide general clauses, the most famous example being § 242 BGB (the so-called good faith provision). Such clauses run the risk of defying the very purpose for which they were drafted; and at times of political instability have been abused by a politically-motivated judiciary. Thus, rather than formulating a test which is equally applied to all cases which fall within the scope of the rule, such general clauses serve as a description of an area of case law. In reality, therefore, it is not the general clause but the case law of the courts which produces the rules. With some justification, the same can be said about § 138 BGB which makes void any legal transaction which offends good morals.

Overall, however, it can be said that the BGB has made fairly prudent use of general clauses, and has generally opted for a mixture of general and special clauses which works well in practice, by covering the typical situations through the specific rules and leaving enough room for development in most other cases.

E. Models and Cross-References

The drafting of rules in concentric circles, in overlapping circles, and through the medium of general clauses occurs by finding the smallest common denominator between situations to which such rules might apply. As a result, each rule is allocated to the largest possible of these circles or situations. Thus, while English law places the rules on duress within the circle "contracts", German law will place duress rules within the much larger circle of "declarations of intention", so allowing the rescission e.g. of letters of resignation or a grant of power of attorney which somebody was required to issue at gunpoint. Such a regime, however, can only function if the smallest common denominator can still serve to exclude cases to which the rationale of the rule does not apply. If this is not the case, the BGB will instead employ a third way of abstraction, i.e. the use of models and cross-references. In applying this technique, the BGB sets out a model of rules which cover an important part of these situations, and then makes selected cross-references to this model of rules for some, but not for all related situations.

Let us take a specific example in order to illustrate this point. There are many restitution-type situations where one person holds assets (e.g., a bicycle) which either belong to another party or should (for other reasons) be returned to him or should be passed on to a third party. Whether or not the party which holds these assets should be liable for any deterioration of these assets (e.g., by continuous exposure to rainwater) will often be influenced by the conduct and knowledge of the party who holds the assets. But the possible categories of situations to which such rules should apply were too diverse to be covered by one set of rules. Here, as in many other situations, the BGB will regulate one particular type of situation. Having done this, it will then make cross-references to these regulations in other parts of the Civil Code where similar situations arise to which the same set of rules can be usefully applied. The following example may help make this point.

Paragraphs 987–1007 BGB regulate situations where one party is in unauthorised possession of property belonging to another party, e.g. if A has bought a bicycle which previously was stolen from B, and which B thus can require A to surrender under para. 985 BGB. Depending on A's knowledge and conduct, §§ 987–1007 BGB may give A the right to recover from B for the costs of repairs, or give B the right to claim from A the value of A's use of the bicycle in money. Once B has sued A in court for surrender of the bicycle, A is liable for any negligently caused deterioration; and, in turn, can claim from B only the cost of emergency maintenance (§§ 989, 994 BGB, with a cross-reference to *negotiorum gestio*). This last situation is similar to that of a person who, while being the owner of the bicycle, must nevertheless surrender the bicycle to another person, e.g. if B has transferred the property in the bicycle to A as a security for an outstanding debt which B has subsequently paid up. Therefore, from the time when an action is pending for the surrender of an object, the defendant will be liable under the very same rules found in §§ 989 *et seq.* BGB by virtue of a cross-reference to § 292 BGB. In addition, § 819 BGB, which forms part of the rules on unjustified enrichment, will make any recipient of a performance which this recipient knows he is not entitled to keep liable "as if an action for return had been pending" at the time of receipt. This is a cross-reference to § 292 BGB which, again, will invoke § 989 *et seq.* Thereby, §§ 989 *et seq.* BGB would also apply to a person who knowingly accepts a mistaken delivery of a bicycle which a neighbour has ordered and paid for, and who happily uses this bike. By these and other cross-references the BGB model of liability in §§ 989 *et seq.* extends its sphere of application to numerous situations which are different, but which nevertheless call for a similar solution.

The BGB has made widespread use of this technique of models and cross-references, but nowhere as much as in restitution-type situations. Happily, however, cross-references are less common in the law of contract, so the reader of this piece need not be particularly worried about them. For the sake of comparative completeness, however, we feel we ought to make him aware of the phenomenon known in Germany as paragraph chains (*Paragraphenkette*).

The arguments in favour of this technique are similar to the ones which support the other techniques of abstraction, i.e. avoidance of repetition and consistency in the treatment of similar situations. Predictably, however, the disadvantages are also the same and, arguably, even worse. This can be illustrated by the following example.

Let us assume that A keeps a bicycle, which A reasonably believes to have inherited from C. When it transpires that C has, instead, left his entire estate to B, B requires A to hand over to him the bicycle. A then repairs a puncture, gives the bicycle to B, and claims from B the costs of parts and of his (A's) own labour. In order to solve this fairly simple case, we have to start our journey in the law of succession (the fifth book) and, in particular, § 2021 BGB, which refers us back to unjustified enrichment in the second book. Since A knew of B's right to the bicycle when A repaired the puncture, § 819 BGB will invoke "the general provisions", which means § 292 BGB which, in turn, refers to the law of property (the third book) and, in particular, to §§ 989 and 994(2) BGB. The latter provision invokes the law of *negotiorum gestio* to find out whether A was entitled to repair the puncture.[36] *Negotiorum gestio*, in turn, calls up the law of mandate (a gratuitous contract of service) to find out what A can claim from B in this case. After a journey through three books and the laws of inheritance, unjustified enrichment, obligations in general, property, and *negotiorum gestio*, we finally arrive at specific contracts and § 670 BGB to learn that A can claim for the cost of the parts used but not for A's own labour. Surely there must be a simpler way to arrive at this unspectacular result! Examples such as these suggest that the German Pandektists may have been, to use the colloquial expression, "too clever by half"; and they have certainly not helped those who, like us, wish to popularise the teaching of German law!

A comparative postscript may not be out of place. The Greek *Astikos Kodikas* (Civil Code), which has often followed the BGB's other abstractions of rules to the letter and the spirit, has, on the whole, eliminated most cross-references. So even what is one of the BGB's closer allies amongst the civil law codifications has deserted the German Civil Code on this issue, and probably for good reasons.

F. *The Use of Concepts*

The preceding pages must have made abundantly clear the fact that German law makes widespread use of concepts *(Begriffe)*, i.e. constructed categories which transcend individual cases, and which are employed to attribute legal rules to a variety of situations. When looking at concentric circles of abstractions, we have encountered two central concepts, namely *Rechtsgeschäft* (legal transaction) and *Willenserklärung* (declaration of intention). When treating the principle of abstraction, we have come across *Verfügung* (disposition). This suffices to show that quite a number of the concepts which German private law employs are gained by the above-mentioned techniques of abstraction. Indeed, in the contract book we are writing, our readers will be confronted with numerous concepts which German law employs for mastering the law of contract. One more example,however, should suffice in this context, namely the *Vollmacht* or grant of authority to an agent. This is a unilateral legal transaction, by which the principal gives to the agent the power to represent the principal towards third parties. This grant of author-

---

[36] The answer is "yes", if B's consent could be presumed, as we shall do here.

ity is abstracted from the underlying contract between agent and principal which gives rise to it, be it a contract for labour, for services, a commercial agency contract, or a binding agreement for gratuitous services (*Auftrag*, or Mandate). As is noted in all discussions of this subject, deficiencies in the underlying contract do not necessarily affect the validity of the grant of authority. This concept has been very influential beyond the borders of Germany; and Zweigert and Kötz[37] go as far as stating that, worldwide, "no subsequent civil code has failed to make the distinction in one form or another between agency as a contract and agency as an authority".

By comparison with the above, English law makes far less use of such concepts. However, it would be wrong to state that concepts are totally alien to this system. What is, arguably, the most powerful and versatile tool of English law—the notion of a trust—is no less of a legal concept than are, say, *Vollmacht* or *Rechtsgeschäft*. The concept of trusts transcends the various aspects of social reality to which it is applied, such as administration of estates, setting up charities, marriage settlements, or simply attributing shares in real property, and can even operate as a mere device for a claim for surrender (constructive trusts). Its broadness can leave continental lawyers gaping with awe and belies misconceptions of English law as a legal order which never rises above the particular in search for greater common principles.

It may have become apparent by now that these concepts are legal inventions which serve the purpose of dealing with a variety of situations by grouping them together and treating them alike. Once invented, however, they tend to start leading a life of their own and wander off into directions which initially they were not expected to pursue. Constructive trusts are, again, a case in point. There was a time when in Germany, courts and scholars seemed to have become more occupied with the concepts themselves than with the solution of cases for which these concepts were designed. This was the time of the so-called *Begriffsjurisprudenz* or legal conceptualism, which peaked during the second half of the nineteenth century and only gradually gave way to *Interessenjurisprudenz* or jurisprudence of interests, which is based on an analysis of the interests of the parties involved in a case. Although the *Interessenjurisprudenz*, referred to above, gained the upper hand between the two World Wars, conceptualism has not become extinct. Rather, it still has considerable influence on German law.

If some writers are to be believed, German private law is a meticulous piece of legal engineering which, by use of concepts, attributes legal solutions to legal problems as precisely and mercilessly as a Swiss chronometer ticks away the years, hours, and seconds of a human life from the cradle to the grave. German law, it has been suggested, is forever prepared to sacrifice notions of justice to the altar of the concept. If this was ever true, it seems to have disappeared in our time. When legal conceptualism reigned, it was true that

---

[37] See above n. 28, at p. 461.

much more time and space were devoted in the drafting of statutes and of decisions to bring out the concepts than were used for explaining the underlying policy reasons, and this still may hold true today. But this does not imply that policy considerations play no role in the decision-making process. Rather, policy reasons are less mentioned explicitly, both in statutes and court decisions. Nevertheless, even at the end of the nineteenth century, those who drafted statutes and judgments alike were generally concerned with finding a solution which they thought just and fair. Indeed, one can go as far as stating that it is very difficult to find a German judgment which the court knew to be unfair on one of the parties, but which the judges nevertheless felt obliged to hand down because the law left them with no choice—something which is not always the case in systems such as the English which take very seriously the doctrine of *stare decisis*.[38] Thus, if all else fails, the German judge is not unknown to resort to the principle of good faith in order to achieve what he believes to be a just solution. A good example can be found in RGZ 84,125, where the *Reichsgericht* criticised the Court of Appeal for being overly conceptual and praised the Court of First Instance for its down to earth reliance on commercial practice and good faith. Thus, time and again, in the area of contracts, torts, and family law, the German courts have invoked general principles or even resorted to *contra legem* interpretations, in order to adjust an old Code to new circumstances. In this respect, therefore, the overall conclusion must be that the German tendency to over-theorize must (and has been) criticised; but the German judicial boldness must equally be praised where this is appropriate.

5. SOME TENTATIVE CONCLUSIONS

We can now, after this abstract intermezzo, attempt to bring together some of the ideas discussed above. Perhaps, the best way to do this is to present our key thoughts in the form of six tentative propositions and indicate some of their wider implications. In some future essay these implications may even be developed further.

First, the solutions reached by German law are, time and again, quite similar to those adopted by English law. The similarities, however, as, indeed, the areas where one system may stand to learn something from the other, are obscured by the effects of a different history and a preference for a deductive rather than an inductive form of reasoning. History (and natural temperament) can explain these differences.[39]

---

[38] It is not difficult to find English judgments which support this observation. Thus, numerous judges have condemned the English third party rule but have proceeded to render judgments which they, themselves, did not regard as satisfactory.

[39] Lord MacMillan's famous speech "Two Ways of Thinking", reprinted in *Law and Other Things* (1938), 76 *et seq.*, thus remains as crucial to the understanding of the Continental legal mind as it was when it was delivered in Cambridge nearly sixty years ago.

Secondly, history in particular can explain what can be found in the German Civil Code where common lawyers expect to find the material they discuss in contract classes. History, however, also explains why much contractual material, relevant to contractual transactions, can also be found in other parts of the Code or, indeed, in other enactments. This may appear to be confusing and, indeed, in many cases it is; but the English lawyers should not complain since their law of contract is scattered into different areas such as trusts, equity in general or, even, tort, for no better reason that the fact that the forms of action have left such deep marks on our law. This often accounts for a chaotic presentation of our material; and in some cases, it can also account for unsatisfactory solutions.

Thirdly, history and, more precisely, recent German history, will also explain the structure of the Code and the way of legal reasoning as well as the kind of legal education which it has encouraged.

Fourthly, an implicit consequence of the above, especially of point three, is the fact that one must "deconstruct" and then "anglicise" German law in order to make it more palatable to an English readership. This "deconstruction" of whichever part of German law is being studied does, of course, entail dangers of different kinds; and it must always be attempted taking into account the entire legal order of which it forms a part.

Fifthly, the "deconstruction" must be attempted in all cases but is particularly essential in the area of contract law (with which this paper is mainly concerned) since in this area the influence of the Pandektist school has been at its most pronounced and, in some instances, not at its most inspired.

Sixthly, the "deconstruction" of German law, coupled with the study of case law and "law in action", will reveal the true extent of similarities between the two systems which we venture to suggest (but have not attempted to substantiate in this piece) is considerable. This "deconstruction" will also reveal in which areas of difference legal borrowing can take place. This is the second phase of a comparative enquiry and, arguably the most exciting; but it will have to await future papers such as this before it is fully demonstrated and its implications fully worked out.

6

*Il Ruolo Della Giurisprudenza Nella Comparazione Giuridica**

I. Sono trascorsi venticinque anni da quando il compianto Otto Kahn Freund lesse la sua prolusione all'Università di Oxford dedicata a "Il diritto comparato come disciplina accademica".[1] Nel 1973 ritornò su questa ampia tematica nella seconda Chorley Lecture[2]; pert anto quando sono stato avvicinato dalla Prof. Harlow per conto della *Modern Law Review* per tenere questa conferenza, il suo suggerimento iniziale fuche analizzassi la situazione alla vigilia di nuovi ed imminenti sviluppi sul fronte europeo. Personalmente, le mie sensazioni verso l'argomento erano di grandi, ma insoddisfatte, aspettative. Il diritto comparato è, a mio avviso, ancora alla ricerca di un pubblico anche dove ha trovato una qualche collocazione nei corsi di studio universitario. Quando dico che il diritto comparato non è riuscito a trovare un pubblico, non intendo, ovviamente, dire che ha mancato di attrarre l'attenzione di eminenti studiosi. Ma ritengo che corrisponda al vero affermare che non è riuscito ad affascinare la fantasia degli studenti e degli operatori, avvocati e giudici.

Se tale conclusione è esatta, credo che gran parte della responsabilità ricada su coloro che manifestano un interesse prioritario verso la disciplina, in quanto nei loro sforzi per promuovere l'interesse nei diritti stranieri e nel metodo comparativo essi hanno *a)* sottovalutato e sotto evidenziato l'importanza della giurisprudenza e *b)* ignorato gli orientamenti delle Corti in casi comuni che abitualmente non vengono pubblicati sulle riviste o sulle rassegne (e, anche, i comportamenti delle parti nel transigere quelle vertenze che non giungono a una sentenza).

In questa conferenza vorrei cercare di spiegare attraverso sei paragrafi connessi tra loro, perchè e come l'attenzione verso la giurisprudenza, le prassi giudiziali e lo studio di problemi specifici potrebbe aiutare a ravvivare un maggiore interesse per la disciplina. In un'altra occasione vorrei forse aggiungere alcune opinioni sulle singole persone: perchè si è scritto molto sul diritto comparato ma poco, credo, sui comparatisti.

* Il testo riprodotto amplia la *Shimizu Lecture* dal titolo "Comparative law—A subject in search of an Audience", resa alla London School of Economics. La traduzione è del Prof. Vincenzo Zeno-Zencovich. Una versione inglese di questo articolo è stata pubblicata dalla *Modern Law Review*.

[1] Pubblicata in (1966) 82 *Law Quarterly Review* 41.
[2] "On Uses and Abuses of Comparative Law", in (1973) 37 *Modern Law Review* 1.

II. L'esperienza di molti anni di insegnamento di diritto comparato e straniero soprattutto, ma non soltanto, a giuristi di *common law* mi ha convinto dell'importanza di presentare un sistema straniero ad un pubblico ancora non iniziato più attraverso la sua giurisprudenza che attraverso una esegesi delle disposizioni del codice. Ho trattato alcune di queste idee nel 1983 a Bruxelles nel corso delle celebrazioni per il 25° anniversario del *Centre Interuniversitaire de Droit Comparé*; e sono assai lieto che questa conferenza (assieme ad un'altra svoltasi presso l'Università di Ghent nel marzo del 1989) mi abbia fornito l'occasione per riesaminare la questione e approfondire la mia riflessione sull'argomento.

Il titolo della mia conferenza allora era "L'inseignement du droit comparé sous l'éclairage de la jurisprudence" ed il mio intendimento era di scoraggiare i comparatisti dall'insegnare la disciplina o, piuttosto, il metodo, ricorrendo ad ampie generalizzazioni sugli altrui sistemi. Invece, spiegavo, si dovrebbe usare come punti di partenza argomenti abbastanza ristretti e da questi gradualmente introdurre gli studenti nello specifico ramo del diritto, spiegare loro la diversa storia, da cui dipendono i diversi concetti e le diverse tecniche utilizzate per risolvere il problema in questione e, infine, l'impatto che le regole procedurali ed il complesso del sistema potevano avere sul risultato finale. Un esempio, che allora non feci ma che creo illusti chiaramente il mio punto di vista, può essere quello del diritto alla riservatezza o, come viene chiamato dai giuristi tedeschi, il diritto generale alla personalità (*allgemeine Persön-lichkeitsrecht*). Una buona scelta in casi giurisprudenziali su questo tema può essere utilizzata per mostrare come: *a)* le corti hanno costruito un nuovo interesse tutelato; *b)* hanno approvato dei rimedi impensati—se non addirittura proibiti—dal codice civile, offrendo così l'occasione al docente di esaminare quanto convincenti sono le opinioni tradizionali sui poteri di legificazione delle corti nei paesi di *civil law*; *c)* questo è avvenuto perchè il retroterra costituzionale ha forzato la mano al giudice civile; *d)* la giurisprudenza è diventata estremamente casistica; *e)* i giudici sono stati obbligati a cercare il delicato equilibrio per conciliare i concorrenti interessi della riservatezza e della manifestazione del pensiero.

In altri termini si potrebbe continuare a spiegare come i giuristi tedeschi hanno superato i problemi posti dalla incerta natura del diritto alla riservatezza affidando la sua configurazione ai giudici sulla base di un procedimento casistico. Sorprendentemente questo procedimento, tipico della common law è stato scartato nell'ordinamento inglese, mentre la stampa è riuscita ancora una volta ad impedire l'approvazione di una legge sul diritto alla riservatezza. Abbiamo pertanto potuto assistere di recente al poco edificante spettacolo di un settore di un grande gruppo editoriale invocare principi libertari contro una proposta di legge sulla riservatezza al fine di consentire alle testate meno rispettabili del medesimo gruppo di continuare a lucrare ingerendosi nella vita di persone spesso innocenti.

Quanto ho indicato sopra può essere fatto utilizzando la giurisprudenza come trampolino; ed anche se l'obiettivo finale del procedimento è imparare prima descrivendo quel che è straniero e poi comparandolo con quel che è conosciuto, l'altezza del salto—se posso continuare con la metafora della piscina—è lasciata a ciascuno studente. Ad esempio, nell'esaminare il caso Schacht[3], ritengo che sia piacevole esporre ai miei allievi alcune considerazioni su quella persona eccezionale e le caotiche condizioni economiche che egli affrontò con tanto successo tra le due guerre mondiali. Condizioni economiche che, sia detto per inciso, fornirono alle corti tedesche la scusa per compiere ancora un'altra delle loro imprese più audaci: lo sviluppo di quella giurisprudenza che avrebbe trovato nell'art. 242 del BGB un sostegno tutt'al più generico e tenue.

III.   In un mio precedente saggio ho confrontato il caso *Dutton* v. *Bognor Regis UDC*[4] con casi tedeschi analoghi[5] e sono giunto alla conclusione che la decisione inglese non era convincente. Nel caso Dutton un'azienda era stata promossa contro un ente locale per avere negligentemente verificato le fondamenta di una abitazione prima che fosse costruita; esso riguardava, però, anche la responsabilità del costruttore. La casa, che era stata negligentemente costruita su una discarica abbandonata era stata acquistata dalla sig.ra *Dutton* non dal costuttore, bensì da un successivo acquirente. Successivamente si manifestarono crepe nei muri, anche se, a quanto consta, essa non fu mai pericolosa per l'uso abitativo. La Corte d'Appello ritenne, a maggioranza, che il danno subito dall'attrice fosse un danno materiale e non—come invece ritenuto in casi simili in Germania—una forma di *economic loss*, e pertanto consentì il risarcimento in via extracontrattuale.

Il principio fu confermato poi dalla Camera dei Lords nel caso *Anns* v. *Merton London Borough Council*[6] e in effetti esteso a casi nei quali le autorità locali avevano omesso del tutto di verificare le fondamenta delle abitazioni. La decisione diede il via ad uno sviluppo della responsabilità civile senza precedenti e, sospetto, non previsto, culminato con la decisione della Camera dei Lords *Junior Book* v. *Veitchi Ltd.*[7]

Sarebbe inutile ripetere qui il punto di vista espresso a suo tempo a questo proposito; mi pare sufficiente evidenziare tre punti.

Innanzitutto ci vollero diversi anni per smantellare i principi affermati nei casi *Dutton* e *Anns*, prima con *Governors of the Peabody Donation Fund* v. *Sir Lindsau Parkinson & Co. Ltd.*[8], poi con *Curran* v. *Northern Ireland Co-Ownership Housing Association Ltd.*[9] e, più recentemente, con *D. and F.*

---

[3] La decisione è pubblicata, tradotta in inglese, in Markesinis, *The German Law of Torts: A Compartive Introduction*, 2 edn. (1990) e accompagnata da ampi richiami

[4] [1972] 1 QB 373.

[5] BGHZ 39, 358 e 39, 266, pubblicate, tradotte in inglese, in Markesinis, in op. cit. alla nota 3.

[6] [1978] AC 728.

[7] [1983] 1 AC 520.

[8] [1985] AC 210.

[9] [1987] AC 718.

Estates Ltd. v. *Church Commissioners*[10], mettendo in luce ancora una volta quel che il Prof. Hamson avrebbe definito "l'elemento accidentale nell'infallibile giudizio delle signorie vostre".

Comunque sia, ciascuna sentenza ha demolito un pezzo dell'edificio difettoso della pronuncia *Anns*, mentre altre decisioni (rese in contesti diversi) ne hanno progressivamente minato il ragionamento di base comunemente attribuito a Lord Wilberforce ma il cui fondamento, in realtà, era stato posto da Lord Reid nella sentenza *Dorset Yacht*.[11] La gradualità, o meglio la crescita per accumulo del diritto inglese, non è solo un dato di fatto almeno per quanto riguarda la *common law* inglese; recentemente ha ricevuto un rinnovato sostegno dottrinale da uno dei nostri più egregi giudici.[12] Per quanto essa sia divenuta radicata in questo secolo, essa non è, a mio avviso, completamente compatibile con le teorie giudiziali di taluni grandi giudici di common law come Lord Mansfield, Chief Justice Holt o Lord Blackburn. Né, credo, sono stati sufficientemente sottolineati i suoi difetti in un mondo in rapido cambiamento. E questi difetti mi paiono ancora più vistosi in taluni settori, come quello ora esaminato, dove vediamo che il gradualismo opera a rovescio (e non sembra che Lord Goff abbia considerato questo aspetto del problema nel suo discorso).

Infatti lo smantellamento della decisione *Anns* è stato lento, inutilmente frammentario, con il risultato di creare una serie di incertezze nel suo cammino. Né credo, che le complicazioni siano terminate, come si può vedere dal progressivo sviluppo del *tort of negligence* nelle decisioni successive a quella *Junior Books* v. *Veitchi Co. Ltd*.[13]

Ci sono dunque volute per il diritto inglese molte costose controversie per giungere ad una posizione approssimativamente simile a quella tedesca. In sostanza questo è quanto risulta dai cinque principi enunciati dalla Corte d'Appello nel caso *Investors in Industrial Commercial Properties* v. *Bedfordshire District Council*.[14]

In secondo luogo, è il caso di ricordare che la decisione tedesca in materia fu resa vent'anni fa e in molto meno spazio delle sentenze inglesi sono enunciate le due regole di base che ora si applicano anche nel diritto inglese, e cioè:

(a) il danno subito dagli attori in questi casi è semplice danno al patrimonio (*economic loss*) e non danno alla proprietà come inizialmente si riteneva;

---

[10] [1988] 3 WLR 368.
[11] *Home Office* v. *Dorset Yacht Co. Ltd* [1970] AC 1004, 1027.
[12] Lord Goff of Chieveley, "The Search for Principle", in *Maccabaen Lecture in Jurisprudence* (1983), p. 69.
[13] [1983] AC 520.
[14] V. la opinione di Neill L.J. in [1986] 1 WLR 1141, a p. 1149.

(b)   lo scopo dei poteri di controllo sulle attività edilizie attribuito dal legislatore alle autorità locali è quello di tutelare gli occupanti di edifici ed il pubblico da pericoli alla salute e all'integrità fisica e nulla più.[15]

Inoltre l'interpretazione teleologica delle leggi tedesche in materia era, fin dal principio, estensibile anche alle leggi inglesi. In effetti Lord Wilberforce cominciò la sua motivazione nel caso *Anns* con parole che suggerivano un ragionamento analogo; tuttavia, inspiegabilmente, non sviluppò l'argomento fino alle sue logiche conclusioni.

In base alle regole di *common law* la domanda avrebbe potuto essere rigettata qualificando correttamente il danno in questione come semplice danno al patrimonio, sia allora che oggi non risarcibile in via di principio. E alla stessa conclusione si sarebbe potuto giungere se l'azione si fosse fondata sulla apposita norma di legge per le ragioni che si sono esposte sopra. Difficilmente si sarebbe potuto immaginare una migliore occasione per applicare il metodo comparatistico. Perchè non fu fatto?

Non si può pretendere che non-giuristi—soprattutto operatori incalzati dalle scadenze—in un paese possano conoscere quale è il diritto in un altro sistema. Ma se i materiali del caso sono resi disponibili la scusa per non utilizzarli diventa assai meno convincente. E nel caso di specie una traduzione di Tony Weir dei casi tedeschi cui ho fatto riferimento in effetti fu messa a disposizione degli avvocati nella causa *Anns*, ma per qualche ragione a me sconosciuta essa non fu utilizzata.

Le mie critiche alla sentenza *Anns* furono pubblicate sia in inglese che in francese ma, ancora una volta, ignorate. E più di recente quando ho, indirettamente, richiamato l'attenzione di materiali stranieri ad un importante avvocato della materia, rallegrandomi per il ripudio della decisone *Anns*, ricevetti, indirettamente, la seguente risposte: "Perchè occuparsi di sentenze straniere quando ne abbiano fin troppe di nostre inglesi?".

Questo tipo di reazione è un isolazionismo vendicativo, che peraltro si rinviene anche nei giuristi di altri sistemi giuridici. Per fare un solo esempio nella sentenza del 18 gennaio 1983 resa alla Corte Federale Tedesca in tema di danno da procreazione[16], la Corte esaminò dei casi inglesi e californiani solo per giungere alla conclusione che "decisioni straniere, per il solo fatto di essere fondate su leggi diverse, sono di limitata importanza per il diritto tedesco". Questa forma di isolazionismo è tanto più sorprendente in quanto la Corte Federale ammetteva che il caso al suo esame presentava delle questioni nuove sulle quali vi erano scarsi precedenti nazionali di qualche utilità.

---

[15] E' al tempo stesso interessante e strano notare che nel caso di danno a beni mobili difettosi in Germania non si è mostrata la stessa chiarezza di visione. Si constata infatti che nel corso di un decennio sono stati proposti ben tre criteri diversi per stabilire se sussista o meno una azione extracontrattuale. Le tre decisioni più importanti—BGZ 167, 359; BGHZ 86, 256; BGHZ NJW 1985, 2420—non sembrano poter essere positivamente confrontate con quella resa dalla Corte Suprema degli Stati Uniti nel caso *East River S.S. Corp* v. *Transamerica Delaval* 106 S. Ct. 2295. Per ragguagli v. Markesinis, op. cit. alla nota 3.

[16] BGHZ 86, 240; ma v. in modo difforme BGH JZ 1988, 150.

E' questo isolazionismo che i comparatisti devono combattere con l'instancabile vigore che è proprio dei giuristi e di riformatori di leggi ma che, per la natura delle loro funzioni, è negato ai giudici. E l'uso della giurisprudenza straniera dovrebbe facilitarne il compito.

IV. I casi in tema di responsabilità per procreazione potrebbero essere utilizzati per illustrare il significato di questo paragrafo; poichè, tuttavia, questo argomento è diventato molto sfruttato dai giuristi di *common law* preferisco concentrare l'attenzione su un'altra nuova questione giuridica che è emersa in parte perchè il diritto non è riuscito a stare al passo con il rapido sviluppo delle tecnologie mediche.

Il caso può essere facilmente illustrato; il medico che per colpa rimuove l'unico rene (sano) di un bambino malato è responsabile per il danno che un parente prossimo (di solito il padre o la madre) subisce per via del trapianto di uno dei propri reni[17]? I giudici tedeschi o canadesi hanno risposto affermativamente a tali domande dei donatori, mentre quelli americani hanno deciso diversamente. Cosa dovranno fare le corti inglesi quando—più presto che tardi—dovranno affrontare simili azioni? Un esame comparato dei diversi casi suggerisce che la decisione del BGH tedesco del 30 giugno 1987[18] ha efficacemente contrastato molti degli argomenti utilizzati dai giudici americani per sostenere il principio di non responsabilità.

Quali sono, dunque, questi argomenti? In primo luogo nelle decisioni americane vi è un accenno, ma non più di questo, che l'intervento del donatore è imprevedibile ed inaspettato.[19] Questo poteva essere vero al tempo in cui il caso *Sirianni* v. *Anna*[20] fu deciso (1967) quando il trapianto era ancora raro[21]. Questo argomento, tuttavia sembra avere scarso perso oggi quando—come affermato da una sentenza canadese *Urbanski* v. *Patel*[22]—"un trapianto di rene è un rimedio comune in caso di deficienza renale".

Un secondo argomento, sviluppato nella sentenza *Moore* v. *Shah*[23] è che la prevedibilità, di per sè, non è sufficiente a dimostrare l'esistenza di un obbligo di diligenza e conseguentemente a imporre una responsabilità per la sua violazione. Ciò può essere vero per quanto riguarda il diritto inglese, ma è piuttosto sorprendente vederlo affermare da giudici americani. Infatti, come è stato detto dal Prof. Fleming[24] "in California la prevedibilità, in gran parte dei casi, è diventato un requisito sufficiente per dimostrare l'esistenza di un

---

[17] A quanto risulta una persona ogni 1100 ha un solo rene, ma pochi hanno occasione di scoprirlo a meno che non insorga qualche emergenza o malattia.

[18] BGH 1988 JZ 150, con nota di prof. Stoll.

[19] *Moore* v. *Shah* 458 N.Y.S. 33, 34 (1982).

[20] 285 NYS 2d 709.

[21] A quanto risulta il primo trapianto di rene umano con esito positivo ebbe luogo nel 1954; il primo trapianto di cuore operato dal dr. Barnard si verificò nel 1967.

[22] 84 DLR 3rd 650, 671 (1978).

[23] 458 NYS 33, 34 (1982).

[24] Fleming, *The American Tort Process*, (1988), p. 118

obbligo di diligenza".[25] Altrettanto sorprendente è il fatto che i giudici amer-icani—i quali nella pratica sono pronti ad usurpare il ruolo (passivo) del leg-islatore—in questi casi sembrano suggerire che se un rimedio è necessario esso debba venire dal Parlamento.[26]

Una terza obiezione trattata nella sentenza *Moore* è che l'attribuzione di responsabilità aggraverebbe la posizione del medico "oltre i limiti governabili" in quanto egli non potrebbe "prevedere chi e quante persone, oltre al proprio paziente, potrebbero ipoteticamente essere colpite dalla sua negligenza".[27] A parte la considerazione che l'argomento della proliferazione di azioni giudiziarie non ha mai presentato molta attrattiva in casi di lesione personale, la verità è che in questi casi ci si deve preoccupare solo di un gruppo ristretto e generalmente identificabile di parenti prossimi i quali, per ragioni mediche (compatibilità degli organi) o per comprensibili spinte morali sono, nella prat-ica, gli unici a farsi avanti per salvare il soggetto passivo primario dell'illecito.

In ogni caso, l'argomento della proliferazione delle cause è stato efficace-mente contrastato dai criteri suggeriti dai giudici tedeschi per una valutazione *ad hoc* prima di giungere alla conclusione che l'intervento del donatore è meritevole di risarcimento.

Pertanto, ad esempio, l'intervento deve essere stato "dettato dal fatto illecito iniziale" e la "accettazione del rischio e la lesione arrecata alla propria integrità deve essere rapportata alle possibilità di successo dell'intervento", la "motivazione dell'atto deve essere accettabile secondo le regole riconosciute di condotta sociale".

Questi criteri, secondo le parole dei giudici tedeschi, sono "definiti in mate-ria molto ampia e devono essere sviluppati con maggiore dettaglio in ciascun caso specifico". Ancora una volta, dunque, è possibile cogliere la piena con-sapevolezza delle corti tedesche della necessità di distinguere, al pari di qual-siasi corte di common law, un caso da un altro, consapevolezza della necessità di chiarezza, ma anche di incoraggiare azioni altruistiche e ricompensare col-oro che le compiono.

La quarta e quinta obiezione si ricollegano ai rimedi che i giudici americani hanno ritenuto inopportuni per siffatti problemi. In parte perchè ritengono che la situazione di fatto sia incompatibile con quanto affermato nella deci-sione del giudice Cardozo nel caso *Wagner v. International Ry. Co*[28]; ed in parte perchè il donatore non ha agito sull'impulso del momento e senza pre-meditazione.

L'interpretazione della frase di Cardozo si fonda, a mio avviso, su di un equivoco lessicale: afferma il celebre giudice che "l'atto di soccorso, purchè

---

[25] Il caso *Moore* fu deciso dai giudici di New York ma le loro argomentazioni furono seguite da giudici del nono distretto della Corte d'Appello: V. ad es. il caso *Ornelas v. Fry* 727 P. 2d 819, 824 s. (1986).

[26] *Sirianni v. Anna* 285 NYS 709, 713.

[27] 458 N.Y.S. 33, 34 s. (1982).

[28] 232 N.Y. 176, 133 N.E. 437, 19 A.L.R. (1921).

non sia 'wanton', è causato dalle circostanze".[29] Il termine "wanton" è stato interpretato nel senso di "internazionale" e successivamente precisato in "voluto, intenzionale, volontario". Ora anche a considerare tali espressioni come sinonimi (il che non sono) mi sembra quanto meno dubbio che Cardozo usando il termine *"wanton"* intendesse attribuirvi questo significato. Poichè ogni atto di soccorso, anche compiuto sull'impulso del momento, è intenzionale e volontario, sarei piuttosto dell'opinione che il termine "wanton" sia stato utilizzato nel significato più tradizionale di "temerario". Una simile interpretazione sembra inserirsi bene nei principi in tema di soccorso che la legge intende incoraggiare purchè ricorrano circostanze appropriate.

Né, ritengo, è convincente tentare di regolare l'applicazione del principio del soccorso argomentando che il donatore ha avuto tempo per riflettere sulla propria azione. Come è stato detto dalla Corte Federale Tedesca[30]:

"Contrariamente a quanto ritiene l'appellante il nesso casuale non può essere negato sostenendo che la madre non si decise a donare un rene in presenza di una grave emergenza, bensì che ebbe a consultarsi con i medici e potè valutare gli elementi a favore e quelli contro. Se si presenta un caso di intervento del donatore, è irrilevante che costui abbia agito per così dire sull'impulso del momento oppure abbia potuto valutare le probabilità ed i rischi del proprio intervento. Questo non modifica assolutamente la 'situazione di emergenza' e lascia immutato il nesso casuale fra il comportamento dannoso di chi compie l'illecito e quello del soccorritore donatore il quale si espone al pericolo o rimane illeso. Non è infrequente che il soccorritore abbia abbastanza tempo per riflettere, soprattutto in circostanze come le presenti dove la donazione d'organo non può essere effettuata subito ma solo dopo un po' di tempo".

Ma la Corte Federale non si è fermata qui, giacchè se lo avesse fatto, avrebbe implicitamente riconosciuto che l'assistenza prestata dopo l'evento dannoso al fine di limitare i suoi effetti dannosi e di riportare la situazione allo *status quo ante* equivale al soccorso. Quindi procedeva ad affermare che

> "la risposta alla domanda su quanto il sacrificio compiuto da una persona che vuole ridurre il danno o cercare di ridurlo costituisce un soccorso o un aiuto d'emergenza richiede una valutazione che tenga in conto il rapporto con la sfida posta dalla situazione ed anche, ovviamente, il rapporto con lo spazio ed il tempo. Da questo punto di vista la donazione di un rene da un vicino parente—nel caso di specie la madre—a vantaggio del minore leso può ancora essere considerato, senza forzare le argomentazioni, un atto, conseguente ad una sfida, volto a salvare il minore la cui vita e salute erano messe in pericolo".

La sesta e ultima obiezione contro la risarcibilità del danno è il consenso del donante. Nel caso *Ornelas* la Corte d'Appello dell'Ariziona ritenne che

---

[29] 133 N.E. 438.
[30] La traduzione inglese della decisione, curata dal Prof. K. Lipstein, è pubblicata in Markesinis, op. cit. alla nota 3.

tale eccezione fosse fondata e quindi fu ritenuto che l'attore/donante non avesse subito alcun "danno giuridicamente rilevante".[31] L'argomento appare, tuttavia, fuorviante: nessuno ha sostenuto che il rene fosse stato trapiantato senza il consenso del donante; se così fosse stato ci sarebbe stata una azione per lesione personale. Quel che si dice, invece, è che la negligenza del convenuto ha posto il donante in una situazione nella quale egli si è sentito, moralmente e socialmente, obbligato a comportarsi nel modo in cui ha fatto. E considerazioni d'ordine più generale dovrebbero incoraggiare tali atti di donazione, piuttosto che penalizzarli lasciandoli senza risarcimento. Nel diritto inglese sappiamo che—ad esempio nei casi di danno al sistema nervoso come *Chadwick* v. *British Railways Board*[32] e *McLoughlin* v. *O'Brien*[33]—la legge premia gli atti meritevoli. I giudici tedeschi, senz'altro influenzati da siffatti argomenti, non hanno dubbi sul fatto che il preteso consenso non potesse essere usato come eccezione. A loro avviso:

> "è prevedibile che, dietro conforme parere medico, una madre sarà disposta a compiere tale sacrificio per il proprio figlio. Il nesso casuale non è interrotto dalla circostanza che la donazione del rene è conseguenza della situazione di pericolo, provocata dal convenuto, che da sola portò all'azione di soccorso. Come la giurisprudenza di questa corte dimostra, anche una causa psicologica può essere sufficiente per affermare la responsabilità del convenuto".

Dunque, non è questa un'area del diritto nella quale la comparazione giuridica offre, come minimo, feconde riflessioni e forse perfino un modello di soluzione?

V.   Il successo delle farse teatrali o le vignette umoristiche sui giornali dipende dalla voluta distorsione, semplificazione o esagerazione della realtà; ma la sostanza deve essere veritiera: un fatto esistente o incontestabile. La stessa sorte sembra spettare agli scritti dottrinali che tralasciano le minuzie di un sistema giuridico e si concentrano sulle sue grandi linee. Il quadro che emerge può sotto taluni aspetti apparire come una caricatura. Tuttavia, poichè si fonda su una certa quantità di fatti veri, esso può anche apparire convincente. Per molti anni questo è accaduto per il diritto comparato. Ma ora, per lo studente del diritto straniero, il quadro generalizzato sta diventando sempre meno attraente, mentre per il professionista o per il giudice esso può essere fuorviante.

Credo che alcuni esempi potranno spiegare il mio punto di vista.

La maggior parte degli avvocati inglesi sanno che il diritto civile continentale è fondato su codici. E' tuttavia fuorviante dire loro—come fece Lord Scarman quale membro della Law Commission—che la codificazione incoraggia uno sviluppo "pianificato" del diritto e può fornire una "formulazione

---

[31] 727 P. 2d 819, 825 (1986).
[32] [1967] 1 WLR 912.
[33] [1983] AC 410.

compatta, accessibile e completa del diritto".[34] E' altrettanto fuorviante sostenere come fece lo stesso autorevole giudice quindici anni più tardi nelle sue celebri Hamlyn Lectures[35], che il diritto inglese trarrebbe un grandissimo vantaggio dall'adozione di un Bill of Rights scritto da invocare in momenti di crisi quali quelli che si verificarono quando il caso *Liversidge* v. *Anderson*[36] fu deciso.

Queste le parole di Lord Scarman:

"Quando i tempi sono normali e la paura non si diffonde nel paese, il diritto inglese protegge con forza i diritti individuali e tutela la personalità umana. Ma quando i tempi sono eccezionalmente minati da paure e pregiudizi allora la *common law* è inadeguata: essa non può resistere al volere—per quanto impaurito e animato da pregiudizi possa essere—del Parlamento".[37]

Quel che si intende dire, cioè, è che l'esistenza di un Bill of Rights garantirebbe la protezione delle libertà civili in momenti di "grave crisi" (uso questo termine, invece di quello di "guerra", perchè vi è attualmente la tendenza a concedere poteri di emergenza non solo durante i periodi bellici ma anche quando si è in presenza di momenti insurrezionali e di gravi disordini interni). L'art. 6 del Bill of Rights canadese, che sostituisce l'art. 6 del War Measures Act[38] consente simili provvedimenti anche nel caso di timore di una insurrezione.

Se questa era l'intenzione di Lord Scarman, essa deve essere considerata la manifestazione di un desiderio piuttosto che la descrizione di quel che accade nella realtà, poichè la storia e lo studio comparato di decisioni straniere dimostra che è vero l'opposto. Lord Scarman avrebbe potuto imparare questo dando un'occhiata alla situazione del diritto canadese o americano.[39]

Ricordiamo come nel 1944 più di 20.000 canadesi di origine giapponese furono coattivamente dispersi nelle province delle praterie e nell'Ontario, e i loro beni furono confiscati e venduti—secondo il parere di molti—a prezzi irrisori.[40] E simili provvedimenti continuarono ad avere efficacia anche nel 1945, quando i giapponesi si erano arresi incondizionatamente, colpendo questa volta i cittadini canadesi di origine giapponese.

---

[34] Lord Scarman, *Codification and judge-made law*, conferenza tenuta il 20 ottobre 1966 presso la Facoltà di giurisprudenza dell'Università di Birmingham, p. 19.

[35] Nello scritto di D.G.T. Williams, "The Constitution of the United Kingdom", (1972), *Cambridge Law Journal* 266 ss. si rinviene una precedente versione dottrinaria di alcune delle sue idee successivamente sviluppate da Lord Scarman nella sua conferenza.

[36] [1942] AC 266.

[37] Lord Scarman, *English Law: The New Dimension* (1974), p. 15.

[38] Approvato nel 1914 sulla falsariga del Defence of the Realm Act inglese dello stesso anno. Esso è stato abrogato dall'att. 80 dell'Emergencies Act del 1988.

[39] Si veda sul punto la decisione *Korematsu* v. *U.S.*, 323 U.S. 214 (1944), un caso in cui le persone di origine giapponese erano state bandite da alcune località della costa occidentale degli Stati Uniti.

[40] Marx, "The Emergency Power and Civil Liberties in Canada", in (1970) 16 *McGill Law Journal* 33, p. 83 ss.

E' vero che ciò avvenne prima dell'approvazione del Bill of Rights canadese. Ma il prof. Tarnopolsky, che ha ampiamente studiato il problema, non ha dubbi che l'esistenza del Bill of Rights "non impedisce in alcun modo che ciò possa avvenite in futuro".[41] L'art. 6 (5) del War Measures Act, nella sua attuale formulazione esclude che qualsiasi provvedimento adottato nella sua applicazione possa essere considerato come violazione del Bill of Rights. Ed anche se così non fosse, poichè il Bill of Rights non è una legge di livello superiore esso può essere derogato da legislazioni speciali. In pratica, dunque, la situazione canadese potrebbe essere considerata non molto diversa da quella che risulta dal recente Emergencies Act inglese del 1988.

Forse la sovraordinazione del Bill of Rights potrebbe essere una soluzione (ammesso che si riesca a superare le obiezioni politiche e giuridiche commesse con i principi inglesi in tema di sovranità parlamentare). O forse il problema potrebbe essere ridotto o risolto eliminando le disposizioni che disciplinano la possibilità di sospendere i diritti civili in periodi di crisi.[42] L'esperienza americana durante la seconda guerra mondiale sembra indicare il senso opposto. E la lezione che si puo' imparare da quella esperienza non è in alcun modo inficiata dalla denuncia, *ex post facto*, di incostituzionalità delle decisioni che furono prese in quel contesto.

Il parere del prof. Tarnopolsky appare convergere sul punto, aggiungendo che la maggior parte delle persone che furono sentite dalla Commissione Speciale Canadese sul Bill of Rights ritenne che tali diritti fossero maggiormente a repentaglio nei momenti di crisi, tuttavia ritenne pure che in tali momenti fosse necessaria una legislazione simile alla War Measure Act.

La particolareggiata disciplina della materia nel Emergencies Act inglese del 1988—che ancora deve essere sperimentata nella pratica—rivela quanto il problema sia complesso. In ogni modo i diritti civili furono notevolmente limitati nel 1970 in Quebec quando si verificarono gravi disordini interni connessi ad un movimento separatista. Infine va evidenziato come la maggioranza degli interpreti ritenga che anche se la carta canadese dei diritti e delle libertà del 1982[43] non contiene una disposizione sui "poteri di emergenza", la sospensione della sua efficacia è tuttavia possibile in base all'art. 1 e all'art. 33.[44] Lo studio della giurisprudenza consentirebbe peraltro di contestare l'affermazione di Lord Scarman secondo cui in momenti di pace la *common law* "protegge con forza le libertà dell'individuo e rispetta la personalità umana," in quanto

---

[41] Tarnopolski, *The Canadian Bill of Rights*, (1975), p. 328.

[42] Opinione sostenuta da Wallington e McBride, *Civil Liberties and a Bill of Rights* (1976), p. 89 ss.

[43] Che, stranamente, non ha mai abrogato il Bill of Rights del 1960 e sembra coesistere con esso: v. la decisione *Sig* v. *M.E.I.* (1985) ISCR 178.

[44] Hogg, "A Comparison of the Canadian Charter of Rights and Freedoms with the Canadian Bill of Rights", in Tarnopolsky (a cura di), *The Canadian Charter of Rights and Freedoms*, (1982), p. 13. Nel suo preambolo l'Emergencies Act del 1988 dichiara che "i diritti fondamentali non dovrebbero essere limitati o soppressi anche in casi di emergenze naturali". Solo l'esperienza potrà dirci se questa è solo una pia intenzione.

essa sottovaluta gli ampi e straordinari poteri che la legislazione inglese attuale concede al governo anche in tempo di pace.[45] Ma essa sembra inoltre ignorare la circostanza che molte decisioni, prese a maggioranza e sulla base di regole generali della *common law* vaghe ed adattabili, potrebbero suggerire a chi non conosce a fondo le istituzioni giudiziarie inglesi che esse sono assai leste a genuflettersi di fronte potere esecutivo.

Lord Scarman, ovviamente, sosterrebbe che l'esistenza di un Bill of Rights "educherebbe" i nostri giudici e favorirebbe i risultati desiderati. Ma potrebbe obiettarsi che il Privy Council ha avuto più di un'occasione per interpretare costituzioni straniere che tutelano libertà fondamentali e non ne ha approf-ittato per accordare ad esse una protezione adeguata. Ad esempio, siamo sicuri che la Corte Suprema americana avrebbe deciso il caso *Att. Gen.* v. *Antigua Times*[46] nello stesso modo in cui fu deciso dal Privy Council?

Oppure che il caso *Spycatcher*, a parte alcune notevoli eccezioni, abbia alzato il prestigio del diritto e dei giudici inglesi?

La mia opinione personale è che se c'è bisogno di "educazione", il processo educativo potrebbe durare molto a lungo prima di cambiare atteggiamenti profondamente radicati. O almeno questo è quello che ci suggerisce lo studio della giurisprudenza.

Gli esempi che ho appena citato—e molti altri se ne potrebbero fare—mostrano come eminenti giuristi possono fare affermazioni inesatte che sono in parte il risultato di una errata rappresentazione (o ignoranza) del diritto straniero, e in parte conseguenza della loro educazione e della inclinazione del momento che, in qualche modo, impediscono loro di vedere o descrivere l'intero quadro. Il contributo del prof. Renè David alla *International Encyclopaedia of Comparative Law*[47] può essere utilizzato come punto di partenza in questa discussione.

Il prof. David concentra la sua attenzione su uno degli aspetti del diritto giurisprudenziale, e cioè in che misura una decisione giudiziale possa o debba utilizzare un precedente come unica propria giustificazione. Ciò porta ad esaminare le regole del precedente e alla ragionevole conclusione che essa non è così vincolante nella *common law* come credono i *civil lawyers*, nè così sconosciuta nella *civil law* come ritengono i *common lawyers*. Una serie di altre questioni connesse al diritto giurisprudenziale come, per esempio, il

---

[45] Sul punto v. D. Bonner, *Emergency Powers in Peacetime*, (1985).

[46] [1976] AC 16. Gli artt. 1 e 10 della Costituzione di Antigua affermavano la tutela costi-tuzionale della libertà di espressione. Una legge di Antigua del 1971 stabiliva che era illecito stam-pare o pubblicare un giornale se non fosse preventivamente stata depositata la somma di 10.000 dollari presso l'ufficio del Procuratore Generale al fine di garantire il pagamento di eventuali con-danne per diffamazione. Questa somma si aggiungeva ad ulteriori 1.000 dollari richiesti da un'altra legge per ottenere la licenza di stampa. Secondo il Privy Council entrambe le disposizioni erano legittime. Con riguardo alla prima espresse l'opinione che il suo scopo era quello di pro-teggere la reputazione e i diritti di soggetti terzi e pertanto non costituiva una limitazione incos-tituzionale della libertà di espressione.

[47] Riprodotto anche in *Revue del la Recherche Juridique—Droit Prospectif*, (1985), p. 775 ss. Le citazioni sono tratte dal testo in francese.

potere creativo dei giudici civili nel campo del diritto sostanziale sono o deliberatamente ignorati o ricevono meno attenzione. Ovviamente, David è un comparatista talmente colto ed un commentatore così esperto da non poter ignorare del tutto questo aspetto. Conseguentemente osserva, in un passo, come il diritto giurisprudenziale ha non solo interpretato le parole del legislatore ma, talvolta, le ha deformate sviando le sue intenzioni.[48] Tuttavia, sorprendentemente, non cita neanche una decisione francese o tedesca in uno scritto che riguarda il diritto giurisprudenziale e contiene 95 note e 27 riferimenti a casi anglo-americani. Come ho detto in precedenza, citando Lord Scarman, queste omissioni certamente non sono dovute ad ignoranza (da escludersi nel caso David) ma largamente dovute alla tradizionale formazione giuridica dell'autore, il suo punto di partenza, il suo stile, le sue prospettive e il periodo in cui scrive: Lord Scarman, per esempio, scriveva quando l'idea di una codificazione, prima, e di un Bill of Rights, poi, era di moda in Inghilterra. Egli scriveva anche avendo in mente testi stranieri, ma probabilmente senza conoscere la pratica. Lo stesso può dirsi, sotto certi aspetti, per il prof. David. Ovviamente egli conosce i casi *Jand'heur* e *Schacht*. E conosce il loro impatto nei due codici. Ma occorre ricordare che, in fin di conti, David benchè sia un comparatista molto noto, scrive come un giurista francese. Ed il giurista tradizionale di *civil law*, anche se occasionalmente possa citare la giurisprudenza a sostegno della propria opinione, difficilmente ammetterà esplicitamente che la sua posizione è resa sostenibile proprio perchè vi è la giurisprudenza sul punto. Questo approccio di *civil law* alla giurisprudenza è evidente anche nel volume di David, *Les grands systèmes de droit contemporains*. Le pagine da 143 a 151 della nona edizione sono dedicate, per esempio, al ruolo della giurisprudenza nei sistemi di *civil law*. La mancanza di qualsiasi riferimento ad una sola decisione è altrettanto significativa del fatto che metà del capitolo è essenzialmente, dedicato al diverso problema della struttura delle corti della giurisprudenza nei sistemi di *common law*, dove su venti, solo otto pagine sono dedicate alla regola dello *stare decisis*, alla logica del giudice e allo stile. E' pertanto davvero un peccato che il perspicace riconoscimento contenuto nella prefazione di David alla 8ª e 9ª edizione.

Forse irriverentemente ma fondatamente vi è la tentazione di adattare il famoso aforisma di Maitland sulle "forms of action", che anche se morte e sepolte continuano a governare, dalle loro tombe, i giuristi inglesi.

In sintesi l'analisi casistica è sostituita da una generalizzazione costruita attorno a disposizioni del codice che possono essere o così astratte da essere prive di significato, o così imprecise da fornite poca informazione pratica su un sistema legale straniero in comparazione con il diritto del proprio paese.

Volendo fare ancora un esempio, si può citare il ruolo delle corti tedesche negli anni '50 e '60 nei loro fortunati tentativi di adattare il testo, ormai datato del Codice civile, in materia di diritto di famiglia alle esigenze dell'ordina-

---

[48] Op. ult. Cit. p. 790.

mento costituzionale del secondo dopoguerra. Esso è importante per i giuristi tedeschi, affascinante per gli studiosi di *common law*, eppure non trova spazio nell'opera di David. Per gran parte degli studiosi di *common law* si tratta di una terra incognita; e si tratta di una ignoranza che alimenta e tiene in vita molti miti e false rappresentazioni che i comparatisti devono eliminare.

La costituzionalizzazione del diritto privato non è un fenomeno unicamente tedesco. Per esempio la *common law* americana in tema di lesione della reputazione ha, a partire dal caso *New York Times* v. *Sullivan*[49], ceduto molto terreno al principio costituzionale caratterizzante l'esperienza tedesca—e in gran parte ignoto a gran parte degli studiosi di common law—è che il fenomeno ha riguardato un vasto spettro di questioni dal diritto di famiglia, alla responsabilità civile, al diritto del lavoro, per citare solo tre esempi.

Quel che portò ala rivoluzione giurisprudenziale degli anni '50 fu il mancato rispetto dell'art. 117 della Costituzione di Bonn del 1949 il quale stabilisce che tutte le disposizioni di legge (comprese quelle del codice civile) che fossero incompatibili con il principio costituzionale dell'uguaglianza fra uomo e donna avrebbero dovuto essere soppresse entro il 31 marzo 1953. Ciò, tuttavia , non avvenne perchè—secondo quanto ci dice il prof. Rheinstein:

"il gruppo politicamente dominante (il partito democratico cristiano) includeva esponenti cattolici e protestanti i quali tendevano ad identificare lo schema della famiglia patriarcale e del predominio dell'uomo all'interno di essa e pertanto non erano particolarmente zelanti nel dare applicazione ad un principio che capitava di trovarsi nella Costituzione".[50]

Con una azione combinata la Corte costituzionale[51] e quella federale[52] dichiararono illegittimi gli artt. 1354[53] e 1387[54] del BGB perchè in contrasto con il principio costituzionale della completa uguaglianza fra i sessi.

Ancora più singolare è il fatto—per quanto ne so unico nei moderni sistemi di civil law—che l'intera disciplina del matrimonio, cioè una consistente parte del BGB si trovò, fra il 1953 ed il 1957, in uno stato di vuoto legislativo nel quale solo le corti stabilivano le regole che ritenevano compatibili con la Costituzione. Una situazione che cessò solo il 18 giugno 1957[55] quando entrò in vigore il Gleichberechtigungsgesetz.

Tuttavia, i vecchi atteggiamenti sono duri a morire ed anche se la nuova legge migliorava, fra l'altro, i diritti patrimoniali delle donne dopo il divorzio

[49] 376 U.S. 254 (1964).
[50] Rheinstein, "The law of Family and Succession", in Yiannopoulos (a cura di), *Civil Law in the Modern World*, (1965), p. 25 ss., ripubblicato nei suoi Gesammelte Schriften 1972, 212 a pp. 219 s.
[51] BVerf. G. NJW 1954, 65; BVerf. GE 3,225.
[52] Nel suo parere consultivo del 6 settembre 1953, in BGHZ 11, 34.
[53] La decisione finale su tutte le questioni concernenti il matrimonio, ivi incluse quelle riguardanti il luogo di residenza o di domicilio, spetta al marito, salvo che abusi del suo diritto.
[54] Sono a carico del marito talune spese giudiziali sostenute durante il matrimonio.
[55] BGBl I 609: Legge concernente l'uguaglianza giuridica dell'uomo e della donna in materia di diritto privato.

introducendo il principio della comunione dei beni acquisiti durante il matri-monio (Zugewinngemeinschaft), "la sua visione dell''uguaglianza' si dimostrò assai più conservatrice di quella mostrata dalle Corti nei quattro anni prece-denti in base alla loro autonoma interpretazione dei principi costituzionali".[56] Ciò non vuol dire che le corti erano disposte ad avvallare abnormi deviazioni dalle disposizioni costituzionali di uguaglianza fra i sessi. Ad esempio in una sentenza del 29 luglio 1959 il Bundesverfassungsricht dichiarò incostituzionale l'art. 1627 del BGB il quale attribuiva al padre l'ultima parola in tema di scelte educative per la prole comune[57]; e due anni prima la stessa corte aveva dichiarato incostituzionale il regime fiscale peggiorativo per le donne lavora-trici.[58] E dieci anni più tardi fu raggiunta un'altra pietra miliare quando la Corte Costituzionale, con la sua sentenza 29 gennaio 1969[59], dichiarò la com-pleta uguaglianza fra figli legittimi e naturali: un risultato ancor più notevole di quelli precedenti considerando che in questo caso la costituzione non poneva—a differenza dell'art. 117 sulla parità fra uomo e donna—alcuna sca-denza. Anche qui, tuttavia, l'intervento era chiaramente fondato sull'art. 65 della Costituzione che richiedeva un intervento legislativo in tal senso. Va tut-tavia osservato che su altre questioni—in particolare sul mantenimento delle disposizioni del codice che identificavano la "moglie" con la "donna di casa" (il c.d. Hausfrauen-und-Versorgungstheorie), le corti assunsero un atteggia-mento assai più prudente, come si vedrà nel prossimo paragrafo.

Uno schizzo di alcuni grandi sviluppi giurisprudenziali, anche se espressi in forma così breve e inadeguata come sopra, sembrava tuttavia sufficiente per giustificare le seguenti osservazioni.

In primo luogo mostra come resoconti quali quello del prof. David sul ruolo della giurisprudenza nello sviluppo del diritto non rendono giustizia all'argo-mento. Al più trasmettono al lettore di *common law* un quadro riduttivo del ruolo delle corti nei sistemi di *civil law* e confermano—almeno tacitamente—il suo erroneo convincimento che i giudici di *civil law* siano soltanto dei buro-crati giudiziari i quali applicano meccanicamente i codici. Potranno forse essere burocrati (nel senso di pubblici impiegati); ma certamente non sono degli automi privi di volontà e di idee che applicano meccanicamente dispo-sizioni del codice.

In secondo luogo lo studio della giurisprudenza smentisce da solo l'affer-mazione che i giudici non sono talvolta fonte creativa di diritto. A mio avviso non è sufficiente dire ai propri studenti che così non è: è necessario fornire esempi e spiegazioni su perchè e come i giudici decidono di intervenire. Ovviamente ciò non vuol dire che il giudice possa creare leggi dando corpo

---

[56] I. Markovitz, "Marriage and the State: A Comparative Look at East and West German Law", in (1971), 24 *Stanford Law Review* 111 a p. 126; si tratta di uno studio interessante che fa un ottimo uso del ricco materiale giurisprudenziale e di altre forme demografiche e sociologiche.

[57] BVerf. GE 10, 59.

[58] FamRZ 4, 82.

[59] BVerf. GE 25, 157; FamRZ 1969, 196.

alle proprie opinioni o a considerazioni di opportunità. Le cose tuttavia si trovano in uno stato diverso laddove il legislatore costituzionale abbia stabilito un principio guida generale ed applicabile (come ad esempio quello di uguaglianza) com'è il caso dell'art. 3, 2° comma, della costituzione tedesca.[60]

In tale ipotesi il legislatore ha, in effetti, "trasferito una parte del diritto affinché sia disciplinato attraverso decisioni giudiziali".[61] Ciò è perfettamente lecito in base alla Costituzione tedesca, la quale benchè attribuisca il ruolo predominante nella produzione legislativa al Parlamento, tuttavia non considera tale attribuzione esclusiva.

Secondo la stessa sentenza "il principio di separazione di poteri, costituzionalmente garantito, non è violato ogni qualvolta al giudice sia attribuito il compito di individuare la norma sulla base e all'interno di una regola generale" (quale quella contenuta nell'art. 3, 2° comma). Infatti, precisa la sentenza, l'art. 117, 1° comma, implica che "dal 1° aprile 1953 il giudice, attraverso il graduale sviluppo della giurisprudenza e del diritto consuetudinario, trasformi progressivamente le regole generali sull'uguaglianza in una serie di norme più precise e vincolanti nei confronti di tutti".

La corte conclude questa parte di sentenza riconoscendo apertamente che il combinato disposto degli articoli della Costituzione prima citati "affida ad essa il compito di realizzare la costituzionalmente richiesta parità fra i sessi attraverso un diritto giurisprudenziale di stampo anglosassone".

Si tratta certamente di affermazioni audaci e la stessa corte, in altre occasioni, ha cercato di occultare un po' il suo ruolo creativo. Ma il velo è davvero assai sottile, come dimostra la seguente affermazione tratta dalla sentenza sul diritto alla riservatezza[62]:

"Eccezionalmente la norma può essere rinvenuta al di fuori delle regole giuridiche positive emanate dallo Stato. Si tratta di una norma che promana dall'ordine costituzionale nel suo complesso ed il cui scopo è la 'correzione' del diritto scritto. Spetta al giudice 'scoprire' la norma e darvi effetto concreto attraverso le sue decisioni. La Costituzione non impone ai giudici di interpretare le leggi in senso letterale quando decidono i casi ad essi sottoposti. Un simile atteggiamento presuppone una assoluta completezza dei comandi legislativi che non è conseguibile nella pratica. La valutazione del giudice può far emergere taluni valori sociali i quali sono implicitamente riconosciuti dall'ordine costituzionale ma che hanno ricevuto una formulazione insufficiente nei testi legislativi. La decisione del giudice può contribuire a realizzare tali idee e a dare effettività a tali valori".

Infine il risultato degli interventi giudiziali appena citati è innovativo e, occorre ribadirlo, applicabile in ordinamenti diversi se solo gli osservatori

---

[60] Si noti il contrasto fra questo articolo e quelli 109, 2° comma e 119, 1° comma della Costituzione di Weimar del 1919. Le proclamazioni di uguaglianza politica e sessuale contenute in esso erano generalmente interpretati come mere norme programmatiche con il risultato che non fu fatto nulla di concreto per migliorare la posizione inferiore delle donne sancita dal codice civile.

[61] BGHZ 11, 34.

[62] BVerf. GE 34, 269.

esterni si fossero mostrati più disponibili a studiare più attentamente la lunga evoluzione del diritto tedesco. Penso, di nuovo, all'istituto della Zugewinngemeinschaft introdotto in Germania nel 1957 al fine di provvedere alla divisione del patrimonio dei coniugi dopo il divorzio. Uno dei fondamenti (se non il fondamento) di tale istituto fu il principio che la equa divisione dei beni dopo il divorzio è raggiunta meglio dalla determinazione di quota fissa, piuttosto che attraverso la discrezionale valutazione del giudice che prenda in considerazione le circostanze di ciascun caso.[63] Un altro modo per risolvere questo problema è invece quello di attribuire al giudice la discrezionalità (con o senza l'ausilio di direttive) di procedere alla divisione dei beni dopo il divorzio. Questo procedimento può conseguire un alto livello di giustizia individuale e la intrinseca flessibilità della discrezionalità giudiziale è molto sentita dai giuristi di *common law*, in particolare in Nuova Zelanda dove l'art. 5 della Matrimonial Property Act del 1963 attribuiva una simile discrezionalità ai giudici. Tuttavia nella realtà le cose si realizzarono in modo diverso da quello originariamente auspicato, e dopo il divorzio le corti dividevano i beni coniugali in base al contributo dato da ciascuna parte. Se lo scopo era quello di valutare il contributo dato dalla moglie alla famiglia, piuttosto che semplicemente dare ad esso un prezzo[64], la discrezionalità giudiziale chiaramente non era equa nei confronti delle donne. Come ha notato un autore "una rassegna dei casi decisi in base all'Act mette in luce una costante attribuzione di limitate quote di patrimonio per le mogli il cui unico contributo alla formazione di tale patrimonio consisteva nel lavoro domestico". E aggiunge [65]: "Retrospettivamente si deve riconoscere che proprio la discrezionalità attribuita all'Act ha affossato gli scopi del legislatore".

Con il Matrimonial Property Act del 1976 (All'art. 11) fu accolta in linea di principio la regola della parità delle quote, offrendo così sostegno alla tesi che la soluzione tedesca, almeno come punto di partenza, era maggiormente nell'interesse della parità fra uomo e donna e preferibile a quella della discrezionale valutazione del "contributo" fornito da ciascun coniuge.

Come è stato detto da Max Rheinstein, in buona sostanza

"prima di adottare questa o quella soluzione legislativa dobbiamo essere consapevoli che vi è un prezzo da pagare. Non possiamo avere nel contempo giustizia individ-

---

[63] Nel senso che la regola generale può essere modificata se la sua applicazione comporterebbe "una grave ingiustizia, tenuto conto delle circostanze del caso". Si v. ad es. l'art. 1381 BGB. In base a questo sistema durante il matrimonio vige la separazione dei beni. Allo scioglimento "gli aumenti che si sono verificati nei patrimoni di ciascun coniuge durante il matrimonio sono confrontati: l'incremento viene sottratto da quello maggiore e la differenza viene divisa per due; quindi la parte che ha avuto l'aumento maggiore deve corrispondere all'altra metà della differenza": così Rheinstein, "Division of Marital Property", in 12 *Willamette Law Journal* 413, 440; pubblicato in *Gesammelte Schriften*, II, 1971, p. 346 a p. 366.

[64] Come fanno i giudici inglesi negli omicidi colposi quando la madre viene uccisa e i figli minori hanno bisogno di assistenza. Recentemente, tuttavia, è stato riferito dalla stampa (*The Independent*, 17. 2. 1989, p. 5) che sono state liquidate 147.000 sterline ad una famiglia per la perdita della madre pur non produttrice di reddito.

[65] Gray, *Reallocation of Property on Divorce*, 1977, p. 93.

uale(o meglio, la speranza di giustizia individuale) e procedure prevedibili, rapide, facili e a poco prezzo in materia di divorzio".[66]

La legge tedesca offre dunque molte idee utili, soprattutto se si analizza la sua esperienza concreta con quella di altre teorie su questo problema spinoso.[67] Essa dimostra che l'ideale di *common law* di adattare la legge ai bisogni individuali è sconfitto dalla pratica dei giudici anglo-americani (e soprattutto di questi ultimi) di riconoscere validità "normalmente agli accordi dei coniugi in questa materia". Secondo la prof. Glendon, il risultato "di queste concessioni di discrezionalità è quello di privare i coniugi e i loro legali di principi chiari che possano servire nella soluzione delle controversie".[68] Inoltre "ogni studio che è stato effettuato in materia dimostra che dopo il divorzio il coniuge al quale non sono stati affidati i minori generalmente ha un tenore di vita superiore a quello del coniuge affidatario".[69] Il tempo ci dirà se questo stato di cose migliorerà a seguito dell'art. 25 del Matrimonial and Family Proceedings Act inglese del 1984 il quale richiede che il giudice nel prendere i provvedimenti economici nei casi di divorzio consideri in primo luogo il benessere dei figli minori; oppure porterà, com'è avvenuto, pure, negli Stati Uniti, ad altre controversie giudiziarie(o alla minaccia di controversie) riguardanti l'attitudine ad essere affidatari dei figli minori. Richard Neely, ora giudice della Corte Suprema della West Virginia, ha riconosciuto che nei suoi anni di pratica forense come avvocato aveva con successo minacciato di iniziare una controversia sull'affidamento dei minori al fine di ottenere un accordo patrimoniale più favorevole per il marito[70], ed altri studi sembrano confermare l'impressione che questo costituisce un periodo effettivo, quantomeno negli Stati Uniti.[71]

VI.   Uno sguardo alle disposizioni del codice civile francese in tema di contratto a favore di terzi chiaramente fornirebbe l'erroneo convincimento che esse costituiscono l'eccezione alla regola generale che il contratto ha effetto solo tra le parti. Nella realtà, come è stato evidenziato dal prof. Lawson, i

[66] Rheinstein, "Division of Marital Property", *op. cit.* p. 365. V. pure Glendon, *The New Family and the New Property*, 1981, p. 93 s. a favore di una "divisione in parti uguali limitata ai beni acquisiti attraverso attività produttrici di reddito durante il matrimonio, in assenza di accordi diversi". Opinioni simili sono espresse nel suo lavoro più recente da EAD, *Abortion and Divorce in Western Law: American Failures, European Challenges*, 1987, p. 86 ss.

[67] Non solo spinoso, ma anche estremamente importantein quanto risulterebbe—secondo quanto riferito nel resoconto del Congresso annuale del 1979 del gruppo "Diritto di famiglia" dell'American Bar Association, pubblicato in (1979) 5 *Fam. L. Repts* 2829, e citato da Glendon, *The New Family ecc. op. cit.* p. 57—che in occasione di divorzio sono trasferiti più beni attraverso la successione testamentaria e intestata.

[68] Glendon, *Abortion ecc., op. cit.* p. 86.

[69] Ib.

[70] Neely, *The Divorce Decision: The Legal and Human Consequences of Ending a Marriage*, (1984), p. 62.

[71] Quantomeno negli Stati Uniti; v. ad es. Chesler, *Mothers on Trial: A Battle for Children and Custody*, (1985).

giudici hanno trasformato l'eccezione nella regola.[72] Parimenti uno sguardo alle disposizioni del BGB sul risarcimento del danno[73] da fatto illecito potrebbe convincerci che esso viene abitualmente e tipicamente liquidato sotto forma di una rendita.

La teoria e la pratica, tuttavia, divergono ampiamente e chiunque si affidi solo o principalmente ai libri omettendo di considerare la giurisprudenza e la pratica delle corti si farà un'immagine errata.

Per certi versi ciò può essere accaduto con la Pearson Commission inglese (sulla liquidazione del danno) anche se è possibile che essa abbia sottovalutato l'erosione che la pratica ha effettuato sulle disposizioni dei codici in quanto all'epoca vi era una diffusa diffidenza verso la liquidazione del danno in un'unica soluzione.

Lo studio della giurisprudenza, gli usi del foro ed il quadro complessivo del sistema possono spesso spiegare queste deviazioni del modello codicistico. Non si può, ad esempio, ignorare la pressione degli avvocati sui propri clienti affinché preferiscano liquidazioni in un'unica soluzione in modo tale che, a loro volta, possano ricevere i loro onorari più facilmente e con minori contrasti con il cliente. Per quanto desiderabile possa essere la libertà di scelta non sembra che essa debba essere sempre incoraggiata. A mio avviso uno studio comparato dell'argomento suggerisce una soluzione di compromesso: liquidazioni in una unica somma nei casi di lesioni meno gravi, rendite annuali per le lesioni più gravi permanenti, anche al fine di tutelare le vittime dalle pressioni, talvolta dei loro stessi avvocati.

Ma lo studio del contesto, sociale ed economico può anche aiutare a spiegare perchè il quadro offerto dalla disposizione legislativa non è sempre una descrizione accurata di quello che accade nella realtà. Un esempio dalla Germania ed uno tratto dal diritto inglese possono servire a spiegare il punto.

Come ho già detto, il Gleichberechtigungsgesetz del 1957 non ha completamente conseguito l'ugualianza dei sessi che il titolo di legge si prefiggeva. Semmai, raffreddò lo zelo riformista che aveva pervaso le corti nei quattro anni precedenti. Ciò è perticolarmente vero con riguardo a disposizioni come quella contenuta nell'art. 1355 del BGB che obbligava la donna, al momento del matrimonio ad assumere il nome del marito[74], e l'art. 1356 del BGB il quale, fondamentalmente, considerava il lavoro domestico come il dovere primario della moglie e consentiva il lavoro esterno solo nella misura in cui fosse compatibile con i suoi obblighi verso il marito e la famiglia.

Questo stereotipo della moglie come madre e casalinga non sembra abbia turbato le Corti tedesche compresa quella costituzionale, la quale nel 1963 poté affermare che

---

[72] Lo stesso si può dire per l'art. 1384 del codice civile francese; a tal proposito si tenga presente l'osservazione di Tunc nei *Essays in Memory of Professor F.H. Lawson*, (1986), p. 71 ss. : "E' saggio non prendere i codici civili troppo sul serio".

[73] Come ad es. l'art. 843 del BGB.

[74] Ritenute costituzionali del Bundesverwaltungsgericht im *FamRZ* 1960, 113.

"il parlamento in consonanza con l'opinione generalmente prevalente, ha stabilito che la gesione della casa familiare costituisce il dovere primario della moglie. Anche una donna che svolga un proprio lavoro, non può senza il consenso del marito, per così dire liberarsi dal proprio obbligo al lavoro casalingo attraverso un contributo monetario".[75]

Ed in un'altra delle molte decisioni analizzate dal prof. Markovits si rinviene questa singolare affermazione dell'Oberlandesgericht:

"La Costituzione tollera l'uguaglianza dei sessi nell'ambito del diritto di famiglia solo nei limiti entro i quali è preservata la nostra concezione del matrimonio e della famiglia, formata nella tradizione culturale e giuridica occidentale e nella fede cristiana".[76]

Questa giurisprudenza ci dice molto di più sul reale stato del diritto tedesco dopo l'approvazione della legge del 1957 sulla parità dei diritti, che lo studio del suo testo o dei suoi lavori preparatori (e, come si è detto, lo stesso vale per la Nuova Zelanda). Ma anche le questioni sottoposte all'esame dei giudici, assieme alle loro decisioni, se osservate nel contesto socio-politico del momento spiegano la retromarcia selettiva delle Corti tedesche. Inoltre, questo ritorno al passato, immediatamente successivo alle interpretazioni evolutive, può essere riscontrato in altri sistemi ed in altre materie, dove l'inerzia del legislatore incoraggia le corti ad assumere iniziative che, a loro volta, si traducono in azione legislativa.[77]

La regressione o il conservatorismo appena descritti sono, credo, comprensibili se ritiene che i giudici si siano abbandonati ad un "attivismo giudiziario" (per usare le parole di Lord Devlin)[78], cioè ad assicurarsi che la legge tenga il passo con i mutamenti nell'opinione maggioritaria, e non in una "giurisprudenza dinamica o creativa" nel senso che le decisioni generano i cambiamenti nell'opinione pubblica. Ho motivo di ritenere, ad esempio, che con riguardo alla libertà della donna di lavorare al di fuori delle mura domestiche, non esistesse nella Germania degli anni '50 e di primi anni '60 un consenso maggioritario. Per esempio, nella sua decisione del 1963, la Corte Costituzionale parla della "opinione generalmente prevalente"[79] che sappiamo essere stata, sia in Parlamento che negli ambienti giudiziari—e probabilmente anche con riguardo alla maggioranza silenziosa—non particolarmente coinvolta in tali problematiche.[80]

[75] Ripubblicata con traduzione inglese di Markovitz, *op. cit.* p. 131.
[76] Fam RZ 5, 326 a p. 328.
[77] L'evoluzione dell'interpretazione dell'art. 1384 del codice civile francese nel caso di infortuni sul lavoro costituisce un parallelo interessante. Le decisioni della Corte di Cassazione del 1896 portarono all'approvazione della legge sull'indennizzo per gli infortuni agli operai che, a sua volta, pose fine alla interpretazione evolutiva dell'art. 1384. l'attenzione per questo articolo ricominciò solo con l'avvento della circolazione automobilistica la quale divenne oggetto di intervento legislativo solo nel 1985.
[78] Lord Devlin "Judges and Lawmakers", (1976) 39 *Modern Law Review* 1, p. 2.
[79] Markovitz, op. cit., n. 75.
[80] Si v. al contrario la situazione della Germania Est dove molte donne su precise indicazioni politiche venivano incoraggiate attivamente dal partito comunista a lavorare per rimettere in piedi

Diversamente nella Germania orientale fu più facile dare attuazione ai proclamati principi di uguaglianza fra i sessi di quanto non lo fosse nella Germania Occidentale dove una serie di circostanze politiche ed economiche rendeva il problema del lavoro femminile meno pressante. Si è quindi portati a ritenere che il testo costituzionale era. semmai, più avanzato dell'opinione pubblica, almeno per quanto riguarda alcune espressioni dell'idea di uguaglianza.

Ma quando i tempi per il cambiamento furono maturi—verso la metà degli anni '70—vi fu un generale sovvertimento del libro del codice civile dedicato al diritto di famiglia. Un mutamento nello stile di vita riallineò dunque, la pratica con la teoria proclamata.[81] Ma fino a quel momento si poteva dire, parafrasando il prof. Honoré[82], che "un marziano si sarebbe tristemente disperso se avesse fatto affidamento sul diritto tedesco per ottenere il suo dottorato in diritto di famiglia tedesco".

L'esempio inglese che intendo fare dimostra la differenza fra quel che è teoricamente possibile secondo la legge ma raramente accade nella realtà. Una divergenza che deve essere spiegata ed anche giustificata. Si pensi ai "compensation orders" che i giudici penali inglesi possono emettere in base al Criminal Justice Act del 1972 (e successive modifiche). In teoria l'istituto presenta alcune somiglianze con quello francese e continentale della costituzione di parte civile.

Nella pratica, però, l'innovazione ha finora incontrato un successo assai modesto. Perchè?

Una spiegazione fornita da giudici—ma non della legge—riguarda il nesso casuale. Questo fu l'approccio assunto dalla Court of Appeal negli anni '70[83], la quale espresse anche l'opinione che i giudici dovessero essere cauti nell'emettere "compensation orders" laddove vi fosse un dubbio sostanziale sulla portata della legge.

Un'altra notevole eccezione si trova nell'art. 31 (3) della legge, in base al quale i "compensation orders" non potevano essere concessi per danni "derivanti da un incidente da circolazione di autoveicoli".

Recentemente alla Commissione per la revisione del codice della strada, costituita nel 1985 e presieduta da Peter North, fu prospettata l'opinione che la regola dovesse essere modificata al fine di aumentare efficacemente i poteri sanzionatori delle corti. Incidentalmente tale soluzione conseguirebbe il principale obiettivo di questo tipo di rimedio, e cioè fornire "un mezzo pratico e

---

una economia gravemente danneggiata ed ulteriormente compromessa da una sfavorevole distribuzione della popolazione in classi di età.

[81] Un commento sulla legge di riforma del diritto di famiglia e del matrimonio del 14 giugno 1976 (BGBI, I, 1421) dall'allora ministro della giustizia H.J. Vogel sembra confermare l'opinione sopra riportata. V. Vogel, "Das Erste Gesetz zur Reform des Ehe und Familienrechts vom 14 Juni 1976", in (1976) 23 *Zeitschrift fur das Gesamte Familienrecht* 481, 482.

[82] Honoré', *The Quest for Security: Employees, Tenants, Wives*, in *Hamlyn Lectures* (1982), 64.

[83] V. ad es. *R. v. Vivian* (1976) 68 Cr. App. R. 53

rapido per evitare di dover ricorrere alla legislazione civile".[84] Ma la proposta fu respinta con la motivazione che essa aggraverebbe il carico—sia in termini di tempo che di denaro—delle Corti.

Quali Corti? Qui si trova un indizio importante dell'atteggiamento ostile del diritto inglese. Infatti la grande massa dei casi del genere viene giudicata dalla Magistates Courts, quell'istituzione tipicamente inglese che benchè assai economica nel suo funzionamento, è resa possibile solo grazie all'impegno gratuito di uomini e donne privi di una formazione giuridica. A tali giudici simili argomenti potrebbero essere attraenti e spiega perchè, in fondo, l'unica eccezione della regola è contenuta nell'art. 104 (2) del Criminal Justice Act del 1988 che consente al giudice di emettere un "compensation order" nel caso di danno derivante dalla circolazione di veicoli quando l'imputato non è assicurato e il Motor Insurance Bureau non provvede all'indennizzo. Dunque il significato pratico dell'eccezione è minimo.

Tuttavia si volga ora lo sguardo alla pratica dei sistemi continentali gestito da giudici di professione che possono giudicare assieme le questioni penali e civili, e che cosa scopre? Un atteggiamento simile prevale nella prassi di alcuni paesi (Germania, Olanda) incoraggiando la vittima del reato a esprimere la sua azione civile davanti ai giudici civili (si veda ad es. l'art. 403 dello Strafprozessordnung). Nei Paesi Bassi l'art. 322 del Codice di procedura penale, richiamando gli artt. 44, comma 3, e 56, comma 5, del codice dell'ordinamento giudiziario, fa divieto al giudice penale di concedere un risarcimento superiore a certe cifre (600 fiorini per le corti inferiori, 1500 per quelle superiori).

In questo caso la ragione per la quale l'azione risarcitoria viene esclusa dall'azione penale non consiste nella natura professionale o non professionale del giudice, ma nel timore che la decisione della causa civile richiederà più tempo e l'esame di prove contrastanti e di consulenze tecniche ritardi la speditezza del giudizio penale. In Olanda è stato manifestato il timore che l'imparzialità del giudizio penale possa venire compromessa da testimoni che cercano di influenzare l'esito dell'istanza risarcitoria.[85]

Attualmente, tuttavia, vi è una spinta a sopprimere le limitazioni esistenti e ad attribuire completa autonomia ai giudici penali nel decidere sulle richieste risarcitorie.[86] Quando una tale riforma sarà attuata il sistema olandese si avvicinerà di più a quello francese, adottando la sua maggiore disponibilità a consentire ai giudici penali di decidere, quando possibile, le questioni risarcitorie.

Quali altre ragioni vi sono dunque per la scarsa utilizzazione di questo rimedio nel sistema inglese? Nel nostro ordinamento, mentre l'iniziativa dell'azione penale è lasciata alla polizia, i diritti della persona lesa di

---

[84] *R. v. Inwood* (1974) 60 Cr. App. R. 70, p. 73 (opinione di Scarman L.J.).
[85] V. De Bosh Kemperer. *Wetbock von Strafvordering* (1840) I, 47.
[86] V. Roording, "De Schadevergoedingsstraf. Rapport von de Commissie Terwee", *Ars Aequi*, (gennaio 1989), pp. 40–7.

intervenire nel procedimento, ottenere documenti e informazioni, quantificare il proprio danno sono incerti e spesso addirittura sconosciuti alla vittima potenziale parte civile.

In altre parole la vittima non sempre sa che dispone di un rimedio civilistico e spesso non vi è nessuno che chiede il risarcimento per suo conto. Forse questa potrebbe essere una spiegazione del perchè i compensation orders sono stati così raramente utilizzati nei casi di violazione del Trade Descriptions Act.[87] Certamente non si tratta di un problema che possa essere risolto in questa sede, ma spero di avere indicato sufficiente materiale comparatistico da giustificare un riesame del problema.

VII.   Si potrebbe obiettare che il titolo di questo paragrafo è talmente ovvio da non dover essere sottolineato. Tuttavia, per almeno tre ragioni, esso merita una particolare attenzione: In primo luogo perchè statistiche precise sul tipo di azioni legali che vengono sottoposte ai giudici possono essere utili per molte ragioni. Potremmo scoprire, ad esempio, i mutamenti nelle tendenze alla controversia giudiziaria, quali azioni hanno maggiori possibilità di giungere ad una decisione e le variabili possibilità di successo; informazioni tutte che potrebbero essere utili sia alle parti, ai loro legali e agli assicuratori. Sfortunatamente in Inghilterra mancano quei rilevamenti empirico-statistici che si trovano in paesi come gli Stati Uniti, finanziati da istituzioni come la Rand Corporation; anche se altri centri di ricerca come il Centre for Socio-legal Studies a Oxford sta fornendo agli avvocati e ad altri operatori dati statistici ed empirici molto utili.

Si consideri, ad esempio, il sorprendente risultato di una ricerca[88] secondo cui il 39% di casi di responsabilità medica viene abbandonato a seguito di consulenze tecniche, svolte dopo l'inizio del procedimento, i quali dimostrano che la lesione lamentata è dovuta a cause naturali. E' vero che si tratta di un campione modesto[89]; ma se si accertasse che si tratta di un fenomeno nazionale, non sarebbe forse ingiustificata la proposta degli autori della ricerca di inserire anche un medico nelle commissioni per l'assistenza legale e il gratuito patrocinio, in modo da chiarire anche gli aspetti medici delle richieste di assistenza. Certamente da studi di questo genere potremmo imparare qualcosa su cosa funziona e cosa non funziona nel nostro sistema.

Inoltre, informazioni del genere sono utili ai fini comparatistici: si pensi ad esempio alla differenza nel numero di cause per responsabilità del produttore promosse in Inghilterra e negli Stati Uniti: 200 qui, 70.000 lì. Oppure ai casi di responsabilità medica: qualche centinaio nel nostro paese confrontato con molte migliaia in America. Anche tenendo conto del diverso numero della

---

[87] V. Borrie, *The Development of Consumer Law and Policy: Bold Spirits and Timorous Souls, Hamlyn Lectures* (1987), p. 67 ss.

[88] Hawkins-Paterson, "Medioco-legal audit in the West Midlands region: analysis of 100 cases", in (1987) 295 *British Medical Journal* 1533, p. 1535.

[89] Fra i 324 casi di controversie legali occorse nei West Midlands—la più grande delle regioni del servizio sanitario inglese—ne sono stati scelti cento a caso.

popolazione (circa quattro volte e mezzo superiore negli Stati Uniti) ci si rende chiaramente conto della crisi dell'istituto della responsabilità civile al di là dell'Atlantico. Scoprirne le ragioni potrebbe contribuire ad evitare che essa si estenda anche al di qua dell'oceano.

Sfortunatamente i dati in nostro possesso sono estremamente approssimatici; la raccolta di dati attendibili riguardanti la Francia si è dimostrata, finora, del tutto impossibile e ho ricevuto l'avvertenza di molti studiosi francesi di considerare con grande cautela le statistiche francesi esistenti. Ad esempio, per quali ragioni (assicurative o di altro genere) le compagnie di assicurazione medica inglesi si rifiutano di pubblicare informazioni precise e dettagliate sulle richieste di indennizzo preferendo invece comunicarci che nel 1987 o nel 1988 vi è stato un aumento dei premi del 71 o dell'87 %? Cosa significa questo? l'aumento è dovuto al fatto che sono state avanzate più richieste oppure che più domande sono state accolte dai giudici, oppure che sono stati concessi risarcimenti più alti?

Secondo il rapporto della Commissione Pearson (basato su dati del 1973) il 60% delle 500 azioni segnalate dalle compagnie di assicurazione medica è stato abbandonato, il 34% è stato risolto transattivamente, il 5% è stato deciso giudizialmente e di questi 25 casi solo uno ha visto l'attore vittorioso.

Non sono riuscito a trovare dati precisi per gli anni 1983–84 e 1987–88. Sembrerebbe tuttavia che nel primo periodo le compagnie di assicurazione per i medici hanno registrato circa 2000 domande, 4000 invece per il secondo periodo.

In una comunicazione non ufficiale ad un gruppo di ricercatori[90] le compagnie hanno affermato che "il numero delle domande soddisfatte è più che raddoppiato fra il 1984 e il 1987". Tuttavia altri dati raccolti dallo stesso gruppo di ricercatori[91] sembrano indicare che la percentuale delle azioni abbandonate è salito dal 60% del rapporto della Commissione Pearson al 75%, anche se vi è un correlativo aumento dei casi che vengono decisi giudizialmente (dal 5 al 10%). Questo sembra indicare che l'aumento dei premi assicurativi—che ha acceso il timore di un propagarsi in Inghilterra della "epidemia" americana di azioni per responsabilità medica, non sia tanto il risultato di decisioni a favore degli attori, quanto di *a)* un aumento delle spese legali nelle fasi preliminari di azioni che successivamente, per una ragione o per l'altra, vengono abbandonate; *b)* l'aumento di alcuni singoli importi risarcitori[92]; *c)* un aumento delle transazioni stragiudiziali in casi di colpa professionale più o meno chiara che precedentemente non venivano perseguiti; *d)* forse la politica delle compagnie di assicurazione.

Tutti questi importanti punti—ed altri ancora se ne potrebbero evidenziare—pongono ulteriori quesiti che necessitano di avere risposte concrete per

---

[90] Hamm, Dingwall, Fenn, Harris, *Medical Negligence: Compensation and Accountability*, (1988), p. 11 (ed. del King's Fund Institute di Londra).

[91] *Op. ult. cit.* p. 12. nonchè Hawkins-Paterson, *op. cit.* p. 1536.

[92] I dati sono forniti da Hamm *et al. op. cit.* p. 11.

sapere se effettivamente vi è una "epidemia" di azioni per responsabilità medica oppure si tratta si una impressione immaginaria; se essa colpisce tutti i medici o solo quelli che svolgono pratica privata (dal 1988 i premi pagati dai medici generici e i due terzi dei premi dei medici che lavorano a tempo pieno per le autorità sanitarie sono coperti dal governo inglese con un costo per il contribuente di circa 50 milioni di sterline); come l'ordinamento debba reagire a questo stato di cose.

Si potrebbe ad esempio sostenere che anche se l'ordinamento inglese, per un verso, favorisce notevolmente il medico, l'orientamento generale attuale incoraggia più persone ad agire contro i medici e che vorremmo modificare l'attuale sistema scoraggiando le pretese non meritevoli e, dall'altra parte, facilitare il successo degli attori meritevoli. In termini più generali, è forse troppo eretico proporre che colui il quale studia oggi la responsabilità medica ha bisogno di un po' meno teoria generale e un po' più di dati di fatto su come il sistema effettivamente funziona?

I dati statistici sul numero dei giudizi iniziati e conclusi potrebbe anche aiutare a dissolvere alcuni timori infondati su possibili liberalizzazioni in altre aree della responsabilità civile. Si prenda ad esempio l'argomento della moltiplicazione dei giudizi utilizzato per avversare il risarcimento del danno al patrimonio. I giudici olandesi, francesi e belgi hanno adottato una soluzione opposta a quella seguita da quelli inglesi.[93] La Corte Suprema olandese è arrivata al punto di affermare che il pericolo di una molteplicità di azioni giudiziarie dovrebbe indurre gli appaltatori di opere pubbliche negligenti (in casi simili a quelli esaminati nella decisione inglese *Spartan Steel & Alloys Ltd v. Martin & Co. Ltd.*)[94] ad essere più attenti, piuttosto che ad esonerarli da responsabilità. La mia impressione dall'esame del problema e da diverse discussioni con studiosi francesi e belgi è che anche in quei paesi il numero di azioni giudiziarie fondate sul risarcimento del danno al patrimonio è ridottissimo. Sicchè, sia che il problema—che tanto preoccupa i giudici inglesi—venga risolto attraverso il risarcimento, autoassicurazione, oppure, semplicemente, riluttanza ad agire in giudizio, la realtà di fatto è che la tanto temuta proliferazione di azioni giudiziarie non si è verificata. E allora perchè dovrebbe verificarsi in Inghilterra dove le spese legali sono più alte ed il procedimento in contraddittorio fra le parti è sicuramente più idoneo a scartare le azioni infondate o pretestuose?[95]

Una osservazione analoga potrebbe essere fatta in casi di responsabilità medica dove viene sollevato il problema del "consenso informato" del paziente. Dati dagli Stati Uniti—dove l'orientamento è più favorevole

---

[93] Si v. Fokkemma—Markesinis, "All or Nothing? The compensation of pure economic loss in English and Dutch Law" in 1987 *Ex Iure* p. 63 ss.

[94] [1973] 1 QB 27.

[95] AR 1 luglio 1977, in N.J, 1978, 449; nonchè HR 14 marzo 1958 in N.H., 1961, 570 A.A. Viii, 72.

all'attore—indicano che il problema si pone in meno del 3% dei giudizi.[96] E occorre anche aggiungere che negli Stati Uniti—le probabilità di successo dell'attore in casi di responsabilità medica sono più basse che in tutti gli altri casi di responsabilità civile. Non sono riuscito a trovare dati tedeschi equivalenti ma ho motivo di ritenere che anche in quel paese i casi sono molto limitati e questo nonostante i giudici tedeschi—con l'incubo nazista al fondo dei loro pensieri—abbiano assunto un atteggiamento ancor più favorevole agli attori imponendo ai medici di comunicare ai loro pazienti, soprattutto se richiesti, anche i rischi minimi.[97] In altre parole, dati esatti sul numero di casi effettivamente giunti davanti ai giudici potrebbero dimostrarsi estremamente utili per disperdere timori infondati.

Infine, dati statistici su quel che effettivamente giunge davanti ai giudici, e che comunque arriva sul tavolo dell'avvocato, possono aiutarci a riformulare il nostro abecedario didattico che spesso è disperatamente antiquato.

Ad esempio, nei miei primi dieci anni alla facoltà di giurisprudenza di Cambridge eravamo abituati a dedicare—sarebbe forse il caso di dire "sprecare"—un numero sproporzionato delle nostre limitate ore di lezione a questioni come la formazione del contratto, la *consideration*, l'errore, la *frustration* anche se nei tempi più recenti esse hanno dato luogo a pochissime decisioni.[98] Lo stesso è vero dell'Animals Act del 1971 o del caso *Rylands* v. *Fletcher*[99] che oggi sono i capostipiti di minuscoli volumi di giurisprudenza.

Ora, sono il primo a riconoscere che tali problematiche presentano un indubbio interesse intellettuale, e vi è stato un periodo negli studi del diritto inglese quando era difficile incontrare un giurista anche modesto che non avesse dedicato un articolo al problema dell'errore. Il comparatista potrebbe anche studiare e, forse, lamentare il danno che Pothier ha arrecato sul punto specifico al diritto inglese. Anche la *consideration* è stato un argomento affascinante per gli studi comparatistici. Certamente è altrettanto difficile spiegare alcune delle sue regole più tecniche ad un giurista straniero, quanto lo è giustificarlo ai giuristi inglesi. O, infine, si prenda un esempio ancor più specifico: la differenza fra l'azione per danni e l'azione per il pagamento di una somma determinata; la distinzione fra le due è stata sottolineata con vigore solo nel magistrale manuale del prof. Treitel. Nella maggioranza degli altri testi la differenza tende ad essere sottaciuta, evidenziandosi piuttosto che i

---

[96] *Making Health Care Decisions*, President's Commission for the study of Ethical Problems in Medicine, US Goverment Printing Offices 1982, 27.

[97] V. OLG Hamm, VersR 1981 68: deve essere comunicato al paziente il rischio pari allo 0,5% di complicazioni in un intervento di diagnostica. La maggior parter delle controversie sorgono in relazione ad informazioni inadeguate in procedure diagnostiche. Nel complesso sembrerebbe che nel 4–5% di tutte le controversie in tema di responsabilità medica viene sollevato il problema , spesso in via subordinata. Sul punto v. Reichenbach "Arzthaftplicht aus der Sicht des Versicherungsmediziners", in 1981 *Vers.R.* 807, p. 809.

[98] E' il solo il caso di ricordare che il Law Reform (Frustrated Contracts) Act 1943 ha trovato una applicazione giurisprudenziale solo nel 1979: *B.P. (Exploration) Libya Ltd.* v. *Hunt*[(1983] 2 AC 352.

[99] (1865) 3 H & C 774; (1866) LR 1 Ex 265; (1868) LR 3 HL 330.

problemi di quantificazione e causalità sono irrilevanti nelle azioni per il pagamento di una somma determinata. Ho quindi l'impressione che pochi studenti colgano tali differenze e sono sicuro che ancor meno si rendono conto del fatto che davanti alla Queen's Bench Division le azioni per il pagamento di una somma sono venti volte più numerose delle azioni di risoluzione contrattuale (i dati esatti erano, per il 1986, 183.191 contro 9.150).

Tutto questo non vuol dire che la scelta di una problematica debba dipendere unicamente in base alla sua importanza pratica. Piuttosto che in un mondo di risorse limitate dedicare troppi sforzi ad argomenti infrequenti alle spese di altri che impegnano il mondo reale può essere un errore costoso. Come si può adattare il corso di studi alla realtà se non si tiene presente quel che giunge davanti ai giudici?

VIII.   In questo scritto ho trattato numerose questioni ma spero non in modo superficiale. Se si volessero formulare delle conclusioni esse potrebbero essere più meno le seguenti.

In casi simili a quelli decisi in Inghilterra da *Dutton* v. *Bognor Regis UDC* mi sembra che i giuristi tedeschi fecero subito la scelta corretta mentre quelli inglesi stanno lentamente recuperando. Nei casi di trapianto del rene le decisioni tedesche e canadesi sono più convincenti dal punto di vista giuridico e più consone ad un principio di giustizia di quelle americane. Nella divisione dei beni coniugali dopo il divorzio il prof. Kahn Freund indicava una soluzione più equa per le donne esprimendo la sua perplessità sul lasciare tutto alla discrezionalità dei giudici.[100] Infine il risarcimento delle vittime del reato in sede penale è meno frequente di quanto si sarebbe sperato. ma vediamo che anche in ordinamenti dove esso apparentemente è maggiormente favorito che in quello inglese le cose non sono molto diverse, spesso per ragioni simili a quelle riscontrare in Inghilterra.

Tuttavia il diritto comparato non è una lista di somiglianze e differenze,e lo scopo di questo scritto era quello, più ampio di dimostrare, attraversp esempi specifici tratti dalla responsabilità civile, dal diritto di famiglia, dal diritto pubblico, dalla procedura e dalla pratica delle corti, che il diritto comparato non può affermarsi attraverso generalizzazioni.

Invece deve attirare lo studente mostrandosi importante per la sua formazione, il ricercatore fornendogli fonti d'ispirazione, l'operatore pratico offrendogli indicazioni per risolvere questioni nuove o complicate.

Mentre stavo riflettendo su come formulare sinteticamente le ragioni per le quali ritengo che il diritto comparato stia attraversando una crisi nonostante il crescente numero di scambi con l'Europa continentale e gli Stati Uniti, ho riletto la prefazione al volume di Mary Ann Glendon, *Abortion and Divorce Law in Western Law*. Le seguenti parole dell'allieva prediletta di Max

---

[100] Kahn Freund, "Matrimonial Property. Where do we go from here?" *The Joseph Unger Memorial Lecture*, University of Birmingham (1971), p. 19.

Rheinstein esprimono esattamente le mie sensazioni e scolpiscono il tema centrale di questo lavoro[101]:

> "Gran parte delle tecniche e dei metodi comparatistici furono sviluppati verso la fine del XIX secolo e, come la scienza giuridica di cui facevano parte, si sono rivelati non del tutto adeguati per l'analisi dei problemi giuridici contemporanei. Il diritto comparato moderno si è formato come disciplina quando studiosi francesi e tedeschi iniziarono lo studio sistematico di altri ordinamenti in coincidenza con la straordinaria mole di attività legislativa che ebbe luogo in questi paesi negli ultimi decenni del secolo scorso. L'apparato concettuale sviluppato nella *belle époque* del diritto comparato era caratteristico della scienza giuridica di quel periodo. Si concentrava su regole formali, istituzioni e procedure. Dava per scontato il ruolo primario del diritto privato, trascurando largamente il diritto pubblico. La sua teoria delle fonti del diritto presupponeva la centralità della giurisprudenza nei sistemi anglo-americani e dei codici civili in quelli romano-germanici".

Come la prof. Glendon ritengo che molti comparatisti hanno ignorato la costituzionalizzazione del diritto privato e hanno iper-concentrato la loro attenzione sull'esegesi del codice e sugli scritti dottrinali trascurando o minimizzando l'importanza della giurisprudenza. Questa scuola di comparatisti è costituita essenzialmente da giuristi tradizionalistie dogmatici i quali hanno sottovalutato l'importanza della ricerca empirica ed interdisciplinare ed ignorato le pratiche dei tribunali. Oltretutto questo tipo di scuola comparatistica mi sembra carica di generalizzazioni spesso prive di significato e con un pesante pregiudizio a favore del diritto delle obbligazioni.[102]

---

[101] Kahn Freund, *op. cit.* p.3.

[102] La riforma del diritto di famiglia è stata già esaminata prima del testo, ma anche i rapporti tra datore di lavoro e prestatore d'opera furono influenzati. Così in BAGE 1, 185 la Corte Federale del Lavoro ha affermato il principio che in determinate circostanze il lavoratore non poteva essere licenziato per avere esercitato il suo diritto costituzionale alla manifestazione del proprio pensiero politico previsto dall'art. 5 della Costituzione. Il principio costituzionale della parità fra uomo e donna ha portato la stessa Corte a invalidare un contratto collettivo che attribuiva un salario inferiore alle donne: BAGE 4, 240 (A partire dal 1980 simili discriminazioni sono state dichiarate illecite con una serie di emendamenti al BGB). La stessa Corte utilizzando l'art. 6, 1° comma, della Costituzione (che tutela il diritto al matrimonio) ha annullato una disposizione di un contratto di lavoro che attribuiva al datore di lavoro il diritto di licenziare il dipendente nel caso di matrimonio (BAGE 4, 274). L'art. 12 della Costituzione (libertà e lavoro) determinò le decisioni in BAGE 13, 168, mentre gli artt. 1 e 2 sui diritti della personalità furono fondamentali per le decisioni BAGE 2, 221 e BAGE 28, 168. Le medesime disposizioni costituzionali portarono la Corte Costituzionale, in una importante decisione del 1983 (B Verf. GE 65, 1) a dichiarare illegittime parti della legge che disponeva il censimento in quanto non tutelavano sufficientemente la riservatezza. Le decisioni sollecitarono il dubbio se la stessa protezione potesse applicarsi nei casi in cui i datori di lavoro privati raccoglievano e distribuivano informazioni sui propri dipendenti. Sul punto v. Simitis, "Die informationelle Selbsbestimmung: Grundbedingung einer verfassungskonformen Informationsordnung", *NJW* 1984 398. Un anno più tardi (BAGE 46, 98) esso fu sciolto positivamente affermando che l'offerente il posto utilizzasse o diffondesse le informazioni contenute nel questionario compilato dall'aspirante. E' notevole che in queste decisioni si sia affermata la *diretta* applicabilità delle disposizioni costituzionali in controversie di diritto privato. In contesti diversi l'opinione prevalente è che in tali casi la Costituzione esercita una influenza indiretta piuttosto che una efficacia diretta. Si v. la decisione della Corte Costituzionale in BVerfGE 7, 198.

La trascuratezza verso altri rami del diritto—come ad esempio quello della procedura penale, dove resta da fare moltissimo lavoro utile ed istruttivo[103]— è pertanto tanto deplorevole quanto inspiegabile.

Sono naturalmente consapevole del fatto che molti miei colleghi, soprattutto quelli francesi, non concorderanno con le mie critiche e difenderanno l'esistenza di corsi generali di diritto comparato con motivazioni "culturali". Ma se questa è la principale giustificazione del diritto comparato allora faremmo meglio a sostituirlo con un corso su un solo ordinamento (francese, tedesco oppure anche romano) pittosto che cercare di coprire troppi sistemi in modo troppo superficiale.[104]

Se i docenti non si rendono conto che l'approccio tradizionale al diritto comparato non attrae più gli studenti, questi invece se ne rendono conto[105] e votano con i loro piedi scegliendo corsi quali diritto urbanistico, diritto industriale, tributario, diritti umani o proprietà intellettuale i quali appaiono più importanti per il loro futuro di lavoro.

Ovviamente molti di questi corsi hanno e possono avere una dimensione comparatistica. Così, per una strana sorte, il metodo comparatistico potrebbe avere un futuro più ampio penetrando altre materie piuttosto che cercando di autoaffermare la propria indipendenza sotto il titolo poco convincente di "diritto comparato". Anche i più rigorosi assertori di quello che ho definito il "vecchio" approccio si rendono conto che questo fenomeno riaccende l'interesse nel diritto straniero.[106] Ed io non la penso diversamente.

Le mie conclusioni dunque sono che i comparatisti devono ripensare al loro atteggiamento verso la propria materia. Studiare un ordinamento straniero può portare ad una migliore comprensione dei problemi che si affrontano ed anche a idee inaspettate su come risolverli, ma ciò accadrà solo qundo anzichè

---

[103] Per esempio recentemente il prof. Spencer dell'Università di Cambridgesi lamentava del fatto che nel campo della procedura penale comparata "ciascun sistema riesce a costruire degli ostacoli che gli ordinamenti vicini ignorano. Ad esempio in Inghilterra esiste il più tremendo (e nemico della verità) sistema probatorio che, ripetutamente fa fallire la richiesta di giustizia. Un pasticcio che in Francia è evitato quasi del tutto attraverso una nozione assai più razionale e meno restrittiva di prova. Ma d'altra parte, nel sistema francese vi è qualcosa che provoca altrettanti problemi e fastidi, cioè le regole in tema di prescrizione le quali consentono a persone manifestamente colpevoli di sottrarsi alla giustizia ritardando le procedure. Un problema che in Inghilterra viene quasi del tutto superato escludendo i termini di prescrizione tranne che per i reati bagatellari. Se tutti i paesi dell'Europa occidentale tenessero una conferenza e decidessero di abbandonare le regole più stupide della procedura e delle prove penali, l'Europa sarebbe un posto più illuminato".

[104] Si v. ad esempio lo scritto del prof. Agostini, in *Droit Comparé*, (1988).

[105] Un incontro fra comparatisti a Parigi ha tentato di minimizzare o giustificare quel che è nel complesso *a)* una bassa produzione di ricerche nel settore del diritto comparato; *b)* un ridotto numero di studenti che seguono i corsi di diritto comparato. Come dimostra il rapporto francese, anche quando il tentativo è intrapreso con l'eleganza e lo stile che contraddistinguono il lavoro del prof. Mouly, la triste realtà non può essere celata all'occhio esperto. Gli atti sono stati pubblicati nella *Revue Internationale de Droit Comparé*, (1988), p. 793 ss.

[106] Anche se questi corsi vengono visti come complementari ad un corso principale introduttivo. A tal proposito si v. le osservazioni del prof. Tallon, "Les perspectives de l'enseignement universitaire du droit comparé", in *Festschrift fur Imre Zajtay*, (1982), p. 479.

allargare il campo visivo, lo si restringerà. Quando si comincerà a fare così lo studente e l'operatore pratico verranno attratti, e quindi crescerà il loro rispetto per la materia. Ed una materia che annoverafra i suoi sacerdoti Ernest Rabel, Max Rheinstein, Otto Kahn Freund, Harry Lawson, Jack Dawson certamente merita maggiore rispetto e riconoscimento di quanto oggi gode.

7

A Matter of Style[1]

1. INTRODUCTION

One of America's leading comparatists rightly remarked not that long ago that:

"The conceptual apparatus developed in the *belle époque* of comparative law was characteristic of the normal legal science of that period. It concentrated on formal rules, institutions, and procedures; it took the primacy of private law for granted, largely ignoring public law; and its sources-of-law theory assumed the centrality of case law in the Anglo-American systems and of civil codes in the Romano-Germanic system."[2]

No book in my opinion has done more to reveal the weaknesses of the old-style works of comparative law than Zweigert and Kötz's *An Introduction to Comparative Law*.[3] Crisp, specific, complete, and reliable, it contrasts markedly with René David's *Les grands systèmes de droit contemporain*[4] which it is rapidly replacing as the leading textbook on the subject. But Zweigert and Kötz have done more than inform the reader about different systems. They have used their rich and focused material to compare and criticise solutions; and, what is for me just as important, they have been quick to emphasise similarities of result and even methodology. Indeed one of their most remarkable chapters is that on "Style", for here they advance the thesis that style more than anything else may set different systems apart. Five particular topics are given as illustrations of the authors' thesis; but notably absent is all discussion about differences in *judicial* style. Why this is so is nowhere explained,[5] so I have chosen this occasion as an opportunity to start a discussion on the subject. Why I think this is important will become increas-

---

[1] An inaugural lecture delivered at University College London on 1 February 1994.
[2] Mary Ann Glendon, *Abortion and Divorce in Western Law* (1987), p. 3.
[3] 2nd edn. (1987) (English trans. by T. Weir).
[4] 9th edn. (1993).
[5] Despite the fact that Professor Kötz has found the subject interesting enough to discuss on at least three different occasions. See "Scholarship and the Courts: a Comparative Survey" in D. S. Clark (ed.), *Comparative and Private International Law: Essays in Honour of John Henry Merryman on his Seventieth Birthday* (1990), pp. 183 *et seq.*; "Einführungsvortrag" in *La Sentenza in Europa: Metodo Tecnica e Stile* (1988), pp. 129 *et seq.*; and "The Role of the Judge in the Court Room: the Common Law and the Civil Law Compared" (1987) 1 *J. of S. Afr. Law* p. 35 *et seq.* A seminal piece on this subject was written by the late Professor Gino Gorla entitled "Lo Stile delle Sentenze-Ricerca Storico-comparative" in *Quaderni de Il Foro Italiano* (1967), 313 *et seq.*; "Lo Stile delle Sentenze-Testi Commentati" in *Quaderni de Il Foro Italiano* (1968), 475 *et seq.*

ingly clear as one reads the text; and it will be stated more succinctly in my conclusions. Before we proceed any further, however, something should be said about the wide meaning I ascribe to the word "style" in the context of this paper.

2. THE MEANING OF "STYLE" IN THIS PAPER

"Style", wrote Edward Gibbon, is "the image of character".[6] In the judicial context it can, I believe, tell the careful observer a great deal about the judicial process, the judge, and the real issues confronting him in a legal dispute. But how a person speaks depends upon whom he is addressing; and we know not in England[7]—let alone in other systems—to whom the judges are addressing their remarks. What we do know for certain, however, is that we find in common law judgments memorable lyrical openings like, "It was bluebell time in Kent"[8] we find thought-provoking apophthegms like "The state of a man's mind is as much a fact as the state of his digestion"[9]; and we come across rhetorical statements such as "The Fourteenth Amendment does not enact Mr Herbert Spencer's Social Statics".[10] Then there are judicial sentences encapsulating pragmatism in a nutshell: "The soundness of a conclusion may not infrequently be tested by its consequences".[11] The capacity for compressive metaphors is also obvious in such famous sentences as "danger invites rescue".[12] Yet it was the same learned judge who, with equal style, warned us that "Metaphors in law are to be narrowly watched, for starting as devices to literate thought, they end often by enslaving it".[13] On other occasions the Anglo-American judge can admirably compress in one sentence a whole legal tradition, as Cardozo did in *People* v. *Defore*[14] when he said: "The criminal is to go free because the constable has blundered". The power of these sentences is so great that, as Judge Posner (himself a judge, jurist, and literary stylist) has remarked, simple substitution of one word with a synonym will not improve but "lame them".[15]

This is because of the use of language that gives the common law judgment its special features and, in my view, its distinctive edge. It simply is not found in the German judgment where judges (to quote Cardozo again but in a

---

[6] *Memoirs of My Life*, edited with an Introduction by B. Radice (1991), p. 39.
[7] For references to different views see Paterson, *The Law Lords* (1982), Ch. 2.
[8] *Hinz* v. *Berry* [1970] 2 QB 40 at p. 42 *per* Lord Denning M.R.
[9] *Edgington* v. *Fitzmaurice* (1885) 29 Ch. D. 459 at p. 483 *per* Bowen L.J.
[10] *Lochner* v. *New York*, 198 U.S. 45 at p. 75 (1905) which is marvellously analysed by Richard Posner in *Law and Literature: a Misunderstood Relation* (1988), pp. 281–7.
[11] *Ostrowe* v. *Lee*, 256 N.Y. 36, 175 N.E. 505 (1931).
[12] *Wagner* v. *International Ry.*, 244 N.Y. 176, 133 N.E. 437 (1921).
[13] *Berkey* v. *Third Avenue Ry. Co.*, 244 N.Y. 84, 155 N.E. 58 (1926).
[14] 242 N.Y. 13, 150 N.E. 585 (1926).
[15] *Cardozo: a Study in Reputation* (1990), p. 56.

different context) seem to "march at times to pitiless conclusions under the prod of a remorseless logic which is supposed to leave no alternative".[16] It has no place in the cryptic judgments of the French Cour de Cassation whose judges are trained[17] to keep their thought to themselves. It is absent from the judgments of the Italian Supreme Court which are uniformly abstract (to the extent that one can ascribe uniformity to a nation as endearingly individualistic as Italy). And yet, of course, one is not saying that English is a richer or more expressive language. Anyone who has read Goethe or Eichendorff, Voltaire or Flaubert, Dante or Pirandello would be crazy even to imply it. All one is saying is that for different (historical) reasons the German, French, or Italian language are not given their full rein in judicial decisions; and this, I shall suggest later, has important consequences for us, both legal and political.

This, then, is what I mean by "style" in this lecture; but I also use the term in a wider sense. Let me explain.

I have on several occasions asked German judges why they quote so much academic literature in their judgments.[18] Of course history should give me a clue; but their answer has been uniform and interesting: "We genuinely consult these writings and whether we follow or not the views of academics we always pay much attention to them. This has always been our style". Habit or tradition might have been here a better word; yet the "dialogue" between judge and jurist is also a stylistic feature of the German judgment, and it has obviously benefited both sides of the legal profession. Indeed, Jack Dawson, one of the leading comparatists of the common law (and one of the few not to be of Germanic origins) has forcefully argued that the common law would also benefit from such a dialogue.[19] This, too, will be part of what will be proposed in this paper. For the more one finds distinguished common lawyers like Professor Goode expressing some doubts about the case law techniques[20] and, on the other hand, eminent colleagues like Professor Kötz arguing that Germanic lawyers are too obsessed with theory,[21] the more one feels inclined

---

[16] Benjamin Cardozo, *The Growth of the Law* (1924); reprinted in *Selected Writings* (1947), p. 215.

[17] See Mimin, *Le style des judgments*, 4th edn., (1978); Schroeder, *Le nouveau style judiciaire* (1978), *passim*. For a recent comparative study see Wells, "French and American Judicial Opinions" (1994) 19 *Yale J. Int. Law* 81.

[18] According to Professor Kötz in Germany, 13 citations to "secondary authority" per case in 1985 compared to 0.77 citations per English case. For fuller details see his "Scholarship and the Courts: a Comparative Survey" in D. S. Clark (ed.), *Comparative and Private International Law: Essays in Honour of J. H. Merryman on his Seventieth Birthday* (1990), pp. 183–95.

[19] Dawson, *The Oracles of Law* (1967), p. 80 *et seq.*

[20] "The European Law School" (1993) 13 *L.S.* 1. The various arguments are so evenly considered that other readers may end up with a different overall impression after having read this stimulating paper.

[21] "A Common Private Law for Europe: Perspectives for the Reform of European Legal Education" in de Witte and Forder (ed.), *The Common Law of Europe and the Future of Legal Education* (1992), p. 31 at pp. 35–6.

to argue that there is, here, room for a reciprocal influence—a legal give and take. To eclectics like myself this is a self-evident starting point.

3. ENGLISH, AMERICAN, AND GERMAN JUDICIAL STYLES: SOME COMPARISONS

The first thesis of this paper is then that the common law judgment can be stylistically attractive and, probably, more informative of what is really going through a judge's mind when he is trying a case. These features make it a device excellent for teaching and suitable for export, both for the purposes of legal training and for ensuring the presence of the English legal culture in the European legal science of the next century. This task is much facilitated by the de facto emergence of English as the new *lingua franca* of international legal transactions—at any rate in commercial settings. So, how different[22] are the common law and German decisions for me to be making this point? And what are their respective strengths and weaknesses? The following observations may help promote further discussion.

A. *The Judge as Literary Stylist*

Naturally, one must again stress that no assertion is made that one language has greater beauty or expressive power than another. Rather, one will ponder over the effectiveness of judicial styles, primarily from the point of the law student. True, this vantage point is in many respects an artificial one since it assumes, without any evidence to support this assumption that the law student is one of the audiences judges have in mind when writing their judgments.[23] On the other hand, judicial styles have been largely shaped by historical factors which may have lost some of their original force; and what is taught to the student of today will be put into practice by the practitioner of tomorrow. There is, therefore, no reason to exclude the possibility that tastes and styles may change as younger lawyers, through increased international contacts, may come to appreciate qualities found in systems other than their own. In any event, for the comparative lawyer the study and comparison of judicial styles can provide many clues about the real factors that determine results but are obscured by legal jargon. My suggestion also has the incidental benefit of leading to a functional approach, playing down differences in concept, and thus facilitating the comparison of legal systems. Two decisions, an American and a German, dealing with the question whether an

---

[22] In what follows one, inevitably, has to generalise. For instance, the judgments of the German administrative courts are much richer in factual detail than the judgments of the Bundesgerichtshof though, if anything, the narrative is even drier!

[23] For whom do judges write their judgments? In England many views have been expressed on this subject; and none seems to have prevailed. For a discussion with references see Paterson, *The Law Lords* (1982), Ch. 2.

injured rescuer can claim damages against the tortfeasor whose fault caused the "primary accident", can prompt many reflections, both on substance and style, and underline the richness of teaching foreign law through cases.

The American decision[24] expresses the crux of the matter with complete confidence: "The wrong that imperils life is a wrong to the imperilled victim; it is a wrong also to his rescuer". On its surface this, together with other key sentences of the crucial quotation, is expressed in totally untechnical language, especially if it is compared with the counter-phrase in the German judgment which tells us "That the finding that the defendant's driving while unfit to drive did not afford an *adequate cause* for the plaintiff's injury cannot be accepted". The simplicity of the language in the American decision ties in with the perception of the policy to be pursued which is equally clearly articulated through such memorable phrases as "Danger invites rescue. The cry of distress is the summons to relief" and "The risk of rescue, if only it be not wanton, is born of the occasion. The emergency begets the man". Here Cardozo does more than give us the policy reason why there should be liability, for he does it through a metaphor which is reinforced by metre. As Judge Posner points out,[25] "the two nouns [danger/rescue] are two syllable words with the emphasis on the first syllable. The first noun ends with an 'r' sound, the second begins with one. This is *law as poetry*". Compare this with the German decision and you will find that incomplete references to "moral duty" is as far as the court is prepared to go[26] towards alluding to the social and moral need to encourage people to rescue endangered fellow human beings; the bulk of the judgment concentrates on abridged repetitions of textbook statements about adequate cause.

As stated, the Cardozo judgment avoids such dryness by avoiding technical concepts; but its "layman's" language is no less precise for that. To the trained eye his use of such words as "normal", "tracing conduct to its consequences", "natural and probable" makes it clear that he, too, is thinking in causative terms, thus making the comparison of the two judgments even more telling that appears at first sight. Nor is the German preference for legal jargon necessarily more precise. German lawyers have, of course, criticised (often convincingly) the literary style of the French Code for having aimed for readability at the expense of precision.[27] But the present decisions (and others like it) show that at the end of the day concepts are not necessarily precise and that everything turns "on the circumstances" of each cases. (And in the common law we know this only too well when we use such terms as "reasonable" and "foreseeable" in order to determine whether particular conduct amounts to a *novus*

---

[24] *Wagner* v. *International Ry. Co.*, 232 N.Y. 176, 133 N.E. 437 (1921)

[25] *Cardozo: A Study in Reputation* (1990), p. 102.

[26] OLG Stuttgart 24. 11. 1964, NJW 1965, 112=VersR 1965, 296, translated into English in Markesinis, *The German Law of Tort*, 3rd edn. (1994), pp. 629–32.

[27] For instance, Zweigert and Kötz, *op. cit.* above n. 3, at p. 93, with well-chosen examples comparing the Code Civil with the German Code.

actus interveniens.) So, in the end, we have to look at the case law, briefly mentioned in the German decision, to discover the true parameters of liability towards interveners and then, of course, we find that the two systems have reached in practice very similar results. In the end, therefore, the *real* difference is not one of result; in this case, not even one of conceputalism, but one of style. And such is the effect of good style that this decision (along with the other Cardozo judgments) has emerged as one of the most cited cases in modern American law. Good style may, after all, impress not only students (for whom judges may express indifference) but also practitioners (on whose work judges depend so heavily). And if to that we add the comments of Professor Kötz, to the effect that a German lawyer feels "submerged in an oxygen bath"[28] when he reads a good common law judgment, we may conclude that in its judicial style the common law possesses an interesting and exportable product. Field Marshal von Moltke's influential reflection that "in war it is often less important what one does than how one does it"[29] may also be appropriate to law and, perhaps, even more to judicial decisions.

B. Abstract Concepts v. Pragmatism

Two decisions, one German and one American,[30] dealing with wrongful birth and wrongful life actions, can illustrate this sub-heading (and also amplify some of the points made under the previous one).

On the substantive level the cases lend themselves to comparison, but also present some interesting differences. Note for example that in German law parental claims for "moral damages" have been limited to the effects of the Caesarean operation whereas, even before the development in *Procanic*, the American case of the pair, American case law had been willing to grant "the dollar value of the parents' emotional suffering" for having been deprived of the right to abort. The German decision denies this more extensive right and, characteristically, stresses in fairly abstract terms that "no pecuniary damages can be awarded. . . in respect of a violation of the 'right to plan a family' as an emanation of the general right to one's personality if a decision involving the personality of the party affected was only frustrated *in fact*—as was the case here".

Another substantive difference worthy of note is the German court's decision to grant only the parents (and not the child) damages for the child's extraordinary medical expenses. Once the parents' have died, the cost of caring for the child will be taken over by the welfare state: the financial consequences of the impairment "must be made good by the community

---

[28] "The Role of the Judge in the Court-room: the Common Law and the Civil Law Compared" (1987) 1 *J. S. Afr. Law* 35 at p. 42.
[29] Kessel, *Moltke* (1957), p. 511.
[30] BGH 18. 1. 1983, BGHZ 86, 240=JZ 1983, 447, translated in Markesinis, *op. cit.*, above n. 26, pp. 142–52; *Procanic v. Cillo*, 97 N.J. 339, 478 A. 2d 755 (1984).

within the bounds of the possible". *Procanic*, by contrast, *tacitly* admitting that in the United States, in the absence of an effective welfare system, the child will be left uncared for if the damages given to the parents cease upon its majority (when the duty to maintain comes to an end), grants the child itself such a claim from that moment onwards.

As stated, both these points concerning the substantive law are made in a markedly more abstract way in the German judgment. But the real conceal-ment of policy through the use of abstract legal reasoning manifests itself most clearly in the parts of the judgment that reject the infant's claim for "general damages" for being born even though, interestingly enough, the German court uses the typically common law terminology of "duty of care". Thus, the Bundesgerichtshof states in somewhat conclusionary terms that "A direct duty, enforceable by an action in tort to prevent the birth of a child on the ground that in all probability it will be affected by an infirmity which makes it appear 'valueless' in the eyes of society or in its own presumed opinion. . . would be alien to the duties sanctioned by the law of tort which are normally centred on the protection of personal integrity. No such duty exists".

The American counterpart is illuminating in its pragmatic admission that the absence of a discernible consensus on the matter means that the courts are forced to hold back from creating a duty of care. The relevant passage thus deserves to be quoted in full since it shows how pragmatism (more than any of the other arguments considered by the court) prevented the recognition of the duty situation:

"Underlying our conclusion is an evaluation of the capability of the judicial system, often proceeding in these cases through trial by jury, to appraise such a claim. Also at work is an appraisal of the role of tort law in compensating injured parties, involving as that role does, not only reason, but also fairness, predictability, and even deterrence of future wrongful acts. In brief, the ultimate decision is a policy choice summoning the most sensitive and careful judgment. From that perspective it is simply too speculative to permit an infant plaintiff to recover for emotional dis-tress attendant on birth defects when that plaintiff claims he would be better off if he had not been born. Such a claim would stir the passions of jurors about the nature and value of life, the fear of non-existence, and about abortion. The mix is more than the judicial system can digest."

C. Codal v. Inter-disciplinary Justifications

Two decisions, this time one German and one Canadian,[31] can illustrate this subheading. They come from a cluster of cases which can be found in English, American, and German law (and, indeed, in other legal systems related to the above three) and deal with claims for lost production resulting from the dam-

---

[31] BGH 8. 6. 1976, BGHZ 66, 388=NJW 1976, 1740=VersR 1976, 1043; *Norsk Pacific Steamship Co. Ltd* v. *Canadian National Railway Co.* [1992] 1 S.C.R. 1021, 91 DLR (4th) 289, dis-cussed by Markesinis, "Compensation for Negligently Inflicted Pure Economic Loss: Some Canadian Views" (1993) 109 *L.Q.R.* 5.

age that the tortfeasor's negligence caused to the property of a third person.[32] In Germany successive attempts to circumvent the exclusion of economic loss from the list of protected interests of § 823 I BGB have met with no success. Thus, an attempt to bring the claim under the judge-made right of an "established and operating business" failed because the loss was "indirect"—a term as notoriously vague as that of "natural" and "non-natural" which also appear in different tort contexts.[33] A similar fate befell a different attempt to argue that the plaintiff could be brought under the protective umbrella of a contract which (in some cases) exists between the defendant and the person who suffered physical interference with his property.[34] It is submitted that this result is perfectly supportable both in law and in logic though no one, to our knowledge, has explained how compatible it is with the considerable expansion of contract remedies that took place in the 1980s in another area of economic loss, this time arising from negligent statements.[35] As stated, however, the reconciliation of the different strands of case law does not appear to be at the top of the list of priorities of German courts.

The leading case[36] reaffirms the above but focuses mainly on a third attempt to circumvent the economic loss rule by invoking § 823 II BGB. The Bundesgerichtshof rejection of the argument that a minor by-law of Baden-Württemberg was a "protective" enactment for the purposes of § 823 II BGB is significant for two reasons. First, it is important because other courts in Germany, Switzerland and Austria reached differing results when required to interpret similarly phrased by-laws, something which must suggest that the solution in these cases does not really depend upon the wording of the enactments.[37] Moreover, the *travaux preparatoires* are, as the Bundesgerichtshof admitted, silent and provide no guidance on this point. As for the distinction between physical damage and economic loss, the court agreed with von Caemmerer (and incidentally and unknowingly with Lord Devlin[38]) that it was "crude". Indeed, beyond a hint at the "floodgates" argument (made by the Court of Appeal and implicitly accepted by the Bundesgerichtshof) we have no real reason offered for the negative result. Instead, and this is the second important feature of this decision, the court focuses on a legalistic analysis of § 823 II BGB *and its position within the wider scheme of things*. This is confirmed by the court's own words, which start with the promising statement that the question whether such a remedy can be granted "must be

---

[32] For fuller comparative reference, see Markesinis, *op. cit.*, above n. 26 at p. 173 *et seq.*

[33] BGH 9. 12. 1958, BGHZ 29, 65=NJW 1959, 479.

[34] BGH 12. 7. 1977, BGH NJW 1977, 2208=JZ 1977, 721=VersR 1977, 1006.

[35] On which see Markesinis and Deakin, "The Random Element of their Lordships' Infallible Judgment: an Economic and Comparative Analysis of the Tort of Negligence from *Anns* to *Murphy*" (1992) 55 M.L.R. 101, with further references to German case law and literature.

[36] Fully translated in Markesinis, *op. cit.*, above n. 26, at pp. 180–4.

[37] For a fully comparative discussion of this case law see Bürge, "Die Kabelbruchfälle" (1981) 103 *Juristische Blätter* 57.

[38] In his speech in *Hedley Byrne & Co. Ltd* v. *Heller & Partners Ltd* [1964] AC 465 at 529–30.

attacked directly". The common law reader at this stage expects some discussion about the opening of floodgates and the insurance consequences of such a decision. Instead he gets the following:

> "In the last resort the question [is whether the] . . . creation of an individual claim for compensation appears meaningful, sensible, and tolerable in the *light of the whole system of liability*. Only by doing this can a development, rightly feared by the Court of Appeal, be avoided, namely that the increasing tendency to base claims on § 823 II BGB might undermine Parliament's ruling against a general liability for purely economic loss."

At one level all this appears not only in tune with German interpretative techniques but also perfectly compatible with the original intention of the draftsmen of the BGB, which was quite openly hostile to the compensation of pure economic loss through tort law apart from certain specific situations (mainly envisaged in §§ 826 and 824 and 839 BGB). But the German student who would like to know why his law differs from, say, that of France, Italy, or the Netherlands, will find no guidance in this decision, little discussion of the issues in the major treatises, and only in his monographs will he find a more wide-ranging discussion of the problem.[39] Our hypothetical student will, however, be greatly stimulated—and I am here speaking from long teaching experience in common law and civil law universities—if given a common law decision such as *Norsk*, the Canadian case of the pair, and asked to consider *his* law in the light of the policy argument given by the justices of the Canadian Supreme Court. Indeed, he need not stop at that point but should, instead, be encouraged to argue whether the *blanket* prohibition of tort damage for pure economic loss is still sensible 100 years after his Code saw the light of day. And more can follow, demonstrating how much can be achieved by teaching foreign law through cases; for as already stated, how is this "conservatism" to be tallied with the very liberal decisions of the 1980s in the areas of damage *to* products or the cases involving liability for negligent certifications? The overall conclusion, therefore, must be that the preoccupation to fit the particular case within the wider legal system is often achieved at the expense of an open discussion of the real reasons which dictate these results and this must be to the detriment of legal education and, arguably, to the handling of future disputes over similar facts.

D. *Defective Products and Judicial Protection of the Consumer*

Two decisions, this time from Germany and California,[40] will complete this selection of examples which are attempting a comparative presentation of

---

[39] For instance, Professor Taupitz, *Haftung für Energieleiterstörungen durch Dritte* (1981) and, most recently, Kessel, *Moderne Entwicklung der Zurechnung für bloße Vermögensschäden im Common Law am Beispiel des Englischen Rechts (dargestellt im Verhältnis zum deutschen Recht)* (1994).

[40] BGH 7. 6. 1988, BGHZ 104, 323 in Markesinis, *op. cit.*, above n. 26, at pp. 514–24; *Escola v. Coca-Cola Bottling Co. of Fresno*, 24 Cal. 2d 453, 150 P. 2d 436 (1944).

judicial styles. Once again, they arise out of analogous (but not identical) facts which facilitate comparisons; and in their own way are regarded as important decisions in their respective countries.

Consumer protection lies behind both and, in this sense, a further comparative dimension can be added by reminding the reader that these days in England the judicial tendency is to leave such matters to the legislator even though it is known that in these matters he tends to intervene rarely and, when he does so, he does so verbosely.[41] Once again, the reading of the two decisions provides ample food for thought, and not only on the matter of style. Note for example, how at one stage the German court is pending over the dangers of being too overt about the objectivisation of liability to the benefit of the consumer. It states: "A generalised form of reversal [of the burden of proof] would turn the manufacturer's tortious liability into a form of objective liability for all consequences *for which it would be necessary to find some specific legitimation in the substantive law*" (emphasis supplied). The problem is thus one of finding a peg on which to hang the judicial decision which, as the other landmark product liability case—the "Chicken Pest" case[42]—shows is not always easy and, in the end, may have to be trenched by considerable judicial boldness. Compare this with Justice Traynor's dissent in the California case: "If public policy demands that a manufacturer of goods be responsible for their quality regardless of negligence there is no reason not to fix that responsibility *openly*".

The italicised last word at the very end of the quotation is the *differentia specifica* between the American and German tort judgments. For in most other respects the results reached by the German and American case law have progressively converged over the years. Indeed, when one thinks of certain types of products—e.g. pharmaceutical products—German law has gone even further than American law by abolishing the defence of state of the art. What, therefore, is lacking in this German judgment, apart from a certain crispness which is very obvious in the Traynor counterpart, is an open acknowledgement of why the court feels that the plaintiff's position must be improved. Traynor gives at least five reasons for this switch: liability should be placed on those shoulders which, effectively, can reduce or eliminate the hazard; insurance and other financial considerations put the manufacturer in a better position to spread the loss; the manufacturer put the product into circulation so he should bear the consequences of his act; public policy has an interest to discourage the circulation of dangerous products; the consumer/plaintiff is badly placed to prove what went wrong. One is unable to find these reasons enunciated in the German judgment even though one can read them tacitly

---

[41] See, for instance, Lord Bridge of Harwich in *D. and F. Estates Ltd.* v. *Church Commissioners for England* [1989] AC 177 at 210.

[42] BGH 26. 11. 1968, BGHZ 51, 91=NJW 1969, 269=JZ 1969, 387= VersR 1969, 155; translated into English in Markesinis, *op. cit.*, above n. 26, p. 493–504.

in most of the points which are given by the Bundesgerichtshof for the pro-plaintiff concession it made in that case.

4. REDRESSING THE BALANCE

All of the points made in section 3 above are variations on one theme. Common law judicial style has many attractions that could be fruitfully studied by foreign students and, perhaps, for different reasons, imitated by foreign practitioners. The flip side of this coin is that, to foreign eyes, the German judgment (and in another article we shall compare the common law judgment with French judgment) can be too abstract, too theoretical, and too preoccupied with fitting concrete problems into a conceptual system. Many of these (real or perceived) weaknesses could be reduced if the authors of German judgments targeted a wider audience than they currently do, paid more attention to the distinctive features of previous decisions (using them as building blocks for the constant development of the law rather as illustrations of a certain position) and placed their cases more overtly in the socio-economic context to which they belong.

Such a change in German judicial style is not likely to come about. A foreign observer who senses the richness of German law might dearly wish to make its "packaging" more attractive so that more people become interested in a product which otherwise frightened them away because of its theoretical complexity.[43] But judicial styles and techniques do not change as a result of such demands by foreign observers, so it is not in the style of the German judgment that the common law is likely to find inspiration.

What then in German law deserves to attract the attention of the common lawyer? Many specific instances could, of course, be chosen for discussion (and over the years this writer has considered many of them), but one *general* area deserves more attention than any other because of its many ramifications. This is the need for a closer co-operation between the different branches of the legal profession charged with the interpretation and adjudication of the law. This "dialogue" is an obvious feature of the German judgment—indeed of the German legal scene as a whole—and it is one which seems to be gaining adherents in this country as well. The arguments for this view were recently put forward by Lord Justice Steyn in *White* v. *Jones*—a judgment concerning the liability of a lawyer towards a non-client—where he complained of counsel's failure to cite relevant academic views and rightly stressed that "it is arguments that influence decisions rather than the reading of pages upon pages from judgments".[44]

---

[43] See Lord Goff of Chieveley's observations in his foreword to Markesinis, *German Law of Torts*, 2nd edn. (1990), p. xxxvi.

[44] *White* v. *Jones* [1993] 3 WLR 730 at 751. Steyn L.J. is not the only judge to make such an observation. In *Rowling* v. *Takaro Properties Ltd* [1988] 1 AC 473 at 500 Lord Keith complained

This was, certainly, true in the context of the case in which the statement was uttered; but other examples can be given to show how an inadequate doctrinal analysis has affected the law (in the sense of both how it is taught and also how it is applied by the courts). For instance, the continuing failure to subject the notion of restitutionary damages to a coherent and systematic analysis offers just such an illustration. Professor Birks, who has written trenchantly on the subject, has observed how the dominant position of compensation for loss is protected by banishing the account of profits from the books on damages, by marginalising the wrongs for which an account is most commonly sought, and by the persistence of the old notion of waiver with its implication that the common law gives restitution for a wrong only when the wrong has been transmogrified into something else.[45] The result, as he explains in detail, is an unsatisfactory dichotomy of treatment of the subject of civil wrongs (under at least two courses: tort and equity); uncertainty as to the existence and ambit of new torts (e.g. is breach of confidence a tort? is "knowing assistance" in a fraudulent misappropriation of fund a tort?); a theoretically under-developed law dealing with the civil liability of accessories; and, on occasion, a rejection of the plaintiff's (just) claim because of the difficulties which our courts are faced with when asked to come to terms with a gain-based rather than a loss-based action for damages.

This point is well illustrated by Lord Justice Nourse's judgment in *Stoke-on-Trent City Council* v. *W. & J. Wass Ltd*[46] where it is clear[47] that the shadow of *Phillips* v. *Homfrey*[48] still covers English law, apparently making it impossible to award *restitutionary* damages for the commission of a tort.[49] Yet one cannot help but notice how this view has been criticised in Australia[50] (as well as in this country[51]) and judicially rejected in the United States[52] and Canada[53] and Germany where, in fact, the *Alte Steinkuhle* case[54] offers a

that "no reference was made in argument to the extensive academic literature on the subject of the liability of public authorities in negligence . . .". Unlike Lord Keith, however, who *judging from his opinion* in this case, in *Murphy*, and in *Woolwich Building Society* v. *IRC* [1992] AC 142 at 148–63, *appeared* to make no use of such literature, Steyn L.J. clearly took account of academic views when preparing his judgment. One can only surmise that we are here faced with a generational attitude and that the trend in favour of a judge/academic dialogue will increase in the future.

[45] "Civil Wrongs: A New World": *The Butterworth Lectures 1990–91* (1992) at p. 74.
[46] [1988] 1 WLR 1406.
[47] See, especially, his words at p. 1415.
[48] (1883) 24 ChD 439.
[49] And it now seems contract, as well. See *Surrey County Council* v. *Bredero Homes Ltd* [1993] 1 WLR 1361, criticised by O'Dair, "Remedies for Breach of Contract: a Wrong Turn" [1993] *Restitution L. Rev.* 31 *et seq.*
[50] By Gummow J. writing extra-judicially: "Unjust Enrichment, Restitution and Proprietary Remedies" in Finn (ed.), *Essays on Restitution* (1990), pp. 60–7.
[51] e.g. by Professor Birks in "Civil Wrongs—a New World", *The Butterworth Lectures 1990–91* (1992), pp. 64–7.
[52] *Edwards* v. *Lee's Administrator*, 96 SW 2d 1025 (1936).
[53] *Daniel* v. *O'Leary* (1976) 14 N.B.R. 2d 564.
[54] RG 27. 1. 1932, RGZ 135, 94; RG 8.9.1938, JW 1938, 3040; cf. von Caemmerer, "Bereicherung und Unerlaubte Handlung" in *Festschrift für Ernst Rabel*, vol. I (1954), pp. 333 *et seq.*

factual equivalent to the "Great Onyx Cave" case.[55] The prolonged German litigation was, in this instance, provoked by the decision of the defendant/lessor of two mines (the *Amatus* and the *Christiansburg*), leased to the plaintiff (owner of an adjoining mine known as the *Alte Steinkuhle*) to mine from the leased mines coal lying at depths which were, in practice, inaccessible from the plaintiff's/lessee's land but were, nevertheless, reachable from other lands belonging to the lessor/defendant. The dispute went twice to the Reichsgericht but, in the end, it was decided in favour of the plaintiff who was—largely due to the special nature of the applicable mining laws— equated with the position of legal owner and thus allowed to rely on §§ 985, 98p and 990 1 BGB[56] and claim all profits made by the defendant/lessor.

Even where the above-mentioned (and usually narrowly construed) provisions of the Code cannot avail the plaintiff, German law will still refuse to follow the English position and will, instead, mobilise some of its other provisions in order to achieve the result reached by the American and Canadian cases in such disputes. Thus, German plaintiffs in the "Great Onyx Cave" type of situation might well be in a position to invoke successfully §§ 687 (2), 681 second sentence and 667 BGB.[57] This combination of rules is, incidentally, particularly advantageous to them since they allow them to claim from the *gestor* even extraordinary profits which have resulted from his (the *gestor*'s) exceptional abilities as "manager". Thus in one case[58] a landlord sued his tenant for repossession of the premises (due to the latter's breach of his contractual obligations). His action was successful; and it also "confirmed" a lien over the tenant's furniture arising by virtue of § 559 BGB. Before this was sold (to satisfy the latter's debts), the landlord let the premises *with* the tenant's

---

[55] *Edwards v. Lee's Administrator*, above n. 52.

[56] BGB § 985: The owner can demand from the possessor the delivery of the thing. § 987 (1): The possessor shall hand over to the owner the emoluments which he derives after the date of filing an action.

(2) If the possessor after the filing of the action fails to derive emoluments which he could derive following the principles of proper management he is obliged to compensate the owner, to the extent that he is chargeable with fault.

BGB § 990 (1): If the possessor was not in good faith when acquiring the possession, he is liable to the owner from the time of acquisition according to sections 987, 989. If the possessor subsequently learns that he is not entitled to the possession, he is liable in the same manner from the time of obtaining the knowledge. (These and the following translations are taken from Forrester, Goren, Ilgen, *The German Civil Code* (1975).)

[57] BGB § 687 (2): "If a person treats the matter of another as his own, although knowing that he is not entitled to do so, the principal may enforce the claims based on §§ 677, 678, 681, 682 . . ." (This is the so-called "impure" *negotiorum gestio*, on which see Stoljar in *Int. Encyclopedia of Comparative Law*, vol. X, Ch. 17, p. 171 (1984).)

BGB § 681: "The agent shall notify the principal, as soon as practicable, of the undertaking of the management of the matter, and await his decision, unless there is danger of delay. For the rest the provisions of §§ 666 to 668, applicable to a mandatory, apply *mutatis mutandis* to the obligation of the manager".

BGB § 667: " A mandatory is bound to hand over to his mandator all that he received for the execution of the mandate and all that he obtains from the charge of the matter".

[58] RG 1. 12. 1922, RGZ 105, 408, 409–10.

furniture. Though the tenant had no right to use the furniture (because of the lien), and had thus suffered no "loss" (in the conventional sense) by being denied its use, he was, nevertheless, allowed to claim from the landlord the *benefit* which the latter had made by letting the flat furnished. One way of achieving this result was by relying on §§ 687(2), 681 second sentence and 667 BGB.[59]

Such complicated reasoning processes—known in Germany as paragraph chains (*Paragraphenkette*)—are typical of the tightly-knit codal provisions which are the product of the sustained kind of academic work which led Maitland to describe the German Civil Code as "the most carefully considered statement of a nation's law that the world has ever seen".[60] But before the common lawyer, Maitland notwithstanding, condemns it as "Germanic", he should consider the advantages of a coherently conceived law of obligations where the component parts of contract, tort, *negotiorum gestio* and unjust enrichment[61] are neatly brought together, avoiding the compartmentalised system of remedies of the common law.

The same result is achieved less obliquely by the new Dutch Civil Code—largely the brain child of Professor E. M. Meijers and, more recently, Professor Arthur Hartkamp's exhaustive comparative efforts—which in Article 104 of Book 6 expressly states that "if a person who is liable towards

---

[59] Another way was through BGB §§ 1213 and 1214 in conjunction with § 99 (3). This meant treating the rent as the "fruit" deriving from the furniture which the landlord should not be allowed to keep without the permission of the owner.

BGB § 1213: (1) The right of pledge may be constituted in such manner that the pledgee is entitled to receive the emoluments of the pledge.

(2) If a thing which may by nature bear fruit is handed over to the sole possession of the pledgee, it is in case of doubt presumed that the pledgee shall be entitled to take the fruit.

BGB § 1214: (1) If the pledgee is entitled to take the emoluments he is obliged to take care of the production of the emoluments and to render account.

BGB § 99: (3) Fruits also include the proceeds which a thing or a right affords by a virtue of a legal relationship.

[60] Maitland's translator's introduction to Otto Gierke, *Political Theories of the Middle Age* (1900), p. xvii.

[61] In cases of negligent invasions of property the above-mentioned provisions would be applicable and plaintiffs would have to rely on the provisions of unjust enrichment, particularly BGB §§ 812 and 818(1). These provisions, if successfully invoked, would produce reduced awards which would usually equal a licence fee. This would go some way towards answering Steyn L.J.'s concern that restitutionary awards might inhibit enterprise and discourage economic activity by retrospectively removing the fruits of one person's labours resulting from an unintentional infringement of another person's property.

Cases which have considered recovery on these grounds include: RG 20. 12. 1919, RGZ 97, 310; (allowed) LG Freiburg 17. 1. 1985, NJW RR 1986, 400. (not allowed on the grounds of §§ 812, 818 BGB). Para. 812 BGB has also been used—usually in conjunction with para. 22 KUG (The Law of Artistic Creations)—to justify the award of restitutionary damages (invariably equalling the amount of a licence fee) in cases of "appropriation of likeness" arising in the law of privacy. Thus see BGH 8. 5. 1956, BGHZ 20, 345; BGH 26. 6. 1979, BGH NJW 1979, 2205; BGH 26. 6. 1981, BGHZ 81, 75; OLG Karlsruhe, 18. 11. 1988, VersR 1989, 259; BGH 14. 4. 1992, NJW 1992, 2084. Full disgorgement of profits, made as a result of the appropriation of one's likeness and claimable under §§ 687 (2), 681 and 667 BGB should, in theory, be possible; but I am not aware of a case that has proceeded on these grounds.

another person on the basis of an unlawful act or a failure in the performance of an obligation has derived profit from that act or failure, the judge may evaluate the damage, upon the demand of this other person [plaintiff] according to the amount of the profit or part thereof".[62] Overall, therefore, one is left with the clear impression that in cases such as the above, plaintiffs (in most systems) are rarely left uncompensated as a result of the "hardening of remedies" which the late Jack Dawson considered as a particularly English disease.[63]

The need for great *open* co-operation between judge and jurist, obvious though it is, could be elaborated further. But if it is to come about, one must first and foremost appreciate some of the reasons why it has not so far been implemented. Apart from the historical tradition, two reasons should be mentioned: judicial mentality and the practising Bar's reluctance to embark on something on which they have had so far no expertise.

True, judicial attitudes towards academic works are changing, as the growing number of references in more recent decisions clearly attests.[64] But the mentality has not yet been transformed, with even "academic" judges being quick to over-stress the different nature of the respective functions of judge and jurist[65] instead of exploring ways in which the respective talents could be brought together in pursuit of those purposes which they have in common. A judge of great distinction who has spent much extra-judicial time on this topic is Lord Goff of Chieveley.[66] But his work is only the beginning, and its influence has not yet filtered down to lower courts. This can be seen most clearly in the decision of the House of Lords in *Woolwich Building Society* v. *IRC*[67] which is important not only in so far as we see the two schools of thought ("to cite or not to cite" academics) in (respectively) the judgments of Lord Goff and Lord Keith of Kinkel, but also—and, perhaps, more importantly— because it underlines the significant role that academic literature can play in the *development of the law*. For, in the words of Judge David Edward, in *Woolwich* the majority of the House of Lords overturned "more than a century of precedent on the basis of reasoning from principle proposed by the Regius Professor of Civil Law at Oxford".[68] Overall, therefore, one can only

---

[62] Haanappel and Mackaay, *Nieuw Nederlandsch Burgerliijk Wetboek* (1990), 271. Professor Hartkamp, with whom I have discussed these cases, had no doubt that they would be covered by Article 104 though he added that Article 104 was drafted with copyright cases mainly in mind.

[63] "Restitution or Damages", (1959) 20 *Ohio State L.J.* 175 at p. 177.

[64] e.g. *Spiliada Maritime Corpn.* v. *Cansulex Ltd* [1987] AC 460 at 488 per Lord Goff; *The Evia Luck* [1992] 2 AC 152. See also Lord Browne-Wilkinson's speech in *Linden Gardens Trust Ltd.* v. *Lenesta Sludge Disposals Ltd* [1994] 1 AC 85 at 112: ". . . the point merits exposure to academic consideration *before* it is decided by this House" (emphasis supplied)—a remarkable open invitation to collaboration with the academic world!

[65] e.g. Sir Robert Megarry V.-C. in *Cordell* v. *Second Clanfield Properties Ltd.* [1969] 2 Ch. 9 at 16.

[66] In "Judge, Jurist and Legislature" (1987) 2 *Denning L. Jo.* 79; "The Search for Principle" (1983) 69 *Proc. British Academy*.

[67] [1993] AC 70.

[68] Markesinis (gen. ed.), *The Gradual Convergence: Foreign Ideas, Foreign Influences and English law on the Eve of the 21st Century* (1994), pp. 263–4.

speak of a trend to take openly into account the views of academic writers, but not yet an accepted practice.

The second reason for the lack of such academic-judicial co-operation can be found in the habits of the practising Bar. In private conversations, expense and lack of time have often been advanced as excuses. In fact, that is what they largely are. For, formidable though the talents of English barristers are, fondness for academic research is not, I venture to suggest, one of them. From private talks and other (admittedly anecdotal) evidence one gets the impression that academic law is dismissed as too theoretical, avoided because it might leave the judges indifferent, and subconsciously played down because it undoubtedly involves a constructive use of national and international developments which successful practitioners do not have high on their list of priorities, except in the narrowest possible way connected with the case they may be handling. But even where academic literature is consulted, the consultation is narrowly within the context of the case to be argued, and marked preference is shown for "practitioners' " treatises where the emphasis is on wealth of citation and technical attempts to reconcile what is often irreconcilable. If an illustration is needed of this point it can, for instance, be found in the discussion which a leading practitioner's treatise[69] gives to the recently discredited decision of *Bognor Regis UDC* v. *Campion*.[70] Thus the text rightly maintains that the decision is reconcilable with the earlier decision of the Divisional Court in *Manchester Corporation* v. *Williams*,[71] where a municipal corporation was denied the right to bring an action for libel in respect of an allegation of "bribery and corruption" in one of its departments. That Carter Ruck wrongly predicted that *Bognor Regis* was "likely to be preferred" over *Manchester Corporation* is, really, neither here nor there. *How* he reached this conclusion is, however, significant for my thesis. For he merely *asserts* that modern conditions in which local authorities have such a wide ranging role in society[72] dictate this choice (i.e. that *Bognor* be upheld). The problem is that the very basis of his assertion is, at the very least, debatable; and Tony Weir did just that in his case note in the *Cambridge Law Journal*[73] where he stressed the competing value of free speech. Yet Carter Ruck contains no reference to this brilliant piece; no evaluation of its different premise; no mention of the possible effect that the European Convention on Human Rights can have on this topic![74] These *extra dimensions* which in able judicial hands can justify new departures or refinements of the law are thus often omitted from practitioners' works, which are always heavy on citation and

---

[69] Carter Ruck, *Libel and Slander*, 4th edn. (1992), p. 73.
[70] [1972] 2 QB 169.
[71] [1891] 1 QB 94.
[72] *op. cit.* above n. 69.
[73] [1992] C.L.J. 238.
[74] Clerk and Lindsell, *Torts*, 16th edn. (1989), §§2–43, 21–18, 21–25, is, if anything, more anodyne, offering no ideas for the future. Likewise Gatley, *Libel and Slander*, 8th edn. (1981), §§ 958, 959.

not infrequently (one is tempted to admit) light on imagination. So I return to my thesis and ask the question: how can practitioner's work help a judge who is trying to discover the limits of the law and determine—to the extent that he can—its rational development? My illustration suggests very little. And yet the judgments in *Derbyshire County Council* v. *Times Newspaper Ltd*,[75] both in the Court of Appeal and the House of Lords, show how much mileage one can get out of scholarly works and the skilful use of foreign experiences, which is precisely what I am advocating in this lecture.

Let me give another example. Can it *really* be argued with conviction that cases like *Wass* could not in the light of the foreign material I have mentioned (both from the common law and the modern civil law) have taken a different turn if the law on the subject had not been approached in such a compartmentalised manner where tort ideas are, through accidents of history, hidden in the interstices of trusts? Or is it really intellectually satisfying to have to rummage around on the fringe of the law of trusts in order to find solutions to contemporary incidents of commercial fraud? There is here a need for a robust academic analysis if the whole law of accessory's liability is to be put on a sound basis; and this cannot, I think, be undertaken by either the practising lawyer or the judge who, given the nature of his work, tends to be more narrowly focused.

Time might also be used more profitably if oral argument was limited to the citation of those cases which were *absolutely* necessary to the case before the court. Perusing the Law Reports and seeing the huge number of cases invariable cited by both counsel and judge convinces one that this does not occur as often as it should. And here, again, in most cases the *giving* of the citation would be sufficient, avoiding the reading of lengthy extracts (except where a particular construction of the words was needed), for this adds nothing of substance, but merely makes both the hearing and the judgments longer than they ought to be. Counsel and judge often succumb to the temptation of long citations as if they could be a substitute to proper reasoning.[76]

At this stage one should pause and say that proposals such as the above, challenging as they do centuries of legal tradition, are likely to be strenuously opposed by those involved in full-time practice. To such probable (hostile) reactions, academic commentators like myself must react with deference though, in counter-argument, one might say that those of us who have witnessed argument before senior American and European courts feel that neither the efficacy of the case nor the cause of justice itself are ill-served by written pleadings which make greater use of academic literature and oral

---

[75] [1992] 1 QB 770; CA 790; [1993] AC 534.

[76] It could be said (with respect) that there is a recent illustration of this tendency in the judgment of Lord Lowry in *Roy* v. *Kensington, etc. Family Practitioner Committee* [1992] 1 AC 624. My objections against long judgments consisting largely of selected citations of earlier cases have been explained in my article with Dr Simon Deakin, "The Random Element of their Lordships' Infallible judgement: an Economic and Comparative Analysis of the Tort of Negligence from *Anns* to *Murphy*", (1992) 55 M.L.R. 619, especially p. 642.

hearings which are considerably shorter than ours. And if this experience were not enough, potential heretics such as the present author are reassured by the fact that if they are to burn in hell for these views they will be doing so in the company of some very senior English Law Lords who are coming around to espousing similar ideas. Thus, to give but one example, Lord Griffiths said not that long ago that:

> "I have discussed this [i.e. time limits on oral argument] with those who practise both before our own appellate courts and at Luxembourg where oral argument is restricted and cases rarely last more than one day, no matter how complicated the issues. They tell me that their written submission is more detailed but they find no disadvantage in the shorter time for oral presentation which is a spur to concentration upon the concise issues in the argument. I believe we are developing an over-indulgent attitude to oral argument for which both the Bench and the Bar are to blame."[77]

But there is another reason why one can even dare to voice such views in a public lecture, let alone express the belief that one day heterodoxy may well become orthodoxy. Quite simply, this is the "European factor", the impact of which has not yet been fully fathomed by the average English practitioner. For, to enter for a moment the related (but treacherous) world of politics, one is tempted to agree with the so-called Euro-sceptics in their belief that European developments are changing the way "things are done" in England. Where, with respect, one is tempted to part company with them is when they argue that this process, already under way, can be arrested. Which brings me to the last point which should be made in this paper.

5. AN INTERESTING PARADOX

In this lecture a number of differences have been noted between the style and contents of the English and German cases which can, ultimately, be traced to fundamental and interrelated decisions taken by these systems in the distant past. The English ones, of course, are well-known: a preference for procedure over principles of substantive law; a neglect of the academic component of the law; the appointment of judges from a small group of leading practitioners; and the adoption of the jury system with all the consequences this has had on procedure and presentation of legal argument. Known though these are, they may well be repeated here since two new developments are seriously affecting the second of the above-named factors and, indirectly, the law that is handed down by our courts. The developments to which I am referring are the greater interaction between English and Continental European universities and the fact that nowadays in England a university training has become an essential ingredient of a legal (including judicial) career. These two developments are,

---

[77] "Civil Litigation in the Nineties" (1991) 57 *Arbitration* 168 at pp. 169–70.

I believe, to determine what we will "take" in future years from Continental systems and, also, what we might be able to "give" them in exchange. Let me explain these points briefly.

When I read law in the 1960s, Treitel's *Law of Contract* had just made its appearance, immediately prompting doubts in my old university as to whether the "market" really needed a third "major" textbook. John Fleming's *The Law of Torts* was an approximate contemporary, but its overt comparative approach failed to impress the English teacher/student market in the way it has (rightly) impressed judges all over the common law world. The same assessment can, I think, be made of the legal literature on other core subjects, so one need not labour this point any further.

Some thirty years later the picture could not be more different. What is significant, however, is not that our students (and our judges) nowadays have a plethora of books and views at their disposal, but that the new books are, in content as much as approach, quite different from the older ones. Treitel, for instance, from the very beginning produced a contract book with a strong systematical and doctrinal element, and his work has greatly enriched the contract debates, especially when read in juxtaposition with that of our other great theorist, Patrick Atiyah. Likewise, Hugh Beale's *Casebook on Contract* (co-authored with Bill Bishop and Michael Furmston) is as rich in its contents as it is new in its approach to its subject in a way that makes one marvel at the conservatism of those teachers who have kept faith with its old competitor still in print. Some of the Law Commission's recent papers are showing similar signs of being as comparative in approach as they are imaginative in content. Thus, in one way or another, the new crop of books, articles, and semi-official papers are providing lawyers with new ideas, more cosmopolitan material and different ways of approaching problems and these are percolating down into the judgments.[78] Needless to say, this literature is likely to have even more of an impact on tomorrow's judges, whose views will have been moulded much more than their predecessors by an academic environment.

If this development is now seen in the context of the even newer "European" perspective—and by that I mean the growing significance for municipal law of the decisions of the European Courts in Luxembourg and Strasbourg *and* the growing contacts under Erasmus-type programmes—it can lead to the conclusions that it is no longer fanciful to predict a steady growth in the impact that European law and doctrine will have on ours. This may not affect the style of judgments—a main theme of this paper—indeed, I hope it does not! But it is bound to strengthen their doctrinal content—the second theme of this paper—combatting the idea that because the tasks of judge and jurist are (in *some* respects) different *they must also be carried out in complete isolation from each other.* In this sense, too, the tide of European ideas will

---

[78] This new trend means that "ideas" books may now influence some of our judges as much as the standard "practitioners" books. See, for instance, Hoffmann L.J.'s judgment in *Ministry of Defence* v. *Ashman* [1993] 2 EGLR 102.

prove difficult to contain. The student of today, who will be the judge of tomorrow, will be unlikely to resist this influence since it will not be alien to him but, on the contrary, will have played a part in his formation and training.

But will the influence be one-sided? I think not and I hope not. If we do not remain in our shells we, too, can and will influence developments elsewhere. Moreover, I believe our *main* contribution may well be something of a paradox since it will come from our universities (which in historical terms were the junior partners in the development of our law) exporting the teaching techniques they have developed relying on the work of our judges. For, though statutory law is increasing in size and complexity, case law is still at the base of common law education. This and the tutorial system (to varying but, by comparison to Continental universities, small numbers of students) are the distinctive features of our legal education. The political tradition of the European universities makes the second feature enviable but totally inimitable. But the first feature, coupled with the emergence of English as the new *lingua franca* of the Western world, gives the common law a powerful instrument with which to make its own contribution to the transnational set of legal rules which many refer to as the new *jus commune*. Let me say just a few more words as to how this could come about.

Though certain features of the common law judgment may come to be imitated by foreign judges (and others rightly avoided), it would be foolish to predict any wholesale European importation of the model. But the study of English judgments *is* growing as more and more young lawyers from the continent of Europe spend short or longer periods of time in common law universities (the Oxford *Magister Juris* being, perhaps, one of the best illustrations). Though particular solutions of our law may often appeal to foreign lawyers, none, I think, return to their countries believing that our doctrinal analyses or theoretical constructions can ever equal theirs. But I do believe that they return to their base impressed by the common law decision, by its grammatical clarity, by the way it has revealed and discussed the issues that in their country are hidden by legal jargon, and—most importantly—by the way it is used as a tool for imparting further legal know-how. Here, I believe, we score heavily over Continental models. And, I hope, we will exploit this strength in the context of many current, private and semi-public schemes aiming to draw up a European law curriculum[79] or, even, design a European law school[80] by becoming involved in such projects rather than rejecting them out of hand. For, behind these projects is not utopian idealism but the growing need *somehow* to harmonise teaching materials and interrelate legal cultures for the world of tomorrow in which lawyers will find

---

[79] On which see Professor Kötz's valuable "A Common Private Law for Europe: Perspectives for the Reform of European Legal Education" in de Witte and Forder (eds.), *The Common Law of Europe and the Future of Legal Education* (1990), p. 31 *et seq.*

[80] Goode, "The European Legal School", (1993) 13 *L.S.* 1.

themselves being as mobile as their clients. (And this is not mentioning the former eastern European countries which are looking westward for ideas for their legal education and for new laws which they need in order to cope with the new kind of economies that they have adopted.)

The English judgment—and the learning of law through studying the judgment—is, in sort, along with our language, one of the two major implements at our disposal in the struggle for shaping the European legal culture of the next century. If we wish to have some impact on this new world we must be prepared to use them. And I say this in full knowledge that none of my friends across the Channel will ever be able to accuse me of nationalistic arrogance. For my approach is and always has been "synallagmatic"—to use Lord Diplock's Graeco-French term—since it is based on the conviction that we need to "take" but we also can "give". It is the duty of holders of chairs like mine to show how this can happen, demystifying comparative law as the subject of the select few and making the comparative method the indispensable tool of all.

8

Richter, Rechtswissenschaftler und das Studium und die Anwendung Ausländischen Rechts

1. DER DIALOG ZWISCHEN DEN RICHTERN

In einem Vortrag, den er vor ungefähr sechs Jahren an der Universität Oxford hielt, ging Lord *Goff* der Frage nach den komplizierten wechselseitigen Beziehungen zwischen Richter, Rechtswissenschaftler und Gesetzgeber nach.[1] Seine Ausführungen zu einem Thema, das, historisch betrachtet, stärker auf dem europäischen Festland als in England diskutiert worden ist, waren verständlicherweise nicht rechtsvergleichend angelegt. Unsere Tagung scheint mir eine vorzügliche Gelegenheit zu sein, diese zusätzliche Dimension des Themas zu untersuchen, auch wenn ich im folgenden nur einige sehr persönliche methodische Überlegungen anbieten kann.

Ich habe bereits an anderer Stelle die Auffassung vertreten, daß—zumindest derzeit noch—das Interesse am deutschen Recht in meinem Land am besten dadurch geweckt werden kann, daß man Richter dazu bringt, sich mehr für das Verstehen und die Anwendung ausländischen Rechts zu interessieren.[2] Auch wenn es verblüffend klingen mag, glaube ich, daß zur Zeit eher unsere Richterschaft als unsere Rechtswissenschaft davon zu überzeugen ist, daß Kenntnisse des deutschen Rechts und seiner Anwendung nützlich für ihre tägliche Arbeit sein können. Es ist anzunehmen, daß ein Zusammentreffen von Praktikern aus verschiedenen Ländern diese Bereitschaft fördern kann. Die Teilnehmer könnten nämlich auf diesem Wege erkennen, daß sie trotz der unterschiedlichen rechtsgeschichtlichen Entwicklung und trotz andersartiger methodischer Vorgehensweisen den gleichen Problemen begegnen, die nach entsprechenden, wenn nicht gar nach identischen Lösungen verlangen.

Darüber hinaus können Richter dank solcher Zusammenkünfte prüfen, in welchem Maße die Ähnlichkeit der sich ihnen stellenden Probleme dazu führt, daß sie zwar nicht ausdrücklich, aber aber *der Sache nach* jeweils die gleichen grundlegenden Wertungsgesichtspunkte in ihre Überlegungen einbeziehen und so in den meisten Fällen zu ähnlichen Lösungen gelangen. Um es mit anderen

---

[1] "Judge, Jurist and Legislator", (1987) *Denning L.J.*, 79.
[2] Markesinis (Hrsg.), *The Gradual Convergence. Foreign Ideas, Foreign Influences and European Law on the Eve of the 21st Century*, (1993), 1. Kap.

Worten und konkreter zu sagen: Der § 823 Abs. 1 BGB und unser "tort of negligence" scheinen zunächst sehr große Unterschiede aufzuweisen. Bei näherer Betrachtung erkennt man jedoch, daß die Richter beider Seiten jeweils bestimmte Tatsachen besonders berücksichtigen. So mag es ihnen etwa beachtenswert erscheinen, daß eine Partei Verbraucher und nicht Kaufmann war; oder daß der gesetzlich vorgegebene Rahmen im Laufe der Zeit zu eng geworden ist und mittels extensiver Auslegung erweitert werden muß; oder auch, welche Möglichkeiten der Versicherung des in Frage stehenden Risikos (durch den Kläger oder durch den Beklagten) bestehen und welche davon vorzugswürdig sind[3], und so weiter. Wenn diese Gesichtspunkte in unseren Diskussionen auftauchen, könnte sich zum Beispiel herausstellen, daß der Verbraucherschutz ein zentrales Anliegen des deutschen Richters ist, von seinem englischen Kollegen jedoch als Sache des Gesetzgebers angesehen wird.[4] Noch wichtiger ist jedoch, daß wir einen echten Dialog ermöglichen, in dem die an der Tagung teilnehmenden Richter über die gleichen Wertungsfragen sprechen und sich nicht in den Sphären verschiedener dogmatischer System- und Begriffsbildungen verlieren. Unser erstes Ziel muß folglich darin bestehen, den Dialog in Gang zu bringen. Das setzt voraus, daß sich beide Seiten darauf einlassen, das Ausmaß der bestehenden Gemeinsamkeiten zu erkennen.

Die Aufmerksamkeit der Common-Law-Juristen (vielleicht sollte ich sagen: erneut)[5] zu gewinnen, wäre ein großer Erfolg für die deutsche Rechtskultur; aber umgekehrt werden deutsche Juristen, meine ich, ebenso davon profitieren, mit dem Denken englischer Richter konfrontiert zu werden. Ich bin davon überzeugt, daß dies nicht bloße Theorie ist. So wird man in meinem Land keinen Richter finden, der etwas dem Beitrag von Dr. *Steffen*[6] über

---

[3] Eine ausführliche Erörterung dieser Frage im Zusammenhang mit reinen Vermögensschäden findet sich in der Entscheidung *Norsk Pacific Steamship Co. Ltd.* v. *Canadian National Railway Co.* [1992] 1 S.C.R. 1021 (Supreme Court of Canada); rezensiert von Markesinis (1993) *LQR* 5–12.

[4] So etwa Lord Bridge in *D & F Estates Ltd. and others* v. *Church Commissioners for England* [1988] 1 AC 177, 210. Cf. *Hayes*, "After Murphy: Building on the Consumer Protection Principle", (1992) 12 *OJLS* 112.

[5] Von den jüngst erschienenen Studien über den Einfluß deutscher Rechtsgelehrter auf das amerikanische Rechtsdenken seien nur einige beispielhaft genannt: Hoeflich, "Savigny and his Anglo-American Disciples", (1989) 37 *The American Journal of Comparative Law* 17; Kegel, "Story and Savigny", (1989) 37 *The American Journal of Comparative Law* 29; Whitman, "Commercial Law and the American *Volk*: A Note on Llewellyn's German Sources for the Uniform Commercial Code", (1989) 37 *The American Journal of Comparative Law* 156; Grossfeld und Winship, "The Law Professor Refugee", (1992) 18 *Syracuse J. of Intern. Law and Commerce* 3—alle mit zahlreichen weiteren Nachweisen. Reimann, "The Historical School Against Codification: Savigny, Carter, and the Defeat of the New York Civil Code", (1989)37 *The American Journal of Comparative Law* 95.

[6] Steffen, "Die Bedeutung der 'Stoffgleichheit' mit dem 'Mangelunwert' für die Herstellerhaftung aus Weiterfresserschäden", *VersR* 1988, 977. Eine rechtsvergleichende Erörterung dieser Frage präsentiert Bungert, "Compensating Harm to the Defective Product Itself—A Comparative Analysis of American and German Products Liability Law", (1992) 66 *Tulane L. Rev.* 1179. Man sollte allerdings nicht annehmen, daß englische Richter nicht in der Lage sind, detaillierte Analysen dogmatischer Fragen vorzunehmen. Ein erst kürzlich erschienenes Beispiel dafür ist der

Mangelfolgeschäden und *Stoffgleichheit* Vergleichbares verfaßt hat. Das liegt zum Teil daran, daß die mit diesen Begriffen assoziierten speziellen Probleme im englischen Recht noch nicht so lange existieren wie in Deutschland. In erster Linie aber hängt es damit zusammen, daß die größten Stärken englischer Richter vor allem darin bestehen, mit umfangreichem Fallmaterial umzugehen und dessen Anwendungsbereich genau abzugrenzen oder neu zu bestimmen, weniger dagegen in der Bildung von Theorien und Systemen oder im deduktiven Denken. Ein englischer Richter würde nämlich instinktiv viel Sympathie empfinden für Goethes Worte: "Grau, teurer Freund, ist alle Theorie, Und grün des Lebens goldener Baum"[7]; freilich nur, bis ihm einfällt, daß es Mephistopheles ist, der sie ausspricht. An diesem Punkt angelangt würde der englische Richter vielleicht zur Vorsicht an den Ausspruch des unverdächtigeren Richter Holmes (der allerdings den gleichen Gedanken anklingen läßt) erinnern: "The life of the law has not been logic; it has been experience".[8] Die analytischen und induktiven Techniken der Rechtsfindung des englischen Richters könnten jedoch einer der (vielen) Bereiche sein, in denen die deutsche Rechtswissenschaft in spezieller Weise vom englischen Recht profitieren könnte (Auch der stärker literarisch geprägte Sprachstil englischer Urteile sollte nicht unerwähnt bleiben; er könnte den oftmals abstrakten Darlegungen deutscher Juristen eine erfrischendere Note geben). Zum Beispiel wird das deutsche Deliktsrecht, um das Gebiet des Zivilrechts zu nennen, das uns hier zum überwiegenden Teil beschäftigen wird, offenbar mehr und mehr zum case law, das in seinem ungeheuren Umfang zumindest für den außenstehenden Betrachter nicht frei von Widersprüchlichkeiten zu sein scheint. Hier könnte man meiner Ansicht nach ein größeres Maß an innerer Ordnung erreichen, indem die Richter die Aufgabe, die Dogmatik dieses Rechtsgebietes fortzuentwickeln, nicht einfach ganz den Kommentatoren überlassen, sondern selbst dadurch mithelfen würden, daß sie frühere Entscheidungen als Bausteine der Urteilsbegründung und nicht bloß zur zusätzlichen Verdeutlichung verwendeten.

2. DER BEITRAG DES RECHTSVERGLEICHERS

Ich wünsche uns allen, daß weitere derartige Zusammenkünfte stattfinden werden und daß die richterliche Tätigkeit im Zentrum des Interesses stehen möge. Darin soll aber, wie bereits erwähnt, keine Schmälerung der Aufgabe und Bedeutung der Wissenschaft liegen. Im Gegenteil, es entsteht so neuer Bedarf für ihre Dienste. Denn der Richter, ob in England oder in Deutschland, kann auf sich allein gestellt keinen Gebrauch von ausländischem Material

Beitrag von Sir Michael (jetzt Lord) Mustill, "Anicipating Breach", *Butterworth Lectures 1989–1990*, (1990)S. 1–78.

[7] Faust, II, 2038–9.
[8] O.W. Holmes, *The Common Law* (1881), S. 1.

machen. Ausländisches Material kann erst dann in einem Rechtssystem Verwendung finden, wenn es zuvor ausgewertet und systemgerecht angepaßt wurde.[9] So lassen sich die Begriffe "common law" und "equity" nicht ins Französische oder Deutsche übersetzen. Umgekehrt kann der Begriff "*ius civile*" die Einordnung in den richtigen Kontext erfordern, damit der englische Jurist ihn richtig versteht. Andere Begriffe können zu einer *wörtlichen* Übersetzung verleiten, die sich als irreführend erweisen kann (z.B. "magistracy" für *magistrature* oder "judge" für *magistrat*).[10] Entscheidet man sich hingegen für eine funktional orientierte Übersetzung, so kann diese bestenfalls ein teilweise korrektes Bild von dem vermitteln, was in der Ausgangssprache mit dem Begriff assoziiert wird (z.B. eine Übersetzung von Master of the Rolls als "*premier président de la cour d'appel de l'Angleterre et de Pays de Galles*"). Das gleiche trifft natürlich auch auf die Übersetzung deutscher Rechtsbegriffe wie dem der *Verkehrspflichten* zu. Die richtige Übersetzung hierfür sollte meiner Ansicht nach nicht "duties in traffic" sondern "duties of care"[11] lauten. Desgleichen sollte der in § 276 Abs. 1 S. 2 BGB gebrauchte Terminus "*im Verkehr*" ("*Fahrlässig handelt, wer die im Verkehr erforderliche Sorgfalt außer Acht läßt.*") richtig mit "in daily affairs" oder "in every-day-life" übersetzt werden. Üblich wird jedoch die genannte Vorschrift so übersetzt, daß man gehalten sei, "to exercise the care required in *ordinary intercourse*", um nicht fahrlässig zu handeln. Aus meiner eigenen Lehrerfahrung weiß ich, daß eine solche Übertragung des deutschen Originals den englischen Leser zu Zweifeln (vor allem dann nicht bloß scherzhaft gemeinten, wenn dem Text erläuternde Anmerkungen fehlen) veranlassen, ob es wirklich nötig ist, daß das deutsche Zivilgesetzbuch sich mit "safe sex" befaßt! Schließlich möchte ich ihre Aufmerksamkeit auf den (für den Zweck unserer Tagung) wichtigen, aber nahezu unübersetzbaren Begriff "*Weiterfresserschaden*" lenken, den nicht einmal die besten Fachwörterbücher[12] zu übersetzen versuchen. Man könnte ihn wohl (in ungefährer Umschreibung) als "insidious loss" (caused by an incon-

---

[9] Siehe Markesinis, "The Destructive and Constructive Role of the Comparative Lawyer", (1993) *RabelsZ* 57, 438–48.

[10] Ein solcher Mißgriff ist Professor David unterlaufen (*English and French Law* (1980), S. 50), weil (a) Richter am Conseil d'Etat streng genommen keine magistrats sind und (b) die magistrature das 'parquet'—eine weitere besondere französische Institution—umfaßt. David hat hier aber insofern Recht, als er magistrature mit bench übersetzt.

[11] Obgleich Professor Rudden sich dazu veranlaßt sah, dies eine starke (zu starke) Anglifizierung des deutschen Begriffs zu nennen; so in [1987] *CLJ* 162. Bei Dietl/Lorenz/u.a., *Wörterbuch für Recht, Wirtschaft und Politik*, Bd. II, 4. Auflage 1992, wird der Begriff übersetzt als "duty to safeguard traffic; duty (or obligation) of occupier to make land or premises safe for persons or vehicles". Meines Erachtens ergibt sich aus den klassischen Monographien zu diesem Thema, wie etwa von Bar's *Verkehrspflichten* (1980), daß diese Definitionen wohl zu eng gefaßt sind und daß 'duties' mannigfaltigster Natur (auch jenseits von 'traffic' und 'premises') unter diesen Begriff subsumiert werden können. Nebenbei gesagt, auch die Verwendung des Plurals weist darauf hin, daß das deutsche Recht, gleich dem englischen, das lateinische neminem laedere nicht als Rechtsgrundsatz anerkennt.

[12] Vgl. etwa Dietl/Lorenz/u.a., *Wörterbuch für Recht, Wirtschaft und Politik*, 2. Aufl. 1986. Die überarbeitete und erweiterte 4. Auflage 1992 bietet folgende Übersetzung: "damage which has spread [into] the defect-free portion of purchased property from a defective part".

spicously spreading and harm-producing defect) bezeichnen. Es erfordert schon einiges an Imagination, um ein Wort, das die Nahrungsaufnahme von Tieren im Gegensatz zu der von Menschen kennzeichnet (*fressen/essen*), als Baustein einer modernen Dogmatik des Haftungsrechts zu verwenden! Ich denke, Professor *Gutteridge* hatte angesichts der skizzierten Probleme nur teilweise recht mit seiner Behauptung, daß "die Fallstricke der Terminologie die größte Hürde für den *angehenden* Rechtsvergleicher"[13] seien. Die terminologischen Schwierigkeiten werden dem Rechtsvergleicher wohl Zeit seines Lebens Mühe bereiten.

Hieraus ergibt sich, daß die Übersetzung, die von Richtern zur Bewältigung ihrer Aufgabe benötigt wird, einer doppelten Anforderung gerecht werden muß: Den Ausgangspunkt bildet die rein sprachwissenschaftliche Übertragung von der einen Sprache in die andere. Daran muß sich anschließen, was ich in Ermangelung eines präziseren Ausdrucks *kreative* Übersetzung nennen möchte. Die Schwierigkeiten, die bei der zuerst genannten Art von Übersetzung auftauchen können, sind bereits angesprochen worden. Die Italiener haben insoweit vielfach recht, wenn sie den *traductore* mit dem *traditore* gleichsetzen. Die zweite, kreative Art von Übersetzung verlangt mehr als bloß sprachliche Fähigkeiten. Man braucht eine Art "feeling" für das andere Rechtssystem; man muß (wie einer meiner Studenten es einmal nannte) gedanklich jonglieren können, um die unterschiedlichen Konzepte und Ideen miteinander in Einklang zu bringen. Professor *Kötz* zitierte vor einigen Jahren einmal *Bernard de Clairvaux* mit dem Ausspruch: "*Res in tantum intelligetur in quantum amatur*".[14] Dieses Gefühl für ein fremdes Recht (und die fremde Kultur) kann nur einer äußerst intensiven Beziehung zu ihm entspringen; einer Beziehung, die allein der wahre Rechtsvergleicher erfahren kann. Diese Erfahrung kann der Rechtsvergleicher seinem nationalen Richter zu vermitteln versuchen. Lassen Sie mich drei Beispiele dafür geben, wie ich mir die Entwicklung dieser Partnerschaft vorstelle.

Wenden wir uns zunächst dem deutschen *Testamentsfall*[15] aus dem Jahre 1965 zu. Problem und Lösung sind im englischen[16], deutschen[17] und amerikanischen[18] Recht identisch: Der Begünstigte eines Testaments, der wegen dessen fehlerhafter Errichtung nichts erbt, kann sich an den Anwalt halten, der den Fehler aus Fahrlässigkeit verursacht hat. Beträchtliche

---

[13] "The comparative aspects of legal terminology", (1938) 12 *Tulane L. Rev.* 401, 403 (Hervorhebung vom Verfasser). In Martin Westons Buch *An English Reader's Guide to the French Legal System* (1991) finden sich, besonders in den ersten drei Kapiteln, einige sehr interessante Ausführungen über die Schwierigkeiten, die sich bei der Überwindung konzeptioneller Unterschiede ergeben.

[14] (1987) 35 *The American Journal of Comp. Law* 857, 8 bei der Besprechung der ersten Auflage meines Buches *The German Law of Torts* (1986).

[15] BGH 6. 7. 1865, NJW 1965, 1955; dazu Anmerkung Lorenz in *JZ* 1966, 143 *et seq.*

[16] *Ross v. Caunters* [1980] Ch. 297.

[17] Siehe oben FN 15 sowie BGH 11. 1. 1977, NJW 1977, 2073.

[18] *Biakanja v. Irving* 320 P.2d 16 (1958); *Lucas v. Hamm* 364 P.2d 685 (1961); *Heyer v. Fleig* 449 P.2d 161 (1969).

Unterschiede zwischen den Rechtsordnungen (und teilweise innerhalb einer Rechtsordnung) bestehen allerdings hinsichtlich der rechtssystematischen Einordnung des geltend gemachten Anspruches: Ist dieser vertraglicher oder deliktischer Art? oder gar beides? Und ist seine Einordung überhaupt notwendig?[19] In Kurzform gebracht lautet die Anwort wie folgt: Der Anspruch ist in Deutschland vertraglicher, in England deliktischer und in den USA von einer Art zwitterhafter Rechtsnatur, die nur durch ein illegales Zusammenleben ("illicit cohabitation") von Vertrag und Delikt entstehen konnte, um *Dean Prossers* Worte aufzugreifen.[20]

Aber nicht nur die systematische Einordnung der Ansprüche divergiert. Auch die Terminologie weist bezeichnende Unterschiede auf. Ein Beispiel bietet der Vergleich zwischen französischem und deutschem Recht, die jeweils das Institut des Vertrages zugunsten Dritter kennen. Überzeugender ist in diesem Fall dank der deutschen Fähigkeiten bei der Theoriebildung die in Deutschland gebräuchliche Terminologie, deren Entstehung man freilich einem Mangel des BGB verdankt.[21] Lange Zeit ist in England das Rechtsinstitut des *Vertrages mit Schutzwirkung für Dritte* mit "contract in favor of a third party" übersetzt worden.[22] Meines Wissens habe ich als erster[23] "contract with protective effects vis à vis third parties" als passenderen englischen Ausdruck für diese Variante des Vertrages *in favorem tertii* vorgeschlagen.

Die abweichende Übersetzung des Rechtsinstitutes ist erklärungsbedürftig; eine Erklärung setzt jedoch ein vertieftes Verständnis des deutschen Zivilgesetzbuches voraus. Dieses Verständnis ist auch in England von Bedeutung. Dort ist zur Zeit die Tendenz[24] zu beobachten, die Fälle, in denen ein deliktsrechtlicher Ausgleich für reine Vermögensschäden gewährt wird, strenger einzugrenzen. Sollte diese Tendenz nämlich weiter anhalten, dann wäre die Entscheidung *Ross* v. *Caunters*[25], in der ein solcher deliktsrechtlicher Anspruch gewährt wurde, möglicherweise nicht mehr so unangreifbar, wie sie

---

[19] In meinem Aufsatz "An Expanding Tort Law—The Price of a Rigid Contract Law" (1987) 103 *LQR* 354 I, gebe ich zahlreiche Gründe an, warum ich die rechtssystematische Einordnung des Anspruches für notwendig erachte. Vgl. auch meinen Aufsatz "Doctrinal Clarity in Tort Litigation: A Comparative Lawyer's Viewpoint" (1991) 25 *The International Lawyer* 953. Professor Kötz hat die gleiche Auffassung vertreten in "The Doctrine of Privity of Contract", (1990) 10 *Tel Aviv Studies in Law* 195.

[20] Prosser, *Handbook on the Law of Torts*, 4. Auflage (1971), S. 634.

[21] § 831 BGB; insbesondere Abs. 1 S. 2 (Exkulpationsmöglichkeit).

[22] Z.B. Zweigert and Kötz, *An Introduction to Comparative Law* 2nd edn. (1987) vol II, S. 145 ff (Übersetzung von Tony Weir).

[23] Lawson and Markesinis, *Tortious Liability for Un-Intentional Harm in the Common Law and the Civil Law*, (1982), Vol. 2, S. 98.

[24] Ein Beispiel hierfür ist *Murphy* v. *Brentwood D.C.* [1991] 1 AC 398.

[25] [1980] Ch. 297. Ross ist tatsächlich kürzlich angegriffen worden, da die Entscheidung nicht mit der Entscheidung *Murphy* v. *Brentwood D.C.* [1991] 1 AC 398 zu vereinbaren sei, vgl. *White* v. *Jones, The Times*, 9 March 1993. Das Berufungsgericht schloß sich der Argumentation jedoch nicht an. Der sehr stark an BGH NJW 1965, 1955 = JZ 1966, 141 erinnernde Fall wird besprochen von W. Lorenz und B. Markesinis in (1993) 56 *MLR* 558 ff.

es bislang war. Wenn also in vergleichbaren Sachverhaltskonstellationen auch künftig ein Ausgleichsanspruch bestehen soll, könnte eventuell die Notwendigkeit entstehen, in irgendeiner Form Vertragsrecht anzuwenden. Wie allerdings die Law Commission kürzlich darlegte, wäre in diesem Fall eine einfache Subsumtion unter die Regeln des Vertrages *in favorem tertii*, wie er herkömmlicherweise verstanden wird, nicht ohne weiteres möglich.[26] Aus unterschiedlichen Gründen könnte somit das englische Recht darauf angewiesen sein, aus den in Deutschland gemachten Erfahrungen den einen oder anderen Schluß zu ziehen. Mit anderen Worten muß man im englischen Recht vielleicht künftig zu einer vertragsrechtlichen Ableitung gelangen, um weiterhin die gleichen rechtlichen Ergebnisse zu erhalten. Auch wenn dies nicht der richtige Ort für eine Erörterung dieser Frage ist, sollte doch festgehalten werden, daß, was ursprünglich ein Übersetzungsproblem zu sein schien, sich rasch als komplizierter und bedeutsamer herausstellte, so daß ein englischer Praktiker zum Umgang mit der Problematik zusätzlicher Hintergrundinformationen und Erläuterungen bedarf. Ich denke, daß dank der (englischsprachigen) Veröffentlichungen der Professoren Lorenz[27], Kötz[28], von Bar[29] und anderen[30] manches davon bereits geleistet ist. Genau das meine ich mit dem Satz, daß der Wissenschaftler dem Praktiker behilflich sein kann.

Lassen Sie mich Ihnen nun ein zweites Beispiel geben, auf das mich der bedeutende Rechtsvergleicher Stefan Riesenfeld aufmerksam gemacht hat. Meiner Meinung nach illustriert es in geeigneter Weise meine Vorstellung davon, wie die Kenntnis ausländischer Rechtsprechung dem inländischen Juristen von Nutzen sein kann. Genauer gesagt zeigt das Beispiel dreierlei: *Erstens*, daß Rechtssysteme, die sich auf den ersten Blick unterscheiden, sich als sehr ähnlich herausstellen können, wenn man ihre Rechtsprechung im Zusammenhang mit der entsprechenden Literatur auswertet. *Zweitens* veranschaulicht das Beispiel, wie grundlegende Ideen zur Lösung gemeinsamer Probleme dank des Einfallsreichtums und der Anstrengungen einzelner, die eine Ausbildung im Ausland genossen haben oder dort Freunde gefunden haben, juristische Grenzen überwinden können. *Zuletzt* macht es auch darauf aufmerksam, daß ein Sachverhalt, bei dem man gewöhnlich an eine Reihe englischer Fälle denkt, sich bereits 60 Jahre zuvor in Deutschland zugetragen hat. Es ist eben oft "nothing new under the sun".

[26] Law Commission, "Privity of Contract: Contracts for the Benefit of Third Parties", *Consultation Paper Nr. 21* (1991). Die Kommissionsmitglieder haben das deutsche Recht offenbar erörtert, brachten ihm aber gemischte Gefühle entgegen, wie man bei J. Beatson, "Reforming the Law of Contract for the Benefit of Third Parties—Another Bite at the Cherry", (1992) *Current Legal Problems*, S. 1 ff, bes. S. 22–6 nachlesen kann.

[27] "Contract Beneficiaries in German Law", in *The Gradual Convergence. Foreign Ideas, Foreign Influence and European Law on the Eve of the 21st Century* (Herausgeber: Markesinis), (1993), Kapitel 3.

[28] "The Doctrine of Privity of Contract", (1990) 10 *Tel Aviv Univ. Studies in Law* 195.

[29] "Liability for information and opinions causing pure economic loss to third parties: a comparison of English and German Law" in *The Gradual Convergence* (siehe FN 27), Kapitel 3.

[30] Markesinis, *The German Law of Torts*, 2. Auflage (1990).

Für den 15. September 1840—der spätere englische König Edward VII war noch nicht einmal geboren -plante Friedrich Wilhelm IV, der romantische und künstlerisch veranlagte preußische König, über den Bismarck einmal sagte, "if you tried to come to grips with him, you would only find a slimy substance"[31], aus Anlaß seiner Inthronisierung einen festlichen Einzug in Berlin. Als diese Prozession später aus Sicherheitsgründen um zwei Tage verschoben wurde, sahen sich diejenigen, die für den ursprünglichen Termin ein "Zimmer mit Aussicht" gemietet hatten, mit derselben Frage konfrontiert wie ein halbes Jahrhundert später Mr. Henry, als er von Mr. Krell auf Zahlung des Mietzinses verklagt wurde, aber nicht zahlen wollte, weil die Krönungsprozession von Edward VII wegen der Erkrankung des Königs verschoben werden mußte.[32] Waren die "Mieter" verpflichtet, die vertraglich vereinbarte Miete zu bezahlen?

Den "deutschen" Festzugfall verdanken wir Rudolf von Jhering, der ihn in eine der wohl ersten deutschen Fallsammlungen aufnahm.[33] Seine verneinende Antwort ließe sich mit Windscheids Theorie von der *Voraussetzung* begründen, die er um diese Zeit in Deutschland entwickelte und schließlich in § 97 seines Lehrbuches zum Pandektenrecht aufnahm.[34] Bekanntlich wurde diese Theorie von den Verfassern des BGB vehement zurückgewiesen mit dem Ergebnis, daß im Gesetz keine spezielle Regelung des Problems zu finden ist, das in England als "frustration of contract" bezeichnet wird. Später jedoch, als die von den wenig vorausschauenden Siegern des ersten Weltkrieges heraufbeschworene extreme Inflation in Deutschland grassierte, zogen die Gerichte den § 242 BGB (Treu und Glauben) zur Lösung der drückenden sozialen Probleme heran. Es war Oertmann, der mit seiner Wiederbelebung der Theorie seines Schwiegervaters in modifizierter Form und unter dem Stichwort "Geschäftsgrundlage" die theoretische Basis für diese Bemühungen lieferte.[35] Der dem deutschen BGB unbekannte Frustrationsgedanke[36] hat in

---

[31] E. Eyck, *Bismarck and the German Empire*, (1968), S. 17.

[32] *Krell* v. *Henry* [1903] 2 KB 740. Mr. Krell vermietete Mr. Henry ein "Zimmer mit Aussicht" auf die geplante Krönungsprozession von König Edward VII zu einem ungewöhnlich hohen Preis. Wegen einer Erkrankung des Königs mußte die Prozession an dem geplanten Tag ausfallen und Mr. Henry verweigerte die Zahlung des Mietzinses. Mr. Krell verklagte ihn auf Zahlung. Die Klage scheiterte jedoch wegen "frustration of contract".

[33] *Civilrechtsfälle ohne Entscheidungen*, 4. Auflage (1881), all Nr. LXX, S. 145. In seiner Einführung sagt Jhering: ". . . ich habe auch die mir obliegende Aufgabe, die Jugend in die Jurisprudenz einzuführen, nicht erfolgreicher lösen zu können geglaubt, als indem ich in meinen Vorlesungen dem casuistischen Element eine unausgesetzte Berücksichtigung geschenkt habe." (S. 5). Ich bin fest davon überzeugt, daß sein Hinweis auf Studenten in einem rechtsvergleichenden Zusammenhang auch auf erfahrene Juristen übertragen werden kann. Anders ausgedrückt besteht der beste Weg, sie in ein fremdes Rechtssystem einzuführen, darin, ihnen Fälle vorzulegen, deren tatsächlichen Umstände ihnen vertraut sind.

[34] Erstmals erschienen in der Ausgabe von 1862. Vgl. jetzt Windscheid (-Kipp), 6. Auflage (1900), § 97 ff.

[35] *Die Geschäftsgrundlage*, (1921). Diese Theorie wird heute nicht mehr vertreten. Ein anderer Rechtsgelehrter, Karl Larenz, hat jedoch eine modernere Variante der Theorie entworfen (*Geschäftsgrundlage und Vertragserfüllung*, (1963)).

[36] Nunmehr bildet die im Jahre 1979 in das BGB eingeführte Spezialregelung § 651 f BGB eine Ausnahme hierzu.

der Folge durch eine überaus große Zahl von Entscheidungen Anerkennung gefunden, die sich auf § 242 BGB in seiner Ausdeutung durch die wissenschaftliche Literatur stützten. In vieler Hinsicht sind die dabei angeführten Begründungen nicht nur denen englischer Gerichte ähnlich und lassen sich auch in unsere juristische Landschaft übertragen. Tatsächlich gibt es zahlreiche Indizien dafür, daß die deutschen Ideen in Form von Section 2-614 des amerikanischen Uniform Commercial Code (U.C.C.) Aufnahme in das amerikanische Recht gefunden haben. Auch wenn er sich selbst nie dazu bekannte[37], müssen diese Ideen von Karl Llewellyn übermittelt worden sein. Lehrte dieser doch just zu der Zeit in Leipzig, als die Theorien von Oertmann allgemein diskutiert wurden. Ferner bediente sich Llewellyn in seinem Werk "Casebook on the Law of Sales"[38] nicht nur der erwähnten Ideen, sondern auch des im ansonsten im Common Law nicht gebräuchlichen Begriffs der "presupposition". Riesenfeld bemerkt hierzu: "Die gedanklichen Strukturen der Architekten des modernen Common Law und die der modernen Pandektisten vereinigen sich bei Llewellyn. Das ist alles, was [mit Sicherheit] gesagt werden kann, aber es sagt doch schon sehr viel."[39]

Mein drittes Beispiel ist etwas komplexer. Ihm liegt die englische Entscheidung *R. v. Reid*[40] zugrunde, in der es in erster Linie darum ging, ob "recklessness" (Leichtfertigkeit) nach objektiven oder subjektiven Kriterien zu bestimmen ist. In seinem Votum wies Lord Goff bemerkenswerterweise und, wie ich meine, völlig zutreffend darauf hin, daß im deutschen Recht bereits eine vergleichbare Fragestellung aufgeworfen worden war. Klugerweise, wenn ich das einmal so sagen darf, warnte er jedoch auch vor den Gefahren, die ein Vergleich des englischen und des deutschen Rechts in sich birgt. Diese bestehen insbesondere deshalb, weil das deutsche Recht, im Unterschied zum englischen, vier Formen des Verschuldens kennt.[41] Es sind sogar fünf, wenn man Leichtfertigkeit als eine von der groben Fahrlässigkeit abzugrenzende Verschuldensform ansieht. Wie lassen sich nun also die von Lord Goff getroffenen Feststellungen überprüfen und aussagekräftige Vergleiche anstellen?

Die erste Schwierigkeit für den Rechtsvergleicher besteht darin, daß er im Gegensatz zum jeweiligen nationalen Juristen nicht so mühelos zwischen den Rechtsgebieten hin—und herwechseln kann. Ein Deliktsrechtler wie ich versucht, vielleicht unter Schwierigkeiten, aber doch mit einiger Zuverlässigkeit, das deutsche Deliktsrecht zu durchdringen. Er sollte sich aber davor hüten,

---

[37] *Grossfeld* and *Windship*, aaO, oben FN 5, geben mehrere Gründe dafür an, warum Llewllyn (und andere Realisten) nicht durchweg gewillt war(en) zuzugeben, daß einige seiner (ihrer) Ideen deutschen Ursprungs sind.

[38] Erschienen 1930, S. 178.

[39] (1989) 37 *The American Journal of Comparative Law* S. 1, 6.

[40] [1992] 1 WLR 793.

[41] Dies sind: direkter Vorsatz (dolus directus), bedingter Vorsatz (dolus eventualis), grobe Fahrlässigkeit (gross negligence) und leichte Fahrlässigkeit (light negligence). Leichtfertigkeit (recklessness) mag eine weitere von der groben Fahrlässigkeit zu unterscheidende Form des Verschuldens sein; sie gehört aber mehr in den Bereich des Strafrechts.

das Strafrecht einzubeziehen, das sich wesentlich vom Deliktsrecht unterscheidet und zuweilen ein wahrhaftiges philosophisches Minenfeld sein kann.[42] Kann er es aber wagen, sich eines zivilrechtlichen Falles anzunehmen, der die Frage der groben Fahrlässigkeit (gross negligence) aufwirft? Als ich mich auf diesem Weg befand, stieß ich auf die Entscheidung des Bundesgerichtshofes vom 5. Februar 1974.[43] Sie weckte mein Interesse, da sich an ihr die Übersetzungsschwierigkeiten verdeutlichen lassen, von denen ich schon gesprochen habe.

Der Erstbeklagte befuhr als Fahrer eines seinem Arbeitgeber gehörenden Wagens (mit dessen Erlaubnis) eine ihm vertraute Straße. Die Geschwindigkeit des Fahrzeugs betrug etwa 70 km/h. Die Außentemperaturen lagen um den Gefrierpunkt und es herrschte stellenweiser Nebel. Etwa zwei Kilometer vor Erreichen des Fahrtzieles kam das Fahrzeug in einer scharfen Kurve von der Straße ab und prallte gegen einen Baum. K, ein Kollege des Erstbeklagten, der ebenfalls im Fahrzeug saß, erlitt dabei schwere Verletzungen. An der Strecke befanden sich unmittelbar vor der Unfallstelle drei Verkehrsschilder: Das erste signalisierte eine Geschwindigkeitsbegrenzung auf 50 km/h, das zweite warnte vor der Kurve und vor Eis auf der Fahrbahn. Ein drittes, etwas dahinter angebrachtes Schild wies auf erhöhte Schleudergefahr hin. Zweitbeklagte war die Kfz-Haftpflichtversicherung des Fahrzeugeigentümers.

Die Klägerin hatte als Trägerin der gesetzlichen Unfallversicherung die dem Unfallopfer (K) zustehenden Ersatzleistungen erbracht und begehrte mit ihrer Klage die Erstattung der verauslagten Beträge von den Beklagten. Sie begründete ihren Anspruch damit, daß der Erstbeklagte bei der Unfallverursachung grob fahrlässig gehandelt habe. Aus später noch zu erläuternden Gründen hing der Erfolg der Klage davon ab, ob tatsächlich ein Fall grober Fahrlässigkeit vorlag. Die zentrale Passage der Entscheidung, die sich mit dieser Frage auseinandersetzt, ist nachstehend wiedergegeben. Sie wird dem englischen Juristen, der allein die Entscheidung betrachtet, ohne dabei die wechselseitigen Beziehungen zwischen den verschiedenen Ersatzansprüchen zu berücksichtigen, nur schwer verständlich sein.

"II. Angesichts dieser Feststellungen läßt sich die angefochtene Entscheidung mit dem in der Rechtsprechung des BGH herausgearbeiteten Begriff der groben Fahrlässigkeit i.S. des § 640 RVO [in seiner geänderten Fassung[44]] nicht vereinbaren.

---

[42] In *R. v. Reid* [1992] 1 WLR 793, 816 sprach Lord Browne-Wilkinson von den "nahezu metaphysischen Abstraktionen des modernen Strafrechts". Vor diesem Hintergrund erstaunt es dann auch nicht weiter, daß in Deutschland (anders als in England, Frankreich oder den Niederlanden) Strafrechtslehrer sehr häufig auch Rechtsphilosophie lehren.

[43] *VersR* 1974, 569 f.

[44] § 636 I RVO: Der Unternehmer ist den in seinem Unternehmen tätigen Versicherten, deren Angehörigen und Hinterbliebenen, auch wenn sie keinen Anspruch auf Rente haben, nach anderen gesetzlichen Vorschriften zum Ersatz des Personenschadens, den ein Arbeitsunfall verursacht hat, nur dann verpflichtet, wenn er den Arbeitsunfall vorsätzlich herbeigeführt hat oder wenn der Arbeitsunfall bei der Teilnahme am allgemeinen Verkehr eingetreten ist. Der Schadensersatzanspruch des Versicherten, seiner Angehörigen und seiner Hinterbliebenen

Nach dieser Rechtsprechung ist freilich nicht nur erforderlich, daß das unfall-ursächliche Verhalten objektiv grob fehlsam war . . . Vielmehr ist weiterhin zu fordern, daß sich der Täter mit diesem Verhalten über Gebote und Einsichten hin-weggesetzt hat, die sich jedem aufdrängen mußten . . . *Daß sich diese wegen der häu-figen Härte des Rückgriffs strengen Erfordernisse auch dann nicht zum Nachteil des Verantwortlichen abschwächen können, wenn er—wie hier der Bekl.—als Kraft-fahrer den Schutz einer Haftpflichtversicherung genießt, bemerkt das Berufungsurteil zu Recht.* Das ändert aber nichts daran, daß der Bekl. nach den Feststellungen des Berufungsgerichts einen typischen Fall der objektiven und subjektiven groben Fahrlässigkeit verwirklicht und dadurch den Unfall herbeigeführt hat. Er hat sich nämlich bewußt und hartnäckig über wichtige Verkehrsgebote hinweggesetzt, die ihm durch die Beschilderung besonders eindringlich nahegebracht wurden und deren Berechtigung offen zutage lag . . ."[45]

Dieses Urteil verlangt geradezu nach dem, was ich als kreative Übersetzung bezeichnet habe. Die hervorgehobene Stelle wird der englische Jurist selbst nach ihrer Übersetzung in passables Englisch nur schwer verstehen, solange nicht auch der prozessuale und materiellrechtliche Hintergrund erläutert wurde.

Zunächst sei noch einmal daran erinnert, daß im vorliegenden Fall der Sozialversicherungsträger den Verletzten bereits entschädigt hatte. Gegenstand des Verfahrens war daher lediglich der Regreßanspruch des Sozialversich-erungsträgers gegen den Fahrer des Unfallfahrzeuges (neben dem Kfz-Haftpflichtversicherer) wegen dessen deliktischen Verhaltens. Offensichtlich versuchte der Sozialversicherungsträger also, durch die Behauptung, der Fahrer habe grob fahrlässig gehandelt, von der Vorschrift des § 640 RVO Gebrauch zu machen, die bei Vorliegen dieser Voraussetzung den Regreß erlaubt. Da die Voraussetzung nach Ansicht des BGH im vorliegenden Fall erfüllt war[46], war der Sozialversicherungsträger berechtigt, Erstattung aller bisherigen Leistungen an den Geschädigten zu verlangen. In Anbetracht der existierenden Rechtsprechung des BGH zur groben Fahrlässigkeit beim Führen

---

vermindert sich jedoch um die Leistungen, die sie nach Gesetz oder Satzung infolge des Arbeitsunfalls von Trägern der Sozialversicherung erhalten.

§ 637 I RVO: § 636 gilt bei Arbeitsunfällen entsprechend für die Ersatzansprüche eines Versicherten, dessen Angehörigen und Hinterbliebenen gegen einen in demselben Betrieb tätigen Betriebsangehörigen, wenn dieser den Arbeitsunfall durch eine betriebliche Tätigkeit verursacht.

§ 640 I RVO: Haben Personen, deren Ersatzpflicht durch § 636 oder § 637 beschränkt ist, den Arbeitsunfall vorsätzlich oder grob fahrlässig herbeigeführt, so haften sie für alles, was die Träger der Sozialversicherung nach Gesetz oder Satzung infolge des Arbeitsunfalls aufwenden müssen. Statt der Rente kann der Kapitalwert gefordert werden.

[45] BGH *VersR* 1974, S. 569.

[46] Das Gericht setzte sich ausführlich mit der Frage auseinander, ob es in Fällen wie dem zu entscheidenden angebracht sei, weniger strenge Anforderungen an das Tatbestandsmerkmal "grobe Fahrlässigkeit" zu stellen, da der volle Schadensersatz letztendlich ja vom Fahrzeughaftpflichtversicherer und nicht vom Schädiger getragen werden würde (siehe hierzu die hervorgehobene Passage im Urteilsauszug). Die verneinende Antwort des Gerichts auf diese Frage führte im Ergebnis jedoch nicht dazu, daß der Schädiger von den gegen ihn geltend gemachten Regreßansprüchen befreit wurde, da der BGH zu der Überzeugung gelangte, daß die vorge-brachten Tatsachen den Vorwurf des grob fahrlässigen Verhaltens stützten.

eines Kraftfahrzeuges mußte dies das Ergebnis des Falles sein. Hätte der BGH jedoch das Vorliegen grober Fahrlässigkeit verneint, wäre die Regreßklage des Sozialversicherungsträgers erfolglos geblieben.

Sofern diese erläuternden Anmerkungen den Text der Entscheidung etwas verständlicher gemacht haben, wäre dies ein gutes Beispiel für das, was ich als kreative Übersetzung bezeichnet habe. Nur durch ein solches Vorgehen kann das oftmals schwierige ausländische Material zur Bestätigung oder als Anregung oder Orientierungshilfe genutzt werden. Fälle wie dieser geben zu zwei Anmerkungen allgemeinerer Art Anlaß. Die erste betrifft die Begriffe "grobe Fahrlässigkeit" und "recklessness", die ein außenstehender Beobachter zu allen praktischen Zwecken gleichzusetzen versucht ist. Hier hat man den Eindruck, daß deutsche Juristen und und das House of Lords den jeweiligen Begriff in annähernd gleicher Weise auslegen. Zweitens fällt auf, daß die Betrachtung des Gesamtzusammenhanges des Falles im deutschen Recht eine im Vergleich mit unserem Recht andersartige und, möglicherweise, sinnvollere Regelung der Rechtsbeziehungen zwischen Arbeitskollegen und des Zusammenspiels verschiedener Ausgleichsansprüche erkennen läßt. Aber das ist eine Frage der Bewertung des jeweiligen nationalen Sachrechts, die von mir hier nicht zu erörtern ist.

Es fragt sich, ob auch unsere deutschen Kollegen etwas von uns lernen können. Selbstverständlich muß hierfür unser Material zunächst in geeigneter Weise für die Übertragung in die deutschen Strukturen aufbereitet worden sein. Dies vorausgesetzt, kann die Antwort auf die Frage meines Erachtens nur positiv ausfallen. Zwei allgemeine Aspekte verdienen jedoch, gesondert gewürdigt zu werden: der Stil von Gerichtsentscheidungen und der Umgang mit vorhandenem Fallmaterial.

Was den Stil von Entscheidungen anbelangt, so bin ich sicher nicht so vermessen zu behaupten, die englische Sprache biete einen reicheren Wortschatz oder subtilere Ausdrucksmöglichkeiten. Ein solches Urteil steht mir nicht nur deshalb nicht zu, weil ich gar nicht in der Lage bin, einen solchen Vergleich anzustellen, sondern vor allem, weil ich bezweifle, daß solche Bewertungen überhaupt möglich sind. Gleichwohl kann man sagen, daß das englische Urteil—auch wenn es allmählich immer länger wird—vom Stil her lebendig und gelegentlich auch humorvoll ist. Durch die Notwendigkeit, den Sachverhalt früherer Entscheidungen in der Urteilsbegründung wiederzugeben, bleibt das Urteil anschaulich und wird nicht allzu abstrakt und dogmatisch. Es würde nicht überraschen, falls einige dieser Merkmale auch deutschen Richtern zunehmend attraktiv erscheinen, je mehr sie in Berührung mit dem Common Law kommen. Selbst wenn es den deutschen Richtern nicht möglich sein sollte, praktische Folgerungen daraus abzuleiten, so gilt dies meiner Ansicht nach nicht für die Wissenschaft. Zusätzlich zu den bereits oben zitierten Worten Jherings möchte ich auf eine von mir bei der Ausbildung ausländischer Juristen gemachte Erfahrung hinweisen: Ich stelle jedesmal eine gewisse Überraschung und wohl auch Freude fest, wenn eine ihnen bereits bekannte Materie von einem weniger erhabenen Standpunkt aus präsentiert wird, als jenem, den meine deutsche Kollegen so bewundern.

Wenden wir uns nun noch dem deutschen Fallmaterial zu, seiner reichen Fülle und den—bei allem Respekt—unzureichenden Versuchen (so jedenfalls wirken sie in den Augen eines Engländers), einander widersprechende Urteile so zueinander ins Verhältnis zu setzen, daß daraus brauchbare Bausteine für die zeitgemäße Anpassung des in die Jahre gekommenen Zivilgesetzbuches werden. Dies sind natürlich gewagte Behauptungen, die durch meinen Status als ausländischer (wenn auch bewundernder) Beobachter der deutschen Rechtsordnung nur teilweise als entschuldigt gelten können. Ich möchte daher zur Begründung meines Standpunktes auf die zahlreichen Entscheidungen und wissenschaftlichen Stellungnahmen hinweisen, die sich mit der Streitfrage der Ersatzfähigkeit des reinen Vermögensschadens befassen, der durch die fahrlässige Erteilung einer falschen Auskunft oder durch ein fehlerhaftes, aber ungefährliches Produkt entstanden ist. Besteht hier nicht eine Kluft zwischen der in der Literatur vertretenen Meinung und den von der Rechtsprechung ausgehenden Initiativen? Könnte man nicht die Auffassung vertreten, daß meine deutschen Kollegen aus der Wissenschaft bei ihrer Kritik der gegenwärtigen Tendenz der Rechtsprechung mehr Wert auf dogmatische Geschlossenheit als auf die Notwendigkeit legen, sich aus den Fesseln von aus dem 19. Jahrhundert stammenden Rechtsnormen zu befreien? Auch wenn ich—bis zu einem gewissen Grade—dogmatische Geschlossenheit ebenfalls für wünschenswert halte—wäre eine solche Befreiung nach so langer Zeit nicht eine Gelegenheit, endlich einzuräumen, daß Vermögensinteressen für die Menschen zu Beginn des 21. Jahrhunderts die gleiche Bedeutung haben wie das Eigentum für die Menschen des ausgehenden 19. Jahrhunderts?

3. EPILOG

Sollte ich eine Zusammenfassung der Punkte geben, die ich herauszuarbeiten versucht habe, würde ich mit der Feststellung beginnen, daß sämtliche von mir in diesem Beitrag erörterten Fälle in der einen oder anderen Weise von angloamerikanischen Gerichten genutzt werden können. Ich hoffe aber, deutlich gemacht zu haben, daß zuvor das jeweilige Material von einem Fachmann übersetzt und dem Gericht in geeigneter Weise präsentiert werden muß. Die schlichte Übersetzung genügt dabei nicht: Das Material bedarf der Erläuterung und Systematisierung und muß in eine Form gebracht werden, die eine Übertragung in ein Common Law Urteil ermöglicht. Das ist zweifellos eine schwierige und zeitraubende Aufgabe und es wird immer Stimmen geben, die sagen: "Unser Recht ist schon viel zu umfangreich. Warum sollten wir uns also mit dem Recht anderer Länder auseinandersetzen, zumal das so viele Gefahren mit sich bringt?" Meine Antwort hierauf lautet, daß unsere Gerichte, allen voran das House of Lords, wesentlich stärkeren Gebrauch von den sich im Ausland vollziehenden Entwicklungen machen könnten, statt—wie man das bisher von ihnen kennt—nur gelegentlich am Rande die eine oder andere aus dem Zusammenhang gerissene US-amerikanische Entscheidung zu zitieren.[47] Die Erkenntnis, daß auch in vielen anderen Rechtsordnungen ähnliche Probleme existieren, könnte meines Erachtens legitimer Anlaß dafür sein, in den Urteilsbegründungen der ausländischen Gerichte nach Ansätzen und Hilfen für die Lösung der eigenen Probleme zu suchen. In vielen Bereichen, in denen das Recht starke wirtschaftliche Bezüge aufweist, könnte die Suche nach harmonisierenden Lösungen ebenfalls ihre Vorteile haben. Dann ist natürlich auch an die Rechtsprechung des Europäischen Gerichtshofes zu erinnern. Es darf nämlich keinesfalls in Vergessenheit geraten, wie wichtig die Kenntnis fremden Rechts und der Gebrauch der Rechtsvergleichung für die Entwicklung des Gemeinschaftsrechts waren und immer noch sind.[48] Diese Tatsache kann freilich kaum überraschen, bedenkt man, daß der EWG-Vertrag, die Quelle des primären Gemeinschaftsrechts, zum Verhältnis zwischen Normen des Gemeinschaftsrechts und einzelstaatlicher Gesetzgebung schweigt und zur Frage nach den Grenzen der durch den EWG-Vertrag zugewiesenen Kompetenzen auch nur wenig aussagt. Hier hat sich die rechtsvergleichende Methode als hilfreich erwiesen, indem der Europäische Gerichtshof rechtliche Konzepte und Prinzipien in den Rechtsordnungen der Mitgliedstaaten untersucht und zu Gemeinschaftsrecht fortentwickelt hat. Der überall diskutierte Grundsatz der Verhältnismäßigkeit ("principle of proportionality") hat so beispielsweise seinen Ursprung im niederländischen und deutschen Verwaltungsrecht. Zwar wird er von manchem englischen Juristen als "novel and dangerous" mit Argwohn betrachtet, andere hingegen erkennen in ihm eine große Ähnlichkeit mit unserem Grundsatz der Angemessenheit ("reasonableness").[49] Derartige Schritte, die, was hier nochmals betont sei, auf dem Studium des Rechts der Einzelstaaten basieren, haben eine ganze Reihe neuer Begriffe entstehen lassen (z.B. "Priorität", "effektiver Rechtsschutz", "Verhältnismäßigkeit", "Waffengleichheit"). Diese Erkenntnis führt mich zu meinem Ausgangspunkt zurück: der Notwendigkeit, die "Verstehbarkeit" des jeweiligen Vokabulars in verschiedenen Rechtsordnungen zu erreichen. Ebenso wichtig ist aber auch, daß dadurch zugleich nach und nach die Funktion sowohl der nationalen als auch der transnationalen Richter verändert und vorangetrieben wird.

Die von mir bislang genannten Gründe, weshalb das Studium des ausländischen Rechts gefördert werden muß, sind natürlich praktischer Natur.

---

[47] *Murphy* v. *Brentwood* DC [1991] 1 AC 398, mit kritischer Anmerkung von Professor Flemming, "Requiem for Anns", (1990) 106 *LQR* 525, 530; Sir Robin Cooke, "An Impossible Distiction", (1991) 107 *LQR* 46, 58–63.

[48] Dies wurde ausdrücklich anerkannt von Generalanwalt Warner in der Entscheidung 17/74, *Transocean Marine Paint* [1974] ECR 1063 und von den Generalanwälten Warner und Slynn in der Entscheidung 155/79, *A.M & S. Europe* [1982] ECR 1575, 1619 und 1642.

[49] Jowell und Lester in Jowell and Oliver (Hrsg.), "New Directions in Judicial Review", (1988) *Current Legal Problems*, S. 51.

Man sollte dabei aber nicht die intellektuelle Befriedigung vergessen, die der Vergleich der eigenen Überlegungen mit denen bietet, die in anderen fortschrittlichen Rechtsordnungen angestellt werden. Wie John Milton einmal sagte:

> " . . . as Wine and oyl are Imported to us from abroad: so must ripe Understanding, and many civil Virtues, be imported into our minds from Foreign Writings, and examples of best Ages, we shall else miscarry still, and come short in the attempts of any great Enterprise".[50]

Juristen mögen nicht so viel Einfallsreichtum besitzen wie Dichter, aber auch sie sollten gelegentlich darum bemüht sein und versuchen, so unvoreingenommen wie möglich zu sein. Tatsächlich gelingt es einigen auch. Sir Thomas Bingham hat in einem Aufsatz in ähnlicher Weise einen über die Grenzen gerichteten Blick befürwortet.[51] Praktiker können es sich leisten, der Wissenschaft keine Beachtung zu schenken. Den Master of the Rolls können sie nicht ignorieren! Teilweise wird die Ansicht vertreten, daß ein englischer Richter, dem ein sorgfältig arbeitender Anwalt in geeigneter Weise aufbereitetes ausländisches juristisches Material präsentiert, weil er es für fallrelevant hält, dieses schon deshalb nicht berücksichtigen sollte, weil es einer ausländischen Rechtsordnung entstammt. Daß diese Meinung überhaupt vertreten wird, wundert mich, und ich kann mich ihr keinesfalls anschließen. Genau genommen bin ich sogar der Auffassung, daß vermutlich der entgegengesetzte Standpunkt richtig ist. Richter, die die Relevanz solchen ausländischen Materials erkennen würden, wären auch in der Lage, es in angemessener Weise zu würdigen. Sollte es darüber hinaus bekannt werden, daß Richter X oder Y bereit ist, solches Material einzubeziehen, dann hätten die Praktiker (und Wissenschaftler) den nötigen Anreiz, entsprechend vorzugehen. Da aber die Richter das erste Glied in dieser Kette sind, sollte die Wissenschaft sie für derartige Überlegungen als die vorrangige Zielgruppe ansehen.

Dies scheint manchem vielleicht ein langwieriger und schwieriger Prozeß zu sein. Er wird viel Geduld erfordern. Der englische Rechtswissenschaftler ist in Gegensatz zu seinem deutschen Kollegen gewohnt, die "*vox clamantis in deserto*" zu sein. Ich jedenfalls bin bereit zu warten, weil ich davon überzeugt bin, daß juristische Anleihen im Ausland sich letztlich als historisch unvermeidbar erweisen werden. Denn, wie Roscoe Pound[52] schon vor rund siebzig Jahren feststellte:

> "In der Rechtsgeschichte haben Perioden des Wachstums und der Expansion Philosophie und Rechtsvergleichung erfordert und sich auf sie gestützt.

---

[50] *The Character of the Long Parliament*, abgedruckt in *The Works of John Milton*, Bd. XVIII, (1938), S. 254.
[51] Sir Thomas Bingham, "There is a World Elsewhere—The Changing Pattern of English Law", (1992) 41 *ICLQ* 513.
[52] In (1921) 34 *Harvard L. Rev.* 34 S. 227, 228.

[Andererseits] beruhen Phasen der Stabilität, in denen eher die Perfektionierung des bestehenden Rechts als seine inhaltliche Weiterentwicklung angestrebt wird, auf analytischen und historischen Überlegungen".

Ich habe keinen Zweifel daran, daß wir uns augenblicklich nicht in einer Ära des Stillstandes, sondern der Veränderung befinden. Nicht Rückzug, sondern Expansion, und nicht inselartige Entwicklungen, sondern kosmopolitische Einflüsse, durch die wissenschaftliche Erkenntnis sich rascher als je zuvor ausbreitet, sind die Zeichen der Zeit. Aus diesem Grunde bin ich überzeugt von dem Nutzen der rechtsvergleichenden Methode und dem Bedarf an "Brückenbauern"—eine Rolle, die ich dem Rechtsvergleicher anvertrauen würde.

9

Learning from Europe and Learning in Europe

Gott grüß Euch, Brüder,
Sämtliche Oner und Aner!
Ich bin Weltbewohner,
Bin Weimaraner

[I greet you, brothers
Partisans of various "isms" and "slogans",
As for me, I'm a world citizen
As well as Weimarian*]

1. THE SEMINAR SERIES AND THE BOOK

Learning from Europe was the title of the seminar series which, as stated in the preface, gave birth to this book. Many of our participants were quick to point out that England was, in fact, part of Europe. Too quick, in fact, for, though geographically this observation is correct, it underestimates the differences in legal history and mentality which were (and, probably, still are) far greater than the distance between Dover and Calais could by itself ever possibly suggest. This insular mentality will, one suspects, survive for some time after the Channel Tunnel technically puts an end to our status as an island off the continent of Europe. It was this "mentality gap" that the title of the series was meant to capture, stress, and attack. For it was further hoped to show—as some comparatists have demonstrated—that attitudes and phobias still constitute the greatest factor that separates this country from the continent of Europe rather than problems, solutions and, even, methodology. Professor Koopmans, the Advocate-General of the Dutch Supreme Court (and formerly a judge in the Court of Justice of the European Communities), put this very same thought in a slightly different way when he wrote in his Harry Street Lecture that "Lawyers in countries like Great Britain and the Netherlands [and the same can be said of other countries on the Continent]

---

* Goethe, Zahme Xenien v, in *Sämtliche Werke* Berliner Ausgame, Bournal, 2: Teil, Poetiische Werke, 687. Trans. by A. Lenhoff. Erasmus of Rotterdam expressed the internationalist spirit even more strongly when he maintained that "for those devoted to studies, it is quite unimportant to belong to one country or another."

still *think* that their legal systems show profound differences, but they are also discovering how much law they have in common".[1] Unashamedly, therefore, the series and the book, while not ignoring the differences, were aimed at the underlying (and at underlining) similarities, common problems, and the advantages of searching together for similar or common answers.

It was at this stage, however, that it became obvious to all who took part in the seminars that the English lawyers (and for obvious reasons I am excluding Scots lawyers who have always struck me as being more internationally-minded) were not only experiencing a Europeanization of their law, which was sometimes conscious but was in other instances unnoticed, but were also teaching European lawyers in more ways than one. For example, one only has to read Professor Kötz's admiring references to English judicial styles,[2] or to listen to foreign lawyers and judges who took part in our seminar series extol the virtues and efficacy of common law advocates when they appear before European courts, or, finally, to read Lord Slynn's Hamlyn Lectures and find some areas of the law where English practice would have a beneficial impact on European law,[3] to realize the most obvious of points, namely that we can both teach in and learn from Europe. Whether one learns from Europe or one learns in Europe, the fact is that these worthy aims can only be pursued through increased contacts and an exchange of ideas of the kind we tried to organise. This is the first and best opening move towards weakening if not destroying what I called the "mentality gap". Most, if not all, of those who took part in the seminar series told us that we had been successful. The papers (and our discussions) also demonstrated a remarkable move towards the Europeanization of our law—something that can also be said (but is not here considered) about the other European systems. Though gradual, this move cannot be surprising to anyone accustomed to taking a longer view of legal developments. After all, not so long ago lawyers in Europe operated a fairly advanced *ius commune* before the modern sovereign state interrupted legal and academic as well as political co-operation. So why should not lawyers move again in that general direction, as greater economic co-operation and a growing similarity in the social environment make the world they all inhabit both smaller and its various parts more interdependent?

The purpose of this introductory chapter is to help bring these papers closer together by developing a theme which, in the eyes of this author (though, perhaps, not of all the readers of this book) could be seen as emerging from our prolonged deliberations.

---

[1] "European Public Law: Reality and Prospects", (1991) *Public Law* 53 (emphasis added).

[2] "The Role of the Judge in the Court Room: The Common Law and Civil Law Compared", (1987–91) *Journal of South African Law* 35, 41 *et seq.* "Einführungsvortrag" in *La Sentenza in Europa: Metodo Techica e Stile* (1988), 129 *et seq.*

[3] *Introducing a European Legal Order*, the Hamlyn Lectures, 43rd series (1992), 155.

2. THE PROBLEMS RAISED BY INTERNATIONAL CONFERENCES

As European integration proceeds apace the need for contacts with our Continental colleagues at different levels increases. Organising such meetings is time-consuming; and turning part or all of them into a book, so that others can get some second-hand knowledge of what took place, can give rise to difficult problems of methodology. We hope that neither of these drawbacks will deter others from following our example. For their benefit, however, and for those who profess a primary interest in comparative law and comparative methodology, this sub-section has been included in the first chapter. The general reader may thus choose to avoid it altogether, though it is not inconceivable that he too, will derive some ideas and benefits from its inclusion.

The following are some of the problems that arose; and though I explain how and why we arrived at particular solutions, I suspect that they will not meet with everyone's approval. Other choices are clearly available.

A. The Co-ordination of the Contributions

It can be argued that the best, closely-knit, truly comparative work on a particular topic remains the classic study in parallel of tort and delict by Catala and Weir.[4] Though nearly thirty years old, and despite the increase in the volume of comparative literature, no one to my knowledge has repeated their remarkable feat. One can advance a number of reasons for this.

First, the partnership was self-created or, at any rate, encouraged by the late Professor Fred Stone who had invited the two co-authors to Tulane.[5] They were colleagues of approximately the same age, with similarly penetrating legal minds, an obsession with an attractive legal writing style, and a caustic sense of humour who combined to produce a piece which, I take it, was substantially written while both authors were in the same location. An organizer of a seminar series (and, subsequently, the editor of the book that emerges from it) can hardly create such partnerships whatever his "casting" powers. If the partnership is "enforced" from above, it can rarely achieve the kind of full co-operation we find in Catala and Weir. Harris and Tallon recently produced an excellent book on the English and French law of contract.[6] Reviewers, including the present writer, expressed some doubts and misgivings about

---

[4] "Delict and Torts: A Study in Parallel", (1963) 37 *Tul L Rev* 573; (1964) 38 *Tul L Rev* 221, 663; (1965) 39 *Tul L Rev* 701.

[5] There is a hint of this in Tony Weir's elegant piece "Friendships in the Law: Essays in Honor of the Life, Legend and Legacy of Ferdinand Fairfax Stone", (1991–2) 6/7 *Civil Law Forum* 61–94. Another example, which Professor Kötz reminded me of when he kindly read the manuscript of this chapter, is Professor Schlesinger's great project entitled *Formation of Contracts: A Study of the Common Core of Legal Systems*, 2 vols. (1968) which Max Rheinstein described as "the most intensive comparison of legal institutions that has ever been undertaken". ((1969) 36 *V. Ch. L. Rev.* 448).

[6] *Contract Law Today: Anglo-French Comparisons* (1989).

it.[7] Overall, however, the book provided a well-organised, informative, and often stimulating insight into the two systems and, one hopes, others like it will follow soon. One suspects much thought went into setting up the teams of contributors who, in essence, came from Oxford and Paris. There again, one notices that the *collaboration* though no doubt *cordiale* was not always *étroite*; and the "paired contributions" were in some instances particularly "independent" whenever one of the partners wrote an overtly comparative piece, while the other merely described and reflected on his or her own legal system.

We could not ignore these lessons from the past—especially since our team was more international, our authors had no chance to get together before or after the seminars, and the time factor was, for different reasons, always working against all of us.[8] If computer-matching of the teams was thus not possible—and sometimes a neglect of the smallest details can impair the combined presentation[9]—the only thing one could do was to assign to pairs of colleagues a common general theme and let them decide between them how best to present it. Inevitably, the two halves reproduced in this book are not as closely connected as one would have liked. But we hoped that the discussions that followed the presentations (and which, in our case, lasted in each session for about two and a half hours) would achieve the desirable unity at the second phase of the proceedings. Thanks to the ability of our chairmen and the warm rapport that our speakers, without exception, established with the audience, we achieved this aim beyond our wildest expectations. This last point, inevitably, leads to the second difficulty that confronted us in this series.

B. *The Discussions: to Publish or Not to Publish?*

The previous paragraph makes the point that the unity of presentation was really achieved at the discussion phase of the seminars. It was then that differences started melting away and the search for workable solutions to common problems began in earnest. Often English practitioners would put to our foreign speakers questions that were currently concerning them and one could not help but admire how, when facing a common problem, experienced lawyers were able to by-pass totally obstacles created by concepts, awkwardly-drafted statutes, or highly specific case law. We had foreign lawyers in the audience and the same feeling of mutual understanding was obvious when they engaged in a dialogue with their English colleagues.

---

[7] [1990] 49 *CLJ*, 152–5; Collins "Methods and Aims of Comparative Contract Law" in (1991) *Oxf. J. of Leg Studies* 396–406.

[8] Nine months elapsed between the invitation to participate at the conference and the actual seminars themselves.

[9] I have, for example, noticed at international conferences the "pairing" of a very senior (in age) with a very junior colleague with the result that the former almost eclipsed the latter in the ensuing discussion. The courtesy, common sense, and great international experience of our keynote speakers ensured that this did not happen in our case.

To deprive the reader of these materials was not an easy decision to take. Yet, on balance, it could not have been otherwise. The increase in size and, consequently, cost was not one the publishers were willing to sanction, and one sympathizes with such an attitude. Harris and Tallon found a partial way round this problem by abridging the discussions and reproducing them in the third person. Some reviewers of their books found the compromise an unsatisfactory one. The vivacity of the oral discussion was lost and the abridgement in places made the text (and arguments) difficult to follow. The amount of extra time needed to prepare these summaries would have delayed further the appearance of this book. Additionally, and most significantly, our sessions were well-attended by many judges who, by speaking candidly, gave us immensely valuable insights into many of these problems. They (and others), however, had informed me in advance that the taping of the proceedings would have an inhibiting effect. Taping was omitted; and the preparation of summaries was made correspondingly more difficult. At the end of the day the discussions had to be omitted from this book.

We have tried to make up for this omission in two ways. The first—and this adds to the unusual features of this book—was by asking the judges who presided over the five sessions to give us in writing some of their personal reactions to the papers presented at their sessions. They have selflessly obliged; and their pieces, especially when combined with the keynote presentations, provide a rich, extra dimension to the comparative discussions contained in this volume.

The second way of replicating the discussions is through this introductory chapter. Though the ideas contained in it are largely mine—and in no way can they be attributed to any of our speakers, chairmen, or participants—the theme of unity and convergence was one that dominated the sessions and I have chosen to make it the leitmotiv of the book. This brings me to our third dilemma.

C. A Joint or Individual "Synthesis" of the Proceedings?

The Harris and Tallon model was, again, one that had to be considered. Some reviewers felt that the inevitable process of compromise had deprived their collaborative conclusions of "punch".[10] In retrospect, one can argue that for the kind of book that Harris and Tallon were writing this may not have been a fatal flaw; indeed, the repeated meetings held by the participants meant that this step towards formulating "common reflections" (if not conclusions) could be undertaken with some ease. We, however, did not have the luxury of many meetings; and (mainly for financial reasons) the whole team never met at the same time and place. These special factors gave me, as organiser and general editor, the opportunity to attempt my own synthesis which, inevitably, has been influenced by the aims and goals that I have pursued in my twenty-five

[10] See above n. 6.

years as a teacher of comparative law. These aims are not necessarily shared by the other participants of the seminar series, though some of the points contained here were discussed with a number of colleagues. If my colleagues do not share in the blemishes that this introduction may have, they do, however, share in such credit as may be due since the synthesis, in fair measure, is based on their papers and what was said at the meetings. In any event, it represents one possible interpretation of the large volume of material which was considered during our five sessions. If readers can draw additional or different conclusions, so much the better. Disagreements with the views expressed can only help to further the dialogue we wish to promote. The "correctness" of our views is very much of secondary importance. After all, there is no claim here of papal infallibility; just a persistent desire for more dialogue and enhanced mutual understanding. On this we all agreed without any reservations.

D. *How Broadly should the Comparative Law Net be Cast?*

It would have undoubtedly been closer to the Centre's interests if all five of the seminar series had focused on the law of obligations. The recent Law Commission Report on the Privity of Contract shows how the willingness of English lawyers to look abroad is growing, and can be developed further.[11] One need not cite other instances to show how fruitful the interchange of ideas can be in the areas of contract, tort, and restitution. So why cast the net wider to include, for example, criminal law, environmental law, and the effect that international conventions (or treaties) can have on municipal law? Our reasons for casting the net widely were mainly two (apart, that is, from the intrinsic interest that these subjects present): one practical, the other theoretical.

The practical aim was to show how international instruments are gradually helping to develop a more Europeanized English law. More is said about this in the penultimate section of this chapter. In the case of criminal law we also wished to expose English lawyers to some foreign views about non-English criminal law. The aim was again practical: to stimulate further debate in this country and make lawyers and, perhaps, laymen appreciate that "the other man's grass is not *always* greener". To put it differently, many comparatists will have been appalled over the last years to read and hear how our media have simplified foreign (mainly French) criminal law, repeatedly indicating that some of our recent infamous miscarriages of justice would not have occurred if we had a system of criminal procedure similar to the French. There can be little doubt that French or, more generally, foreign ideas, could help us rethink our own legal solutions (and incidentally, stop us seeing our police through rose-tinted spectacles). The idea of whole-hearted transplantation is

---

[11] "Privity of Contract: Contracts for the Benefit of Third Parties", Consultation Paper No. 121 (1991).

utopic at best, ludicrous at worst. We needed comparative criminal lawyers to make these points and to respond, with appropriate authority, to the specialists of the English Bar who attended that particular session.

Practical considerations have always been paramount in our minds. Yet, at the end of the day I am among those who have expressed grave doubts about the orientation that comparative law seems to have taken from the 1960s onward. Like Dante in the first tercet of the *Inferno* I felt that in its middle-age comparative law was losing its sense of direction. These doubts were advanced forcefully in the 1989 Shimizu Lecture at the London School of Economics;[12] and ever since the lecture was delivered I had hoped for the chance to organise a conference on comparative law in England which would, in a sense, provide an English answer to the French conferences organized by the Institut de Droit Comparé de Paris.[13] Over the years a number of aims have been defined for comparative law for the turn of the century.[14] They are discussed briefly in the next sub-section, but among them was the need to make municipal lawyers more comparatively minded rather than leave comparative law as the exclusive domain of the small coterie of comparatists. Criminal law seemed an obvious and topical candidate; and John Spencer, whose essay complements perfectly Professor Marty's contribution, has recognized this fact and has responded by setting up a course on comparative criminal procedure at Cambridge University after spending a year as a Visiting Professor in Paris. A great service will have been rendered to comparative law if other national lawyers were to follow John Spencer's example. This book offers yet another incentive in that direction.

E. *The Language as a Barrier to Greater Co-operation*

Any organiser of an international conference has to face the dilemma of either (a) inviting the speakers to talk in their mother language, (b) making one or two languages the official languages of the sessions, or (c) asking everyone to use the language of the forum. Each approach has advantages and drawbacks, but our opting for English as the language of the seminar series was largely prompted by practical considerations—not linguistic chauvinism.

---

[12] "Comparative Law: A Subject in Search of an Audience", (1990) *MLR* S3 1. In that article I complained of the platitudinous generalities that some comparatists use in presenting their subject. Alas, they show no sign of abatement so that for example a senior colleague in the field was recently telling a *mature audience* that "The term 'civil law' system is a convenient shorthand for those Western legal orders that arose out of the legal culture that began to develop in 1095 with Irnerius' lectures at Bologna on the newly rediscovered *Corpus Iuris Civilis* of Justinian" and that "The common law emerged in England in the course of the twelfth and thirteenth centuries". Arthur von Mehren, "The Comparative Study of Law, Essays in Honor of Ferdinand Fairfax Stone", (1991–2) 6/7 *Civil Law Forum*, 43, 44.

[13] A. Tunc and others, "L'Enseignement de Droit Comparé", (I 98 8) (1988) 4 *Rev Int de droit comparé* 703 *et seq*.

[14] In addition to the article mentioned in above n. 11, see my inaugural address at the Royal Belgian Academy, "The Destructive and Constructive Role of the Comparative Lawyer" to be published in the summer 1993 issue of the *Rabels Zeitschrift*.

By presenting their papers in English and continuing in the same language during the tiring question and answer sessions, our foreign visitors made their linguistic talents obvious and enviable! In the course of listening to them and subsequently editing their texts—in some cases constantly comparing the English version to the original—one had cause to reflect on a number of issues, two of which might provide the themes of future joint seminars.

It can be argued that English lawyers labour under a considerable disadvantage by not having access to foreign legal literature. The phenomenal success that the central European *émigrés* had in this country and in the United States in the 1940s, 1950s, and 1960s was in large part due to their linguistic abilities which enabled them to combine European (especially Germanic) doctrinal analysis with common law pragmatism in a way that was not seen before in the New World and (alas) may never be seen again in the future.[15] The measure of their success is that they made comparative law and the comparative method a recognised, even admired, topic at a time when there was really little practical need for it. It is a measure of the failure of this generation of comparatists (and the one immediately preceding it) that they have allowed the subject to flounder at a time when a shrinking world needs it more than ever. The immigration from Europe has stopped; the Rabels, the Rheinsteins, the Kesslers, the Ehrenzweigs, the Kahn-Freunds have died; the Dawsons and the Lawsons, their indigenous counterparts, have proved difficult to replace. With one or two notable exceptions, the study of foreign and comparative law experienced a "dip" in the mid-1970s and early 1980s.

Yet if we are lacking in the knowledge of foreign languages, how rich is our own; and to what effective use it has been put by the great judicial masters of the common law. Along with others, I have on timeless occasions introduced foreign audiences to the economy and confidence of Blackburn and Willis; and time and again I have recited Denning texts or declaimed those of Cardozo. Astonishingly, they may have their critics in their own countries;[16] but they have never failed to impress, even move, civilian lawyers. How much we ceded to the French, even without a legal battle, when through our absence from Europe in the 1950s we allowed them to shape the procedure and even the style of the European courts. Yet the ground is not totally lost, since the common lawyer's training and ability to refine and constantly redefine

[15] For a collection of interesting essays on the central European *émigrés* see Mosse (ed.), *Second Chance: Two Centuries of German-speaking Jews in the United Kingdom*, (1991). The immigration of the German intellectuals is discussed in different contexts by, among others, Göppinger, *Juristen jüdischer Abstammung im "Dritten Reich": Entrechtung und Verfolgung*, 2nd edn. (1990); Freyermuth, *Reisen in die Verlorengegangenheit: Auf den Spuren Deutscher Emigranten* (1990); Stiefel, "Die deutsche juristische Emigration in den USA", 1988 *JZ*, 421. American accounts include Kent, *The Refugee Intellectual. The Americanization of the Immigrants of 1933–1941* (1953) and, more recently, Grossfeld and Winship, "The Law Professor Refugee" (1992) 18 *Syracuse Journal of International Law and Commerce* 3. The multiple difficulties these scholars encountered makes their achievements even more remarkable.

[16] For a recent sympathetic and well-written appraisal see Posner, *Cardozo: A Study in Reputation* (1990).

evolving case law may prove of great use to the modern civilian lawyers, who find their law developing and adapting through cases rather than through an apparently deductive reasoning from codal article to disputed case. The study of the ways we analyse and reconcile cases, as well as the style of our judgments, could, I think, have some beneficial effects on the way foreign lawyers handle their decisional law. A jurist arguing the "English case" in Europe, should make this a key point in his presentation.

Yet, as always, the learning process is a two-way road; and it would appear that our stylistic superiority in the area of judge-made law is seriously eroded in the domain of legislative drafting, be it because of our lack of a solid legal tradition,[17] or because of our determination to be mathematically precise and exhaustive.[18] Our legislative drafting techniques could learn a thing or two from the continent of Europe. This statement could be seen as an attempt to be even-handed in one's praise and criticism of the various legal systems. It was Sir William Dale who, after a remarkable study of comparative drafting techniques, argued in favour of a style of draftmanship that would come closer to the Continental style by defining first the appropriate *general principle* and then following it up with only so much detail as order and clarity required.[19] This is no place to go into this topic, beyond repeating the claim that it would, on its own, justify a comparative conference and warrant an open mind on behalf of English lawyers who tend to assume that immutability is not only a feature but also an advantage of English law.

But let us return briefly to the impact our language can have on foreign lawyers. Take three German student text books on the law of tort written by Professors Kötz,[20] Deutsch[21] and Medicus.[22] Each of these authors is highly respected in his country for his learning, and rightly so. Yet look at the books, and if you are an English (or indeed a non-German) lawyer you will probably rank them in terms of *readability* in the order in which they were named (and German students—when asked—have always agreed). Has the obvious comparative training of the first of these jurists and his frequent exposure to common law audiences had an obvious effect? I venture the thought—and no conclusive proof can, in the absence of a "confession", be advanced—that it

---

[17] Professor Honoré's view expressed in *The Quest for Security: Employees, Tenants, Wives*, the Hamlyn Lectures, 34th series (1982), 119.

[18] "English statutes", claimed Sir Charles David, Legal Adviser to the House of Commons Select Committee on European Secondary Legislation, are "customarily drafted with almost mathematical precision, the object (not always attained) being in effect to provide a complete answer to virtually every question that can arise". Evidence submitted to the Renton Committee, Cmnd 6053, para. 52. The draftsmen of the gargantuan (and unsuccessful) Prussian Land Code of 1794 would have heartily endorsed such a statement. Sir Michael Kerr, "Law Reform in Changing Times" (1980) 96 *LQR*, 515, 527–8 thought this was "a basic and apparently ineradicable feature of our constitutional philosophy".

[19] *Legislative Drafting: A New Approach* (1977), 335.

[20] *Deliktsrecht*, 5th edn. (1991).

[21] *Unerlaubte Handlungen und Schadensersatz: Ein Grundriß* (1987).

[22] *Bürgerliches Recht*, 15th edn. (1990). This last book, however, is not limited to tort law.

has. And, more immediately, look how important this attribute is when one reads Professor Lorenz's contribution on third party beneficiaries or Professor Kötz's recent lecture[23] on (roughly) the same area of the law. The reader should note how these jurists adapt their writing for an English-speaking audience. No long sentences, no endless discussion of theory, but a masterly use of factually similar cases; those are the characteristics of their written work. They manage to make their law look more similar to ours; and make us ponder about theirs when it appears superior. For does not Professor Kötz's piece add further significance to the judgment of Lord Justice Goff (as he then was) in *The Aliakmon*[24] and make Lord Brandon's hasty rejection of it (arguably) even less convincing?[25] One may not, at the end of the day, be convinced of the superiority of German law as a result of such writings; but one will have at least been persuaded to look at it and, re-think one's own law in the light of such foreign observations, thus closing what I called the "mentality gap".

Much more comparative work remains to be done in the area of legal styles and legal translations; and, one hopes, the masterly treatise of Zweigert and Kötz, which rightly considers matters of style as forming the most substantial differences between the common law and civil law systems, will devote in its next edition more space to this neglected yet important aspect of comparative law.

3. THE ROLE OF THE EXPOSITOR OF FOREIGN LAW

A. *The Art of Making One Legal System Intelligible to Lawyers of Another*

All of us, at one time or another, will have listened to lawyers explaining a legal point to a layman using legal jargon and causing more confusion than enlightenment. Equally we will have witnessed and admired the reverse ability, possessed by some commentators, to minimise the use of jargon, go to the heart of a legal point, and make it easy for a lay audience to follow a fairly sophisticated legal argument. Some experienced legal journalists have this gift;[26] but it has not been totally denied to all law professors either.[27]

Comparative law and the use of the comparative method raise similar difficulties. It is a question of talent and deep understanding of what is being compared rather than professed expertise that gives some authors the ability

---

[23] "The Doctrine of Privity of Contract", (1990) 10 *Tel Aviv University Studies in Law*, 195.
[24] [1985] QB 350.
[25] *Leigh and Sillivan Ltd.* v. *Aliakmon Shipping Co. Ltd.* [1986] AC 785, 820.
[26] Berlins and Dyer, *The Law Machine*, 3rd edn., is a book in point. Joshua Rosenberg's television presentations of current legal affairs offer another example. Bagehot's *The British Constitution* may be the best example of a book which attained great fame largely, I believe, because of its very readable style.
[27] Professor Brian Simpson's *Invitation to Law* (1988), Professor Glanville Williams' *Learning the Law*, 11th edn. (1982), and even his quite unusual (in style) *Textbook of Criminal Law*, 2nd edn. (1983), offer good illustrations.

to present intelligibly to their own colleagues intricate aspects of foreign law. Professor Gray's *Re-allocation of Property on Divorce*[28] is one of the best (fairly) recent monographs in comparative family law; moreover, not only was this the author's first book; the author had never professed a primary interest in comparative law. By contrast, books or articles written by "professional" comparatists—and for obvious reasons it is best not to be specific—have fallen between the Scylla of excessive conceptualism and the Charybdis of almost condescending simplification. In comparative law, the absence of an impeccable legal pedigree in one system may not be a disadvantage; the qualities of a mongrel may be highly valued.

Professor Lorenz's piece is, arguably, a model of what the presentation of foreign law should be. His written style uses the shorter sentences that appeal to the English rather than the more complicated, grammatical structure associated with the German language. In this paper, though the code is not ignored, the law is presented through cases; and, wherever appropriate, the English counterparts are given. The essay not only describes German law; by giving us its answers to questions that are still vexing us, it subtly makes the reader think about his own law and its rationality. So successfully is this presentation made, that it lulls the reader, who otherwise may know nothing about German law, into thinking that it is easy, clear, and conceptually totally uncluttered. It takes a quick glance at the major treaties and the interminable discussions in the legal literature[29] on how the *Vertrag mit Schutzwirkung für Dritte* differs from the notion of *Drittschadensliquidation* to crash-land him back into reality.

But a teacher, or come to that an expert witness, who starts his presentation in such a manner, who emphasizes notions rather than actual case law, who stresses differences in classification rather than proceeding with a functional comparison of the system, will end up putting off his audience from foreign law. He will be feeding what we have called the "mentality gap", and

---

[28] Published in 1977.

[29] The German law can be found discussed in all the classic treatises as well as in the shorter but respected text books of Larenz, *Lehrbuch des Schuldrechts*, vol I, 13th edn. (1982), 201, esp. 208 *et seq.*; Esser-Schmidt, *Schuldrecht*, vol I, 6th edn. (1984), 562 *et seq.*; Fikentscher, *Schuldrecht*, 7th edn. (1985), 179 *et seq.*; Medicus, *Bürgerliches Recht*, 15th edn. (1991), 508 *et seq.* The following articles have also proved useful; von Caemmerer, "Verträge zugunsten Dritter", in *Festschrift Wieacker* (1978), 311 et seq.; Krause, "Untermieter und Mieter im Schutzbereich eines Vertrages", 1982 JZ, 16 *et seq.*; Lorenz, "Note to BGH 6. 7. 1965", 1966 JZ, 143 *et seq.*; Ries, "Grundprobleme der Drittschadensliquidation und des Vertrags mit Schutzwirkung für Dritte", 1982 JA, 453 *et seq.*; Schlechtriem, "Deliktshaftung des Subunternehmers gegenüber dem Bauherrn wegen Minderwerts seines Werks: Eine neue Entscheidung des House of Lords", (1983) *Karlsruher Forum*, 64 *et seq.*; Schwerdtner, "Verträge mit Schutzwirkung für Dritte", 1980 *Jura*, 493 *et seq.*; Sonnenschein, "Der Vertrag mit Schutzwirkung für Dritte und immer neue Fragen", 1979 JA, 225 *et seq.*; Ziegler, "Personale Abgrenzungskriterien beim Vertrag mit Schutzwirkung zugunsten Dritter", 1979 JuS, 328; Strauch, "Verträge mit Drittschutzwirkung", 1982 JuS, 823; Assman, "Grundfälle zum Vertrag mit Schutzwirkung für Dritte", 1986 JuS, 885. All of these articles contain extensive references to the rich case law.

encouraging the attitude that has kept us apart for so long: "why should I look at German law which is so obscure and different?" Professor Lorenz (and indeed some of the other contributors) show that foreign law need not be obscure; and, if it is suitably clarified, it comes closer to our own. It takes considerable exposure to international audiences to achieve such clarity.

B. *The Need to Destroy Myths*

In my inaugural address to the Royal Belgian Academy I spoke of the need to destroy myths before the work of comparative reconstruction can begin.[30] The interested reader will find there many examples of this. Here let me provide two particular illustrations, the first of which emerged during the lucid presentations made by Professors Delmas-Marty and Spencer, while the second surfaced during the discussion that followed Professor Tallon's essay.

Professor Delmas-Marty's paper is brief. Even in its English version it retains the lightness of touch that so often characterises French writing. It is uncluttered by footnotes. Yet from the very outset it explodes a leader in *The Times*[31] and other assertions similarly made in the English media about the undiluted merits of the inquisitorial system in general and the French *juge d"instruction* in particular. The Germans and the Italians had such an institution but they have abolished it. The French are having serious doubts about it. A book edited by Professor Delmas-Marty shows how comparative law should be used in such instances.[32] As Sir Robin Auld and John Spencer note, English law can be improved by using foreign ideas to adapt and reshape English institutions (for example the Crown Prosecution Service), but to talk of a wholehearted importation of foreign institutions can be naive. In this instance, for example, who would do the *"instruction"*? Sir Thomas Bingham, in a lecture delivered in the Institute of Anglo-American Law of the University of Leiden, talked of the English criminal law—warts and all.[33] This was an impressive public statement by a jurist in a position of authority who courageously admitted that we could learn from others but rightly doubted whether we were setting about this task in the right way.

The discussions initiated by the papers presented by Professor Delmas-Marty and John Spencer suggest that English criminal law may have defects but that it also has its strengths. More importantly, the borrowing of foreign ideas must be done in a subtle way that fits in with the existing environment, and does not cause more upheaval than benefit. We see this in other areas of the law. The Nordic institution of ombudsman had to be Anglicized before it was allowed to immigrate successfully. Sir David Calcutt's Report of the

---

[30] See above n. 13.
[31] *The Times*, 8 March 1991.
[32] *Procé Pénal et Droits de l"Homme* (1992).
[33] *The English Criminal Trial. The Credits and the Debits* (Leiden Institute of Anglo-American Law, 1990).

Committee on Privacy and Related Matters[34] likewise recommended the introduction of greater privacy protection, but in a way that may have made it more palatable to the English environment.[35] Our press is, of course, still flexing its formidable muscles to oppose such moves; but in the long run its current practices, sanctimoniously defended under the banner of public interest, will have to change. This is another area where foreign law and practice will show the way.

The second myth—perhaps more accurately described as a distorted picture—that foreigners have about our law concerns our techniques of statutory interpretation. Different drafting techniques have, especially in the past, undoubtedly led to a more literal interpretation of statutes by English courts. The purposive or teleological interpretation that one finds so often in the civil law system was, when not frowned upon, attributed to their more open-ended, principle-oriented, legislature drafting. For example, in *Customs and Excise Commissioners* v. *ApS Samex*,[36] Mr Justice Bingham (as he then was) said of Community law (but his views apply equally to codal provisions of Continental systems):

"The interpretation of Community instruments involves very often not the process familiar to common lawyers of laboriously extracting the meaning from words used, but the more creative process of supplying flesh to a spare and loosely constructed skeleton. The choice between alternative submissions may turn not on purely legal considerations but on a broader view of what the orderly development of the Community requires."

Though this statement presents clearly the orthodox position, it must not be allowed to conceal three important and interrelated developments. First, let us not forget the widely-phrased discretions that English statutes are increasingly vesting in judges. There may, of course, be nothing strange in "restor[ing] to the judges . . . the task of interpreting law according to statements of principle, rather than by painfully hacking their way through the jungles of detailed and intricate legislation".[37] But this may not only be happening more frequently; it may be done so broadly as to invite the application of the broader principles of interpretation which Lord Justice Bingham thought appropriate to a broad and loosely-constructed codal enactment. At any rate, common-law lawyers might be interested to read Professor Kötz's views on the discretion given by section 33 of the Limitation Act 1980 to English judges allowing them to "disapply" time-limits for actions involving

[34] Cmnd. 1102 (1990).
[35] I have elaborated this point in "Subtle Ways of Legal Borrowing: Some Comparative Reflections on the Report of the *Calcutt* Committee 'on Privacy and Related Matters' ", in *Festschrift für W. Lorenz zum siebzigsten Geburtstag* (1991), 717 *et seq.*
[36] [1983] 1 All ER 1042 at 1056. See, also, *Henn and Darby* v. *DPP* [1981] AC 850 at 905 per Lord Diplock.
[37] Lord Wilberforce speaking on the Law Commissions Bill in the House of Lords, H. L. Debates 264, 1175–6 (1 April 1965).

personal injury or death. Having "spared" the audience of his Chorley Lecture "the many words used by the parliamentary draftsmen in section 33(3) to tell the judge what factors he ought to consider in determining whether or not it is 'equitable' to disapply these time limits", Professor Kötz concluded that the discretion was so widely phrased "that a similar rule would, in this particular field of law, be unacceptable to German lawyers and, I believe, to lawyers from other Continental countries as well".[38]

Such drafting clearly makes the literal rule of interpretation redundant. But even where the legislator has spoken and spoken clearly, courts seem to be increasingly moving towards purposive interpretation. One cannot think easily of a more dry or more narrowly-conceived statute (enacted to rectify a gap in the common law) than the Employers' Liability (Defective Equipment) Act 1969, yet look what the courts did to the literal rule in *Coltman* v. *Bibby Tankers Ltd.*[39] which involved the sinking of a vessel with much of its crew. The plaintiff (the widow of a seaman), sued the defendants under the Employers' Liability (Defective Equipment) Act 1969 to be met, inter alia, by the argument that a ship could not be considered as "equipment for the purposes of this Act". Indeed, section 1(3) of the Act defined equipment as including "any plant and machinery *vehicle, aircraft* and clothing" (emphasis added). Ships were conspicuously absent from this list; and, in any event, as the Court of Appeal pointed out, "equipment" was ancillary to something else and could not be taken to refer to the workplace itself. The House of Lords reversed this judgment; and though the omission of ships from the definition of section 1(3) was described as "certainly curious", the view was taken that Parliament could not have intended to exclude ships from the ambit of the Act. The purposive construction of the Act thus won the day.

Yet these changes in the English scene, brought about by new drafting techniques and likely to increase as our courts have to interpret more European-emanating statutory material, are only one side of the coin. The reverse, and equally misunderstood (by us this time and not by our foreign colleagues) situation is the increasingly technical and detailed language used by German (and other European) enactments that have added to or otherwise affected the Civil Codes. For example, section 11(l) of our Unfair Contract Terms Act 1977 may have a counterpart in the German Standard Terms Act of 1976;[40] but the complexity of the other provisions of the German statute, and their close interrelationship with various paragraphs in the Civil Code is so great, that it would be foolish to deny that the German judge who has to apply them does not have to pay very close attention to the text of the statute.

A variety of drafting techniques may call for a variety of rules of interpretation. Whatever judges may say they do, they must, at the end of the day, strive to reach a common sense solution when interpreting statutory law. In

[38] "Taking Civil Codes Less Seriously", (1987) 50 *MLR* 1, 5.
[39] [1988] AC 276.
[40] Translated and discussed in (1978) 26 *Am J Comp L* 551.

this sense, English and Continental judges are not so very different whatever the books may say to the contrary.

C. *The Importance of Using Foreign Material to Further a Greater Understanding of One's Own Law*

From the days of the late Professor Gutteridge, if not before, this has been accepted as a significant aim of comparative law. The way in which Professor von Bar pursues it in his erudite contribution makes his piece worthy of study and not just casual reading.

Case law dominates his presentation on negligent misstatements and economic loss. In one sense this is not surprising, given the relative paucity of codal and other statutory provisions on the subject in German law. Yet what is really surprising—arguably troublesome for the reasons which I shall give below—is the excessive wealth of the German case law. Nearly 120 decisions figure in this heavily annotated text—many more than I believe can be found in English law. These are truly American proportions, incontrovertibly proving a point which some comparatists have laboured to stress when combating the "René David way of teaching comparative law": one cannot begin to understand a foreign legal system simply by studying its codes, its statutes, its text books; one must tackle and understand its case law before one can start acquiring a clear picture of the law.[41] One of the questions Professor von Bar's paper raises is how can one do this in the absence of a visibly practised system of *stare decisis*?

Falling back on the codal or statutory background is, I think, only a partial answer given the fact that, as we have already noted, the statutory signposts are few and far between. Of course, that is how the European courts start their reasoning process, using previous case law merely for illustration or supporting purposes and, in any event, much more loosely than an English court would have to do.[42] Moreover, the reference to the earlier case law does not seem to be either exhaustive or particularly analytical. My own impression—obviously that of a foreign observer of German law—is that the internal consistency of the cases is neither strong nor obvious. For the teacher who is interested in detail as much as the practitioner who is trying to obtain a focused view of the law, this must be something little short of a nightmare. Yet order may come in a different way; and one which holds out useful comparative insights both to the foreign observer and the German jurist.

The *deus ex machina* must, in part, be the German academic. Like his predecessor in the ancient Greek tragedies, his intervention may be contrived and the solution he provides only partially convincing. Yet an answer of sorts he

---

[41] My theory is elaborated in my article in (1990) *MLR* S3, 1, and put into practice in my *The German Law of Torts*, 2nd edn. (1990).
[42] See Kötz, "Einführungsvortrag" etc., above n. 2, to which add "Scholarship and the Courts: A Comparative Survey", in *Comparative and Private International Law, Essays in Honor of J. H. Merryman on his Seventieth Birthday* (1990), 183, 194.

does provide, thereby and—incidentally—continuing the long-established dialogue between judges and academics which is one of the hallmarks of German
law. What comparative lessons can one draw from this thesis, assuming it is
at least plausible?

Professor von Bar's paper is as rich in ideas as in its citation of primary
material. He offers a number of interrelated explanations that could provide
a unifying theme that would work as a guideline for future disputes. But are
the German courts likely to take advantage of such guidance? Traditionally,
of course, the interaction between German judge and jurist was constant and
close; certainly closer than one finds in other systems. The latter's theories on
numerous occasions were taken over by the former to provide a manageable
synthesis and a solid foundation of the ever-increasing case law. For example,
the BGB was still in its infancy when Staub in his monumental *Positive
Vertragsverletzungen*[43] provided the theoretical underpinnings for the most
important category of breach of contract (i.e. bad performance) which the
Code, misled by nineteenth century Romanists,[44] had omitted to regulate
alongside the other types of breach—impossibility and delay—for which codal
provisions were provided.[45] Some twenty years later, Oertmann's theory of
"basic assumption of the parties" (*Geschäftsgrundlage*),[46] reviving the
doctrine of "presupposition" (*Voraussetzung*) of his famous father-in-law
Bernhard Windscheid,[47] again provided some semblance of order to a hyperactive Reichsgericht[48] which was trying to cope with the consequences of
hyperinflation provoked in Germany by the narrow-sightedness of the victors
of the First World War. Another thirty years later and Karl Larenz was to find
the codal regulation of contracts in favour of third parties (*Vertrag zugunsten
Dritter*) lacking and was thus forced to elaborate[49] the notion by creating the
variant of contracts with protective effects *vis-à-vis* third parties (*Vertrag mit*

---

[43] *Die positiven Vertragsverletzungen* (1904).

[44] Mommsen, "Die Unmöglichkeit der Leistung in ihrem Einfluß auf obligatorische
Verhältnisse", *Beiträge zum Obligationenrecht* (1853) I. It was not until the 1920s that the wider
notion of *Leistungsstörungen* entered the scene, again under the influence of academic writers.

[45] e.g. §§ 275, 279, 280, 323–5 BGB (impossibility); 284–7, 326 BGB (delay).

[46] *Die Geschäftsgrundlage* (1921). The theory has nowadays lost some of its wide appeal; but
another academic, K. Larenz, *Geschäftsgrundlage und Vertragserfüllung*, 3rd edn. (1963) has
come up with a usable alternative.

[47] *Pandektenrecht* (1862) para. 97. It is highly likely that the Windscheid-Oertmann theories
influenced Llewellyn's drafting of section 2-615 UCC even though the latter makes no express references to the former. For Llewellyn taught in Germany when the Oertmann theory was at its
height; and in his *Casebook on the Law of Sales* (1930), 178 Llewellyn talks of "the contract
[being] abrogated by the failure of a *presupposition* upon which it was founded" (emphasis
added). The unusual (for the common law) term "presupposition" is an accurate rendering of the
German term "Voraussetzung" and this strengthens the view that Llewellyn was drawing strongly
on German ideas. The Germanic influence on Llewellyn is discussed by, among others, Whitman,
"Commercial Law and the American Volk: A Note on Llewellyn's German Sources for the
Uniform Commercial Code", (1987) 156 *Yale L J* 97.

[48] RG 3. 2. 1922, RGZ 103, 328, 332.

[49] *Schuldrecht*, I, lst edn. (1953), § 16, p. 139 *et seq.*; *idem* in 1956 *NJW*, 1193 in a note to BGH
25. 4. 1956; 1960 NJW, 77, 78 *et seq.*

Schutzwirkung für Dritte) to which both Professors von Bar and Lorenz allude in their papers. Here then—and in our present context of economic loss the third illustration is the key one—are examples where academics can provide (and have provided) the courts with theories which, if not quite as effective as the doctrine of *stare decisis*, have established a rallying theme, an anchoring point, for the purposes of bringing some sense and order to the massive case law. In practice however, things have not always worked out like that.

To an outside observer, the German courts have, in recent times and especially in the context of economic loss, broken loose from academic tutelage, ignored its criticisms, and set themselves on a course which has proved them—at least so it seems to me—more literally-minded than their English counterparts. The spreading defect theory (*Weiterfresserschaden*) offers one example,[50] the expansion of the ambit of the contract with protective effects *vis-à-vis* third parties is another.[51] Both developments hold out lessons for English law. Here, because of lack of space, a few words will be said only about the second as it has a close connection with Professor von Bar's paper.

This expansion of the ambit of the contract has taken place largely as a result of the weakening of the requirement of *Wohl und Wehe*. This has been explained elsewhere;[52] and some references are made to this "controlling device" by Professor von Bar in his paper. The courts, by ignoring it or watering it down, have struck out on a course of their own, rapidly making the compensation of pure economic loss more widely available than ever before. Whether this is the result of the availability of insurance, the possibility of contractual limitation of liability, or a sense of consumerism (far greater it would seem than is currently found in the House of Lords),[53] one cannot be sure. For present purposes it does not matter, other than to show that it has made the reconciliation of numerous decisions difficult if not impossible.

In this context, the German academic, it seems to me, has a crucial role to play, not so much in criticizing the BGH whenever its solutions offend academic purists, but in finding ways to help make its case law more consistent and more predictable. If Professor von Bar shows that German tort law is almost unpresentable and unintelligible without its case-law component, he also indirectly makes a case for the need for a greater sense of order to be brought into this case law. In his Chorley Lecture Professor Kötz quoted[54]

---

[50] On which see Hager, "Zum Schutzbereich der Produzentenhaftung", (1984) 184 *AcP*, 413; Steffen, "Die Bedeutung der 'Stoffgleichheit' mit dem 'Mangelunwert' für die Herstellerhafung aus Weiterfresserschäden", 1988 *VersR*, 977; Kullmann, "Die Rechtsprechung des BGH zum Produkthaftpflichtrecht in den Jahren 1989/90", 1991 *NJW*, 675. The academic literature that opposes these judicial trends is given in Kötz, *Deliktsrecht*, 5th edn., 28 and 29.

[51] On which see literature in above n. 29.

[52] "The Random Element of their Lordships' Infallible Judgment: An Economic and Comparative Analysis of the Tort of Negligence from *Anns* to *Murphy*" (co-authored with S. Deakin) (1992) 55 *MLR*, 621, 640 n. 115.

[53] Discussed and criticised by Jane Stapleton in "Duty of Care and Economic Loss: A Wider Agenda", (1991) 107 *LQR*, 249–97.

[54] See above n. 38, at 14.

Karl Llewellyn (who, it must not be forgotten, was a great Germanophile) who wrote in 1938:[55]

> "No one who has never seen a puzzled Continental lawyer turn to his little library and then turn out at least a workable understanding of his problem within half an hour will really grasp what the availability of the working leads packed into a systematic Code can do to cheapen the rendering of respectably adequate legal service."

One wonders, with the greatest respect to both these masters (Llewellyn and Kötz) of comparative law, to what extent this statement is still true today. Unless "workable understanding of [the] problem" is taken at the most simple level, my own feeling is that a German lawyer asked to advise on the potential liability for negligent statements towards third parties, has to do almost as much research as an American lawyer in order to find the relevant case law and to come up with a moderately workable answer. Moreover, whereas the American lawyer will have some sense of how to determine binding and persuasive precedents, his German counterpart will have to take his cue from what he finds in the standard treatises. The richness of the case law may, however, be subject to a different interpretation, justifying different and rich variations. It could thus be argued that an English lawyer—uninhibited by language barriers—could present some very intriguing possibilities to a German court as a result of the training he has received in handling cases. If I am right in this, German judges might stand to learn a great deal from the common lawyer's training in handling cases. This, then, is an area where German law can learn from our law; but the argument has not, apparently, been proved.

If the above offers an area of potential interest to German lawyers, what can we learn from them in this area of the law? Professor von Bar offers a number of ideas; indeed, he suggests that we have already picked up something from them via Lord Haldane's German education. It is, however, the wider questions that again concern me here; and the question which deserves to be considered most is how can our courts, also faced with a growing and rapidly changing case law, benefit by enlisting academics in their cause?

Clearly in the English context the role that the academic lawyer will have to play if he is to help a court of law will be new and different from that played by his German counterpart. The role here will not be one of finding a substitute to *stare decisis*, but one of assisting the judge in his research and—equally important—assisting him in placing the isolated instance of litigation that is before him against a more logical and consistent general background. The idea may be anathema to traditional common lawyers who rejoice in talking of "experience" not "logic", stressing pragmatism over theory, emphasising the *casus* over principle. For reasons that have been explained

---

[55] "The Bar's Troubles, and Poultices—and Cures?" 5 *Law and Contemporary Problems*, 104, 118.

elsewhere,[56] and which a growing number of jurists seem to acknowledge,[57] I think this combination of different talents may have to take place. I think it will; and the growing Europeanisation of English law which is currently afoot and to which the next section is devoted will make this change more rapid.

4. THE EUROPEANISATION OF ENGLISH LAW

A. *Some General Comments*

The title of this sub-heading needs some explanation to avoid creating too many misunderstandings. Thus, the reader must first be reminded yet again that these are my own conclusions or interpretations from what went on during nearly twenty meeting-hours and that none of my colleagues are in any way bound by anything other that what they included in their respective papers. Secondly, though I am talking of the Europeanisation of English law, since I have taken the vantage point of English law, I have no doubt that some of the factors discussed in this section and elaborated in some of the papers apply equally to French law, German law, and the laws of other European states. They, too, are in other words subject to the same transforming pressures. That development, however, is best left to others to document in another paper and it has thus been omitted from their account. Thirdly, one talks of the Europeanisation of English law because, as a result of multiple influences, one can argue that a new corpus of law, a kind of European *ius commune*, is gradually developing and, indeed, it may be developing faster than one is prepared to acknowledge. The Court of the European Communities may be playing a crucial role in this development, but it is not the only one. Nevertheless, the term Europeanisation may indicate the particular importance that the Luxembourg Court is having on national law and, in this sense, it seems to me even more appropriate. Having said this, however, one must stress that this was a legal conference which avoided, at least overtly, political and ideological issues or emotive terms such as sovereignty. I stress this because, even though I am not willing to hide my own bias for "things European", I think the aim that we all had was to discuss developments that were actually taking place whether we (or the majority of our compatriots) liked them or not. It thus seems to me that whereas the first four papers (Delmas-Marty, Spencer, Lorenz, and von Bar) discussed similarities— obvious or not yet discovered—and differences—real or apparent—between our various national systems, the next six speakers (Bonell, Tallon, Schermers, Francioni, Bocken, and Stephen Tromans' additional essay) have focused

---

[56] See above n. 11 and n. 13.
[57] e.g. Lord Goff in "Judge, Jurist and Legislature", (1988) 2 *Denning L Journ*, 79; "The Search for Principle" Maccabean Lecture in Jurisprudence, (1983) 69 *Proceedings of the British Academy*, 169.

wider influences or pressures on English law. Once again my colleagues' eloquent presentations speak for themselves. For my part, however, I feel there is enough material here to support the thesis that English law is progressively being Europeanised. For those who are refusing to accept it here are some points for further thought; and for those for whom the result is a sign of potential weakness, the following thought made by an historian[58] but, in my opinion, equally valuable for law could be considered:

> "in the conflict of cultures, it is more blessed to receive than to give; and the real quality of any civilisation is shown less perhaps by its indigenous products than by the way in which it constantly grafts new shoots on to its own trunk, to stimulate further growth and to achieve richer and more differentiated products".

B. From Where do These Unifying or Harmonising Pressures Stem?

To this question I would give a list of five headings. The more I think of them, the more I feel they deserve a paper of their own so that these views do not become too deformed through compression. Here I shall merely give the list, in ascending order of importance, and will only elaborate on two of them which are arguably particularly significant *at this stage of evolution of our law*.

1   Academic work in universities
2   Judges and practitioners
3   International conventions
4   EC Directives
5   The case law of the Luxembourg court

Academic work in Universities

Academia could play a very significant role in the process described in this paper and, more generally, in ensuring a stronger British presence in Europe. In reality, however, its contribution has been modest. For the research/writing currently taking place in England is, in terms of volume at least, rather meagre. Teaching offerings in comparative law, though rich in some universities, have low student attendances. Finally, exchange programmes of real academic merit are, if one is to be honest, limited to the four-year Anglo-French Programme, organised by King's College, London and Paris I for over a decade now. Four-year courses (with a one-year foreign component) are springing up; but their real impact in raising European awareness has yet to be properly measured. Other currently operating Erasmus-inspired exchanges tend to be labour-intensive to organise and of low immediate returns (since the students' stay abroad is so brief). As a long-term public relations exercise in European affairs these programmes may have their merit. But their

---

[58] Sir Hamilton Gibb, "The Influence of Islamic Culture on Medieval Europe" in Thrupp (ed.), *Change in Medieval Society: Europe North of the Alps, 1050–1500*, (1964).

short-term effect on our curriculum is limited; and on the development of our law in the European direction it must be close to nil.

Judges and practitioners

We find under this heading an intriguing development of potentially great practical significance. Given that in England there is not the close co-operation between judges and academics, it is not surprising to note that, on the whole, our judges have shown little interest in foreign legal developments (unless the case before them obliges them, so to speak, to take into account foreign law). Academic speculation about foreign law also leaves them indifferent. It is therefore particularly interesting to note that in recent times some of them have broken from the ranks and manifested an open interest in both academic and foreign law attempting, whenever possible, to make use of both of them in their judgments. In his Child Lecture in Oxford, for example, Lord Goff made the outstanding claim that comparative law was the subject of the future![59] Lord Justice Bingham, in his Francis Mann Lecture, catalogued a host of areas where English law had learned (and could continue learning) from foreign (including Scottish) law.[60] In his 1986 Denning Lecture Lord Slynn forcefully reminded his audience that:[61]

> "In the early days the impact of Community law tended to be confined to certain specialised areas and outside those areas it was unusual for points of Community law to be taken other than by specialised practitioners. What I have said shows, I think, that Community law now applies to such a variety of different areas of law that a practitioner cannot afford to ignore it. He cannot regard it as a marginal field of law to be left to specialists".

Lord Slynn's statement refers, of course, to Community law; but one must never forget that much comparative work is done both by the court's judges and Advocates General before some of their decisions are finally reached. There used to be (and still is) a symbiotic relationship between comparative law and the conflict of law; there is now a *ménage à trois*, with Community law having joined the other two. Together they are changing our law in the way described in this sub-section.

Enlightened judges with strong academic credentials are not the only practitioners' who can "internationalize" our law. Practitioners with an international practice before courts such as the International Court of Justice in the Hague, the Court of Human Rights in Strasbourg, or the Court of the European Communities in Luxembourg are accustomed to handling foreign material—indeed obliged to do so by the nature of their work—in appropriate circumstances combining it with purely English law. These working habits

[59] "Judge, Jurist and Legislature" above n. 57, at 92.
[60] "There is a World Elsewhere: The Changing Perspectives of English Law", (1992) 41 *ICLQ*, 513.
[61] Quoted by Lord Griffiths in "Civil Litigation in the Nineties", (1991) 57 *Arbitration* 7 (Aug.). 168, 171. So far as I have been able to ascertain this lecture was never published.

must, inevitably, find their way back into England when more traditional English work is being handled. Their input, however, on the Europeanisation of English law comes from their exposure to the procedure and practices of the international courts. Two examples will help bring out my point more clearly.

Civil procedure in European courts is, as everyone knows, more geared towards a written than an oral presentation of the material and pertinent arguments. Cross-examination may be, as Wigmore once wrote, "the greatest legal engine ever invented for the discovery of the truth",[62] yet the oral proceedings of the common law trial, of which cross-examination is an integral part, also has its drawbacks. Recently Lord Griffiths claimed extra-judicially that "whilst there is value in oral argument and cross examination the presentation of the trial materials and its assimilation by the judge is more quickly and efficiently performed through the written rather than the spoken word".[63]

It is difficult to imagine statements such as these coming from the lips of senior English judges thirty or even twenty years ago. In my opinion they have become acceptable (and will become commonplace) as time pressures and increased workloads, in conjunction with exposure to European trial techniques, are forcing us to review the efficiency of our methods of civil trial. Likewise our more umpire-oriented way of defining judicial duties may, in the end, give way to "court-controlled case management techniques" which are so typical of the continental European method of trial.[64]

Another topic which may soon succumb to foreign influences, (and if it does it will, again, be supported by those of our practitioners who have practised before international courts), is that of oral argument. A hallmark of the English trial since its inception may thus, once again, fall under the pressures created by time and experience acquired abroad. Lord Griffiths, again, could not have been clearer when he said that:

"I have discussed this with those who *practise* [emphasis added] both before our own appellate courts and at Luxembourg where oral argument is restricted and cases rarely last more than one day, no matter how complicated the issues. They tell me that their written submission is more detailed but they find no disadvantage in the shorter term for oral presentation which is a spur to concentration upon the crucial issues in the argument."[65]

These are remarkable changes, not least because they refer to the law of procedure which is so closely linked to the *modus operandi* of practitioners that traditional comparative lawyers regarded them as being beyond the pale of comparative law and the comparative method. It is, therefore, all the more

---

[62] *On Evidence* (1940) para. 1367, p. 28.
[63] "Civil Litigation in the Nineties", (1991) 57 *Arbitration*, 7 (Aug.), 168, 169.
[64] *Ibid.* at 169.
[65] *Ibid.* at 169–70.

significant to read a senior Law Lord express his vision of tomorrow with such confidence:[66]

> "As we have closer and closer commercial links and possibly monetary and political links as well, we shall be working with ever-increasing frequency with European lawyers. We shall have to familiarise ourselves with their practices and procedure and, of course, when working with them in Luxembourg or Strasbourg we shall all be using the same procedure. Would it not be a great step forward if we could work towards a common procedure for use by all European lawyers? Some countries who try cases through the inquisitorial procedure are now suggesting that they should make a move towards our adversarial procedures. I have suggested that the morality of our adversarial procedure needs modifying, which is perhaps a step towards the inquisitorial procedure. Can we together with our European colleagues find an acceptable middle ground?"

International Conventions
Professors Bonnel, Tallon, and Schermers provide rich material about various aspects of international conventions and how they can, directly or indirectly, mould municipal law. Their erudite discussions, when combined with the comments supplied by the judges who presided over the respective sessions, should provide much food for thought. Here I should like to continue with the harmonisation/convergence theme that I have been pursuing throughout this paper and which has been described as the Europeanisation of English law.

The warning was given earlier on that the emphasis in this chapter is on the Europeanisation of *English* law (though French, German, Italian, and the other Continental systems have been experiencing similar convergence prompted by supra-state factors such as the activities of the two European Courts). The European Convention on Human Rights, as fleshed out by the Commission and the Court, is having just such an effect, especially in the majority of the European countries which treat it as an integral part of their national law.[67] But from the English side, the old doctrine of "dualism", "*cette doctrine satanique*" as the French have called it, has provided English judges with a brake, or at least a negative excuse, whenever asked to consider its effects in cases that come before them. Once again, however, the legal explanation for the reluctance to make full use of the Convention provides only part of the answer. The English judge's hesitations on the subject can, no doubt, be traced to deeply ingrained fears about *the political* implications such an activity might have on their functions.

---

[66] *Arbitration*, 7 (Aug.), at 171.
[67] For example, Francioni, F. Francioni (ed.), "Italy and the EC: The Legal Protection of Fundamental Rights" in *Italy and EC Membership Evaluated* (1992), 191 *et seq.* Koopmans, "Judicial Review of Legislation in the Netherlands" in Cartin and O"Keeffe (eds.), *Constitutional Adjudication in European Community and National Law, Essays for the Hon. Mr. Justice T.F. O'Higgins*, (1992), 273.

Professor Jacobs, among others, has rationally confronted these fears in his excellent "The Convention and the English judge";[68] but the mentality gap remains, albeit weakening by the day.

The true situation is, in fact, much more complex as those who have studied the attitude of the courts towards the Convention have clearly shown.[69] Our courts have thus been in two minds as to what effect they should give to the Convention. The problem has divided judges, with some like Lord Scarman,[70] Lord Reid,[71] Lord Wilberforce,[72] and, most recently, Lord Goff[73] for example, arguing with varying degrees of conviction that it was hardly credible to interpret English legislation in isolation from the Convention, whereas others[74] opted for the more orthodox view that the Convention is not, technically speaking, part of the law of the United Kingdom and could thus be ignored. More dramatically, it has led distinguished judges to take contradictory views on the subject[75] or reach truly paradoxical conclusions. Professor Jacobs, it is submitted rightly, brings into this category Sir Robert

---

[68] *Protecting Human Rights: The European Dimension (Studies in Honour of Gerard J. Wiarda)* (1988), 273.

[69] For example, Duffy, "English Law and the European Convention on Human Rights" (1980) *ICLQ* 585; McCouch, "Implementing the European Convention on Human Rights in the United Kingdom", (1982) *Stanford LJ*, 147.

[70] For example in R v. *Secretary of State for the Home Department ex p. Phansopkar* [1976] QB 606; *Att-Gen.* v. *British Broadcasting Corporation* [1981] AC 303; *Whitehouse* v. *Lemon* [1979] AC 617.

[71] *R. v. Miah* [1974] 1 WLR 683.

[72] *Blathwayt* v. *Baron Cawley* [1976] AC 397.

[73] *Attorney-General* v. *Guardian Newspapers Ltd. (No. 2)* [1990] 1 AC 109, 283–4. This approach is, in turn, having an important impact on national law as *Derbyshire C. C.* v. *Times Newspapers* [1992] 1 QB 770 clearly shows. In the latter case Balcombe L.J. following *R v. Secretary of State For the Home Department, ex p. Brind* [1991] 1 AC 477, was of the view that [Article 10 of the Convention] may be resorted to in order to help resolve some uncertainty or ambiguity in municipal law (*ibid.* at 812). But he also went beyond established wisdom in arguing that "even if the common law is certain the courts will still, when appropriate, consider whether the United Kingdom is in breach of article 10" (*ibid.* at 812). Commenting on this decision Professor Fleming has asked "Why should it need a quasiconstitutional text of supranational origin to vindicate democratic values, in [the] teeth of the traditional boast that the common law is a trusted protector of such values in no need of constitutional reinforcement, such as by adoption of the very Convention here invoked?" (1993) 109 *LQR*, 12, 14. Comparative lawyers have often doubted the validity of the boast; and the case in hand demonstrates the practical significance of the international instrument. No wonder increasing numbers of senior national lawyers are advocating the formal incorporation into our law of the European Convention.

[74] R v. *Chief Immigration Officer, Heathrow Airport ex p. Salamat Bibi* [1976] 1 WLR 979, 988 (per Lane L.J.); *Malone* v. *Metropolitan Police Commission* [1979] Ch. 344, 378, (per Megarry VC); *Cheall* v. *Association of Professional, Executive, Clerical and Computer Staff* [1983] QB 126, 146 (per Donaldson L.J.). Contrast, however, Lord Denning's views in the same case at 137.

[75] e.g. Lord Denning in R v. *Secretary of State for the Home Department, ex p. Bhajan Singh* [1976] QB 188 in favour of taking into account the Convention; R v. *Chief Immigration Officer, Heathrow Airport ex p. Salamat Bibi* [1976] 1 WLR 979 (back-tracking from the earlier pronouncements); *Cheall* v. *Association of Professional, Executive, Clerical and Computer Staff* [1983] QB 126, 137 reverting to his earlier, more robust position. Compare, however, Crawford, (1982) 50 *BYIL*, 253, 282–5.

Megarry's judgment in the *Malone* case,[76] for in that case the learned judge at the outset of his judgment declared his willingness to "give the convention due consideration in discussing English law on the point". Yet when he comes to the point and finds that there is no English law, he considers himself "unable to apply the Convention".

Reviewing English law on this topic might lead one to the over-pessimistic conclusion that the Convention has had no effect on English law except to divide its judges as to how it should be handled. Such a conclusion, however, would be misleading for three reasons.

First, it implies that our difficulties with the effects that international conventions can have on municipal law are not shared by other countries. That is not true. Professor Tallon's paper, for example, refers to the contradictory attitudes taken by the two French Supreme Courts on the relationship of conventions and municipal law, a division which once led judge Pierre Pescatore to remark that we "must free ourselves from the idea of the French Republic being "une et indivisible", as contradictory positions on an identical problem of vital importance are taken on the left and on the right banks of the Seine".[77]

Secondly, excessive emphasis on our "dualist" approach might lead us to underestimate (a) the "atmospheric" effect the Convention has had on our law and (b) the indirect but obvious effect the Convention has had on law via the jurisprudence of the *Luxembourg* Court and this despite the fact that there exists no formal link between these two European Courts. More is said about this in the last subsection.

Finally, if the courts have been unable (or unwilling) to give a decisive effect to the Convention, the Convention has, through the combined activity of Parliament and administrators, in the end resulted in significant changes in our law, bringing it ever closer to European law and practice. Quoting Professor Jacobs[78] again, examples include:

> "In the field of freedom of expression, the enactment of the Contempt of Court Act 1981 in purported compliance with the *Sunday Times* case;[79] in relation to Article 3 of the Convention, the abandonment of certain interrogation techniques for detainees in Northern Ireland, and the non-use (but not the repeal) of the sentence of birching in the Isle of Man. Corporal punishment in state schools has been abolished in Scotland, and proposals made allowing an element of parental choice in England. The legislation prohibiting homosexual behaviour between male consenting adults in Northern Ireland has been amended, as have the rules governing

---

[76] [1979] Ch 344, critically discussed in "The Impact of the European Convention on Human Rights on judicial Decisions in the United Kingdom" in Turp and Beaudouin (eds.), *Perspectives Canadiennes des Droits de la Personne*, (1986), 80, 86–8.

[77] i.e. by the Conseil d''Etat and the Cour de Cassation. See Pescatore, "Conclusion" in Jacobs and Roberts (eds.), *The Effect of Treaties in Domestic Law*, (1987), 273, 281.

[78] "The Impact of the European Convention", above n. 76, 89.

[79] *The Sunday Times* case, judgment of 26 April 1979, Series A, No. 30.

prisoners' rights of access to the courts, rights of correspondence and right to marry. Legislation on the rights of mental health patients has been amended by the Mental Health (Amendment) Act 1982, the Mental Health Act 1983 and the Mental Health Review Tribunal Rule 1983. Provision has been made for compensation for employees dismissed as a result of the closed shop. The immigration rules concerning finances have been amended and further changes are in prospect as a result of cases currently in Strasbourg, as are changes in the rules of telephone tapping in the light of the *Malone* case. The overall effect that fundamental human rights can have in the processes of European integration is one that deserves closer study and proper credit."[80]

EC Directives
The enormous importance of this source of Europeanisation of our law is obvious. It can justify many articles but can clearly not be discussed here. It is mentioned merely for the sake of completeness of my list of "harmonising factors". By contrast a few words may be needed to place in its proper perspective the last and, in my opinion, most important of harmonising elements.

The jurisprudence of the Court of the European Communities
More than twenty years have gone by since Lord Denning, with his usual vision and power for imagery, described the arrival of European law.[81] In those twenty years the European Court of Justice has been hyperactive in shaping Community law not only in the way it has effected a common market but also in the way it has affected common people by promoting free movement of workers (and their families), by affecting the professions, by strengthening the legal rules of equality between men and women, and much more. Treatises and case books have multiplied over the years, but this invasion is revolutionising the contents and substance of the common law, just as the other European invasion, over eight hundred years ago, led to its emergence. The impact, in my opinion, has not been adequately studied; and this is no place (nor am I the right person) to undertake such an awesome task. Yet two illustrations might set the reader's mind in the direction I would like it to take.

What the Court has done with Article 119 of the Treaty—which addresses itself to equal pay between men and women[82]—is remarkable not only

---

[80] For further discussion see Frowein, Schulhofer, and Shapiro, "The Protection of Fundamental Human Rights as a Vehicle of Integration" in Cappalletti, Secombe, and Weiler (eds.), *Integration through Law*, Series A, i: 3 (1986), 300.

[81] "The Treaty is like an incoming tide. It flows into the estuaries and up the rivers. It cannot be held back". *Bullmer Ltd.* v. *Bolinger SA* [1974] 1 Ch. 401, 418.

[82] "Each Member State shall during the first stage ensure and subsequently maintain the application of the principle that men and women should receive equal pay for equal work . . . For the purpose of this Article, 'pay' means the ordinary basic or minimum wage in salary and any other consideration, whether in cash or in kind, which the worker receives, directly or indirectly, in respect of his employment from his employer."

through its wide interpretation of "pay" but also by then declaring it to have direct effect. The combined effect has been not only to extend equal opportunity law in general but also to provide, in Lord Slynn's words, an excellent example of the way in which Community law can have an impact on English law".[83] The same has happened with the Court's broad interpretation of Article 48 of the Treaty, especially the words "worker" and "activity as an employed person".[84] National judges have, in this respect, followed Community law definitions rather than national legal definitions, and the harmonising effect achieved in this and related areas of the law has been, again, considerable throughout the Community states.

The second way in which the Court's jurisprudence has affected our law was by its taking over the European Convention on Human Rights, making it part of Community law, and in this way openly penetrating countries (like England and Denmark) which have refused to give direct effect to the Convention. *Johnston* v. *Chief Constable of the Royal Ulster Constabulary*[85] offers a good illustration of this.

Mrs Johnston was in full service with the Royal Ulster Constabulary. When the Northern Ireland police were instructed to carry arms, the Chief Constable decided that women should not be allowed to do so lest they become terrorists targets. Mrs Johnstone was thus dismissed. She considered her dismissal as contravening the Northern Ireland equivalent of the British Sex Discrimination Act, but the police relied on its article 53[86] which expressly stated that nothing in the Order could render unlawful anything done for the purposes of national security and public order. For good measure it added that a certificate from the Secretary of State 'shall be conclusive evidence that these conditions are fulfilled". The Industrial Tribunal which heard Mrs Johnston's case referred the case to the European Court under Article 177 of the Treaty seeking a preliminary ruling as to whether the dismissal, though in conformity with the Northern Ireland Order, contravened the 1976 Directive

---

[83] *Introducing a European Legal Order*, the Hamlyn Lectures, 43rd series (1992), 127.

[84] But the "interference" with national law has come in other ways as well as the *Van Duyn* v. *Home Office* case—[1974] ECR 1337—shows. That dispute stemmed from a decision taken by the British Government in 1969 to consider Scientology as socially harmful and, henceforth, to deny to foreign nationals the right to enter the UK and work for that Church. When in 1973 Miss van Duyn was denied entry, she sought a declaration in the High Court that the refusal was contrary to Article 48 of the EC Treaty and Article 3 of Directive 64/221. On an Article 177 referral, the European Court held, inter alia, that "By providing that measures taken on grounds of public policy shall be based exclusively on the personal conduct of the individual concerned, Article 3(l) of Directive No. 64/221 is intended to limit the discretionary power which national laws generally confer on the authorities responsible for the entry and expulsion of foreign nationals" and, further down, the Court added: "It should be emphasised that *the concept of public policy* in the context of the Community and where, in particular, it is used as a justification for derogating from the fundamental principles of freedom of movement for workers, *must be interpreted strictly, so that its scope cannot be unilaterally determined by each member State without being subject to control by the institutions of the Community*" (emphasis added).

[85] Case 222/84, [1986] ECR I-1663; [1987] QB 129.

[86] Sex Discrimination (Northern Ireland) Order 1976, SI 1976 No. 1042 (N.I. 15).

seeking to establish equal treatment for men and women with regard to employment. For the European Court of Justice the crucial question was whether article 53 could effectively bar English judges from ensuring effective compliance with the Directive. The Court took the view that "Article 6 of the Directive requires Member States to introduce into their internal legal systems such measures as are needed to enable all persons who consider themselves wronged by discrimination to pursue their claims by judicial process".[87] It followed, in the Court's reasoning, that Member States had to take all measures necessary to ensure "that the rights thus conferred may be effectively relied upon before the national courts by all persons concerned". This need for effective *judicial* control reflected nothing other than a general principle of law found in all Member States and, in fact, reflected in Article 6 of the European Convention on Human Rights.[88] The conclusion, bringing these different strands of thought together was, inevitably, that article 53 was contrary to the Directive as it "allow[ed] the competent authority to deprive an individual of the possibility of asserting by judicial process the rights conferred by the Directive". Judge Koopmans has summarized this as follows:[89]

> "The Court's judgment illustrates the force of the combined effect of different lines of legal evolution in Europe. It extrapolates a provision of the European Convention into a Community Directive because it embodies a general principle. The Directive is not only to be implemented by legislative or administrative action: national courts are to respect its provisions when interpreting and applying their national law. European legal developments have a kind of dynamics of their own."

How right judge Koopmans is when talking about the European "dynamics"! A glance at the developing law of European environmental protection makes this obvious, for the protection of the environment was conspicuously absent from the original Treaty of Rome. Then, as those halcyon days receded into the background, and the (largely) self-inflicted destruction of the environment became increasingly apparent, the era of EC activity was ushered in under the general principles of the Community or on the basis of "Implied powers". As Professor Francioni shows in his thoughtful piece, the foundations were thus firmly laid for future, more specific, regulatory measures. And now, on the eve of the Single European Market and, who knows, one day of some form of European Union, this European activity is seen by many as a necessary component of the Single Market, and with inevitable harmonising effects on domestic environmental standards.

---

[87] Quotations from [1986] ECR I-1680, 1682–3.

[88] Traditionally seen as guaranteeing a fair trial but since the *Golder* case—*Golder* v. *UK* [1975] 1 EHRR 524—increasingly having shaped rights of access to courts—an excellent example of judicial creativity which has ultimately affected national laws.

[89] "European Public Law: Reality and Prospects", (1991) 53 *Public Law*, 61.

5. ARE THE COMMON LAW AND CIVIL LAW
SYSTEMS CONVERGING?

The preceding paragraphs should leave the reader in no doubt that convergence is taking place. The convergence is gradual and, indeed, patchy (i.e. more obvious in some areas than in others despite the dynamics of the case law of the European Court which, I believe, has accelerated the convergence process). There is thus a convergence of solutions in the area of private law as the problems faced by courts and legislators acquire a common and international flavour; there is a convergence in the sources of our law since nowadays case law de facto if not de jure forms a major source of law in both common and civil law countries; there is a slow convergence in procedural matters as the oral and written types of trials borrow from each other and are slowly moving to occupy a middle position; there may be a greater convergence in drafting techniques than has commonly been appreciated and this is bound to lead English law closer to purposive interpretations; there is a growing *rapprochement* in judicial views (the abolition, for example, of the old prerogative writs brought English law much closer to its continental counterparts); and, I think, the apparently amorphous concepts of "proportionality" and "just expectations" may be creeping into English law (assuming that on proper analysis they were not there already). Judicial styles may remain more different since common law judges still seem to talk to everyone who is prepared to listen (or must listen), German judges only talk to intellectual equals, and French judges (at the highest levels) keep their thoughts to themselves!

This assessment is not, I think, shaped by my international background and European-oriented outlook. The points raised in our various papers and in this first chapter will, I think, if further pursued, substantiate the convergence theory even though it is gradual (as indeed it should be) and the title of the book acknowledges. But I think it is also justified by the underlying socio- economic similarities one finds these days in most of Europe (and this despite the current craze of ethnic separation and violence). Increased travel, enhanced communications, greater urbanisation, and closer interdependence of national economics, have all combined to make the kind of problems that have to be resolved by the law similar, to weaken or discredit more traditional ways of resolving such disputes, and to raise (at times unreasonably) the expectations that citizens have of the state and the law. All these factors have, in my opinion, favoured growing assimilation—increasingly through court activity.[90]

Take the first point: similarity of problems. It would be wrong to assume that this was always as strong as it is today. Look, for example, at the French

---

[90] See, more generally, Koopmans, "The Future of Legal Systems", The David Hume Institute, Hume Occasional Paper No. 13 (1990).

law of contract or, more particularly, the topic we call frustration. At the turn of the twentieth century or during the First World War, though intellectually French law had an uninterrupted link with Roman law and medieval philosophy, thus presenting impeccable intellectual credentials, its case law was simple, agrarian, and at times very quaint in appearance. When contrasted with the English law of the time, predominantly commercial and maritime in flavour, it leaves one in no doubt that the kind of cases that were shaping the developments of the law in these two countries were as often as not very different in their factual content. Yet look at our law of contracts now and you see in all European countries how the kind of problems that face all our courts are very similar, I suspect to a large extent as a result of the appearance in the 1960s, or thereabouts, of the consumer as a litigating party. To be sure, the richness of national case law is such that there is evidence to support any contrary theory. One should, however, be intrigued by the growing similarity of problems that are litigated by national courts and, indeed, I have made this a central theme of a new methodological approach to comparative law.

The second factor I mentioned—the weakening of family ties, religion, neighbourhood bonds, and the growing distrust of authority—also contribute to the assimilation process I have stressed. As traditional ways of coping with the vicissitudes of life are weakened,[91] citizens tend to become more willing to seek their remedies in a court of law. This, combined with the third factor—the growing awareness of entitlements—makes modern citizens more anxious to assert their rights in court. Differences of mentality—for example, is litigation the first or last resort in the dispute resolution process—are changing attitudes and, in the process, reducing long-standing differences with other systems such as that of the United States.[92] The growth of litigiousness is equally provoked by the State's increased hyperactivity in favour of the citizen. For more administration inevitably brings more maladministration and more rights generate a greater willingness to assert them. Growing distrust in the political and administrative process can only enhance in the minds of many citizens the importance of the courts in the establishment and protection of rights and entitlements. The task the modern courts face is formidable; the responsibility awesome; their opportunity to harmonise legal systems indisputable (even if not always very obvious). The European Courts are, I think, showing how legal assimilation can by-pass political differences and

---

[91] Cf. the observations of the former Chief Justice of the United States Supreme Court Warren E. Burger: "One reason our courts have become overburdened is that Americans are increasingly turning to the courts for relief from a range of personal distresses and anxieties. Remedies for personal wrongs that once were considered the responsibility of institutions other than the courts are now boldly asserted as 'entitlements'. The courts have been expected to fill the void created by the decline of church, family and neighborhood unity." "Isn't there a Better Way", (1982) 68 *American Bar Association Journal*, 274, 275. As I tried to argue in my "Litigation Mania in England, Germany and the USA: Are we so very different?" [1990] 49 *CLJ* 232 *et seq.*, those trends may be arriving in Europe as well.

[92] On which see my "Litigation Mania in England", above n. 91, at 233 *et seq.*

slowly guide Europe towards a new era of a more internationally-based system of law and order. Time only will show if power politics will cause cracks in the edifice of the rule of law as they have done so many times in the past. But until that happens, the harmonisation made in Europe seems, to me at least, unstoppable.

10

Bridging Legal Cultures

1. THE INTERNATIONALIST MENTALITY

The main object of the Cohen Lecture is to promote and encourage learning in the subject of English law at the Hebrew University. I would like to approach this task in a different and somewhat unorthodox way by emphasising a virtue that English law arguably had more in the nineteenth[1] century than in the mid-twentieth century and which, in any event, it will be forced to develop more on the eve of the twenty-first century. I shall call it "the spirit of open-mindedness and internationalism". Some, with current English Europhobia in mind will, no doubt, find this approach un-English; a few might even resent it. Yet flexibility has, I think, always been a virtue admired by the English and espoused by their law; and, generally speaking, in the conflict of cultures throughout the ages it has, invariably, been a sign of strength to receive as well as to give. For, in my view, the quality of any civilisation can be seen not only in its indigenous products but also in the way it constantly grafts new shoots onto its own trunk, in order to stimulate further growth and to achieve richer and more differentiated products. In any event, adopting this angle seems to me particularly appropriate on this occasion since it admirably links the English and Jewish components of my lecture and also sets it firmly in the central European, mainly Germanic, context which has always held for me a great intellectual appeal.

No one who has even the slightest idea of the international exchange of ideas has, of course, ever doubted the significant role played by Jewish/Central European lawyers.[2] But it is the mentality and personal characteristics of some of these jurists which have attracted me as much as their work, but which has not yet been adequately studied. Certainly, in the field of comparative law, most of those whom I have been lucky enough to meet combined Germanic education and thoroughness with Jewish tenacity and

---

[1] In *Cox* v. *Troy* (1822) 5 B & All. 474, at 480; E.R. 1264, Best J. boldly asserted that the authority of Pothier's *Treatise on the Law of Obligations* was "the highest that can be had, next to a decision of a court of justice in this country". Pronouncements such as this continued throughout the 19th century, and by its close Savigny (and other Germans, such as Gierke) were exercising a considerable intellectual influence on both English and American jurists.

[2] See K. Lipstein, "The History of the Contribution to Law by German-speaking Jewish Refugees in the United Kingdom" in W. Mosse (co-ordinating ed.), *Second Chance: Two Centuries of German-speaking Jews in the United Kingdom* (1991) 221–7 and, more recently, M. Lutter, E.C. Stiefel, M.H. Hoeflich (eds.), *Der Einfluß deutscher Emigranten auf die Rechtsentwicklung in den USA und in Deutschland* (1993).

resourcefulness, as well as being possessed of the wide culture of Renaissance humanism (something which *planners* of modern legal education seem to underestimate and, even, downgrade). They were also, in terms of outlook, citizens of the world, being Jewish and English, Jewish and German, Jewish and American, astute in taking what was best in other people's laws while preserving, where it was desirable, the salient features of their own culture. Goethe's lines[3] could, I think, be applied to them as they may well apply to the next generation of European lawyers:

> "I greet you, brothers
> Partisans of various 'isms' and 'slogans'
> As for me, I am a world citizen
> As well as Weimarian."

I honestly believe that the cosmopolitan education and outlook of these scholars must be borne in mind when assessing the significance of their work; and it holds the key to the kind of attributes and attitudes which will be relevant to the lawyers of tomorrow who, in my view, will be shaping a new *genre* of *ius commune* and will be aided in this task by the work of the Court of European Communities. But if a *ius commune* existed in the past and is likely to appear again within the European context, this will in the future (as it was in the past) be in no small measure due to the kind of jurists who will develop it: devoid of nationalistic arrogance, extrovert in disposition, able to withstand the special kind of isolation that their approach often brings in its initial phases. That, in my opinion, is the definition of the modern comparatist who, whether he is an academic or an open-minded judge, is thus forced to realise that he *has* to study more than he can ever fully digest. This leads to an intense, omnivorous erudition; but it also comes with a sense of desperation as he realises early on in his career what Socrates proclaimed towards the end of his: that the more one reads the less one really knows. Yet the quest for understanding others as much as learning about them must and will continue, especially in our shrinking world. And often, by accident rather than by design, it leads to some unique insights into the law and its rules, as well as underscoring the commonness of human suffering and the universality of the basic notions of justice which one's nationalistic schooling has done so much to blur.

2. A DIALOGUE WITH JUDGES AND A DIALOGUE BETWEEN JUDGES

So how does one set about encouraging such an internationalist approach? In my view by promoting, among other things, a greater partnership between

---

[3] *Gedichte, Zahme Xenien* V, in *Sämtliche Werke*, Deutscher Klassiker Verlag, I Abteilung, 2. Band (Gedichte 1800–1832), (1988), p. 661.

academic and judge, and then ensuring that they meet their colleagues from other jurisdictions as often as possible. The first part of this proposal is, of course, largely a Continental and not an English idea; but it can be made more palatable to English lawyers, if one begins by giving prominence to the English judge and then encourages him to increase his contacts with judges from other systems. This is based on the belief that in England (and, perhaps, elsewhere) interest in foreign law will grow if our judges can be persuaded that its knowledge will help them in their work. This interest is bound to be stimulated whenever practitioner meets practitioner and sooner rather than later realises that despite a different legal history and different methodology, the problems they both face are similar, calling for analogous if not identical solutions.[4]

Not only that. Through such meetings judges can also ask themselves to what extent the similarity of the problems they face may be forcing them to consider implicitly, but not explicitly, the same underlying policy factors, thereby in most cases being pushed towards similar solutions. To put it differently and in a more specific tort context, the regulation of tort liability provided by section 823(1) BGB may appear to be very different to our tort of Negligence; but in the interpretation of its constituent elements judges may, for example, be paying special attention to the fact that the plaintiff (or defendant) may be a consumer rather than a commercial entity; whether the statutory framework has been rendered too restrictive with the passage of time and has to be bypassed by means of bold interpretations; which type of insurance (first or third party) is available or preferable,[5] and so forth. If these points surface in discussions between judges from different systems, as I think they will if the approach adopted is functional rather than conceptual, one may discover that, for example, consumer protection is more in the mind of the German judge, but, as of late, left to the legislature by his English counterpart.[6] More importantly, however, this way of proceeding will have succeeded in establishing a judicial dialogue between judges from different legal families. For in this way judges will end up talking about the same things and will not be lost in a paradise (or hell) of legal ideas and concepts. Our first aim, therefore, must be to get a dialogue going; and for this to happen we must make the two sides realise how much they have in common.

---

[4] In this paper my comments will focus mainly on English and German law, not only because these systems have, in recent times, represented my own prime interests, but also because they formed the basis of the legal learning of many of the comparatists whose work I admire. But most of my observations also apply to other legal systems (e.g., the French) which have just as much to offer to the English lawyer.

[5] A good discussion, in the context of pure economic loss, can be found in *Norsk Pacific Steamship Co. Ltd.* v. *Canadian National Railway Co.* [1992] 1 S.C.R. 1021 (Supreme Court of Canada), discussed by Fleming, (1993) 1 *Tort L. R.* 68–74; Markesinis, (1993) *L.Q.R.* 5–12.

[6] See, for example, Lord Bridge in *D & F Estates Ltd and Others* v. *Church Commissioners for England* [1988] 1 AC 177, at 210. Cf. Hayes, "After Murphy: Building on the Consumer Protection Principle" (1992) 12 *O.J.L.S.* 112.

Capturing (or should I say recapturing)[7] the imagination of the common lawyer will be a great coup for German legal culture; but the reverse will also occur and, in my opinion, the jurists from the Roman-German world also stand to be enriched by exposure to the English judicial mind. To be sure, this is not cast in a theoretical mode. One cannot, for example, find in my country a judge matching Dr. Steffen's piece[8] on *Mangelschäden* or *Stoffgleichheit*, partly because the particular problems connected with these terms are more tender in age in English law than in Germany, but largely because the English judicial mind is at its best when handling, defining, and re-defining complex case law rather than when it is forced into system building and deductive reasoning. For the English judge would, instinctively, feel much sympathy for Goethe's famous words *"Grau, teurer Freund, ist alle Theorie, Und grün des Lebens goldner Baum"*[9] until, that is, he is reminded that these words are put into the mouth of Mephistopheles at which stage judicial caution may lead him to invoke the words of the more respectable Mr. Justice Holmes who, nevertheless, echoed the same idea when he claimed that "the life of the law has not been logic; it has been experience".[10] But in the analytical and inductive techniques of the English judge one may find one of the (many) areas where English law can make a particular contribution to continental European legal science; and this is not to mention the refreshing flavour that the literary style that English judgments can bring into the often abstract law of, say, the German jurist.[11] For German tort law, to take the area of private law which will receive particular attention in this lecture, strikes me as being increasingly case law oriented; and this massive raw material is not free from contradictions—at least to an outside observer. A greater sense of order could, I think, be brought to it if the task of analysis and synthesis could come not only from the practitioners' treatises, but also from the judge, himself, using earlier decisions as building blocks rather than as supporting ornaments.

[7] Among recent studies describing the influence of German scholars on American legal thought see Hoeflich, "Savigny and his Anglo-American Disciples" (1989) 37 *Am. J. Comp. L.* 17; Kegel, "Story and Savigny" (1989) 37 *Am. J. Comp. L.* 29; Whitman, "Commercial Law and the American Volk: A Note on Llewellyn's German Sources for the Uniform Commercial Code" (1989) 37 *Am. J. Comp. L.* 156; Grossfeld and Winship, "The Law Professor Refugee" (1992) 18 *Syracuse J. of Intl L. and Commerce* 3—all with rich further references. Reimann, "The Historical School Against Codification: Savigny, Carter, and the Defeat of the New York Civil Code" (1989) 37 *Am. J. Comp. L.* 95. See, also, the more recent literature quoted above n. 2.

[8] Steffen, "Die Bedeutung der 'Stoffgleichheit' mit dem 'Mangelunwert' für die Herstellerhaftung aus Weiterfresserschäden" 1988 *VersR*, 977. For a German-American discussion of the topic, see Bungert, "Compensating Harm to the Defective Product Itself—A Comparative Analysis of American and German Products Liability Law" (1992) 66 *Tulane L. R.* 1179. One must not assume, however, that English judges are incapable of very sophisticated analyses of doctrinal issues. For a recent illustration of my point, see Sir Michael (now Lord) Mustill's "Anticipatory Breach", *Butterworth Lectures 1989–1990* (1990) 1–78.

[9] Faust, II, 2038–9 ("Grey, my dear friend, is all that theory is, and green the golden tree of Life").

[10] O. W. Holmes, *The Common Law* (1881) 1.

[11] Discussed in my inaugural lecture at University College London under the title "A Matter of Style", to be published in the October 1994 issue of the *Law Quarterly Review*.

3. HELPING THE JUDGE

A. *The Problems of Language*

By wishing upon us future meetings and a judge-orientated approach I am not, as stated, betraying or belittling the role of the academic scholar. On the contrary, I am creating a new and real need for his services. For the judge alone, be he English, German, or Israeli, cannot utilise, without assistance, the foreign material in which he has been induced to develop an interest. Recently Mr Justice Barak confirmed that "language boundaries impair [the Israeli and Roman-Germanic systems] from cross-fertilizing one another". He continued: "The developments in Roman-German law, both in judicial decisions and the academic literature, are a closed book to the vast majority in the Israeli legal community".[12] In my opinion, in intellectual terms this is a great loss not only because contemporary German "decisions" and "literature" are very rich in ideas, but also because, as the learned Justice stressed in the same lecture, "In nature, purpose and content, our [i.e. Israeli] codification process was heavily influenced by Continental law".

The first task which thus faces the lawyer—academic or practitioner—who wishes to interest the judge in foreign law is the task of interpretation and (which is more difficult) an appropriate adaptation of the foreign material in order to make possible its immigration into his national law.[13]

Thus, starting at the most basic level, the very terms "common law" and "equity" are untranslatable in French or German; and, conversely, *ius civile* may call for a contextual rendering. Other terms can tempt the translator into a literal translation which is misleading (e.g. *magistrature* into magistracy or *magistrat*[14] into judge) or a superficially obvious functional rendering which, at the very least, may give in the translation language only a partially correct picture of the notion or office as it is understood in the "source language" (e.g., Master of the Rolls as *premier président de la cour d'appel de l'Angleterre et de Pays de Galles*). The same is, of course, true when we are faced with German legal terms such as *Verkehrspflichten* which should not, I think, be translated as "duties in traffic" but as "duties of care".[15] More generally, the

---

[12] Aharon Barak, "The Israeli Legal System—Tradition and Culture" (1992) 40 *HaPraklit* 197.

[13] The institution of Ombudsman, and its reception by English law, offers a good illustration of this process.

[14] As Professor David has done (*English Law and French Law* (1950) 50) since: (a) judges at the Conseil d'Etat are not, strictly speaking, *magistrats* and (b) the magistrature includes the *parquet* (which is another distinctive French institution). Here David is right in translating magistrature as the bench.

[15] Though Professor Rudden, in [1987] *C.L.J.* 162, was inclined to call this a "bold" (too bold?) Anglicisation of the German term. The *Wörterbuch für Recht, Wirtschaft und Politik*, II, 4th edn. (1992) by Dr. Erika Dietl, Professor Egon Lorenz (and others) renders the term as a "duty to safeguard traffic; duty (or obligation) of occupier to make land or premises safe for persons or vehicles". In my opinion classic monographs such as Professor von Bar's *Verkehrspflichten* (1980) suggest that the dictionary definitions may be too narrow and that nowadays "duties" in

same is true of the term *im Verkehr* which appears in § 276 BGB ("*Fahrlässig handelt wer die im Verkehr erforderliche Sorgfalt außer Acht läßt*") and which should, I think, be rendered "in daily affairs" or "every-day life". Instead, the second sentence of this article of the Code is commonly translated in such a way as to advise human beings to "exercise the care required in *ordinary intercourse*" or else they will be regarded as being negligent. From my teaching experience I know that such a rendering of the German original can make the English reader wonder (not entirely tongue in cheek, especially if the text is unaccompanied by a contextual explanation) whether it is really necessary for the Code to be concerned with "safe sex"! Finally, consider the important but almost untranslatable term *Weiterfresserschäden* which even the best specialised dictionaries[16] do not even attempt to translate but which could be (circuitously) rendered as "insidious loss" (caused by an inconspicuously spreading and harm-producing defect already existing in a chattel). Indeed, it takes a good deal of imagination to use the word that describes how animals (rather than humans) eat (*fressen/essen*) as a basis of conceptual thinking for modern product liability law! The late Professor Gutteridge was thus, it is submitted, only partially correct when he maintained that the "pitfalls of terminology are the greatest difficulty and danger which the student of comparative law encounters in his novitiate"[17] since these terminological difficulties are, in my opinion, bound to haunt the comparatist throughout his life.

B. *The Problem with Concepts*

I have already hinted at the fact that the interpretation that we must attempt in order to help our judges in their task must be a double one. First is the linguistic interpretation. Then comes what, for lack of a better term, I call the creative interpretation. The difficulties of the first type have already been alluded to; and I think the Italians are frequently right when they equate the *traductore* with the *traditore*. But the second type of interpretation—the creative one—requires more than linguistic skills; it requires the acquisition of a "feeling" for the other system, the mastery of a form of intellectual juggling (as one of my students once put it) which allows the matching of different concepts and notions. Professor Kötz once quoted Bernard de Clairvaux who

---

multifarious situations (beyond traffic and premises) can be brought under the heading. Incidentally, the use of the term in the plural is also indicative of the fact that German law, like English law, does not accept that the latin-phrased exhortation *neminem laedere* constitutes a legal principle.

[16] For example, the *Wörterbuch für Recht, Wirtschaft und Politik* by Dr. Clara-Erika Dietl, Professor Egon Lorenz (and others) (1956). The expanded and revised 4th edition of 1992 defines the term as "damage which has spread [into] the defect-free portion of purchased property from a defective part".

[17] "The Comparative Aspects of Legal Terminology" (1938) 12 *Tulane L. R.* 401, at 403. Martin Weston's *An English Reader's Guide to the French Legal System* (1991) makes, especially in its first three chapters, some very interesting points about the difficulties of overcoming conceptual differences.

said: "*res in tantum intelligetur in quantum amatur*".[18] This feel for *foreign law* (and the foreign culture) can only spring from an intense love affair with it; a love affair which only a true comparatist can experience; and it is this experience which the comparatist can try to transmit to his national judge. Let me give you one illustration which shows how I see the partnership developing.

The example comes from tort law: and the starting point is the German *Testamentfall* case of 1965.[19] The problem and the solution are identical in English,[20] German[21] and American law,[22] all of which allow a frustrated beneficiary of a badly drawn-up will to sue the lawyer who drafted it negligently. Where there is considerable disagreement between the systems (and, sometimes, within one system) is as to the nature of the cause of action: is it contractual or tortious or both, and does the characterisation really matter at all?[23] The quick answer, of course, is that it is contractual in Germany, tortious in England and, in the United States the kind of hybrid which, in the late Dean Prosser's words, is the result of the illicit cohabitation of contract and tort.[24]

The cause of action is not the only thing that is different; the terminology is also different and revealing when compared to, say, French law which, like German law, recognises contracts in favour of third parties. For then the superior Germanic ability to theorise, borne in this instance from a defect in the Civil Code,[25] becomes apparent. For years the concept of *Vertrag mit Schutzwirkung für Dritte* was, in England, rendered as contract in favour of a third party.[26] I am inclined to believe that I was the first[27] to coin a more appropriate English term for this variation of the contract in *favorem tertii* by calling it a contract with protective effects *vis-à-vis* third parties, though my paternity has not, I think, been publicly acknowledged!

---

[18] (1987) 35 *Am. J. Comp. L.* 857, at 858 reviewing the first edition of my book *The German Law of Torts* (1986). The third edition will appear in 1994.

[19] BGH 6. 7. 1965, NJW 1965, 1955; JZ 1966, 143 *et seq.*, note Lorenz.

[20] *Ross* v. *Caunters* [1980] Ch. 297.

[21] To above n. 19, add: BGH 11. 1. 1977, NJW 1977, 2073.

[22] *Biakanja* v. *Irving* 320 P.2d 16 (1958); *Lucas* v. *Hamm* 364 P.2d 685 (1961); *Heyer* v. *Fleig* 449 P.2d 161 (1969).

[23] In my "An Expanding Tort Law—The Price of a Rigid Contract Law" (1987) 103 *L.Q.R.* 354 I gave my reasons why I think the proper characterisation of the cause of action has practical significance. See, also, my "Doctrinal Clarity in Tort Litigation: A Comparative Lawyer's Viewpoint", (1991) 25 *The International Lawyer* 953. If my approach is heretical, I am happy to know that I shall burn in good company since similar views have been expressed by Professor Kötz in his "The Doctrine of Privity of Contract" (1990) 10 *T.A Studies in L.* 195.

[24] Prosser, *Handbook of the Law of Torts*, 4th edn. (1971) 634.

[25] Para. 831 BGB. For further details in English see Markesinis, *The German Law of Torts: A Comparative Introduction*, 2nd edn. (1990) 499–502; 576–606.

[26] For example, Zweigert and Kötz, *An Introduction to Comparative Law*, 2nd edn. (1987) vol. II, 145 *et seq.* translation by Tony Weir.

[27] Lawson and Markesinis, *Tortious Liability for Unintentional Harm in the Common Law and the Civil Law* (1982) vol. II, p. 98.

But why a different term? The different rendering requires an explanation; and the explanation requires a broader understanding of the German Code. This is important in England, as well. For if the present trend[28] to cut down the incidents of tort recovery for pure economic loss continues, *Ross* v. *Caunter*,[29] the English case which allowed tort recovery in such cases, may not be as unassailable as it has hitherto been. If, therefore, this factual situation is to continue justifying recovery, as I think it must, it may somehow have to be handled under contract. But, as the Law Commission recently showed in my country, this may not be so easily done by subsuming this case under the more traditional notion of contracts in *favorem tertii*.[30] Thus, for different reasons, English law may be forced to draw some lessons from the German experience. To put it differently, it may have to use some kind of contractual thinking if it wishes to preserve the legal result that it currently adopts; and if this is too much for any English judge to attempt, then he must be quick to stress that the tort action he is more accustomed to, is determined in scope and extent by the underlying contract between testator and attorney. This is not the place to discuss this issue in any great detail; but you will have noted, however, that what started as a translation problem, was quickly turned into something more complicated and more significant, requiring a "background" explanation before it can be used by an English practitioner.

I have compressed here much material and quite a few ideas but I think I can claim that as a result of the work done (in the English language) by Professors Lorenz,[31] Kötz,[32] von Bar[33] and others,[34] much of all this has become quite recognisable to English lawyers. And this is exactly what I have in mind when I say that the academic can help the practitioner.

C. *The Unpublicised Movement of Ideas*

The movement of ideas is not always obvious or publicly acknowledged. Revealing these concealed migrations must be of interest to those with a historical "bent"; it also provides further evidence for my thesis that knowledge of foreign law can be (and has been) of use to national lawyers even when it

---

[28] Exemplified by *Murphy* v. *Brentwood DC* [1991] 1 AC 398.

[29] [1980] Ch. 297. Ross was, in fact, recently challenged in *White* v. *Jones* [1993] 3 WLR 730, as having become untenable after *Murphy* v. *Brentwood D.C.* [1991] 1 AC 398; but the Court of Appeal refused to accept this argument. This English decision, factually similar to BGH NJW 1965, 1955=JZ 1966, 141, is discussed by Lorenz and Markesinis in (1993) 56 *MLR* 558–63. An appeal against this decision will be heard by the House of Lords on 7 March 1994.

[30] "Privity of Contract: Contracts for the Benefit of Third Parties", Consultation Paper No. 21 (1991).

[31] "Contract Beneficiaries in German Law", Ch. 3 in B. S. Markesinis (Gen. ed.), *The Gradual Convergence: Foreign Ideas, Foreign Influences and English Law in the 21st Century* (1994).

[32] "The Doctrine of Privity of Contract", above n. 23.

[33] "Liability for Information and Opinions Causing Pure Economic Loss to Third Parties: A Comparison of English and German Law", Ch. 3 in B. S. Markesinis, (Gen. ed.), *The Gradual Convergence*, above n. 31.

[34] Markesinis, above n. 31, at 43–51; 233–9.

has not been publicly acknowledged. Many illustrations could be given under this heading,[35] but this time I shall take as an example the law of contract. It was first brought to my attention by the distinguished comparatist Stefan Riesenfeld when I visited Berkeley many years ago.

On 15 September 1840, when the future King of England, Edward VII, was not yet born, Frederick William IV, the romantic and artistic King of Prussia, about whom Bismark, however, once said that "if you tried to come to grips with him, you would only find a slimy substance",[36] planned a ceremonial entry into Berlin to mark his ascension to the throne. When the procession was later, for security reasons, postponed for two days, those who had rented "rooms with a view" for the originally fixed day were faced with the same problem that confronted Mr. Henry when he was sued for the rent by Mr. Krell.[37] Were the "lessees" obliged to pay the contractually agreed rent?

We owe to Rudolf von Jhering this example which he included in what must be one of the earliest German casebooks.[38] The negative answer could be explained by reference to the theory of "presupposition" (*Voraussetzung*), which Windscheid was developing at about this time in Germany, and which was finally incorporated in § 97 of his *Pandektenrecht*.[39] As is well-known, the theory was substantially rejected by the draughtsmen of the BGB, with the result that the Code contains no specific regulation of the problem we, in England, call frustration. Later, however, when hyper-inflation—induced by the short-sighted victors of the First World War—ravaged Germany, § 242 BGB (good faith) was to be used by the courts to provide an answer to pressing social problems; and Oertmann was able to provide the theoretical answer to their endeavours by resurrecting the theory of his late father-in-law under the modified form of "basic assumption of the parties".[40] "Frustration" which

---

[35] For example, Professor von Bar, in B. S. Markesinis, (Gen. ed.), *The Gradual Convergence*, above n. 31, believes that Lord Haldane, who studied in Göttingen, may have been influenced by Germanic ideas in his judgment in *Nocton* v. *Lord Ashburton* [1914] AC 932. In his Autobiography, 3rd edn. (1921) 21, he certainly admits to studying the works of influential jurists like Jhering. See, also, Honoré in his comments on *Hedley Byrne* v. *Heller* published in (1965) 8 *J.S.P.T.L.* 284, at 295.

[36] E. Eyck, *Bismark and the German Empire* (1968) 17.

[37] *Krell* v. *Henry* [1903] 2 KB 740.

[38] *Civilrechtsfälle ohne Entscheidungen*, 4th edn. (1881), case no. LX, p. 145. In his introduction to the book, especially p. 5, Jhering argues that he has "always believed that [he] could introduce his students more effectively to the law by paying special attention in his lectures to its casuistry". He continues: "Nobody who has had any experience as an examiner will doubt that a student is only able truly to comprehend those ideas which he can conceptualise in the concrete form of actual cases". I strongly believe that, in the comparative context, his reference to students can be taken to refer even to mature lawyers. To put it differently, the best way to introduce them to a foreign system is through the medium of cases dealing with factual situations with which they are familiar. Von Jhering's book reached its ninth edition by 1901—surely a sign that his case law method had struck a sensitive chord, even though nearly one hundred years later this little book is unknown to most contemporary German lawyers.

[39] First appeared in the 1862 edition. See Winscheid,(5th edn. (1882) para. 97 *et seq*.

[40] *Die Geschäftsgrundlage* (1921). The theory has, nowadays, lost its appeal, but another academic, Karl Larenz, in his *Geschäftsgrundlage und Vertragserfüllung*, 3rd edn. (1963), has come up with a more modern alternative.

is thus absent from the German Code can be found in the most elaborate case law that has been built around § 242 BGB, as it has been explained by academic writers. In many respects, the reasoning is both similar to our own and transplantable into our environment. Indeed, there is circumstantial evidence to support the view that the Germanic ideas were transplanted into American law in the form of section 2–614 of the Uniform Commercial Code. The medium for this transplantation must have been Karl Llewellyn. Though Llewellyn does not make such an acknowledgment[41] he was teaching in Leipzig at the time when Oertmann's theories were widely discussed. Moreover, in his *Casebook on the Law of Sales*,[42] he uses not only the idea but also the otherwise unusual (for the common law) term "presupposition". As Riesenfeld observes: "The thought pattern of the modern common law architects and that of the modern Pandectists merge in Llewellyn; that is all that can be said [with certainty], but it says a lot".[43]

Can one draw more specific conclusions from this example? I believe at least three are possible. First, we see how systems, very different on the surface can, in fact, turn out to be very similar in practice once their case law is examined in conjunction with the relevant academic literature. The German law of "frustration", non-existent in the Code is, in fact, immensely rich with nuance in the books and the cases, and contains many interesting ideas of potential use to others. This is not surprising, of course, when one remembers that Germany is the only country with a major legal system that actually experienced in the 1920s conditions of severe economic dislocation which forced its law to develop and acquire its present sophistication. Secondly, my example illustrates how *basic* ideas (not detailed concepts or solutions) can travel across legal boundaries thanks to the efforts of imaginative individuals who have acquired training and/or friends abroad. Finally, it shows how a factual situation, traditionally associated with an English set of cases (the *Coronation* cases) was, in fact, anticipated by a lively German mind some sixty years earlier. So, if nothing else, it confirms the view that in law (as in other aspects of human activity) there is nothing new under the sun.

4. THE DANGERS OF IGNORING THE CONTEXTUAL BACKGROUND

From foreign case law and academic literature the national lawyer can glean interesting, often exciting ideas. By studying them he may come to realise that his own way of "doing things" is not the only way of producing the desired

---

[41] Grossfeld and Winship, above n. 7, suggest a number of reasons why Llewellyn (and the Realists) were not always willing to refer openly to the German parentage of some of their ideas.
[42] (1930) 178.
[43] (1989) 37 *Am. J. Comp. L.* 1, at 6.

result.[44] This process helps him understand his own law better—always an important role performed by the study of foreign law. Alternatively, he may be inclined to "experiment" with a new idea and the study of the foreign law may then give him some clues, perhaps even answers, as to the kind of consequences that may flow from his experiment. Yet in other cases the study of foreign law may open his eyes to problems which have not yet confronted him and thus prepare him for the day this type of situation comes before the courts.[45] In all these instances, however, the study of decisions or the use of examples given in books must be undertaken with caution, bearing in mind the contextual background that prevails in the system which is about to be imitated.

This is particularly crucial when studying the law of the United States. Common lawyers often tend to think that the law on the continent of Europe is all, more or less, the same and that it is based on Roman law. Likewise, modern civilians assume no substantial differences between the common law systems or, as they tend (inaccurately) to refer to them, the "Anglo-Saxon" countries. Neither perception is, of course, true. But the interesting thing to grasp when comparing English and American law is that the differences between these two systems are not explicable by reference to a different history (since, in the main, American law derives from English law) but can be traced to important differences in the "structural" or "contextual" background.[46] Here are some—and the list is by no means exhaustive—which "bridge-builders" must constantly bear in mind when attempting to move ideas from the American common law background to another related system.

(a)   *The United States has a written, legally 'superior' Constitutional document—England does not.* This presence of a *Grundnorm* (in its technical sense) is not only important for constitutional and administrative law; it also

---

[44] Karl Llewellyn's words are particularly apposite. Over sixty years ago he wrote: "What is striking and mysterious in comparing two legal systems is the ways they are similar and the ways they are different. Much of what follows will be of immediate use to German lawyers only insofar as the contrasts between German and American law make them more sharply aware of the fundamental character of their own legal system. By seeing how another . . . advanced culture can make entirely different arrangements for things they have always supposed to be matters of course—things that obviously must be this way and not the other—they also may gain a critical outlook and an expanded capacity for adapting their own system's traditional institutions to the practical needs of real life as they evolve. On the other hand, much in this book addresses problems that are virtually identical in both systems. Recognising and solving a problem becomes remarkably easier when it shows up wearing a peculiar foreign costume". P. Gewirtz and M. Ausaldi, *The Case Law System in America*, (English edn., 1989) 1.

[45] An interesting example involving the donation of human organs discussed by American, Canadian, and German courts but not yet tackled by English courts is given in Markesinis, *The German Law of Torts*, above n. 25, at 461–9 and 486–8. In Professor Mary Ann Glendon's words (*Abortion and Divorce in Western Law: American Failures, European Challenges* (1987) 1): "The hope is that history and comparison will give us insight into our own situation and that they may occasionally help us find, as John P. Dawson once put it, 'our own paths through the forest' " (the quotation from Dawson comes from his *Unjust Enrichment: A Comparative Analysis* (1951) 111).

[46] Fleming's main thesis in his excellent *The American Tort Process* (1988) vi.

has important effects on private law in general, and the law of torts in particular. The American law of defamation and privacy are obvious examples; and since I have made comparisons elsewhere,[47] I shall only stress here the importance of "constitutionalisation" of private law which, I believe, is happening in most legal systems but has not yet attracted adequate attention.[48]

(b) *The size and geographical diversities that exist in the United States— especially when compared to England—has also had significant effects on the development of private law*. The doctrine of *stare decisis* is not, for example, taken as seriously in the United States as it is in England, and this has, undoubtedly, made the law in the former more "adaptable" than it has in the latter. In tort law, too, we see variations in rules determined by geographical and economic conditions obtaining in one particular locality but not found in another. In the nineteenth century, for example, when it was still fashionable in America to imitate developments in English law, the famous rule in *Rylands* v. *Fletcher*[49] had a mixed reception in the United States.; and whether it was accepted or rejected depended not on legal arguments but on the kind of industrialisation and geographic conditions which prevailed in one state but not, perhaps, in another.[50] Legalistic reasoning in favour or against transplants is, in such cases, clearly of little value since the final result is determined by other factors.

(c) *The method of financing litigation*. Every advanced legal system is anxious to ensure that access to justice is not limited only to those who can afford it; but *how* they pay for those who cannot chance litigation may also have effects on the substantive rules of its tort system. The contingent fee system in the United States, as a method of financing tort plaintiffs, has affected American tort law in many ways. Such rules as untaxed damages, punitive damages (including punitive damage for breach of contract), and the American collateral source rule may, in part at least, be justified by reference to the fact that the court knows that up to 45 per cent of the award will, in fact, not reach the deserving plaintiff, but will end up in the pocket of his attorney. The alleged enrichment of the plaintiff if, for example, following his injury he is allowed to "cumulate" sums from different sources, may thus simply not be there. Some evidence that this rule may be due to this type of reasoning rather than to abstract, legal arguments about the theoretical desirability of cumulation can, in fact, be found in a surprisingly frank judgment by Justice Tobriner of the California Supreme Court in *Helfend* v.

---

[47] e.g., Markesinis and Deakin, *Tort Law*, 3rd edn. (1994) Ch. 8.

[48] I coined this term (and discussed the phenomenon in the context of German family law) in the Shimizu Lecture delivered at the L.S.E. under the title "Comparative Law—A Subject in Search of an Audience" and published in (1990) 53 *M.L.R.* 1, esp. 7–13.

[49] (1866) LR 1 Ex. 265; (1868) LR 3 HL 330.

[50] See Lawson and Markesinis, *Tortious Liability for Unintentional Harm in the Common Law and the Civil Law*, above n. 27, p. 57 *et seq*.

Southern California Rapid Transit District,[51] which thus deserves a closer look.

(d)   *The "abuse" of the democratic element in the United States.* At first sight and, perhaps, on closer analysis, the United States is more "democratic" than England. Certainly, it seems less obsessed by the official secrecy that prevails in England; and, undoubtedly, it protects the freedom of expression more effectively than English law. The fact that judges in most state courts are elected can also be seen as a further manifestation of the "democratic" ideal; and so, arguably, is the continued use of juries in civil trials. In reality, however, the last two notions seem highly questionable, though it would be over-simplifying matters in the extreme if one were to argue that, say, the continental European (or English) way of appointing judges is flawless. Clearly, this is a vast problem that cannot be dealt with within the confines of this lecture. Yet two consequences that these two "democratic" institutions—elected judges and juries—have on the law of torts must be noted here, since they are relevant to my thesis.

A notable aspect of the elected judiciary is its election on its political manifesto.[52] It is closely related to the way an American (state) judge sees his role and the resulting judicial activism—more often than not in favour of plaintiffs—can be explained (if not justified) by the relative inactivity of the legislators in tort matters.[53] The result is clearly seen in the area of tort law where this subject experienced in the post-Second World War years a remarkable modernisation and, in certain areas, an irrational expansion which has ignored the essential question: "who picks up the bill?".[54] Certainly, the contrast with England is quite remarkable where the modernisation of tort law has been very largely achieved by statutory intervention.[55] Thus many, especially continental European, observers are surprised when told that England has more tort statutes (and substantially longer in size at that) than any other

---

[51] "Generally the jury is not informed that plaintiffs' attorney will receive a large portion of the plaintiff's recovery in contingent fees or that personal injury damages are not taxable to the plaintiff and are normally deductible by the defendant. Hence the [plaintiff] rarely actually receives full compensation for his injuries as computed by the jury. *The collateral source rule partially serves to compensate for the attorney's share and does not actually render 'double recovery' for the plaintiff* . . . In sum, the plaintiff's recovery for his medical expenses from both the tort-feasor and his medical insurance programme will not usually give him 'double recovery', but partially provides a somewhat closer approximation to full compensation for his injuries". 2 Cal. 3rd 1, 12–13, 465 P. 2d 61 (1970) (emphasis added).

[52] See, for example, Mr Justice Neely's comments in *How Courts Govern America* (1981). The point is discussed in a more scholarly manner by Fleming, above n. 46, at Ch. 2.

[53] The comparison with England is interesting: and I have attempted it briefly in my "The Constructive and Destructive Role of the Comparative Lawyer" (1993) 53 *RabelsZ* 438–48.

[54] Professor Fleming's masterly depiction of this trend deserves careful reading. He states: "the new ideology betrays little concern for the cost of its judicial welfare programme, in the insouciant or naive belief that insurance and deep pockets will have taken care of the problem. The tort system has thus become about the only segment of the economy not subject to the discipline of prudent resource allocation: it is a programme without a budge". See above n. 46, at 13.

[55] See above n. 53. Fleming, above n. 46, at 38–40, rightly suggests that this judicial interpretation of the legislator's role may, in part at least, be due to legislative inertia.

continental European state, and this despite the "myth" that continental European law is statutory in origin and the English common law emanates from cases.

The at times desirable and at times excessive expansion of American tort law was brought about partly by its judiciary and partly by its jury system. The jury's contribution to the complexity and unpredictability of American tort litigation has come largely (but not entirely) in the area of quantification of damages where, surprisingly, the continued use of juries does not seem to be *required* by the Constitution. As would be expected, the literature on this subject is huge; and though opinions on the available statistical data differ greatly, there seems to be a fair amount of consensus on the fact that the size of awards can vary significantly from state to state, or can be affected by the nature of the defendant (individual, government entity, corporate defendant), and even how the complaint is formed (e.g., the case is pleaded as an accident at work, traffic accident, product liability accident, etc.).[56] Thus, whatever view one takes of details and, as stated, there exists no consensus on the matter, the fact is that the operation of tort law *in practice has* been greatly shaped by the use of civil juries. Clearly this is a point which cannot be laboured further in this paper, but it is one which presents considerable importance both to the academic tort lawyer and to his practising counterparts.

5. A NEW EUROPEAN IUS COMMUNE?

If I were now to sum up the points I have tried to make, I would start by maintaining that all the cases I have discussed in this paper can be used in one way or another by Anglo-American courts. I hope, however, that I have also shown that before this can happen, the material has to be translated by counsel and presented to the court. Indeed, more than translated since it must also be explained, qualified, and moulded into a shape and form that makes it transplantable into a common law judgment. This is, undoubtedly, a difficult and time-consuming task; and there will always be those who will say "we have too much law of our own, why bother with other people's law, especially since its use entails so many dangers?"

My answer to that objection comes in two parts. The first is addressed to my Israeli friends, and here I can do no better than repeat the words of Mr Justice Barak who recently said: "We must not enslave ourselves to other legal families; but we also must not reinvent the wheel. *We must draw interpretive inspiration from any proper source*".[57] The second part of my answer, though I think relevant to Israeli law as well, has the English system primarily in mind. For I believe that a court of the stature of the House of Lords should

---

[56] For further statistical details see my "Litigation Mania in England, Germany and the U.S.A.: Are We So Very Different?" (1990) *C.L.J.* 233–76.

[57] Aharon Barak, above n. 12.

be giving an intellectual lead to other courts; and it should certainly not be exposed to the accusation that it is prone to selective (and, indeed, misleading) use of American material.[58] To put it differently, as an English lawyer I do not wish to have to say to my students, as I have done in the recent past,[59] that, for example, the Canadian Supreme Court is nowadays producing more thought-provoking analyses than the House of Lords to problems that are common to us both. (The excuse, sometimes given, that foreign Supreme Courts benefit from the use of clerks is, I think, too spurious to receive any attention in a lecture such as this one!)

The realisation that similar problems are being faced in many jurisdictions should, I think, also legitimately encourage a search for help in the reasoning of the courts of other countries. In many areas where the law has a commercial flavour, the search for harmonising solutions must surely have its advantages. And then, of course, there is the law that is coming out of the Court of the European Communities. For we must not forget how important the knowledge of foreign law and the use of comparative law has been in the development of Community law.[60] This, of course, is not surprising given that the Treaty, which is the main source of Community law, is silent on the relationship of Community rules and national legislation, and is rather brief on the question of limits imposed on the exercise of powers conferred by the Treaty. That is where the use of the comparative method has come in hand as the Court discovered legal ideas and notions in the systems of Member States and then recycled them back into the Member States in a new form and under the label "Community law". Thus, to give but one example, the widely discussed principle of proportionality, widely feared by some English lawyers as "novel and dangerous" while regarded by others (including myself) as akin to our notion of "reasonableness",[61] in fact owes much to Dutch and German administrative law. This kind of activity by the European Court, based on the study of the laws of the national states is creating a new corpus of law and with it a whole new vocabulary (e.g., priority, effective remedy, proportionality, equality of arms, etc.) which, once again, brings me back to my starting point: the need to make it "intelligible" in different jurisdictions. Just as importantly, however, the work that Community law is requiring national courts to do (including the difficult task of re-interpreting or even setting aside national legislation) is also progressively modifying and energising the func-

---

[58] *Murphy v. Brentwood DC*, above n. 28, criticised by Professor Fleming, "Requiem for Anns" (1990) 106 *L.Q.R.* 525, at 530; Sir Robin Cooke, "An Impossible Distinction" (1991) 107 *L.Q.R.* 46, at 58–63.

[59] For example in (1993) *L.Q.R.* 5–12. Equally critical of the House of Lords and admiring of the Canadian Supreme Court's decision is Fleming, (1993) 1 *Tort L. R.* 68–74.

[60] And acknowledged in the opinion of Advocate General Warner in Case 17/74, *Transocean Marine Paint Assn. v. Commission* [1974] ECR 1063 and the opinions of Advocates General Warner and Slynn in Case 155/79, *AM. & S. Europe v. Commission* [1982] ECR 1575, at 1619 and 1642.

[61] Jowell and Lester in Jowell and Oliver (eds.), "New Directions in Judicial Review", (1988) *Current Legal Problems* 51.

tions of national judges. There is here, in short, a phenomenon that needs to be studied carefully not only because Community law is now affecting almost every branch of municipal law, but also because in various ways it is forcing national systems to converge in their solutions to particular problems. In short, with the help of the comparative method, a new *ius commune* is thus in the making; and to those supra-nationalists who worry unduly about it, one could say that the old *ius commune* worked out an effective way of coexisting with local variations, so that the problem of preserving (in some areas) local individuality is not, in theory at least, insoluble.

6. COMPARATIVE LAW IN TIMES OF TRANSITION—AN EPILOGUE

All the above are, of course, practical reasons why the study of foreign law must be encouraged. Yet one must not also forget the purely intellectual satisfaction of testing one's own reasoning against that found in other, advanced systems. As John Milton once put it:

> "as Wine and oyl are Imported to us from abroad: so must ripe Understanding, and many civil Virtues, be imported into our minds from Forreign Writings, and examples of best Ages, we shall else miscarry still, and come short in the attempts of any great Enterprise".[62]

Lawyers may not be as imaginative as poets; but, occasionally, they must strive to attain such goals and to remain open-minded. In fact, some of them do. For example, writing extra-judicially, Sir Thomas Bingham has advocated a similar, outward look.[63] Practitioners may choose to ignore academics; but, in the long run, they cannot ignore the Master of the Rolls! I cannot believe, and will certainly not accept, the view that if counsel do their work properly and present pertinent and suitably "anglicised" foreign legal material to an English judge, he will refuse to consider it simply because it emanates from a different legal system. In fact, I am convinced that the opposite is likely to be true. Such materials would be accorded the respect they deserve, from judges who would recognise their relevance. And if it became known that Judge X or Y would be willing to have such material cited to him, practitioner (and academic) would have to follow suit. But the beginning of the "chain' is the judge which is why academics should target them for their ideas.

This may strike some as a long and complicated process. It may involve much patience. The English academic lawyer, unlike his German counterpart, is used to being a *vox clamantis in deserto*. However, I for one am prepared

---

[62] *The Character of the Long Parliament*, reproduced in *The Works of John Milton*, (1938) vol. XVI, p. 254.
[63] Sir Thomas Bingham, "There is a World Elsewhere—The Changing Pattern of English Law" (1992) 41 *I.C.L.Q.* 513.

to wait, convinced that, in the end, legal borrowing is an historical inevitability. For, as Roscoe Pound[64] put it some seventy years ago:

> "In legal history, periods of growth and expansion call for and rely upon philosophy and comparative law. [On the other hand] Periods of stability, striving for perfection of the form of the law rather than for development of its substance, rely upon analysis and history".

I have no doubt that ours is an era not of stability, but of change; not of retrenchment, but of expansion; not of insular developments, but of cosmopolitan influences where scientific knowledge of all types travels better than it did in the past. That is why I am confident about the utility of the comparative method and the need for bridge-builders—a role which I would venture to entrust to comparative lawyers possessed of the virtues which the German-Jewish comparatists of the 1930s, 1940s and 1950s had in such abundance.

[64] In (1921) 34 *Harv. L. R.* 227, at 228.

11

Conceptualism, Pragmatism and Courage: a Common Lawyer Looks at Some Judgments of the German Federal Court

1. THE FORM OF THE JUDGMENT

A judgment of the German Federal Court (Bundesgerichtshof) presents some marked differences both in style and form from the judgments (opinions) of the House of Lords or the French Cour de cessation. In terms of length, the contrast is greater with the French decisions (especially those of the Cour de cassation), which are unparalleled in terseness and peculiarity of grammatical style.[1] For example, a typical German judgment dealing with a contractual or delictual matter will run to 2,000–2,500 words—in a minority of cases reaching the 5,000 word range. On the other hand, judgments of the Federal Constitutional Court (Bundesverfassungsgericht), which can deal with topics overlapping with civil law, tend to be much longer. In length the judgments of the Federal Court thus tend to be closer to the average American decision than to the longer judgments of the House of Lords or the English Court of Appeal. One also acquires the impression, though to my knowledge no empirical study has been conducted on this matter, that the average decision of the Reichsgericht was shorter during the nineteenth century and the earlier part of this century than those of its successor, the Bundesgerichtshof, since the end of the Second World War.

Like French decisions, but unlike Anglo-American equivalents, the decisions of the German Federal Court are unanimous, anonymous[2] decisions of the entire court, though dissenting judgments are allowed in the Federal Constitutional Court, and the judges make frequent use of this right.[3] Clearly,

---

[1] And criticized even by French lawyers. See, for example, the seminal article of Touffait and Tunc, "Pour une motivation plus explicite des decisions de justice notamment de celles de la Cour de cessation", (1974) *Rev. Trim. Dr. Civ.* 487.

[2] No names of judges are given in the published version of the judgments. But in accordance with para. 313 I, nr. (2) of the ZPO the names of the participating judges are on a separate document kept in the original file.

[3] In the famous *Mephisto* case, for example (BVerfGE 30, 173), Justices Stein and Rupp-v. Brunneck delivered dissenting judgments, the latter citing with approval *New York Times* v. *Sullivan* at 225. See, also, BVerfGE 28, 36, 50 and 28, 55, 66, both decided on 18.2.1970).

this does not mean that there are never any disagreements between the judges trying a particular case; but it does mean that divergencies or disagreements are not visibly displayed in the published decision. The court decides by simple majority—judges voting in inverted order of seniority, the presiding judge voting last. Thus, on occasion, the phrasing of the judgment requires very careful drafting in order to express the compromise formula agreed upon by the members of the court. The possibility of reaching the same conclusion via different routes which, according to Lord Diplock, is "the beauty of the Common law",[4] is thus simply not there: all judges take the same road, negotiating the same obstacles in the same way even though in practice one of them—known as the *Berichterstatter*—may have imperceptibly had a firmer hand on the wheel.

Unlike French law, however, the absence of dissent does not conceal developing or uncertain areas of the law. When the Federal Court wishes to rule only on the facts before it and not go further than is necessary it will say so clearly. This leaves room for manoeuvre for subsequent courts; it displays an increasing tendency for casuistry, usually associated with the common law; and, perhaps, also suggests the minimum common ground that the judges are willing to accept. The decision of the BGH of 28.1.1976 shows this most clearly.[5] There, a child, accompanying her mother shopping in their local supermarket, slipped on a vegetable leaf, fell and injured herself. The injury happened while the mother was queueing at the till to pay for the goods she had already selected and her daughter (the plaintiff) went round the packing counter to help the mother pack the goods. In a double-jump—evident whenever the judges wish to avoid the narrow rule of para. 831 BGB[6]—the court held (a) that the mother was in a "relationship" with the shop that "bore a character similar to a contract" and was therefore covered by the doctrine of *culpa in contrahendo* and (b) the child was also included in the protective umbrella of this quasi-contractual situation. This double-jump is dangerous in that if left unchecked, it could lead to a complete blurring of contract and tort. Would the same protection be given, for example, to someone who was merely window-shopping? Or, seeking shelter from the rain by entering the shop? Or, even, entering it in order to steal? One suspects that not all members of the court would countenance such extensions. Yet, they were fully aware of the consequences of their ruling; and by mentioning these instances in their judgment, without ruling on them, they were making clear to the world that the remaining uncertainties would have to be clarified by future courts.

---

[4] *Morris* v. *C.W. Martin & Sons Ltd.* [1969] 1 QB 716, 730.

[5] BGH NJW 1976, 712. The contractual point was raised since the tort action had been statute barred by the period of limitation. See also RGZ 78, 239.

[6] See Zweigert and Kötz, *An Introduction to Comparative Law*, vol. II at 129 (English trans. by Weir, 1977).

But let us return to the form of the judgment. Typically the report will begin with a couple of paragraphs containing in abstract form the propositions of the law supported by the decision. This section of the report forms no part of the decision though in practice it can offer a useful summary of the points at issue. These paragraphs will be followed by references to the articles of the Civil and Criminal Code (or other enactments) that had to be construed and applied in the case. The Section (or Senate)[7] of the court that had to decide the case will then be given, followed by the date on which the trial was concluded and the initials of the parties to the action.[8] This is the form adopted in the official reports quoted as BGHZ (which is an abbreviation for *Entscheidungen des Bundesgerichtshofs in Zivilsachen*—decisions of the civil section of the Federal Supreme Court) and the abbreviation will be followed by the number of the volume and the page on which the decision is reproduced.[9] Other reports—the NJW,[10] for example—follow a slightly different order of presentation.

The facts of the case (*Tatbestand*) will then follow, usually abbreviated from the judgment of the Court of Appeal. Quite frequently, sections of the legal reasoning of the Court of Appeal will also be reproduced and the court will then state whether it agrees or disagrees with the reasoning and/or the result. It will then proceed to consider the grounds for appeal advanced by the appellant and give its own reasons for its conclusions.

The extent to which the facts will be given in detail will vary from case to case; sometimes the court merely states that the facts, as found by the lower court, are inadequate, then gives its opinion on the question of law and, finally, refers the case back to the lower courts to discover the relevant facts in the light of the law as stated by the court. But the statement of facts, though much more extensive than that found in the judgments of the French Court of Cassation, is rarely as detailed (and as colourful) as it is in some English (or American) judgments, the court not being obliged to indulge in the kind

---

[7] The Federal Court is divided into ten civil sections and five criminal sections (or Senates), each specialising in a different matter. Tort problems are in most cases dealt with by the sixth civil Senate.

[8] The frequent use of the word *die Klägerin* might lead an inexperienced foreign observer to believe that in Germany women tend to litigate more than men. In fact the feminine designation refers either to the Social Security carrier (*die Berufsgenossenschaft*) or the private insurance company (*die Gesellschaft*) who typically meet most of the claims and then exercise a subrogation right against the tortfeasor. Terminological precision thus underscores the fact that the bulk of personal injury litigation is nowadays (in Germany and elsewhere) undertaken by these two types of subrogees.

[9] The court, itself, decides which of its decisions will be included in the official series. To a foreign observer this practice could be taken to suggest two things: first, which decisions the judges, themselves, regard as particularly important; and secondly, an omission of a decision from the official series might also imply that the judges themselves may have some doubts about some aspect of the decision. It must be emphasized, however, that the author has found no positive evidence to support the second supposition.

[10] *Neue Juristische Wochenschrift* (NJW) which, in addition to reporting leading cases, also publishes learned articles.

of detailed consideration of material which is necessary in the common law in order to decide whether the case before it is covered by an earlier authority, or whether, on the contrary, the facts of the case before it are materially different and thus justify distinguishing it from earlier precedents. To put it differently, previous cases may be considered and distinguished but the court is not required to discover the "case in point" since the search is invariably not for precedents but for examples. The constant refining and redefining of the cumulative experiences of past judges, so typical of the common law, is thus absent from the German judgment.

The legal arguments that follow are usually presented in an abstract manner which is not always easy for a common lawyer to follow or even to translate accurately. For first of all, the tone of the argument can be highly conceptual, even metaphysical. Sections of the leading judgment dealing, for example, with the protection of human personality in privacy, pre-natal injuries cases, and wrongful life decisions[11] are just that; they can, in turn, generate academic literature which can reach heights of abstraction unthought of in the common law. An important, though now rather "forgotten" decision of the Great Civil Senate, provides another interesting illustration.[12] Clearly, this decision is almost incomprehensible (perhaps even to a young German lawyer); and it can only be understood if it is accompanied by an excursus into the meaning of the concept of unlawfulness and its particular relevance to the law of vicarious liability (para. 831 BGB).[13]

Another difference, especially from English decisions, is the detailed consideration of the view of contemporary (and past) academic writers dealing with the subject before the Court.[14] In particular, what is usually referred to as the "dominant opinion" (*Herrschende Meinung*), which is the opinion on a certain matter as reflected in the majority of writings and decisions, will enjoy strong persuasive authority. As we shall see in the next section, judgments sometimes contain more than a mere reference to academic literature; they can produce an admirably lucid summary of the views of the academic world, and then proceed to state why and to what extent they find them unsatisfactory.

The "chicken-pest" case,[15] which is probably the leading decision on the modern product liability law, furnishes an excellent example of the court's willingness to take into account the views of academic writers, if only to reject

[11] BGHZ 8, 244; 58, 48 (pre-natal injuries). BGHZ 86, 240 (wrongful life); BGHZ 13, 334; 26, 349; 35,363 (privacy).

[12] BGHZ 24, 21 reproduced in translated form in Lawson and Markesinis, *Tortious Liability for Unintentional Harm in the Common Law and the Civil Law*, (1982) Vol. II at 177–83.

[13] For a good short account see Kötz, *Deliktsrecht*, 3rd edn. (1983) 54 *et seq.* and 129 *et seq.* For a short account in English see Lawson and Markesinis, above n.12, vol. I at 99 *et seq.*

[14] Cf. Lawson, "Doctrinal Writing: A Foreign Element in English Law," in *Ius Privatum Gentium-Festschrift für Max Rheinstein*, (1969) Vol. I at 191–210.

[15] BGHZ 51, 91, which can be found translated and annotated in Lawson and Markesinis, above n.12 at 84–100.

them and then come up at the end of its judgment like a *deus ex machina* with its own solution. This judgment is, in fact, a teacher's dream insofar as it offers an excellent spring-board for any teacher of German law from which to consider the various theories behind modern product liability law.

Professor Rudden, in an excellent article published in the *Tulane Law Review*, described the four dialogues that an English judge has to conduct: with counsel, with his fellow-brothers; with the "dead" (previous case law); and the "unborn" (i.e., to consider the consequences of the judgment for the future).[16] The second dialogue is, as stated, absent from the final record of the German decision; the others tend to be muted and their place is, more often than not, taken up by a dialogue with the people responsible for the development of the modern civil law—academics. Bismarck apparently had little patience with academics[17]; but in the world of law their prestige appears to equal if not exceed that of the most distinguished judge. Strangely, perhaps, no rivalry seems to flow from this. On the contrary, the interesting thing about this dialogue between court and academics is that it helps perpetuate this interaction from which, apparently, both branches of the profession stand to gain. For writers will respond to such judicial criticism and often come up with new theories or modifications of existing theories that may well be later accepted by the court. The overall impression that one obtains is one of mutual respect and reciprocal influence and it is not uncommon to find the court expressly adopting the views of a certain writer on a particular problem even if this means revising its own early views. Thus, to give but one example, the whole doctrine of contract with protective effects *vis-à-vis* a third party (as a variant of the classical contract in favour of third parties regulated by the BGB in paras. 328 *et seq.*) was largely taken over by the courts from the writings of Professor Larenz. Another example of this close co-operation between academic writers and the courts can be found in the judicial development of the para. 242 BGB (good faith)[18]—an area of the law which reveals the German judges at their most adventurous and, incidentally, also at their most humane.

As indicated, the previous case law—especially that of the Supreme Court itself—is also considered and quoted in the judgments but again in a manner different from that adopted by the Anglo-American courts. More often than not the previous case law will be given to show what the established practice of the court is on a particular matter and to reinforce the present argument. Many of the differences with Anglo-American law are obviously due to the

---

[16] Rudden, "Courts and Codes in England, France and Soviet Russia", (1974) 48 *Tul. L. Rev.* 1010, 1014.

[17] At least when they entered into politics since he, apparently, once expressed the view that "zwei Professoren Vaterland verloren". Heine, on the other hand, who is responsible for the full quote, mistrusted lawyers in general for, in his words: "zwei Professoren Vaterland verloren, drei Advocaten Vaterland verraten".

[18] See RGZ 103, 328, 332 expressly following Oertmann's views in *Die Geschäftsgrundlage* (1921).

doctrine of *stare decisis*, which is unknown in German law. This is not to say, however, that an inferior court will easily depart from the line taken by the BGH, especially if there is a series of decisions (*standige Rechtsprechung*) substantially to the same effect. But technically these are not (in most cases) treated as binding law. Statutes and custom are the only true sources of law (though published preparatory works can be used in order to discover the intention of the legislator as part of the technique of interpretation of any law). Thus, it is not unknown for the various State Courts of Appeals to "rebel" against a particular decision of the Federal Court. Sometimes, as in the case of the recognition of the general right to one's personality, the rebellion will be short-lived and within a relatively short period of time the Federal Court (perhaps with some help from the Constitutional Court) will manage to assert its will; in other instances, however, the reaction of the Courts of Appeal may be strong and persistent, forcing the Federal Court to reconsider its own decision.[19]

2. ABSTRACTION, COMMON SENSE AND BOLDNESS

A. *Abstraction*

It is instructive to move from a general description of the form of the judgments of the Federal Court to some important features which do not always receive adequate attention from foreign observers.

An important characteristic is the tendency to be abstract and conceptual. This is certainly a feature which has not escaped the attention and criticism of the foreign student of German law though, more often than not, the foreign observer will have formed his opinion on the basis of academic writings rather than judicial decisions. Abstraction and conceptualism is, however, a feature of both, and with a long tradition.[20]

A decision of the Court of Appeal of Stuttgart of 24 November 1964 clearly elucidates these points.[21] The defendant, while driving under the influence of alcohol, drove into a stationary lorry and, as a result, his car burst into flames. The plaintiff, who saw the accident, hurried with an extinguisher and, together with a passer-by, rescued the defendant and his passengers from the burning car. In the process, however, he suffered severe burns and was unable to work for two weeks. His claim for his economic loss (presumably under the German Road Traffic Act of 1951) was immediately met by the defendant's insurers; but his claim for pain and suffering (based on paras. 823 I, II

---

[19] See, for example, BGH NJW 1976, 1740 where the earlier decision of BGH NJW 1968, 1279 is overturned in the light of persistent opposition from various State Courts of Appeal.

[20] See Lawson's general review in *A Common Lawyer Looks at the Civil Law* (1953) 138 *et seq.*

[21] OLG Stuttgart, NJW 1965, 112 = VersR 1965, 296.

and 847 BGB) was turned down by the lower Court. The decision on this point was reversed on the following reasoning:

"Contrary to the view of the Landgericht, the plaintiff is also entitled to be paid for his pain and suffering in delict under §§ 823 1, II and 847 BGB. The finding that the defendant's driving while unfit to drive did not afford an *adequate cause* for the plaintiff's injury cannot be accepted. Admittedly, it is not every *conditio sine qua non* that constitutes an adequate cause, but only such a one as, generally and in accordance with an objective judgment or experience, is apt to produce such a consequence, or one that in general appreciably enhances the possibility of its occurrence, and therefore adequate causes do not include conditions which according to general human experience are completely irrelevant to its occurrence . . . that according to common opinion they cannot reasonably be taken into account. All the same, the finding cannot be accepted that in the present case the bodily injuries to the plaintiff lay outside what was to be normally and objectively expected as a consequence of the accident. It is of course true that it occurred here only because of a further act, due to the free decision of the plaintiff, namely his intervention in order to rescue the defendant and his passengers. That does not however exclude an adequate causal connection between the unlawful act and the consequences. It is not correct that where there is an independent and voluntary intervention by a third party an adequate causal connection can only be recognized to exist if the intervention served to ward off an especial danger to the public and therefore was in performance of a legal or moral obligation. Admittedly in RGZ 29, 121 and 50, 223, where an adequate connection was held to exist between the insufficient securing of a team of horses drawing a vehicle and the injuries to a person who tried to hold them up, attention was directed to the fact that the rescuer had acted in performance of a legal or moral duty. In RGZ 50, 223 attention was also expressly directed to the fact that the injured party had intervened to avoid a threatened accident to persons in the village street, and especially children coming out of school precisely at that moment. Nevertheless the Bundesgerichtshof in NJW 64, 1363, when holding that 'an adequate causal connection existed between the conduct of a hit and run driver and an accident to a pursuing driver caused by an increase of speed', expressly said that the recurrent allusion in those decisions of the Reichsgericht is the fact that the rescuer's intervention of the self-sacrificing third person is nearly always automatic, so that the injuries suffered in doing so were undoubtedly adequate consequences of the wrongful act. In the above-mentioned decision the Court drew the conclusion that in less threatening situations it turns on the circumstances whether the situation produced by the wrongdoer is generally to be considered apt to produce rescues by third persons and, if so, in the present form. In the case then decided the Court went on to say that after a sufficiently serious traffic accident it is not at all unusual for other drivers to take up the pursuit of a hit and run driver independently, and that such traffic camaraderie, even if it may not reach the level of moral duty, is a fact which prevents us from regarding such a pursuit of the escaping driver as the quite improbable and gratuitous intervention of a third party in the causal continuity. Thus, one may start from the position that even where such an intervention is the immediate cause, an adequate connection may be held to exist between the damage and the event that was the initial occurrence, if the conduct of the third person was justifiable. It is therefore irrelevant that in the present case the plaintiff was not expected to assist and, therefore, under no legal duty to help. It can also be left undecided whether there was a moral duty to rescue. In any case there was justification. Indeed morally his conduct was of a high standard. Although in the circumstances his intervention required considerable courage and intrepidity, one cannot agree with the Landgericht that the possibility of it must have appeared to an observer so remote that it could not reasonably have been taken into account . . ."[22]

The case is a typical rescue case in which the courts consider when a rescuer has any rights against the person who initiated the harm. The problem is well-known to common lawyers and their solutions are quite similar to the ones canvassed in this decision.[23] But in terms of style, the judgment invites comparison with *Wagner* v. *International Railway Co.*[24] There the plaintiff was hurt while trying to rescue a relative who had fallen from the defendant's train due to the negligence of the crew. The court of first instance took the view that negligence towards the relative would not lead to liability to the rescuer unless the jury found that the train conductor had invited the plaintiff to take part in the rescue and had accompanied him in this task. Rejecting this approach, Judge Cardozo uttered the following memorable words:

> "Danger invites rescue. The cry of distress is the summons to relief. The law does not ignore these reactions of the mind in tracing conduct to its consequences. It recognizes them as normal. It places their effects within the range of the natural and the probable. The wrong that imperils life is a wrong to the imperilled victim; it is a wrong also to his rescuer. The state that leaves an opening in a bridge is liable to the child that falls into the stream, but liable also to the parent who plunges to its aid (*Gibney* v. *State of N.Y*, 137 N.Y. 1). The railroad company whose train approaches without signal is a wrongdoer toward the traveler surprised between the rails, but a wrongdoer also to the bystander who drags him from the path (*Eckert* v. *L.I.R.R. Co.*, 43 N.Y. 502. Cf., *Matter of Waters* v. *Taylor Co.*, 218 N.Y. 248) . . . The risk of rescue, if only it be not wanton, is born of the occasion. The emergency begets the man. The wrongdoer may not have foreseen the coming of a deliverer. He is accountable as if he had."

The comparison of the two judgments is particularly illuminative of comparative judicial styles; it also reveals the tendency of the common lawyer to think in terms of duty rather than legal cause. The difference, however, is one of terminology rather than substance; even the terminological differences are very slight when one notes how Cardozo emphasizes "the natural and probable" nature of the rescuer's conduct. In other words, the common lawyer also could have achieved the same result through legal cause,[25] and did, in fact, rely on "remoteness" rather than "duty", especially before the latter concept

---

[22] The full text of the decision is reproduced in Lawson and Markesinis, above n.12 at 131–5.
[23] Cf., for example, *Haynes* v. *Harwood* [1935] 1 KB 146 and *Baker* v. *Hopkins & Son* [1959] 3 All ER 225.
[24] 232 N.Y. 176, 133 N.E. 437 (1921).
[25] Cf. *Socony Vacuum Oil Co.* v. *Marshall*, 222 F.2d 604 (lst Cir. 1955).

came into fashion. But that is another matter that has been discussed else-where.[26]

B. *Pragmatism and Common Sense*

Common lawyers expect German lawyers to be abstract and conceptual; sometimes they also mistakenly think that these qualities make for opaque texts and theorizing at the expense of a common sense approach. Causation is a subject that springs to mind and yet it is from this area that the following extract comes and challenges this widely held assumption.

The facts of the dispute that gave rise to the decision of the Federal Supreme Court need not concern us here. But the following review of the relevant causation theories is noteworthy, not only because it represents a remarkably clear summary of some very complicated theories; but also because at the end the court openly accepts that these theories are but tools which may help the judge to formulate his decision but in no way dictate the result. Here is the relevant extract of the judgment[27] (with references to academic literature omitted):

"Adequate cause has been formulated mainly by von Kries, Rumelin and Traeger . . . Common to these formulations is the valuation of a concrete *conditio sine qua non* on the basis of its tendency to favour the consequence according to general standards. They differ according to the point of view from which the valuation is undertaken. While von Kries, the creator of the concept of adequate cause, prefers to undertake a valuation on the basis of all circumstances known or knowable individually to the originator of the condition at the time of its entry (*ex ante*), and also taking into account general practical knowledge *ex post* based on experience, Rumelin puts forward the theory of 'objective hindsight'. For the formation of a judgment of possibility he prefers to have regard to the whole empirical knowledge of mankind and all the circumstances anywhere to hand at the time the condition occurred, whether they were recognizable by the most superior discernment or had first become recognizable *ex post* from events following the condition in question.

Von Kries's individual foresight proved to be too narrow for private law cases of objective strict liability and contractual liability, Rumelin's objective hindsight too wide, to exclude with certainty the inequitable results of the condition theory. Rumelin, himself, accordingly found it necessary to curtail his doctrine, in so far as by the condition in question the injured party was brought into contact in time or in space with the damage-producing event. Traeger avoided the defects in both formulations with the following formulation . . . An event is an adequate condition of a consequence if it has in a general and appreciable way enhanced the objective possibility of a consequence of the kind that occurred. In making the necessary assessment account is to be taken only of:

---

[26] See Fleming, "Remoteness and Duty: the Control Devices in Liability for Negligence", (1953) 31 *Can. Bar Rev.* 471.

[27] BGH 23. 10.1959, BGHZ 3, 261= VersR 1952, 128. The full text of this decision, originally translated for inclusion in vol. II of Lawson and Markesinis but excluded for reasons of space, is reproduced in my *A Comparative Introduction to the German Law of Tort* (1986).

a)   all the circumstances recognizable by an 'optimal' observer at the time the event occurred,

b)   the additional circumstances known to the originator of the condition.

   The factual situation so established is, according to Traeger, to be examined by applying the whole human experience available at the time a decision is made, to see whether it appreciably favoured the occurrence of the damage-producing event . . . Traeger's formulation has been followed in essentials by the Reichsgericht since the decision in RGZ 133, 126, 127, more recently in the form that there is an adequate connection 'if a fact in general and not under special peculiar quite improbable circumstances, to be disregarded according to the regular course of things, was apt to produce a consequence'. This formulation expressed until now unaltered in essentials in many decisions . . . has also been followed by this Senate, maintaining the grounds for decision laid down by Traeger. *Admittedly as Lindenmaier points out . . . one must not forget the starting point of the inquiry. namely, the search for a corrective that restricts the scope of the purely logical consequences, in order to produce an equitable result to the imputable consequences. Only if the courts are conscious of the fact that it is a question here not really of causation but of the fixing of the limits within which the originator of a condition can equitably be presumed liable for its consequences, and therefore establishing in reality a positive condition of liability . . . will the danger of a schematization of the formula be avoided and correct results be guaranteed.*"[28]

C. Creativity

Not every common lawyer would dream of generalising about the difficulties of German judicial style; but most would hold to the belief that civil law judges in general, and German judges in particular, tend to apply the Code, rather than make law. Interestingly enough, legal orthodoxy even in Germany would deny judges any pure law-making powers. The truth of the matter is, however, different. The 1900 Civil Code could not have survived without some very daring judicial interventions which, if not hallowed by the term judicial law-making, come as close as any common law judge has come into making new law.[29] The creation of the general right of privacy and its ranking among the other protected interests of para. 823 I BGB is, of course, an obvious (though not unique) example. But the boldness and courage of the German judiciary is evident not only in the creation of the new interest but also in its balancing against the competing right of free speech. The *Lebach*[30] decision of the Federal Constitutional Court fully underscores this point.

   The plaintiff (Lebach) was convicted as an accessory to an armed robbery and was about to be released from prison after having served most of his sen-

---

[28] Emphasis added. For a similar "policy" pronouncement, see BGHZ 30, 154.

[29] For an interesting attempt to bridge theory and practice, see BVerfG of 14.2.1973, BVerfGE 34, 269. The relevant section is translated in Markesinis, *The German Law of Torts: A Comparative Introduction*, 3rd edn., 31.

[30] BVerfGE 35, 202. The translation of the extracts given in this article is largely by Lawson. The full text is reproduced in my *A Comparative Introduction to the German Law of Tort*.

tence. At that time the defendants, the publicly-owned television corporation, were about to screen a film which they had commissioned, describing the robbery, clearly identifying the plaintiff and also alluding to his homosexual tendencies. Lebach complained that the film violated his right to privacy but his claim was dismissed by the District Court of Mainz and the Court of Appeal of Koblenz on the grounds that he was "relatively a personality of contemporary history" and that his interest in his privacy should give way to the interest of the general public to receive a truthful account of the incident in question which had undoubtedly received much public attention. The clash was clearly between two constitutionally protected interests: the freedom of speech and freedom of the press and the interest in one's privacy and personality. The Federal Constitutional Court, in a bold and lucidly expressed opinion, took the bull by the horns, weighed the competing interests and, in the present case, came down in favour of Lebach's claim. The full judgment of this seminal decision is reproduced in my *The German Law of Torts: A Comparative Intorduction*. Here suffice it to provide a fairly extensive quotation from this important decision (the numbering of the paragraphs is that of the Court):

"For the present case the Court of Appeal has held correctly that several fundamental rights affect the application of private law and that they lead in opposite directions. The right to one's personality guaranteed by Article 2 § 1 in conjunction with Article 1 § 1 of the Fundamental Law [the Constitution of Bonn] conflicts with the freedom of broadcasting stations to provide information, in accordance with Article 5 §1 sentence 2 of the Fundamental law.[31]

I.   On the one hand a televised broadcast of the kind in use here concerning the origins, execution and detection of a crime which mentions the name of the criminal and contains a representation of his likeness necessarily touches the area of his fundamental rights guaranteed by Article 2 § 1 in conjunction with Article 1 § 1 of the Fundamental Law. The right to the free development of one's personality and human dignity safeguard for everyone the sphere of autonomy in which to shape his private life by developing and protecting his individuality. This includes the right 'to remain alone', 'to be oneself' within this sphere [reference]. This includes the right to one's likeness and to one's utterances [reference] and even more to the right to dispose of pictures of oneself . . .

However, according to the constant practice of the Federal Constitutional Court the entire sphere of private life does not enjoy the absolute protection of the above mentioned fundamental rights [references]. If an individual in his capacity as a citizen living within a community enters into relations with others, influences others by his existence or activity and thereby impinges upon the personal sphere of other people or upon the interests of communal life, his exclusive right to be master of his own private sphere may become subject to restrictions, unless his sacrosanct innermost sphere of life is concerned. Any such social involvement, if sufficiently strong may, in particular, justify measures of public authorities in the interest of the public as a whole such as the publication of pictures of suspect persons in order to

---

[31] For translations of these provisions, see Finer, *Five Constitutions*, (1979) 198–9.

facilitate a criminal investigation (§ 24 KUG).[32] However, neither the interest of the State in clearing up crimes nor any other public interest always justifies an infringement of the personal sphere [reference]. Instead, the pre-eminent importance of the right to the free development and respect of personality, which follows from its close connection with the supreme value enshrined in the Constitution, i.e., human dignity, demands that any intrusion of the right of personality which may appear necessary to predict such interests, must always be balanced against the protective rule laid down in Article 2 § 1 in conjunction with Article 1 § 1 of the Fundamental Law. Accordingly it must be determined in the individual case by weighing the particular interests whether the pursuit of the public interest merits precedence generally and having regard to the features of the individual case, whether the proposed intrusion of the private sphere is required by this interest in this form and extent; and whether it is commensurate with the importance of the case [references] . . .

II. In this respect the consideration is decisive, as the Court of Appeal has pointed out correctly, that the broadcast in dispute serves a function, the free exercise of which on its part is directly protected by a provision in the Constitution. Freedom of information by broadcasts in accordance with Article 5 § 1 second sentence of the Fundamental law (freedom to broadcast), like the freedom of the press, of expression and information is a basic constituent element of a liberal-democratic order [references . . .]

Only when the exercise of the freedom to broadcast conflicts with other protected legal interests, the purpose by the individual broadcast, the manner of its presentation and its actual foreseeable effect may become relevant. The Constitution has regulated possible conflicts between the freedom to broadcast and the interests of individual citizens, of groups and of the community as a whole, by referring to the legal system as a whole; according to Article 5 §2 of the Fundamental Law the emission of broadcasts is subject to the restrictions imposed by the general law. According to the constant practice of the Federal Constitutional Court the need expressed by this provision to take other protected legal interests into account must not render the freedom to broadcast a relative one; instead the laws which restrict the freedom to broadcast must in turn be interpreted in the light of the constitutional guarantee and must, if necessary, be equally restricted in order to ensure that the freedom of broadcasting is safeguarded adequately [reference]. Consequently the opposing protected legal interests must be balanced against each other in each individual case in the light of general and specific considerations . . .

II. In solving this conflict it must be remembered that according to the intention of the Constitution both constitutional concerns are essential aspects of the liberal democratic order of the Fundamental law with the result that neither can claim precedence in principle . . . In case of conflict both concerns of the Constitution must be adjusted, if possible; if this cannot be achieved it must be determined which interest must be postponed having regard to the nature of the case and to any special circumstances. For this purpose both concerns of the Constitution, centered as they are on human dignity, must be regarded as the nucleus of the system of Constitutional concerns. Accordingly the freedom to broadcast may have the effect of restricting any claims based on the right to personality; however the damage to

---

[32] *Kunsturhebergesetz* (Law for the Protection of the Copyright in Works of Art and Photographs).

"personality" resulting from a public representation must not be out of proportion to the importance of the publication upholding the freedom of communication [reference] . . .

IV.1.   In the light of these general principles the following criteria are relevant from the point of view of Constitutional law in assessing televised broadcasts of the kind in issue here.

a)   A public report of a crime in which the name, a likeness or a representation of the culprit is provided will always constitute a severe intrusion of his personal sphere, seeing that it publicises his misdeed and gives from the outset a negative slant to his person in the eyes of those to whom the report is addressed. It may be different if the report is designed to create sympathy for the culprit, as for instance in order to achieve a new trial, a pardon or some other assistance . . .

b)   Disregarding the possibility of an additional infringement by the manner of the representation (polemics, falsification), even a report which seeks to be objective and factual if televised constitutes normally a much greater invasion of the private sphere than an oral or written report published in the press or over the radio. This is so, in the first place, because the visual impression and the combination of a picture and word is much stronger, but mainly because television commands a much greater audience than the cinema and the theatre, resulting in a special position. Consequently there is a special reason 'for watching over the observation of the limits established by the law and to prevent an abuse [sic] of the right of personality which has become more vulnerable. In this respect the law must not give way to technical developments' [reference].

c)   If for the above mentioned reasons alone a special need exists for protection against violations of the right to personality by televised broadcasts reaching such a wide audience, it must be remembered that the broadcast performance of a documentary play entails specific dangers . . .

In conclusion it can be stated that television broadcasts reporting on a crime naming, depicting or representing the culprit, especially in the form of a documentary play, will normally constitute a serious invasion of his sphere of personality.

2.   On the other hand weighty considerations suggest that the public should be fully informed of the commission of the crimes, including the person of the culprit, and of the facts which led to them. Crimes, too, are part of contemporary history, the presentation of which is altogether the task of the media. Moreover the violation of the general legal order, the infringement of protective legal interests of the citizens involved or of the community, sympathy with the victims and their relatives, fear of the repetition of such crimes and the desire to prevent them create a fully justified interest in receiving detailed information concerning the deed and the criminal. This interest will be all the greater the more the criminal act is unusual, having regard to the special features of the object of the attack, the manner in which it was carried out or the severity of the consequences. Where serious crimes of violence are involved, such as that represented in the film in issue, the interest in receiving information is based not only on general curiosity and sensationalism but on serious reasons for asking who were the perpetrators, what were their motives, what was done to detect and to punish them and for preventing similar crimes. For this purpose the desire to know only the facts will be predominant, but as time passes

the interest in receiving a more searching interpretation of the deed, its background and its social setting increases. Not least is the legitimate democratic desire in determining control of the organs of the State and public authorities responsible for security and order, the prosecution and the criminal courts . . .

3.   In balancing generally the interest in receiving information . . . against the invasion of the sphere of personality of the culprit which must follow inevitably, the interest in receiving information must generally prevail in so far as current reporting of crimes is concerned. He who breaks the peace established by law, attacks or violates by his act and its consequences his fellow citizens or legally protected interests of the community, must not only suffer the criminal punishment provided by the law. He must also accept, as a matter of principle, that the public interest in information caused by himself by his own deed is being satisfied in the usual manner in a community which observes the principle of freedom of communication. Moreover the control of the prosecution and of the criminal proceedings which is assured thereby also benefits the culprit. However, the interest in receiving information does not prevail absolutely. The importance of the right to personality, which is a cornerstone of the Constitution, requires not only that account must be taken of the sacrosanct innermost personal sphere [reference] but also a strict regard for the principle of proportionality. The invasion of the personal sphere is limited to the need to satisfy adequately the interest in receiving information, and the disadvantages suffered by the culprit must be proportional to the seriousness of the offence or otherwise to its importance for the public. Consequently, it is not always admissible to provide the name, a picture, or any other means of identifying the perpetrator.

It is obvious that the right of personality is only postponed if the reporting is objective and if the interpretation is serious; it is different if the account seeks to be sensational, is intentionally one-sided or misleading. On the other hand, objective reporting of a serious crime justifies not only the publication of the name or of a likeness of the perpetrator; it also includes his personal life insofar as it is directly connected with the act, provides clues about his motive or the setting and seems relevant for assessing the guilt of the perpetrator in the light of more criminal law. The actual question as to where the limits are to be drawn in fact seeing that in principle the interest in receiving information by reports of contemporary events must prevail, can only be answered having regard to the circumstances of the individual case.

4.   The reflex effect of the constitutional guarantee of personality does not, however, allow the media of communication, apart from contemporary reporting, to deal indefinitely with the person of the criminal and his private sphere. Instead, when the interest in receiving information has been satisfied, his right 'to be left alone' gains increasing importance in principle and limits the desire of the mass media and the wish of the public to make the individual sphere of his life the subject of discussion or even of entertainment. Even a culprit, who attracted public attention by his serious crime and has gained general disapproval, remains a member of this community and retains his constitutional right to the protection of his individuality. If, with the prosecution and conviction by a criminal court, the act attracting the public interest has met with the just reaction of the community demanded by the public interest, any additional continued or repeated invasions of the personal sphere of the culprit cannot normally be justified."

Lebach is a monumental decision. It is a tribute to the courage and ability of the German judges to tackle rather than evade controversial issues. It is thus a clear example of what courts and lawyers are meant to do: decide about competing values and interests. Moreover, it invites comparison with similar decisions in the United States and can form the basis of an excellent comparative study on a specific issue of great importance. Lack of space prevents a detailed consideration of the American parallels. We shall return to this elsewhere.[33] Here suffice it to note the following points.

First, the courageous approach of the German Court must be compared with the more timorous approach adopted by the American Supreme Court in *Cox v. Cohen*.[34]

Secondly, the possibility of prohibiting the publication of the offensive material in Germany must be contrasted with the American preference for punitive damages if the right of privacy is allowed to prevail.[35] This type of tort of privacy, however, seems almost to have been eliminated by an (arguably) exaggerated preference for free speech.

Thirdly, the detailed consideration of all the surrounding circumstances in the *Lebach* case must be compared with the briefer examination of the issues in *Briscoe v. Readers' Digest*[36]—the Californian decision most closely related to the *Lebach* facts. The facts in these two cases appear to be so similar that they offer excellent material for a comparison of judicial styles and techniques.

Fourthly, it is important to stress the impact that the constitutional background has had in both systems (German and American) on the evolution of their law of torts. A further dimension to this problem can be added when one considers how English law (without any constitutionally protected freedom of speech) could develop if a wider right of privacy were ever to be recognised.

3. CONCLUSION

The cited German decisions come from part of the law of obligations. In the absence of the notion of a "leading case", as we understand the term in the common law, the selection is more than usually "personal"; and the eyes looking at these decisions belong to someone who professes an interest in German law but cannot claim to have a real feeling of how things are done in that

---

[33] "The Right to be Let Alone Versus Freedom of Speech", to be published in *Public Law* (1986).

[34] 420 U.S. 469; 95 S.Ct. 1029 (1975), persuasively criticised by, among others, Hill, in "Defamation and Privacy Under the First Amendment", (1976) 76 *Colum. L. Rev.* 1205.

[35] See, for example, *Diaz v. Oakland Tribune, Inc.*, 139 Cal. App. 3d 118, 188 Cal. Rptr. 762 (1983), but contrast the somewhat unusual *Commonwealth v. Wiseman*, 356 Mass. 251, 249 N.E.2d 619 (1969), where limited injunctive relief was granted by the court.

[36] 4 Cal. 3rd 529, 93 Cal. Rptr. 866 (1971).

system. And yet, despite these limitations, it is submitted that some themes do emerge from this essay and some common myths can be challenged if not dispelled. In my book, *The German Law of Torts: A Comparative Introduction*, I have reproduced some ninety decisions of German courts translated by a team of distinguished scholars. The interested reader is therefore able to draw his own conclusions and make his own comparisons. What follows are some tentative conclusions on the subject under review.

A reader of German judgments expecting them to be abstract, conceptual and difficult to follow will, on the whole, not be disappointed in this expectation. Logic is often taken to extremes, legal details relentlessly pursued; as Harry Lawson once told me, "they leave nothing to the imagination". The Denning-type of judgment—admittedly unusual even by English standards—is simply not known. Yet from my experience in teaching German students or discussing this issue with German colleagues, it is almost universally admired. The lively, staccato phrase is simply not there, its place taken by the well-known long sentences. Humour is also conspicuously absent from the German judgments; one could never imagine a judge of the Supreme Court ending his judgment with a reflection on strawberries, as Lord Hailsham did with great style and effect in a complicated case dealing with frustration of leases.[37] Lack of space has prevented me from quoting many examples, but the above-mentioned rescue case contrasts clearly with Cardozo's romantic imagery. Cardozo could almost have been thinking of Arthurian fair damsels in distress rather than the poor victim of the railway accident that was the cause of the litigation. Yet the mundane nature of the accident did not frustrate his taste for literary style. His German colleagues will not allow themselves such escapades but instead prefer to pursue relentlessly their scientific approach which (they are taught to believe) is bound to produce the right result and may even lead them into the *Paradise of Legal Ideas*.

On the other hand, a common lawyer may be surprised to see a German judge being much less theoretical and more pragmatic than the general image would have it. Causation was chosen as an illustration since the French have caustically suggested that if the subject did not exist it would have to be invented to exercise the German legal mind![38] There is some truth in this statement, though in fairness, it could have been equally directed against the Americans. Moreover, it seems to describe better doctrinal rather than court attitudes towards causation. The courts will, of course, "converse" with their academic brethren; and, as we have seen, such a dialogue not only takes into account views expressed by academics but also helps to shape future developments in a way which has no parallel in England. But as the causation case

---

[37] *National Carriers Ltd* v. *Panalpina (Northern) Ltd.* [1981] 2 WLR 45 at 5556: " 'Doubtless God could have made a better berry, but doubtless God never did'. I only append to this observation of nature the comment that it does not follow from these premises that He never will, and if it does not follow, an assumption that He never will becomes exceedingly rash".

[38] Marty, in (1939) *Rev. Trim. Dr. Civ.* 685, 689.

quoted above shows, theories are taken up to a certain point. Beyond that, policy and common sense determine the result. Here, as elsewhere, the systems appear to meet in the middle. English judges, who delight in stating that causation is a problem of common sense, have nonetheless produced some very long judgments discussing theoretical aspects of the problem. Their German brethren, imbued with theories from their university days, feel the need to start with theories only to end with declarations that common sense and policy dictate the final outcome.

But the common lawyer who studies German law will be most impressed by the boldness of some decisions. One prevalent myth, which must be dispelled, is that the civilians find their law in their books. Roscoe Pound, comparing in the 1950s English and American law, felt confident enough to distinguish these systems from the continental European systems on the grounds (inter alia) that the latter were the "products of universities", treating professors as their "oracles", whereas the former were the products of the courts.[39] Historically this statement is, of course, correct. But today its unqualified acceptance would be wrong, not least because it would perpetrate the myth, still accepted by a remarkably large number of common lawyers, that the civilian judge is a timorous creature compared with his all-powerful common law brothers. One can quote many instances of modern common law judges openly expressing the view that reform of the law-however badly needed—can only come from Parliament.[40] This is the kind of reaction one would expect from German judges. Instead, they have often done the opposite. They have adapted codal provisions to meet new needs, often interpreting them contrary to their literary meaning, and though criticized they seem to have won the day. The history of the new right of privacy is one such example. And in their balancing of the competing values of free speech and the right to be left alone the German judges have shown themselves bolder than their American counterparts and, arguably, even more just.

---

[39] "The Development of American Law and its Deviation from English Law", (1951) 67 *L.Q.R.* 49. Pound's point was accepted as correct eleven years later by Kahn-Freund in "English Law and American Laws—Some Comparative Reflections", in *Essays in Jurisprudence in Honor of Roscoe Pound* (1962) 362–3.

[40] See, for example, *Morgans* v. *Launchbury* [1973] AC 127, 37 (per Lord Wilberforce); 138 (per Viscount Dilhorne); 142 (per Lord Pearson); 145–6 (per Lord Cross). *Malone* v. *Metropolitan Police Commissioner* [1979] Ch. 344, at 372 (per Sir Robert Megarry V.C.); *Pirelli General Cable Work Ltd.* v. *Oscar Faber & Partners (A Firm)* (1983] 2 AC 1, at 19 (per Lord Scarman).

12

Policy Factors and the Law of Tort

1. INTRODUCTION

American scholars have, for some time now, been arguing that "the courts cannot and should not escape taking into consideration in the determination of tort or other cases the interests of 'we the people' at large, or important groups whose interests are identified within the interests of the social order".[1] This "third phase" of the judicial process, which goes far beyond the interests of the immediate parties to the litigation, is dominated by wider considerations of policy which, until recently, were deliberately obscured behind such elusive concepts as duty, unlawfulness, *faute*, foreseeability, remoteness and the like.

In England, ideas not dissimilar to these have, from time to time, been echoed by a number of academics.[2] Dennis Lloyd, for example, in his monograph on *Public Policy* argued that it is "difficult to resist the conclusion that the law of tort has been developed by the English judges very largely on the basis of their feelings as to what the public interest demands".[3] Yet, he excluded from the scope of his comparative monograph the law of torts on the ground that it was only in the law of contract that judges (both in England and France) were prepared to admit *openly* that their decisions were based on public policy.[4] His reasons for this omission, valid some twenty-five years ago, seem to have lost some of their force since, in recent years, certain members of the judiciary have become increasingly willing to refer to various reasons of "policy", the "public interest", the "demands of society" etc. when formulating their judgments.

---

[1] Notable amongst them is Leon Green, in "Tort Law Public Law in Disguise" (1959) 38 *Texas L.R.* 1, 2 (from which the quote in the text is taken); *idem.* "Duties, Risks, Causation Doctrines" (1962) 41 *Texas L.R.* 42, 45. For a similar approach see J. G. Fleming, "Remoteness an Duty: The Control Devices in Liability for Negligence" (1953) 31 *Can. Bar Rev.* 471; A. M. Linden, "Down with Foreseeability! Of Thin Skulls and Rescuers" (1969) 47 *Can. Bar Rev.* 545; cf. M. A. Millner's more cautious approach in "Growth and Obsolescence in Negligence" (1973) 26 *Current Leg. Prob.* 260, 280.

[2] Most recently by C. R. Symmons in his useful discussion of a number of leading cases decided in the 1960s and early 70s in "The Duty of Care in Negligence" (1971) 34 *M.L.R.* 394, 528. See, also, M. D. A. Freeman, "Standards of Adjudication, Judicial Law-Making and Prospective Overruling" (1973) 26 *Current Leg. Prob.* 166 and, more broadly, Neil MacCormick, *Legal Reasoning and Legal Theory* (1978) *passim* and B. Rudden's comments in *The Juridical Review* (1979), 193–201.

[3] *Public Policy* (1953), xi–xii.

[4] *Ibid.*

This "judicial legislation or interpretation founded on the current needs of the community"[5] is, undoubtedly, helping develop both the civil law and the common law and bring it in tune with the economic and social demands of our times. However, differences in judicial styles,[6] as much as anything else, make it difficult to find in civil law *judgments* the type of explicit and, it is submitted helpful, pronouncements that one can find in many modern common law decisions (though in France the annual reports of the Cour de cassation, submitted to the Garde des Sceaux since 1968, throw a great deal of light on the importance the Supreme Court attaches to these wider policy factors in its attempts to adapt the law to the demands of modern society). But, whether admitted or not, considerations of wider policy and social advantage play a decisive role in the determination of a quantitatively small but qualitatively crucial number of cases. Discovering and evaluating these policy factors involves an inquiry into, amongst other things, the whole method of judicial thinking and style. It is thus a topic which does not lend itself to facile generalisations; nor is it within the scope of this work. Yet, it is desirable to look, however briefly, at some of these policy factors which appear to have played an unusually important role in the determination of negligence litigation. Three reasons can be advanced for this.

One reason for wishing to bring into the open some of the policy reasons which lie behind these judgments is the belief that this can lead to a more intelligent discussion of the real issues involved. A second reason is purely didactic since a policy-orientated approach can help students realise that the various concepts they encounter in their books and in judgments are often little more than verbal devices, "means of formulating conclusions"[7] but not the reasons that dictate them. This in turn can help students appreciate the considerable equivocation that exists between many of these concepts; and it can also minimise their use—especially in circumstances where it is clear that they have become little more than judicial fictions. (The term "foreseeability" immediately springs to mind as a most apposite illustration of such use.) For present purposes, however, the most important reason for emphasising this policy-orientated approach is the belief that it can facilitate the comparison

---

[5] This is how Winfield, rather hesitantly, defined public policy in "Public Policy in the English Common Law" (1928) 42 *Harv. L. Rev.* 76, 92.

[6] The literature on this subject is immense. The following may be particularly useful for what follows: Lord Devlin, "Judges and Lawmakers" (1976) 39 *M.L.R.* 1; A. Tunc, "Methodology of the Civil Law" (1976) 50 *Tul. L. Rev.* 459; J. L. Goutal, "Characteristics of Judicial Style in France, Britain and the U.S.A." (1976) 24 *Am. J. of Comp. L.* 43; F. H. Lawson, "Comparative Judicial Style" (1977) 25 *Am. J. of Comp. L.* 364; B. Rudden, "Courts and Codes in England, France and Soviet Russia" (1974) 48 *Tul. L.R.* 1010; A. Touffait and A. Tunc, "Pour une motivation plus explicite des décisions de justice notamment de celles de la Cour de cassation", (1974) *Rev. trim. dr. civ.* 487 (an article of seminal importance); P. Perrot, "Le rôle du juge dans la société moderne", (1977) *GP* I. 91; J. Déprez, "A propos du rapport annuel de la Cour de cassation", (1978) *Rev.trim.dr.civ.* 504.

[7] J. G. Fleming, above n. 1, at 497–8. This was acknowledged by M. Bellet, the first President of the Cour de cessation in a speech delivered on 19 December 1979 to the Société de Legislation Comparé published in (1980) *Rev.int.dr.comp.*, p. 293.

of the various legal systems. For it can prevent the student from adopting a barren comparison of different abstract concepts and encourage him, instead, towards a functionally-orientated method of examination of the different legal systems.

Two additional observations must be made at this stage. The first is that it would appear that nowadays lawyers seem to have recourse to these policy factors whenever their aim is to *limit* rather than *expand* delictual liability. Since in the law of torts in general and the law of negligence in particular the crucial problem is that of limitation of liability, the study of policy reasons that help achieve this goal thus acquires an added dimension. The above is increasingly true of the common law and, in many instances, of German law as well. French law, on the other hand, already broader in its conception of delictual liability than the other two systems, appears to be utilising broader policy arguments in order to extend its law of delict even further. The decisions of the Chambre mixte of the late 1960s and early 1970s bear witness to this tendency and, as the court itself put it in its annual report to the Garde des Sceaux of 1975:

> "la Cour marque aujourd'hui moins d'hésitation et prend moins de temps que par le passé, à revenir sur telle ou telle décision de principe, dés lors qu'il lui apparaît que cette décision n'est plus adaptée à l'évolution générale des moeurs, de l'ordonnancement social ou des institutions".

Secondly, to return to the common law, policy may intervene to prevent the imposition of *all liability,* or it may affect the right of a *particular plaintiff* to recover, or to recover a *particular item of loss.* Different concepts are, more often than not, used to give effect to these different aims but here, for reasons of space, we shall concentrate on the first aspect of this problem.

2. A CLOSER LOOK AT SOME OF THESE POLICY FACTORS

It could be argued that amongst the most frequently encountered policy factors are the following: the "administrative factor"; the "superior value" factor; the "environmental" factor and the "insurance" factor. None of them are mutually exclusive and, more often than not, there is considerable overlap.

A. The "Administrative Factor"[8]

Courts, especially though not exclusively in countries with uncodified systems, are notoriously fearful of the risk of being flooded by large numbers of

---

[8] The "administrative factor", as explained and illustrated in the text above, appears to have played a very limited role in the French law of *responsabilité civile,* its most obvious applications to be found in the decisions of the Chambre criminelle of the Cour de cessation when deciding on the "*recevabilité de constitution de partie civile*" in a criminal action. Further illustrations can be found in decisions limiting the circle of persons who can claim "*dommage moral par ricochet*",

claims—some of them, no doubt, fictitious—which the legal and economic system would not be able to support. This is what MacCormick[9] calls a "consequentialist" type of argument and it is not limited to negligence actions only. It could, for example, be argued that the gradual erosion of the imaginative rule in *Rylands* v. *Fletcher*[10] is, surely, as much due to the traditional dislike of the idea of no liability without fault as it is to the fear that the new right of action might, if not carefully circumscribed, get out of control.[11] The courts' treatment of nervous shock and economic loss, however, offers better and more appropriate examples of how such fears can help defeat claims.

The number of persons who can suffer some form or other of mental distress through seeing or hearing an accident can be clearly greater than the number who can be injured in the accident itself, hence the anxiety of the courts both in common law and civil law jurisdictions to find effective means of keeping potential liability under control.

> "As a policy decision this may be intelligible. In a small crowded island (like England), on whose 200,000 miles of road some seven or eight thousand people are killed every year, and another 100,000 are seriously injured, it is obvious that many people must witness some very distressing scenes on the roads . . . It would probably be undesirable to attempt to compensate all those who suffer some small degree of distress, even if some slight pecuniary loss were suffered as a result—for instance if a person witnessing an accident had to go home and lie down for the afternoon instead of going to work. Certainly the claims of such a person must have a low priority when it is remembered that thousands of victims with physical injury go uncompensated every year because they are injured in accidents not caused by negligence."[12]

To this problem the "impact theory",[13] widely accepted by common law systems, originally provided a crude but effective solution. But, as the social pressures to increase the number of persons entitled to claim damages grew, and the "impact theory" was progressively questioned, the search for new

especially whenever this appears *a priori* to be negligible. For another illustration, see the revealing comments of M. le Conseiller Ponsard in his Rapport in the decision of the Assemblée Plénière of 12 January 1979, (1980) *JCP* 11, 19335.

[9] See above n. 2, at 129 *et seq*. In brief, MacCormick's thesis is that in complicated cases "the adduction of the principle . . . although necessary to is not sufficient for a complete justification of the decision. The ruling which directly governs the case must be tested by *consequentialist* argument as well as by the argument from 'coherence'. . ." *Ibid.* at 250 (italics supplied).

[10] (1865) 3 H and C 774 (Court of Exchequer); (1866) LR I Ex 265 (Court of Exchequer Chamber); (1868) LR 3 HL 330, HL.

[11] See, for example, Lindley L.J. in *Green* v. *Chelsea Waterworks Co.* (1894) 70 LT 547, at 549 and cf. G. H. L. Fridman, "The Rise and Fall of *Rylands* v. *Fletcher*" (1956) 34 *Can. Bar Rev.* 810.

[12] P. S. Atiyah, *Accidents, Compensation and the Law*, 3rd edn. (1980), 80. Cf. J. Harvard, "Reasonable foresight of nervous shock" (1956) 19 *M.L.R.* 478.

[13] Exemplified in this country by *Dulieu* v. *White and Sons*, [1901] 2 KB 669 and other authorities given in *Clerk and Lindsell on Torts* 14th edn. (1975) (Gen. ed. R. W. M. Dias), § 872. For American authorities see Prosser, *Law of Torts* 4th edn. (1971), 327 *et seq*. See, also, F. Stone in (1974) 48 *Tul. L.Rev.* 782.

means of control intensified. For English lawyers, the answer seemed to lie in the use of the concept of duty and foreseeability.[14] The advantage of such an approach is that it involves the use of known concepts which are flexible enough to yield the desired results; and it also confers an *appearance* of consistency since it gives the *impression* that whenever a person can foresee damage to another (be it physical injury or mental distress) he is under a duty to take care. These advantages, however, are bought at the price of using these notions in an extremely artificial manner which prevents the intelligent discussion of the true policy issues that lie behind these cases. So, for example, our courts appear to have been more concerned to prevent such actions in general getting out of hand—and in the process imposing arbitrary limitations—than to try to distinguish the more serious consequences of shock (such as were experienced in *Bourhill* v. *Young*)[15] which deserve compensation, from the more trivial forms of distress which are commonly experienced by the witnessing or hearing of tragic accidents. One wonders, however, if the time has not come to say that if the plaintiff, as a result of the defendant's conduct, has suffered some kind of serious and "recognisable psychiatric illness"[16] he should be allowed to recover damages irrespective of his relationship with the victim, his physical position at the time of the accidents, or even his personal propensities towards such type of injury.[17] Indeed, the law may be slowly moving in that direction.

The fear that a chain reaction of claims may follow an isolated negligent act has been voiced even more strongly in cases of pure economic loss. This anxiety lay behind the rule in *Winterbottom* v. *Wright*[18] and was echoed in *Donoghue* v. *Stevenson* by Lord Buckmaster when he said "If one step, why not fifty?"[19] Perhaps too much has been made of this consequentialist argument since it is, after all, the function of the courts to draw the line and distinguish the deserving from the undeserving case. But however over-emphasised this fear may be, it has, nevertheless, been voiced with some measure of frequency during the last fifteen years in important "pure economic loss" cases both in England and in Germany. In *Weller & Co.* v. *Foot and Mouth Disease Research Institute*,[20] for example, Lord Widgery stressed the fact that in an agricultural community (such as the one involved in this case) the escape of foot and mouth virus could be a tragedy which could fore-

---

[14] The Germans, fully conscious of the nature of the problem, have opted for an *apparently* mechanical application of the adequate cause theory. There is little doubt, however, that it is applied in a normative and not factual manner. On this, see E. von Hippel, "Haftung, für Schockschäden Dritte", NJW 1965, 1890, 1891–2; U. Huber, "Verschulden, Gefährdung und Adäquanz", in *Festschrift E. Wahl* (1973), 301, 318.

[15] [1943] AC 92.

[16] *Hinz* v. *Berry* [1970] 2 QB 40, 42 (per Lord Denning M.R.).

[17] For a strong criticism of the English law see P. Atiyah, *op. cit.* above n. 12, at 77 *et seq.*

[18] (1842) 10 M & W 109, and in *Cattle* v. *Stockton Waterworks* (1875) LR 10 QB 453, the first modern case of pure economic loss.

[19] [1932] AC 562, 577.

[20] [1966] 1 QB 569, 577.

seeably affect *almost every* business in that area. Yet how decisively this fear weighed in his mind and led him to decide the case in favour of the defendants can be only a matter of conjecture since he cautiously added that such fears "should not be allowed to deprive the plaintiffs of their rights".[21] In *Spartan Steel and Alloys, Ltd.* v. *Martin & Co. (Contractors), Ltd.*,[22] on the other hand, Lord Denning M.R. was more forthright

> "if claims for economic loss were permitted for this particular hazard, there would be no end of claims. Some might be genuine, but many might be inflated, or even false. A machine might not have been in use anyway, but it would be easy to put it down to the cut in supply. It would be well-nigh impossible to check the claims . . . . Rather than expose claimants to such temptation and defendants to such hard labour . . . it is better to disallow economic loss altogether, at any rate when it stands alone, independent of any physical damage".[23]

Whatever the value of such fears, the fact is that they are voiced not in this country alone. So, for example, in one of the leading "cable cases" in Germany, the courts had to decide whether Article 18 III of the Baden-Wurttemberg Building Code (a local by-law) was a *Schutznorm*, i.e. a rule intended to protect an individual against the infliction of pure economic loss. This was necessary since the claim was based, inter alia, on section 823 II BGB. The Court of Appeal held that the by-law was not a *Schutznorm*. In the absence of a clear legislative indication to the contrary, the Federal Supreme Court refused to assume that

> "Art. 18 III entitles individual electricity consumers to compensation claims for which no provision is made by the general stipulations, *particularly in view of the fact that this would be bound to result in a considerable and unreasonable extension of liability*".[24]

A year later the BGH,[25] once again, relied on this type of consequentialist argument. The facts were very similar to those of the earlier case though this time the argument proceeded on a different basis. The negligent worker was here employed by a local body and had been warned against the risk of

---

[21] *Ibid.*

[22] [1973] QB 27. The same fears were voiced by Lord Kissen in the factually similar Scottish case of *Dynamo Ltd.* v. *Holland and Hannen and Cubitts (Scotland) Ltd.* [1971] SC 257, at 263.

[23] *Ibid.*, at 38–9. Lawton L.J., on the other hand, while admitting that policy accounted for the different treatment of economic loss, was unwilling to elaborate further on the subject. *Ibid.*, at 49. See, also Geoffrey Lane J. in *Electrochrome Ltd.* v. *Welsh Plastics Ltd.* [1968] 2 All ER 205, at 208. In *Hedley Byrne and Co. Ltd.* v. *Heller and Partners Ltd.* [1964] AC 465, some of the Law Lords attributed the different treatment accorded to negligent acts and negligent words to the greater propensity of the latter to provoke unlimited litigation. Thus, Lord Pearce, at 534 and Lord Reid, at 482–3. Others, however, could see no logic in the distinction. So, for example, Lord Devlin, at 517.

[24] The italicised words come from the judgment of the Court of Appeal as quoted in the judgment of the Federal Court: BGH NJW 1976, 1740, and Emmerich, JuS 1977, 120. Similarly, OLG Karlsruhe, 10.7. 1974, NJW 1975, 221.

[25] BGH NJW 1977, 2208.

damaging submerged electricity cables. Since all earlier attempts to found a claim in tort (based on either §§ 823 I or 823 II BGB) had been, for a variety of reasons, repeatedly rejected by the Federal Supreme Court,[26] the plaintiff, in this case, tried to put his claim on a contractual basis. His argument was that the worker had, by ignoring the warning given him, breached his contract with his employer. It was further contended that this contract should be treated as one with "protective effects with regard to third parties", including the plaintiff. The court rejected this argument, adding that if the plaintiff's contention was correct then not only he but a further 1,300-plus electricity consumers, who had been affected by the same incident, should be allowed to recover. However, to ascribe protective effects to a contract *vis-à-vis* so many persons was clearly absurd, not only because it would be overstretching the notion of contract to intolerable limits; but also because it would be indirectly undermining the broad policy of the Code not to recognise (outside the normal boundaries of contract) the compensability of pure financial harm.

In *Rondel* v. *Worsley*,[27] one finds yet another and, for present purposes, the last illustration of this policy factor though formulated in an interesting variation. The "opening of the floodgates" argument is to be found emphasised in varying degrees in some judgments[28] but policy appeared to militate against the plaintiff in another, and stronger way. For the judges were not only anxious to spare the courts from other, *similar,* actions but also eager to shield them from the otiose task of having to re-try the *same* case. As Lawton J. put it at first instance:

> "many who have been convicted of criminal offences and who had unsuccessfully exhausted all their rights to appeal would seek, maybe years later, to get a retrial by means of action for negligence against the advocate who had defended them. There would be no end to litigation".[29]

This argument must have carried a great deal of weight in the Court of Appeal for its members opted for a more radical solution to the problem before them by holding that this was a situation where policy prevented the rise of *any* duty of care. The alternative approach, proposed by the plaintiff's solicitor,[30] that a duty should in principle be recognised to exist and the control of the court limited to an investigation in each case whether it had been breached, was thus rejected, presumably on the ground that it was a less efficient measure for giving effect to the courts' decision of policy. The case is

---

[26] BGHZ 29, 65; BGH NJW 1976, 1740.See, also, OLG München of 21. 3. 1956, NJW 1956, 1719.

[27] [1969] 1 AC 191.

[28] [1965] 2 WLR 300, 317 (per Lawton J.); [1967] 1 QB 443, 504 (per Lord Denning M.R.); [1969] 1 AC 191, 251 (per Lord Morris).

[29] [1965] 2 WLR 300, 317; [1967] 1 QB 443, 503, (per Lord Denning M. R.); 519 (per Salmon L. J.); [1969] 1 AC 191, 230 (per Lord Reid); 248 (per Lord Morris).

[30] The plaintiff was unrepresented on the appeal but his solicitor (instructed before the appeal came on for hearing) tendered to the court a written brief setting out the arguments against barristers' immunity.

therefore interesting not only because it illustrates how policy (and the administrative factor in particular) can be openly invoked to decide a particular claim; but also because it shows how (and why) the courts decide through which abstract concept they will exercise their controlling function.

B. The "Superior Value" Factor

A prime concern of any legal system is the protection of certain things (tangible or not) which are of value to human beings. Not all these things can have the same value; nor can they always be given efficient protection against all invasions. A hierarchy is thus dictated by moral, economic and other considerations with the result that the law affords better protection to the better things in life. We can, in fact:

> "see how highly the legal system rates a thing by checking how much protection the law gives to it relatively to other good things. We know, for example, that liberty is more highly rated than property because *habeas corpus* is a better remedy than detinue. We know that the integrity of a person is more important than the integrity of property because the victim of assault can claim from the Criminal Injuries Compensation Board whereas the victim of theft cannot, and because you must have insurance against liability for causing personal injury with your car but need not have insurance against liability for causing property damage. The carrier by air must pay more for killing or injuring a passenger than he need pay for losing or damaging his property; and since he need pay nothing at all for mere financial loss, as by delaying the passenger or his property, we can infer that wealth is in fact rated lower than property or person. This last point is evident also from the fact that taxation, or the imposition of financial loss, is more acceptable than expropriation, or the taking away of property. It is clear also from the relative strength of the remedies which protect tangible property, namely conversion and detinue, as compared with the remedies for unjustified enrichment".[31]

This kind of hierarchy, which is not necessarily immutable, not only determines the degree of protection afforded to the various interests; it also resolves potential clashes between them. A few examples can show how this kind of reasoning, concealed behind abstract legal terminology, has often dictated the outcome of negligence litigation.

This first example comes from France and it involves a clash between the idea of "sanctity of marriage", which every civilised society accepts as one of its cornerstones, and the right to be indemnified for loss suffered as a result of another person's harmful conduct (Art. 1382 CC). In France this clash reached quite considerable proportions and, perhaps, one could even say that no other system has felt so strongly in its law the effects of fluctuations in ideas about marriage and extra-marital relationships. The reasons for this last-mentioned phenomenon, quite widespread in practice, are far too complex to relate here but may, paradoxically, be partly due to the simultaneous idealisation and repression of women during the peak of the romantic

---

[31] J. A. Weir, "Abstraction in the Law of Torts", *City of London L. Rev.*, Oct. 1974, 15, 20.

movement in the nineteenth century. For, in practice the flowering of the romantic ideal separated rather than brought closer together man and wife, while the Catholic Church preaching an austere conception of marriage with the procreation of children as its main if not sole aim, unwittingly contributed to adultery becoming what a distinguished scholar has described as an "almost inevitable" institution.[32] Such adulterous relations had some bearing on the criminal law and some parts of the civil law (mainly family law, legitimisation and, to a lesser extent, the law of succession) but, on the whole, left the law of civil responsibility untouched. The position, however, was very different in the case of more permanent relationships with "kept women" (concubinage), for here serious financial loss could be proved by such women when deprived through accidents of the financial support of their paramours. Initially, such claims were tolerated (so long as the relationship was long and the damage *certain*)[33] but by the early 1930s fears were expressed that such extra-marital cohabitations were on the increase and that compensation of mistresses only helped undermine the sanctity of marriage.[34] This "*hommage posthume au concubinat*" as Josserand branded it in 1932 was, to him at any rate, legally indefensible and represented "*la victoire du fait sur le droit, de l'union libre sur l'union légitime*".[35] Five years later Josserand, who by then had joined the Cour de cessation, was able to give effect to these ideas by prompting the Supreme Court to adopt his views and to deny a mistress's claim for compensation on the grounds that she did *not* possess an "*intérêt légitime juridiquement protégé*".[36] This requirement that the plaintiff's claim be "*juridiquement protégé*" was clearly a gloss on the basic text (Art. 1382 CC) introduced solely in order to frustrate the mistress's claim and it was not until 1970 that this extraneous requirement was excised, no doubt under the pressure of altered social and economic conditions.[37]

---

[32] Th. Zeldin, *France 1848–1945, 1* (1973), 307. (This erudite work contains at pp. 285–314 a brief but most interesting description of the social and economic background of the time.) Adultery even became the subject of "serious" monographs, e.g. P. Vernon, *Paris vicieux: le guide de l'adultère* (1883); E. Cademartori, *L'Adultère de Marseille* (1886)!

[33] Crim. 28 févr. 1930, D.P. 1930.1.49 and note Voirin; Paris, 5 juin 1923, GP 1923.2.417; Montpellier, 24 juin 1924, D.P. 1924.2.145 note Savatier; Paris, 2 juin 1928, motifs, S. 1928.2.125 etc.

[34] Thus, L. Josserand, "L'avènement du concubinat", D.H. 1932.1.45; M. Nast, "Vers l'union libre, ou le crépuscule du marriage 1égal", D.H. 1938.1.37. As these dramatic titles suggest for many the phenomenon had reached cataclismic proportions. The alarmists put the figure of "faux ménages" at 40% of the population whereas a study conducted by the Church put the figure at 16–29%. (Le Bras, *Revue d'histoire de l'Eglise de France* (1945), 328 *et seq.*). The most recent sociological study by R. Thery, "Le Concubinage en France", (1960) *Rev. trim.dr.civ.* 33 *et seq.*, puts the figure at a much more modest 3%. Yet its author admits that since his figure is based on information supplied at the population census of 1954 it may err on the optimistic side.

[35] *Ibid.*, at 48.

[36] Civ. 27 juil 1937, S. 1938.1.321 and note Marty; D. 1938.1.5 and note Savatier. The view that the words "*juridiquement protégé*" were really another way of saying that the *intérêt* must be *légitime* (Civ. 26 janv. 1954, D. 1954, 217 and note Levasseur) was never widely accepted.

[37] Cass. 27 févr. 1970, D 1970, 201. The English Fatal Accidents Act 1976, still refuses to recognise a mistress as a "dependant in law". But the woman's children with the deceased may have a claim for the loss of dependency.

The clash between property and its free enjoyment on the one hand and the right to be indemnified for damage caused by such uninhibited use of land offers a different and equally interesting setting for potential clash of values. Nowadays such a competition has a frightening ring about it though more and more people would, almost certainly, be inclined to favour the latter value rather than the former. But in days gone by, and certainly during the eighteenth and nineteenth centuries the balance was often tipped in favour of property and its free exploitation. For it was felt that any other solution would, above all, place a heavy burden on business by obliging land owners to incur great expense in order to take preventive action. Though not without force, especially in its day, this argument is nevertheless unsatisfactory in so far as it implies that the courts would expect landowners to ensure the safety of entrants rather than take reasonable precautions to protect them against injury. No doubt, control through the concept of reasonable care would have meant a more flexible standard, lower perhaps in the nineteenth century, higher in the twentieth. But, as in *Rondel* v. *Worsley*,[38] the courts obviously felt that the concepts of reasonableness or careless breach of duty were not as effective a way of bolstering the prevailing policy as was the complete denial of any duty in the first place. It was thus not until the early 1970s when as a result of a considerable change in the environment, the harsh rule towards trespassers was finally overruled. Lord Reid frankly acknowledges this when he declared that "legal principles cannot solve the problem (of child trespassers). How far occupiers are to be required by law to take steps to safeguard such children, must be a matter of public policy";[39] and Lord Pearson openly referred to the changes in the social environment which, in his opinion, dictated the abandonment of the old, harsh, rule.[40]

A not dissimilar clash of competing values can be found in the development of the doctrine of abuse of rights in French law—particularly in the area of the so-called *"troubles de voisinage"*.[41] In France this term covers the ground which the common lawyers include in their law of nuisance. For the common lawyer, with his forms of action abolished only the other day, the emphasis is, understandably, on the wrong rather than the right; and it also reflects his suspicion of hollow declarations of rights unaccompanied by effective remedies. But to the French (and, indeed, the civilian) eyes what is in issue in these

---

[38] [1969] 1 AC 191.

[39] *British Railways Board* v. *Herrington* [1972] AC 877, 897.

[40] *Ibid.* at 929.

[41] A selection from the vast literature on the subject can be found in Mazeaud and Tunc, *Responsabilité civile*, 6th edn. nos. 547 *et seq.*, especially notes 547(i) and 593(2). The pioneering French work is L. Josserand's *De l'Ésprit des droits et de leur relativité (theorie dite de l'abus des droits*, 2nd edn. (1939) and *Cours de droit civil positif français* (1933). For an eloquent opposition see, G. Ripert, *La règle morale dans les obligations civile* (1949), esp. 157 *et seq.* For a stimulating comparative study see Catala and Weir, 38 *Tul.* L.R., 221 *et seq.* See, also, Gutteridge, 5 *CLJ* 22–45; Scholtens, "Abuse of Rights" (1958) 75 *S.A.L.J.* 39; M. Rolondi, *Inchieste di Diritto Comparato* vol. 7 (1979) (a collection of essays on abuse of right), and generally, C. K. Allen, *Legal Duties* (1931), 95–118.

cases is the proper ambit of *ownership* and not the personal duty of a neighbour not to commit a delict of encroachment. The subject is thus treated in the section of property, where one finds in Article 544 CC a definition of ownership[42] which is modelled on the lines of the Roman law concept of *dominium* and which in its absolute character reflects the aspirations of an era which treated private selfishness as a public virtue. So conceived, the right of ownership inevitably predominated over the other important right—the right to be indemnified for harm culpably caused—enshrined in Article 1382 CC.

This situation could not, in fact, last for ever and, surprisingly, the break with the past came earlier than one might have expected.[43] The way the change was effected was also, to some extent, predestined. For if a system (for example, the English) avoids conferring rights in broad terms, the need for controlling their limits is not felt so strongly. But if rights are conferred in sweeping terms, the control of their excessive and antisocial use becomes imperative. A notion of abuse of rights becomes almost inevitable and the first way of fixing the limits of the permissible use of rights was by making their malicious exercise actionable. The decision of the Court of Colmar in 1856[44] marked this turning point and the idea was subsequently enshrined in the famous *Schikaneverbot* of the German Civil Code.[45] But it did not go far enough since it is rare that a man will act out of sheer spite or malice in order to hurt his neighbour; more often than not he may be trying, like the defendant in *Mayor of Bradford* v. *Pickles*,[46] to put pressure on the plaintiff which, though it may not bring the defendant immediate benefits, is clearly calculated to benefit him in the long run. A further step had thus to be taken and when it was, the emphasis was switched further towards Article 1382 CC. This was, in fact, quite easy to achieve once attention was concentrated on the abnormal character of the defendant's exercise of his right. Of course, one still had to find a suitable test for determining what was normal and what was abnormal, but academics were quick to come up with suggestions. The most elab-

[42] "*La propriété est le droit de jouire et disposer des choses de la manière la plus absolue. . .*"
[43] The change came with the decision of the court of Colmar in 1855 (see n. 44). On the other hand, one must remember that the older French jurists, probably under the influence of canon law, had come to regard as actionable any purely malicious exercise of rights. Thus, in 1577 the Parlement of Aix condemned a wool-carder for singing continuously solely in order to annoy his neighbour. Mazeaud and Tunc, I, no. 556. This break with the Roman law tradition can also be found in Scots law which, from about the seventeenth century onwards, apparently accepted the doctrine of abuse of rights within its law of real property. See B. W. Napier, "Abuse of Rights in British Law", in M. Rotondi, *Inchieste di Diritto Comparato*, 267 *et seq*. But this came to an abrupt end when Lord Watson agreed (it is submitted erroneously) with the English Law Lords in *Mayor of Bradford* v. *Pickles* [1895] AC 587, 598, that Scots law was the same as English law.
[44] D.P. 1856.2.9.
[45] Paragraph 226 BGB: "The exercise of a right is inadmissible if it can only have the purpose of causing damage to another". In practice, better results have been achieved by relying on § 826 BGB which requires of malicious damage not that it be against the law but merely *contra bonos mores*—a formulation which sidetracks the defence that the damage was done in the exercise of a right.
[46] [1895] AC 587. French courts have penalised conduct identical to that of Mr. Pickles. See D.P. 1902.1.454; S. 1903. 1.1 I.

orate of those proposed came from Josserand[47] and, though no longer widely accepted,[48] it earned itself a quite unique reputation. According to it, every right has its own spirit and every act which is consistent with this spirit is normal; all other acts are abnormal. Rights, in other words are not absolute but relative or, to use a more English terminology, they are more in the nature of powers of which the repository is a trustee. Of course, some rights are, in Josserand's terminology egotistical, established in the interest of those persons on whom they are conferred; and property rights should be classed in this group. To exercise them without malice was, of course, essential; but was this "minimum" requirement sufficient? With the passage of time it was felt that it was not. But the further search for a solution within the context of the social aims or objectives of the right of property was unpalatable, especially since its socialistic flavour had quickly earned it some influential enemies.[49] The answer was finally to be found in the standard of behaviour of the hypothetical *bon père de famille*; if he would not have exercised his right in this way neither should the defendant do so with impunity.[50] The integration with the fault system of Article 1382 CC was now complete. Indeed, in the context of the "*troubles de voisinage*" the courts moved even beyond liability based on fault to stricter forms of liability determined by what can be reasonably tolerated in neighbourly relations.[51] The final outcome of the cases is thus nine times out of ten quite similar to that reached by common law courts in similar circumstances and, indeed, as the number of dicta that are prepared to take into account bad motives increase in the English law,[52] the similarity of *results* may spread from "neighbour disputes" to other areas of the law of torts. But in terms of technique the two systems are poles apart and will remain so for as long as English law (unlike French law) chooses to place the emphasis on the commission of a "wrong" rather than the existence of a "right". That the techniques are diametrically opposed can be shown clearly by two cases which cry out for comparison. In *Christie* v. *Davey*[53] the defendant, annoyed by his neighbour's piano lessons, started to produce loud noises with the intention of making life intolerable for the neighbour (plaintiff). The defendant's malice was decisive in characterising the disturbance to the

---

[47] *Cours de droit civil positif français*, 2nd edn. (1933), nos 428–37; *De l'ésprit des droits et de leur relativité, passim.*

[48] For an up-to-date account of the doctrine in France see Antoine Pirovano, "L'abus de droit dans la doctrine et la jurisprudence françaises", in M. Rotondi, *Inchieste di Diritto Comparato*, vol. 7, 313 *et seq.*

[49] Notably by Ripert in *La règle morale dans les obligations civile* (1949) esp. 157 *et seq.*

[50] Mazeaud and Tunc, 1, nos 568 *et seq.*

[51] Cass 29 mai 1937, D.H. 1937.393; S. 1937.1.244. Cass. civ. 4 fév. 1971, *JCP* 1971, 16781 and note Lindon; cass. civ. 18 juil. 1972, *JCP* 1972, 17203 and rapport Fabre.

[52] Lord Denning M.R. has been one of the most persistent exponents. See, for example, his dissenting judgment in *Chapman* v. *Honig* [1963] 2 QB 502; *Morgan* v. *Fry* [1968] 2 QB 710, 729; *Secretary of State for Employment* v. *ASLEF (No 2)* [1972] 2 All ER 949, 967; *Re Brocklehurst* [1978] 1 All ER 767, 775.

[53] [1893] 1 Ch 316.

plaintiff as unreasonable. In a parallel French case[54] the defendant hired an orchestra to play loudly near his neighbour's boundary whenever the latter organised a hunting party on his own land. His bad motive was used to characterise the exercise of his right as abusive and he was then held liable. The comparison of these two cases is interesting not only because the same results were achieved in what were substantially similar factual situations but also because they demonstrate that whenever nuisance is linked to fault fault plays a different role in each system: in France it characterises the defendant's conduct as "abusive"; in England, in view of the fact that in nuisance one looks at the effect on the plaintiff and not the defendant's conduct, fault is an element which, taken with others, may render unreasonable what might otherwise be regarded as reasonable.

C. The "Environmental" Factor

Though there is clearly a considerable overlap between this and the previous policy factors, in this present type the emphasis is not so much on "moral" or "value" considerations but on the exigencies of the economic environment. Once again, lawyers and judges have, on the whole, avoided mentioning these factors in public and, instead, have chosen to conduct their argument on the basis of abstract concepts and legal doctrine. But unexpressed though these considerations may be, they are there nevertheless. Indeed, few are the cases which, once stripped of their legal technicalities, do not reveal the environmental forces that dictated their outcome. Leon Green, for example, has analysed *Rylands* v. *Fletcher*[55] as a case having to decide which of two industrial users of land (the milling or the mining industry) should bear the loss of the type of hazard encountered in that case.[56] Analysed in such a way the case can only produce the result actually reached by Blackburn (and the House of Lords) not only because the surface industrialist alone could provide protection for the mine beneath; but also because to decide otherwise would be tantamount to striking a severe blow to the mining industry and, in the nineteenth century, to harm the mining industry would be to harm England. Such an analysis is attractive but, displaying as it does concern for loss-spreading ability and accident preventive procedures, it could be accused of telescoping into the nineteenth century ideas and methods of reasoning more appropriate to the twentieth. On the other hand, there is no evidence to suggest that judges did not think in this way even though they did not openly

---

[54] Amiens 7 févr. 1912, 1913 D.2.177, at 179. For what is probably the leading case see Req. 3 août 1915, *D.P.* 1917. 1. 79.

[55] (1866) LR I Ex 265; (1868), LR 3 HL 330.

[56] "Tort Law Public Law in Disguise" (1959) 38 *Texas L. Rev.* 1, 5. Harper and James, *The Law of Torts, 11* (1956), 14.3, though putting forward a slightly different view, also explain the case by reference to its economic and political environment. Similarly, F. H. Bohlen, in *Studies in the Law of Torts* (1926), 359. This kind of interpretation, however, is rejected by Roscoe Pound in (1940) 53 *Harv. L. Rev.* 365, 383–4. Cf., Fridman, 34 *Can. Bar Rev.* 810, 812.

express it in judgements which were more anxious to appear to be relying on analogies. And comparison with the eastern United States at that time would lend *some* indirect support for this for, as Green, once again, has observed,

"in a new country like Atlantic seabord, where industrial enterprise was just getting on its legs and where water storage was so important for its uses, it is quite understandable that American courts should reject the doctrine (of *Rylands* v. *Fletcher)* *as* unsuitable to our economic situation".[57]

It was thus only after the economic and industrial environment changed that the *Rylands* v. *Fletcher* doctrine came to be accepted and, in some instances, even to be extended.

It could be argued that a similar concern for the land-owning classes encouraged the common law to adopt the varying and confusing standards of care owed by occupiers of land towards lawful entrants.[58] The emphasis on the plaintiff's status rather than on the nature of the defendant's land, the risks attendant to it, and his ability to prevent them, was clearly in tune with the economic demands of the time and the desire not to hinder or burden the free exploitation of one's property. But it also gave judges the extra bonus of being able to control the findings of juries on the issue of carelessness by enabling them, through the "proper" characterisation of the plaintiff, to raise or lower the standard of care due to him. With the passage of time, however, the vagueness if not outright artificiality of these distinctions became an asset which judges were prepared to utilise in response to the exigencies of a changed economic and social environment. The use of the "implied licence" concept thus became the "most palpable fiction ever employed in order to impose legal responsibility"[59] and recently Lord Denning openly admitted the utility of such fictions as a means of avoiding the rigidity of the old law.[60]

The law related to industrial accidents and workers' compensation can provide us with our last example of environmental factors influencing the development of the law of torts. In the rise and fall of the doctrine of "common employment" we can find a neat illustration of these forces at work.[61]

---

[57] *Ibid.*, at 5. The early milldam cases in the United States could, arguably, be used to support this. *Shrewsbury* v. *Smith* (1853), 12 Cush 177 *(Mass.); Livingston* v. *Adams* (1828), 8 Cow. 175 (N.Y.). This attitude remained unaltered even after *Rylands* v. *Fletcher.* Thus, *Losee* v. *Buchanan* (1873), 51 N.Y. 476, 10 Ann. Rep. 623; *Marshall* v. *Welwood* (1876), 38 N.J.L. 339, 20 Am. Rep. 394; *Brown* v. *Collins* (1873), 53 N.H. 442, 16 Am. Rep. 372. With some exceptions (e.g., *Sanderson* v. *Pennsylvania Coal Co.* (1878), 86 Pa. 401, 27 Am. Rep. 711; *Ball* v. *Nye* (1868), 99 Mass. 582) the new doctrine was thus avoided by many courts and liability was made to rest on nuisance or negligence. The principle, however, is nowadays accepted by a majority of jurisdictions. For details see Prosser, *Law of Torts* 4th edn. (1971), 508 *et seq.*

[58] Fleming, *The Law of Torts* (5th edn. 1977), 432 *et seq.* Leon Green, "Landowner v. Intruder—Intruder v. Landowner. Basis of Responsibility in Tort" (1923) 21 *Mich. L.R.* 495.

[59] Green, *ibid.*, 508.

[60] *Pannett* v. *P. McGuinness & Co. Ltd.* [1972] 2 QB 599, 606.

[61] L. M. Friedman and J. Ladinsky, "Social Change and the Law of Industrial Accidents" (1967) 67 *Colum. L. Rev.* 50.

Priestley v. *Fowler*[62] is commonly regarded as the *fons et origo* of this doctrine[63] though this must be qualified before being accepted. For, first, there is nothing in the plaintiff's declaration about an act of another servant; instead the attempt is to make the employer liable for breaking his own duty to provide a safe conveyance. Secondly, since at this period of time the tort of negligence has not yet acquired a foothold in English law, the case could not really have been decided in tort. Certainly, counsel for the plaintiff argued his case on the basis of an implied term in the contract of employment; Chief Justice Shaw, in the almost contemporaneous decision in *Farwell* v. *Boston & Worcester Railroad Corp.*,[64] spoke the language of contract; and subsequent decisions rationalised the immunity on the basis of an implied term in the contract of employment.[65]

At this juncture, the comparative lawyer can pause for thought. A moment's reflection will remind him that about this time French lawyers, too, started to experience similar problems. In those days actions against employers had to be brought under Article 1382 CC and this requires the plaintiff (employee) to prove his employer's (defendant's) fault which was (and is) more often than not, impossible. For practical purposes, therefore, French law was very close to English law; for, though it recognised the existence of a "duty" in tort (if we may use the English terminology) it did not accept easily its careless breach. Progressive lawyers tried to avoid this result—iniquitous as far as the workmen were concerned—by trying (unsuccessfully) to expand the contents of the contract of employment by implying in it a term of "security" and "safety" for the benefit of the worker.[66] The point at issue is not identical to that considered in the above-mentioned cases of the common law; but the cases do show how, in the absence of an "amenable" law of tort, civilian lawyers are tempted to expand their law of contract in order to afford a remedy to "deserving" plaintiffs.

But let us return to *Priestley* v. *Fowler*.[67] In his judgment Lord Abinger had no doubt that the plaintiff's claim should fail; the consequences of deciding the case otherwise were too horrible even to contemplate. In fact he gave a series of hypothetical instances to illustrate the multiplicity of actions that might ensue from the adoption of a different rule. These examples have been selected from an "engagingly domestic"[68] scene and the author of the standard monograph on *Employer's Liability* wonders whether Lord Abinger's

---

[62] (1837) 3 M & W 1, 7 LJ Ex 42.

[63] Thus, Windfield and Jolowicz, on *Tort*, 11th edn., 169; J. Muncman, *Employer's Liability at Common Law*, 7th edn. (1971), 7. *Contra*, F. H. Newark, "Bad Law" (1966) 17 *N.I.L.Q.* 469, 477.

[64] (1842), 45 Mass (4 Met.) 49. For a fuller discussion of this important case see Friedman and Ladinsky, (1967) 67 *Colum. L. Rev.*, 54 *et seq.*

[65] *Bartonshill Coal Co.* v. *Reid* (1858) 3 Macq. 266, HL.

[66] For example, Marx Sauzet, "De la responsabilité des patrons vis à vis des ouvriers dans les accidents industrialise", (1883) *Rev. crit. leg. et jur.* 596 *et seq.* and 677 *et seq.*

[67] See above n. 62.

[68] B. Rudden, *The Juridical Review* (1979), 198.

mind was not dwelling at that moment on his own immense household as master of Inverlochy Castle near Ben Nevis![69] Of course, one should not carry this kind of thinking too far. Roscoe Pound,[70] for example, has warned against the danger of explaining such decisions *solely* by reference to the conscious or unconscious desires of the economically-dominant class of the time. But there seems little doubt that the immunity, once accepted, could be transplanted into the industrial context and there become a potent shield for employers against all legal consequences of industrial accidents. In *Hutchinson v. York, Newcastle & Berwick Ry.*,[71] Alderson B. did precisely this and it is hard to believe that this and the other cases that followed do not reflect a conscious decision *to allocate the risk* in such cases in the *economically* most suitable manner.

The result was harsh on poor workers; and some judgments reveal this preference for strong economic logic to any feelings of compassion.[72] But the decision was harsh not because it refused to hold the employer liable but because the welfare system was pitifully inadequate. For, if the social welfare system works properly, it can even today be argued that "broader social responsibility" is preferable to one which taxes a particular industry for the claims of its workers.[73] Of course, which of these two possibilities is preferable, in economic and political terms, is not relevant for present purposes.

Industrial accidents posed similar problems for the civil law. In France, attempts to improve the lot of workers through the law of contract met with little success with the courts and for the better part of the nineteenth century the possibilities offered by Article 1384 CC remained unused. In a decision delivered in 1870,[74] for example, the Chambre civile of the Cour de cassation refused to apply Article 1384 CC to a case involving the explosion of a boiler installed in a laundry and, instead, insisted that recovery in such cases depend upon the plaintiff producing evidence of the defendant's fault. Commenting on this decision in Sirey in 1871,[75] Labbé let the cat out of the bag by admitting that the case simply could not have been decided otherwise. Industry, he argued, had its dangers, but it also benefited the community at large which should therefore carry such risks. The implication is, once again, that one

[69] Muncman, *op. cit.* above n. 63, at 6. "These instances seem to show personal apprehension rather than any principle" per Lord Wright in *Radcliffe* v. *Ribble Motor Services Ltd.* [1939] AC 215, at 239.

[70] "The Economic Interpretations and the Law of Torts" (1940) 53 *Harv. L. Rev.* 365.

[71] (1850) 5 Exch. 343. This was a tort case under Lord Campbell's Act 1846. It was later said that "Lord Abinger planted the doctrine of common employment. Baron Alderson watered it and the Devil gave it increase".

[72] For example, Bramwell B. in *Dynen* v. *Leach* (1857) 26 LJ (NS) Ex 221.

[73] Friedman and Ladinsky (1967) 67 *Colum L. Rev.* 50, 56.

[74] D.P. 70.1.361.

[75] S. 1871.1.9. It must be said that it is not clear from the "*arrat*" whether the plaintiff was an employee of the defendant's or not. The headnote to the *Sirey* report talks of injury "*d'un tiers*" but the facts of the case are quite similar to some of the "boiler-explosion" cases decided a few years later and indisputably dealing with injured employees. In any event, Labbé's case-note is couched in sufficiently wide terms to be able to cover both kinds of situation.

should not hamper unduly the gradual industrialisation of the country. Those who favoured greater protection for the working classes were still very much in the minority and the pressure for legislative reform remained weak throughout the first two decades of the life of the Third Republic. But by the end of the century increased mechanisation and a steady growth of industrial accidents demanded some modification in the approach and, through the medium of more efficient insurance, industry was becoming increasingly able to shoulder such risks. Equally important, perhaps, is the fact that this is the era of the growing strength of the socialist movements which began to generate strong pressures on the Parliaments of the day to intervene. In actual fact, the change came first from the courts[76] and some thirty years later M. le Conseiller le Marc'Hadour, in the celebrated *Jand'heur* case, admitted that this was the result of the "*nécessité chaque jour plus impérieuse de protéger l'ouvrier contre les consequences des accidents survenues au cours du travail*".[77] And, lest France should be regarded as being backward with other European countries, he added: "*Déjà, à l'étranger des lois speciales avaient réglé la matière des accidents du travail; la jurisprudence française ne pouvait d'être impressionnée par des tendances qui correspondaient à un souci évident de justice sociale . . .*". Incidentally, the admiring reference to foreign legislation (the English Compensation Act of 1897 and the German laws of the 1870s and 1880s) is partly misconceived, for Professor Kahn-Freund amongst others has shown that the prime purpose of this legislation—which was based on inquiries which the German Consulate in London made in voluntary schemes established by the trade unions in this country—was not meant to assist the German workers but to "take the wind out of the sails of the Social Democracy" by satisfying in advance some of its more pressing demands.[78]

D. The "Internal Balance of the Code" Factor

Lon Fuller has pointed out that judges are

> "confronted by a problem of system. The rules applied to the decision of individual controversies cannot simply be isolated exercises of judicial wisdom. They must be brought into, and maintained in, some systematic interrelationship; they must display some coherent internal structure."[79]

This need to interrelate results is both strong and obvious in codified systems, where the outcome of a particular case may often be determined or justified by the structure of the Code. In such cases to sanction a result other than that

---

[76] First from the Conseil d'Etat, 21 juin 1895, *D.P.* 1896.3.65 and then the Cour de cessation 16 juin 1896, *D.P.* 1897.1.433 and note Saleilles; S. 1897.1.17 and note Esmein. A year later the legislator intervened in a manner similar to our 1897 Workmen's Compensation Act. The relevant law can now be found in the Social Security Code.

[77] *D.P.* 1930.1.57.

[78] K. Renner's *The Institutions of Private Law and their Social Functions* (1949), 238 (English edn. with an introduction by O. Kahn-Freund).

[79] *Anatomy of the Law* (1971), 134.

actually reached would disturb the internal balance of the Code and run counter to the wider policy decisions embodied in it. The various rules on cumulation of contractual and delictual actions, invariably worked out by courts and jurists rather than by legislatures, offer a very good illustration. The German rule allowing cumulation of actions is, for example, very largely the result of §§ 253 and 847 BGB and the German attitude towards damages for pain and suffering (*Schmerzensgeld*) which are only available in tort actions.[80] To prohibit cumulation would, for example, be tantamount to holding that a negligent driver would be liable to pay such damages to an injured pedestrian (suing him in tort) but not to his injured passenger (who would normally sue him in contract). Yet the driver's conduct amounts to a breach of contract as well as tort and to allow the passenger to sue in tort means allowing him to recover for pain and suffering which he would not be allowed to claim if he were suing in contract. Such a solution is, in practice, just and perfectly acceptable in a system such as the German which provides only for impossibility for performance and delay but not for positive breaches of contracts and thus clearly envisages the possibility of contractors suing each other in tort.

The opposite solution obtains in French law where most authors accept the principle of *non cumul des actions*. Once again, the internal structure of the Code makes this solution desirable if not, indeed, inevitable. The reason for this is that Article 1382 CC is extremely wide and Article 1384 CC is extremely strict. To allow cumulation in such circumstances would sap the law of contract of all its content since every breach of contract could be treated as a tort. "The same risk does not arise in West Germany or the Common law where economic harm, the typical consequence of the typical breach of contract, gives rise to no liability in tort if it is caused by mere 'negligence'. Thus in Germany admission of concurrence still leaves much to the exclusive regulation of the law of contract . . . In France on the other hand, the admission of concurrence would have a very different and much more serious effect, for it would mean the effective abolition of the special rules of contractual liability except in so far as they benefited the victim only."[81] Secondly, the admission of concurrence would, in effect, make such persons as doctors and bailees liable to the patients and their bailors respectively under Article 1384 CC and this would be clearly contrary to the kind of duty imposed on such persons by the law which is invariably an *obligation de moyens* rather than an *obligation de résultat*. It is, therefore, necessary for French law to prevent recourse to the articles on delict by reserving those articles to the exclusive use of strangers or third parties.

The internal structure of the Code argument can also be found in some of the economic loss cases in Germany. Thus in the leading "cable case"

---

[80] Tony Weir, *International Encyclopaedia of Comparative Law*, XI, Ch. 12 § 24, 63; RGZ 88, 317.
[81] *Ibid.*, at p. 54.

mentioned earlier[82] the Supreme Court did not allow compensation for pure economic loss under § 823 II BGB by refusing to hold that the violation of an article of a building statute of Baden-Wurttemberg gave a right of action to factory owners affected by a power cut which was the result of damage to a near-by electricity cable. To do so, reasoned the court, would be tantamount to allowing a *state legislator* to sanction the recovery of pure economic loss despite the contrary provision of the basic, Federal, enactment (§ 823 I BGB). This could clearly not have been in the mind (or the competence) of the state legislator and this was therefore an additional argument in favour of the view that the violated rule (Article 18 III of the Baden-Wurttemberg Building Code) was not a *Schutznorm*.

To a common lawyer the above-mentioned policy factor may sound unduly restrictive—in so far at any rate as it ties down developments in the law to the pre-arranged structure of the Code. To some extent this is correct though, on the other hand, one should not take the civil codes too seriously since often those who have to live under them do not. Thus, for example, the French courts have so disturbed the balance between Articles 1119 and 1120 of the Civil Code as to make the recognition of third party rights in contract normal instead of exceptional, as was assuredly the intention of the compilers. The German Code, too, has received some mauling at the hands of the courts, and that too before the two world crises had placed an exceptional strain on it. Thus, the courts allow a debtor to charge his stock-in-trade in favour of a creditor without actual delivery, and without the registration which English law would require for a bill of sale. This is certainly *contra legem*. The old practice, permitted by Roman law, of alienating a thing by *constitutum possessorium*, i.e. by attorning to the alienee, has maintained itself in defiance of § 1205 BGB, which insists that a pledge be accompanied by a transfer of physical possession to the pledgee. This may not worry common lawyers unduly, but the Germans are certain that the Code is being at least evaded. However, the principal way of evading inconvenient provisions of the Code is to have recourse to other provisions which establish what Professor Gutteridge once called super-eminent principles, such as § 242 BGB, which provides that the performance of an obligation must be in accordance with the requirements of good faith, having regard to business usage. Obviously such a provision enables the courts to cut through many difficulties by operating on the conscience of contracting parties as the old Chancellors would have done in similar circumstances. And the courts have taken advantage of it especially in relation to the repayment of mortgage debts in inflated currency and in the handling of frustration cases.[83]

---

[82] BGH NJW 1976, 1740.
[83] F. H. Lawson, *A Common Lawyer Looks at the Civil Law* (1955), 56.

E. The Insurance Factor

It is a well known fact that insurance companies nowadays meet the vast majority of claims for damages for personal injury and death.[84] It is not surprising, therefore, that liability insurance has had a great impact on the law of tort which, at the very least, is now obliged to reconsider familiar problems in a new perspective. So much we can say without any hesitation. But it is less easy to be precise as to the exact way in which this influence is manifested, given a certain reluctance on the part of judges to make public what they may well be thinking in private. Certainly English, and for that matter French and German, legal theory has it that the presence or absence of insurance should have no bearing on the imposition of liability in the case actually before the judge. Viscount Simmonds, for example, has expressed himself clearly in this respect in two leading tort cases;[85] and legal orthodoxy would, undoubtedly, be on his side. It would be idle, however, to deny that judges are not aware of the fact that defendants are insured, particularly against third party traffic risks and just as futile to pretend that the law has not altered to take into account the spreading of insurance practice. But in the United States they have gone even beyond such simple "awareness" and many courts and authors would agree that:

"if loss administration rather than deterrence is the principle aim (of the law of torts) ... then lack of insurability should be considered an important factor in *its own right* and also a reflection of the difficulties that face enterprises forced to become self-insurers by the unavailability of insurance on the market".[86]

Professor Tunc has spoken in the same vein, writing a few years ago[87]:

"Les problèmes de responsabilité civile ne doivent . . . plus être envisagés comme s'ils se posaient entre deux individus. La plupart du temps, aujourd'hui, l'assurance en transformes les donné. Et si la solution d'un procès ne peut guère dépendre du fait que l'une ou l'autre des parties soit assurée . . . ce serait condamner le droit à un contenu singulièrement artificiel que ne pas en élaborer les règles en tenant compte, selon les circonstances, de ce qu'une catégorie de personnes a la possibilité de s'assurer, ou est couramment assurée ou même est obligatoirement assurée".

[84] According to the Pearson Report, vol. 11 no. 509 "It is estimated that claims on insurers represent about 88 per cent of the total number and about 94 per cent of the total value of all personal injury claims in tort".

[85] In *Davie* v. *New Merton Board Mills* [1959] AC 604, 627; *Lister* v. *Romford Ice and Cold Storage Co. Ltd*. [19571 AC 555, 572.

[86] Fleming James Jr., "Limitations on liability for economic loss caused by negligence: a pragmatic appraisal" (1972–73) 10 *JSPTL* 104, 113. See also, *Rowland* v. *Christian* (1968), 69 Cal. 2d 89, 94, 443 P. 2d 561, 564, 70 Cal. Rept. 97, 100. Among the scholars who have for many years advocated the substitution of the fault principle by the risk insurance approach is A. Ehrenzweig, "Assurance oblige—A Comparative Study" (1950) 15 *Law & Contemp. Prob.* 445. See, also, his "Negligence without Fault" (1966) 54 *Cal. L.R.* 1422. In this country the case for the risk approach has been made by, amongst others, J. A. Jolowicz, "Liability for Accidents", (1968) *CLJ* 50.

[87] In *Dalloz Chr.* 1975, 83, 86 and *Archiv. de Philosophie du droit,* vol. 22, 31.

The same is now true in some of the Scandinavian systems where a distinguished member of the Danish Supreme Court has said extra-judicially that in his country judges while expressing themselves in terms of fault, are actually thinking in terms of who is in a better position to bear the risk.[88]

This *open* approach has yet to acquire respectability in this country[89] even though many of the controversial cases lend themselves very easily to such an analysis. The "cable cases", for example, can be approached either in the conventional, abstract, way (presence or absence of duty; remoteness etc.) or they can be seen as deciding who is in the better position to bear the risk they involve. To put it differently, the answer to these cases can be made to turn:

> "on the practicability of insurance against various types of risk, whether of loss or liability, which can only be described in the policy in general terms. If, for example, it is a practical proposition for a business to insure against 'loss of production, however, caused', there would be more to be said for a general rule of non-liability for such losses than if it is in practice necessary to specify the causes of any loss of production covered by the policy".[90]

In fact, consequential losses of the kind suffered by the plaintiffs in these "cable cases" have come to be regarded as usual insurable risks, and loss insurance rather than liability insurance seems to be more practicable and economical.[91] It is, therefore, not surprising that the courts have so far resisted the temptation to extend tort liability to this type of situation. Whether insurance was the dominant consideration when they reached these conclusions is, however, difficult to say since they have given little away in their judgments.[92] But, as Professor Atiyah has pointed out, "whatever motives have actuated the courts, there seems no doubt that their instincts have been sound".[93]

There are other instances which show that a particular plaintiff may, for reasons of insurance, be regarded as a better loss distributor. Though not openly acknowledged, this factor may, nevertheless, have influenced the courts to decide against liability for water companies who failed to keep their water pressures up and thus contributed to the spreading of fires.[94] Similar reasons

---

[88] Trolle, *Risiko og Skyld* (1960) (quoted by S. Jorgensen, *Scandinavian Studies in Law* (1963) (ed. F. Schmidt) at pp. 47–8). For the Swedish Law of 1972 see J. Hellner, "The New Swedish Tort Liability Act" (1974) 22 *Am. J. Comp. L.* 1, at 6–7.

[89] The same is, more or less, true of French law even though, once again, much of the development of the law can only be understood against the background of insurance. Thus, see, Cass. civ. 2 mai 1968, *GP.* 1968.2.109 and, more generally, A. Tunc, *International Encyclopedia of Comparative Law,* vol. XI, Ch. 1. n. 304 and in JCP 1966.1.1983.

[90] J. A. Jolowicz, "The Law of Tort and Non-Physical Loss" (1972–73) 10 *JSPTL* 91, 98.

[91] D. Riley, *Consequential Loss Insurance and Claims*, 4th edn. (1977) 306. A. V. Alexander, "The Law of Tort and Non-Physical Loss: Insurance Aspects" (1972–73) 10 *JSPTL* 119.

[92] But see Lord Denning M.R.'s judgment in *Spartan Steel* v. *Martin* [1973] QB 27, 38, and Lawton L.J.'s remarks at p. 48.

[93] *Accidents, Compensation and the Law*, 2nd edn. (1975), 87. Prof. M. A. Millner, however, in "Growth and Obsolescence in Negligence" (1973) 26 *Current Leg. Prob.* 260, at 272, is not so sure of the result nor happy with "the pure policy approach adopted by Lord Denning".

[94] *Atkinson* v. *Newcastle and Gateshead Waterworks Co.* (1877) 2 Ex D 441; *H. R. Moch Co.* v. *Rensselaer Water Co.* (1928), 159 N.E. 896 (N.Y. Ct. of Appeals).

lie behind the so-called "New York fire rule" "which exempts tortfeasors (usually railroad companies) from liability for all but the first building set alight"[95]
though, once again, open acknowledgement of this is more than lacking.[96]
Finally, to give one last example, this time from France. The more modern
tendency of the Court de cessation to make, where possible, each and every
member of a group liable *in solidum* for the damage caused by one of them
who cannot be discovered, can also be attributed to modern insurance practice. Originally, none of the members of the group were held liable and this
was explained by reference to the theory *of conditio sine qua non* which was
the theory of causation which prevailed at that time. Then the courts changed
their policy and had recourse to a multitude of causal and non-causal concepts to justify this change. It is only rarely however that one finds an open
allusion to the insurance factor which must have played a dominant role in
this judicial *volteface*.[97]

By contrast we find some acknowledgement of the insurance factor in some
recent road accident cases, probably because here insurance is compulsory. In
Launchbury v. *Morgans*,[98] the majority of the Court of Appeal were prepared
to incorporate insurance arguments in their attempt to expand the area of
responsibility in total disregard to the traditional reticence on the subject,
though the House of Lords in that same case was much more cautious. In
Nettleship v. *Weston*[99] Lord Denning was, once again, clearly of the opinion
that in these cases the question to be asked was not whose fault had caused
the damage but who was in a better position to carry the risk. "Morally the
learner driver is not at fault", he said, "but legally she is liable to be because
she is insured and the risk should fall on her".[100] *Nettleship* v. *Weston*[101]
presents an additional interest in so far as it reveals yet another influence of

---

[95] *Ryan* v. *New York Central Ry. Co.* (1866), 35 N.Y. 210.

[96] J. G. Fleming, "More Thoughts on Loss Distribution" (1966) 4 *O.H.L.J.* 161, 166. See, also,
Fleming James Jr., "Accident Liability Reconsidered: The impact of liability insurance" (1947–48)
57 *Yale L.J.* 549, reprinted in Harper and James, *The Law of Torts*, vol II, §§13.2 *et seq.*

[97] Since 1966 the Fonds de garantie will idemnify victims of hunting accidents where it is
impossible to discover which of the hunters involved caused the damage or where they are not
covered by private insurance. The problem discussed in the text will thus no longer arise in the
context of *hunting* accidents. On this and its consequences see Durry, (1971) *Rev.trim.dr.civ.* 377.
A decision of the Court of Grenoble of 16 May 1962 (D. 1963, 137 and note Azard; (1963)
Rev.trim.dr.civ. 555, note Tunc) offers, however, an excellent example of how the insurance factor operated before *the* Fonds de garantie were brought into the picture. In that case, two hunters,
insured with the same insurance company, negligently discharged their guns but only one pellet
hit the victim. Since it was impossible to discover from which gun it had come, the court (ignoring the tendency prevailing at the time to hold both defendants responsible) refused to hold either
of them liable to the plaintiff. Nevertheless, it obliged their *common insurer* to indemnify the victim in the amount specified by the terms of the insurance contract most favourable to the insurer.
The plaintiff was thus compensated even though *neither* of the defendants was held liable for his
hurt.

[98] [1971] 2 QB 245; [1973] AC 127.

[99] [1971] 2 QB 691. The implications of insurance were also taken into account in *Ministry
of Housing* v. *Sharp* [1970] 1 All ER 1009, 1019 and *White* v. *Blackmore* [1972] 2 QB 651, 667.

[100] *Ibid.*, at p. 700.

[101] [1971] 2 QB 691.

insurance on traditional tort thinking: the willingness of modern courts to objectivise the standard of care to near strict liability standards. For since the damages are not going to be met by the defendant but by his insurer, one can afford to ignore the defendant's personal shortcoming and, instead, focus attention on the plaintiff and the consequences of his not being adequately compensated. The same is true of the tendency to approach contributory neg-ligence in a more subjective way and anyone reasonably familiar with the Law Reports will notice how judges often describe conduct as negligent but are most reluctant to describe the very same conduct as contributory negligence.

One could go on listing examples of tort rules which bear strongly the marks of insurance thinking but it would serve no further purpose. It should be noted, however, that insurance has affected rules of procedure as well as substance and of course, the overall preventive function of the tort rules. And it has almost certainly affected the size of awards. To what extent this has actually occurred is difficult to say, though such empirical evidence as exists in the United States would support the view that juries tend to award higher dam-ages in cases of insured defendants.[102] The value of such surveys is, of course, small as far as our system is concerned though, on the other hand, it cannot be entirely ruled out that even judges are not influenced by this factor. And yet, despite all the above, the influence of insurance on the law of tort still tends to be "invisible"[103]in the sense that it is not, as a general rule, openly discussed or admitted by the common law and civil law courts. True, the insis-tence of judges to formulate their judgments in abstract and rather conven-tional terms has not prevented liability insurance from having the kind of effect on torts rules which we have described above; but, it is submitted, it has, on occasion, hindered the intelligent discussion of the policy issues that lie behind all these cases. The prevailing view must, therefore, be regretted for, if the law of tort is, as most would nowadays accept, concerned with the allocation of risks and the best way to absorb them, one should be prepared to discuss in public the bearing of liability insurance and the ways in which it can help achieve these aims.[104] And it has been argued, it is submitted correctly, that this would, among other things, bring a greater degree of certainty in the law:

"for once the allocation of the most frequently recurring kinds of risk had been determined there would be little litigation. Disputes on fact would be very rare and the remaining litigation would be concerned with the question of law—on which of the parties did the risk in question lie".[105]

---

[102] Kalven, "The Jury, the Law and the Personal Injury Damage Award" (1958) 19 *Ohio St. L.J.* 158. The position in France may not be different. See, for example, A. Tunc, "Logique et politique dans l'élaboration du droit, spécialment en matière de responsabilité civile", (1963) *Mélanges Jean Dabin*, 317, 324.

[103] The expression comes from G. Williams and B. Hepple's *Foundations of the Law of Torts* (1976), 141 *et seq.*

[104] See A. Tunc, "Le droit en miettes", 22 *Archives de Philosophie du Droit* (1977), 31, 34 and references given above in nn. 101 and 102.

[105] J. A. Jolowicz, *op. cit.* above n. 86, at 63.

3. SOME TENTATIVE SUGGESTIONS

The prime aim of this paper was to discuss some of the real policy factors that seem to determine the outcome of some important tort cases. One could follow this up with a discussion of the wider implications that this method of approach can have not only for the purposes of the comparative exposition of different legal rules, but also for the teaching and development of one's own legal system. At this stage, however, some tentative suggestions are all that one can offer in the hope that they may lead others to develop them even further.

That the comparative exposition of the law can be facilitated by this kind of approach has, I hope, been made reasonably clear. For how else can a common lawyer explain to his German counterpart the notions of, say, "duty" or "duty owed to the plaintiff"? Certainly, the fact that he, himself, had, until recently at least, doubts about these concepts hardly makes his task any easier. Conversely, how can you direct the common law mind towards an approach based on a list of enumerated interests (such as has been adopted by § 823 I, BGB) rather than a number of legal relationships? And how can you compare "unlawfulness" (*Rechtswidrigkeit*) with "faute" and "duty" without becoming involved in a nightmarish dialogue on abstract concepts? On the other hand, belief in the idea that all these notions are simply verbal *formulae* which enable judges to express their value judgments in particular situations can lead to a proper understanding of their *common* basis. For the real issues that lie behind many of these cases are remarkably similar—at any rate in countries with similar socio-economic structures and comparable levels of industrial development.

This manner of approach will also lead the student to realise that in most cases it matters little which concept one chooses to rely upon in order to produce a particular result for there is, truly, a remarkable possibility of equivocation between all of them.[106] Does it matter, for example, if you deny an owner of a silver fox farm the right to claim damages for harm caused to his foxes by over-flying airplanes by saying that there is "no duty" (as a Canadian court has done)[107] rather than by saying that his damage is not "adequately caused" (which is the reason given by a German court)?[108] Does it matter if you deny the plaintiff in *Bourhill* v. *Young*[109] her right by saying that no duty was "owed to her" rather than by saying (as the French courts have come

---

[106] According to Leon Green, *Judge and Jury* (1930), 19, which concept is selected is often "a matter of taste and finesse". Cf., J. A. Weir in Catala and Weir, "Delict and Tort: A Study in Parallel", 39 *Tul. L. Rev.* 705. ("It is a question of aesthetics as much as anything else whether one feels that the acceptable solution is better produced by emphasizing causation or duty or damage.")

[107] *Nova Mink Ltd*. v. *T.C.A.* [1951] 2 DLR 241.

[108] RGZ 158, 34, 38–9.

[109] [1943] AC 92.

close to doing) that her damage is "indirect"?[110] Does it matter if you say that a rescuer should be allowed to recover for his hurt because his intervention is causally "adequate" (which is what German courts do)[111] rather than by reaching the same result through the medium of "duty"?[112] Does it, finally, matter if you say that a particular plaintiff cannot claim damages for her nervous shock because the harm was "not foreseeable"[113] or because no duty was owed to her,[114] personally, or finally, because it was not adequately caused?[115] The answer to all these questions must be "no". However, what does matter is the realization that in all these instances the common results were dictated by similar considerations of policy. Similar, and similarly concealed behind abstract concepts. If this is correct, however, is it not desirable and useful to discover these policies? To bring them out into the open and discuss them rationally rather than fudge the issues behind terminology which is misleading and can only lead to inconsistencies?

Finally, this kind of analysis will help the comparative lawyer in yet another way. For it will help him understand why the common results sometimes have to be achieved by reliance on different concepts. It is clear, for example, that in the common law systems, where the notion of damage was in the province of the jury, judicial control had to be exercised through some other concept. Causation proved initially a suitable vehicle and, in fact, the first nervous shock cases and pure economic loss cases were decided on causal grounds.[116] Causation, here was, in fact, understood in a strongly normative sense. And where this is so, the logical progression seems to be towards something like the notion of "duty". This is especially true for systems like the common law which tend to fix the limits of extra-contractual liability for negligence by reference to defined relationships. Yet the same trend can be found even in German law. There, the list of enumerated interests made, and to some extent still makes, the notion of duty redundant. But when we move to omissions (which can only be made actionable if a pre-existing duty to act can be discovered) the picture changes. The *Verkehrssicherungspflichten*[117] prove this,

---

[110] Cass. 17 mai 1973, GP 1974.1.71 and note H.M.; Cour de Lyon, 26 juin 1973, *GP* 1974.1.4; Durry, 1974 *Rev. trim. dr.civ.*, 409.

[111] e.g., RGZ 50, 219, 223.

[112] *Wagner* v. *International Railway Co.* (1921), 232 N.Y. 176, 133 N.E. 437; *Haynes* v. *Harwood* [1935] 1 KB 146.

[113] *King* v. *Phillips* [1953] 1 QB 429, 442, per Lord Denning.

[114] *King* v. *Phillips* [1953] 1 QB 429, per Singleton and Hodson L.JJ.

[115] This is, invariably, the German approach. Thus, see, RGZ 133, 270; OLG Freiburg, *VersR* 1953, 322; OLG München, NJW 1959, 819; LG Frankfurt, NJW 1969, 2286 (with an interesting note by Berg, NJW 1970, 515)—though in all of these disputes the harm was held to have been "adequately caused". But many authors stress that this apparently causal approach really conceals policy decisions. See E. von Hippel, "Haftung für Schockschäden Dritter", NJW 1965, 1890, 1891–2; U. Huber, "Verschulden, Gefährdung und Adäquanz", in *Festschrift für E. Wahl* (1973), 301, 318.

[116] *Victoria Rty. Commrs.* v. *Coultas* (1888) 13 App Cas 222; *Cattle* v. *Stockton Waterworks* (1875) LR 10 QB 453.

[117] For a short but excellent account see D. Medicus, *Bürgerliches Recht*, 9th edn. (1979), nos 641 *et seq.* For a more detailed consideration of some of these problems, E. von Caemmerer,

and they have brought German law closer to the English duty-based approach. All these, however, are issues which are too complicated to be discussed at the end of this paper, so they had better wait for its sequel.

Wandlungen des Deliktsrechts (1960), reprinted in his *Gesammelte Schriften, 1*, 452 *et seq.* and, most recently, Christian v. Bar, *Verkehrspflichten* (1980) (the most exhaustive monograph on the subject). For an English summary, B. S. Markesinis, "The not so dissimilar tort and delict" (1977) *LQR* 78, 120–122.

13

An Expanding Tort Law—The Price of a Rigid Contract Law

1. INTRODUCTION

Judicial decisions dealing with the compensability of pure economic loss do not and never will rival in terms of volume the litigation arising from road traffic accidents, defective products and injuries at work (in those systems that deal with this subject under the heading of tort). Nevertheless, the theoretical difficulties associated with some of the recent economic loss cases place them indisputably in the first rank of problem areas of modern tort law.[1] This case law is not unique to England. Courts in the United States,[2] Canada,[3] Australia,[4] New Zealand[5] and Germany[6] have all in the last two decades been

---

[1] This is an enlarged version of an inaugural lecture delivered in the University of Leiden on 3 April 1987. The theme of this lecture owes much to the following works: Fleming, "Comparative Law of Torts" (1984) 4 *O.J.L.S.* 235; Lorenz, "Some Thoughts about Contract and Tort", *Essays in Memory of Professor F. H. Lawson* (1986), pp.86 *et seq.*; *idem*, "Verkehrspflichten zum Schutze fremden Vermögens?" in 25 *Jahre Karlsruher Forum* (1983), pp.48 *et seq.*; Reynolds, "Tort Actions in Contractual Situations", 11 *New Zealand Universities Law Review*, 215 (1985) and Weir, "Complex Liabilities" in *International Encyclopedia of Comparative Law* (1976), vol. xi, Torts, Ch. 12. I also wish to express my thanks to Professor David Robertson of the University of Texas at Austin with whom I discussed many of the points made in this article.

[2] Cf. for instance, *J'Aire Corp.* v. *Gregory*, 24 Cal. 3rd 799, 598 P. 2d 60 (1979); *State of Louisiana* v. *M/V Testbank*, 752 F. 2d 1019 5th Cir. (1985); *People Express Airlines* v. *Consolidated Rail*, 100 NJ 246, 495 A. 2d 107 (1985); *East River Steamship Corp.* v. *Transamerica Delaval, Inc.*, 476 U.S. 858, 106 S.Ct. 2295 (1986).

[3] The most recent interesting case is *B.D.C. Ltd.* v. *Hofstrand Farms Ltd.* [1986] 1 SCR 228. For general discussions of the common law from a Canadian perspective see Smith, *Liability in Negligence* (1984), Chs. 4 and 11; Feldthusen, *Economic Negligence: The Recovery of Pure Economic Loss* (1984).

[4] *Caltex Oil (Australia) Pty Ltd.* v. *The Dredge "Willemstad"* (1976) 136 CLR 529 probably contains one of the most exhaustive analyses. See, also, *Shaddock (L) and Associates Pty Ltd.* v. *Parramatta City Council* (1981) 36 ALR 385; *Minister of Environmental Planning* v. *San Sebastian Pty Ltd.* [1983] 2 NSWLR 268; *Jaensch* v. *Coffey* (1984) 54 ALR 417; *Sutherland Shire Council* v. *Heyman* (1985) 59 ALJR 564.

[5] *Rowe* v. *Turner Hopkins and Partners* [1982] 1 NZLR 178; *Gartside* v. *Sheffield, Young and Ellis* [1983] NZLR 37; *Allied Finance and Investments Ltd.* v. *Haddow and Co.* [1983] NZLR 22. See also, Sutton and Mulgan, "Contract and Tort" [1980] *N.Z.L.J.* 366; Dugdale, "Solicitor's Liability to Third Parties: (1) The Disappointed Beneficiary" [1984] *N.Z.L.J.* 316. See also, French, "The Contract Tort Dilemma", (1983) 5 *Otago L. Rev.* 239.

[6] A number of leading decisions can be found in translation form in Markesinis, *The German Law of Tort: A Comparative Introduction* (1986), pp.112–160. More is reproduced in a companion volume (currently in preparation) dealing with the German law of contract, Some extracts from these decisions—translated by Kurt Lipstein (indicated as KL) or Tony Weir (indicated as TW)—have been included in this article.

called upon to decide when and on what basis pure economic loss should be compensated. In the process some important judgments have been handed down which deserve, at the very least, a glance from those, who in other systems, are asked to resolve similar disputes.

The difficulties associated with pure economic loss stem from many causes. One may result from the tendency to regard no compensation as the only alternative to excessive compensation (both in numbers of successful claims and in size of awards). The real problem with this "all or nothing" approach is that it no longer gives an accurate picture of the positive law of any legal system. For alongside judicial dicta proclaiming continued faith in legal orthodoxy—which denies a tort action for negligently inflicted economic loss—there is an ever-increasing number of exceptions plunging both teachers and practitioners into a confusing, if not unparalleled, state of uncertainty. The "easy" way out would be to revive in a more modern context the old debate about a law of tort or a law of torts. More stimulating and potentially more useful, however, is the attempt to reconcile some of these cases by trying to find a doctrinal explanation for the "deviations" from the rule.

A second and related cause for the difficulties surrounding pure economic loss may be the continued reluctance of judges to acknowledge the fact that often the "right" result does not depend entirely on purely legal reasoning but is influenced by a proper economic analysis of the individual situation which, of course, includes the incidence of insurance. Rare exceptions apart, English judges are still reluctant to consider—in public at least—such factors, while some of their American colleagues at times[7] seem to assume that the insurance factor always favours the non-liability rule.

A third source of difficulty seems to be particularly English and more about this will be said in section 4 below. Briefly, however, one could say that it stems from the fact that some situations resulting in pure economic law defy rigid categorisation, straddling the traditional boundaries of contract and tort. The problem, as will become obvious, is more acute in English law where we still operate on the basis of a fairly rigid demarcation line between these two parts of the law of obligations. This has not been the case in either the United States, or Germany—the two other systems which form the subject of this article—where tort law is more often seen as part of the wider category of obligations; and contract law, especially in Germany, has, for historical reasons,[8] often proved the point of least resistance for expansion when new problems called for the discovery of hitherto unknown remedies.

---

[7] This, apparently, was the view of the majority in *State of Louisiana* v. *MIV Testbank* 752 F.2d. 1019, 1029 (1985).

[8] Four reasons account for this expansion of the law of contract at the expense of the law of tort: the unfortunate tort rule concerning vicarious liability (§ 831 BGB); the refusal to compensate negligently inflicted pure economic loss (§ 823 I BGB); the more extensive period of limitation generally provided for contracts (§ 195 compared to § 852 I BGB); and the more favourable (for the plaintiff) burden of proof provided by § 282 BGB. Of these, the first was probably the most important.

In my opinion it is this boundary zone of contract and tort that we must look at more closely in order to understand some of the recent decisions in English law, criticise them where criticism is due, and praise them where praise has not been forthcoming. In this article I shall concentrate on three factual situations exemplified by the decisions in *Ross* v. *Caunters*,[9] *Junior Books Ltd.* v. *Veitchi Co. Ltd.*[10] and *Leigh and Sillivan Ltd.* v. *Aliakmon Shipping Co. Ltd., The Aliakmon.*[11] Thus, in section 2 below I shall set out some of the salient points of German law. In section 3 the main features of American law will be given, while in section 4 I shall focus on modern English trends. This comparative article will close with some tentative suggestions contained in section 5.

2.   GERMAN LAW[12]

A.   *Contracts in Favour of Third Parties and Contracts with Protective Effects vis-à-vis Third Parties*

Thoroughness, this characteristic feature of the German mind, is particularly obvious in the subject under discussion. To understand it better, we must start by looking at the facts of three well-known common law decisions. Not all are related with economic loss, but they provide a convenient starting point. Moreover, though the cases come from the common law they have exact equivalents in German law.

In *Cavalier* v. *Pope*[13] the wife of a tenant was injured due to the defective state of the leased premises caused by the negligence of the landlord. Her action against him framed in tort as well as contract failed—the first because (as the law then stood) there was no duty in tort, the second because any con-

---

[9] [1980] Ch 297.

[10] [1983] 1 AC 520.

[11] [1986] AC 785. The judgment in the House of Lords must be read in conjunction with the decision of the Court of Appeal in [1985] QB 350.

[12] The German law can be found discussed in all the classic treatises as well as in the shorter but respected text books of Larenz, *Lehrbuch des Schuldrechts, I*, 13th edn. (1982), 201, esp. 208 *et seq.*; Esser/Schmidt, *Schuldrecht, I*, 6th edn. (1984), 562 *et seq.*; Fikentscher, *Schuldrecht*, 7th edn. (1985), 179 *et seq.*; Medicus, *Bürgerliches Recht*, 12th edn. (1984), 483 *et seq.* The following articles have also proved useful: von Caemmerer, "Verträge zugunsten Dritter" in (1978) *Festschrift Wieacker*, 311 *et seq.*; Krause, "Untermieter und Mieter im Schutzbereich eines Vertrages", *JZ* 1982, 16 *et seq.*; Lorenz, note to BGH 6. 7. 1965, NJW 1965, 1955 in *JZ* 1966, 143 *et seq.*; Ries, "Grundprobleme der Drittschadensliquidation und des Vertrags mit Schutzwirkung für Dritte", *JA* 1982, 453 *et seq.*; Schlechtriem, "Deliktshaftung des Subunternehmers Gegenüber dem Bauherrn wegen Minderwerts seines Werks—Eine neue Entscheidung des House of Lords", 25 *Jahre Karlsruher Forum* (1983), 64 *et seq.*; Schwerdtner, "Verträge mit Schutzwirkung für Dritte", *Jura* 1980, 493 *et seq.*; Sonnenschein, "Der Vertrag mit Schutzwirkung für Dritte und immer neue Fragen", *JA* 1979, 225 *et seq.*; Ziegler, "Personale Abgrenzungskriterien beim Vertrag mit Schutzwirkung zugunsten Dritter", *JuS* 1979, 328; Strauch, "Verträge mit Drittschutzwirkung", *JuS* 1982, 823; Assman, "Grundfälle zum Vertrag mit Schutzwirkung für Dritte", *JuS* 1986, 885. All of these articles contain extensive references to the rich case law.

[13] [1906] AC 428 and cf. RGZ 102, 231.

tractual duties owed by the landlord were owed to the tenant only (co-contractor) and not to his wife.

In *J'Aire Corporation* v. *Gregory*,[14] Sonoma County in California had leased premises to be used as a restaurant to the plaintiff. The air-conditioning equipment having broken down, the owner/lessor entered into a contract of repair with the defendants, the restaurant obviously having to close during the repair period. The defendants took a long time to fulfil their contractual obligations to the owner, with the result that the lessee's (plaintiff's) business remained idle for a long time leading to a substantial loss of income. This economic loss was successfully claimed in tort from the defendants.

In *Junior Books* v. *Veitchi*,[15] factory owners employed contractors who, in turn, employed sub-contractors to lay the floors of the building. The work was carried out defectively and, though it presented no danger to human beings or to other goods, it had to be repaired and stock temporarily stored elsewhere. The resulting economic loss, consisting of cost of repair, cost of storage and wages paid to laid-off staff, was deemed recoverable in tort.

The common law in these cases is now likely to allow a tort action; but the possibility of framing the action in contract has also crossed the minds of many lawyers. As stated, *Cavalier* v. *Pope* considered but rejected this point on the grounds that the wife was not a party to the contract of lease. In *J'Aire* the case was initially also pleaded in contract on the ground that the plaintiff could be regarded as an intended beneficiary of the contract between the owner of the premises and the defendants. This point, however, was later abandoned by the plaintiff's attorney in the belief that it would not have succeeded in court. Nevertheless, a Californian commentator has come out in favour of the contractual approach arguing that it would have been less drastic to discover a contract in favour of the plaintiff than to grant his claim by extending tort to cover negligently inflicted economic loss.[16] Finally, *Junior Books* v. *Veitchi* has also been seen by an English tort expert as supportable "in a legal system which admits that [a third party] beneficiary of a contract can sue".[17]

It must be noted that in all these instances common law commentators are envisaging a contract *in favorem tertii* similar to that recognised by section 302 Restatement (Second) Contracts, article 4 of the 1982 Contracts (Privity) Act of New Zealand, and advocated by the 1937 (English) Law Reform Committee. As similar treatment can also be found in section 328 of the German Civil Code (BGB), such terminology, however, in the cases described above, is misleading as German lawyers have clearly demonstrated.

[14] 24 Cal. 3rd 799, 598 P. 2d 60 (1979).
[15] [1983] 1 AC 520, cf. BGH NJW 1981, 1779 (*obiter*).
[16] Schwartz, "Economic Loss in American Tort Law: The Examples of J'Aire and of Products Liability", 23 *San Diego L. Rev.* 37 at 40 *et seq.* Contrast Rabin's view in "Tort Recovery for Negligently Inflicted Economic Loss: A Reassessment", (1985) 37 *Stanford L. Rev.* 1513.
[17] Weir, *A Casebook on Tort*, 5th edn. (1983), 34.

The reason why it is wrong is, on closer reflection, obvious. In the classic contract in favour of third parties, which the above-mentioned enactments envisage, the third-party beneficiary (plaintiff) is given the right to demand from the debtor/promisor the performance of the *primary* obligation. This is not, however, the case in the three instances we have been looking at. Instead, what has happened in Germany is that in these cases the third party can—through judicial creativity—be brought under the protective umbrella of the contract so that he can entertain an action if injured as a result of a breach of one of the *secondary* obligations in the contract. For example, in the German equivalent of *Cavalier* v. *Pope*, the wife/plaintiff is not entitled to demand that the lessor deliver the leased premises (the primary obligation); but she is entitled to claim damages if she is injured as a result of a breach of one of the *secondary obligations* (e.g. to keep the premises in good repair).

This German refinement of the classic notion of contract in *favorem tertii* is of little practical use to the common lawyer, insofar as it represents a conscious attempt to by-pass the unfortunate rule of section 831 BGB which, in effect, makes masters liable only for *culpa in eligendo* or *vigilando*.[18] Indeed, even German lawyers have criticised it for leading to the misleading categorisation of tort cases as contractual.[19] To put it in other words, our *tort* law is nowadays more often than not adequate to deal with most cases involving *physical injury* which in German law are brought under this *contractual* heading. Thus, to give but some illustrations, we do not need this construction in order to protect a child injured on a slippery floor of a supermarket while helping her mother do her shopping;[20] a charlady injured in her employer's house as a result of a defective gas installation made by an independent contractor;[21] an employee injured by defective equipment sold to his employer by an independent supplier[22] or, finally, a member of an association injured on defective premises rented for a special occasion by his association.[23]

But the German concept of a contract with protective effects *vis-à-vis* third parties may be of interest where economic loss is at issue as was the case in *Junior Books* v. *Veitchi* and *J'Aire Corp.* v. *Gregory*. True, German practice has found an even better way round the type of problem that faced the

---

[18] For a fuller discussion in English, see Markesinis, *op. cit.* above n. 6, p.357 *et seq.*

[19] e.g. Zweigert and Kötz, *An Introduction to Comparative Law* (1977) 11, (English translation by Tony Weir), 129.

[20] BGH NJW 1976, 712 (translated in Markesinis, *op. cit.* above n. 6, 434 *et seq.*); cf. *Ward* v. *Tesco Stores Ltd.* [1976] 1 WLR 810.

[21] RGZ 127, 218 (translated in Markesinis, *op. cit.* above n. 6, 444 *et seq.*); cf. *Green* v. *Fibreglass* [1958] 2 QB 245.

[22] BGH NJW 1956, 1193 (with a note by Larenz). (The court here thought that the expansion of the contract was a theoretical possibility was for imposing liability but, in the event it did not do so for reasons unconnected with the discussion in the text above.) BGH NJW 1959, 1676—though here the injury was due to a failure to warn about the inflamable nature of the supplied goods rather than a defect. (For a more detailed discussion, see Heiseke and Larenz in NJW 1960, 77). Cf. Employers Liability (Defective Equipment) Act 1969. For further references, see Sonnenschein, *op. cit.*, note 11, above, p.227.

[23] RGZ 160, 153.

common law courts in these cases; and, I believe, the R.I.B.A. might do well to study them carefully. For it is, I understand, common practice in Germany in respect of the General Conditions of Trade in the building business, for contractors to assign in advance all claims they may have against their sub-contractors arising from breach of warranties, rather than structure the relationship of the parties in such a way as to make it difficult if not impossible to make the sub-contractor liable to the employer for the bad quality of the work.[24] Indeed, so common this practice appears to be that the *Junior Books* type of case apparently has not been litigated in the courts.[25] Well-known academic writers, however, have speculated that, if no assignment had taken place and/or the main contractor was not worth suing, a result similar to that reached by the House of Lords would be achieved by German courts through the medium of contract with protective effects *vis-à-vis* third parties.[26] The advantages of this contractually-flavoured action will be considered more carefully below in section 4 below. Here suffice it to state that the contract with protective effects *vis-à-vis* third parties makes contractual protection possible while avoiding all the consequences of a fully-fledged contract in favour of third parties.

B. The Problem of Keeping the Expansion of Contractual Liability Within Workable Bounds

The doctrine of contractual relativity is as firmly established in German law as it is in the common law. If the ambit of contract is to be enlarged—as it is by constructions such as the contract with protective effects *vis-à-vis* third parties—special care must be taken so that the expansion is kept under control and the dividing line between contractual and tortious liability is not blurred or, even, abolished. The way German lawyers have grappled with these, at times, incompatible aims is instructive for a number of reasons.

Noteworthy is first of all the fact that we are here faced with a judge-made doctrine. True, courts and academics have tried—as is customary in German law—to pin their views on some article of the Code. Thus, sometimes the expansion of the contract has been based on the implied intentions of the parties (or the end-aim of the transaction)[27] whilst in others § 157 BGB or the

---

[24] Schlechtriem, *op. cit.* above n. 12, pp. 64–5. But a building owner accepting such an assignment does not thereby lose his claims against the main contractor. For details see BGHZ 62, 251; 67, 101; 74, 258, 270: see also, § 11 no. 10(a) of the AGB-Gesetz of 1976 (i.e. the German equivalent to our Unfair Contract Terms Act).

[25] BGH 23. 4. 1981, NJW 1981, 1779 (in what appears to be an *obiter dictum*) denies a main contractor's direct action against the sub-contractor; but the relation of Bauherr/employer-sub-contractor is not discussed. But see next note.

[26] Schlechtriem, *op. cit.* above n. 12 at p.65 (especially in view of BGH, NJW 1965, 1955 and BGH NJW 1982, 2431 (neither of these two cases, however, deals with building contracts). Lorenz, in *Essays in Memory of Professor F H. Lawson*, p.97, seems to agree with Schlechtriem.

[27] RGZ 87, 289, 292; 98, 210, 213; 106, 120, 126; 127, 218 (an interesting decision); 152, 175, 177. For a time this practice was continued by the BGH. Thus see BGHZ 1, 383, 386; 5, 378, 384; BGH NJW 1956, 1193 (*obiter*).

even more amorphous § 242 BGB (good faith) have been invoked to render respectability to what is a clear example of judicial activism.[28] This problem has greatly exercised academics,[29] but the courts, in what I have elsewhere called fits of "pragmatism",[30] have refused to resolve this "theoretical" issue, preferring to focus on the narrow aspects of each action before them.[31]

A second interesting feature is, as we shall see, the emphasis on the relationship between contractual creditor and plaintiff/third party (which is known to the defendant/debtor) rather than on the foreseeability of the plaintiff/third party by the contractual debtor/defendant. The weakness of the latter (tort) approach is the potential open-endedness of the liability; an open-endedness which could, given the vagueness of the foreseeability test, lead to the blurring of contractual and tortious liability.

Turning then to the conditions required for the opening of the contractual umbrella we note that they are three.[32] *First*, the third party must come into contact with the performance of the contractual debtor and be endangered (or otherwise affected) by any misperformance in (roughly) the same way as the contractual creditor. This is commonly known as the requirement of proximity of performance (*Leistungsnähe*). *Secondly*, according to what is probably the better view, the contractual creditor must have some *interest* in protecting the third party; and *thirdly*, the above two elements must be known to the debtor/defendant at the time of conclusion of the contract (or the commencement of the contractual negotiations).

This, as stated, is a subject rich in case law where most generalisations are dangerous; not all decisions are clearly reconcilable with one another (as German lawyers readily admit); and where the only discernible trend is for the courts—despite academic doubts—to move towards an expansion of the contractual umbrella. This last point is particularly obvious from recent decisions (taken from what one might describe broadly as the banking/financial area) in which the second (and, in one sense, most important element) of the above requirements has been given a rather too generous interpretation.

The existence of any type of relationship between the creditor and the third party will not automatically bring the latter within the protective scope of the

---

[28] Larenz, *Schuldrecht I*, 1st edn. (1953), 16, III (emphasis placed on § 157 BGB); *idem* in NJW 1956, 1193, note to BGH 25. 4. 1956 and NJW 1960, 78—a joint essay with Professor Heiseke entitled "Zur Schutzwirkung eines Schulvertages gegenüber dritten Personen"—by which time the emphasis has shifted to § 242 BGB. Larenz's work changed not only the theoretical foundation of the new concept but also helped distinguish it from the traditional contract in favour of third parties regulated by § 328 *et seq.* BGB.

[29] For fuller references, see Sonnenschein, *op. cit.* above n. 12, 226 *et seq.*; Strauch, *op. cit.* above n. 12, 823 *et seq.*

[30] "Conceptualism, pragmatism and courage: A Common lawyer looks at some judgments of the German Federal Court", 34 (1986) *The American Journal of Comparative Law* 349.

[31] Thus in BGHZ 56, 269, 273 the theoretical basis of the concept was deliberately left undecided; and in BGH NJW 1977, 2073, 2074 it was regarded as irrelevant!

[32] Rich references to the case law illustrating these requirements are given by Sonnenschein, *op. cit,* above n. 12 227 *et seq.*

creditor's contract with the debtor. On the whole, the relationship between creditor and plaintiff/third party must be sufficiently close so as to create an interest in the former to safeguard the rights of the latter. This is particularly obvious whenever the creditor is himself under a duty of care towards the third party. Thus, parents are responsible for the well-being of their children (§ 1626 BGB) and employers for the safety of employees (§ 618 BGB). Such a close "personal" relationship (as the courts often describe it) has also been found in the contract of lease where the lessor (defendant) is deemed to have an interest in the well-being of not only the lessee (co-contractor) but also of his family (potential plaintiffs) and some at least of his employees. Here, for example, is how the BGH stated this point in its judgment of 16 October 1963:[33]

> "the circle of persons entitled to enjoy the protective effects of a contract has been drawn very narrowly by the Bundesgerichtshof—[BGH NJW 1959, 1676] . . . such contracts are certainly not intended to give a contractual claim for damages to any-one who may suffer harm as a result of the debtor's breach of a duty of care. It accords with the sense and purpose of the contract and the principle of good faith that the only persons to whom the debtor owes his contractual duty of care and protection are those who are brought into contact with his performance by the cred-itor and in whose welfare the creditor has an interest because he himself is bound to take care and protect them, like the members of a man's family or the employee of an entrepreneur. To extend the contractual debtor's responsibility in this way is justified because he must know that the safety of the limited and compact group of persons to whom the contractual protection enures is of as much concern to the creditor as his own."

The same ideas were repeated by the Bundesgerichtshof in, inter alia, an interesting judgment delivered on 19 September 1973[34] where the court, after repeating the by now expected exhortation "that it is essential not to over-extend the circle of persons also brought within the protective ambit of the contract", went on to say:

> "However, there can be no objection to including within this ambit, along with the tenant's family, at least those employees also who are, in accordance with the lease on the property with the tenant or on his behalf."

If these three conditions are satisfied the same rules can be applied to con-tracts of services. The problem of deciding who is to be included within the protective umbrella is, again, crucial. The difficulties it entails can be com-pounded when, because of the nature of the harm, pure economic loss is in issue.

The first case that extended the concept of contracts with protective effects *vis-à-vis* third parties to cover pure economic loss was a testament case where, because of the negligence of the lawyer, an intended beneficiary of a will was

---

[33] NJW 1964, 33, 34 (trans. T.W.).
[34] BGHZ 61, 227, 234 (trans. T.W.).

deprived of a substantial amount of money. In this context the relationship between testator (creditor) and beneficiary (third party) was both close and known to the debtor (lawyer) so there was little difficulty in this respect. There was, however, another problem and this stemmed from the fact that in that case (unlike *Ross* v. *Caunters*) the lawyer was not guilty of misfeasance but of complete inaction, with the consequence that no will was drafted before the testator's death. Not unexpectedly the decision was subjected to much discussion[35] and some criticism, but the Federal Court has refused to abandon its position of giving, in appropriate circumstances, a claim to frustrated beneficiaries. Thus, in a more recent case[36] the defendant was an attorney who represented the plaintiff's father in divorce proceedings. The plaintiff's parents in due course signed a divorce agreement drawn up by the defendant whereby it was agreed that a certain percentage of the parents' property would be transferred to the children after the pronouncement of the divorce. The attorney failed to inform fully his client (the plaintiff's father) how to implement this agreement, as a result of which the plaintiff was no longer able to demand from her mother the transfer of her half of the said properties. The plaintiff's argument that she was included in the protective umbrella of the contract made between the attorney and her father was accepted. The Court reasoned:

> "Now the contract between client and attorney is such, given its nature and structure, that it can only be very seldom, whether one interprets the contract extensively or invokes § 242 . . . that the duties it generates can be sued on by third parties, for the fiduciary relationship between client and attorney makes it strongly bilateral and self-contained. Thus the fact that third parties have an interest in what an attorney does will not normally lead to any extension of his liability, even if those persons are named or known to him. However, an exception must be made where a contract drafted by the attorney is to vest rights in third parties specified therein, especially third parties who, as in the present case, are represented by the client . . . In drawing the line here one must certainly apply an especially stringent test: the circle of persons to whom the protective effect of a contract extends is to be narrowly drawn, so as to avoid blurring the line between contractual and tortious liability in an unacceptable manner. It must always be borne in mind, in claims of purely eco-

---

[35] BGH 6. 7. 1965, NJW 1965, 1955 = JZ 1966, 141 (with a note by Lorenz). The 1965 case is thus identical to *Gartside* v. *Sheffield, Young and Ellis* [1983] NZLR 37 and Hof.Amsterdam, NJ 1985, 40 except that the latter two decisions based the action on tort not contract. I am unhappy at the acceptance of an action in a case of *total inaction* (as opposed to a bad action) on the part of the lawyer, whether this is justified in the German or the New Zealand way. Nor do I think the problem is solved by describing the lawyer's inaction as a *bad act* (breach of duty) rather than as an *omission* as McMullin J. seemed to do in *Gartside*. For *vis-à-vis* the third Party/beneficiary there is no duty to act; and to "discover" one in tort represents a further blurring of the contract/tort dichotomy. In Germany Medicus, among others, used to share my doubts, though in the 12th edition of his book (1984, p.491) he has become reconciled with this result. Reynolds in (1985) 11 *New Zealand L. Rev.* 215, 230 is equally sceptical; but in *Gartside* Sir Robin Cooke took a different view (*ibid.*, pp.40–43).

[36] BGH NJW 1977, 2073, 2074 (trans. T.W.).

nomic loss, that the debtor is not to be made liable for the mere ricochet effect of his conduct on third parties."

What is clear from the above-mentioned cases (and many more could be quoted in this context) is that according to traditional wisdom, the interest to protect the third party/plaintiff is based on a close if not personal link between the third party and the creditor and that this requirement ensures that the contract/tort divide is not excessively eroded.

As indicated previously, however, there is a recent tendency to enlarge the group of protected persons. The widening of the protective ambit of the contract is obvious not only in the fact that the courts no longer insist that the protected third party be specifically identified in advance but also and mainly in the fact that the third party no longer stands in a close, *personal* relationship with the creditor. No longer, it seems, is it necessary (in these financial/banking cases) for the creditor to be responsible for the third party "for better or for worse"—("*Wohl und Wehe*"); instead the paramount question is "in what circumstances the *objective interests involved [sic]* permit the inference that the parties [debtor/creditor] have [even] implicitly stipulated a duty of care towards third parties".[37]

The facts of the case, from which this statement comes, were as follows: the defendant, a professional valuer of land, was asked by S to advise him on the value and rental income of a particular building. The instructions were given at a meeting attended by a banker, S, and the plaintiff who subsequently bought the premises. The defendant did not know whether S and the plaintiff were intending to purchase the building jointly; but in a subsequent letter (addressed to another party but placed before the court) he accepted that he believed that S had probably made the inquiry on behalf of a consortium interested in purchasing the premises. The defendant's valuation concerning the rental income proved greatly exaggerated, due to the fact that he had failed to realise that some of the apartments in the building were subject to rent control restrictions. When the error was discovered the contract of sale was rescinded by a new contract; but the purchaser/plaintiff, in trying to effect the unfortunate transaction, had also incurred considerable expenses which he now claimed as damages from the defendant/valuer.

The BGH first agreed with the Court of Appeal that there was no question here of a contract in favour of third parties (§ 328 BGB) since only S had a right to demand the performance of the *primary* obligation to supply the expert valuation. The Court then continued:[38]

> "[However] this consideration alone does not exclude the *locus standi* of the plaintiff to pursue his claim for damages since it is necessary, in addition, to consider

---

[37] BGH NJW 1984, 355, 356 (trans. K.L.).
[38] It will be noticed that from the reported facts an English lawyer would be hard-pressed to discover a contract between S and the defendant/valuer let alone accept that the plaintiff could demand the protection of this contract.

whether the plaintiff is included in the area protected by the contract. [For] it is recognised today . . . that a contractual obligation may create duties of care towards third parties who themselves are not entitled to demand performance of the principal obligation. As this Senate has stated (references) this consideration applies also to contracts with officially appointed and sworn experts . . . duties of care can also be created in favour of those persons who are not mentioned by name to the other contracting party [debtor]. Nor is it necessary that the contracting party [debtor] should know the exact number of persons to whom a duty of care is owed. The Federal Court has recognised in its case law a duty of care towards third parties even if the [debtor] owing the duty of care was ignorant of the number and the names of the persons to whom the duty was owed (references). It is essential, however, that the group to whom the duty of care is owed should be capable of being determined objectively . . ."

The Court then went on to consider the desirability of including the plaintiff within the list of protected persons, given that S—the person who has asked for the valuation—was not, himself, under any duty towards the plaintiff. The Court's opinion deserves, again, to be quoted fully:

"The District Court was of the opinion that the present contract did not include a duty of care towards third persons for the reason that the witness S did not himself owe a duty of care and protection towards the plaintiff. This consideration, too, does not exclude the *locus standi* of the plaintiff. In principle the parties are free to fashion a contract; they are only restricted in their freedom of choice by the binding rules of law and by the moral requirements to be observed in accordance with § 138 BGB. The parties are therefore at liberty to determine which persons are to be included in the duty of care owed by the contract; they can even extend this duty of care to persons who are not in the charge of either 'For better or for worse' (reference). This cannot be doubted in so far as the parties have inserted express provisions. Where the extent of the duty of care is to be implied from the unequivocal conduct of the parties, the conclusion must be the same; for in the absence of rules requiring the observance of particular formalities an implied declaration of intention is equivalent to one which is express. It is true that in several instances the Federal Supreme Court, in deciding whether a certain person is owed a duty of care by virtue of a contract, has examined whether the other contracting party, to whom the duty of care was owed, was in charge of that person 'for better or for worse' (references). These decisions must not, however, be interpreted in the sense that the Federal Supreme Court affirmed the legality of this type of contract only in these circumstances. Instead they only concern the question in what circumstances the objective interests involved permit the conclusion that the parties have implicitly stipulated a duty of care towards third parties—i.e., where neither any express statements by the parties nor their conduct otherwise offer any concrete evidence. (Even within this approach, which relies on typical situations, the practice of the Federal Supreme Court (references) requires only that normally, but not always, a contracting party should have been in charge 'for better or for worse' of the person to whom the duty of care is owed). It is another question, however, whether an extension of the duty of care arising from a contract beyond the contracting parties must be presumed having regard to the special circumstances of the particular case. It often happens when an expert is being engaged that the opinion to be supplied is to serve as a basis for a decision by persons who are not linked to the expert by contract (reference). In such a case the court ascertaining the facts must examine in accordance with the general principles of interpretation in the light of the circumstances whether the contracting parties intended to create a duty of care in favour of that person. In this connection, too, it may be relevant whether the instruction party was charged with the care of the third party in question; it is not, however, a necessary prerequisite for holding that such a duty of care exists. In the present case it will have to be considered that an interested party who asks for an expert opinion to form the basis of a decision by a certain group, will normally seek to protect not only his personal interests but also those of the other members of the group; consequently it will not normally be his intention, in entering into the contract, to limit the duty to pay compensation to damage which he suffers personally."

The erosion of the requirement of "personal", "intimate" link between creditor and third party, and the corresponding blurring of contract and tort, is seen even more clearly in the next decision.[39]

In that case the plaintiff sold limestone to F who had agreed that the defendant V (who was F's banker) would pay submitted invoices by directly debiting F's account. The plaintiff—who had a giro account with bank G—presented through them at five different dates invoices for goods delivered to F during May–June 1973. None of these invoices were paid since F's account was by that time overdrawn and, in fact, he soon after was declared bankrupt. Worse still, the defendant failed to return the unpaid invoices until the end of June and it was only then that the plaintiff realised that none of his invoices had been paid. He sued the defendant complaining that had the first unpaid invoice been returned to him promptly he would have made no further deliveries of limestone. In the court's view the direct-debiting agreement did not create a contractual link between the plaintiff and the defendant. But, by a separate agreement, banks G and V had agreed to notify each other promptly of any non-payment of presented invoices that exceeded a certain amount. This agreement included within its protective umbrella the plaintiff, so his claim succeeded. The main obstacle that the court had to overcome was the objection that the relationship between plaintiff (third party) and his bank (creditor) was not such as could justify the application of the concept of contract with protective effects *vis-à-vis* third parties. This is how the court handled this crucial objection:

"In order to avoid a flood of claims of this kind to an incalculable extent and to establish limits beyond which the protection of third parties is restricted to the law of tort, the practice of the courts has stated repeatedly that such an inclusion of third parties can normally be considered only if the internal relationship between the creditor and the third party discloses aspects of a personal law character and

---

[39] BGHZ 69, 82, 85 *et seq.* (trans. K.L.). For a discussion of this recent case law see Assman in *JuS* 1986, 885 (above n. 12). The most recent important decision of the BGH on economic loss is reported in *JZ* 1986, 1111.

show that the creditor acts on behalf of a third party for whom he shares responsibility and to whom he owes a duty of care. In so far as characteristics of a personal
law nature are thus required, the principles developed in the light of individual
agreements as to what should apply according to good faith, are unnecessarily narrow whereas in the present case—bulk transactions of a certain type are in issue
which follow a uniformly practised procedure provided on a general scale for legal
transactions based upon the confidence that they will be settled properly and with
due regard for the interests involved. In these circumstances the inclusion of third
parties in the protective sphere of the contractual relations in issue may be possible
and indicated according to good faith, if the mechanism entails for the third party
who employs it certain risks inherent in it and if the participants charged with handling the mechanism can be called upon without further discussion to keep these risks
down. Such is the case in so far as in direct debit proceedings the debtor bank must
return invoices because the payments cannot be made in the absence of funds.
According to the Agreement of the Banks concerning direct debits, invoices exceeding 1,000 DM not met by payment must be returned together with a notice of dis-
honour to the bank at the latest on the second working day by the reverse process
of claiming payment from the first payor, accompanied by a notification by
telegram, telephone or telex . . . This solution may have been adopted primarily in
the interest of the creditor bank [G] concerned. When the invoices are submitted to
it, it credits the creditor's [i.e., plaintiff's] account with the amount to be debited
(subject to a proviso) and normally allows the creditor to dispose of it. Therefore
it runs the risk of losing that sum when the invoices are not honoured if the customer had disposed of the amount in the meantime and is no longer able to repay
it. Consequently the creditor bank has an interest that the 'critical' interval between
crediting the amount and a possible failure to honour the invoices is kept short; . . .
The interest of the creditor is, however, involved to an even greater extent since he
issued the instruction to collect the debt. Firstly, . . . Secondly, if he employs the
procedure of direct debiting for the purpose of collecting outstanding monies, he
will normally be engaged in current business relations with the debtor. If these relations extend over a longer period he has a considerable interest which goes beyond
collecting whatever amount may have fallen due, to receive early notice of any difficulties in the operation of these relations. The fact that invoices are not honoured
is often an alarm signal that the debtor is in payment difficulties . . . While not sharing an identical interest, the creditor bank and the creditor nevertheless share what
is at least an equal interest, based on a similarity of risks, in the immediate return
of unpaid invoices after having received and examined them, or in immediate notification . . . For these special reasons and because legal relationships rely upon the
observance of the practice of the banks confirmed by the Agreement in Direct
Debits, the duty to return dishonoured invoices constitutes not only a contractual
obligation of the debtor bank towards the creditor bank . . . but also a protective
obligation of the debtor bank, based on good faith, in favour of the particular creditor claiming a direct debit."

C. The Theory of "Transferred Loss"

Older, analogous, but not identical to the institution of a contract with protective effects *vis-à-vis* third parties is the theory of "transferred loss"

(*Drittschadensliquidation*). Two English cases could, in German law, be solved by the application of this theory. *Ross* v. *Caunters* is the first. There, it will be remembered, the solicitor's negligence in connection with the attestation of his client's will deprived the intended beneficiary of the intended legacy. The frustrated beneficiary's action has, as already been stated, been upheld in German law and of the various contractually-flavoured explanations that have been proposed, the theory of "transferred loss" probably is the best.

The Aliakmon offers another excellent illustration. Simplifying the facts, one notes that there the buyer, who had the risk but not the property in the purchased goods, failed in his action against the shipowner whose negligent storage had damaged the goods resulting in the plaintiff's economic loss. BGH VersR 1972, 1138 was a decision involving land transport and the Federal Court, following established case law[40] had no difficulty in resorting to the theory *of Drittschadensliquidation* and giving the plaintiff a contractually flavoured action. The separation of risk and property, in the context of carriage of goods, is also envisaged by section 447 BGB and, again, the theory of "transferred loss" provides the plaintiff/buyer with a successful remedy.

What unites the large miscellany of cases which the Germans have systematically brought under the theory of "transferred loss" are two common elements.[41] First is the fact that in these cases the invocation of the floodgates argument—the "shop-soiled" argument of the timorous as Professor Fleming calls it[42]—is inappropriate since one person only suffers loss. Secondly, the co-contractor of the defaulting party—in our two examples the testator or the seller of the goods—will have no incentive to sue (or may simply no longer be around to sue!). As German lawyers argue, in these cases the person who has suffered the loss has no remedy, while the person who has the remedy has suffered no loss. If such a situation is left unchallenged, the defaulting party may never face the consequences of his negligent conduct; his insurer may receive an unexpected (and undeserved) windfall; and the person on whom the loss has fallen may be left without any redress. The question to my mind is not whether the plaintiffs should be allowed to recover—I believe the answer must be in the affirmative—but whether the defaulting defendants should run the risk of incurring greater liability towards these plaintiffs than they would have incurred had they been sued by their co-contractor. The German reply is negative; and their contractually-flavoured solutions offer a neater explanation of this result than the tentative English attempts to harness tort for an answer. (We shall return to this point in section 4 below.)

---

[40] Starting with RGZ 62, 331. See, also, BGH VersR 1979, 906. In German law the plaintiff in *The Aliakmon* would also succeed by relying on § 281 I BGB. In practical terms this produces the same result as the *Drittschadensliquidation* but a very different result to that reached by the House of Lords.

[41] Tägert, *Die Geltendmachung des Drittschadens* (1938) was the first to classify the various instances of transformed loss under various headings. Illustrations are also provided by Ries, *op. cit.* above n. 12. Lange, *Schadensersatz, Handbuch des Schuldrechts 1* (1979) pp.274–97.

[42] *An Introduction to the Law of Torts*, 2nd edn. (1985), 3.

D. *Some Preliminary Reactions to the German Approach*

The comparatist must first describe a foreign system to his readership and then see what conclusions can be drawn from it to benefit his national law. The picture of German law given thus far is, inevitably, a simplified one. The reality is infinitely more complex, if not inscrutable to the foreign observer who treads on perilous ground when expressing a critical view of this system. But even the potentially distorted appreciation of foreign law by the comparatist may be of use to the national lawyer. Four points should, thus, be made at this stage.

First, the test that will determine who is to be included within the protective umbrella of the contract is crucial if the concept of contract with protective effects *vis-à-vis* third parties is to be employed. Most German lawyers agree that the list of such persons must be limited; but they differ greatly as to the criteria that must be employed to achieve this aim and, as a result, as to who precisely enjoys such protection. The traditional emphasis on the creditor's interest to protect the third party/plaintiff seems to me to be the most precise test without being excessively restrictive. In any event in my opinion it is probably more workable to place the emphasis on the relationship between creditor and third party/plaintiff (which is *known* to the debtor/defendant) than to operate, as the common law does, on the basis of the amorphous foreseeability test applied to the plaintiff/defendant relationship.

Secondly, one might venture the thought that the more recent attempts to enlarge the circle of contractually protected persons threatens to undermine the security and (relative) predictability provided by the older tests. If the current trend remains limited, however, to the banking/financial services, it is understandable if not necessarily justifiable. For in these cases the German courts are essentially faced with variations of the *Hedley Byrne* problem which they cannot solve through tort law because of the restrictive provision of § 823 I BGB. The way they expand contract is thus, essentially, as arbitrary as our own attempts to limit tort duties in similar factual situations. Though the pressures are exerted in different directions in the two systems, the problem is the same: discovering the proper bounds of liability which modern insurance practices tend to expand outwardly.

Thirdly, the concept of contract with protective effects *vis-à-vis* third parties and the theory of transferred loss originally had a different area of application: the first was used in cases of physical injury and property damage (mainly in order to avoid the problems created by § 831 BGB); the latter applied to cases of pure economic loss which had not always received full and adequate regulation by the positive law. In this original context the two notions presented one further difference. In the former, the risk of the contractual debtor was widened by the inclusion of a third party within the contractual umbrella. For example, in the *Cavalier* v. *Pope* type of situation, the landlord's liability was *extended* to cover injury suffered by the tenant's family as well as by the tenant himself. On the other hand, in the "transferred loss" type of case all that happens is a "fortuitous" shift of liability as the loss is transferred from the contractual creditor to the third party. As stated, however, the concept of contract with protective effects *vis-à-vis* third parties was extended in 1965 by the legal malpractice case (concerning the defective will) to cover pure economic loss. In *theory*, therefore, one now has two essentially contractual ways of dealing with these cases of economic loss. In *practice*, however, I see little or no difference as to which one applies and my inclination is to suggest that the more clearly defined theory of "transferred loss" can best solve the problems raised by *Ross* v. *Caunters*, *The Aliakmon* and, arguably, *Junior Books*. It is by no means clear, however, how many German colleagues would share this inclination of an "outsider".

Fourthly, and most importantly, I am inclined to think that German law, once stripped of its many technicalities and competing theories, is characterised essentially by one central idea that could be useful to both English and American common lawyers, and this is that these actions are contractual not tortious in nature.[43] No matter that this approach grew out of the necessity to avoid defective or narrow tort provisions. No matter which theory is used to accomplish the end aim (contract with protective effects *vis-à-vis* third parties or "transferred loss"). In the end, what matters is that the result achieved through the medium of contract ensures that the plaintiff succeeds in these cases but that the defendant's liability remains similar to that which he had agreed to with his co-contractor. This is not the right approach for all instances of pure economic loss; but it seems to be eminently suitable for those cases that straddle the traditional contract/tort divide.

3. AMERICAN LAW

American law being better known to English readers than German law need not be discussed in the same detail. I shall, instead, concentrate on some of the points that have also been raised by the English cases. The discussion will proceed under three headings: (i) the possibility of founding an action in tort and/or contract; (ii) consequences that may flow from the proper characterisation of the cause of action; (iii) a bird's-eye view of the wider issues of economic loss with special reference to the position of the plaintiff with a

---

[43] This is, certainly, the position *de lege lata*. *De lege ferenda*, however, some German lawyers (e.g. von Bar, *Gutachten und Vorschläge zur Überarbeitung des Schuldrechts—herausgegeben vom Bundesminister der Justiz*) who have studied the Anglo-American scene believe that the answer may lie in expanding tort law. This is no place to look at these arguments (which, in my opinion, do not take into account some of the objections raised in this article against the use of tort law in the three instances examined here); however, they do give the impression that the well-known saying "the other man's grass is greener" seems to have a strong appeal to comparatists!

relationship to physical property that falls short of legal ownership or a possessory title.

A. *The Possibility of Founding an Action in Tort and/or Contract*

Courts in the United States have shown a healthy disregard for legal tradition where a case before them seemed to require a solution different from that dictated by received legal wisdom. In *Webb* v. *McWowin*[44] for example, a grateful rescuee promised his rescuer a sum of money for the duration of the latter's life. The promise was made after the rescue was over and kept by the promisor but not by his heirs. The plaintiff/rescuer's action to enforce the agreement was upheld by the court even though such an agreement would have been unenforceable under traditional contract thinking since it involved past consideration. After an uncertain start[45] the rationale of *Webb* has found favour in most jurisdictions in the United States and is now substantially codified in section 86 of the Restatement (Second) of Contracts (1981).

American law has also freed itself from the shackles of consideration in the topic of revocability of offers. Through the medium of court decisions such as *Drennan* v. *Star Paving Co.*,[46] the Uniform Commercial Code,[47] or the Restatement (Second) of Contracts,[48] the offeree of a prematurely revoked offer may, under differing conditions, be entitled to at least some compensation for his loss. For our purposes, however, it is the third instance of diluting the doctrine of consideration that is most significant. One is, of course, referring to the erosion of the doctrine of contractual privity by the conferment of rights on third parties to the contract, starting with the decision of *Lawrence* v. *Fox*[49] and consolidated some sixty years later by the decision of the New York Court of Appeals in *Seaver* v. *Ransom*.[50] It is this development that has led many courts to apply the doctrine to two out of the three instances of economic loss considered in this article: the legal malpractice suit brought by the frustrated beneficiary and the action of the general employer against the sub-contractor. The extent to which this reasoning has been used has, however, varied a great deal depending on the courts' willingness to treat these plaintiffs as "intended" beneficiaries of the contract between attorney and testator or contractor and sub-contractor.

In the legal malpractice area the first decision to grant an intended beneficiary a right of action[51] relied on negligence doctrine to achieve its result. But

---

[44] 27 Ala. App. 82, 168 So. 196 (1935).

[45] See, for example, *Harrington* v. *Taylor*, 225 N.C. 690, 36 S.E. 2d 227 (1945).

[46] 51 Cal. 2d 409, 333 P. 2d 757 (1958) which, coincidentally, adopts reasoning similar to that found in French and pre-codification German law.

[47] §2-205.

[48] §87(2).

[49] 20 N.Y. 268 (1859).

[50] 244 N.Y. 233, 120 N. E. 639 (1918).

[51] *Biankanja* v. *Irving*, 49 Cal. 2d 647, 320 P. 2d 16 (1958).

in its next seminal judgment[52] the court ruled that the plaintiff could also recover on the ground that he was intended third-party beneficiary of the attorney-client agreement. Since much effort has been expended by American courts over the years to determine who is an intended beneficiary, it is, perhaps, worth noting that in this case the plaintiff was brought into this category not so much because he was *explicitly* designated as a third-party beneficiary but because the "end and aim" of the entire agreement with the attorney was meant to benefit not the testator but the beneficiary.

Some eight years later, however, this reasoning which, incidentally, entirely conforms with German thinking, was doubted (if not actually abandoned) by the Supreme Court of California in its decision in *Heyer* v. *Flaig*.[53] Justice Tobriner, delivering the majority opinion, argued that the contractual "theory of recovery . . . is conceptually *superfluous* since the crux of the action must lie in tort in any case; *there can be no recovery without negligence*" (italics supplied).

It is not entirely clear—at any rate to a non-American observer—what were the real reasons for the casting of serious doubts on this contract and/or tort approach which, incidentally, can even trace its origins to the celebrated judgment of Cardozo J. in *Glanzer* v. *Shepard*.[54] One reason—perhaps the most pressing one given the facts of *Heyer* v. *Flaig*—will be considered in the next section. Here we can discuss briefly two other possible explanations for this doctrinal shift.

The first *may* be the court's (unexpressed) view that under the multi-criteria test enunciated in *Biakanja* v. *Irving* future courts might have more room to expand the liability of attorneys to other persons who could not so easily be brought under the narrow heading of "third-party beneficiaries". This has, indeed, happened in other jurisdictions, but has not gained universal favour in California.[55] But, quite apart from what has actually happened in California and elsewhere, the fact remains that the contractual theory espoused by *Lucas* v. *Hamm* is: (a) more definite in its fixing of the boundaries of liability; (b) easier to apply compared with the multi-criteria balancing test of *Biakanja* v. *Irving*; and (c) less likely to cause serious disruption in the lawyer-client relationship.

The second reason for the abandonment of the contractual explanation is, in fact, the only one given by Justice Tobriner: the contractual doctrine is "superfluous" since in any event there can be no recovery in the absence of negligence. Now, if that means that an action for breach of contract is not necessary since there is an action based on the tort of negligence, then it is unconvincing. For not only does the narrower contractual test arguably present certain advantages over the vaguer tort criteria; but a contractually-flavoured action, as we shall

---

[52] *Lucas* v. *Hamm*, 56 Cal. 2d 583, 364 P. 2d 685 (1961).
[53] 70 Cal. 2d 223, 449 P. 2d 161 (1969).
[54] 233 N.Y. 236, 135 N. E. 275 (1922).
[55] See, for example, *Goodman* v. *Kennedy*, 19 Cal. 3rd 335, 556 P. 2d 737 (1976).

see, helps explain better some other consequences that flow from the granting of a right of action.[56] Thus, for one thing it avoids the rather awkward formulation that "the duty grows out of the contract [but] it is *ex delicto*".[57] In other words, the tort-based action can never be completely separated from the underlying contractual link between lawyer and client.

Justice Tobriner's statement, however, could be given a second meaning. The words "there can be no recovery without negligence" could be taken to mean that the lawyer must be found to be negligent whether the action against him is framed in contract or in tort. To put it in other words: the lawyer's contractual obligation is, to use the felicitous French expression, an *obligation de moyen* not an *obligation de résultat*. This interpretation is unobjectionable; and it may well have been the one the court had in mind. But the fact that no action for breach of contract is maintainable (in some instances at least of legal malpractice) in the absence of negligence does not explain why the contractual action is "superfluous". From what has been said and from what will follow later the opposite seems to be true, namely that a contractually-flavoured action can best explain some of the little-studied consequences that may flow from the granting of such actions and, therefore, should not be dismissed out of hand.

If we now turn our attention briefly to the *Junior Books* v. *Veitchi* analogues, we note the same general willingness to cope with this factual situation either under contract or tort. That contract theory should have been used to resolve some of the problems that arise in the construction business is understandable, since a typical construction situation will involve at least three closely interrelated contracts, namely that between owner and main contractor; main contractor and sub-contractor; and sub-contractor (or main contractor) and suppliers of materials. In such a complex series of "eternal triangles" the doctrine of third-party beneficiaries seems, at first sight at least, well suited to provide a solution and, indeed, its invocation could be attempted by both sides in such possible disputes: the sub-contractor (for his expenses, etc.) against the owner and the owner against the sub-contractor for the latter's delayed or bad performance of his contract with the main contractor.

Though American courts have repeatedly turned to the doctrine of third-party beneficiaries, they seem to have been unable to work out a clear and consistent attitude towards its usefulness in this type of factual situation. In this context, a clear pattern has emerged only in cases involving actions by workmen and suppliers of materials attempting to recover the value of their services as beneficiaries of the surety bond given by the contractor to the owner of the proposed building. Initially, such actions, too, were viewed with suspicion; and nice distinctions were made depending upon whether the con-

---

[56] For an amplification of this statement see §4.
[57] 449 P. 2d 161 at 164 (1969).

tract was a "private" or "public" construction contract. But for some time now it appears to have been settled that "such persons [can] sue as beneficiaries on the surety's promise, which is regarded as one made to the owner to pay claims in discharge of the contractor's obligation".[58] But in the *Junior Books* v. *Veitchi* type of "situation", which serves as the English model for this discussion, no such agreement has been reached. Many—perhaps most—American lawyers have up to now refused to treat the owner as an intended beneficiary of the sub-contractor's agreement with the main contractor.[59] And according to Professor Farnsworth[60] the same reluctance to use the third-party beneficiary doctrine may continue, given the new wording of section 302(l)(C) of the Restatement (Second) of Contracts (1981).[61] Other lawyers, however, have refused to follow such an approach adopting, instead, differing ways of solving this problem.

The first is characterised by a willingness to invoke the third-party beneficiary doctrine by construing (liberally where possible) the contract between contractor and sub-contractor. Cases like *Oliver B. Cannon* v. *Dorr-Oliver, Inc.*[62] suggest how courts can treat the general employer/owner as a third-party beneficiary whenever the sub-contractor's contract with the main contractor envisages some—even limited—liability directly to the employer/owner in the event of bad performance of the subcontractor's duties. The judgment followed closely the earlier decision in *Sears, Roebuck and Co.* v. *Jardel.*[63]

---

[58] Comment, (1971) 40 *Fordham L. Rev.* 315, 316.

[59] See, for example, *Vogel* v. *Reed Supply Co.*, 277 N.C. 119, 177 S.E. 2d 273 (1970); *Port Chester Elec. Constr. Co.* v. *Atlas*, 40 N.Y. 2d 652, 357 N.E. 983 (1976)—often invoking an argument put forward by Corbin, *Contracts*, (1951) Section 779D, that the main contractor's duty to produce the completed building is different from the sub-contractor's duty to do parts of the work (e.g. the electrical installation).

[60] *Contract* (1982), 725.

[61] A very recent decision of the Court of Appeals of New York appears to confirm this: see *Fourth Ocean Putnam Corp.* v. *Interstate Wrecking Co., Inc.*, 485 N.E. 2d 208 (1985).

[62] 336 A. 2d 211 (1975).

[63] 421 F. 2d 1048 (3rd Cir. 1970) where the complicated facts may, for present purposes, be summarised as follows. Jardel, a property owner, employed a contractor (Robbins) for the construction of a shopping centre. Robbins in turn employed Hirsch, as sub-contractor to do part of the work. The work was badly done so the owner of the building, after he had been sued by one of his lessees, himself sued (in a third party action) the sub-contractor for failing to comply with the specifications contained in his contract with Robbins (the main contractor). The court, analysing the contractor/sub-contractor contract, and in particular a provision that stated that Hirsch agreed to "indemnify and save harmless the owner . . . against all claims . . . growing out of the execution of [his] work" (p.1054, n. 20), decided that Jardel could be properly regarded as a third-party beneficiary of this contract. But the court's reasoning may, arguably, go further than that. For it stated that the contract in any event "*explicitly* contemplated the provision of services by Hirsch [sub-contractor] to Jardel, [employer/owner]". This is an important statement in so far as the "explicit" contemplation of services was discovered in a provision of the sub-contract which, apparently, can be found in the Standard Form of Subcontract of the American Institute of Architects. Where, therefore, similar provisions have been included in the relevant contracts the court's task in treating the employer/owner as a third-party beneficiary must be considerably facilitated. On this and further details, see Comment, (1971) 40 *Fordham L. Rev.* 315, 331–2.

A second way of approaching these cases has shown a clear willingness to circumvent the "intent to benefit" requirement by ignoring it altogether and concentrating, instead, on wider and, it must be admitted, vaguer concepts such as "equity" and "justice". *Flintkote Co.* v. *Brewer Co.*[64] is such a case, also invoking the pragmatic argument that any refusal to recognise the plaintiff as a third-party beneficiary would lead to multiplicity of suits (owner suing contractor and then contractor suing subcontractor, etc.).

The complicated and uncertain picture described above may be an important reason why plaintiffs failed to develop the contractual argument in *J'Aire Corp.* v. *Gregory*, thus forcing the Supreme Court of California to resort to negligence theory as the only way left to satisfy such demands. The facts of the case are fairly similar to those of *Junior Books* v. *Veitchi* and the decision has been analysed in some detail by two Californian tort law specialists. Further discussion here is, therefore, unnecessary except to stress that arguably greater problems arise by the application of tort doctrine, than by the extension of the third-party beneficiary doctrine to this type of situation. English law has experienced (and will continue to experience) similar problems, so we shall return to this point in section 4 below. One observation, however, can be made at this stage and it emerges from the study of German law (sketched out in the previous section). Could it be that the reluctance to expand the third-party beneficiary doctrine stems from the fact that we are thinking in terms of the classical doctrine of contract in favour of third parties which, as regulated both in § 328 BGB and the American Restatement, envisages a right of action that would lead to the enforcement of the *principal* contractual obligation? Such an action carries with it *all* the incidents of contract including, for example, the right to sue for an omission as well as the right to expect the (possibly) higher (strict) contractual standard of care. But in most of these cases we are not really concerned with such a sweeping broadening of the contract but only with the imposition of contractually-flavoured duties of care for breach of secondary obligations. In German terms we are thinking of contracts with protective effects *vis-à-vis* third parties which extend the liability of the contractual debtor only to a limited extent.[65] The contractual flavour of this action helps, as German law shows, keep it within workable limits; it avoids an unnecessary extension of tort (of the kind that we saw in *J'Aire* and *Junior Books*); and it helps explain in an effortless way why the debtor's liability towards the plaintiff is not more extensive than it would have been had he been sued by his co-contractor. This, of course, may not be the way an American lawyer would reason. But it could, perhaps, be tested by asking the following question: if in the *J'Aire* case the defendant had refused to perform altogether his contractual obligations, would the court have allowed the plaintiff a *tort* action? No doubt, some American lawyers would see no problem in

---

[64] 221 So. 2d 794; *cert. denied*, 225 So. 2d 920 (1969) and *County of Giles* v. *First US Corp.*, 445 S.W. 2d 15 (1969).

[65] See Lorenz *JZ* 1966, 143, note to BGH 6. 7. 1965.

this, even though in this way the difference between contract and tort would be completely (and, it is submitted, unnecessarily) destroyed.

B. *Consequences that may Flow from the Proper Characterisation of the Cause of Action*

American law, having abandoned the nineteenth century English notion of privity of contract, has expended most of its energies either trying to explain the departure or, more frequently, trying to identify the classes of beneficiaries. This task has in many instances been accomplished, and when (one hopes rather than if) English law takes a similar path it will, no doubt, profit from this learning. But the next stage refers to a relatively uncharted territory for the American and, *a fortiori*, English courts. The learned authors of a leading American case book have admitted as much when stating that ". . . it may be anticipated that in the future the courts will be less concerned with the metaphysics of privity and purpose and more concerned with the by no means simple problem of the effectiveness of defences, modifications and rescissions against the beneficiary".[66] Even that is not the end of the story. The proper characterisation of the action in the kind of cases we are considering can have a number of consequences which, to my knowledge, have at best only been described. The precise nature of the action—contractual or tortious—against the negligent lawyer, sub-contractor or carrier is crucial for such varied questions as limitation, standard of care, defences, damages, liability for omissions and jurisdiction. Courts in England and in the United States have often been so quick to stretch tort to provide a remedy where contract appeared to offer none, that they have almost completely ignored these questions.

These issues will be discussed briefly in section 4 below as they seem appropriate to both common law systems. Here only one—that of limitation—will be considered since it could have a bearing on some cases. *Heyer* v. *Flaig*[67] offers an interesting illustration.

In December 1962 Doris Kilburn retained the defendant (Flaig) to prepare her will. She told the defendant that she wished all of her estate to go to her two daughters—the plaintiffs in this action. She also told the defendant that she was planning to remarry, which, in fact, she did at the end of that year, ten days after she had executed the will.

The attorney (Flaig) apparently failed to warn his client of the consequences of post-testamentary marriage and included no provision in the will as to the intended marriage.[68] Further, subsequent to her marriage and up to her death

---

[66] Kessler, Gilmore and Kronman, *Contracts: Cases and Materials*, 3rd edn. (1986) p.1419.

[67] 70 Cal. Reptr. 225; 449 P. 2d 161 (1969).

[68] According to section 70 of the Californian Probate Code: "If a person marries after making the will, and the spouse survives the maker, the will is revoked as to the spouse, unless . . . the spouse is provided for in the will, and in such a way mentioned therein as to show an intention not to make such a provision; and no other evidence to rebut the presumption of revocation can be received".

he failed to advise of the need to re-draw her will if she still wished all her estate to go to her daughters. Upon Mrs. Kilburn's death her husband lawfully claimed a portion of her estate and her two daughters sought damages against the defendant for the corresponding reduction of their share in their mother's estate.

An English lawyer might try to explain *Heyer* v. *Flaig* in this way. In contract the limitation period starts to run from the moment of the breach whereas in tort the cause of action accrues when damage is inflicted. Since in the instant case the will remained freely revocable until the time of Mrs. Kilburn's death, the harm to the plaintiffs did not occur until that time. A tort theory of recovery could thus offer, if one were so inclined, the frustrated beneficiary a longer period within which to bring his action. In many instances this may be so. (I say "may" because: (a) the death may ensue soon after the making of the will, in which case there may be little practical difference between the two limitation periods; (b) in some states in America malpractice statutes provide the same limitation period for legal malpractice actions irrespective of whether they are founded in contract or tort; (c) it is theoretically possible to argue that the lawyer's obligation, especially in factual situations similar to those of *Heyer* v. *Flaig*, could be treated as a continuing one and thereby prolong the contractual limitation period.) But the fact that the tort limitation period may be more advantageous to the plaintiff does not explain why the contractual theory of recovery is, *as a matter of law*, "superfluous".

The above explanation of *Heyer* v. *Flaig* does not appear to be correct in the Californian context of the case. That the court there was anxious to establish that the cause of action accrued at the time of the testatrix's death is beyond doubt. But this was more the result of the wish to mitigate the "occurrence rule", that then prevailed in California, and had no connection with the contract/tort controversy. For according to the "occurrence rule" the limitation period "commences to run upon occurrence of the essential facts constituting the cause of action . . . The traditional . . . rule is that nominal damages coincide with the occurrence of the attorney's act or omission, and thus accrual of both cause of action and the statute of limitations is simultaneous".[69] Further, it is asserted that "the occurrence rule applies equally to a theory predicated upon either breach of contract or upon tortious conduct".[70] In the limitation part of its judgment the court in *Heyer* v. *Flaig* was thus not so much interested in contract or tort theory as establishing different periods of limitation, but in adopting the *actual damage* rule in order to mitigate the rigours of the "occurrence rule" in this type of factual context.[71] Thus the preoccupation with the limitation period still does not explain why the contract theory of recovery was challenged by the court.

---

[69] Mallen and Levit, *Legal Malpractice*, 2nd edn. 1981 (with 1985 supplement), pp.446–8.
[70] Mallen and Levit, *op. cit.*, p.450.
[71] Mallin and Levit, *op. cit.*, pp.451–3, 481.

C. *A bird's-eye view of the wider issues of pure economic loss*

This section gives special reference to the position of the plaintiff with a relationship to physical property that falls short of legal ownership or a possessory title. This enormous topic has been the subject of so many articles and notes that it would be an affront to repeat in summary form the many interesting views expressed by other colleagues on both sides of the Atlantic. My comments will, therefore, be limited to some general observations which can be grouped under three headings.

First is the persistent tendency to return to the ruling of the Supreme Court in *Robins Dry Dock & Repair Co.* v. *Flint*[72] and to try to subsume under it subsequent cases dealing with different factual configurations. This application or extension of the *Robins Dry Dock* ruling is by no means obvious in all cases;[73] but, subject to what is said below, it tends to prevail in practice.[74]

Second is the continued tendency to invoke the "floodgates argument". However, the fact that the "floodgates argument" is not relevant in many pure economic loss cases has not received equal attention. Nor has much attention been paid to the fact that it is slowly falling into disfavour in another area of negligence liability (nervous shock) where it once played an equally important role. And, finally, it all too often seems to be forgotten that the proposed distinction between physical and economic harms—based on their respective natures—is losing much of its force as courts are increasingly called upon to resolve issues of liability involving massive disasters. One hopes that no court would decline to consider the actions of persons suffering physical injury as a result of a nuclear accident or toxic waste contamination on the ground that hundreds or even thousands of claims could be involved. If that is so, the distinction between physical and economic harm is drawn not so much on the propensity of the latter to be more extensive but on the ground that the interest of physical integrity is more valued by the legal order than the protection of the economic interests of the members of society—an assumption which is by no means appropriate in all cases.

Not unrelated to this is a third argument often advanced by courts favouring the non-liability rule. In the *Testbank* case Judge Higginbotham spoke of the need to adopt a "bright line rule". The requirement that the plaintiff suffers material damage to his property may be arbitrary; but it does provide such a "bright line rule" that can reduce litigation and encourage settlements out of court. There is some force in this argument; and certainly many recent decisions have adopted it as an essential part of their reasoning.[75] Three

---

[72] 275 U.S. 303.

[73] As the minority suggested in *State of Louisiana* v. *M/V Testbank* 752 F. 2d 1019 (5th Cir. 1985) *en banc.*

[74] See, also, *Barber Lines* v. *M/V Donau Maru.* 764 F. 2d (lst Cir. 1985).

[75] See, for example, *Barber Lines* v. *M/V Donau Maru*, 764 F. 2d So. (1st Cir. 1985); *Getty Refining and Marketing Co.* v. *MT Fadi*, B 595 F. Supp. 452 (1984); *Candelwood Navigation Corp.*

points, however, could be made against it. First, that this kind of argument, however sound it may be from an "administrative point of view" is not conducive to justice. Judges are there to decide disputes and not to think of reasons, however plausible, in order to reduce their work-load. Secondly, those who advocate the retention of the non-liability rule lest the courts be flooded with claims, seem to forget that the same kind of argument has been invoked in the past. For example, something not very dissimilar was advanced against the modern products liability law but, in the end, did not stop the common law from developing the rule that society seemed to demand.[76]

By far the most important criticism against the "bright line rule", however, is that it totally fails to reflect the actual state of the law both in England and the United States. For, not only do we have important decisions given before the *Testbank* case[77] which clearly thought otherwise; but we are also faced with crucial decisions delivered afterwards[78] which openly reject this "bright line rule". Indeed, the *Testbank* ruling has even failed to influence the state courts of one of the states in its circuit about the wisdom of its solution.[79] Even more important is the objection that the non-liability rule is riddled with numerous exceptions which make it more than ever necessary to try to reconcile the cases rather than to try to simplify the law by re-imposing a rule which is quite manifestly not acceptable in many situations. Thus, among the numerous exceptions to the "bright line rule" one can mention the liability for pure economic loss where the action can be framed in nuisance; the liability of attorneys for third-party economic losses; the liability for economic loss flowing from negligent statements; the cases which compensate economic losses using contractual clothing; the slowly growing trend to allow tort law in cases involving damage to products (rather than damage caused by products); and, finally, a group of shipping cases allowing recovery for loss suffered by persons who have a relationship to physical property that falls short of legal ownership as a possessory title.

These cases, the subject of the third observation in this paragraph, deserve closer attention since the issues they raise present a certain factual affinity to *The Aliakmon*. (I have not been able to find in the United States an exact factual equivalent of *The Aliakmon*, I suspect because in "shipment contracts"

Ltd. v. *Mitsui OSK Lines Ltd. and others (The Mineral Transporter)* [1986] AC 1; *Leigh and Sillivan Ltd.* v. *Aliakmon Shipping Co. Ltd., The Aliakmon* [1986] AC 785, 816–7.

[76] The chaotic state of modern product liability law, especially in the United States, cannot, of course, be attributed to the granting of an action against a manufacturer and the setting at rest of the ghost of *Winterbottom* v. *Wright* (1842) 10 M & W 109, 152 ER 402.

[77] e.g. *Petition of Kinsman Transit Co.*, 388 F. 2d 821 (2nd Cir. 1968); *J'Aire Corp.* v. *Gregory*, 24 Cal. 3d 799, 598 P. 2d 60 (1979).

[78] e.g. *People Express Airlines, Inc.* v. *Consolidated Rail Corp.*, 100 N.J. 246, 495 A. 2d 107 (1985).

[79] For further details see D. Robertson, (1986) 46 *Louisiana State University Law Review* 737.

"the title to the goods and the risk of loss passes to the buyer when the goods are properly delivered to the carrier for shipment to the buyer".[80])

In *Amoco Transport Co.* v. *S/S Mason Lykes and others*[81] the *Mason Lykes* left New Orleans half-laden with cargo destined for the Far East. Its first port of call was Galveston, where it was planned to load further cargo and then proceed to its ultimate destination. In the Galveston Channel a collision took place between the *Mason Lykes* and another vessel. The responsibility negligence of the *Mason* for this was attributed 90 per cent to the *Mason Lykes* crew and 10 per cent to the crew of the other vessel. The owners of the *Mason Lykes*, having surveyed the extent of the damage to their vessel, decided that it would take sixty days to be repaired. So, without obtaining instructions on the part of the cargo owners, they discharged the cargo (which was undamaged) at Galveston and subsequently offered to transport it in another vessel to the port of destination. A "freight earned clause" in the bill of lading entitled them to retain the freight originally paid for the uncompleted voyage with the *Mason Lykes*. They subsequently also charged new freight for the transportation of the goods in the substituted vessel. This the cargo owners claimed successfully partly from the owners of the *Mason Lykes* and partly from the owners of the second vessel. The reasoning on the first part of the claim is entirely based on shipping law rules and need not concern us. But the claim against the second vessels[82] which had contributed to the damage to the *Mason Lykes*, was faced with the *Robins Dry Dock* argument: the loss of the cargo owners was purely economic in nature and could not be recovered in the absence of any physical damage to property. The argument was rejected, the court holding that the recent *Testbank* case had not disturbed the long-standing admiralty exception that allowed recovery in such cases on the well-known grounds of "community of venture".

Venore Transportation Company v. *M/V Struma*[83] is less easily reconciled with the non-liability rule. In that case the time charterer of a vessel was required to pay charter hire during the period that the chartered vessel underwent repairs as a result of colliding with defendants' vessel. The charterers' tort claim against the defendants succeeded, notwithstanding the *Robins Dry Dock* ruling. The United States Court of Appeals for the Fourth Circuit avoided the *Robins* rule by giving it a very narrow ambit: in *Robins*, reasoned the Court in *Venore*, the plaintiff/charterer paid no charter hire for the period during which the vessel was out of service. The claim there was essentially one for loss of anticipated profits. In *Venore* by contrast, payment of the charter hire was provided for contractually, even during such periods of immobility of the vessel. The court held that:

[80] *Ladex Corp.* v. *Transportes Aereos Nationales*, 476 So. 2d, 763 at 765 (1985). See, also, UCC sections 2-320; 2-401(a); 2-504. Thus, in the "shipment contract" which is regarded as the "normal contract", American law seems to have avoided *The Aliakmon* problem.
[81] 768 F. 2d 659 (1985).
[82] *Ibid*. at p. 665 *et seq.*
[83] 583 F. 2d 708 4th Cir. (1978).

"when there has been no suspension in the payment of charter hire during the period when the vessel is out of service, the time charterer who has paid the charter hire is entitled to recover what the owner would have been entitled to recover had those payments been suspended".

As stated, the judgment is an interesting one: *first* because it interprets the *Robins* case in a narrow way;[84] *secondly* because its approach has been followed by other courts in other jurisdictions[85] showing, at the very least, a relative unease with the *Robins* ruling which, however, was not shared by the majority in the *Testbank* case; *thirdly*, because the fate of such cases, not even considered in *the Testbank* decision must, in theory at least, remain undecided in the light of the sweeping contrary dicta in the *Testbank*. Conversely, of course, one could argue that they remain unaffected as depending on their own facts—an argument that could be strengthened by the observation that, as already stated, the *Testbank* itself does not appear to have had much impact on the state case law within its own circuit.

The third case, *Domar Ocean Transportation Ltd.* v. *MIV Andrew Martin*[86] is particularly worth quoting, since it was decided by Judge Higginbotham *after* he had delivered his *Testbank* opinion. In this case the plaintiff *owned* a barge (*Domar*) and *chartered* a tug (*Cindy Cenac*) to tow it. The barge was damaged, primarily as a result of negligent navigation by the defendant's tug. The damaged barge had to undergo repairs lasting over 1,000 hours and the magistrate who tried the case at first instance awarded the plaintiff "detention damages of US$ 373 per hour, [this being] the average rate charged for the *Domar* [barge]-*Cindy Cenac* [tug] combination".[87] The defendants contested this method of calculation of the plaintiff's loss. They argued that "much of this award represents *Domar*'s loss of the optimal use of the *Cindy Cenac*, which, deprived of its partner the *Domar*, earned less than it would have otherwise. Andrew Martin [the defendants] argues that because the *Cindy Cenac* itself suffered no physical damage, *Domar* cannot recover for the loss of its use under *Robins Dry Dock*". In simple language the plaintiff could recover the loss he suffered as a result of the damage to his barge, but not that which he suffered by not using the tug (which he did not own and which was undamaged) in combination with his barge. Judge Higginbotham disagreed, holding that *Testbank* "is not so restrictive".[88] True, *Testbank*, reaffirming the *Robins* case, wished to insist on the presence of "physical damage to a *proprietary* interest" before economic loss could be compensated. In this case, however, barge and tug operated "as a unit" and, therefore, the plain-

---

[84] "In *Robins Dry Dock,* Mr. Justice Holmes wrote broadly, as he customarily did": *ibid.* at p.711.

[85] e.g. *Standard Navigazione* v. *K.Z. Michalos*, 1981 A.M.C. 748 (S.D. Tex. 1981).

[86] 754 F. 2d 616 (1985). The court describes the charter as an open-ended "evergreen" charter. It is not clear to me whether this could be treated as an equivalent to a charter by demise. But even if that were so, the judge did not seem to base his judgment on that point.

[87] *Ibid.* at p.618.

[88] *Ibid.* at p.619.

tiffs "had the requisite *proprietary* interest in the combination".[89] English lawyers, reading the case with *La Société Anonyme de Remorquage à Helice* v. *Bennetts*[90] will find the reasoning intriguing; American readers may be excused for wondering what happened to the "bright line rule"; and academic writers may well wonder whether there is not yet another factual type of situation which represents an exception to the non-liability rule. To put it differently, did not Judge Higginbotham engage in this case in what he had termed in his *Testbank* opinion "management" rather than "adjudication"?[91]

4. ENGLISH LAW

A. General Remarks

In the introduction I gave some reasons why I think the compensation of pure economic loss is in such a state of chaos. Now we can add another reason which is particularly appropriate to English law. Quite simply it is this system's tendency to operate on the basis of a rigid demarcation between contract and tort. In *this apparently* neat divide, unintentionally inflicted economic loss should, in principle, be left to the law of contract. Tony Weir has encapsulated this philosophy by stating that: "Contract is productive, tort law is protective . . . tortfeasors are typically liable for making things worse, contractors for not making them better". The statement is phrased in a descriptive way—"this is what has been happening"—and in that sense it is correct. I suspect, however, that Weir also would like it to be taken prescriptively: that is how things should remain. His frequently expressed opposition to the use of tort law as a way of compensating negligently inflicted economic loss is well known and lends credence to this interpretation. We have here, therefore, a *theoretical* reason why we should leave the compensation of pure economic loss to contracts, which buttresses some of the more *pragmatic* objections offered against the abandonment of the non-liability rule.

One wonders, however, whether economic loss can be really placed on one side of the divide? Weir is conscious of the difficulties of his proposed division so he cautiously adds the word "typically" in his above-quoted statement. In fact he goes further by admitting that "a man who makes a thing worse is also not making it better". This, however, does not go far enough since it does not seem to face a primary tort problem which is: "is a man who is not making a thing better making it in any sense worse?" We do not have to quibble with these tongue-twisters but only think of the types of cases we have been discussing. In the legal malpractice situation has the intended beneficiary been made poorer or not made richer? And what if he had bought a house

[89] *Ibid*. at p.619, italics supplied.
[90] [1911] 1 KB 243.
[91] This "jurisprudential" argument of Judge Higginbotham's can be found on pp. 1028–9 of his opinion; Judge Wisdom's reply is on p. 1052.

intending to pay off a mortgage with the proceeds of the expected legacy? Similarly in the construction contracts has the negligence of the sub-contractor made the employer poorer or failed to make him richer? The same arguments can be made in the context of the shipping cases; and other illus-trations could be given.

Examples such as these suggest, if not actually prove, that the produc-tive/protective dichotomy is often unworkable. These cases also show, espe-cially when contrasted with some American and German counterparts, how rigid English contract law has been by refusing to bring them within its ambit. But if contract has been rigid, tort law has been obstinately simplistic in its animosity towards pure economic loss with the result that many of these cases, until recently at least, remained beyond the pale of law. Weir attacked the *Junior Books* judgment inter alia on the grounds that it is "unfair".[92] To me it would be unjust if the plaintiffs in the three cases under review were not allowed an action, *given* that the co-contractor of the defaulting defendant will have no incentive to sue (or he may simply no longer be around to sue!). The unfairness becomes even more obvious in cases involving bulk shipments which are bound to be affected by *The Aliakmon* ruling. For such a buyer of a bulk shipment may have the risk—hence he will be unable to sue the seller. But he does not have the ownership in goods nor any contract with the car-rier so he cannot sue him either. This iniquitous result flows from *The Aliakmon* and the fact that in this type of factual situation the buyer does not get the ownership in the goods until the bulk is split on delivery; and he gets no contract with the carrier because he (the buyer) provides no consideration (freight having been prepaid and no demurrage being due under the bill of lading). The upshot of all this is, as a learned academic with great practical experience has remarked,

> "that one who takes a bill of lading covering an unidentified part of a bulk cargo may find that if the cargo is lost or damaged through the negligence of the ship he has no right to sue the carrier either in contract or in tort and is entirely dependent on the co-operation of his seller in the pursuit of proceedings".[93]

In *The Aliakmon* Lord Brandon does not appear to have contemplated the consequences of his ruling in the bulk cargo situation. Nor, apparently, did he consider its repercussions on international banking and the law of docu-mentary credits. For buyers are not the only possible victims of *The Aliakmon*. Issuing banks (acting for the buyers), when faced with insolvent clients in a situation where insurance is unavailable (or inadequate), have, themselves, the right to present to the carrier the shipping documents and

---

[92] *A Casebook on Tort*, 5th edn. (1983), 33.
[93] Goode, *Proprietary Rights and Insolvency in Sales Transactions* (1985), 64. But even if the buyer somehow acquires ownership during transit, he would still face the formidable difficulty of having to prove that he has ownership at the time of the loss. See *The Nea Tyhi* [1986] 1 Lloyd's Rep. 606. This would certainly be the case where, as a result of bad storage, minor damage occurred but was not discovered until arrival. See Clarke in [1986] *C.L.J.* 382.

demand possession of the goods. Now if these goods have been damaged or lost during the voyage the bank will not be able to take advantage of section 1 of the Bills of Lading Act 1855 since they have only obtained special (and not general) property as pledgees of the goods. Their only remedies therefore will be on the basis of an implied contract[94] or tort. The first course of action, however, may, for a variety of reasons, not be available;[95] and the tort remedy has now been foreclosed by the House of Lords.

In view of the above it can be asserted that Lord Brandon failed to consider adequately the full implications of his negative ruling. But was this ruling fair at least in the specific factual situation of *The Aliakmon?* Lord Brandon obviously considered that it was, since he clearly thought that the particular buyer's misfortune was the result of his own failure to stipulate that the seller exercise his contractual rights against the carrier or for failing to have the seller transfer such rights to him by means of assignment. With great respect, even this solution, in addition to being commercially inconvenient,[96] does not always adequately protect the buyer. For a buyer who follows Lord Brandon's advice will only obtain such rights as the seller himself had under the contract of carriage. This means that he (like the seller who is the original shipper) would not be able to claim that the goods (or part of them) were already damaged at the time of shipment where a clean bill of lading had been issued. (This was, in fact, the case in *The Aliakmon*). If, on the other hand, the buyer is allowed to sue in contract under the Bills of Lading Act 1855 he would then have the benefit of any estoppels arising from the false statements in the bill of lading.[97]

The question, therefore, is not whether the plaintiffs in all these cases should be allowed to recover from the tortfeasor. Rather the real issue is to make sure that their defendants are not placed in a worse position than they would have been in had they been sued by their co-contractors. Finding the proper doctrinal explanation seems infinitely more important than trying to re-establish the shaken authority of the non-liability rule. As the Supreme Court of New Jersey put it in its most recent decision: "In the end, the challenge is to fashion a rule that limits liability but permits adjudication of meritorious claims".[98] We shall discuss this point in section C below of this

---

[94] On the lines of *Brandt* v. *Liverpool Brazil and River Plate S.N. Co.* [1924] 1 KB 575.

[95] e.g. *The Wear Breeze* [1969] 1 QB 219 and *The Aliakmon* [1986] AC 785 situations.

[96] Practice does not seem to like the suggestion that the buyer makes it a term of the variation that the seller sues personally or assigns his actions to the buyer. The inconvenience of adding extra terms in standard-form transactions becomes particularly obvious not in single sales but in chain transactions. "The very essence of a bill of lading is the negotiability, and one-off terms could be very inconvenient . . . in bulk commodity sales, where the goods may be sold many times while at sea." Todd, "Actions by Banks Against Carrier—An update of the Tort Position", (1986) 2 *Journal of International Banking Law*, 127, 130.

[97] *Silver* v. *Ocean SS Co. Ltd.* [1930] 1 KB 416. In this sense Treitel, "Bills of lading and third parties" (1986) 10 *L.M.C.L.Q.* 294, 304–5 (adding, however, that an action of misrepresentation may be available in this case).

[98] *People Express Airlines* v. *Consolidated Rail*, 100 N.J. 246, 495 A. 2d 107 at p.2, 11 (1985).

paragraph after we have commented in section B below upon the House of Lords' recent attempts to return tort law to its old simplistic narrow-mindedness.

B. *The Aliakmon*

The Aliakmon[99] is a remarkable case but for all the wrong reasons. At the Court of Appeal three learned judges spoke with three different voices. This diversity of reasoning came at the end of three years after *Junior Books* was decided—three years filled with judicial decisions expressing dissatisfaction with *Junior Books* or, more likely, its wide *dicta*, but agreeing on little else. The judgment of the House of Lords was thus awaited with an interest that probably exceeded the significance of the facts of that particular case. The tone of the one opinion judgment that was finally delivered by the House of Lords carries the infallibility doctrine to extremes. Yet one wonders whether an opinion that at times displays an inadequate consideration of the repercussions of the decision, opts for a solution that clearly is utopic, and unforgivably misses the opportunity to bring some order into the prevailing chaos, will prove the last word on this matter.

The dubious logic is evident, inter alia, in the part of the judgment that advocates strict adherence to the non-liability rule. A prime reason given for this is that "where a general rule . . . has been established by a long line of authority over many years . . . the law should [not] allow special pleading in a particular case within the general rule to detract from its application".[100] This is a remarkable declaration to the effect that however questionable a legal rule may be, however much the circumstances may have changed since its inception, it must remain fossilised and immutable. Since it cannot be judicial laziness that prompted such a pronouncement it must be something else. Lord Brandon gives two further reasons: one is that "the rule [of non-liability which he prefers] is simple to understand and easy to follow".[101] But assuming a rule is bad or inappropriate, should it still be applied because it is "simple to understand and easy to follow"? Lord Brandon realises that this must be untenable for he buttresses this first bad reason with a second. If one exception were to be made, others might follow and this would undermine certainty in the law which is "of the utmost importance".[102] But this is precisely the problem academics and practitioners are trying to work out: the rule of non-liability is already riddled with exceptions. The observations made

---

[99] [1986] AC 785. Such notes as have appeared so far have varied from the mildly disapproving to the severely critical. Thus, see Clarke [1986] *C.L.J.* 382; Jacobs (1985) 135 *N.L.J.* 285 (criticising mainly the majority in the Court of Appeal); Pearce and Tomkin (1986) 136 *N.L.J.* 1169; Shaw [1987] *Journal of Business Law* 55; Todd [1986] *Journal of International Banking Law*, II *et seq.*, 127 *et seq.*; Treitel, (1986) 10 *L.M.C.L.Q.* 294 *et seq.*

[100] *Ibid*. at pp.816–7.

[101] *Ibid*. at p. 816.

[102] *Ibid*. at p.817. On the argument of certainty in this context, see Treitel's sceptical views in (1986) 10 *L.M.C.L.Q.* 294, 301.

about American law on this point apply equally to English law. Those teaching this branch of the law are nowadays forced back into the old debate about a law of tort or a law of torts. Have all these exceptions vanished by judicial fiat?

The means proposed to effect a return to the simple non-liability rule are equally novel. The early cases on economic law were decided before the law of negligence had—for better or for worse—moved into forward gear. *Hedley Byrne and Co., Ltd.* v. *Heller and Partners, Ltd.*,[103] with its many direct and indirect offshoots, was the first forward step. Then came the adoption of the famous "two-phased" approach, commonly linked with Lord Wilberforce's opinion in *Anns* v. *Merton London Borough*[104] but in fact first shaped in present form by Lord Reid in *Dorset Yacht Co., Ltd.* v. *Home Office*.[105] This approach had been used by the Court of Appeal (though it led the learned judges to different conclusions). It had been relied upon directly or indirectly by numerous lower courts; it has been used by the House of Lords itself though, admittedly, warnings were voiced about it not being treated as a hard and fast rule.[106] Lord Brandon felt otherwise. This useful test—and no-one treats it as being more than just a test to determine whether a duty should exist—was appropriate *only to* "*novel*" factual situations. The facts of *The Aliakmon* not being novel, the test had no role in resolving this dispute. As stated, this "two-phased" approach has been used in many cases up to now which did not involve "novel factual situations". It would be a great blow to certainty—which Lord Brandon rates so highly—if litigants were to use his dicta successfully in order to reopen issues which appear to have been settled. It is this type of reasoning, which aims at re-establishing the authority of a rule that has clearly broken down in practice, that makes me doubt the longevity of the judgment.

The Aliakmon judgment, however, is just as remarkable for what it failed to do as for the way in which it tried to achieve its aims. The main omission lies in its failure to consider adequately the imaginative judgment delivered by Robert Goff L.J. in the Court of Appeal. But the Court, in its own words, was too "fainthearted" to attempt the task of elaboration. It thus took the view that it was impossible to shape a duty of care in tort that would reflect the contractual duties owed by the carrier to the shipper.

The task was seen as near impossible given the intricate blend of rights, immunities and responsibilities contained in the Hague Rules. The German theory of *Drittschadensliquidation* would provide an answer here, and from what has been said up to this point its similarity with the reasoning of the

---

[103] [1964] AC 465.
[104] [1978] AC 72–8.
[105] [1970] AC 1004.
[106] *McLoughlin* v. *O'Brian* [1983] AC 410 (at pp.420–1); *Tate and Lyle* v. *G.L.C.* [1983] AC 509 (at pp.529–31); *Governors of the Peabody Donation Fund* v. *Sir Lindsay Parkins and Co. Ltd.* [1985] 1 AC 210 (at pp.240–l).

judgment of Robert Goff L.J. must be obvious. The third party who had suffered the loss is given the *contractual* action of the creditor against the debtor.
The difficulties that Sir John Donaldson M.R. and Lord Brandon experienced
in this respect have, apparently, been resolved by Scandinavian and Dutch
lawyers,[107] and they would also vanish into thin air if one were prepared to
adopt the German reasoning. But traditional English lawyers would object,
however, that such a contractually-flavoured action, even though it does not
amount to a fully-fledged contract in favour of third parties, remains impossible while English law adheres to its own notion of privity of contract. The
main contribution of Robert Goff L.J. in *The Aliakmon* was his attempt at
the end of his judgment to circumvent this difficulty by showing how the *permissible tort action could be fashioned by the underlying contractual relationship*. In this he identified the real problem in *The Aliakmon*. For surely what
matters is that the carrier's liability in tort is no greater than his liability in
contract under the Hague/Visby Rules rather than whether he can be sued by
the buyer. Why could not the standard and ambit of the tort duty be determined by the contract? Why could not the exclusion clauses in the Rules apply
in the tort action? In fact, Article IVbis of the Hague/Visby Rules expressly
states that the carrier's defences shall apply "whether the action be found in
contract or in tort".

The wording and the history of this Rule could be taken to envisage tort
actions, *whether or not the claimant had a contract with the defendant/car-
rier*.[108] Courts have limited a tort action in terms of a contract between the
same parties.[109] Why should this not be also possible when the terms are
found in a contract between different parties but are clearly known to all the
world? Why not a tort action which must be brought within a year and for
no more than a certain sum? True, the onus of proof under the Hague Rules
is different from those in a tort action; but a tort action is harder to make, so
at the end of the day the carrier is not really prejudiced. In fact the Dutch
legislator has, in this context, adopted Lord Goff's theory. For articles 321(3)
and 473(a) of the Dutch Commercial Code (as interpreted by academic writers) allow the buyer of goods (who has the risk but not the property in the
goods) to sue the negligent "operator of the vessel" (*reder; armateur*) or carrier for damage to the goods. The action is in *tort;* and the carrier/defendant
can invoke against the plaintiff all the limitation and exclusion clauses embod-

---

[107] See Clarke [1986] C.L.J. 382. See, also, BGHZ 56, 269, 273 (notation clause); 33, 247, 250
(contributory negligence). For Dutch law, achieving similar results through statute, see below n.
10.

[108] This is the view taken by an experienced practitioner: Diamond, "The Hague-Visby Rules"
(1978) L.M.C.L.Q. 225, 248–9. Treitel, in 1986 L.M.C.L.Q. 294, 304, following Scrutton, *On
Charterparties and Bills of Lading*, 19th edn., 458, is inclined to think that the rule merely means
"that a person who is a party to the contract of carriage cannot improve his position by disregarding the contract and suing in tort". In the Court of Appeal Lord Justice Goff was implicitly
prepared to accept the Diamond view; and Treitel, though disagreeing with it, in no way suggests that it is untenable. Reynolds, in (1986) L.M.C.L.Q. 97, 108 also leaves the point open.

[109] *The Tai Hing* [1986] AC 80.

ied in his contract with the seller which, in the case of carriage of goods by sea, is governed by the Hague/Visby Rules.[110] As I see it, therefore, the real difficulty lies in the unwillingness to undertake this "blending" operation rather than in its impossibility. That this result—through tort—may be conceptually inelegant is the price we have to pay for our rigid adherence to antiquated notions of privity and/or our unwillingness to amend the 1855 Act.

C. *Problems Unsolved or Partially Solved*

We have so far noted how German law has opted for contractual solutions for the three types of cases considered in this article; American law has experimented with both contract and tort answers and English law has adopted the tort reasoning. The advantages of the contractual explanation become even more obvious when one turns to consider the following issues that depend on the choice of contract or tort as the basis of these actions.

(a) *Jurisdiction.* The choice-orientated approach adopted by conflicts rules in cases of contract seems more appropriate in these types of cases than the *locus* of the accident tort approach. In any event, it would be odd if the dispute between plaintiff and defendant/debtor were subject to one rule and the relationship between defendant/debtor and creditor were governed by a different law. We can, of course, again allow the contractual relationship to influence the tort action;[111] but why not opt more openly for the more straightforward contractual reasoning?

(b) *Liability for omissions.* Traditional tort theory would deny liability where the debtor/defendant has remained inactive rather than acted badly. A contractual solution could make the defendant/debtor liable both for nonfeasance and misfeasance. Should this be regarded as excessively onerous for the defendant/debtor it may still be avoided through the use of *Drittschadensliquidation* or the German notion of contract with protective effects *vis-à-vis* third parties, since this, it will be remembered, makes the debtor liable only for the bad or delayed performance of the *secondary* obligations of the contract.

(c) *Measure of damages.* The tort and contract measure of damages probably remains different despite Lord Denning's attempt to propose a compromise in *H. Parsons (Livestock) Ltd.* v. *Ottley Ingham & Co., Ltd.*[112] A

---

[110] Article 321(3) Dutch Commercial Code: "In respect of loss or damage caused to persons or goods carried by a ship, the operator's (*reder*) liability to third parties shall not exceed the amount for which he would be liable to the other party to the contract of carriage or affreightment made by him".

Article 473(a) Dutch Commercial Code: "In respect of loss or damage caused to goods carried by him the carrier's liability to third parties shall not exceed the amount for which he would be liable to the other party to the contract of carriage made by him".

[111] As Tobriner J. suggested in *Heyer* v. *Flaig*, 70 Cal. 2d 223, 449 P. 2d 161 (1969).

[112] [1978] QB 791.

contractual solution would favour the award of full expectation damages to the plaintiff/third party and this, again, is supported by German law.[113]

(d)   *The limitation period*. Both the length and starting point of the limitation period differ in contract and tort. It is submitted it would be impractical if one relationship (plaintiff/defendant/debtor) were subject to one rule and the other relationship (debtor/creditor) governed by a different rule. This appears to be in principle the correct starting point but it must be admitted that in some cases it may cause problems. Thus, in the frustrated beneficiary type of case the right of the beneficiary to sue the testator lawyer is not identical to that of the testator since the harm suffered by each is different. Also, if the contractual period of limitation were to apply in exclusion of all tort remedy, it could harm the beneficiaries' interests in those systems where the contractual period of limitation is not substantially longer than the tort period of limitation.

(e)   *The standard of care*. Few lawyers in England seem to have considered points (a)–(d). More concern, however, has been shown about the standard of care that would be appropriate to the tort action and whether it would be different from that found in the debtor-creditor (contractual) relationship. German law, proceeding on contract theory, has not experienced this difficulty; and German writers, considering a hypothetical (for them) tort action had had no difficulty in saying that the tort standard of care should be determined by the contract.[114] American courts have taken a similar view; and both Lord Roskill (in *Junior Books*) and Robert Goff L.J. (in *The Aliakmon*) saw little difficulty in adopting this reasoning in English law. Of course, the contractual solution avoids at a stroke these real or imaginary difficulties.

(f)   *Exemption clauses/defences*. It has never been doubted in German law that the contractual debtor can oppose against the third party/plaintiff all defences, etc., he may have against the contractual creditor. The contractual solution makes this answer indisputable. In an *obiter dictum* in *The Aliakmon* Robert Goff L.J. suggested that something similar should happen where the action was founded in tort[115] but details have not been worked out. Strangely enough, at least one First Instance judgment has considered a variant to this problem. In *Southern Water Authority* v. *Carey*[116] the court was not asked to decide whether the defendant sub-contractor (debtor) could oppose against the owner/plaintiff (third party) the exemption clauses that he (the sub-contractor) had in his contract with the main contractor (creditor); instead the court was faced with a claim by the sub-contractor to oppose against the owner a clause which the main contractor had in his contract with the owner. The court thought he could do so and, I believe, the solution displays a mis-

---

[113] A tort solution may also give rise (especially in the United States) to a claim for punitive damages. See *Heyer* v. *Flaig*, above n. 111.

[114] e.g. Schlectriem, *op. cit.*, above n. 12, at p. 66.

[115] [1985] QB 350 at 397–8.

[116] [1985] 2 All ER 1077.

understanding of how this triangular relationship should work. It is submitted that had a contractual explanation been used this misunderstanding would not have occurred.

In *Carey* the plaintiffs (or, rather, their predecessors in title) engaged the first defendants as consulting engineers and the second defendants as main contractors in the building of certain sewage works. The second defendants in turn engaged the third and fourth defendants as sub-contractors. Clause 30 of the work contract between the plaintiffs and the second defendants (main contractors) contained an exemption clause. Subsection (VI) of this clause stated that "for the purposes of this sub-clause the Contractor contracts on his own behalf and on the behalf of and as trustee for his sub-contractors, servants and agents". The main contractors having ceased trading, the action for defective workmanship and materials proceeded against the two sub-contractors. At this stage it is worth noting that while the fourth defendant/sub-contractor had in his contract with the main contractor a term almost identical to Clause 30 of the main contract, the third defendants/sub-contractors, when negotiating with the main contractor, had insisted on their own, different limitation clause. (Though we are nowhere told in what respect the two sets of terms differed, one must assume that the contractor's terms were more advantageous to the defendants/sub-contractors than their own terms, for otherwise why did they try to invoke their protection?) The Court, applying the tort reasoning of *Junior Books*, accepted that the plaintiff had a cause of action. Unlike *Junior Books*, however, the plaintiff was faced with a defence put forward by the defendant. This was based on an exclusion clause contained not in his (the sub-contractor's) contract with the main contractor (in which case the position could have been similar to *The Aliakmon*), but on the exclusion clause contained in the contract between the plaintiff and the main contractor (and which the third defendant/sub-contractor had, as stated, rejected). Diagrammatically the difference from *The Aliakmon* case can be demonstrated as shown in Diagram 1.

As stated, the court was prepared to allow a tort action by the employer against the sub-contractor but was also willing to give the latter the protection of the clause contained in the contract between employer and main contractor. One reason was that the nature of this limitation clause was relevant in defining the scope of the duty of the sub-contractor in tort. Another explanation was the use of the notion of volenti. The judge expressly excluded the latter concept;[117] but later in his judgment he appears to have come very close to accepting it (or something very similar to this concept) since he said: "As the plaintiffs . . . did . . . choose to limit the scope of the sub-contractor's liability, I see no reason why such limitation should not be honoured".[118] Is the reasoning of this decision and its result acceptable? I confess I have doubts as to both.

[117] *Ibid.* at p. 1085a.
[118] *Ibid.* at p. 1086f.

Situation 1: *Ross* v. *Caunters*
              Junior Books
              The Aliakmon

Situation 2: *Carey*

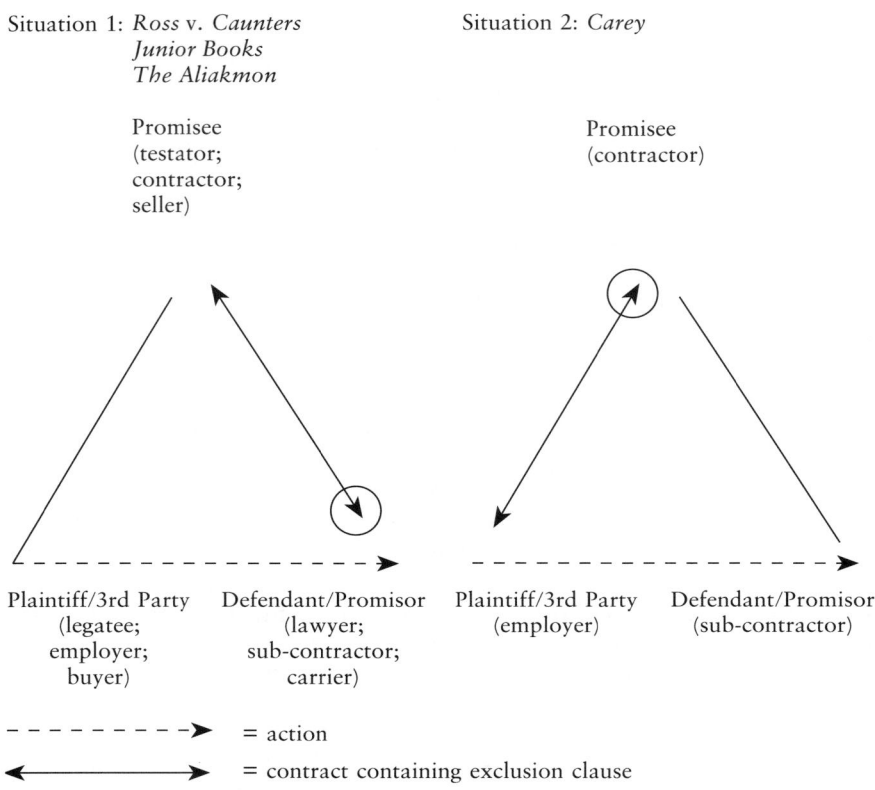

Diagram 1: Position in Carey and The Aliakmon Contrasted

It is first of all interesting to note that in *Carey* the court did not follow *The Eurymedon*[119] reasoning in order to achieve its result. The artificiality of the contractual reasoning in that case has been noted by many lawyers; but it was reaffirmed by the Privy Council in *Port Jackson Stevedoring Pty Ltd., The New York Star* v. *Salmond and Spraggon (Australia) Pty Ltd.*[120] so the judge in *Carey* was, obviously, anxious not to challenge it openly. On the other hand, it was not used either, so those opposed to *The Eurymedon* result and reasoning might be able to argue that in future it may be limited to the special shipping context of such cases. This still, however, leaves open the question of how to explain *Carey*.

One could, *de lege ferenda*, construe *Carey* as a case of contract in favour of third party (and, for brevity's sake I include in this term the contract with

---

[119] *New Zealand Shipping Co. Ltd.* v. *A. M. Satterthwaite and Co. Ltd., The Eurymedon* [1975] AC 154.

[120] [1981] 1 WLR 138.

protective effects *vis-à-vis* third parties). After all, *Carey* is, in one respect, very similar to *Junior Books*: the owner could be seen as the third party beneficiary of the contract between sub-contractor (promisor) and main contractor (promisee). This construction, of course, is unacceptable *de lege lata* given the English notion of privity. But even if it were accepted it would still not explain the second part of *Carey*, namely allowing to the promisor the defences that the promisee had against the third party. For in contracts in favour of third parties it is the reverse that is allowed: namely the promisor can oppose against the third party the defences he has in *his* contract with the promisee.

Can one then justify the outcome through tort reasoning? The judge in *Carey* did so by allowing the tort action to be shaped by the contract to which the plaintiff was a party but the defendant was not. In this he was clearly influenced by certain dicta contained in Lord Roskill's judgment in *Junior Book v. Veitchi*.[121] With respect I do not find Lord Roskill's *dicta* as obvious as that, my inclination being to interpret them as referring to the *second* contract (sub-contractor-main contractor) and *not* to the *first* contract (between contractor and owner). I incline in favour of this view largely because Lord Roskill seemed to rely heavily in his relevant passage on *Hedley Byrne*; and there, apart from the fact that there were no contractual relations *stricto sensu*, the exemption clause was inserted by the second bank/defendant when replying to the plaintiff's bank and not by the plaintiff's bank (which was merely transmitting the information) to the plaintiff. The clause, in other words, was in the second not the first relationship. My own understanding of the Roskill *dictum* is also shared by the Court of Appeal in *Muirhead* v. *Industrial Tank Specialities Ltd*.[122] On the other hand, it must be admitted that this is not how the judge understood it in *Carey*; and his interpretation also has the important support of Professor Treitel.[123] Clearly, therefore, the dictum has led to some confusion and should be clarified at the earliest possible opportunity. Nevertheless, even if it were eventually to be classified in the way it was understood in *Carey* it still does not, in my opinion, justify the actual outcome *in that case*. For in that case we were in fact faced with an interesting variant to the problem we have been discussing. Because in *Carey* the judge was faced with two sets of exemption clauses, one in the contract between owner and main contractor and one in the contract between main contractor and sub-contractor; and he allowed the sub-contractor the benefit of the first clause even though at the time of conclusion of the relevant contracts the sub-contractor had rejected it in favour of his own clause. I see no commercial reason justifying this result; nor do I think we can say that the plaintiff assented to a limited liability when the defendant, at the time of the making of the contracts, rejected the relevant limitation clause.

[121] [1983] 1 AC 520, 546. Lord Roskill refers there to "a relevant exclusion clause in the *main* contract" (italics supplied).
[122] [1986] QB 507 and, it seems, by Reynolds in (1986) 10 *L.M.C.L.Q.* 97, 106.
[123] (1986) 10 *L.M.C.L.Q.* 294, 302.

5. CONCLUSIONS

In all three systems under review, case law and legal literature on pure economic loss show no signs of abating. The nature of the problem—the overlap between contract and tort—may, ultimately, be an important cause for this continuing controversy; it is also what gives this topic its unique theoretical attraction. Given such richness of material, it is unlikely that any one article or even monograph could provide satisfactory solutions to most types of problems of economic loss. Certainly, this was not the aim of this paper which was limited to examining the theoretical foundations of certain types of situation often subject to litigation. The aim was more modest and more closely limited to the interests of someone who professes an interest in comparative law. I should be satisfied if the following suggestions which, I believe, are supported by the material of this article, were given closer attention.

First and foremost this paper along with most of my work, is a *cri de coeur* about how comparative law should be taught; for the need, both practical and theoretical, to apply the method of exegesis and comparison to relatively narrow and manageable problems[124] avoiding those over-worked accounts of "les grands systèmes de droit contemporains".

Secondly, I tried to stress my belief that here as elsewhere an awareness of foreign law and its proper comparison with one's own law can yield new insights and, perhaps, solutions to problems which seem otherwise almost impossible to understand. Knowledge of what the American and German lawyers have done in the three situations discussed in this article can have precisely that effect. For they can reveal important problems which we in England have not even considered; and suggest answers that have much to commend themselves to all who are prepared to approach these problems with an open mind. In particular the contractual flavour of the solutions adopted especially by German law in the three types of cases considered in this article seems preferable to the tort alternatives tried by the common law. These contractual explanations are not appropriate for other instances of pure economic loss. In my opinion, however, this does not diminish their usefulness since I believe that, as things stand now, it is impossible and, perhaps, even undesirable to try to construct a generalised principle which will justify liability for all instances of negligently inflicted pure economic loss.

Thirdly, inadequate or inelegant though the common law tort solutions may be, they must not be abandoned; and they can still be explained by the remarkable reluctance of English law to move in the direction suggested fifty

---

[124] I advocated this approach in "L'enseignement du droit comport sous l'éclairage de la jurisprudence" (1985) 3 *Revue de la Recherche Juridique Droit Prospectif*, 866 *et seq.*, and applied it in "Tort Damages in English and German law: A Comparison" 1985 *Studi Senesi, 7 et seq.*; "The Right to be Let Alone versus Freedom of Speech," [1986] *Public Law*, 67 *et seq.*; "Conceptualism, Pragmatism and Courage: A Common Lawyer Looks at Some Judgments of the German Federal Court" (1986) 34 *The American Journal of Comparative Law*, 349 *et seq.*

years ago by the Law Reform Committee.[125] Professor Fleming, reviewing a book I wrote with the late Professor Lawson, wrote that:

> "Before resorting to tort, in order to correct perceived inadequacies of contract law, should we not ask whether the privity requirement itself should be modified . . . in short whether it is wise to let tort intrude into so complex a relationship as that of the various participants in a building project under the umbrella of long-tested standard contracts?"[126]

Professor Fleming is right. On the other hand, however, no one could accuse English courts of *rushing* to intrude into such complex relationships that are best left to contract. On the contrary, the courts appear to me to have been excessively restrained in the handling of the doctrine of contractual privity given the "long period of Parliamentary procrastination"[127] over this subject. Had their oft-expressed dissatisfaction with this doctrine been matched by a willingness to modify it, some of the courts' tort solutions, which are causing so much debate, might have been avoided.[128] The comparative approach furnishes, I hope, yet another reason why contract should be expanded (here and elsewhere) and tort correspondingly restricted. The way tort is getting out of control in the United States, furnishes a further reason why we should be wary of the unexplored consequences of allowing tort actions where none previously existed. But until our contract law is re-examined, the courts will, I think, continue experimenting with a vague and expanding tort law, providing academics with food for thought and litigants with cause for concern.

---

[125] 6th Interim Report, Cmnd. 5449.

[126] "Comparative Law of Torts" (1986) 4 *O.J.L.S.* 235 at 241, reviewing Lawson and Markesinis, *Tortious Liability for Unintentional Harm in the Common Law and the Civil Law*, 2 vols. (1982).

[127] Per Lord Reid in *Beswick* v. *Beswick* [1968] AC 58, 72. See also Lord Scarman's strong words in *Woodar Investment Development Ltd.* v. *Wimpey Construction UK Ltd.* [1980] 1 WLR 277 at 300 ("I hope the House [of Lords] will reconsider *Tweddle* v. *Atkimon . . .* and the other cases which stand guard over this unjust rule").

[128] Partial improvements can, of course, be achieved by means of limited reforms, either intended (as Mr. Reynolds' wise recommendations for rewording the Bills of Lading Act: (1986) 10 *L.M.C.L.Q.* 97 *et seq.*); or unintended (which may have come about as a result of section 3 of the Latent Damages Act 1986. In this sense Griew in (1986) 136 *N.L.J.* 1206). It is submitted, however, that the problems discussed in 4C above, will never be fully solved until we take the bull by the horns and reconsider the proper relationship between contract and tort in general and the utility of the English doctrine of privity in particular.

14

The Random Element of their Lordships' Infallible Judgment: an Economic and Comparative Analysis of the Tort of Negligence From Anns to Murphy

1. INTRODUCTION

In 1977 the House of Lords handed down its seminal judgment in *Anns v Merton LBC*.[1] The immediate question that their Lordships had to decide was whether a local authority, whose agents and servants had failed to inspect or had inspected negligently the foundations of a building under construction, could be liable in tort towards an ultimate purchaser of that building when it developed defects which posed an imminent threat to safety and health. But the decision, while apparently not openly stated by the House of Lords, also had a great bearing on the question whether negligently inflicted economic loss could be compensated through the law of torts. Finally, at its most abstract level, *Anns* also contained some very important dicta about the notion of duty of care and when and how the courts should decide that it came into existence.

In the years that followed *Anns* our highest court has returned to some or all three of these issues (as well as the question of limitation) on at least twelve different occasions.[2] Thus, in the space of fifteen years, nineteen Law

---

[1] [1978] AC 728.

[2] *Junior Books Ltd* v. *Veitchi Co Ltd* [1983] AC 520 (henceforth: *Junior Books*); *Pirelli General Cable Works Ltd* v. *Oscar Faber and Partners* [1983] 2 AC 1 (henceforth: *Pirelli*); *Tate and Lyle Food and Distribution Ltd* v. *Greater London Council* [1983] 2 AC 509 (henceforth: *Tate and Lyle*); *Governors of the Peabody Donation Fund* v. *Sir Lindsay Parkinson and Co Ltd* [1985] AC 210 (henceforth: *Peabody*); *Candlewood Navigation Corp Ltd* v. *Mitsui* [1986] AC 1 (henceforth: *Candlewood*); *Leigh and Sullivan Ltd* v. *Aliakmon Shipping Co Ltd* [1986] AC 785 (henceforth: *The Aliakmon*); *Wallace Edward Rowling* v. *Takaro Properties* [1988] 1 AC 473 (henceforth: *Takaro*); *Yuen Kun Yeu* v. *AG of Hong Kong* [1988] AC 175 (henceforth: *Yuen Kun Yeu*); *D & F Estates*; *Smith* v. *Eric Bush*; *Harris v Wyre Forest DC* [1990]1 AC 831 (henceforth: *Smith* v. *Bush*); *Caparo Industries plc* v. *Dickman and others* [1990] 2 AC 605 (henceforth: *Caparo*); *Murphy* v. *Brentwood DC* [1991] 1 AC 398 (henceforth: *Murphy*). For present purposes, we feel we can exclude from this list the decisions of the House of Lords in *Ketteman* v. *Hansel Properties* [1987] AC 189 and *Curran* v. *Northern Ireland Co-Ownership Housing Association Ltd* [1987] AC 718, even though they can be linked to the *Anns* rationale.

Lords[3] have given us the benefit of their views on questions that have vexed lawyers from the common law and Germanic worlds, but have left almost totally unexcited their colleagues from the Romanistic group of systems (such as France, Italy, Belgium, the Netherlands, Spain and the Latin American world). This learning has come in the form of 298 pages of law reports or (approximately) 180,000 words, or the equivalent of two average-sized doctoral theses. In this sea of ink, which does not include the judgments of almost double the number of decisions from the Court of Appeal,[4] our highest judges divided heavily against *Anns*. Thus while two of them (Lords Wilberforce and Roskill) can clearly be described as proponents of the forward-looking approach of *Anns*, the rest have, in varying degrees, played a key role in its demolition. Lord Keith has led the attack on *Anns* with four major opinions against it,[5] to be followed by Lords Bridge[6] and Oliver[7] with three, and Lords Fraser,[8] Templeman[9] and Brandon,[10] with two each, the remaining Law Lords having generally contributed brief (or very brief) concurring judgments. One could argue, therefore, that the currently prevailing thesis, first robustly propounded in Lord Brandon's dissenting judgment in *Junior Books*, is, in most respects, the brainchild of Lords Keith, Bridge and Oliver, the last mentioned of whom has proclaimed extra judicially[11] his intellectual antipathy for *Anns*.

Such growing opposition to *Anns*, arguably fuelled by its expansive treatment in *Junior Books*, was bound to lead to the invoking of the 1966 Practice Statement (Judicial Precedent)[12] and the formal overruling by the House of Lords of one of its most important recent decisions. One may disagree with the decisions of the late 1970s and early 1980s. One might even feel that it was wrong to take so long to "correct an error", given that the present position has, essentially, been foreshadowed since the *Peabody* decision in 1985. Yet, arguably, the most disturbing feature of these rich pronouncements is not so much that they display a change of heart but an unsystematic and not fully thought-out series of shifts without proper regard to what was said earlier or what may follow in the future. This criticism can, of course, itself be criticised as confusing the role of the judge and the jurist, both defined and

---

[3] In alphabetical order: Lords Ackner, Brandon, Bridge, Brightman, Diplock, Fraser, Goff, Griffiths, Jauncey, Keith, Mackay, Oliver, Russell, Salmon, Scarman, Simon, Templeman, Wilberforce and Sir Robert Megarry.

[4] For example, there were over eight in 1989 alone. See Huxley, "Economic Loss in Negligence—The 1989 Cases" (1990) 53 *MLR* 369.

[5] Namely in *Peabody, Takaro, Yuen*, and *Murphy*.

[6] In *D & F Estates, Caparo* and *Murphy*.

[7] In *D & F Estates, Caparo* and *Murphy*.

[8] In *Pirelli* and *Candelwood*.

[9] In *Tate and Lyle* and *Smith* v. *Bush*.

[10] In *Junior Books* and *The Aliakmon*.

[11] "Judicial Legislation: Retreat from *Anns*" (1988) 1 SCJ 249 (the Malaysian Supreme Court Journal); also published in [1989] *Leiden Journal of International Law* under the shorter title "Judicial Legislation".

[12] [1966] 1 WLR 1234.

elegantly defended by Lord Goff in his Maccabean Lecture.[13] But after twelve, often long, decisions of the House of Lords it is time that even the judges abandoned their usual "intense view of the particular"[14] and, taking a leaf out of the book of academic training, occasionally strove for a more "diffused view of the general". In this article, we examine their Lordships' tergiversations from the complementary vantage points of economic and comparative analysis. These perspectives highlight the extraordinary degree to which argument in our supreme appellate court has been carried on in isolation from outside influences. In our conclusion we suggest that the law will benefit if judges continue with the slowly emerging practice (adopted by some of them) of talking with academics and not ignoring their criticisms.

However, before moving on to the economic and comparative analysis of our theme, let us point out some of the doctrinally weak points of the cases. This can be done briefly, since others have carried out the task in greater detail.[15] First, the nature of the loss: following *Dutton* v. *Bognor Regis UDC*,[16] *Anns* characterised the plaintiff's loss as "material, physical damage" even though Lord Denning had, extra-judicially,[17] made it clear that this was a misdescription—one presumes in order to help a "deserving" plaintiff. For a time the House of Lords persisted with this notion[18] but, eventually, it came to accept that the loss was purely economic. As we shall see, later German law avoided this mistake from the beginning.

Secondly, in *D & F Estates* their Lordships toyed with the idea of complex structures, namely the notion that "one element of the structure should be regarded as distinct from another element so that damage to one part of the structure caused by a hidden defect in another may qualify to be treated as damage to "other property".[19] In *Murphy* one of them, at least, regarded this theory as totally "artificial".[20] Yet others came up with examples which made it unclear whether the complex structures approach has still any life left in it.[21] If it has, it will only promote more litigation, as German law again demonstrates. Thirdly, *Hedley Byrne* survives; indeed, Lord Oliver in *D & F Estates* thought it would explain *Junior Books*.[22] *Pirelli*, severely dented by *D & F Estates*, has also been revived as a *Hedley Byrne* case. The result may be

---

[13] "The Search for Principle" (1983) 69 *Proceedings of the British Academy* 169.

[14] *Ibid.*

[15] See Fleming (1990) 106 *LQR* 525; Weir [1991] *CLJ* 24; Cooke (1991) 107 *LQR* 46; Howarth [1991] *CLJ* 58; Duncan Wallace (1991) 107 *LQR* 228; Stapleton (1991) 107 *LQR* 249; O'Dair (1991) 54 *MLR* 561; Cane, *Tort Law and Economic Interests* (Oxford, Clarendon Press, 1991) 511–18; Grubb and Mullis [1991] *Conv.* 225; Giles and Szyszczak (1991) 11 *Legal Studies* 85.

[16] [1972] 1 QB 373.

[17] *The Discipline of the Law* (London: Butterowrths, 1979) at pp 225–61.

[18] See *Tate and Lyle* [1983] 2 AC 509, 530.

[19] See, for example, Lord Bridge [1989] AC 177, 207.

[20] Lord Oliver [1991] 1 AC 398, 484.

[21] For discussion of these examples and their weaknesses, see Grubb and Mullis, *op. cit.* above n. 15, at pp. 229–33.

[22] [1989] 1 AC 177.

that architects and consulting engineers who give bad advice leading to the construction of shoddy buildings may be liable to their owners, but the builders, whose negligence produces the same result, will not.[23]

Fourthly, *D & F Estates* and *Murphy*, when read together with *Smith* v. *Bush*, have also resulted in the differential treatment of builders on the one hand and surveyors on the other. For, leaving aside for a moment the statutory regime set up by the Defective Premises Act 1972, and focusing simply on the internal inconsistencies of the common law, we see that the second purchaser of a building has no action against the local authority or the builder but may still have an action against the surveyor who has been employed by the building society to value the premises in question prior to granting a mortgage to the second purchaser/mortgagor. A technical explanation for this could be found by invoking the notoriously vague notion of proximity and arguing that it is not satisfied in the case of local authority inspector and house owner/mortgagor. But that, surely, would not be so where the house owner pays a fee to the local authority for the inspection needed when an extension of his house is being planned.

Fifthly, builders may still be liable for the anticipatory cost of repairs "if a building stands so close to the boundary of the building owner's land that after discovery of the dangerous defect it remains a potential source of injury to persons or property on neighbouring land or on the highway".[24] If this is justified by the distinction between negligence and nuisance, it must be absurd. In any event, as Cane has pointed out, if maintained it "could drive a ten-ton truck through the basic principle: [for] is there not always the chance that a building or chattel which is known to be dangerous will cause injury or damage for which the owner might be legally liable?"[25]

Finally, *Murphy* by extending *D & F Estates*, may have targeted the wrong defendant. The argument that runs through both cases is roughly the following: if the builder is not liable, neither should the local authority be liable. The wisdom of the first part of this argument may be doubtful on policy grounds; but the linkage of the two liabilities, in a manner that makes them co-extensive, is seriously questionable and, it is submitted, has yet to be properly justified.[26]

2. ECONOMIC ANALYSIS AND THE HOUSE OF LORDS

Techniques of economic analysis, for so long the preserve of academic lawyers, are now finding their way into the courts.[27] The use of these

[23] For lucid discussion of these problems, see McKendrick (1991) 11 *Legal Studies* 326, at p. 328 *et seq.*

[24] See Lord Bridge in *Murphy* [1991] 1 AC 398, 475.

[25] *Tort Law and Economic Interests* (Oxford: Clarendon Press, 1991) at p. 517.

[26] *Ibid.*, at p 513.

[27] On the growing influence of economic analysis, see Ackerman, *Reconstructing American Law* (London, Harvard UP, 1984).

techniques to shape the development of the common law is nonetheless controversial, not least because of the widespread association of "law and economics" with the values and approach of the Chicago school. However, there is a danger here of throwing the baby out with the bath water. Even one of Chicago's most forceful critics has written that "economic analysis by itself, unencumbered by value choices, can be an effective aid in analyzing the issues presented in legal disputes, clarifying when a value choice must be made, and identifying what choices are available".[28]

It may be that, as Hoffman J. recognised in *Morgan Crucible Co Plc v. Hill Samuel & Co Ltd*,[29] "courts do not have the information on which to form anything more than a broad view of the economic consequences of their decisions. For this reason they are more concerned with what appears to be fair and reasonable than with wider utilitarian calculations". But at the same time, his Lordship recognised that "economic realities" inevitably enter into the prevailing conception of what is "fair, just and reasonable". Allowing the appeal in *Morgan Crucible*, Lord Justice Slade did "not think it right by reference to economic considerations to dismiss as unarguable an otherwise arguable case".[30] But the case law concerning the boundaries of negligence is full of references to the supposed economic consequences of particular liability rules, and it is for academics to attempt to put them in some kind of order.

Some of these references are more explicit than others. Traditional arguments, such as the "floodgates" and the need to maintain commercial certainty, make strong assumptions about the economic impact of liability rules; new concerns about the implications of insurance and the particular effects of liability upon public and governmental bodies have also been raised. The fact that many judges (and commentators) use policy arguments of this kind is justification in itself for subjecting them to critical economic analysis; all the more so, since the question of recovery for financial loss has given rise to a considerable theoretical literature which the English courts have not used adequately. It is arguable that had they chosen to do so, they would have had, at the very least, a clearer perception of some of the policy issues involved.

A. Restrictive Arguments: "Bright Line Rules" and "Floodgates"

After *Caparo* and *Murphy* there is a perception that economic loss is not just ranked differently from physical injury and property damage in the hierarchy of interests, but that it is so fundamentally different in kind as to justify a wide rule excluding liability at the outset in all but the most exceptional cases.[31] The claim that economic loss is fundamentally different from physi-

---

[28] White, "Coase and the Courts: Economics for the Common Man" (1987) 72 *Iowa Law Review* 577, at p. 579.

[29] [1991] Ch 295, 303.

[30] [1991] Ch 295, 321.

[31] See, in particular, dicta in *Reid v. Rush & Tompkins Ltd* [1990] 1 WLR 212, 231 (Ralph Gibson L.J.); *The Morning Watch* [1990] 1 Lloyd's Rep 547, 557 (Phillips J.); *R v. Islington Health*

cal and property loss is not, however, an argument that the former is intangible or only a "phantom loss". Such an argument could not possibly succeed; for example, the courts regularly compensate plaintiffs for economic or pecuniary losses which arise directly out of personal injury. These futures losses are no easier to quantify than many of the losses claimed in the "pure" economic loss cases. Moreover, the courts will protect pecuniary interests in the context of the intentional torts of inducing breach of contract, interference with trade and business by unlawful means, and so on, if necessary by computing the expected future earnings or business profits of the plaintiff.

Rather, in its most developed form the argument involves an explicit reference to the nature of market activity as the origin of financial gains and losses alike:

> "what exactly *is* [the plaintiff's] interest in earning? How should it be analysed? We can hardly say that there is a legal *right* to one's living in the way that there is a right to property, because although neither interest is unqualified, the former is qualified almost to the point of extinction by the existence of a similar right in one's competitors".[32]

In a competitive market, then, business gains and losses are being incurred all the time; under such a system, losses caused by superior competition cannot be the subject of compensation. Even an intention to inflict losses on another will not (in English law) ground liability, unless the defendant knowingly acted to interfere with the plaintiff's existing legal right or employed independently unlawful means. It follows that the merely negligent (as opposed to intentional) infliction of pure economic loss will not normally give rise to liability.

In economic theory, this rule of limited recovery is explained by the idea that the plaintiff suffers a personal or private cost as a result of the defendant's activity, but that there is no social cost to the community as a whole which would justify the court's intervention. A "pure economic" loss will not always be a social cost because the plaintiff's loss will be counterbalanced by gains made by his competitors elsewhere. It is therefore preferable to let the loss lie where it falls, than engage in a wasteful income transfer.[33]

To appreciate this point it is necessary to recall that economic analysis of law focuses upon the net cost to society of a particular activity and of any legal intervention designed to offset it. Income transfers, whether made through the tax and social security systems or through the liability rules of

---

Authority [1991] 2 WLR 501, 506 (Potts J.); *Topp* v. *London Country Bus (South West) Ltd*, *The Times*, 8 November 1991 (May J.); *Glen-Mor Fashions Ltd* v. *Jaeger Company Shops Ltd* (unreported), Court of Appeal, 20 November 1991 (transcript available on Lexis) (Glidewell L.J.).

[32] Weir, *A Casebook on Tort*, 6th edn. (London, Sweet & Maxwell, 1988) at p. 485. See also Lord Oliver in *Murphy* [1991] 1 AC 398, 487, discussed by Howarth, "Negligence After *Murphy*—Time to Rethink" [1991] *CLJ* 58, at pp. 88–91.

[33] Bishop, "Economic Loss in Tort" (1982) 2 *Ox J Leg Stud* 1; Landes and Posner, *The Economic Structure of Tort Law* (London, Harvard UP, 1987) at p. 251.

tort law, are not necessarily seen in welfare economics as value-enhancing in the same sense that free exchange is. The normal mechanism of resource allocation will ensure that resources are exchanged until they reach their most efficient use. On the assumption that both parties to an exchange are acting rationally to pursue their own self-interest, and that their contract is not vitiated by force or fraud, the exchange will by definition make them both better off than they were before. Tort may affect the relative distribution of resources between the two parties, and in that sense will alter their relative wealth. However, an income transfer from one party to the other will not normally create a surplus as a contract would. Because of the administrative costs of income transfers, they are more likely to create a net cost to society.

Tort is therefore supplementary to contract in ensuring an optimal resource allocation. This idea is familiar to lawyers who refer to the "primacy of contract" in the field of obligations.[34] However, the primacy of contract does not hold in a situation where transaction costs, or barriers to exchange, are so great as to outweigh the parties' mutual gains from trade. Where high transaction costs prevent certain exchanges from taking place, the price structure of any given market will not necessarily reflect the true costs of particular activities. Under these circumstances, it is appropriate for liability rules to operate so as to "internalize" the costs of dangerous and harmful activities to those responsible for them. In this sense the law is a "giant pricing-machine" which uses liability rules and the assignment of property rights to influence economic behaviour.[35]

This focus of economic analysis on the net cost of harmful activities is illustrated by Posner's explanation of the American case of *Rickards* v. *Sun Oil Co*,[36] in which the defendant negligently destroyed the only bridge between an island and the mainland. The court rejected claims by businesses on the island for loss of profits. According to Posner, "if the island merchants had been allowed to sue, Sun Oil might have ended up being liable for more than the total damages [*sic*] it had caused, since those merchants' losses may well have been gains to mainland merchants to whom consumers switched when they no longer could reach the island.[37]

However, not every case of pure economic loss can be analysed so straightforwardly. In *Union Oil Co* v. *Oppen*[38] an oil spill led to the destruction of fishing stocks; local fishermen successfully sued for loss of business. The Ninth

---

[34] On this, see Cane, *op. cit.* above n. 15, at p. 489 *et seq.*

[35] See Veljanovski, *The Economics of Law: An Introductory Text* (Hobart Paper 114, London, IEA, 1990) at p. 15; Harris and Veljanovski, "Liability for Economic Loss in Tort" in Furmston (ed.), *The Law of Tort: Policies and Trends in Liability for Damage to Property and Economic Loss* (London, Duckworth, 1986) at p. 48.

[36] (1945) 41 A. 2d 267.

[37] Posner expresses this opinion in his judicial capacity in *Grip-Pak Inc* v. *Illinois Tool Works Inc*. 694 F.2d 466, (1982), and in an academic capacity in Landes and Posner, *op. cit.* above n. 33, at p. 251.

[38] 694 F.2d 466 (1982).

Circuit Court of Appeals applied Calabresi's test of the "least cost avoider" to impose liability on the defendants. Landes and Posner provide a somewhat different interpretation, namely that as the oil spill led to a net reduction in the number of fish caught, the plaintiffs' losses were not directly offset by gains made by their competitors. The case was not the same as one in which the fish were netted by a rival. As a result, there was a genuine social cost— an uncompensated externality—which could only be internalised by allowing the fishermen an action.[39]

Most commentators agree that the decision in *Oppen* can be justified on economic theoretical grounds, if not necessarily those put forward by the court itself. *Oppen* could be seen as an exceptional situation of liability.[40] However, Harris and Veljanovski have suggested that "in most of the leading cases the economic loss is a real social cost and that the distinction is therefore of little value to understanding the law or economics of the situation".[41] This is because it is only in a few cases—such as *Rickards*—that the plaintiff's economic loss can be seen or assumed to be offset by gains made by his competitors. The important result of this is that a "bright line rule" which restricts recovery for economic loss as such—a rule of the kind advocated by Lord Brandon in *The Aliakmon* and by Lords Keith, Bridge and Oliver in *Murphy*—cannot be justified through economic analysis.

Economic analysis also casts doubt on the validity of the "floodgates" argument in this context. Extensive liability to a wide number of potential plaintiffs raises the prospect that the administrative costs of processing large numbers of small claims will outweigh the potential benefits, in terms of incentives for performance, of a liability rule.[42] This may explain cases such as *Stevenson* v. *East Ohio Gas Co.*,[43] in which the court rejected the plaintiff's claim for lost wages following an explosion which prevented him from getting to work.

The fear of the floodgates is expressed repeatedly in the judgments in *Caparo*.[44] Yet it is striking how little resemblance *Caparo* bears to the stereotypical floodgates situation. Far from there being large numbers of potential plaintiffs, Caparo had concentrated the loss on itself by buying out the other shareholders; after the take-over it held over 90 per cent of Fidelity's shares. In this respect, *Caparo* is no different from most of the other major economic loss cases of the 1980s. In practically all of them the plaintiff was in a close

---

[39] *op. cit.* above n. 33, at p. 252. Landes and Posner also suggest that the extent of recovery of economic losses in *State of Louisiana, ex rel Guste* v. *M./V. Testbank* 752 F.2d 1019 (1985) should have been wider than the 5th Circuit Court of Appeals allowed.

[40] See Bishop, *op. cit.* above n. 33.

[41] *op. cit.* above n. 35, at p. 49. See in particular their analysis of the *Spartan Steel* case ([1973] 1 QB 27) at pp. 62–4.

[42] Landes and Posner, *op. cit.* above n. 33, at p. 254.

[43] (1946) 73 N.E.2d 200.

[44] See in particular Lord Bridge [1990] 2 AC 605, 619–21, and Lord Roskill, *ibid.* 628–9.

relationship with the defendant and was either the only potential litigant or one of a very small number.[45]

B. Deterrence, Self-reliance and the Tort-Contract Divide

An argument made in many economic loss cases is that the plaintiff should look after his own interests, normally by contracting for protection against the loss in question, rather than rely on a tort claim. Where the plaintiff can contract at low cost to do this, he is likely to be the "least cost avoider". Imposing liability on the defendant would then send the wrong signals to both sides, on the one hand inviting the plaintiff to under-protect himself and on the other giving the defendant an incentive not to continue the activity in question. In misstatement cases the result would be to increase the costs of disseminating information.

In practice, however, the costs to the plaintiff of contracting elsewhere for the relevant information (or for protection against loss) may be high. In addition, the plaintiff may be the intended third-party beneficiary of a contract between the defendant and another party. In this case the defendant will not be a volunteer, and it is potentially wasteful for the law to require the plaintiff to enter into a further contract with him. This is even more clearly the case in a situation where the defendant is unlikely to be sued in contract for the consequences of his negligence. In the absence of a tort action he would have, in effect, an immunity from liability for negligence.

Caparo illustrates both these points, as do most of the decisions in the *Hedley Byrne* line of cases. In *Caparo* there was an extreme asymmetry of information between the directors and auditors of the company on the one hand, and the shareholders on the other. There was no market for the information about the company, and so the plaintiff could not have contracted for it elsewhere. It is because of this asymmetrical relationship between the controllers of a company and the shareholders that legislation requires the appointment of independent auditors in public companies. A large body of economic literature attests to the importance of controlling the agency costs which arise between the owners and managers of corporations, and to the role of the stock market in disciplining corporate management;[46] in each case, accurate pricing depends on the steady flow of information out of the company *via* the auditors.

Nor, clearly, were the auditors volunteers. They were contracted to the company (Fidelity). At the same time, it is unlikely that the company, as opposed to the shareholders, could have successfully sued the auditors for damages for the breach of contract arising from their negligence, for the

---

[45] See generally Markesinis, "An Expanding Tort Law—the Price of a Rigid Contract Law" (1987) 103 *LQR* 354; Harris and Veljanovski, *op. cit.*, above n. 35.

[46] See generally Easterbrook and Fischel, *The Economic Structure of Corporate Law* (London, Harvard UP, 1991).

reason that the loss was concentrated on the shareholders who either purchased or held on to shares as a result of what was, in effect, an overvalua-
tion of the company.[47] Any loss suffered by Fidelity as a result of the auditors'
misjudgment—such as under-investment stemming from Caparo's losses—
would most likely be too remote to be recoverable in a contract action.

Caparo illustrates the constraints of the rigid privity rule in English contract law. Using similar language to that employed by Lord Devlin in *Hedley
Byrne*,[48] Lord Justice Bingham argued that "certainly as between the shareholders as a class and the auditor, the relationship seems to me to be very
close indeed to contract . . . As between the shareholders individually and the
auditor, the analogy with contract is less compelling, but in my view it
remains close".[49] In economic terms, a liability rule is needed here to provide
incentives for the effective performance of an exchange designed, essentially,
for the benefit of a third party; "we should not be blinded by legal categori-
sations and forms as to the true nature of the underlying problem and its economic basis".[50]

It may be that triangular relationships of this kind could best be dealt with
by regarding the third party's cause of action as contractual, rather than tortious; this has a number of advantages, in terms of clarifying both the standard of performance required and the application of exclusion and limitation
clauses.[51] At the very least, the contract should define the scope of any tort
duty owed by the "promisor" to the third party. This was the central issue in
The Aliakmon. If, for the purpose of the tort action, the carrier could not take
advantage of the limitation of liability inserted for his benefit into the contract of carriage, the allocation of risk made by the parties themselves would
be upset. The doctrinal solution proposed by Lord Goff—namely, using the
doctrine of transferred loss to ensure that the benefit of the limitation clauses
extended to the tort action—proved unacceptable to the House of Lords.[52]
And yet, a solution based upon this idea—or upon the notion that the scope

[47] See Bingham L.J. in *Caparo* in the Court of Appeal [1989] QB 653, 682–3. Although the
company might have an action against the auditors if, for example, their negligence failed to alert
it to the fraudulent activities of one of its employees, an action by the company would not cover
the loss of the shareholders in terms of the diminished value of their stock. In truth, it is clear
that reliance on the report will be principally by the shareholders and not the company. It is difficult to agree with Lord Bridge who said "I find it difficult to visualise a situation arising in the
real world in which the individual shareholder could claim to have sustained a loss in respect of
his existing shareholding with reference to the negligence of the auditor which could not be
recouped by the company" ([1990] 2 AC 605, 626). An action is being brought by Fidelity, under
its new name of Intersound Consumer Electronics against the auditors: see Percival, "After
Caparo—Liability in Business Transactions Revisited" (1991) 54 *MLR* 739, at p. 743.

[48] [1964] AC 465, 529.

[49] [1989] QB 653, 685.

[50] Harris and Veljanovski, *op. cit.* above n. 35, at p. 47.

[51] See Markesinis, *op. cit.* above n. 45; "Doctrinal Clarity in Tort Litigation: A Comparative
Lawyer's Viewpoint" (1991) 25 *The International Lawyer* 953. See also the Law Commission,
Consultative Paper No 121, *Privity of Contract: Contracts for the Benefit of Third Parties* (London,
HMSO, 1991).

[52] See Lord Brandon [1986] AC 785, 815; cf. Robert Goff L.J. [1985] QB 350, 399.

of the tort duty is either defined by the underlying contract or limited by the defence of *volenti*[53]—would have enabled the court to give legal effect to the three-way exchange between buyer, seller and carrier. As it was, the latter was relieved from the normal legal incentives to perform his contract.[54]

The strict application of the privity rule may be appropriate in a case where the parties in a potential duty relationship can make their own contract at low cost. In building cases, collateral warranties are frequently agreed between the site-owner and the subcontractor, or the architect or designer and the intended vendor or user of the building; they have become more common recently in response to the restriction of *Anns*. In the interesting pre-*Murphy* decision of *Portsea Island Mutual Co-Operative Society Ltd v. Michael Brashier Associates*, in which a tenant under a full repairing lease sued an architect in tort for the costs of repairing certain defects in the property, the Official Referee disallowed claims for pure economic loss the on grounds that:

> "Portsea was in effect seeking to recover in negligence sums which they might well have been entitled to claim under a collateral agreement. Portsea could have invited Brashiers to enter into a collateral warranty in respect of the superstore when, for suitable consideration, they might have agreed to do so".[55]

Similarly, in *Greater Nottingham Co-Operative Society v. Cementation Piling and Foundations Ltd*,[56] where a contract had actually been agreed between the owner of the site and the subcontractor, its mere existence led the Court of Appeal to reject a claim for economic loss arising from the sub-contractor's negligence. This was because the contract contained warranties as to the quality of the materials to used and to the specification of the design, but no warranty as to the execution of the building work itself. As it was defective performance of the building work which caused the owner to suffer the economic losses in question, there was held to be no claim in either tort or contract. Here, the absence of a contract term which could have been agreed proved fatal to the tort claim, in contrast to *Tai Hing Cotton Mill Ltd v. Liu Chang Hing Bank Ltd*,[57] where terms actually present in the contract were used to cut down the scope of any duty of care in tort. In these cases, the priority of contract seems to be the right result.

---

[53] On this, see the dissenting judgment of Lord Denning in *Scruttons Ltd v. Midland Silicones* [1962] AC 446, 488–9.

[54] In cases coming after *The Aliakmon*, courts have used the restrictive test of recovery of economic loss in tort to extend the benefit of exclusion (as opposed to limitation) clauses beyond the immediate contractual nexus of promisor and promisee. See *Southern Water Authority v. Carey* [1985] 2 All ER 1077; *Norwich City Council v. Harvey* [1989] 1 WLR 828; *Pacific Associates Inc v. Baxter* [1990] QB 993. The fact that these cases are argued in tort rather than contracts has, however, produced a number of doctrinal confusions: see Markesinis, "Doctrinal Clarity in Tort Litigation", *op. cit.* above n. 51, pp. 959–64.

[55] (1990) 6 *Const LJ* 63, 70.

[56] [1989] QB 71: see Webster, "Implied Exclusion Clauses—The *Cementation* Case" (1990) 6 *Const LJ* 7.

[57] [1986] AC 80.

Yet it will not be every case in which a collateral warranty is either possible or effective in achieving an extension of contractual liability. Collateral warranties granted to the initial vendor will not help subsequent purchasers, unless the first vendor makes an assignment of the benefit of the warranty. Even then, it is not clear whether the assignee can sue for substantial damages. In doctrinal terms, he is unlikely to be able to do so unless the benefit of the warranty forms part of the consideration for the subsequent sale.[58] But the complexity of this point illustrates the high costs of contracting and the risks involved in trying to reach a solution through the collateral warranty route. While such costs can probably be overcome where two business parties are contracting with one another, it is very unlikely that consumers can be protected in the same way. They are unlikely to have the same access to information and contracting expertise as business contractors, and may be unable to insist upon a collateral warranty in the first place. These factors suggest that while *Peabody* (in a slightly different context) drew a perfectly valid distinction between business and consumer interests, the combined effect of *D & F Estates and Murphy* goes too far by denying consumers an effective remedy for loss of what for many will be their single most valuable financial asset.

The judgment of Hoffman J. in *Morgan Crucible* v. *Hill Samuel* contains an eloquent exposition of the economic factors which could determine a selective approach to the imposition of liability for negligent misstatements. The differences between *Caparo* and *Smith* v. *Bush* "consist in the different economic relationships between the parties and the nature of the markets in which they were operating".[59] In *Smith* the mortgagor "is a person of modest means and making the most expensive investment of his or her life", in contrast to the take-over bidder in *Caparo* who "is an entrepreneur taking high risks for high rewards". The vulnerability to economic risk of the consumer in *Smith* provides a good reason for the imposition of tort liability even in a case where he is faced with a disclaimer.

In *Caparo*, by contrast, not only were the plaintiffs themselves a corporation; as shareholders in a company, they were shielded from economic risk to a significant degree by the legal institution of limited liability. This may provide the best explanation of the outcome. Incorporation and limited liability protect the shareholders of a company from economic risks which they would face if they contracted directly with the suppliers and customers of the firm; they have a form of statutory immunity from normal tort and contract liability.[60] Just as the shareholders gain the benefit of this immunity, so it might be said that they should share some of its burdens, including the lack

[58] See generally Cartwright, "The Assignment of Collateral Warranties" (1990) 6 *Const LJ* 14.
[59] [1991] Ch 295.
[60] See Wedderburn, "Freedom of Association and Philosophies of Labour Law", Ch. 8 in *Employment Rights in Britain and Europe* (London, Lawrence & Wishart, 1991) at p. 207 for discussion of this point in the context of labour and company law.

of capacity to sue the company's contractors (including, here, the auditors) for their personal losses. In this respect, it is perhaps significant that the English courts have recently reaffirmed their reluctance as a matter of general principle to pierce the veil of corporate personality.[61]

Even if this argument is seen as having some force, however, it is not one which the House of Lords chose to make directly. The judgments of the House contain little more than broad assertions to the effect that the auditor's function is limited to assisting the shareholders in the performance of their internal function of corporate control.[62] The historical development of the auditing requirement in the Companies Acts certainly does not support such a view.[63] Even if the legally privileged position of shareholders is recognised, economic arguments in favour of providing incentives for the flow of information still apply. One of these is the need for "an orderly and flourishing market in company shares".[64] As Lord Justice Bingham put it:

> "it is a truism that possession of adequate information is a necessary condition of effective decision-making. It would not be realistic to expect shareholders to exercise their powers of control on the basis only of such information as the directors chose to give them. But I think these provisions also reflect a wider and more commercial intention. The growth and development of limited liability companies over a relatively short period have been phenomenal. Their proliferation and expansion have depended on their acceptance by the investing public as an advantageous and (on the whole) reliable medium of investment. The statutory requirements that companies should account to their members and that auditors express an independent opinion to shareholders on the truth and accuracy of company accounts are in my view designed (in part at least) to fortify confidence in the holding of shares as a medium of investment by enabling shareholders to make informed investment decisions. There are obvious reasons, both economic and social, why this end should be regarded as desirable".[65]

C. Insurance, Public Liability and Public Good

English courts have traditionally chosen to play down the availability of insurance as a factor determining the extent of tort liability. In both *Caparo* and *Murphy*, however, arguments over insurance were, for once, openly addressed. Before the Court of Appeal in *Caparo*, the defendants alleged that there was "already extreme difficulty in obtaining professional indemnity cover". The results of extending liability would therefore include "defensive" or self-protective accounting and, as an extreme solution, an unwillingness on the part of accountants to undertake audit work. Lord Justice Bingham found

---

[61] *Adams* v. *Cape Industries* [1990] BCC 786.

[62] Lord Bridge [1990] 2 AC 605, 626–7; Lord Oliver, *ibid.* 650–4; Lord Jauncey, *ibid.* 658–63.

[63] See Howarth, *op. cit.* above n. 32, at pp. 84–6; and see the essays in the November 1991 issue of the *Modern Law Review*, "Law and Accountancy," in particular McGee, "The 'True and Fair View' Debate: A Study in the Legal Regulation of Accounting" (1991) *MLR* 874.

[64] [1989] 1 QB 653, 682.

[65] [1989] QB 653, 681–2.

the insurance argument "hard to assess in the absence of evidence or inquiry", and drew no conclusions from it;[66] none of the other judges in either the Court of Appeal or the House of Lords referred to the point.

In *Murphy*, the availability to the house-owner of first party insurance appears to have played an important part in Lord Keith's judgment. The plaintiff's insurance company had settled most of his claim and were now bringing the action with him.[67] Lord Keith did not spell out the clear implication, which has been expressed by Weir:

> "Now it hardly needs saying (any more) that a local authority does not normally have to pay companies which suffer merely pecuniary loss as a result of their care-lessness, as the Norwich Union did in this case, and it is hard to imagine anybody less deserving of a dip in the public trough than the insurer who profits taking the risk that houses may collapse . . . But our absurd law on subrogation to tort claims means that the public must bail out private insurers".[68]

If the plaintiff can insure more cheaply than the defendant, the "least cost avoider" argument would suggest a no-liability rule: let first party insurance meet the loss, with no liability and therefore no possibility of subrogation. If loss insurance is widely available, a court which imposes liability is creating the conditions for a potentially wasteful double insurance. In practice, double insurance is not uncommon in some areas, such as road traffic accidents, but this is the consequence not of common law liability rules but of statutory intervention making liability insurance compulsory with the aim of securing maximum coverage of compensation for accident victims.[69]

In theory, the party best equipped to take out insurance is the one best placed to control the risk and to calculate in advance both the probability of the loss occurring and its likely magnitude.[70] This approach points to imposing liability upon both auditors, in *Caparo*, and builders, in *D & F Estates*, since in each case they will have superior access to the relevant information and the greater capacity to avoid the loss than those relying upon them. In practice, few insurance markets will reflect this economic calculus in a perfect fashion. Indeed, counsel in *Warner* v. *Basildon Development Corp.* argued that "it is difficult for builders to obtain insurance cover in respect of liability for defective parts of a structure because of the difficulty in assessing the nature and extent of the risk and the appropriate premium".[71] The actual as opposed to theoretical availability of insurance will be influenced by long-standing practices, by legislation which makes certain kinds of insurance

---

[66] [1989] QB 653, 688.

[67] See Lord Keith's judgment, [1991] 1 AC 358, 458–9, 472.

[68] "Governmental Liability" [1989] *PL* 40, p. 43.

[69] See Cane, *Atiyah's Accidents, Compensation and the Law*, 4th edn. (London, Weidenfeld & Nicholson, 1987) at p. 226 *et seq.*

[70] Posner and Rosenfield, "Impossibility and Related Doctrines in Contract Law" (1977) 6 *J Leg Stud* 83; O'Dair, "*Murphy* v. *Brentwood District Council:* A House with Firm Foundations?" (1991) 54 *MLR* 561, at p. 564.

[71] (1991) 7 *Const LJ* 146, 154.

compulsory, and upon the willingness of insurers to underwrite emerging forms of liability. The latter will depend, in part, upon the degree of spare capacity in the insurance industry at any given time. Although a few years ago it was suggested that there was considerable spare capacity in the insurance markets,[72] this appears no longer to be the case, in part because of the pressure placed on the markets by recent large-scale liability settlements in the United States.[73]

First party insurance for house-owners is very widespread in Britain, in part through the insistence of lenders, but the normal type of insurance does not necessarily cover all the consequences of latent defects of the kind in *Anns* and *Murphy*. Mr Murphy's next door neighbour, whose house also suffered structural damage as a result of the defective construction of Mr Murphy's house, was unable to persuade his insurance company to accept liability. Nor will property insurance necessarily cover the whole of the plaintiff's loss; the Norwich Union would not cover Mr Murphy's costs of moving to another house.[74] It is unclear whether such a loss would also be too remote to recover in tort.

These points are sufficient to indicate the uncertainty surrounding some of the central questions arising out of insurance. Very often a court will not be able to make a clear judgment on the insurance implications of a liability rule, because it will not have before it the necessary information on insurance markets and practices, or because the arguments are finely balanced. However, in seeking to load the burden on to first party insurance in a generalised way, there is a great danger of leaving plaintiffs under-compensated and defendants under-deterred. It should also be borne in mind that subrogation is an important means of overcoming the enormous risks and expense of litigation for non-corporate plaintiffs, and thereby of providing more effective deterrence against defective performance on the part of builders and manufacturers.[75]

Murphy also raises the special position of public bodies as defendants. *Anns* marked a potentially considerable extension of governmental liability, which was then whittled down in *Yuen Kun Yeu, Curran, Peabody, Hill*[76] and *Murphy*. One basis for granting special status to public bodies is what Harris and Veljanovski refer to as the danger of the "asymmetric treatment of gains and losses".[77] Their theory can be applied to the situation in *Anns* and *Murphy*. Local councils charged with the administration of the Public Health Acts are creating a "public good" in terms of a cleaner and healthier envir-

---

[72] Hitcham, "Some Insurance Aspects" in Furmston (ed.), *op. cit.* above n. 35.

[73] See Davies, "The End of the Affair: Duty of Care and Liability Insurance" (1989) 9 *Legal Studies* 67; Percival, *op. cit.* above n. 47, pp. 734–45.

[74] See the judgment of Lord Keith in *Murphy*, [1991] 1 AC 398, 458. Latent defect insurance has until recently been comparatively rare in the commercial property sector: see Gloyn, "Latent Defects Insurance" (1987) 87 *Law Soc Gaz* 2034.

[75] O'Dair, *op. cit.* above n. 70, at p. 565.

[76] *Hill* v. *Chief Constable of West Yorkshire* [1988] QB 60.

[77] *op. cit.* above n. 35, at p. 53.

onment. Individual householders and companies gain a benefit from the council's activities but they do not pay for it as individuals; if they do so at all, they pay for it collectively as taxpayers. It would only be efficient for the law of tort to allow individuals to bring actions against the council for their particular losses arising from the negligent performance of the council's public duties, if the council could charge the plaintiffs on an individual basis for the gains they receive in terms of a cleaner environment. The result of breaking the symmetry of collective goods being paid for collectively is to load excessive costs, in terms of liability and litigation, on to the council (and hence on to the general body of taxpayers). In effect, Messrs Anns and Murphy (not to mention corporate plaintiffs such as Sir Lindsay Parkinson & Co) obtained the benefits of a clean environment free of charge, "but now want damages for losses imposed by the body which had conferred these unrewarded benefits".[78]

There is a case then for treating public (local authorities) and private (builders) defendants differently in this type of case. And yet, in *Murphy* just the opposite line is taken; there is no attempt in the judgments of Lords Keith, Bridge and Oliver to draw any distinction between the liability of the builder (for constructing a defective house) and that of the local authority (for failing effectively to check what the builder had done). Indeed, Lord Oliver considered that "the liability of the local authority and that of the builder are not . . . logically separable".[79]

The effect of restricting the tort liability of the builder/manufacturer of a defective house/chattel is quite different (and, it is submitted, less justifiable) from restricting the liability of a public, regulatory authority. The negligence of the builder imposes a cost on the house-owner who has to take steps to remedy the defect to the house. This expenditure—or its equivalent in terms of the diminution in the market value of the house—is correctly classified as "pure economic loss", but this is no reason as such to deny recovery. Where the product is or may become dangerous and the owner incurs loss or expenditure in order to prevent it causing physical damage either to persons or to property, the result is clearly to impose an externality. Even where the product is merely defective and will at no stage pose a danger to persons or property, it is by no means clear that the law should avoid imposing a liability rule. Defective products put into circulation may in this respect be analogous to mis-statements which impose costs on those who rely on them.

After *Caparo* and *Murphy*, the distinction between negligently making or building something (no liability), and negligently misinforming someone (liability) is already proving difficult to apply in any rational way. It is hard to perceive any clear economic rationale for the distinction. Economic analysis indicates that more meaningful distinctions were available to the courts;

---

[78] *ibid.* at p. 66, discussing *Weller* v. *Foot and Mouth Disease Research Institute* [1966] 1 QB 569.
[79] [1991] 1 AC 398, 483.

indeed, there is judicial support for an approach which distinguishes between consumers, business entities and public authorities in term of their differing capacity to control economic risk. This approach is more clearly expressed in *Smith* v. *Bush*, a case which, together with Hoffman J.'s judgment in *Morgan Crucible*, deserves further elaboration.

3. COMPARATIVE LAW AND THE HOUSE OF LORDS: A GERMAN EXCURSUS

In the introduction to her book, *Abortion and Divorce in Western Law*,[80] Glendon observes that:

> "Since controlled experimentation in law is hardly ever possible, legal scholars often use comparative law, just as they sometimes consult history, to see how legal systems of the past or present have dealt with problems similar to ours. The hope is that history and comparison will give us insight into our own situation and that they may occasionally help us to find, as John Dawson once put it, 'our own paths through the forest'."

To legal scholars one should add the courts, especially when they are called upon to interpret international conventions, where uniformity of interpretation may be an added incentive for them to undertake such comparative studies.[81]

This task, worthy if not at times essential, is fraught with obstacles. The first is related to the judge's mentality and, in particular, his willingness to be guided by foreign experiences. Reluctance may be the result of a certain type of intellectual arrogance, or it may stem from the genuine belief that a foreign system, because it is (or is believed to be) very different from the judge's own system, is unlikely to be of any practical use.[82] This is not the place to explore this fascinating subject of judicial attitudes and preconceptions; but one can make the (paradoxical) suggestion that this insular mentality may have been greater in the twentieth century than it was in the nineteenth, though it may now, again, be about to give way to a greater degree of internationalism.[83]

Another reason for the reluctance to undertake any comparative examination of the issue under consideration is, undoubtedly, the fact that both judge and counsel are nowadays under enormous pressures produced by lack of

---

[80] London, Harvard UP, 1987, at p. 1.

[81] Reynolds, *The Implementation of Private Law Conventions in English law: The Example of the Hague Rules*, 5th Butterworths Lecture (London, Butterworths, 1992).

[82] Our judges are not, of course, alone in committing this error. For a German example, see BGHZ 86, 240 reproduced in translated form in Markesinis, *The German Law of Torts*, 2nd edn. (Oxford, Clarendon Press, 1990) 120, at p. 126.

[83] See Lord Justice Bingham's observations in his Francis Mann Lecture " 'There is a World Elsewhere'—The Changing Perspectives of English Law" (1992) 41 *ICLQ* 513.

time, volume of work, and clients ever-more watchful of expenditure (including research expenditure) deemed to be unnecessary or, at any rate, an avoidable luxury.

As far as judges are concerned, the answer to this pragmatic objection is threefold. First, one is not asking all judges to employ the comparative method at all times. One is, primarily, thinking of the Law Lords who are, undoubtedly, under less pressure than the High Court or Court of Appeal judges; and, again, we have in mind so-called *arrêts de principe* like *Murphy* where the problem is difficult and its consequences far-reaching. Secondly, in most cases one need not seek the exact foreign precedent or study foreign law in all its minutiae but simply ensure that their Lordships are made aware of trends, tendencies and solutions to broadly equivalent problems. Thirdly, one should note that Supreme Courts of other countries are, in varying degrees, showing an increased interest in foreign law and our judges could, surely, do the same. And if it be objected that our judges do not have clerks, are not presented with Brandeis briefs, nor benefit from the kind of work that *avocats généraux* perform in some systems, then a partial solution lies in the greater use of the academic's ability to collect and synthesise information. The greater willingness of American courts to utilise academic distillations of primary material may, in part, be due to the existence of a huge and diverse case law which no one judge can handle on his own.[84] If our law is getting unmanageable, and our judges are increasingly overworked, a partnership with the academic profession could thus provide more benefits to judges than many have hitherto been willing to recognise. After all, anyone who has followed the *Murphy* debate will have noticed how two "outsiders" presented American law more comprehensively than their Lordships did in their judgments![85]

Foreign law can thus be used by our courts; and German law, sharing as it does the traditional common law hostility towards pure economic loss, seems an obvious system for study and comparison. For, in its constant attempts to escape from shackles more rigid than our own, we may find things to imitate and things to avoid. A further reason for examining German law is the ever-increasing pressure for the harmonisation of national laws within the European Community. For this to be successfully achieved, it will be necessary for our courts to pay greater attention to civilian concepts and techniques of reasoning. We shall thus look briefly at German law in three particular contexts: (i) the proper characterisation of the nature of the harm in the *Anns* case; (ii) the notion of complex structures; and (iii) the solution to the wider problem raised in *Caparo* of liability for negligent statements.

[84] Kötz, "Scholarship and the Courts: A Comparative Survey" in *Essays in Honour of Henry Merryman on his Seventieth Birthday* (Berlin, Duncker and Humblot, 1990) 190, with further references.

[85] e.g. Cooke, *op. cit.* above n. 15; Fleming, *op. cit.* above n. 15.

A. *The Proper Characterisation of the Harm*

Where *Anns* went badly wrong was in its characterisation of the plaintiff's loss as "material, physical damage" whereas, as we have seen, it is best seen as pure financial loss. The second critical error in *Anns* was the failure to say that, the plaintiff's loss being purely financial, it was not the kind of mischief that the relevant statute (the Public Health Act 1936) was designed to avoid. (As the law then stood, a claim under purely common law principles could also have been defeated on the ground that the loss in question was not recognised by the law.) It is tempting to see in those two errors most of the reasons for the subsequent confusion of our law. In any event, these errors were avoided by the Supreme Court of the Federal Republic of Germany in two decisions published as far back as 1963.

In one of them,[86] a site owner failed to make liable in tort the builder who negligently used defective cement in the construction of the building, with the result that it subsequently developed cracks in its ceilings. The court reasoned that:

". . .there is no question of a claim for damages under § 823 I BGB[87] on the basis that the plaintiff's property (*Eigentum*) has been damaged by fault . . . [for] to make someone the owner of a defective building is not to invade an already existing ownership".

Intriguingly, the court then went on to address a point which concerned Lord Denning in *Dutton*,[88] for it added:

"Nor is the claim for those damages [to repair the ceilings before they collapsed] justified by the consideration that the replacement of ceilings which are in danger of collapse is necessary to save the users of the rooms from imminent danger. It still remains the case that the cost of rendering the ceilings represents a harm which affects only the pecuniary interests of the plaintiff. This is evident if one imagines that a ceiling collapses and injures an individual; then certainly the harm attributable to the personal injuries must he compensated under §§ 823 II BGB[89] and 330 Criminal Code; but there would still remain the material harm requiring the replacement of the ceilings, and this would still affect only the economic interests of the plaintiff".

We must stress here that we are not questioning the rule that prevails both in English and German law which prohibits the compensation through tort of

---

[86] BGHZ 39, 366: also BGH NJW 1981, 2248 (III) and BGH NJW 1981, 2250; Markesinis, *The German Law of Torts, op. cit.* above n. 82, at p. 392.

[87] "A person who wilfully or negligently injures the life, body, health, freedom, property or other right of another contrary to law is bound to compensate him for any damage arising therefrom."

[88] [1972] 1 QB 373, 396.

[89] "The same obligation [to pay compensation] attaches to a person who infringes a statutory provision intended for the protection of others. If according to the purview of the statute infringement is possible even without fault, the duty to make compensation arises only if some fault can be imputed to the wrongdoer."

negligently inflicted pure economic loss. We are merely saying that trying to evade this rule by characterising the loss suffered by the *Dutton* and *Anns* plaintiffs in an erroneous way will only lead to further complications, and that is precisely what happened in the post-*Anns* case law.

In that same year, the Federal Court[90] seized upon another opportunity (that was equally available to our highest court but ignored by it) and absolved a local authority of all liability in circumstances similar to *Anns*. This was achieved by means of a teleological interpretation of the German equivalent of our Public Health Act 1936. The starting point of the German decision bears a striking resemblance to Lord Wilberforce's assertion that the 1936 Act "was enacted in order to provide for the health and safety of owners and occupiers of buildings, including dwelling houses, by *inter alia* setting standards to be complied with in construction".[91] The German court, however, took this approach to its logical conclusion:

> "The provisions requiring the verification of the calculations concerning the load-bearing capacity of buildings are directed to the dangers which threaten the public from the collapse of unsafe constructions. While these provisions and the official duties which they impose serve the protection of the public . . . they also protect every individual member of the public who might be threatened by its unsafe condition . . . The owner or developer may also be a beneficiary of this protective function if he suffers damage to his body, health, or property as a result of a collapse while he is visiting the building or inhabiting it, but only if the harm is a consequence of the danger from which it is the function of the official verification of the technical specifications to protect the public and hence the individual endangered. This is not the case here".[92]

The comparative juxtaposition of these sections with the pertinent paragraphs of *Dutton*, *Anns* and our subsequent case law, shows that the German analysis was not only more convincing than ours but also transplantable— indeed, on both issues our law has broadly come into line with the analysis and the results advocated by the German Supreme Court. But one should be more than intrigued by such comparative study; one should ask why the German analysis was ignored by our judges. In this instance, the reason (or excuse) that the foreign material was unavailable is not applicable since the translations of these cases were, apparently, communicated by Mr Weir to counsel in *Anns*; and they have been made public in a number of subsequent publications.[93]

---

[90] BGHZ 39, 358, Markesinis, *op. cit.* above n. 82, at p. 390.
[91] [1978] AC 728, 753.
[92] Markesinis, *op. cit.* above n. 82, at pp. 391–2.
[93] For example Markesinis, "A Comparative Look at Certain Problems of Pure Economic Loss" in Eastham and Krivy (eds.), *The Cambridge Lectures* (London and Toronto, Butterworths) at p. 45 *et seq.*

B. *The Problems of Complex Structures*

The Germans were also the first to experiment with the notion of complex structures as a way of neutralising the prohibition upon compensating pure economic loss through tort law. Since there is, already, some information in English about the details of German law,[94] we need only make three points.

First, the notion of complex structures made its appearance in a decision of the Federal Court of 1976;[95] and it was couched in terms that were quite similar to those used by Lord Bridge in *D & F Estates*. The 1976 decision has been followed by a stream of academic criticism,[96] but that has not deterred the Supreme Court from refining its formulations and constantly re-applying the main idea.[97] For the comparatist, the phenomenon is not without interest. Not only does it give the lie to the idea so widely held among common lawyers that in Germany the oracles of the law are the universities and not the courts; it also demonstrates yet again the need to focus mainly on cases and court practice (rather than Codes and academic literature) if one is trying to find out what the foreign law actually is on a particular point.[98]

Secondly, the complexity (and wealth) of the German case law must also be noted by the municipal lawyers. It provides telling empirical support for Duncan Wallace's prediction, first made after *D & F Estates* was decided, that the notion of complex structures would prove difficult to apply and would increase litigation.[99] The warning has not been heeded, perhaps because, consistent with the thesis of this article, their Lordships ignore (or attach little importance to) academic literature and the experiences of foreign systems. Thus in *Murphy*, though the complex structure theory was doubted by Lord Bridge[100] and condemned by Lord Oliver,[101] it nevertheless seems to have survived if one is to judge by the series of "complex structures" examples which Lords Bridge, Keith and Jauncey[102] were willing to accept as capable of giving rise to liability in the event of "spreading loss". The lessons of German law have thus been missed not once, but twice. It took years and much wasted

---

[94] Fleming (1989) 105 LQR 508; Markesinis, *op. cit.* above n. 82, at pp. 368–409; Bungert (1992) 66 *Tui. L. Rev.* 1192.

[95] BGHZ 67, 359.

[96] For instance. Hager, "Zum Schutzbereich der Produzentenhaftung", *AcP* 184 (1984), 413. But cf. Steffen, "Die Bedeutung der 'Stoffgleichheit' mit dem 'Mangelunwert' für die Herstellerhaftung aus Weiterfresserschäden", *VersR* 1988, 977; Kullmann, "Die Rechtsprechung des BGH zum Produkthaftpflichtrecht in den Jahren 1989/90", *NJW* 1991, 675.

[97] BGH NJW 1978, 2241; BGHZ 86, 256; BGH NJW 1985, 2420. BGH VersR 1990, 1283 (and note by E. Lorenz); OLG Köln, VersR 1991, 348.

[98] See Markesinis, "Comparative Law—A Subject in Search of an Audience" (1990) 53 MLR 1.

[99] In "Negligence and Defective Buildings: A Confusion Confounded" (1989) 105 *LQR* 46, at p. 77. See also Grubb and Mullis, *op. cit.* above n. 15.

[100] [1991] 1 AC 398, 476.

[101] [1991] 1 AC 398, 484.

[102] [1991] 1 AC 398, 478 (Lord Bridge), 470 (Lord Keith), 497 (Lord Jauncey).

expenditure to correct *Dutton*'s mis-description of the loss; do we need the same waste of time and energy before we correct this one?

Thirdly, the German case law can be seen as "a means to an end"—a costly means, to be sure, but a means worth adopting in the worthy cause of breaking loose from a rigidly-phrased code and an analytical tradition characterised by considerable doctrinal rigidity. A common lawyer with unique insights into German law was thus right to say that what is really at issue in these cases[103]

> "is the German willingness, indeed eagerness, to extend tort protection for damage to the defective thing itself. It is the more remarkable because of the Civil Code's categorical exclusion of tort damages for purely economic loss and the great weight reputedly given by German law to theoretical orthodoxy over pragmatism. Clearly, English law would not have to go to the same pains to justify similar results: only traditionalists have to seek refuge in abstractions".

C. *Caparo, Hedley Byrne and Liability for Negligent Certifications*

This subject, too, confirms Professor Fleming's observations about German courts trying to escape the straitjacket of dogmatic orthodoxy in order to enlarge the scope of compensation of pure economic loss. But two points must be borne in mind. First, German lawyers have yet again been forced to invoke (and even deform) their flexible law of contract in order to avoid their more rigid law of delict. Secondly, the problem receives its solution partly by statute and partly by case law. The two, however, as is so often the case, are not imbued with the same philosophy. For the statutory German regime, complex and often shaped by EC legislation and lobby pressures, is more protective of accountants and auditors. On the other hand, the more modern and liberal law is the product of the Federal Court which, quite obviously, is less susceptible to lobby influence.

Caparo itself would in Germany be subject to the statutory regime and the result would be similar to that reached by the House of Lords. This is because the *Atkiengesetz*, by reference to § 323 of the Commercial Code (HGB), specifically regulates the legal position of auditors in the case of "mandatory audits" (*Pflichtprüfungen*), namely annual, formation, and special reports, by restricting the auditor's liability for negligent breach of his duties to the company only.[104]

Shareholders (and potential shareholders) are thus excluded from the purview of this paragraph and are also denied an action under § 823 II BGB on the ground that § 323 HGB is not a norm enacted to protect *their* interests (*Schutzgesetz*).[105] This restrictive interpretation is reinforced by § 340b (5)

---

[103] Fleming, *op. cit.* above n. 94.

[104] Article 323 HGB. For an English version, see *Business Transactions in Germany*, Ruester (gen. ed.) (New York, Matthew Bender, 1990). Thus, liability under this Article towards third parties for negligent reports is excluded. See, among others, Ebke, *Wirtschaftsprüfer und Dritthaftung* (1983), 37–44; 56–60.

[105] On this A. Baumbach, G. Hueck and J. Schulze, *Aktiengesetz Kommentar*, 13th edn. (München, Verlag F. Vahlen, 1968), § 168, no. 7; Gessler, Hefermehl, Eckardt and Kropff,

of the *Aktiengesetz*, which deals with the potential liability of auditors in the event of mergers. Here, liability is expressly extended towards "the companies participating in the merger and their shareholders" (italics supplied).

Since the loss typically suffered by shareholders in all these cases is pure economic loss (*reiner Vermögensschaden*), it cannot be recovered under § 823 I BGB which is the main tort provision of the Code, since this has not included economic loss among its list of protected interests. However, an affected shareholder can seek recovery under § 823 II BGB (which allows tort recovery for breach of statutory duties intended for the protection of the plaintiff) whenever § 403 of the *Aktiengesetz* has been violated.[106] Since § 403, however, deals with intentional misreporting, its usefulness is limited in practice.

Once we move outside the statutory regime designed for public stock corporations, the picture changes and the courts become more adventurous. Paragraph 826 BGB, which imposes liability on anyone who causes harm to another "intentionally and morally (*contra bonos mores*)", may be brought into play, given that the Federal Court has progressively widened the scope of its two essential requirements. Nowadays, the courts may treat reckless behaviour as amounting to immoral behaviour. For example, the following activities have been brought under this rubric: a bank manager's giving of false information concerning the soundness of a client;[107] a surveyor's favourable report about a building which he had not fully checked for dry rot, thereby leaving the person who made the loan with a mortgage secured by a worthless property;[108] and the over-estimation by a reckless witness of the value of machinery.[109]

Additionally, the courts have widened the meaning of *intention* to include not only *dolus directus* but also *dolus eventualis* (a notion that approximates to our understanding of reckless behaviour). Thus, in one recent decision, the Federal Court[110] cased the fault requirement stating that it will suffice to show (for the purposes of liability under § 826 BGB) that the auditor expected his report to be used in connection with credit negotiations and would cause harm to the relying creditor. Professor von Bar has, in fact, gone further by stating that "a person who gives information off-the-cuff must . . . recognise that it could be false; and the very fact that he still goes ahead and gives that

Aktiengesetz Kommentar vol. III (1973) § 168, no. 31 *et seq.*, esp. no. 36; W. Zöllner (ed.), *Kölner Kommentar zum Aktiengesetz* vol II (Köln, Berlin, Bonn, München, Carl Heymanns Verlag KG, 1971), § 168, nos. 16 and 17. These are commentaries on § 168 of the older version of the Aktiengesetz which is now to be found as § 323 of the Commercial Code (HGB), quoted in the text above.

[106] See W. Zöllner (ed.), *Kölner Kommentar zum Aktiegesetz* vol II (1971) § 168, no. 17; vol III (1983) § 403, no. 5, *Dolus eventualis* will suffice: *ibid* § 403, no. 39.

[107] RG JW 1911, 584.

[108] BGH WM 1966, 1150.

[109] BGH WM 1960, 1323. See, also, BGH WM 1962, 933, 935 (characterising as reckless behaviour the superficial investigation of the business transactions carried out by a company's Chief Executive Officer, leading to false accusations).

[110] BGH NJW 1987, 1958, 1759.

information demonstrates that he has reckoned with the possibility of damage to others and accepts it. This at least is the view adopted by the German courts, which, as a result, end up by elevating what is essentially careless behaviour to the level of *dolus eventualis*".[111] The possibility of third parties suing auditors under § 826 BGB may thus, in appropriate circumstances, give third parties a plausible cause of action.

In all cases not covered by the statutory regime of § 323 HGB, the courts have utilised the notion of contracts with protective effects *vis-à-vis* third parties which have been explained briefly elsewhere.[112] The result: the auditor's liability towards third parties may be extended even beyond § 826 BGB to include purely negligent behaviour. The liability in this case, however, will be treated as, essentially, contractual, and, whether it extends to third parties or not, will depend upon whether their reliance on the report can be considered as reasonable. This will largely depend on the contract (commissioning the auditor report) as well as the surrounding circumstances—all of the above determining the subject, scope, procedure and prospective use of the report. Thus, third parties may be able to sue for damages under contracts to which they are not signatories,[113] their protection under the contract commissioning the report in some cases arising by necessary implication.[114] The Federal Courts have also made it clear that for protective effects *vis-à-vis* third parties to arise, it is no longer necessary that the requirement "*Wohl und Wehe*" ('for better or for worse')[115] be fulfilled. The BGH moved away from this restrictive requirement for the first time in its decision of 28 February

---

[111] "Liability for Information and Opinions Causing Pure Economic Loss to Third Parties"—lectures given at Queen Mary and Westfield College as part of a series of seminars organised by the Centre for Commercial Law Studies, now published in *The Gradual Convergence* (Oxford, 1994).

[112] Markesinis, *op. cit.* above n. 82, at pp. 43–51.

[113] BGH JZ 1986, 1111.

[114] BGH NJW 1987, 1758, 1759. The rich case law is considered critically by, among others, Lang, "Die Rechtsprechung des Bundesgerichtshofes zur Dritthaftung der Wirtschaftsprüfer und anderer Sachverständiger", WM 1988, 1001; Ebke, "Die Haftung des Wirtschaftsprüfer für fahrlässig verursachte Vermögensschäden Dritter", WM 1991, 389. Müller, "Wirtschaftsprüfer und vereidigte Buchprüfer als Sachverständige und Gutachter", WPK-Mitt 1991, 3 and, more generally, Damm, "Entwicklungstendenzen der Expertenhaftung", JZ 1991, 373.

[115] Traditionally, the opening of the contractual umbrella to include third parties depended on three factors. First, the third party came into "contact" with the performance of the contractual debtor and was affected by it in roughly the same way as the contractual creditor. This is commonly known as the requirement of proximity of performance (*Leistungsnähe*). Secondly, the contractual creditor must have some interest in protecting the third party. This would typically be the result of some internal relationship between the creditor and the third party, more often than not of a personal law character, which would show that the creditor acts on behalf of a third party for whom he has responsibility or to whom he owes a duty of care. This is the "*Wohl und Wehe*" requirement mentioned in the text above, which is now being watered down. Finally, these two factors must be known to the debtor/defendant at the time of conclusion of the contract or the commencement of the contractual negotiations. See BGH NJW 1959, 1676; BGH NJW 1964, 33; BGH NJW 1965, 1955. *Ross* v. *Caunters* [1980] Ch 297 illustrates clearly the operation of these complex factors with the testator standing in the position of the creditor, the attorney/defendant in that of contractual debtor and the beneficiary/plaintiff being the third party.

1977[116] and subsequently, inter alia, in other decisions handed down in the mid-1980s.[117] The BGH also departed from the argument that third party protection has to be denied because of the conflict between the interests of the principal of the commissioning report and the interests of the third parties.[118] The inclusion of third parties within the protective umbrella of the contract between company and auditor has thus become easier in recent times, despite the fact that the courts themselves insist that the range of the third parties must be objectively definable (*objektiv abgrenzbar*) or, to put it differently, the inclusion under the protective umbrella must be reasonable (*zumutbar*) or recognisable (*erkennbar*).

Of particular interest is a decision of the Federal Court of 1985,[119] where one reason given for enlarging the scope of the auditor's liability was the existence of mandatory liability insurance according to § 54 of the Accountants' Regulations (*Wirtschaftsprüferordnung*, WPO). Also relevant may be the fact that under the WPO the auditors are allowed to make use of the General Commissioning Terms for Chartered Accountants (*Allgemeine Auftragsbedingungen für Wirtschaftsprüfer*) which restrict or eliminate the liability. Statutes such as the General Conditions of Business 1977 (the German Unfair Contract Terms Act) may also help define the ambit of liability[120] and thus, *de facto*, limit litigation by reference to the amount of insurance coverage. One should also add that if third parties are entitled to sue auditors, they can be opposed by all defences that may be available to the latter in their contract with the company. The contractual nature of the action of the third parties makes this obvious, whereas it would not be so obvious if the action had been based on tort.

One may conclude that, in the context of the *Hedley Byrne* type of case, the liability of providers of information has, in recent years, been widened by the German courts (despite recurring academic criticism) more or less in the direction advocated by some of the most liberal American decisions; indeed, this move may not have reached its outer legal limits. The profession of accountants and auditors, however, shielded by insurance and a variety of protecting terms found in their standard terms of practice, still continues to flourish.

---

[116] BGHZ 69, 82, 86 *et seq*. In a subsequent decision—BGH NJW 1984, 355—the court (on p. 356) expressly downgraded the significance of the "*Wohl und Wehe*" requirement (at any rate in the context of cases dealing with banking and financial matters) and stressed, instead, that the paramount question for consideration was whether "the *objective* interests involved permit the inference that the parties [debtor/creditor] have [even] implicitly stipulated a duty of care towards third parties".

[117] The rich case law is considered, inter alia, by Assmann, "Grundfälle zum Vertrag mit Schutzwirkung für Dritte", *JuS* 1986, 885.

[118] BGH NJW 1987, 1758, 1759.

[119] BGH WM 1985, 450, 452 (nos. 6 and 8).

[120] See BGH NJW 1987, 1758, 1760.

4. CHANGING THE LAW AND THE HOUSE OF LORDS

The twelve House of Lords cases we have been considering in this article, especially if compared with the current expansive case law in a country like Germany (which, in principle, shares our system's dislike for pure economic loss), also contain some interesting clues as to how their Lordships see their role in changing the law, either positively in the sense of expanding it or negatively in the sense of restricting or overruling what they themselves have done in the past. A few words about these two aspects of judicial "law-making" may not be out of place; and this section will conclude with some observations about current judicial styles.

A. *Expanding the Law*

In *D & F Estates*, Lord Bridge provides us with an indication of his approach. After referring to the decision of the New Zealand Court of Appeal in *Mount Albert Borough Council* v. *Johnson*,[121] where the court held that a development company which had employed independent contractors to build a block of flats owed a duty of care towards one of the purchasers whose flat was damaged by subsidence, he said:

> "As a matter of social policy this conclusion may be entirely admirable . . . As a matter of legal principle, however, I can discover no basis on which it is open to the court to embody this policy in the law without the assistance of the legislature . . . it is a dangerous course for the common law to embark upon the adoption of novel policies which it sees as an instrument of social justice but to which. unlike the legislature, it is unable to set carefully defined limitations".[122]

But, apart from the fact that the last part of the statement itself is "disproved by the carefully limited and crafted rule laid down in *D & F Estates*",[123] the proposition that the House of Lords cannot (or should not) develop the common law further will strike modern civil lawyers (and, we suspect, some common lawyers as well) as representing a sorry state for the "Common Law in an Age of Statutes".[124]

In fact, the more one reflects on this kind of statement, the more one comes back to the idea that judicial and academic roles are not only different but also deliberately kept apart. Here is how a lawyer (wearing his judicial and not his equally distinguished academic hat) put this point:[125]

> "The process of authorship is entirely different from that of a judicial decision. The author, no doubt, has the benefit of a broad and comprehensive survey of his

[121] [1979] 2 NZLR 234.
[122] [1981] 1 AC 177, 210.
[123] Cane (1989), 52 MLR 200, at p. 211.
[124] The title of a monograph by Dean Guido Calabresi, *A Common Law for the Age of Statutes* (London, Harvard UP, 1982).
[125] Megarry J. in *Cordell* v. *Second Clanfield Properties* [1969] 2 Ch 9, 16.

chosen subject as a whole, together with a lengthy period of gestation, and intermittent opportunities for reconsideration. But he is exposed to the peril of yielding
to preconceptions, and he lacks the advantage of that impact and sharpening of
focus which the detailed facts of a particular case bring to the judge. Above all, he
has to form his ideas without the aid of the purifying ordeal of skilled argument on
the specific facts of a contested case. Argued law is tough law".

This statement emphasises the distinctness of the two thinking processes.
Yet the distinctness should not preclude combination. Moreover, it seems
unconvincing to suggest that judges (unlike academics) are not exposed to the
peril of giving in to preconceptions. In the economic loss cases, the entire judicial approach seems based on preconceptions which academic and empirical
literature have seriously questioned if not rejected, namely: that compensation
of economic loss will open the floodgates of litigation, that proper economic
analysis militates against recovery of such losses, and that on the eve of the
twenty-first century economic interests are still of lesser significance to the law
than wrongful interference with limb and tactile forms of property.

Yet, as we have seen, neither *Caparo* nor *Murphy* are floodgates cases, as
most commentators clearly demonstrate. The huge increase of tort litigation
has, if anything, come from physical injury cases both in the common law and
the civil law systems. Asbestos, Dalkon Shield, massive toxic torts, traffic accident or medical malpractice injuries have been the generators of extensive litigation. The floodgates argument has rarely, if ever, been invoked in these
cases. Yet those who, like us, advocate the need to adapt the law towards a
more flexible position on economic loss are accused, sometimes with (exaggerated) indignation, of either having lost simple common sense[126] or of advocating this expansion because we are "closet imperialists". Our critic
continues:

> ". . .if [our] theme is liability, the theme must be the empire. The more liability the
> better. On no *other* [sic] basis can I [the critic] explain the extraordinary predomi-
> nance of plaintiff's lawyers among the intelligentsia, or its substitute, in English-
> speaking countries".[127]

Incidentally, why limit this to the English-speaking countries, given that
civilian systems, like the French and German, can actually boast rates of litigation, pro-plaintiff judgments and amounts of damages which are often
comparable to the American?

Those of us who criticise the recent attempts to restrict the impetus given
to the law of tort by *Anns* do so not out of "closet imperialism" but because
we are concerned that tort law should continue to perform its traditional
function of protecting vital interests from wrongful interference. In this
regard, we do not accept the argument that economic interests can always be

---

[126] Weir [1991] 50 *CLJ* 553 (reviewing Peter Cane's book, *Tort Law and Economic Interests*).
[127] Weir, "Loss of a Chance—Compensable in Tort? The Common Law" in *Neuere
Entwicklungen im Haftpflichtrecht* (Zürich, Schulthess Polygraphischer Verlag, 1991), 111, 112.

ranked as having a lower value than tactile forms of property and even some forms of physical interest; nor do we accept that economic interests can always be efficiently protected through contract law alone. We do not rigidly oppose subrogation claims by insurers, in particular where reductions in costs can be passed on to the insured. Finally, we envisage at least as much uncertainty in the law arising from the attempts to limit *Anns* as its critics felt *Anns* itself brought into the system.

B. *Limiting the Expansion of the Law*

Their Lordships may feel cautious about using their traditional powers for expanding the law. Indeed, civil lawyers are surprised when they are told how much of our law of tort has been modernised by statute or as a result of judicial abdication. But were they bolder in putting down the "judicial revolution" in *Anns*? The twelve cases discussed here suggest not. Consider, for example, the treatment of Lord Wilberforce's formulation of the duty of care,[128] which to us followed the lead given earlier by Lord Reid in the *Dorset Yacht* case, where the great judge had stressed "the time has come when we can and should say that it [the Atkinian principle] ought to apply unless there is some justification and valid explanation for its exclusion".[129]

In *Peabody*, Lord Keith was unhappy with the "tendency" to treat Lord Wilberforce's words "as being themselves of a definitive character".[130] "The true question in each" he said, "is whether the particular defendant owed to the particular plaintiff in the case, a duty of care having the scope which is contended for". But this is obvious; and since it does not take us any further with our enquiry on the main question, Lord Keith had to explain it by adding that: "in deciding whether or not a duty of care of particular scope was incumbent upon a defendant, it is material to take into consideration whether it is just and reasonable that it should be so".[131] Would not Lord Oliver, who described *Anns* as a case involving judicial legislation, feel that this statement of Lord Kelth's is, similarly, an enticement to judicial legislation? And was not Lord Oliver involved in judicial legislation when he "discovered" the precise ambit of the statutory rule in *Yuen Ku Yeu* and *Caparo*? In fact, the wider the tort rule is, the closer the discovery of its proper scope and ambit resemble judicial legislation.[132]

Semantics apart, however, the significance of the new approach was that it was putting the brake on the forward-looking test of *Anns*. So, at least, one could have thought after *Peabody*'s shadow fell on *Anns*. Yet a year later, in

---

[128] [1978] AC 728, 751–2.
[129] [1970] AC 1004, 1027.
[130] [1985] AC 210, 240.
[131] *Ibid.* 241.
[132] Honoré, "Causation and Remoteness of Damage", Ch. 7 in A. Tunc (ed.), *International Encyclopedia of Comparative Law* (Tübingen, JCB Mohr, and London, Martinus Nijhoff, 1983) Vol XI.

The Aliakmon, Lord Brandon could be taken to suggest that the Wilberforce test (presumably with its restrictive element in the second limb rather than the first as Lord Keith had stated in *Peabody*) was still appropriate, at any rate "in a novel type of factual situation".[133] So, were their Lordships simply too polite to overrule openly the Wilberforce test? Or were they "adrift on the limitless seas of the common law"[134] as Sir Robert Megarry had felt (and openly admitted) when delivering his judgment in *Ross* v. *Caunters*? Or were they inadvertently allowing the Wilberforce test to remain alive for the most novel and, by their nature, more interesting type of cases? Of course, there is a third possibility, and that is that academics are making heavy weather of such linguistic divergences. Yet if only they could be explained away that easily! Proof, however, that this cannot be done is the decision of the Court of Appeal in *Hill* v. *The Chief Constable of West Yorkshire*[135]—a case which involved physical luxury and, therefore, not *prima facie* subject to the restrictive tendencies of modern courts. The various judges were distinctly unsure which test to apply and whether preference of one over another would, at the end of the day, really make any difference. So, in the end, policy dictated the (right) result and one feels grateful to Lord Justice Glidewell for having articulated it so convincingly in that instance.[136] But the question remains: are we left with a one-pronged, two-pronged or three-pronged test? And does it matter?

So where do we stand now? The answer is in a state of uncertainty, enhanced not reduced by the notions of justness, fairness and reasonableness which must guide our judges to decide if there is a duty. We know that these terms (more than any others before them) are shorthand expressions for policy. At the same time, we see that the judges are not willing (in most cases) to discuss openly these policy considerations or to consider the discussions of policy by academic writers. The ultimate result cannot be in doubt; the uncertainties of the *Anns* decision are removed and are replaced by those created by *Murphy*, to the dismay of teachers, students and litigants but, no doubt, to the delight of some practitioners.

C. *The Style of the Demolition*

This is no place to go into the merits and demerits of the multiple-opinion judgments. However, one of our points is that the multiple judgment, coupled with the inevitably narrow judicial focus, has resulted in a plethora of contradictions which might have been avoided if the disputed facts had been looked at in terms of the wider picture of our tort law. There must be times when, to quote Lord Goff again, "the diffused picture of the general" must be

---

[133] [1986] AC 785, 815.
[134] [1980] Ch 297.
[135] [1988] QB 60.
[136] *Ibid.* 74–6.

combined with the "intense study of the particular".[137] But the judgments we have been looking at are just as notable for their expansive style as they are for their neglect of academic authority and lack of boldness. What has happened to those Victorian judges—the Willes, the Jessels, the Blackburns— "whose statements of principle, precise, economical and profound, still influence, where they do not control, much of our common law and equity over a century later".[138] One finds, instead, in the judgments we have studied, an absence of a general plan, a lack of economy and an abuse of citation. Lord Bridge's judgment, for example, in *D & F Estates*, consists of 477 lines of quotations (or, approximately, 6,200 words) compared to 463 lines of personal contribution (or, approximately, 6,000 words). Lord Keith's ratio is only slightly better. In *Peabody*, his judgment runs to 253 lines of personal text (or, roughly, 3,300 words) compared to 144 lines of cited material (or, roughly, 1,900 words); a ratio which is only slightly improved in *Murphy* where 525 lines of text (or 6,825 words) compare with 260 lines (or 3,380 words) of quotation. Compare this with Lord Atkin's 689 lines of text (or 7,500 words) and 78 lines (or 850 words) of cited material in *Donoghue* v. *Stevenson*[139]; or Lord Justice Denning's famous dissent in *Candler* v. *Crane Christmas & Co*,[140] where one finds 374 lines of original text (or 4,100 words) as against 22 lines (or 240 words) of quotation.

To whom are our highest judges addressing their remarks?[141] For whom are these copious citations intended? These questions, important for both substance and style, have often been asked but never conclusively answered. We doubt that litigants who, ultimately, pay for the delays that result from such extensive citations in court, or students, who have to read such voluminous materials, feel grateful for them. The nineteenth century judgment, invariably crisper and often full of the kind of conviction that inspires admiration is, quite simply, no longer there; and it would be facile to suggest that the length of the opinion is, nowadays, determined by the volume of existing law, for this would, inter alia, ignore the fact that the ultimate size of the judgment is largely determined by repetitive and excessive quotations.

5. CONCLUSIONS

One of the main themes in this article has been the extent of the inconsistencies and the new uncertainties that can be found in the case law of the House

---

[137] *op. cit.* above n. 13, at p. 184.
[138] *Ibid.* at p. 172.
[139] [1932] AC 562.
[140] [1951] 2 KB 164.
[141] Paterson, *The Law Lords* (London, Macmillan, 1982) at p. 9, mentioning possible different audiences and giving further references. More generally on judicial methods, see Murphy and Rawlings, "After the Ancien Régime: The Writing of Judgments in the House of Lords 1979/1980" (1991) 44 *MLR* 617 and (1982) 45 *MLR* 34.

of Lords on economic loss between *Anns* and *Murphy*. It has been argued that this is, partially at least, caused by the fact that the judge's intensely focused view of the facts of the case he is deciding has not been aided by the academic's broader approach to specific problems. The degree to which our courts ignore or neglect academic literature is more fully appreciated if put in a comparative perspective. For instance, Professor Kötz recently looked at the decisions published in 1985.[142] Volume One, for example, of the All England Law Reports of that year reproduced 93 judgments which contained 72 citations to "secondary authority" or 0.77 citations per decision. On the other hand, Volume 95 of the official reports of the German Federal Court (BGHZ) for the same year contained 41 judgments with 533 citations to "secondary authority", or 13 citations per case. We do not suggest that this different German attitude makes their judgments better than ours.[143] Nor are we asking our judges to increase dramatically their citations from academic literature. What one is asking for, however, is an increased dialogue between judges and academics, in the hope that it could reduce the kind of weaknesses that have been pointed out in this article. This dialogue is unfortunately in a fairly basic state if one is to measure the extent to which judges consult academic works by the overt use they make of them.[144] It is difficult to say whether this is because, for the more traditionally-minded judges, "academics are not a *part* of the legal order, but are merely commentators on the work of those who are a part of it" or because it may "challenge assumptions which have reigned supreme for generations" and thus prove "unsettling. . . to those who have learned a subject by practising it".[145]

As this article has attempted to demonstrate, the academic contribution could take many forms. It could inform our judges of how their decisions were received by those who have to train future generations of lawyers. It could point out the true position of a foreign legal system (thus sparing our courts the embarrassment that follows the kind of selective use they made of American law in *Murphy*[146]); and it might even be able to inform them of how the law actually works in practice. Let us provide an illustration of this

---

[142] *op. cit.* above n. 84, at pp. 183, 188, 193.

[143] Thus, Professor Kötz has criticised the Federal Court's tendency to discuss with "too much enthusiasm learned views which are not, in the end, relevant" to the point under discussion. See "Einführungsvortrag", 129, 138 in *La Sentenza in Europa: Metodo Tecnica e Stile*, Cedam-Casa Editrice Dott. A. Milani, (Padova, 1988). One must further note that Professor Kötz's comparisons must be approached with some caution since the BGHZ series reproduces only Supreme Court decisions whereas the All England Law Reports are not so limited.

[144] Lord Goff is so notable an exception that a distinguished foreign commentator (Kötz, *op. cit.* above n. 84) has referred to him as the *vox clamantis in deserto*. See for example his judgment in *The Evia Luck* [1991] 4 All ER 871. See also his judgment *Spilada Maritime Corp* v. *Causuler Ltd* [1986] 3 All ER 843, 863. Compare these judgments with *Murphy* where only one judge (Ralph Gibson L.J.) out of ten (three in the Court of Appeal and seven in the House of Lords) felt the need to buttress his arguments with four citations—one to a classic textbook and three to leading practitioners' works. See [1991] 1 AC 398, 408–9, 423, 425.

[145] Atiyah, *Pragmatism and Theory in English Law* (London: Stevens, 1987) at p. 139.

[146] See for example Cooke, *op. cit.* above n. 15.

last point which lies at the core of the *D & F Estates* and *Murphy* problem: the applicability of the Defective Premises Act 1972.

Now that the common law remedies granted by *Anns* have been taken away, the significance of the 1972 Act is much enhanced.[147] But when, exactly, does it apply? In *Warner* v. *Basildon Development Corporation*,[148] Ralph Gibson LJ stated that "About 97 per cent of houses constructed in any year are built under the N.H.B.C. Scheme approved under section 2 of the Defective Premises Act 1972 and, *in consequence, the section 1 remedy is eluded*". If, in *Murphy*, their Lordships shared this view, they ought to have realised that the 1972 Act (by which they set great store) afforded insufficient protection to purchasers of houses, and this not only by virtue of its unworkably brief limitation period. On the other hand, their Lordships may have known what the Court of Appeal did not know in *Warner*, namely, that at some time before 1988, as a result of an agreement reached between the N.H.B.C. and the Secretary of State, the action envisaged by section I of the 1972 Act did become available even for houses built under the N.H.B.C. scheme. If they were aware of this little-known change,[149] then the protection given to purchasers through section I of the 1972 Act had become more significant. Unfortunately, the relevant sections of their Lordships' judgments[150] give us no clue as to whether their view of the 1972 Act was the same as, or different from, that expressed in the contemporaneous decision in *Warner*. What we do get, however, in their Lordships' judgments is a repetition of the currently prevailing view that consumer protection reform should be left to Parliament and not handled by the courts.[151]

The question that arises, but which has not been addressed by our courts, is whether this is the best way to afford efficient consumer protection. Our comparative study would suggest that statutory protection of consumer rights can turn out to be very strictly circumscribed by legislative drafting, and one can only hazard the guess that this must partly be due to the fact that the professionals whose liability is in question (accountants, builders) tend to be more organised and effective lobbyists than consumers as a general and amorphous group. It may thus not be a coincidence that a more liberal law was adopted and a wider protection given whenever courts (in the German system and others) have had a chance or the courage to move outside the bounds of

---

[147] On this see Duncan Wallace, *op. cit.* above n. 15, at p. 242 *et seq.*

[148] (1991) 7 *Const LJ* 146.

[149] Duncan Wallace, highly experienced in this area of the law, describes the scheme as "unknown to the Bar" and the surrounding secrecy as "extraordinary", *op. cit.* above n. 15, at p. 243. In *Murphy*, the arguments of counsel for the defendants are so abbreviated in the Law Reports ([1991] 1 AC 398, 440) that it is not clear whether this charge was fully appreciated. The judgments suggest that the point was probably missed. Thus, Lord Oliver complains [1991] 1 AC 398, 491 that "one of the curious features of [*Anns* is that it makes] no mention even of the existence" [of the 1972 Act]. But why should *Anns* have done so given that *at that time* the Act did not apply to the bulk of houses covered by the N.H.B.C. scheme?

[150] Lord Keith [1991] 1 AC 398, 472; Lord Bridge, *ibid.* 491.

[151] On this see Stapleton's impressive discussion, *op. cit.* above n. 15.

particular statutory schemes. The liability of accountants in Germany and builders in this country seems to support this view. If all this—as we believe— is so, then a court which abandons a common law remedy and invites the legislator to give it instead, must realise the extent to which the lobbying process may succeed in diluting the desired protection.

We have also argued that, in the development of our law, greater attention should be paid to foreign laws (especially those of our major European trading partners) which have traditionally been neglected at the expense of Commonwealth and American case law. Here, the blame must be shared with most law faculties which have, until recently, failed to grasp the significance of the European challenge; with academic writers, who have not done enough to make foreign material available in a digestible form to English practitioners; and with the practitioners themselves, who have not sensed the growing interest that a new generation of judges seems to have in European law.

A more comparative approach to problems of this kind can, and often should be, combined with an open economic analysis of the question confronting a court. Of course, one might object that the relevant policy considerations are so "highly general and abstract" that it would be unfair to ask judges who "lack the empirical information that would allow measurement of the force of magnitude [of these considerations] to apply [them] on a case-to-case basis".[152] However, the uncertainty is not so real as to justify the courts retreating behind a "bright line" rule which accepts nothing as the only alternative to accepting everything. Thus, to give an example from one area of the law of negligence, systems with wider rules on accountants' liability than ours have not faced, as a result of adopting such rules, either legal uncertainty or economic dislocation. In the *Caparo* context, for example, Dutch law has devised extra-judicial techniques for discovering what, if anything, went wrong in the auditing process and then, while not excluding liability in principle, encouraging a settlement or defeating (or reducing) claims employing techniques that resemble Lord Justice Bingham's views in *Caparo*.[153] Posner has made similar comments about the American situation by stating that: "The principle of *Ultramares* has been rejected in most states, yet the sky has

---

[152] *Barber Lines A/S v. Donau Maru* (1985) 764 F 2d 50, 1st Circuit Court of Appeals, per Breyer J.

[153] In the Netherlands, it is fairly common to refer a dispute first to the Accountants' Disciplinary Board (composed of accountants and lawyers) to determine in a procedure which is, apparently, both informal and quick whether the accountant has violated the rules of his profession (but not the issue of civil or criminal liability). If the accountant is absolved, that is the end of the story. But if he is found in breach of the professional rules, a compromise is usually worked out. If this does not happen and litigation ensues, it will not necessarily lead to a judgment for the plaintiff, since the few reported cases that exist suggest that the courts can use against him causation and contributory negligence and thus deprive him of a final or complete victory. Liability in theory thus does not mean liability in practice; though the Dutch accounting profession is increasingly weary of the growing size of claims. See Nieuwboer, "De beroepsaansprakelijkheid van de accountant" in *Nederlands Juristen Blad* 1990, no. 43, 1682; Jansen, *Enkele Aspecten van beroepsaansprakelijkheid Recht op een scheme schaats* (essays edited by F. H. A. Arisz, 1991).

not fallen on the accounting profession".[154] And, as we have already noted, German case law has also moved towards a more liberal position whenever it is not clearly hemmed in by statute. If overworked counsel cannot help unearth information of this kind and the use of an *amicus curiae* seems alien to our system, the use of academic works might provide the desired information and even a sense of direction. Our thesis is that economic and empirical work could aid, not hinder, the work of our highest courts.

This leads on to a further underlying theme of this article: economic loss does not deserve to remain the pariah of tort law. Nor will the problem disappear by means of *Murphy*, and the attempt to close the sluice gates that remain ajar. The solution, it is suggested, will come only when we find a way for a "controlled opening of the gates, permitting the flooding of a reasonably foreseeable area".[155] Though this is not the place to make specific suggestions, we believe that the courts should be more sensitive to the different nature of economic relationships. Rules which operate well where relationships between business entities are concerned should not necessarily be transplanted to situations involving consumer interests on the one hand, or governmental liability on the other. We also believe that the courts could control liability adequately through such devices as carelessness, causation and remoteness, by treating (whenever possible) these concepts as raising issues of fact rather than turning them into questions of law. Insurers, in our opinion, would be able to adjust to such a new approach, as they have in countries such as France, Belgium, Italy, the Netherlands and, indeed, Germany. Finally, such a change should be aided by the fact that judicial costs, uncertainties, and a practice that would soon become apparent to practitioners, would ensure that frivolous or unmeritorious claims were not brought before the courts. Indeed, in *Caparo*, Lord Justice Bingham indicated that these factors would have defeated the plaintiffs' claims even if the issue of duty had been decided in their favour.[156]

Anyone who has read the literature on *Murphy* will be mindful of the extent of condemnation meted out to the judgments, and conscious that the uncertainties that the decision has created may well exceed its virtues. In 1953, Mr Justice Jackson of the United States Supreme Court uttered a phrase which has, justly, become well-known. He said of himself and his fellow judges: "We are not final because we are infallible but we are infallible only because we are final".[157] Without expressing a conclusive view about their Lordships' infallibility (beyond that implied in the title of this article[158]), we venture the prediction that their judgments in *Murphy* do not represent the final word.

[154] *Cardozo—A Study in Reputation* (Chicago, U of Chicago Press, 1990) at p. 112.

[155] [1985] QB 350, 393.

[156] [1989] QB 653, 689–90.

[157] *Brown* v. *Allen* (1953) 344 US 443, 540. We are grateful to Professor Charles Alan Wright of the University of Texas School of Law for the reference.

[158] And first coined by the late Professor C. J. Hamson in his Cambridge inaugural lecture, *The Law: Its Study and Comparison* (Cambridge, CUP, 1955), at p. 12.

6. POSTSCRIPT

In *Canadian National Rly Co.* v. *Norsk Pacific Steamship Co.* the Supreme Court of Canada returned to the troubled question of pure economic loss and by a four to three majority held the owner of a tug liable to the plaintiffs when a barge, pulled by the tug, damaged a bridge, owned by a third party but primarily used by the plaintiffs on the ground that "pure economic loss is *prima facie* recoverable where, in addition to negligence and foreseeable loss, there is sufficient proximity between the negligent act and the loss". Since the fourth judge of the majority reached the same conclusion on a narrower *ratio* (liability was here justified because the defendant knew or ought to have known that a specific individual, as opposed to the general public, was likely to suffer the foreseeable harm), and the third member of the majority was the Quebec judge, the end result may, from the point of view of the common law, be even more narrowly balanced than appears at first sight. La Forest J.'s dissent, a veritable *tour de force*, confirms the view that there is no indisputable answer to this problem. But if we cannot claim that the case fully supports our more liberal view towards pure economic loss, we regard the case as an excellent application of the other points advocated in our article. For the judgments of both the majority and the minority demonstrate a keen interest in foreign law, an obvious predilection towards economic and policy-oriented arguments, and an impressive command of the relevant academic literature. It is anyone's guess what our Supreme Court will make of this decision; but tort teachers may wish to use it as an excellent introduction to the real issues that have to be faced by the courts when dealing with the compensation of pure economic loss.

15

Five Days in the House of Lords: Some Comparative Reflections on White *v.* Jones

1. INTRODUCTORY REMARKS

I became professionally involved in this case probably as a result of Steyn L.J.'s decision to quote some of my works in his judgment in the Court of Appeal in *White* v. *Jones*.[1] This prompted Mr James Quirke, junior counsel for the plaintiffs, to enter into a protracted correspondence with me which concluded with a formal request to join the plaintiffs'/respondents' team in the House of Lords led by Mr John Mitting QC. The appellants' team, led by Mr Duncan Matheson QC, included Professor Jolowicz QC (a newcomer to this litigation like myself) and Ms Teresa Rosen Peacock (who had argued the case at the lower levels appearing against Mr Quirke). My late inclusion in the respondents' team meant that my side could not guarantee my fees unless they could convince their Lordships at the end of the hearing to extend a crucial condition imposed on the defendants before granting them leave to appeal. This was that the appellants would agree to "indemnify" the respondents for all their costs irrespective of the outcome of the appeal. I agreed to this condition without hesitation, mainly because I was anxious to help implement a long-held belief that judicial decisions could, in appropriate circumstances, be enriched if both counsel and judges were persuaded to pay more attention to academic writings. The decision of the House of Lords, handed down on 16 February 1995[2] has, I feel, only partially vindicated my views as a teacher of comparative methodology. As a result, colleagues like myself, who believe that in appropriate circumstances foreign material can be of use to our practitioners (be they barristers or judges), will have to refine further their presentation of foreign ideas before they can ensure their greater use by British colleagues. But two preliminary observations may not be out of place. First, *White* v. *Jones* demonstrates that some of our judges, contrary to the views expressed by colleagues such as Professor Jolowicz,[3] are prepared to

---

[1] [1993] 3 All ER 481 at 501; [1993] 3 WLR 730 at 752.

[2] [1995] 1 All ER 691; [1995] 2 WLR 187. The citations in this article come from the latter report.

[3] In an article entitled "Les professions juridiques et le droit comparé: Angleterre", published in (1994) no. 3 *Revue Internationale de Droit Comparé* 747 at 753. For some recent instances that

look at and be influenced by foreign material where this has some bearing on the issues before them (even where the case is not one involving a conflicts of law problem). Secondly, the hearing of *White* v. *Jones* in the House of Lords has also prompted a number of reflections which I have decided to commit to writing in the belief that they may be of some interest, mainly to colleagues working in the fields of foreign and comparative law. If, in addition, some of these observations also persuade my English colleagues (practising or academic) to reflect further on the unexplored interaction of judicial and academic work in English law, especially where there is an inter-action with foreign law, then my decision to invest much effort (in fact, nearly 100 hours) in the practical side of this case will have been well- (albeit in an unorthodox way) rewarded.[4]

The above introductory remarks are, I feel, necessary so that the reader is from the very outset made fully aware of the nature of my *interest* in this case, both as an academic and as a member of the English bar. I hope, however, that this will not be allowed to belittle the importance of my main theme which is the development of a proper interrelationship of the different but complementary tasks of judge, counsel, and academic, especially where foreign law may be of use to a national lawyer. That much at least was achieved by the presence of two professors of comparative law in the hearings before the House of Lords even though, in my view, more remains to be achieved.

2. THE DRAMATIS PERSONAE

For the present writer the chance to appear before the Appellate Committee of the House of Lords was a novelty. (Professor Jolowicz, I believe, had done this once before.) On reflection, the proceedings presented a strange combination of formality and informality that foreign lawyers in particular would find intriguing if not perplexing.

First the setting. Though counsel are robed and wigged, their Lordships are not. Apart from the use of such quaint expressions as "if it pleases your Lordship" or "as it has been held by your Lordships' house", the atmosphere is informal, the presentation of arguments carried out in a remarkably low key and unrhetorical fashion. For those accustomed to the film versions of the English trial, it is a disappointment. On the other hand, for those who have

---

weaken Professor Jolowicz's theory see: *Smith* v. *Littlewoods Organisation Ltd* [1987] AC 241 at 271; *Kaye* v. *Robertson* [1991] FSR 62, CA (reproduced in the *Report of the Committee on Privacy and Related Matters* (Cmnd 1102, 1990), p. 103); *Ellis* v. *Wallsend District Hospital* (1989) 17 NSWLR 553 at 564; *London Drugs Ltd* v. *Kuehne & Nagel International Ltd* [1992] 3 SCR 299; *Norsk Pacific Steamship Co Ltd* v. *Canadian National Railway Co* [1992] 1 SCR 1021 passim; *Woolwich Equitable Building Society* v. *IRC* [1993] AC 70 at 174; *Henderson* v. *Merrett Syndicates Ltd* [1994] 3 WLR 781; *White* v. *Jones* [1994] 2 WLR 187 at 194–5; 201–3.

[4] In the event, the House of Lords decided that I should be remunerated, so my time in this case proved doubly profitable.

experienced an Oxbridge tutorial, an interesting parallel can be drawn, subject to the crucial difference that counsel is in the position of the solitary student interrogated by five tutors (rather than one tutor interrogating three or four students). Notwithstanding the informality, the atmosphere can be tense, the pressure put on counsel considerable. For the Law Lords are latter-day inquisitors, to be sure low-key in tone, benevolent in their motives, courteous in the extreme, but no less persistent in their avocation. The aura of unreality that thus permeates the highly ornate Committee Room only temporarily distracts the visitor's attention from the strength of the judicial personalities and their occasional desire to score points with counsel or, even more crucially, with each other. Disagreeing with such inquisitors is an exquisite art, requiring utmost self-control, an ability to think quickly while on one's feet and, if necessary, alter one's strategy on the spur of the moment.

Advocacy in an English court is thus not for the faint-hearted; and an aggressive pursuit of a particular point (prompted, perhaps, by a great "ego") may not be to the advantage of counsel or the client. On the contrary, a skilful concession can earn a respite, as can the ability to inject a measured sense of humour when the cross-examining becomes oppressive. However, such judicial pressure, when applied by one judge, can also bring another judge into the fray, throwing to the embattled counsel a much-needed lifeline. All of these things occurred in this case; and the "observing" academic is bound to be even more favourably impressed by this ritual, especially in comparison with a "trial" in one of the Continental supreme courts where the atmosphere is more cerebral, the judges robed and in an elevated position, manifestly performing their duties as high-powered civil servants benevolently administering justice to their citizenry and a rather subdued bar. No signs here of past tutorials, or the kind of *camaraderie* stemming from the fact that today's judge was yesterday's counsel. The background is different and so is the end product—at least as far as form is concerned. I discussed this last point recently in my inaugural lecture at University College London so I shall say no more about it.[5]

Apart from their Lordships' interventions, the presentation of the argument proceeds in a highly structured, indeed rigid, fashion. Counsel for the appellant speaks first, followed by counsel for the respondent; and then the former has the chance to close the proceedings. A structure must, obviously, exist; but it can also become something of a straitjacket. For, in practice, the inability to intervene means that dubious, even misleading statements can be made and left unanswered. At one stage, for instance, the case of *Ministry of Housing and Local Government* v. *Sharp*[6] was described as a case dealing with physical damage. If it is, many tort books and their successive editors have totally missed this point. To provide a riposte to such statements at a later

[5] "A Matter of Style" (1994) 110 *LQR* 607.
[6] [1970] 2 QB 223.

(often much later)—stage is not the most effective way of handling them, not least since the delay which intervenes may make it pointless to engage in an argument which may have become "stale". No doubt, this can also, on occasion, hinder the judges when writing their opinions with little other than their notes to help them see their way through the jungle of arguments that have been developed over a substantial period of time. The fact that despite these "shortcomings" the appeal process works well must, no doubt, be largely due to the impressive working techniques which the judges have acquired during their days as practising lawyers. In my view, this sharpens their style, questioning techniques, and ability to think in terms of concrete problems, which is rarely matched by professionals operating in other, especially Continental, legal systems.

In contrast to the restraints placed on counsel, their Lordships enjoy a complete freedom to interrupt, question, and construct hypotheticals, often of a highly improbable variety. The way they were taught law in their youth is, again, obvious and bears its strong marks. For reasons which I have explained in my (aforementioned) inaugural lecture it also represents one of the greatest contributions English lawyers could make to the emerging law of the new Europe which seems to lie ahead.

Their Lordships' interventions contain more than signs of the tutorial system. As the presentation of the case progresses, the open-mindedness of the early days is gradually, at the beginning almost imperceptibly, reduced and the sensitive observer begins to detect a judicial temptation to substitute helpful interventions in lieu of searching or even "aggressive" questions. Counsel, however, acts very much at one's peril if one allows oneself to be encouraged by such a change of tone, for often a reassuring or confirmatory remark does not really represent judicial conversion to one's point of view, but the judge's own way of making sure that counsel's argument has been understood.

A judge who has spoken or written extra-judicially about a related topic may have a heightened interest in the dispute. A well-prepared counsel will, inevitably, receive these signals; and may even choose to adapt the team's strategy during the mini-conferences that take place at the end of each day's hearing. Jurisprudentially, however, this phenomenon also raises an interesting question: to what extent does a judge who has given prolonged thought to a problem in a lecture room or a conference room become the captive in the court room of theories developed elsewhere? More about this, however, in ss 7 and 10 below.

One final point should be made under this heading; and it is again appropriate to a paper such as this which initially was addressed to a foreign audience. It concerns the use of language and the obstacles this poses (and will pose) as the move towards increasing rights of audience in courts of the European Union gains momentum. For someone like the present author who has had English as a parallel but not sole language, the problems which language poses in the legal context are truly formidable. One of them has already been addressed in an article published in the *Law Quarterly Review*;[7] and it involves the need to anglicise and not merely translate foreign material. The problem is not yet acute in English courts since open contact with foreign (non-common) law remains the exception and not the rule, though there are some signs that in difficult cases attitudes may be changing. The second difficulty, however, which will become relevant as rights of audience are extended in the future, is the art of expressing a disagreement or criticism in another (or second) language. This is as difficult as becoming numerate in another language; and will, clearly, require local adaptations (inside the court room and outside) as lawyers eventually become as mobile as their clients. There is more in this point than mere language technicalities that might be of interest to professional translators; and I hope some other author will return to this topic, perhaps under the heading of legal education, sometime in the future.

3. TIME, COSTS AND EFFICIENCY

Most Continental (and, perhaps, some English) lawyers would be surprised to hear that the hearing of a case like *White* v. *Jones* could take five full days in the House of Lords. In other systems cases of similar complexity would take up less time, in some jurisdictions considerably less time, perhaps one morning at most. Why is our system so much more cumbersome? And is the resulting cost of litigation—in this instance over a quarter of a million pounds for the sake of two legacies totalling £18,000—disproportionate to the benefit (real or assumed) gained by such thoroughness? In the absence of a specific empirical study, the last point must be left open. But this author's view is that much of the delay (and resulting costs) are not caused by activities *that necessarily* help qualify the English trial as either "user-friendly", efficient, thorough, or exceptionally illuminating. For much of the delay comes from the volume of material which counsel (or, if one wishes to phrase this more impersonally, tradition) requires to be placed before the court. Thus, in the instant litigation both parties produced photocopied material which, when stacked up on the table, probably amounted to about five feet of paper! Some of it was "just in case" it might be needed; other reported decisions were included in the various batches even though they received only a passing reference; and one is here referring only to judicial decisions placed before the court and one is not including the sizeable bundle of academic writings which were also submitted for the consideration of their Lordships but, in terms of the hearing, occupied in total less than half of one morning.[8]

But let us return to the use made of previous case law which, in some instances, involved reading aloud lengthy passages from earlier judgments.

[7] "Judge, Jurist and the Study and Use of Foreign Law" (1993) 109 *LQR* 622.

[8] Library facilities in the Lords apparently are neither extensive nor user-friendly and that is another reason why counsel have to cart with them everything they think they may need.

Steyn L.J. complained of this practice in the Court of Appeal;[9] but the tradition he is fighting against obviously needs repeated onslaughts before it can be changed in a way that makes sense to modern conditions. In the meantime litigants bear the cost of such verbosity.

Unlike Continental systems the common law, especially the English common law, pretends that our judges know no law. *Iura novit curia* is not a maxim known to our system; if anything, the opposite seems to be true, with lawyers frowning upon judges who do (as Lord Denning used to) their own research. The late Francis Mann, one of the most learned comparatists of recent times, was thus right in maintaining that "the most spectacular feature of English procedure is that the rule *curia novit legem* has never been and is no part of English law".[10] So the relevant material must be presented to the court. But does this mean that it must also be read to the judges?

Established practice has given a positive reply to this question. Thus, in the instant case (and according to my notes and recollection) many extracts were read out by Mr Matheson, including, for instance, some five to six pages from the judgment at first instance (even though the transcript was described on several occasions as unsatisfactory due to technical omissions); and over ten printed pages were read out from *Seale* v. *Perry*,[11] even though no particular textual point was being made by counsel for the appellants.[12] By my reckoning, and because of such practices, the hearing time in this case was extended by about 40 per cent. If I am right in this observation (and my comments must, of course, be treated with caution), much delay and extra cost were generated for no proper reason other than habit and tradition.

I was told in this case, as I have been told in other instances by other more knowledgeable practising colleagues, that if the material is not read out there is no guarantee that the judge may have the time or inclination to read it personally. This strikes one as a joke, albeit a bad one, until one is reminded of the huge volume of material both sides put before the judges and then one acquires much sympathy for our over-worked judiciary. But apart from the fact that the overall material can (despite the temptation of the photocopier) in many instances be reduced in volume, one could, surely, argue that it would be better digested by our judges if they read it on their own rather than having it read out to them, often almost at dictation pace.[13] To put it differently,

---

[9] "[I]t is arguments that influence decisions rather than the reading of pages upon pages from judgments": [1993] 3 All ER 481 at 500; [1993] 2 WLR 730 at 751.

[10] "Fusion of the Legal Professions?" (1977) 93 *LQR* 367 at 369.

[11] [1982] VR 193.

[12] Contrast the selective use of earlier material made by Lord Mustill in *White* v. *Jones* and his remark—at 221C—that "[e]xtensive quotation from previous judgments is not usually productive". This point was made forcefully by Markesinis and Deakin in "The Random Element of their Lordships' Infallible Judgment: An Economic and Comparative Analysis of the Tort of Negligence from *Anns* to *Murphy*" (1992) 55 *MLR* 619 esp at 642–3.

[13] Apparently judges, as well, are bored by "the slowness of the intensely oral procedure". Thus, Lord Devlin's surprise resignation from the House of Lords in 1964, a mere three years after his appointment to that high office, was, largely, caused by boredom! Lady Devlin wrote to

I think a good case could be made in favour of the view that time and money could be saved by not reading out extensive parts of judgments unless a textual point was being made. Ideally, money thus saved could be channelled to provide their Lordships with research assistance giving them background legal material, empirical studies, summaries of arguments etc, since this would ease their task and, arguably, improve the product of their labours. *Amici curiae, judge référendaire,* Advocates General, judicial clerks, different though their respective roles may be, are all institutions which may save time, money, and, most importantly, better prepare judges for the task of judging. However, the chance of persuading a highly conservative profession and a tight-fisted government even to consider such ideas is so remote that it must be pointless to labour these points any further. Yet a comparatist can muse about such matters, knowing that the "talking" time allowed to counsel by such important courts as the United States Supreme Court, the Court of the European Communities in Luxembourg (not to mention the German or French Supreme Courts) is infinitely more restricted than it is in the House of Lords without the quality of "justice" dispensed by these courts being inferior to ours.[14]

Of course one could argue that the flip side of this coin is that the product that emerges from such hearings—the judgment—is, in its final shape and form, more readable and more informative in the common law world. To some extent reading in juxtaposition the international case law—say, *Seale* v. *Perry,*[15] *White* v. *Jones,*[16] *Biakanja* v. *Irving*[17]—and comparing these judgments with the decision of the BGH of 6 July 1965[18] and the decision of the Court of Cassation of 23 November 1977,[19] confirms such an observation. However, we in England must not, I believe, rush to use this assertion (to the extent that it is correct) as an argument in favour of retaining counsel's prolonged oral presentation of the case. For, first, other *common law jurisdictions* are coming up with judgments at least as intellectually exciting as ours even though they spend less time reading, citing, and recycling well-known decisions. (The common law cases I mentioned above can, again, if read in parallel, serve as an illustration of my point.) Secondly, we must not forget the cost of such real or alleged advantages.

The length of the oral presentation of particular points is not only striking; it can also appear exceptionally wasteful. Consider, for instance, the fact that Professor Jolowicz was given close to one *full* day's hearing to present his

---

Professor Heuston on 21 June 1993: "[I]t was boredom and *boredom of the way in which time was wasted reading judgments*" (emphasis added). See R. F. V. Heuston, "Patrick Arthur Devlin" (1994) 84 *Proceedings of the British Academy* 247 at 256.

[14] Cf. Lord Griffiths' remarks on precisely this point in "Civil Litigation in the Nineties" (1991) 57 *Arbitration* 168 at 169–70.

[15] [1982] VR 193.

[16] [1995] 2 WLR 187.

[17] 320 P 2d 16 (1958).

[18] NJW 1965, 1955.

[19] 1979 JCP (Jurisprudence) 19243.

336 Foreign Law and Comparative Methodology

views on the "exclusive domain of contract"; and then note that his argument received minimal attention in the judgments. *Henderson* v. *Merrett Syndicates Ltd*[20]—a case heard just after *White* v. *Jones* but decided almost immediately after its hearing—may be partly accountable for such judicial neglect of Professor Jolowicz's meticulously presented argumentation.[21] Yet the persistent questioning to which Professor Jolowicz was subjected during the presentation of his argument was, to some observers at least, an indication that his thesis was being received with caution rather than enthusiasm. If such impressions are, indeed, correct (and, as stated, the written judgments do not disprove them),[22] why allow the court's time to be used in this way? Neither courtesy nor tradition, in my view, provide a fully satisfactory response.

4. *WHITE* V. *JONES*: FACTS AND LEGAL PROBLEMS

For present purposes the facts of the case can be simply stated. Following a family quarrel the testator, on 4 March 1986, had a will drawn up by Mr Jones (his family solicitor and defendant in this case) excluding his two daughters (Carole and Pauline) from his inheritance. The bulk of the estate was left to his first son-in-law (Carole's first husband) and the two daughters she had from that marriage. When later the family relations were restored, the testator asked his solicitor (over the telephone around mid-June 1986) to prepare a new will ensuring that his two daughters should receive £9,000 each. The five grandchildren (two from Carole's first marriage, one from her second to Mr White, and two of Pauline's) were to receive a legacy of £1,600 each. The testator destroyed the will he came to regret having signed; and his daughter Carole, and his other son-in-law (Pauline's husband), repeatedly informed the solicitor/defendant of the need to draw up a new will. Three attempts to arrange a meeting between the testator and solicitor failed because Mr Jones never turned up. July and August 1986 came and went, but the solicitor did nothing about the matter other than dictate an internal memo on 16 August to a member of his firm's probate division suggesting the drawing up of a new will. On 17 August 1986 the solicitor left for his annual holiday and returned on 1 September. The testator's daughter then arranged for him to see

---

[20] [1994] 3 WLR 761.
[21] There is a touch of irony here for *Henderson* admiringly approved (at 783) the judgment of Oliver J. (as he then was) in *Midland Bank Trust Co* v. *Hett, Stubbs and Kemp* [1978] Ch 384 which, 15 years ago, Professor Jolowicz had praised as a "useful contribution" to the progressive "demolition of the barriers between contractual and tortious liability"! See [1979] *CLJ* 54.
[22] Lord Goff's opinion simply contains summary allusions to it. See, for instance, at 196E, 197F, 200G. Lord Nolan, at 321E, is sterner by stating that, "it would be highly artificial to treat the appellants' responsibility to Mr Barratt [the testator] in contract as excluding their responsibility to the respondents under the law of tort" (emphasis added). Lord Mustill's opinion, which favours the appellants' overall position, is briefly dismissive of the "exclusive domain" theory, in the *post-Henderson* era: see at 217A–B. Lords Keith and Browne-Wilkinson do not even refer to it.

her father on 17 September, but it was not to be. On 6 September the testator had an accident. A week later he suffered a heart attack and died before the new will was prepared. The testator's estate thus devolved according to the contents of the first will, and the frustrated beneficiaries (of his final and true intentions) sued for their lost legacies. Their action in the High Court failed, largely because the intervening publication of *Murphy* v. *Brentwood DC*[23] seemed to cast a shadow over the authority of *Ross* v. *Caunters*.[24] The precise reasons given by the judge at first instance for rejecting the plaintiffs' claims were two. First this was a case of nonfeasance and not malfeasance. It was thus distinguishable from *Ross* v. *Caunters*. Secondly, in the opinion of the judge, the plaintiffs' loss was too speculative. A unanimous Court of Appeal thought otherwise[25] and decided the case in favour of the plaintiffs. Permission to appeal to the House of Lords was granted by their Lordships in July 1993. Argument was heard early in March 1994; and the judgment under consideration was delivered on 16 February 1995.

The impressive array of arguments advanced by the defendants and their refutation by the Court of Appeal can be found discussed in the Law Reports and in the notes that appeared subsequently in learned journals and thus need not be repeated again.[26] Here suffice it to say that at the House of Lords hearing some of them were either half-heartedly pursued, while others were regurgitated in a slightly different way. Thus, in the first group we find the argument that *White* v. *Jones*, unlike *Ross* v. *Caunters*, was a case of an omission rather than of a bad act.[27] An example of the second category was the argument that a pro-plaintiff decision leads, in effect, to the doubling of the will. This second argument, which was effectively disposed of by the German courts well before our Court of Appeal had a chance even to confront it[28] was raised in a slightly different form at the House of Lords where it was said by the appellants that the result sanctioned by the Court of Appeal meant that the person receiving the estate under the (unrevoked) will ended up with an undeserved windfall. But apart from the fact that the law of torts does, on occasion, tolerate such enrichments (cf., for instance, our law on punitive damages which allows the successful plaintiff to cumulate the punitive and

---

[23] [1991] 1 AC 398.

[24] [1980] Ch 297. Academic commentators at the time did not think so; and neither did Lord Nolan, the only judge in this case to refer to this point: see at 229 F.

[25] [1993] 3 All ER 481; [1993] 3 WLR 730.

[26] Fleming, "The Solicitor and the Disappointed Beneficiary" (1993) 109 *LQR* 344; Lorenz and Markesinis, "Solicitors' Liability Towards Third Parties: Back into the Troubled Waters of the Contract/Tort Divide" (1993) 56 *MLR* 56; Barker, "Are we up to Expectations? Solicitors, Beneficiaries and the Contract/Tort Divide" (1994) 14 *Ox J of Leg Studs* 138.

[27] "That argument cannot, to my mind, have any force where the omission occurs after the duty of care has been assumed by the defendant": at 231–2 per Lord Nolan. This way of analysing facts *such as these* has prevailed since Roman times. Yet contrast Tony Weir's *jeu de mots* in favour of the opposite view: "It was wrong of him [i.e. the solicitor] to do nothing, but he did nothing wrong". See *La responsabilité des prestataires de services* (1994) 125 at 135. Lord Goff's reference to this argument was even briefer: see at 197D.

[28] Lorenz and Markesinis, *op. cit.* above n. 26 at 560.

compensatory damages of the award), the point received little attention at the hearing in the House of Lords where, instead, the appellants' strategy was, essentially, based on three different arguments: first, that the respondent in this case only had a *spes successionis* and such *spes* was, in itself, unprotected by the law. Secondly, and relatedly, that there were, in law, certain situations which were (and should remain) the exclusive domain of the law of contract and the instant case was one of them. Thirdly, that this factual situation was unlike any other where a tortious duty had been recognised, especially since no legitimate reliance on the part of the plaintiffs could be shown. The case thus did not warrant an "incremental" extension of existing principles. Overall, the conceptual difficulties that cases such as this one raise are well-summarised by Lord Goff;[29] and his judgment in this context is profitably read in juxtaposition to that of Lord Mustill.

5. THE PRINCIPLE OF GRADUALISM IN PRACTICE: A HURDLE FOR THE RESPONDENTS

Early on in the proceedings the respondents reached the conclusion that it would be tactically unwise to invite their Lordships to approach this case on a contractual basis by trying to chip away at the doctrine of privity of contract, beleaguered though the doctrine appears to be these days. This left them with the tort option which, in turn, presented two major difficulties. First, how to present the facts of this case as justifying an incremental expansion of existing rules.[30] Secondly, how to fashion a tort duty which would not make such defendants more extensively liable towards a third party/plaintiff than they might be towards their co-contractors and do so without having to invoke the underlying contract.[31] It is submitted that both counsel and their Lordships dealt with this latter point less fully than it deserves with the result that unresolved problems will have to be addressed in future cases. Having said this, however, one must also note that Lord Goff for the majority was prepared to state that the tortious remedy he was prepared to fashion for the plaintiffs would:

> "of course [*sic*] be subject to any term of the contract between the solicitor and the testator which may exclude or restrict the solicitor's liability to the testator under the principle of *Hedley Byrne*".[32]

---

[29] At 195–7.

[30] Mainly *Hedley Byrne & Co Ltd* v. *Heller & Partners Ltd* [1964] AC 465 and *Smith* v. *Eric Bush* [1990] 1 AC 831.

[31] In his questioning of both counsel Lord Mustill demonstrated persistent unease over this point and it is noteworthy that this is also evident in his extra-judicial writings about which more in section 10 below. This issue was recently discussed by Professor John Fleming in an article entitled "Tort in a Contractual Matrix" (1993) 5 *Cant L Rev* 269 (see also (1995) 3 *Tort L Rev* 12). His approach coincides largely with the views of the present author.

[32] See, also, Lord Nolan's similar views at 321E. This is what I have called a tortious remedy

So let us focus on the main hurdle that confronted the respondents.

Throughout the hearing at least three of their Lordships (Lords Goff, Browne-Wilkinson and Nolan) refused to accept that as a matter of principle it was not open to them to fashion a new duty situation if considerations of practical justice required such a result.[33] Equally, however, two Law Lords (Lords Keith and Mustill) also indicated early on in the proceedings the difficulties they were experiencing in justifying an increment. For the respondents this meant that a formulation had to be devised that would indicate the case on which *White* v. *Jones* could be added as an increment. The absence of reliance was, in this instance, an obstacle that had to be overcome; but the view was taken early on by the respondents that it was at least arguable that reliance was a controlling device of liability which was related to the notion of causation and not duty and which could be dispensed with where, as in this case, the nexus between the defendant's fault and the plaintiffs' hurt was particularly close.[34] This was a point that had to be put across to their Lordships as forcefully as possible.

Half way through the hearing the present writer was asked to prepare a first draft and the following text was produced:

> "If a *professional person undertakes* vis-à-vis another person to confer a specific benefit upon an identified or identifiable third party and through his negligence fails to do so, then he will be liable towards the said third party *to the extent that the third party's loss is not recoverable by the person towards whom the professional assumed the undertaking*".

The italicised sections were each inserted for different reasons.

The whole tenor of a series of exchanges between Lord Mustill and senior counsel for the appellants left the respondents in no doubt that the formulation of the "new" duty had to be limited to "professional" men and women hence the limitation of the proposed rule to professionals. Likewise, the word "undertakes" was meant to be understood to include a non-contractual assumption, of a duty to do something for the beneficiary. This was a point that kept "creeping" into Lord Mustill's questions which suggested that the result should not be different where the solicitor had acted in the absence of a contract. The concluding italicised clause was inserted with a view to limiting the new duty to the type of situation before the court in which there had been a shift of the loss from the person who had the right to sue (but has suffered no loss) to the person who had suffered the loss (but had no right to

with a "contractual flavour"; and as far as I am concerned this is the second best answer to an openly contractual remedy which Lord Goff—at 204–5—and Lord Mustill—at 218–19—felt was impossible without overturning the current doctrine of privity of contract.

[33] Their opinions accept this. Thus, see, Lord Goff at 206 H; Lord Browne-Wilkinson at 213F–G; Lord Nolan at 230B.

[34] This view is not without strong academic support. Thus, see Cane, *Tort Law and Economic Interests* (1991), p. 193. For an additional reason why reliance is not necessary in these cases, see Lord Browne-Wilkinson's opinion at 210H to 211A.

sue). This is a key notion of German law (known as *Schadensverlagerung*) which had also been a notable feature of Lord Goff's theory of transferred loss in *The Aliakmon*,[35] which the respondents were, obviously, keen to revive.[36]

For a variety of reasons senior counsel for the respondents took the view that the last section of the draft definition should be omitted, and after some further, minor, textual alterations (my French "*vis-à-vis*", for instance, was replaced by the words "to another"!), the following text was submitted to their Lordships on the morning of 10 March:

> "If a professional person undertakes (to another) to perform work in order to *permit* that other to confer a benefit on an identifiable third party, then he owes a duty to the third party to perform that work with the care, skill and dispatch reasonably to be expected of a man of his calling".

Apart from the word "permit", which was subsequently changed on Lord Goff's suggestion to "enable", the text was then circulated to all present along with a further note prepared by Mr Mitting which defined the existing categories of duty of professional persons. These were submitted to include the following:

(i)   a duty to perform professional work with care and skill—owed to a contractual client;

(ii)   as above but to a non-contractual client;

(iii) a duty not to make careless misstatements to a third party who foreseeably relies on it;

(iv)   a duty to perform professional work with care and skill, so as to ensure that when the results of that work are reported to a third party who foreseeably relies on the report, it is accurate;

(v)   a duty to perform professional medical and related work so as to treat a patient with care and skill either to prevent the patient getting worse or to make the patient better.

In the respondents' contention the proposed new duty was an increment to (i) and (ii), was, arguably, within (iv) (deleting the mechanics by which the loss is caused) and was analogous to (v).

The reaction of the House of Lords to the above strategy will be discussed more fully in the next section though here one may briefly state that Lord Goff, essentially, accepted this formulation[37] while Lord Mustill did not.[38] Here suffice it to stress that the preceding observations have been included in this lecture in order to give "outsiders" some idea of the way in which the

---

[35] *Leigh and Sillivan Ltd* v. *Atiakmon Shipping Co. Ltd* [1985] QB 350; [1986] AC 785.

[36] Especially since Lord Goff had indicated both judicially—*in Smith* v. *Littlewood Corp* [1987] AC 241 at 280—and extra-judicially—in B. S. Markesinis (gen. ed.), *The Gradual Convergence* (1994) p. 130—that he hoped that it would, eventually, be resurrected.

[37] See especially at 207.

[38] See his comment at 217 *et seq.*

strategy of the respondents evolved in response to real or perceived hints received from the judges at the time of the hearing. It may also give some idea of how practising lawyers try to handle the facts of their case in an environment that favours incremental growth of the law. This "evolving" strategy must, I suspect, be more of a feature of systems which adopt an oral rather than a written type of procedure where the advocate's strategy seems to crystallise at a much earlier stage.

<h2 align="center">6. MAJORITY AND MINORITY</h2>

Overall and for obvious reasons this author can find little fault with the *result* reached by the majority. It is, however, fair to add that the expansion of the law proposed by the majority through the notion of "assumption of responsibility" is intellectually troublesome; and though it appears to have gained a renewed foothold in our law as a result of some recent decisions of the House of Lords,[39] it is not likely to appeal to academic lawyers because of the inherent vagueness of the notion.[40] Deciding the case on classic tort principles—dare one say of the kind that one finds in the now discarded Wilberforce test in *Anns*[41]—might have produced a more sound doctrinal basis for the decision. Neater still, in the opinion of this author, would have been the contractual explanation which he has always advocated (though, as already stated, this was not even argued by the respondents who did not regard this as the case that could breach the traditional privity doctrine). The basing of the decision on the notion of assumption of responsibility may thus prove the Achilles heel of the majority judgments. Notwithstanding such hesitations, however, the result of the litigation (if not the entirety of the arguments of the majority) appears compelling. Arguably, therefore, it might be more conducive to further discussion of this case if the limited space available is used to explain why this commentator remains troubled by some aspects of the dissenting judgments. So it is to Lord Mustill's opinion that we must now turn our attention, limiting the discussion to fundamentals.

Lord Mustill's opinion begins with a heroic overture in which its composer asserts, one suspects with some relish, his decision to disagree with the basic assumptions of almost all of the academics and judges who have spoken on the subject before him.[42] Yet the next few bars—if one may continue with the same musical metaphor—seem to be in a different key! For his Lordship starts by attacking the notion of fault which he is anxious to exclude from his

---

[39] Notably *Spring* v. *Guardian Assurance* [1994] 3 All ER 129, *Henderson* v. *Merrett* and, now, *White* v. *Jones*.

[40] Yet the notion is capable of further refinement as Lord Browne-Wilkinson's opinion shows: see at 212.

[41] *Anns* v. *Merton London Borough Council* [1978] AC 728.

[42] At 214H.

subsequent inquiry as an irrelevant distraction. The thesis here is based on the belief that "legal fault cannot exist in a vacuum; the person who complains of it must do so by virtue of a legal right".[43] Puzzling stuff to say the least, even though it has the advantage of starting one thinking! Perhaps, it is best to start at the beginning.

Initially, fault indicated moral blameworthiness. Nowadays, it indicates that the defendant has failed to attain the requisite standard of behaviour. This, on its own, entails no further legal consequences in the *civil law* field, though it may, along with the appropriate *actus reus*, constitute a criminal offence. Thus, if I carelessly or recklessly drive through red traffic lights I commit a criminal offence. For civil liability to be found, additional factors will have to be satisfied: damage, proximate cause (between the fault and the damage) and a "proximate plaintiff" or, as the common lawyer would put it: "It is not enough that there is in such cases a general (or notional) duty to drive carefully; it must also be owed to the plaintiff".[44]

In *White* v. *Jones* the elements of causation and damage were easily satisfied. Whether a tort duty to the beneficiaries (alongside the undoubted contractual and tort duty to the testator) could also be found to exist was the subject of the whole inquiry. This should depend upon a variety of policy factors; but the presence of fault—which is again indisputable in facts of this sort—is prima facie the traditional (*though not sufficient*) reason for shifting the loss from the innocent plaintiff to the careless defendant. This has always been an important role of fault and to treat it, therefore, as a distracting factor, is not very convincing. Nor, it is submitted, is it convincing to attribute the plaintiffs' loss to the peculiarities of the law of successions.[45] If the solicitor had acted in a timely manner, but the testator had died prematurely before the new will had been drafted, no-one would have even dreamed of claiming redress. If a legal action came even to be contemplated in this case it was, *precisely*, because the solicitor behaved in such an irresponsible way. In this sense, the solicitor's fault was not only a key factor but the starting point of the entire thinking process for it took the matter out of the law of wills and into the law of torts. It is submitted, therefore, that the reasoning process would be weakened by leaving this element aside (as Lord Mustill seems to be suggesting) instead of making it its starting point.[46]

The next part of the "score" is devoted to contract.[47] Here one finds an

---

[43] At 215H.

[44] That is the reason why Lord Mustill's hypothetical negligent driver (mentioned at 215 E), who runs down the testator, is not liable to the latter's beneficiaries. For though the motorist is at fault, no duty is owed to them. The famous *Palsgraf* v. *Long Island Ry Co* 248 NY 339, 162 NE 99 (1928) litigation has always been treated as authority for this proposition; and it has been as much part of our law as it has been accepted in the United States. Incidentally, the majority and dissenting judgments in that case illustrate the equivocation between the concepts of duty and proximate cause.

[45] At 216C.

[46] This analysis is shared by Lord Nolan: see his observations at 229H.

[47] At 216H–220D.

interesting motif; but one suspects that the main theme will not become ingrained in the collective memory. The reasons for this last observation are two. First, Lord Mustill is very conscious of the fact that "no claim in contract has been advanced, and no direct argument has been addressed upon it".[48] Secondly, despite expressing a variety of views on the contractual approach, including an (intriguing) throwaway statement that "English law may be inching towards the direct enforcement of contracts . . . by persons standing outside the mutual obligations",[49] Lord Mustill scrupulously avoided "expressing a final conclusion about a contractual claim".[50] This section of his judgment is thus *purely obiter*; and if and when it is relied upon by future generations of lawyers, it will have to be used with great caution.

What about the interesting "motif" that we said can be found in this part of the opinion? It refers to Lord Mustill's rigorous analysis of the meaning of "transferred loss"[51] which he finds in *The Albazero*[52] and the *Linden Gardens* case[53] (and, he might have added, *The Aliakmon*), but he does not see in the instant case. He is, of course, right; and that is why the German literature (which in his judgment he tells us that he has consulted even though he chose not to cite it) in the instant type of case has *not* used its version (*Drittschadensliquidation*) of what we call "transferred loss" but used more frequently the kindred *but also subtly different* notion of contract with protective effects towards third parties. This part of Lord Mustill's judgment is best read in conjunction with Lord Goff's opinion,[54] where Lord Mustill's concerns are shared. At the end of the day one is thus left with the impression that where the two Law Lords differ is in their willingness to use existing law as a spring-board for further expansion. Whether they do this or not depends on the view they take on "incrementalism"; and this, in Lord Mustill's view, expressed extra-judicially in his "Kuala Lumpur Lecture",[55] is a matter of "social engineering" which the judges are reluctant "to accept inwardly, and afterwards to acknowledge outwardly". This, it is submitted, is the better way of explaining the fine differences (if, indeed, there are any) that exist in the opinions of the two learned judges on the true meaning and future potential of the notion of "transferred loss". This, too, may explain why the tort increment was denied by Lord Mustill in the last and most interesting part of his opinion,[56] to which we must now turn our attention.

Notwithstanding the preceding observation, which in the view of the present writer holds the key to Lord Mustill's philosophical stance, this (last) part

---

[48] At 218D.

[49] At 218–19.

[50] At 220C (emphasis added).

[51] At 219D–220B.

[52] [1977] AC 774.

[53] *Linden Gardens Trust Co Ltd* v. *Lenesta Sludge Disposals Ltd* [1994] 1 AC 85.

[54] At 201–6.

[55] "Negligence in the World of Finance" (1992) 5 *The Supreme Court Journal* 1. This piece will, henceforth be referred to as the Kuala Lumpur lecture.

[56] At 220–8.

of his opinion is based on an impressively rigorous examination of the opinions in *Hedley Byrne*, which in his view contain four themes: mutuality, reliance, special relationship and undertaking of responsibility. In *White* v. *Jones* the first two of these factors were, according to this analysis, lacking.[57] To assert that this analysis of earlier case law is *objectively* more accurate than that of Lord Goff's or Lord Browne-Wilkinson's would, I think, be tantamount to attempting to insert into the analysis of texts a degree of "certainty" and "self-assurance" that words, alone, are not capable of supporting. Reading the Browne-Wilkinson/Mustill analyses of the key elements of "mutuality" and "reliance" leaves one in no doubt of the inability to argue that the words in *Hedley Byrne* are capable of one—*and only one*—interpretation. Though I am confident that this part of Lord Mustill's opinion will find both future users and supporters, I submit that its real significance becomes obvious only if one: (a) sees it as part of his wider judicial philosophy as expressed in his Kuala Lumpur lecture and (b) constantly bears in mind that in *Hedley Byrne* their Lordships were consciously effecting what is now known as an incremental enlargement of the law.[58] So what are the central themes of the Mustill opinion which I, for one, regard as traceable to the Mustill lecture? I believe they are two.

The first is his search for symmetry, "rationalisation", "orderly development of the law", "principled expansion of the law"; the second is his narrow interpretation of incrementalism.[59] His attitude towards these two issues can be enhanced by the reading of his Kuala Lumpur lecture; and they give clear insights into the social, economic, and philosophical points from which he starts and the lengths to which he goes in his opinion in order to remain faithful to them. This, I hasten to add, is not the wrong way of dissecting the opinion of the learned judge since he, himself, tells us in the Kuala Lumpur lecture that this is how judges think and decide cases! Legal concepts are thus, in the by now famous statement of Professor John Fleming, little more than the verbal devices that help formulate judgments but do not actually give us the real reasons for them.[60]

Lord Mustill's repeated emphasis on "rationalisation" and a "principled" and "orderly" expansion of the law makes him sound more like a continental European academic than the traditional common law judge. From a jurist

---

[57] Contrast, in this respect, Lord Nolan's analysis of the facts (also summarised above), where he states, inter alia (at 231F): "In the particular circumstances of the case, the degree of proximity to the plaintiffs could hardly have been closer. Carole White, the first plaintiff, had spoken to Mr Jones about the revised wishes of Mr Barratt and the letter setting out those wishes was written for Mr Barratt by Mr Heath, the husband of the second plaintiff [daughter]. It would be absurd to suggest that they placed no reliance upon the appellants to carry out the instructions given to them". Cf. Lord Mustill's views at 228G.

[58] Lord Browne-Wilkinson's lucid analysis of the judgments in both *Nocton* and *Hedley Byrne* brings this out most clearly: see especially at 210–13.

[59] See his observations on the *Linden Garden* case, above n. 53.

[60] J. G. Fleming, "Remoteness and Duty: The Control Devices in Liability for Negligence" (1953) 31 *Can Bar Rev* 471 at 497.

who received his first training in the modern civil law this is, of course, a compliment. Notwithstanding this, however, one may be allowed to wonder how comfortably the Mustill approach sits with the traditionally accepted view of the role of the common law judge. Moreover he, himself, seems to accept the fact that a "principled" and "orderly" expansion of the law is something of a chimera since he tells us in his Kuala Lumpur lecture that in the "space of 60 years [i.e. since *Donoghue* v. *Stevenson*[61] was decided], our courts have successively embraced six mutually *inconsistent* [*sic*] doctrines in a matter of great theoretical and practical importance".[62] One could, of course, counterargue "why not start putting things in order"? This is a perfectly reasonable proposal though, as stated, in the light of the immediate past history of the tort of negligence, it is not one which holds out much promise of being adopted. The prescriptive force of the suggestion thus appears to be of limited value however laudable its motives may be.

Yet what seems even more worrisome about the "principled approach" is not the small chance of success of it being adopted but its tendency to lead to a very narrow understanding of the incremental factor. The comparison with Lord Goff's judgment is, again, useful. Of course, there are differences from existing decisions. The comparisons with *The Aliakmon, The Albazero* or the *Linden Gardens* case show this; and as already noted, Lord Mustill rightly pointed them out. But the differences may also be consciously (or unconsciously) magnified to such an extent as to prevent the creation of an increment if the judge is already philosophically opposed to an expansion of the law. *By definition an increment is bound to take matters further than they are already.* Where the difference from the earlier case is drawn is, at the end of the day, largely a matter of personal preference, confidence, and courage. The history of the tort of negligence proves as much. For was Lord Devlin's powerful expansion of the law in *Hedley Byrne*—the cornerstone of Lord Mustill's analysis—inhibited by the kind of hesitations which obviously haunted his successor? Would the present Law Lord, given his proclaimed mentality, have felt able to expand the limits of the tort of intimidation so as to include threats to break a contract as well as threats to assault another, as his illustrious predecessor did in *Rookes* v. *Barnard*?[63] And where would our administrative law have been today if, instead of the Denning and Reid approaches of the 1960s and 1970s, the Mustill caution had ruled the day?

If "rationalisation" and "orderly development of the law" become more than a "desirable" feature of the legal system and are, instead, elevated to a "basic aim" of judicial law, why then not abolish *Hedley Byrne* or, even, *Nocton* v. *Lord Ashburton*[64] (which started it all)? Indeed, why stop at

---

[61] [1932] AC 562.

[62] A result which the learned judge describes with paradigmatic self-restraint as being "not one of unqualified success".

[63] [1964] AC 1129, the other "expansive" judgment of that great judge.

[64] [1914] AC 932.

economic loss and not discredit totally the remaining vestiges of the nervous shock rule which some ultra-conservative academic lawyers dislike just as much as the exceptions to the non-liability rule of economic loss?[65] The problem with this approach is that it resolutely refuses to accept that, despite repeated predictions of the imminent demise of tort law, the subject is very much alive and kicking. Those who are concerned with some of its (undoubted) excesses are thus best advised to seek methods of alternative dispute resolution, to devise ways of streamlining litigation, to invent ways of keeping monetary compensation within reasonable and workable limits (and synchronised with the social security system), rather than urge our judges to tell citizens that they should stoically endure the varied harms that modern society is increasingly inflicting upon them. But that is material for another lecture!

7. JUDICIAL PRECONCEPTIONS

In *Cordell* v. *Second Clanfield Properties*[66] the former Vice-Chancellor Sir Robert Megarry said:

> "The process of authorship is entirely different from that of a judicial decision. The author, no doubt, has the benefit of a broad and comprehensive survey of his chosen subject as a whole, together with a lengthy period of gestation, and intermittent opportunities for reconsideration. *But he is exposed to the peril of yielding to preconceptions*, and he lacks the advantage of that impact and sharpening of focus which the detailed facts of a particular case bring to the judge. Above all, he has to form his ideas without the aid of the purifying ordeal of skilled argument on the specific facts of a contested case. Argued law is tough law."

This is a well-phrased and perceptive thumb-nail sketch of the roles played by two parts of the legal profession—the academic and the judicial. It is submitted, however, that it is also unconvincing in so far as it suggests (as the italicised section of the quotation does) that academics but not judges can be captives of their own preconceptions. In this section one common source of judicial preconceptions will be discussed; and in section 10, below, another and potentially more important one will be examined.

The first misconception runs throughout the law of torts and is associated with the floodgates argument in all the various forms in which this appears. Cases of pure economic loss, nervous shock, and medical malpractice disputes connected with the doctrine of patient consent, are but instances. In all of them our judges start from the premise that if they find for the plaintiff the

---

[65] Happily, the Law Commission does not share such views and its recent Consultation Paper, *Liability for Psychiatric Illness* (No. 137, 1995) has recommended the relaxation of some of the traditional limitations of liability. Interestingly enough, the paper also contains lengthy references to French and German law.

[66] [1969] 2 Ch 9 at 16 (emphasis added).

floodgates of litigation will be thrown wide open and the consequences on various professions will be truly cataclysmic.

The judicial starting point is what many would call a "common sense" approach but one which often seems to be based on unsubstantiated assumptions or self-serving rumours spread by interested parties. Thus, the view that a wider medical liability would lead to defensive medicine has never, to my knowledge, been empirically substantiated.[67] Moreover, the "defensive tests" ordered by one doctor might well be seen as "good practice" by another. All one may suggest of the huge American literature on the subject is that whenever it is not evidently self-serving it is inconclusive. Yet the ghost is difficult to exorcise!

With economic loss, the adverse consequences on certain professions provide the parallel. Indeed, Lord Mustill has alluded extra-judicially to some of these points several times in the context of accountants' liability; and he also dropped such hints during the present hearings.

As already stated, the problem is that much of the evidence relied upon for the making of such statements is either incomplete or self-serving, or disseminated by the interested parties. For instance, one can juxtapose Lord Mustill's view of what would happen to the accounting profession if the *Hedley Byrne* and *Caparo Industries Plc v. Dickman*[68] rules were relaxed, with Judge Richard Posner's opinion that in the United States the reduced importance of the *Ultramares*[69] (limiting) principle has not caused the sky to cave in on the accounting profession.[70] In the absence of complete and hard evidence to support such statements, which of the two learned judges is to be preferred? Selecting one over the other for some unexplained, idiosyncratic, or unscientific reason is not a satisfactory way of resolving this kind of dispute!

Alternatively, one can base one's belief on even more unsubstantiated evidence: newspaper reportings. News reports and leading articles are legion. But do they advance the debate in a scientific manner? The truth of the matter is that journalistic writings do not represent solid enough evidence for a judge to use as the starting premise which is then bound to colour the entire argumentation that will follow. For instance, why should one pay more attention to writings suggesting that accountants can no longer "afford" to be insured and ignore others which claim that the accounting profession (or, at least, specialised departments within it) is one of the few that has done well during the recent recession by handling liquidation proceedings and the like? That is why many authors (and even judges speaking in private) admit that they would be greatly aided in their work if English law made greater use of *amici curiae* or, in appropriate cases, introduced Brandeis-type briefs. But until that is done,

---

[67] On the other hand, economic incentives, e.g. the ability to charge separately for each, extra, test ordered, may be a partial reason for the American tendency to encourage excessive tests which thus increase the cost of treatment.

[68] [1990] 2 AC 605.

[69] *Ultramares Corp v. Touche, Niven & Co* 255 NY 170; 174 NE 441 (1931).

[70] *Cardozo. A Study in Reputation* (1990), p. 112.

anecdotal evidence (even when coupled with mature intuition) will be a very poor basis for informed decision-making.

We all know of course that none of the above reforming suggestions are likely to be accepted by our system in the foreseeable future. The problem, however, is that even if they were, they would only further the discussion in a partial way. For it is by no means obvious to everyone that even if scientific evidence were to prove a judge's preconceptions to be correct, it would also justify, *without more*, the non-liability rule. Tort law after all is not just about administrative expediency, easing the burden on over-worked courts, or making sure that commercial firms (especially the badly run variety) are kept in business. It is also (or, perhaps, more importantly) concerned with justice, compensation, deterrence, and devising a system for the efficient spreading of losses. A blanket acceptance of the non-liability rule in all cases of economic loss does not serve those needs. To put it differently, a liability rule that risked destroying financially an entire profession should prompt lawyers (especially legislators) to come up with workable compromises: capping damage awards; liability insurance (perhaps with limits); pre-trial attempts for alternate dispute resolution. Variations of all of these ideas can be found in many systems of the common law and civil law variety; and should, perhaps, also be considered by us. But it does not justify the judicial fashioning of legal rules that "nip all liability in the bud without more ado".

In *White* v. *Jones* such "alarmist" arguments were, understandably from their point of view, openly advanced by the appellants; they were even, though faintly, echoed by some of their Lordships in their questioning.

This argument was put by the appellants in the guise of a list of pending complaints against solicitors which stood to be influenced by a judgment adverse to the interests of the appellants. Huge economic consequences and, possibly, uninsurability were the dangers waved at the court. Lord Goff's opinion was the only one that dealt at some length with this point; and it deserves to be quoted in full. He said:[71]

> "Mr Matheson (who was instructed by the Law Society to represent the appellant solicitors) placed before the Committee a schedule of claims of the character of that in the present case notified to the Solicitors' Indemnity Fund following the judgment of the Court of Appeal below. It is striking that, where the amount of claim was known, it was, by today's standards, of a comparatively modest size. This perhaps indicates that it is where a testator instructs a small firm of solicitors that mistakes of this kind are most likely to occur, with the result that it tends to be people of modest means, who need the money so badly, who suffer".

Lord Goff was thus not impressed by this argument. But what his extract does not show (nor, indeed, is it obvious from the other judgments) are two further factors which suggest that the Law Society (through Mr Matheson) might have been disingenuously crying wolf by invoking this variant of the

---

[71] At 199C.

floodgates argument. For first, when the list of cases mentioned by Lord Goff was reviewed by their Lordships, the vast majority proved to be different from *White* v. *Jones* in that some other person did, in fact, exist who could have claimed damages for the solicitor's negligence. Secondly, one can reproduce (without further comment) a statement attributed to Ms Karen Aldred, head of the property and commercial services of the Law Society. This came at the end of a brief account of the decision in *White* v. *Jones*, in which Ms Aldred was reported to have said:

> "We [at the Law Society] are pleased to have the law clarified. Solicitors are already urged in guidelines to deal with wills in a 'timely' manner.[72] There are a number of similar cases which have arisen *but we are not anticipating a large number*".[73]

In the accompanying words of the legal correspondent of *The Times*: "The Law Society yesterday said the impact [of *White* v. *Jones*] would not be huge"!

One further observation, related to this argument of the appellants, needs to be made. Mr Matheson's list of cases prompted leading counsel for the respondents to attempt a different economic/insurance approach. For he calculated how much each solicitor in England and Wales would have to pay if all these (pending) claims were met in full. The amount was £67! Neither the Law Lords nor counsel for either side treated this part of the debate as being anything more than indicative, containing rough speculation. Yet it did show that a liability rule, resulting as it would in *different* insurance coverage from what currently prevails, could also lead to a *small* increase in insurance premiums which, in any event, would be spread among the profession as a whole (and, of course, eventually passed on to those using the services of solicitors). I stressed "different" and "small" since the insurance market would, no doubt, respond to a liability rule in a more subtle way than the above calculations suggest. For in the first place repeated "offenders" would end up by paying more and this would (rightly) "penalise" firms or individuals who were particularly and repeatedly sloppy in their work. Secondly, there is no reason to believe solicitors could not adjust their insurance coverage along the lines of current German practice. Thus, according to this system, attorneys can exclude their liability up to the minimum insurance coverage which they are obliged by law to carry. This insurance coverage can, however, be extended prior to taking up a case which involves particularly large amounts or significantly increased risks. The details of this coverage are, of course, individually negotiated; and one assumes that the higher premium involved goes a long way towards covering eventual claims without affecting the remainder of the profession. If this is right, then a liability rule would affect even less radically

---

[72] If the Law Society needs costly litigation to prompt it to remind its members that they must act timeously, who said that tort law cannot also perform a useful deterrent function? Law and economics experts argued this long ago. See Veljanowski and Whelan, "Professional Negligence and the Quality of Legal Services—An Economic Perspective" (1983) 46 *MLR* 700 at 708.

[73] *The Times*, 17 February 1995, 7 (emphasis added).

the entire profession. Is there something in this practice which merits, perhaps, a closer look?

8. THE UTILITY OF FOREIGN LAW

The appellants, unlike the respondents, played down the importance of foreign law and this even though their team included the last holder of the Chair of Comparative Law in the University of Cambridge. The decision was, no doubt, a deliberate one founded partly on the (very plausible) belief that this was to be won or lost on the strength of technical arguments based on English case law and partly on the realisation that the bulk of foreign law did not favour their arguments. As a result their senior counsel devoted only a very short part of his closing statement to American, French, and German law. Such reliance as the appellants chose to place on non-British material tended to come from Australia, *Seale* v. *Perry*[74] having received particular (arguably excessive) attention, especially given the subsequent reception that the decision has had in its own country. More precisely: (i) American law received scant attention from the appellants (a) because, as a result of a statement read out from *Seale* v. *Perry* and coming from the American Law Reports 3rd series,[75] the claim was made that the various jurisdictions in the United States were more or less evenly divided on the matter; and (b) because some American courts had come up with contractual answers which were not available to English law. The position is, of course, much more interesting than the appellants implied and this for two reasons.

First, as the American Law Reports 4th series (published in 1988) demonstrates, the position on wills cases has, if anything, hardened during the last ten or twenty years in favour of the position taken by the respondents. The ALR put the point thus:[76] "In cases involving will drafting, courts have ruled every case with an incorrect attestation to have at least stated a cause of action." And, interestingly enough, the last Restatement of the American Law Institute on *The Law Governing Lawyers*, 7th Tentative Draft, 1994, also goes in the same direction. Additional research by the respondents suggested that only four jurisdictions had remained faithful to the privity doctrine and had refused frustrated beneficiaries any cause of action. The law in the United States was, thus clearly, not helpful to the appellants' cause.

Secondly, the position of American courts is particularly significant in the sense that practising lawyers have, through such organisations as the ATLS, a strong influence over the attitudes of trial judges. Lawyers in the United States have repeatedly invoked many of the arguments raised by the appellants in *White* v. *Jones* and particularly stressed the dangers that could arise

---

[74] [1982] VR 193.
[75] Published in 1972! See Annot 45 ALR 3rd 1181.
[76] Annot (1988) 61 ALR 4th 464 at 474.

from liability rules that might create situations with conflicting duties. As stated, however, these fears have been rejected by the vast majority of American courts on the grounds, inter alia, that at least in wills cases the interests of the testator and the beneficiary coincide.

I.   American law has divided between tortious and contractual approaches to this problem. Now, while it is true to say that in England it would take an exceptionally bold court to bypass our doctrine of privity, Lord Goff's and Lord Nolan's opinion has produced (most of) the beneficial effects of a contractual action by accepting that the solicitor's tort duty to the beneficiary will be shaped by the underlying contract with the testator.[77]

II.   French law, with a constant case law in this matter since 1910, was also cavalierly rejected by the appellants on the ground that "it did not recognise a duty of care" (*sic*). This is true; and presumably it was meant to suggest that it is so much more liberal than English law that it holds out no lessons for the latter. The second part of this sentence (admittedly not stressed but only implied by the appellants) is wrong. For French law, though widely conceived in the Code, is severely restricted in practice through the use of causative devices and a normative understanding of the notion of damage. So much so that in another type of situation of pure economic loss, involving ricochet damage in the case of fatal injuries, the open-ended provisions of the Code have been so tightly circumscribed by the courts that Professor Durry, until recently President of the University of Paris 11, was prepared to admit that "our law follows a well-known dialectical pattern: in theory it allows extensive compensation but in practice it limits it to a closed list of relatives".[78]

III.   German law was also downgraded on the ground that it proceeded on contract. Why German law has to resort to such techniques has been explained elsewhere; it was known to their Lordships as was made clear by their interventions; and is effectively summarised in Lord Goff's opinion.[79] Four additional points should be made to complete the presentation of the foreign law[80] as given to their Lordships. First, in German law tortious liability is also possible when notaries are being sued for notarial work subject to the requirements of § 839 BGB in conjunction with § 19 of the BNotO (Regulations for Public Notaries). Second, in German law the duty—whether in contract or tort—is owed to those persons who were identified or identifiable at the time of the contract (of drawing up the will). Thirdly, German law,

---

[77] See at 207D. A statement by Lord Browne-Wilkinson in *Henderson* v. *Merrett Syndicates Ltd* [1994] 3 WLR 761 at 800B–C could be read to favour the same view.

[78] (1976) *Rev trim dr civ* 132 at 134.

[79] At 201–3.

[80] The one and only Dutch case that was found by the appellants which was to the point was cited by them to the House and appears in Lord Goff's opinion at 195 A. On the other hand, no Italian law was cited to the Lords. However, during the course of my lectures in Rome, I was informed by Professor Vincenzo Zeno-Zencovich that the *notarial* liability toward third parties is now governed by statute and, on the whole, is not in doubt. Older case law, dealing with facts similar to those of *Ross* v. *Caunters*, apparently reached the same result. For further details see Angeloni, *La Responsabilita del Notaio* (1990), especially Chs. 6 and 12.

despite its strong doctrinal foundation and its interest in legal theory, has not tolerated "black holes" in its legal system. As a result, in cases such as these where (a) the interests of the testator and the beneficiary are co-terminous and (b) the beneficiary is identified in accordance with the above test, German law is prepared, through a variety of legal constructions, to allow a remedy in order to ensure that the separation of the loss from the right to sue does not lead to injustice. Lord Goff considered this "a point of cardinal importance".[81] Fourthly, German case law has in this context (as in many others) refused to succumb to pressure groups who have paralysed Parliament and thus prevented it from acting on the matter. On many occasions, whenever this has proved to be the case, the German courts have taken matters into their hands and provided an answer.

Which brings me to my fifth and last point and perhaps the most significant one in favour of using foreign material in the present case. The point can be made briefly for I, for one, think it is self-evident. One is not trying to persuade English courts to adopt foreign reasoning, though sometimes one has to explain to the English courts why the reasoning or the concepts are different. But one is legitimately entitled to draw to the attention of our courts the position in a large variety of jurisdictions, both common law and civil law, which prove (as far as it is humanly possible short of commissioning an ad hoc empirical survey) that the answer favoured by one party (here the respondents) has worked in other systems and has not produced the consequences that are feared by English lawyers by instinct or tradition but on the basis of no hard evidence. Such points, if fully argued, must surely have *some* persuasive force for an open-minded English judge; but they must also have some bearing in giving concrete effect to the vague notions of "fair" and "reasonable" which have to be considered at the concluding phases of the inquiry that will determine whether or not there should be a duty of care. Certainly the number of German higher court decisions in circumstances similar to the one under investigation has been limited, suggesting that the solution that was favoured by the respondents has worked well in other systems where similar financial and insurance markets are at work.[82]

9. COURTS, PARLIAMENT AND LAW REFORM

This is a complicated topic with interesting comparative dimensions and, clearly, it cannot be discussed here at any great length. Yet questions touching upon it were raised by some of their Lordships in the course of the hear-

---

[81] See at 199.

[82] The leading German cases are: BGH JZ 1966, 141; BGH NJW 1977, 2073; OLG Hamm MDR 1986, 1026; BGH NJW 1986, 581; BGH NJW 1987, 1266; BGH NJW 1988, 200; BGH NJW 1991, 32 (action failed because the contract had no protective effects towards third parties). The latest decision to follow this trend was published on 13 July 1994: see NJW 1995, 51.

ing so a few words may be appropriate even though these discussions are not evidenced in the judgment.

Counsel for the appellants drew their Lordships' attention to the fairly recent Consultation Paper issued by the Law Commission advocating the introduction of third party rights in contracts along lines similar to those found in other systems. The Law Commission, conscious of the Germanic distinctions between contracts in favour of third parties and contracts with protective effects *vis-à-vis* third parties (as well as the Germanic equivalent of transferred loss),[83] also realised that the *Ross* v. *Caunters* type of case did not fall squarely within its remit and, consequently, invited reactions as to how this particular type of problem should be dealt with. For counsel for the appellants this, clearly, called for special legislation, additional to the one envisaged by the Commission for their main topic. Judging from some of the questions put to counsel, one had, at the time, the impression that some of their Lordships seemed concerned by the danger of solving the instant case on an ad hoc basis and thus, indirectly, pre-empting the possibility and content of the proposed legislation. This raises the question about the proper interrelationship of the courts and Parliament in the role of reforming the law. The possible solutions are three.

First one can ascribe to the legislator a semi-exclusive role in such matters. This has the advantage of wider consultations before any decisions—especially when economic (e.g. insurance) consequences are taken.[84] The difficulties with this approach are two (not including the objection that this is not the common law way of doing things). First, it assumes that the legislator will address the problem, which is not borne out in many (if not most) instances where this possibility has arisen; the second is that if legislation ensues, its content may well be determined by the pressure groups with most clout and greater interest in the proposed law. An instance can be found in the Defective Premises Act 1971 (UK); and, no doubt, the same would occur if legislation regulating accountants' liability was ever contemplated. In both instances, consumer interests are likely to suffer.

The second approach would be to leave it to the courts to reform the law. This they have, of course, been doing for centuries; and the fact that it tends to take time to occur incrementally is not, necessarily, a drawback. Strangely, however, our courts in the 1980s and 1990s seem to have lost their appetite for this way of reforming the law. We see instances of this in the area of privacy and also where consumer protection is involved. This attitude must, for the time being at least, be taken as a fact of life; though, as stated, it contrasts strongly with the 1960s and 1970s when, for instance, our administrative law acquired, almost exclusively as a result of judicial initiative, its modern character.

---

[83] Yet another sign that foreign law is being noticed in my country. This undermines further Professor Jolowicz's thesis mentioned at above n. 3.

[84] See, for instance, the diverging views of the Court of Appeal and the House of Lords in *Morgans* v. *Launchbury* [1971] 2 QB 245 and [1973] AC 127.

The third and final approach is to accept law reform coming concurrently from the courts and the legislator. Two major areas of tort law have experienced this phenomenon: the area of negligent misstatements which was regulated by *Hedley Byrne* and the Misrepresentation Act 1967 (UK); and the area of defective premises, where for a long time one had to cope with *Dutton* v. *Bognor Regis UDC*[85] and its progeny and the Defective Premises Act 1972 (UK). Since both of these instances have created a complex and often not easily reconcilable regime of concurrent rights and duties, it could be objected that this way of addressing problems of law reform is not particularly successful. Yet the problems largely stem from the fact that the respective attempts of courts and legislator have been *uncoordinated* rather than because they have originated from two different sources.

In the instant case, the invocation of the Law Commission's proposals as a reason for non-judicial intervention appeared more as an attempt to stop this case being decided in favour of the plaintiffs than as a logically unassailable argument in favour of proper law reform. Two arguments seem to support this assertion. First, there was no evidence at the time of the hearing (1994) that the Law Commission's recommendations (already two years old) were likely to be implemented in the near future; and one year later (1995) the prospects of imminent legislative reform do not appear substantially greater. Indeed, when one thinks of early suggestions for reform in this area of the law, and one reminds oneself of Lord Reid's judgment in *Beswick* v. *Beswick*,[86] one cannot but feel pessimistic about such chances. Secondly, a judicial resolution of the *Ross* v. *Caunters* dispute would remove from the Law Commission proposal this "dubious" instance and thus allow the legislative implementation of the Commission's main suggestions to proceed (if it ever happens) by concentrating on the paradigm type of case of contract in favour of third parties.

10. THE JUDGE AS JURIST

This subsection is concerned with the effect that research and academic writing done extra-judicially by a judge may have on the outcome of particular litigation. By this I do not mean that the judge who wrote such a piece has henceforth a closed mind with regard to specific applications of the issues which are discussed in the article, let alone that the judge is "unfit" to try a case that touches on the points of the previous academic endeavours. It is not unknown for academics to fall in love with a particular theory they have developed (usually in the laboratory), but this does not mean that their minds are necessarily closed to other views; and it is less likely to happen to judges

---

[85] [1972] 1 QB 373.
[86] [1968] AC 58.

who spend much of their life listening to conflicting arguments before decid-ing disputed points.

Yet these extra-judicial musings of our judges can take two forms; and their long-term effect might be different on the judges themselves, depending on whether the piece falls into one category or another of legal writing. This is a topic which, in my opinion, academic commentators have inadequately con-sidered; and yet with more and more judges assuming the academic mantle the topic awaits an authoritative exposition.[87]

The first category includes work which consists of editing, or re-editing practitioners' treatises. Here the work, demanding though it is, is not missionary or thematic in its character but consists largely of collecting all the available material, presenting it in a systematic way and resolving, to the extent that this is possible, existing contradictions so that busy practi-tioners and business people can use the book in their professional dealings. *Scrutton on Charterparties*, the practitioners' bible on its subject, co-authored and co-edited (in the past) by Lord Mustill (among others), falls into this category.

But then there also exists a second category of extra-judicial writing. This can take the form of a learned monograph (Lord Mustill's seminal work on *The Law and Practice of Commercial Arbitration in England* (co-authored with Stewart Boyd QC) and Lord Goff's pioneering work on *Restitution* (co-authored with Professor Gareth Jones) immediately spring to mind); alterna-tively, such concentrated intellectual effort could appear in the form of an article, typically the result of an important, named lecture given by the judge. Lord Mustill's Kuala Lumpur lecture is such a piece; and it has already been referred to on several occasions in this paper.

The Kuala Lumpur lecture Lord Mustill has described, with characteristic modesty, as a talk mainly addressed to a lay audience. Yet, like another piece he authored on "Anticipatory Breach",[88] it is an elaborately thought-out text, as anyone who has read it and has tried to follow his complex diagrams will be quick to agree. Both lectures suggest that a great deal of thought has gone into their texts, containing deeper reflections on the wider aspects of the judge's chosen topic. This, in itself, gives the piece particular significance; but it also gives some evidence of the judge's "philosophy" of his chosen topic and, more generally, the state of our law. In both respects it comes close to the typical academic work (with the characteristics of prolonged gestation and intermittent re-examination) and thus differs from the judge's usual intellec-tual product: the judgment. These characteristics, however, may subcon-sciously also tie judges unduly to a given philosophical point of view and give

---

[87] In this paper I have, understandably, focused the attention on Lord Mustill's academic works; but many of my more general comments can be applied to other judges (such as Lords Goff and Woolf) who also have an impressive publication record.

[88] *Butterworth Lectures 1989–90* (1990), pp. 1–78.

them the kind of intellectual leanings which Sir Robert Megarry attributed to academics.[89]

When one is faced with such a piece one may thus be allowed to ask to what extent the judge's mental vision has been narrowed to exclude *judicially* solutions which run entirely counter to the *extra-judicially* expressed philosophy? Lord Mustill would, probably, discard the validity of this comment by arguing that in, say, his Kuala Lumpur lecture he was careful not to advance a particular solution or specific thesis. This is perfectly true.[90] Yet, as already stated, his article reveals a fully developed philosophy about the role of tort law in a modern society. Such pieces thus pose a challenge both for counsel and for the academic; and it would, I think, be wrong to exclude them from one's purview when analysing a judicial opinion coming from such an author simply because no-one has, until now, explored this relationship.

A. The Challenge to Counsel

This is not idle speculation. For the respondents, who had studied Lord Mustill's Kuala Lumpur lecture, it was obvious from the very first day that many of his questions harped back to the points and examples he had discussed in his lecture.[91] The aforementioned challenge was thus subconsciously if not consciously constantly in their mind even though it is more than likely that this possibility may never have occurred to the learned judge himself! In such cases, therefore, the judge, wearing the hat of jurist, can have a great bearing on the attitudes and preconceptions of counsel.

---

[89] Sir Robert may, himself, not have been immune to this temptation since eighteen years before he decided *Ross* v. *Caunters* he had commented approvingly (on the liability side) of the California decision in *Lucas* v. *Hamm* Cal Rptr 583; 364 P. 2d 685 (1961): see (1965) 81 *LQR* 478 at 480. Nor is the thesis advanced in the paragraphs that follow limited to English law. The famous decision of the French Court of Cassation of 27 July 1937, S 1938, 1, 321 and note by Marty, which denied a "mistress" tortious claims against the tortfeasor who injured or killed her paramour, was justified by Josserand (speaking as a judge) in legalistic terms (*"une absence d , un intérêt légitime juridiquement protégé"*) but was really foreshadowed by Josserand's earlier article (written while he was still an academic) in *Dalloz Hebdomadaire* (1932), 1, 45. Since similar examples can be found in other legal systems, it is submitted that the thesis advanced in the text merits further consideration.

[90] For instance, his article is meticulously phrased so as to leave "open" the contractual door to the kind of cases he is considering. Yet even here his text (e.g. at 31, second full paragraph; at 32, second paragraph) can be read as containing the necessary elements that will allow him to "close" the door when he is next given the chance to do so judicially.

[91] Even his opinion contains allusions to points which are so pithy that they only acquire their full significance if read against the background of his Kuala Lumpur lecture. For instance, Lord Mustill refers at 217C–D to the difficulties that may arise in "commercial networks", where there may be situations where the parties have erected a structure which leaves no room for any obligations other than those which they have expressly chosen to create. These cases are discussed in his lecture (see at 20 *et seq.*) and also form the subject of diagrams (group F at 39) the sheer complexity of which shows how much thought Lord Mustill has given to the problems raised in these factual configurations. Here, however, it is notable that he stops short of giving an answer, probably in order to avoid the kind of "criticisms" levelled against him in this article!

B. *The Effect on Academic Writing*

This is the second effect that extra-judicial musing can have. The high standing of the author guarantees that the writings will be noticed and scrutinised. This is certainly true of the piece in question. For Lord Mustill, effectively, nailed to the door of the academic cathedral a series of propositions which deserve a closer look since, as I have already stated, they shed further light on his opinion. At the risk of being crass, those parts of his thesis which are relevant to this piece could be summarised as follows.

First, he proceeds to analyse his material under six different headings (illustrated, at the end of the lecture, by some increasingly complicated diagrams). The author admits that such categories "have a false air of precision",[92] but also insists that they are helpful in so far as "they impose some semblance of order on an otherwise chaotic 'wilderness of single instances'". Does not this sound like an academic ordering decisional law for the purposes of teaching? More significantly, however, is the acceptance that these categories "call for very different legal analysis". This means that in some of these instances recovery for pure economic loss will be allowed. It also follows that it is up to the ingenuity of those who believe that the English common law has taken an excessively hostile view towards economic loss to find ways to expand the categories incrementally, legislatively, or otherwise. So far then, so good.

After a careful reading of the judgments in *Donoghue* v. *Stevenson*, Lord Mustill proceeds to enquire why the decision did not immediately "detonate an explosive increase in successful claims".[93] His reasons are basically three; and they are indicative of the philosophy which will come to dominate his article. First is the argument that "resignation not litigation" is the response to the vicissitudes of life. Second, is that "delictual rights [have in the English common law] grown by accretion, like coral". Finally the "duty argument" was circuitous and thus meaningless—a damnation which is, again, followed by the important assertion that "[n]ot for the first or last time in the history of the common law a principle is stated in terms which conceal the fact that the process of deciding on liability begins with an answer which is largely intuitive, and reasons backwards from it".[94]

The remaining ten pages of Lord Mustill's article contain three main ideas, two of which will detain us here.

First, the English common law is in such a state of confusion that probably only legislation can extricate it from the mess. One must contrast this approach with that taken by other systems. The foreign audience to which these lectures were addressed would have been perfectly entitled to ask what has happened to the common law when it constantly puts up its hands in

---

[92] At 3.
[93] At 10.
[94] At 10–11.

despair and calls for legislation? Certainly, there is much food for thought here for comparatists if not for English lawyers.

Secondly, there is the resurfacing of his main philosophy: "resignation is better than litigation". This approach the judge calls "Victorian"; and he contrasts it with "the interventionist". The terms here are emotive; and they call for two observations.

The first observation must be that this is a strong policy stance, no doubt shared by many and opposed by others just as numerous. But the open allusion to the philosophy (which underlies the legal solutions provided in cases of this kind) must be forcefully stressed. For not only have too many lawyers, for too long, ascribed a political neutrality to tort law which is simply not there;[95] but also it is crucially important to ask to what extent such deeply held philosophical views effectively predetermined Lord Mustill's attitude towards incrementalism?[96] For this underlying philosophy is not a matter of detail on which counsel's argument, however carefully crafted, can have any impact whatsoever. When Lord Mustill, himself, courageously tells us that judicial decision-making is largely intuitive, involving social engineering and retrospective legal justification, then articles such as his acquire paramount significance for they provide the best explanation for subsequent judicial opinions written by their authors.

The second observation refers to Lord Mustill's attachment to the "Victorian" value of "resignation [over] litigation". He may like it as, indeed, many a jurist (and politician) did on both sides of the Atlantic in the 1980s. But does it remain a workable proposition for the future? A review of the development of tort law as a whole in this country (and elsewhere) during its last 60 years or so[97] yields the incontrovertible general conclusion that, despite temporary tergiversations, tort law has demonstrated a forward momentum. This is entirely compatible with the law's overall growing social awareness and its reduced belief in the merits of private ordering (even in the area of contract). Seen against this trend, a narrow approach to incrementalism, seems, in the long run at least, bound to fail. It is, however, to Lord Mustill's credit that in his article he seems to accept that it is no longer possible to put the genie back into the bottle![98]

---

[95] This view was recently challenged by J. Conaghan and W. Mansell, *The Wrongs of Tort* (1993), a provocatively interesting book.

[96] For Lord Goff in this case was just as aware that its facts were not identical to earlier ones where a duty of care had been discovered; but he was, nevertheless, willing to fill the lacuna by paying attention to wider considerations of justice. Nor is this sensitivity to social realities unique to *White* v. *Jones*, for *Smith* v. *Bush* provides another illustration of precisely this phenomenon. Thus it will be remembered that in that case much attention was paid to the fact that the transaction involved a "modest dwelling" and that the woman in question could not have been credited with great business acumen.

[97] The period which he, in fact, covers in his article.

[98] At 28.

11. CASE LAW AS A SOURCE OF IDEAS AND AS A TEACHING TOOL

In my inaugural lecture at University College London I discussed comparative judicial styles and maintained that the common law judgment is, in stylistic terms, superior to its civilian counterparts. I also argued that it is a rich source of ideas and can thus serve as an excellent teaching tool. My points are, I believe, validated by the study and use made of foreign law in the present dispute and even by a quick glance at a representative sample of judgments among which I would include *Biakanja* v. *Irving*,[99] *Lucas* v. *Hamm*[100] and *Heyer* v. *Flaig*[101] from the United States; *Cassation Civile* of 23 November 1977 from France; BGH JZ 1966, 141 and BGH NJW 1977, 2073 from Germany; *Seale* v. *Perry*[102] from Australia; *Gartside* v. *Sheffield*[103] from New Zealand; and *White* v. *Jones* from England.

Selecting cases is always difficult;[104] but for my purposes the above sample is, I believe, illustrative of the points I wish to make; and they are the following:

Starting with the French case law one must, I think, admit that it is rich but singularly uninformative. Its significance lies more in the fact that its richness attests to the reality that the cataclysmic consequences of a pro-liability rule feared by the English profession have not materialised in France, and also because its case law demonstrates that in France not all plaintiffs necessarily win.[105] As stated, those who argue that the absence of a notion of duty of care makes French law open-ended are wrong. The same is probably true of Dutch law. The one case found on the subject was more discursive than the French but focused on matters of evidence, assuming all along the existence of liability. Thus, though the imaginative academic can draw some conclusions from these decisions, the student will have learnt little—or nothing—from reading them. Their style is simply too opaque.

To a European observer (and I am using the term in its geographical sense to include the British) the law in America deserves special attention; but it will also occasion despair and caution. The first is obvious once one realises that here, as indeed elsewhere, the United States courts have pioneered developments. The trilogy of Californian cases selected for my list also show a wide appreciation of many of the underlying problems, a keen emphasis on the crucial issue in these cases (i.e. that the beneficiary is the end and aim of the entire transaction which leads to litigation), a flexible resort to contract and tort

[99] 320 P 2d 16 (1958).
[100] 56 Cal 2d 583; 364 P 2d 685 (1961).
[101] 70 Cal 2d 223; 449 P 2d 161 (1969).
[102] [1982] VR 193.
[103] [1983] NZLR 37.
[104] One wonders how case-book writers will reproduce *White* v. *Jones*!
[105] For details see *Jurisclasseur*, art. 1382–6. Fasc 420–5.

and, even, a considerable similarity with German law which has been stressed by German comparatists.[106] The last point is, of course, particularly important to teachers who strive to show that the different conceptual apparatus conceals considerable similarities between apparently very different systems.

The disappointment with American law stems mainly from two facts. First is the volume of the case law which must be looked at before any view is expressed about the law in the United States in general. Such a survey, however, soon reveals that the bulk of the decisions are unimaginative repetitions of a handful of leading judgments. Thus, much material has to be sifted before any gold nuggets are discovered.

The second cause for disappointment represents the reverse side of the American willingness to move freely between contract and tort and not be bound by traditional classifications. This has already been seen as a source of intellectual strength; but it also leads to doctrinal untidiness and terminological uncertainties which American judges do not seem to be keen to address. More importantly, it seems to ignore some practical consequences which can be attributed to the correct characterisation of the cause of action.[107] Noteworthy in this respect is the latest draft of the American Restatement of the Law Governing Lawyers which, while approving the *Lucas* v. *Hamm* rule, has deliberately left the nature of the cause of action open. As Professor Leubsdorf, the chief draughtsman of the section, informed me, this was deliberate, the general view being that for some purposes the cause of action could be seen as contractual and for others as tortious. I used my position as counsel in *White* v. *Jones* to pass on a copy of the Restatement to the House of Lords; and as a member of the American Law Institute, I was delighted that judicial note was taken of it. Conversely, I have attempted to inform my colleagues in the American Law Institute of some of the issues discussed in *White* v. *Jones* but not expressly considered by them. The give and take, which comparatists so treasure, was thus evident in yet another form.

American law (as this expression, which is not a term of art, suggests) should, finally, make European lawyers approach it with caution. Its immense richness is the reason. The variation between state practices can be considerable, though the trend is nowadays settling in favour of the *White* v. *Jones* solution. But state law changes, as even a brief comparison between the 3rd and 4th series of the American Law Reports clearly shows; and variations are often determined by local and political factors which the foreign practitioner can hardly appreciate and almost never follow in detail. The undoubted benefit acquired from new ideas thus has to be earned through hard work and extensive research; and when it comes to American law our courts have not proved

---

[106] See, for instance, Kötz, "The Doctrine of Privity of Contract" (1990) 10 *Tel Aviv University Studies in Law* 195; Lorenz, "Some Thoughts About Contract and Tort" in *Essays in Memory of F. H. Lawson* (1986). Both these pieces were cited by Lord Goff.

[107] On this see my "Doctrinal Clarity in Tort Litigation" (1991) 25 *The International Lawyer* 953.

themselves particularly adept at this task, partially, perhaps, because of lack of time and lack of research assistance. Once again, therefore, one is thrown back on a theme already discussed because of its multifaceted importance.

Moving now to the German decisions and the supporting literature, one is struck by those features one least expects to find in them. Clearly, the German cases raise linguistic and terminological problems of the highest order and these, probably, account for the fact that the German case law has received so little attention outside the systems that belong to the German legal family. Yet when one compares the cases with the literature they have generated one is confronted with an interesting paradox (and one which does German judges great credit). For unlike the academic writings on this topic, the decisions themselves have not been bogged down by sterile dogmatics. Notable, for instance, is the fact that the decision which started it all in 1966 found the defendants liable without going into too much detail as to whether the result was based on the idea of a contract in favour of third parties (as expressed in the Code), a contract with protective effects towards third parties (as shaped by the late Professor Larenz), or the German notion of transferred loss. Though the second seems to be the prevailing view, in a subsequent important decision[108] the German Supreme Court seemed to brush such disputes aside in a way that would endear it to any common lawyer, and chose, instead, to extend the 1966 ruling in what we would call an incremental way. Yet the academic debates on the theoretical justification of the result, neatly summarised recently in an article written by an English and German Assistant to Professor von Bar of the University of Osnabrück,[109] are not devoid of value since they show why the contractually-flavoured solution has a practical bearing on this problem. In short, German law is full of pointers of things to follow, of things to avoid, of things simply to think about provided one can make the intellectual effort to surmount the language and, above all, the mentality barrier which confines lawyers to their local patch! Comparatists will thus once again find themselves in Lord Goff's debt for giving such prominence to foreign solutions.

Last but not least we must turn to the English and Commonwealth decisions. Four of them are included in my present list for the purposes of comparison; others could have been included. For the teacher as well as the practitioner, these decisions are veritable gold mines. True, they tend to be long; certainly longer than they need to have been. But not only are they written with an elegance which simply is not found in their foreign counterparts—after all it was a famous German lawyer who said that he felt "submerged in an oxygen bath" every time he read a common law judgment[110]—they also

---

[108] BGH NJW 1977, 2073.

[109] Middleton and Rogge, "Anwaltshaftung gegenüber Dritten im Englischen und Deutschen Recht" *VersR* 1994, 1027.

[110] H Kötz, "The Role of the Judge in the Court-Room: The Common Law and Civil Law Compared" [1987] 1 *Journal of South African Law* 35 at 42.

represent the common law's answer to the Germanic learned article. For these judgments could also be seen as short articles, with ideas and a structure all of their own. *Seale* v. *Perry* and *Gartside* v. *Sheffield* thus represent an intellectual tennis match, with the ideas flying to and fro across two countries and then re-assembled and refined by the House of Lords in *White* v. *Jones*. Academics may doubt this answer or that. Practitioners may bemoan a particular result. But the teacher—and it is the teacher who is now speaking—can see in these judgments a partial redemption of other features of the English legal procedure which was criticised earlier on in this paper. Adapting Oscar Wilde, one is thus forced to admit that the art of comparing legal systems is rarely plain and never simple but it is always rewarding!

12. BEYOND WHITE V. JONES: SOME TENTATIVE CONCLUSIONS

For an academic an appearance before one's supreme court is both an impressive and a disappointing affair. The intellectual rigour of the "interrogating" Law Lords is what impresses most, with reasoning power obviously given a premium over mere knowledge of the existing material. The drawbacks are mainly determined by a system which has functioned for centuries and thus makes the questioning of its efficiency in all respects a heresy. Here are four areas which the academic observer finds capable of improvement.

First, is the slow tempo of the process made even slower by the tradition of reading out large sections of judgments and the attempt to reconcile, by hook or by crook, all previous judicial authority cited to the court. True, this is an essential part of the fabric of the common law system; yet it reinforces an in-built tendency to stick with existing rules, often for no better reason than that they have been unchallenged for a very long time. To put it differently and, perhaps, more strongly: the foreign observer (perhaps, even, the English observer) is nowadays likely to find more intellectual excitement in Commonwealth decisions than in the courts of the former "metropolis". That is a subject on its own; but a marker can be laid at this point, indicating that a comparative examination of common law decisions on tort (and other) matters might yield some interesting conclusions.

Secondly, and related to the above, is the willingness of contemporary English judges to surrender all reforming power to the legislator. The justification sometimes put forward, that legislators have a political mandate and judges do not, is not very convincing, not least since many tort problems do not always have a strong political content but also because English legal tradition militates against this trend. The reluctance to adapt the law to new circumstances is all the more remarkable when the Law Commission or other official review body has had a chance to look at the state of current law, found it wanting, and recommended changes which, nevertheless, remain, for various reasons, unimplemented. In any event, if this timorous inertia is justified in the eyes of English lawyers, it will come as a total surprise to foreign observers—and this lecture was originally addressed to them—who have been taught that the common law is more flexible than their own, and owes its flexibility to its courts. This is not a picture one can easily recognise in the English legal scene today though, admittedly, it is different in other common law systems.

Thirdly, *White* v. *Jones* marked yet another step in the growing trend to take into account the views of academic writers even though it was only two Law Lords who openly acknowledged their debt to the ideas of others. Related is the fact that *White* v. *Jones* is one of a number of decisions which have shown an interest in a civilian solution. If the glance in that direction was brief, professional comparatists (like myself) must take a fair share of the blame. Our main shortcoming, as I have stressed repeatedly, is not only our reluctance to proclaim the relevance of our subject to modern English law but also the fact that we have not found a satisfactory way of proving this relevance to our judges and practitioners.

Finally, comes the question of the precedential value of the decision. This, it must be admitted, is difficult to predict. For, as stated earlier on, Lord Goff's opinion is stronger in stressing the reasons of practical justice for expanding the law than in enunciating a principled reason for such an expansion. Lord Mustill's dissent, on the other hand, though intellectually very powerful (notwithstanding the objections mentioned against it), suffers from the drawback that it could be seen as encouraging ossification of the law through its narrow understanding of incrementalism. Since both approaches will find supporters among practitioners and academics,[111] it is difficult to predict what future generations of judges will make of such diametrically-opposed views. Two thoughts can be advanced here, albeit in tentative form.

The first refers to the precedential value of this decision. Clearly, this will be considerable in factual configurations similar to those encountered in *White* v. *Jones*. It is possible (but, at present not likely) that the ratio of the majority could be extended to cover further factual situations where the plaintiff has no remedy and the court feels that the defendant's culpable behaviour must not be allowed to go scot free. In theory, the re-emerging doctrine of assumption of responsibility could be stretched even further. This last possibility, however, would have a number of drawbacks not least of which in my opinion would be the fact that it would leave the legal world with two clusters of decisions from our Supreme Court, each pulling in different directions: *D & F Estates*[112] and *Murphy*[113] proclaiming the non-liability rule, and

---

[111] The first signs are already there. Thus see W. Lorenz, "Anwaltshaftung wegen Untätigkeit bei der Errichtung letztwilliger Verfügungen", *JZ* 1955, 317 (favouring the majority) and J. Stapleton "Duty of Care: Peripheral Parties and Alternative Opportunities for Deterrence" (1995) III *LQR* 301 (inclining in favour of the dissent).

[112] *D & F Estates Ltd* v. *Church Commissioners* for England [1989] AC 177.

[113] *Murphy* v. *Brentwood DC* [1991] 1 AC 398.

Spring, Henderson, and *White* v. *Jones* adopting a formula that enlarges the areas of exception that are born out of the *Hedley Byrne* rule. One way out of this confused state would be to solve, as I have always maintained, the *White* v. *Jones* type of cases by abandoning the English doctrine of privity. An alternative way might be for a bold court to revert to an *Anns*-type of formulation and shed its long-held fears about the potential problems of pure economic loss. In my view, neither possibility is very likely, at any rate in the foreseeable future.

Secondly, one must re-emphasise the willingness of some of our top judges to fashion new remedies when circumstances seem to require them. This, in itself may, in the fullness of time, lead to an expansive view of the decision in *White* v. *Jones.* If this were to prove correct, it would be in tune with other indications (here and in the Commonwealth) which suggest that our cyclical law of torts may be about to re-enter the expansionist phase that characterised the 1970s and abandon the 1980s, which proved to be years of retrenchment. But like all prophesying of the future this, too, may contain more wishful thinking than an element of sound prediction. Time, alone, will thus show how true it is.

16

La Pervesion des Notions de Responsabilité Civile Délictuelle par la Pratique de l'assurance

1. INTRODUCTION

On sait que les compagnies d'assurances satisfont à la majorité des demandes d' indemnisation, en particulier pour les décès et dommages corporels, dans les situations de responsabilité civile délictuelle. Il n'est donc pas surprenant que la pratique dans le domaine de l'assurance ait eu une grande influence sur le droit de la responsabilité civile qui, au minimum, est maintenant contraint de reconsidérer des questions familières dans une nouvelle perspective. Il est indiscutable que cela a entraîné une tendance croissante à déclarer les gens responsables des dommages causés par eux. L'expansion de ce que les Américains appellent la responsabilité de l'entreprise, la responsabilité du fabricant et, en France, l'interprétation jurisprudentielle de l'article 1384, alinéa 1 du Code civil, résultent largement des mécanismes modernes et ont été rendues possibles par l'assurance moderne. Autrement dit, l'extension de la responsabilité objective ou quasi-objective est étroitement liée au développement de l'assurance de responsabilité.

Il est toutefois moins facile de préciser la facon exacte dont cette influence s'est manifestée et devrait se manifester, compte tenu de la réticence des magistrats à discuter publiquement ce qu'ils peuvent penser en privé. Les allusions ouvertes à l'assurance sont rares, même dans les pays de la *common law,* les juges préférant déguiser leurs jugements de valeur (y compris leurs idées concernant l'assurance) derrière des concepts aussi éprouvés et impersonnels que le " devoir" (*duty of care*), la "faute", l'"illicéité" ou la "cause légale". Une telle attitude renforce certainement le détachement olympien que les tribunaux cultivent toujours; et elle masque dans une certaine mesure leur créativité. Mais elle a aussi imposé une adaptation et une extension considérables, et allant jusqu'à la perversion de concepts qui n'étaient absolument pas prévus pour l'environnement socio-économique que nous connaissons. L'effort, souvent tortueux, pour justifier une décision au moyen des notions de responsabilité civile vagues et abstraites, peut cacher le rôle de la politique judiciaire[1]

---

[1] Pour une étude comparative de ce phénomène, v. B.S. Markesinis et. Ch. von Bar, *Richterliche Rechtspolitik im Haftungsrecht* (Tübingen, 1981).

dans cette matière ainsi que d'empêcher la libre discussion des aspects économiques de ces affaires. Bien qu'il soit parfaitement correct de poser, comme le font tous les systèmes, que la présence ou l'absence d'un contrat d'assurance ne doit aucunement affecter la décision du juge dans une espèce[2], certains suggèrent de tenter plus fréquemment et plus ouvertement de discuter l'aspect de l'assurance. Comme le dit un auteur américain[3]:

> "Si l'administration des pertes plutôt que la prévention est l'objet principal du droit de la responsabilité civile . . . alors l'absence d'assurance devrait en tant que telle être tenue pour un facteur important, ainsi que le reflet des difficultés rencontrées par les entreprises qui ne trouvent pas à s'assurer et sont contraintes de s'auto-assurer".

En Europe, cette approche franche n'a pas encore droit de cité, bien qu'elle devienne plus populaire. Mlle Viney a eu beau parler il y a presque vingt ans du "déclin de la responsabilité individuelle"[4] à cause de l'assurance, il n'en reste pas moins que, dans son pays comme dans le mien, nous enseignons et nous appliquons un droit de la responsabilité conçu pour une société pré-industrielle et n'ayant pas de système d'assurance développé. Notre collègue André Tunc s'est également élevé contre cette séparation artificielle entre le droit et les usages en matière d'assurance dans la croisade impressionnante qu'il mène depuis des années pour réformer le droit des accidents de la circulation. Il y a plusieurs années qu'il écrivait[5] fort justement, ayant de nombreuses fois tenté de faire valoir cet argument pour réformer le droit de la responsabilité en matière d'accidents, que:

> "Les problèmes de responsabilité ne doivent . . . plus être envisagés comme s'ils se posaient entre deux individus. La plupart du temps, aujourd'hui, l'assurance en transforme les données. Et si la solution d'un procès ne peut guère dépendre du fait que l'une ou l'autre des parties soit assurée . . . ce serait condamner le droit à un contenu singulièrement artificiel que ne pas élaborer les règles en tenant compte, selon les circonstances, de ce qu'une catégorie de personnes a la possibilité de s'assurer, ou est couramment assurée, ou même est obligatoirement assurée".

Mon impression est que les tribunaux sont, pour toutes sortes de raisons, incluant celles mentionnées ci-dessus, quelque peu réticents à suivre ce con-

---

[2] V. par exemple l'opinion de Viscount Simmonds dans *Davie* v. *New Merton Board Mills* [1959] AC 604, 627 et *Lister* v. *Romford Ice and Cold Storage Co Ltd.* [1957] AC 555, 572; aussi Tunc dans D. *Chron.* [1975] 83,86. Plus généralement von Bar, dans AcP 181 (1981), 289.

[3] Fleming James Jr., "Limitations on Liability for Economic Loss Caused by Negligence: a Pragmatic Appraisal" 10 (1971–2) *J.S.P.T.L.* 105, 113. V. aussi les observations du même auteur dans "Accident Liability Reconsidered: the impact of Liability Insurance", (1947–48) 57 *Yale Law Rev,* 549 et s.

[4] Cette thèse remarquable a été publiée en 1965. V aussi sa contribution dans le *Traité de droit civil* (sous la direction de J. Ghestin), t. IV, *Les Obligations, La Responsabilité: Conditions* 1982, surtout pp. 24–33.

[5] "Les causes d'exonération de la responsabilité de plein droit de l'article 1384, al. 1, du Code civil", D. *Chron.* 1975, 83, 86. V. aussi par le même auteur, "Le droit en miettes", *Archives de Philosophie du Droit,* t. 22, 1977, 31.

seil et à admettre l'influence de l'assurance. Et dans le cas de la France, où les arrêts ne contribuent pas particulièrement à éclaircir la situation, je crains qu'il ne faille pour quelque temps encore chercher dans les conclusions des avocats généraux qulelques indices de ce qui se passe derrière la facade. Mais, même s'il existe des raisons spécifiques qui expliquent (sans, à notre avis, les justifier toujours) cette réticence juridique, il n'existe plus de raison convaincante à la tendance qu'ont qulelques enseignants d'ignorer ou de minimiser l'influence de l'assurance sur les mécanismes de responsabilité civile.

Le problème est peut-être plus complexe encore que nous le suggérons. Peut-être y a-t-il plus, dans cette idée de se référer ouvertement aux pratiques des assurances , que de simples modifications de style et de motivation d'arrêts. On pourrait, comme cela a été avancé en Angleterre à plusieurs reprises, suggérer qu'un tel équilibre entre des intérêts économiques opposés serait plus facilement atteint par des organes exécutifs ou législatifs, mieux équipés que le judiciaire pour les apprécier[6]. Une telle objection n'est pas sans valeur, mais l'admettre, telle quelle, est un moyen sûr de prolonger l'actuelle passivité; et l'expérience dans les pays de *common law* prouve que les reformes judiciaires provoquées par des considérations économiques ou d'assurance ont assez correctement réussi et n'ont pas entraîné les dangers que redoutaient certains. Nous avons l'impression qu'on peut dire la même chose de la jurisprudence francaise dans le contexte de l'article 1384, alinéa 1 du Code civil, même si chaque étape novatrice a été fortement critiquée par une partie de la doctrine. En tout état de cause, le maintien du *statu quo* ne fera pas disparaître les problèmes d'assurance en les cachant derrière des notions abstraites; il ne fera qu'aggraver leur usage artificiel, même abusif, et retarder l'allocation logique des risques. Si, en revanche nous arrivons à admettre l'importance du facteur "assurance", nous pourrons discuter les problèmes de facon plus significatif; et nous pourrons essayer de faire coincider, dans la mesure du possible, l'obligation de réparation avec les possibilités du recours à l'assurance; nous pourrons faire prendre conscience à nos étudiants de ce que les concepts juridiques ne sont que les outils qui doivent être mis au rebut quand ils deviennent inutiles. Ce que je suggère n'a rien d'une tâche secondaire et ne peut être fait dans un exposé si bref. Notre but immédiat est donc plus modeste: il s'agit de montrer comment la pratique de l'assurance a influencé la decision rendue dans certaines affaires; comment, malgré son rôle crucial sur le résultat final, l'assurance a été proscrite du texte des arrêts; et en quoi les raisonnements juridiques de ces arrêts sont obscurs, voire même insatisfaisants à cause de ces omissions Ainsi, nous avons choisi trois exemples (aux États-Unis, en Angleterre et en France), couvrant l'ensemble des notions de *tort*, de *negligence* (si on peut utiliser pour l'instant la terminologie du droit anglais)

---

[6] Telles étaient, par exemples, les opinions des juges de la Chambre des Lords dans l'affaire *Launchbury v. Morgans* [1973] AC 127, pp. 136–7 (per Lord Wilberforce); pp. 142–3 (per Lord Pearson); pp. 145–6 (per Lord Cross); p. 151 (per Lord Salmon).

de facon à montrer comment le facteur "assurance" opère derrière les différents éléments de la résponsabilité.

Nous verrons donc, dans le premier exemple, des considérations d'assurance cachées derrière la notion de "faute" (dans le sens de *negligence, carelessness*) et dans le troisième, derrière des notions causales.

2. DEVOIR (DUTY OF CARE) ET ASSURANCE

Depuis de nombreuses années, la jurisprudence aux États-Unis a eu à répondre des actions intentées contre les compagnies de distribution d'eau qui avaient conclu des contrats avec les municipalités pour la mise en place et l'entretien de bouches d'incendie. Dans toutes ces affaires, les bouches d'incendie n'avaient pas été correctement entretenues ou la pression d'eau n'était pas suffisante et, en cas d'incendie, les pompiers n'avaient pu combattre le feu avec l'efficacité voulue, en raison de la mauvaise exécution des obligations assumées par ces compagnies. Toutes les actions avaient été intntées par des propriétaires dont le domicile avait, de ce fait, péri par le feu.

A notre connaissance, dans tous les États des États-Unis sauf quatre[7] les tribunaux ont refusé de faire droit au demandes[8], se fondant sur quatre arguments, dont le second et le troisième étaient, apparemment, les plus décisifs: (i) la négligence de la compagnie n'était pas la cause immédiate du dommage (*proximate cause*); (ii) l'absence de relation contractuelle (*privity*) entre les parties[9]; (iii) l'absence de devoir dû au demandeur, qui n'était ni partie au contrat de services principal, ni un tiers bénéficiaire pour le profit exprès duquel le contrat avait été passé[10]; et (iv) le fait que la compagnie était coupable d'une omission et non pas d'un acte positif[11], et que l'omission n'est pratiquement jamais de nature à créer en *common law* une responsabilité en l'absence de contrat.[12] En réalité, tous ces arguments sont insatisfaisants.

L'argument de causalité n'est pas convaincant, puisque, dans le droit des ÉtatsUnis, c'est une question qui est de la compétance du jury. Il n'est cepen-

---

[7] Floride, Kentucky, Caroline du Nord et Pennsylvanie, V. *Mugge v. Tampa Water Works Co*, 52 Fla. 371, 42 So.81 (1906). *Paducah Lumber Co v. Paducah Water Supply Co.*, 89 Ky 340, 12 S.W. 554 (1889); *Gorrell v. Greensboro Water Supply Co.*, 124 N.C. 328,32 S.E. 720 (1899); *Doyle v. South Pittsburgh Water Co.*, 414 Pa. 199, 199 A. 2d 875 (1964). Dans cette dernière décision, qui est en même temps la plus importante, deux juges exposent une opinion différente.

[8] V. ainsi, *German Alliance Ins. Co. v. Home Water Supply* Co. 226 U.S. 220 (1912); *Anderson v. Iron Mountain Water Works* 225 Mich. 574, 196 N.W. 357 (1923); *H.R. Moch Co. v. Rensselaer Water Co.*, 247 N.Y. 160, 159 N.E. 896 (1928).

[9] Ainsi, *German Alliance Ins. Co. v. Home Water Supply Co.*, *supra*; *Bush v. Artesian Hot and Cold Water Co.*, 4 Idaho 618, 43 Pac. 69 (1895).

[10] Ainsi H.R. *Moch Co v. Rensselaer Water Co.*, *supra*. V. aussi Williston, *Contracts*, 3e éd.,Jaeger 1959, § 373, p. 942.

[11] *Restatement, Torts* (1934), § 288 et *comment* c.

[12] Pour une brève étude comparative et des références supplémentaires, v. Lawson et Markesinis, *Tortious liability for unintentional harm in the Common Law and the Civil law*, (1982), t. I, pp. 71–80.

dant pas douteux qu'en principe le mauvais entretien de la bouche d'incendie *peut être* une cause directe et que ceci suffirait pour justifier un renvoi devant un jury.

L'argument d'omission/acte positif, mis dans un langage archaïque (*malfeasance/non feasance*), trahit la réticence traditionelle de la *common law* à admettre l'existence d'obligations d'agir en faveur d'un tiers en dehors de situations contractuelles. Cela n'est pas plus convaincant, car la jurisprudence (surtout aux États-Unis[13]), admet de plus en plus volontiers l'existence de telles obligations en faveur des tiers. De plus, les arrêts que nous considérons n'étaient pas vraiment des cas d'omission, mais de mauvaise exécution.[14] Pour utiliser l'excellente terminologie française, c'étaient des cas *d'abstention dans l'action* et non pas *d'abstention pure et simple*, et une responsabité aurait parfaitement pu être retenue, même en *common law*.

L'effet relatif des contrats comme fondement de l'absence de devoir dû au demandeur, qui était le troisième argument, ne tient plus, au moins depuis la décision rendue dans *Mcpherson* v. *Buick*, où Cardozo J., dans sa célèbre opinion, déclara nettement que[15]:

> "l'existence d'un danger connu, qui résulte d'un comportement ou d'un usage quelconque, doit imposer un devoir de diligence. Quand les conséquences d'un comportement imprudent sont prévisibles, on ne dit plus que le devoir d'agir pour protéger la vie ou le corps émanent seulement d'un contrat valable. On a mis la source d'une telle obligation là où elle devrait être trouvée: la loi elle-même".

Que ces raisons ne soient que de mauvais prétextes, on peut s'en convaincre en observant d'autres arrêts. Il suffit de regarder les affaires de bouches d'incendie dans lequelles les biens des municipalités furent endommagés pour voir que les compagnies d'eau ne furent pas non plus jugées responsables.[16] Dans ces cas-là on ne pouvait pas poser le principe d'effet relatif du contrat: le contrat de mise en place et d'entretien des pompes avait été conclu entre les parties à l'instance; malgré cela, le résultat était le même: pas de responsabilité. Enfin, la même solution était retenue dans les quelques affaires où les contrats avaient spécifiquement prévu qu'ils étaient destinés à la protection des tiers propriétaires de maisons[17]. Ainsi, le langage employé par les arrêts ne donne aucune indication de la vraie raison qui a dictée le résultat; et ceux qui ne l'ont pas découverte ne sont pas en position de critiquer le résultat final. Tout ce qu'ils peuvent faire, c'est de condamner abstraitement l'usage de

---

[13] V. l'arrêt remarquable de *Tarasoff* v. *Regents of the Univ. of California* 17 Cal. 3rd 425, 551, P. 2d 334 (1976) et le commentaire intéressant dans (1978) 31 *Stan. L. Rev* 165.

[14] V. Seavey, "The Waterworks Cases and Stare Decisis" (1952) 66 *Harv. Law Rev*. 84.

[15] 217 N.Y. 382, 390, 111 N.E. 1050, 1053 (1916).

[16] *Town of Ukiah City* v. *Ukiah Water and Improvement Co*,. 142 Cal. 173, 75 Pac. 773 (1904); *Inhabitants of Milford* v. *Bangor Ry. and Elec Co*., 106 Me 316, 76 Atl. 696 (1909).

[17] *Trustees of Jennie De Pauw Memorial Methodist Episcopal Church* v. *New Albany Water Works*, 193 Ind. 368, 140 NM.E. 540 (1923); *Eaton* v. *Fairbury Water Works Co*., 37 Neb 546, 56 N.W. 201 (1893).

notions abstraites[18]—analyse hautement satisfaisante pour les juristes germanistes du XIXᵉ siècle , mais aujourd'hui peu productive!

L'explication de ces arrêts repose, selon nous, dans la pratique de l'assurance moderne, qui n'est pas obligatoire dans l'espèce, mais qui est en pratique très étendue. Ainsi , les cours surtout dans les arrêts les plus rècents, ont dû tenir compte du fait que l'assurance—incendie[19], même si elle n'est pas obligatoire, est en fait répandue au point que dans la grande majorité des cas la victime sera indemnisée. Si la règle de non-responsabilité était modifiée, les seuls bénéficiaires en seraient les assureurs, qui seraient subrogés aux droits de la victime en cas de sinstre et bénéficieraient donc d'une aubaine, touchant des primes pour le cas où le risque se réaliserait et pouvant agir en indemnisation en cas de sinstre. Mais une telle modification bénéficierait-elle aussi aux propriétaires? La réponse est probablement négative, car le nombre de sinstres dus au mauvais entretien de bouches d'incendie est statistiquement faible. Il serait donc statistiquement insignifiant pour les assureurs de pouvoir se retourner contre les compagnies de distribution d'eau et les primes d'assurance n'en seraient pas modifiées en faveur des propriétaires de maisons. En revanche et à l'opposé, la modification de la règle actuelle changerait la situation des compagnies d'eau: car les compagnies attaquées en responsabilité devraient contracter des assurances et ce coût spplémentaire serait sûrment répercuté dans le prix de l'eau. Les seuls bénéficiaires d'un revirement de jurisprudence seraient donc les assureurs et les victimes—assez peu nombreuses—qui auraient omis de s'assurer contre l'incendie. Mon premier exemple est donc une illustration claire de la tendance des cours à faire coincider autant que possible l'obligation de réparation avec la pratique de l'assurance. Notons aussi qu'ici on pense à une assurance directe qui, *dans ce cas-là*, paraît moins coûteuse et plus efficace que l'assurance de responsabilité (l'assurance "adverse").[20]

3. ASSURANCE ET "FAUTE"

Les considérations d'assurance ne se cachent pas seulement derrière la notion de *duty of care*. La notion de "faute" (dans le sens de *negligence*) peut, également, servir d'écran à ces considérations, comme le montre l'exemple suivant, tiré cette fois de la jurisprudence anglaise.

---

[18] V. Prosser, *The Law of Torts,* 4e éd. (1971), pp. 625–6.

[19] Peu d'arrêts ont, à notre connaissance ouvertement reconnu le facteur "assurance". Les arrêts suivants constituent l'exception: *German Alliance Ins.* v. *Home Water Supply etc., supra* note 9 et *H.R. Moch Co.* v. *Rensselaer Water co.* etc., supra, n. 8.

[20] V. les observations de A. Tunc "dans Responsabilité civile et assurance" *Hommage à René Dekkers*, (1982), pp. 343, 351 et s. Mais v. aussi nos observations dans "La politique jurisprudentiele et la réparation du préjudice économique en Angleterre: une approche comparative", 1983 *Revue Internationale de Droit Comparé,* pp. 31, 34, 38 et 49.

Dans *Henderson* v. *Jenkins*[21], les freins du camion du défendeur tombent en panne et le camion tua le conducteur d'une camionnette. La panne résultait d'une fuite du liquide de système de freinage, qui ne pouvait être découverte à l'examen *de visu*. Le défendeur entretenait son camion toutes les semaines, l'examinait régulièrement et, de facon générale, en prenait son soin correct. Ni le ministère des Transports, ni le constructeur ne recommandaient le démontage du système de freinage pour examen; on pensait qu'une telle opération risquait de le briser. Il fut suggéré dans l'espèce que la fuite aurait pu être causée par une substance corrosive transportée par le camion ou par une circulation en bord d e mer ou sur de la neige salée. La Chambre des Lords, à une faible majorité, cassa l'arrêt d'appel qui confirmait l'exonération prononcée en première instance et jugea qu'il y avait eu négligence et que le défendeur était tenu en responsabilité. Le niveau de diligence (*standard of care*) demandé à l'homme raisonnable est dans de tels cas fixé si haut qu'il; est hors de portée. La responsabilité est officiellement fondée sur la faute; elle est en fait presque objective.

Deux autres arrêts, toujours en matière d'accidents de circulation, confirment qu'une telle solution est dans ce domaine presque la règle plutôt que l'exception.[22] Dans *Nettleship* v. *Weston*[23], la Cour d'appel jugea qu'une conductrice inexpérimentée était responsable du dommage causé par sa conduite. L'accident résultait d'une erreur qu'un conducteur aguerri. Cela n'est pas une excuse, comme le dit Lord Denning, M. R.[24]:

"Le conducteur débutant d'une voiture peut essayer de fair de son mieux, mais cela ne suffit pas si son mieux le laisse toujours dans l'incompétance. Il devrait conduire comme un conducteur adroit, expérimenté et prudent, sain de corps et d'esprit, qui ne commet pas d'erreurs de jugement, qui a une bonne vue, l'oreille fine et n'a aucune infirmité".

La déduction est que, si le conducteur débutant ne satisfait pas à ces exigences auxquelles pratiquement, par définition, il est incapable de satisfaire, il sera considéré comme négligent et donc responsable sur ce fondement. A moins de s'absentir de conduire, le débutant ne peut éviter d'être responsable s'il cause un dommage en raison de son inexpérience; et il ne pourra acquérir d'expérience qu'en conduisant. Mais le droit peut être encore plus strict, comme le prouve l'arrêt suivant.

Dans *Roberts* v. *Ramsbottom*[25], un homme souffrant à son insu d'une

---

[21] [1970] AC 282.

[22] Mais v. l'affaire tragique de *Snelling* v. *Whitehead*, *The Times*, 31.7.1975.

[23] [1971] 2 QB 691.

[24] *Ibid*. p. 700. V. aussi des observations analogues par le même juge dans *Dutton* v. *Bognor Regis Urban District Council* [1972] 1 QB 373, 397. Mais v. *Pearson Committee Report*, Cmnd. 7054, vol 1, n. 986.

[25] [1980] 1 WLR 823 (cf. Grenoble, 4 décembre 1978, J.C.P. 1980, II, 19340 et note Dejean de la Batie). Mais si le comportement d'un piéton est la cause du dommage les cours hésitent à le caractériser comme faute, même quand il cause des blessures à un cycliste innocent. V. *Green* v. *Hills* (1969) 113 Sol. Jo. 385.

légère hémorragie cérébrale monta dans sa voiture et pris une route autre que celle qu'il voulait prendre. Il percuta une voiture de livraison en stationnement et s'arrêta derrière elle. Il sortit de la voiture, manqua de se faire écraser en traversant, puis revint à la voiture, redémarra et faillit percuter de nouveau la même camionnette. Repartant en marche arrière, il manqua d'écraser deux piétons, renversa unc cyclister et percuta une autre voiture en stationnement. Il fut transporté à l'hôpital avec sa victime, et l'on découvrit alsors seulement son hémorragie cérébrale. Le juge anglais le jugea responsable du dommage causé. S'il avait été complètement inconscient et avait agi par rèflexe, la solution eût été différente, mais le fait qu'il ait été partiellement conscient permit à la cour de le déclarer en faute. La distinction me semble fort délicate et, dans l'espèce, peu convaicante.

Les arrêts anglais concernant les accidents de la circulation, qui tiennent responsables comme négligents les conducteurs défendeurs, ne sont pas plus satisfaisants dans leur utilisation du mot "négligence" appliqué des affaires où l'accident est statistiquement inévitable. D'après notre collègue Geneviève Viney, cette fusion des deux notions nous fournit encore une illustration de l'influence "déformante" de l'assurance. Pour nous, c'est une vraie perversion du concept de faute pour des raisons de politique judiciaire. Cette confusion des concepts entre la négligence et l'erreur statistiquement inévitable a été largement critiquée par André Tunc[26] et je n'ai rien à ajouter. Mais est-il possible que les tribunaux emploient consciemment une terminologie inadéquate, parce que leur jugement est influencé par d'autres facteurs? A notre avis, leur tendance à abandonner toute clarté d'analyse à chaque fois que l'assurance joue un rôle preponderant ou obligatoire, et à revenir à la distinction correcte dés lors que l'assurance manque ou que le coût de la responsabilité serait prohibitif, suggère qu'il se passe autre chose dans l'esprit des juges. L'arrêt récent *Whitehouse* v. *Jordan*[27] suggère que des considerations économiques et sociales jouent toujours un rôle important dans la détermination des litiges.

Dans *Whitehouse* v. *Jordan*[28], la Cour d'appel jugea qu'un médecin effectuant un accouchement difficile ne devait pas être tenu responsable de la malformation de l'enfant à cause d'un accouchement maladroit. Le demandeur soutenait que le docteur, tentant un accouchement au forceps, avait tiré trop fort et trop longuement, entraînant une déformation de la tête de l'enfant en lui causant de lésions intracrâniennes. La preuve de l'excés de force, avec laquelle le docteur avait tiré l'enfant, ne fut pas considérée satisfaisante et fut considérée comme ne corroborant pas les affirmations de la mère. On a demandé à plusieurs experts médicaux de déterminer le sens d'un terme médical assez vague, employé dans un compte rendu hospitalier, écrit peu après

---

[26] *La Responsabilité Civile* (éd. Economica 1981), p. 114 et s.V. aussi, *Pearson Committee Report, supra*, n. 24.
[27] [1981] 1 WLR 246.
[28] [1980] 1 All ER 650.

l'accident, et que la cour de première instance avait interprété comme suggérant que la tête avait été bloquée et que cela ne pouvait être imputé qu'à l'usage imprudent des forceps par le docteur. Après de longues audiences— onze jours en instance, quatre en appel et cinq devant la Chambre des Lords— occupant neuf juges et plusieurs avocats, et coûtant au contribuable anglais une petite fortune, les cours jugèrent que le docteur était coupable d'erreur professionnelle, mais non pas de négligence. Invoquant cette distinction en appel, Lord Denning M.R alla même plus loin, suggérant que "dans les professions libérales, une erreur de jugement ne constitue pas une négligence". Pour la Chambre des Lords, cela allait trop loin. Comme le dit Lord Fraser[29]:

"Le principe correct, c'est qu'une erreur de jugement pourrait ou ne pourrait pas être une faute, cela dépendant de la nature de l'erreur. S'il s'agissait d'une erreur que n'aurait pas commise un homme raisonnable et compétent qui exerçait une profession libérale et déclarait avoir le niveau de compétence que prétendait le défendeur lui-même, alors il y a faute. Mais si, au contraire c'est une erreur qu'aurait pu commettre un tel homme, agissant avec une diligence raisonnable, ce n'est pas une faute".

A notre avis, cette réserve de la Chambre des Lords pose simplement que l'erreur de jugement n'exclut pas la negligence. Ceci est vrai, mais la clarté de l'expression voudrait que le terme "erreur" ne soit utilisé que pour ces malheureuses confusions ou inadvertantes statistiquement inévitables qui ne sont pas de vraies fautes. Et, comme l'admettent les juges de la Chambre des Lords, même des professionnels soigneux peuvent commettre de telles erreurs.

On admit donc la distinction entre l'erreur et la négligence, on la poussa même trop loin, pour obtenir une exonértion de responsabilité. La distinction a cependant totalement disparu du domaine des accidents de circulation. Cette facon d'agir pourrait-elle, encore une fois, être due à la présence de l'assurance obligatoire qui, dans le domaine des accidents de circulation, facilite— voire même rend souhaitable—le transfert du risque du défendeur "innocent" au demandeur "innocent" comme le seul moyen d'assurer une indemnisation complète? Dans *Nettleship* v. *Weston*[30], Lord Denning M.R., direct comme toujours, allait au moins jusque-là en déclarant:

"Moralement, la conductrice débutante d'une voiture n'a commis aucune faute; mais, dupoint de vue de la loi, elle peut être considérée comme étant en faute puisqu'elle est assurée et doit donc assumer le risque".

En revanche, dans les affaires médicales, les choses sont moins simples.[31] Compte tenu des faits, la situation est moins claire et moins prévisible.

---

[29] [1981] 1 All ER 267, 281.
[30] [1971] 2 QB 691, 700.
[31] La responsabilité médicale est un sujet complexe et controversé. Parmi la vaste littérature, on peut citer les oeuvres suivantes: États-Unis: Rubsamen, "Res Ipsa Loquitur in California Medical Malpractice Law", (1962) 14 *Stanford Law Rev.* 251; Project, "The medical Malpractice Threat: A Study of Defensive Medicine", (1971) *Duke Law Journal* 939; Burstein, "Medical

Chaque fois qu'il est possible de comparer un diagnostic humain à diagnostic fait par la machine sur la base de tous les symptômes et éléments pertinents, le pourcentage de diagnostics humains exacts est apparu dangereusement faible. Tenir toutes ces affaires pour des affaires de vrais fautes pourrait avoir des conséquences économiques insupportables, surtout dans un système où l'État lui-même prend d'une manière ou d'une autre une très grande partie des frais médicaux à sa charge[32]. Dans un remarquable paragraphe de son jugement, Lord Denning M.R. dit ceci à propos de telles affaires, en faisant en même temps une observation comparative très importante[33]:

> "Si l'on tenait les mèdecins responsables chaque fois qu'ils ne guérissent pas un malade ou chaque fois que se passe quelque chose de malcontreux, on rendrait un mauvais service à la médecine elle-même. A vrai dire, cela rendrait un mauvais service non seulement au corps médical, mais à la société tout entière. Il faut tenir compte de ce qui est arrivé aux États-Unis. Les arrêts de responsabilité médicale sont très troublants, en particulier parce qu'ils sont jugés par les jury qui ont de la compassion pour les malades, mais n'en ont aucune pour les médecins qui sont assurés. Les dommages-intérêts sont énormes. Les médecins s'assurent, mais les primes deviennent très élévées et, evidemment, ce sont les clients qui, finalement, doivent les payer. Il existe même ds cas où des médecins expérimentés ont refusé de traiter des

Malpractice A Move Toward Strict Liability" (1975) 21 *Loyola Law Rev.* 194; Reder, "Medical Malpractice: An Economist's View", (1976) *Am. Bar Foundation Research* J. 511; Blaut, "The Medical Malpractice Crisis—Its Causes and Future" (1977) *Insurance Counsel Journal* 114; Roth "The Medical Malpractice Insurance Crisis" (1977) *Insurance Counsel Journal* 469; Schwartz et Komesar, "Damages and Deterrence: An Economic View of Medical Malpractice", (1978) 298 *New Eng. J. Med.* 1282; Wadlington, Waltz et Dworkin, *Cases and Materials on Law and Medicine* (1980); Angleterre: Jackson et Powell, *Professional Negligence* (1982), chapitre 6. Pour la France, v. Penneau, *La responsabilité médicale* (1977). Droit allemand et comparé: Giesen, *Arzthaftungsrecht* (*Medical Malpractice Law: A Comparative law Study of Civil Responsibility arising from Medical Care*) (1981).

[32] L'Angleterre est un exemple évident et le lecteur intéréssé peut trouver un apercu général de ce système fort complexe dans le livrre du professeur Atiyah, *Accidents, Compensation and the Law*, 3e éd (1980).

[33] [1980] 1 All ER 650, 658. Le danger que le médecin puisse refuser de traiter n malade a été souligné pour la première fois par McCardie J. dans *De Freville* v. *Dill* (1927) 96 L.J.K.B. 1056 mais, à notre connaissance, il n'existe aucune étude empirique en Angleterre qui supporte une telle conclusion (même si une telle attitude est toujours possible en pratique). Mais le danger qu'une responsabilité accentuée peut entraîner ce que l'on appelle aux États-Unis "defensive medecine" (les médecins prenant toutes les précautions possibles, même si elles sont inutiles ou coûteuses, afin de minimiser leurs risques) est, apparemment, réel. "Negligence and Forceps Delivery" (1979) 1 *British Medical Journal* 763. v. aussi Altschule, "Bad law, bad medicine", (1977) *Amer. J. of Law and Med*, 296–7. Dans ce contexte on doit noter *Helling* v. *Carey*, 83 Wash. ed 514, 519 P. 2d 981 (1974). Dans cette affaire un opthalmologue a été condamné à payer des dommages-intérêts parce qu'il a été considéré comme étant en faute quand il a omis de faire un test de pression interoculaire à la jeune demanderesse pour découvrir si elle souffrait de glaucome. Sa défense était qu'en évitant le test il a suivi la conduite normale des opthalmologues raisonnables puisque la chance de découvrir un glaucome chez une personne de l'âge de la demanderesse était minime. La défense était rejetée et malgré une loi postérieure votée afin de minimiser les efets de cette décision, plusieurs tribunaux continuent à imposer une responsabilité dans de pareils cas, obligeant ainsi les médecins à multiplier le nombre des tests médicaux. V. *Gates* v. *Jensen* 92 Wash. 2d. 246, 595 P. 2d. 919. Cf. Giesen, *Arzthaftungsrecht* (1981), p. 162, et notes 65b–67.

malades,ayant peur d'être accusés de négligence. De jeunes hommes sont même découragés de devenir médecins cause de tels risques. On doit éviter, dans l'intérêt public, un tel développement en Angleterre".

4. ASSURANCE ET NOTIONS CAUSALES

La pratique de l'assurance et des considérations économiques jouent également un grand rôle dans la solution des problèmes de causalité. Tous les systèmes qui font l'objet de cette étude nous fournissent des illustrations, mais nous nous concentrerons cette fois sur le droit francais.

A notre avis, un grand nombre d'arrêts francais pourraient être interprétés à l'appui de notre thèse. Ainsi les vieux arrêts des affaires d'accidents de chasse donnent des exemples tragiques, mais pittoresques, de la facon arbitraire dont on peut appliquer les théories de la cause.[34] On se souvient tout d'abord que, selon la théorie de la condition *sine qua non*,aucune des personnes impliquées dans les accidents ne fut jugée responsable. Par la suite l'application de la théorie de cause adéquate et quelques moyens liés à l'article 1384,alinéa 1 du Code civil permirent aux juges et aux commentateurs de se rendre compte que l'on pourrait arriver au résultat contraire et tenir tout le monde pour responsable. A l'exception d'un cas très particulier, toutes les autre affaires furent traitées par l'application presque mécanique des théories de la causalité.

Il se passe *a priori* quelque chose de semblable en matière de responsabilité de fait des employés—domaine du droit francais qui est toujours une source d'étonnement et d'amusement pour les juristes anglais. Amusement, parce que quelques arrêts (peu nombreux à la verité) ont interprété la phraséologie de l'article 1384, alinéa 5, du Code civil de facon si large qu'ils conduisent à des résultats qui fournissent de merveilleux exemples au professeur, mais constituent un droit assez grotesque[35] (on pense bien sûr à l'arrêt qui tint le propriétaire d'une salle de cinéma civilement responsable du viol d'une cliente par un de ses employés, au motif que c'était pendant les heures du travail!) Étonnement, parce que nous nous émerveillons de voir la Cour de cassation conserver une jurisprudence double et contradictoire, malgré les tentatives désespérées de l'Assemblée plénière de fournir une jurisprudence claire aux cours du fond.

La jurisprudence des Chambres civile et criminelle en la matière est bien connue et nous nous bornerons à livrer les réactions qu'elle nous inspire. Si

[34] civ. 29 sept. 1941, 437; Montpellier, 8 Nov. 1949 J.C.P. 1950, 2, 5519: Orléans, 17 janv 1949, D. 1949, 502; Civ. 4 janv. 1957, d. 1957, 264; Crim. 22 mars 1966, G.P. 1966, 2 46; Grenoble, 16 mai 1962, D. 1963, 137; Cour d'Appel d'A.E.F. 5 avr. 1957, J.C.P. 1957, 2 10308; civ. 5 fév 1960. d. 1960, 365; Civ 18 mai 1955, 520; Civ 6 mars 1968, Bull. civ. II, no 76 p. 52, *Rev trim dr. civ.* (1968), 718 obser. Durry; Civ 19 mai 1976, J.C.P. 1978,2, 18773; Rennes, 14 janv. 1971.J.C.P. 1971, 16733; Durry, *Rev. trim. dr. civ.* (1971), 377.
[35] Crim. 5 nov. 1953, D. 1953, J. 698.

nous nous sommes trompés dans l'interprétation, nous rappelons à nos collègues francais qu'évidemment ce sont les réactions d'un *"Common lawyer looking at the civil law"*.[36]

Les mots "dommage causé par leurs domestiques et préposés dans les fonctions auxquelles ils les ont employés" à l'article 1384, alinéa 5 du Code civil ont toujours recu une interprétation large de la part de la Chambre criminelle, pour laquelle—selon la théorie de l'équivalence des conditions—il est constant que le commettant est responsable même lorsque le préposé a agi en dehors de son travail et dans son propre intérêt, tant que la victime ignore cet abus et qu'il existe quelque lien entre le travail et le fait dommageable. Ce lien existe dès lors que le fait dommageable est par exemple accompli pendant les heures de travail ou que la situation de l'employé lui a donné la possibilité de le commettre. La deuxième Chambre civile, au contraire, adoptant la théorie de la cause adéquate, s'en tient à une interprétation plus restrictive[37]. La première tentative de résolution de ce conflit, faite en 1960[38] par les chambres réunies en faveur de la solution de la Chambre civile, fut un échec. La rédaction de l'arrêt était telle qu'il; fut généralement pris pour un arrêt d'espèce et non pour un arrêt de principe. L'Assemblée plénière confirma cette jurisprudence par un arrêt du 10 juin 1977[39], de formulation beaucoup plus générale. Malheureusement, il s'agissait d'un accident de la circulation et l'arrêt se limita donc à ce domaine. Ce fait s'avéra crucial, car la Chambre criminelle, dans ses arrêts ultérieurs, semble avoir été atteinte par un virus anglais et s'est mise à distinguer les espéces selon les faits et à adopter—au fond, sinon dans la forme—la terminologie de *ratio decidendi* et *obiter dictum*. Ainsi, comme l'a très correctement remarqué notre collegue Georges Durry, l'intervention de l'Assemblée plénière en 1977 n'e eu pour résultat que de faire rebondir le débat au lieu de le clore.[40]

Il est intéressant quand même de noter que, dans ses arrêts récents, la Chambre criminelle admet la position restrictive de l'Assemblée plénière quant à la responsabilité du commettant *dans les accidents de circulation* causés par son préposé.[41] Mais dans les affaires ne concernant pas ls accidents de la circulation, la Chambre, récusant l'autorité de l'Assemblée plénière, est revenue à son interprétation de la causalité et continue de déclarer responsable le malheureux commettant.[42]

[36] C'est le titre d'une remarquable série de conférences prononcées aux États-Unis en 1955 par le professeur F.H. Lawson d'Oxford.
[37] Pour plus de détails, v. Viney, *La responsabilité* (*op. cit., n. 4, supra*, p. 893 et s.); Hassler, "La responsabilité des commettants", *D. Chron.* 1980, 125.
[38] Ch. réunis, 9 mars 1960, d. 1960, 329, note Savatier; J.C.P. 1960, II, 11559, note Rodière.
[39] D. 1977, 465 note Larroumet; J.C.P. 1977, II, 18730, concl. avocat général Gulphe.
[40] V. ses observations dans la *Rev. trim. dr. civ.* 1981, 159.
[41] Ainsi, v. Crim. 18 juill. 1978, Bull. crim n. 237, 627: crim. 15 mars 1978, d. 1978, 412, mais v. aussi Crim. 13 mai 1980, J.C.P. 1980, IV, 281 et observ. Durry dans *Rev. trim. dr. civ.* 1981, 159.
[42] Crim. 3 mai 1979, *Bull. crim* n. 157, 447 : d. 1979, I R 530, obs. Puech; Crim. 26 juill. 1977, *Bull. crim.* n. 275, 687; D. 1978, I.R. 109, obs. Puech; Durry, *Rev. trim. dr. civ.* 1978, 144.

Ces arrêts en matière de responsabilité du commettant peuvent être expliqués par référence à l'assurance et à des arguments économiques. Autrement, il semble, en fait, impossible de concilier les jurisprudences divergentes et d'introduire un semblant d'ordre dans cette matière. Mais l'explication économique, quelque insatisfaisante qu'elle puisse être pour les juristes francais, permet d'expliquer (sinon de justifier) ce résultat. En tout cas, le résultat serait plus acceptable si la motivation de la Cour de cassation était plus claire et complète. Cela est un autre, vaste, problème. Mais dans l'espèce, il paraît que la jurisprudence a adopté une notion restrictive de l'article 1384, alinéa 5 du Code civil, dans les accidents de la circulation, car les victimes peuvent être indemnisées par le Fonds de Garantie Automobile lorsque le commettant est exonéré et que le conducteur est insolvable ou n'est pas assuré. En revanche, dans les cas d'abus de pouvoir, la victime ne recevrait qu'une indemnisation partielle, car la loi du 3 janvier 1977, sur l'obligation de l'État d'indemniser certains préjudices corporels résultant de crimes, est limitée dans sa portée. Bien que ces dispositions soient d'application générale, couvrant tous les crimes en général, sa mise en application est assortie de strictes conditions: la victime doit avoir été incapable de travailler pendant plus de trois mois et doit être dans une situation critique. Et, dans tous les cas où la loi ne s'applique pas ou dans les cas anterieurs à son entrée en vigueur, la victime ne serait pas indemnisée du tout si le commettant se trouvait exonéré de responsabilité, par suite de l'application d'une conception juridique correcte de l'article 1384, alinéa 5 du Code civil.

Nous n'avons ni la compétence ni l'intention de traiter en détail le célèbre arrêt de la Seconde Chambre civile de juillet dernier dans un article qui, dans l'essentiel, ne touche qu'indirectement le problème que cette Cour devait trancher. Mais un arrêt, qui avait été décrit comme "un événement"[43], "une révolution"[44], "un retour au néolithique"[45] ou comme "un précurseur"[46] (en même temps que les conclusions de l'avocat général ont été saluée pour leur "clarté" et leur "courage"), provoque évidemment la tentation spéciale, même pour un juriste étranger, de faire trois brèves observations, liées avec la thèse générale que nous avons soutenue dans cette conférence.

Tout d'abord, il nous semble nécessaire de souligner que cet arrêt comme, en effet, tout l'édifice jurisprudentiel de l'article 1384 du Code civil, repose largement sur la pratique de l'assurance moderne. Des références de telle sorte souvent explicites—existent dans les conclusions fameuses de M. l'avocat général Schmelck, maintenant premier président de la Cour de cassation, dans les arrêts de la Chambre mixte de 1968[47] concernant le transport bénévole,

---

[43] Par le Garde des Sceaux. V. Tunc "La réforme du droit francais des accidents de la circulation", cette Revue 1983 *Revue Internationale de Droit Comparé*, p. 143 et s. Pour une bibliographie plus complète, v. G.P., doctrine, 18–19 mars 1983.

[44] Par G. Durry, *Rev, trim. dr. civ.*, 1982, 606.

[45] Par Y. Bigot, *J.C.P.* 1982, I, 3090.

[46] Par Y. Lambert-Faivre, *D. Chron.* 1982, 207

[47] 20 déc. 1968, D. 1969, 37.

ainsi que dans les conclusions de M. l'avocat général Charvonier dans l'arrêt *Demares*[48]. Mais le facteur "assurance" n'en est pas moins important même s'il a été caché par toute une série de décisions semblables qui paraissaient l'ignorer. Cela me rappelle, par exemple, la théorie dite de "faute virtuelle", avant le revirement de la jurisprudence en matière de transport bénévole. Cette jurisprudence n'était -elle pas influencée par le désir d'améliorer la situation de la victime? N'est-ce pas l'assurance moderne qu la rend possible? N'est -il pas aussi possible de dire, avec notre collègue Jean Bigot[49] (qui critiqua l'arrêt *Demares*) que les tribunaux "se montrent particulièrement circonspects pour admettre la faute du piéton ou du cycliste, généralement écartée lorsqu'il s'agit d'enfants ou de vieillards"? A vrai dire, dans de tels cas, on pourrait soutenir que les victimes étaient dépourvues de la maîtrise psychique qui caractérise avant tout la faute. Il nous paraît, cependant, qu'une telle explication n'offrait souvent qu'une simple méthode pour éluder, voire nier, des fautes d'imprudences de la part de la victime afin de préserver le droit d'indemnisation de celle-ci et d'eviter les conséquences inéquitables qu'entraînerait une application de la jurisprudence établie à partir de 1934.[50]

La seconde observation que nous voudrions faire, c'est que le facteur assurance n'est pas le seul facteur économique qui aura une influence sur les développements futurs de ce sujet. Des conséquences économiques de l'arrêt, surtout en ce qui concerne le montant des primes d'assurances, peuvent avoir un effet retardateur sur l'intervention législative généralement envisagée. Elles peuvent aussi être utilisées ou exploitées par ceux qui souhaiteraient le revirement de cet arrêt. Ainsi, le directeur à l'Union des Assurances de Paris, M. Margeat, a suggéré[51] avant l'arrêt *Demares* que la pratique des cours favorise tellement les victimes (surtout les cyclistes et les piétons) que "nous sommes proches de la finalité du 'système Tunc', sans réforme et sans la modulation indispensable du coût du préjudice". Cela est parfaitement correct; et la loi du 7 janvier 1981 a également comblé des importantes lacunes du système francais. Mais que le prix reste énorme! Les cours sont encombrées de litiges et, en ce qui concerne l'Angleterre (et nous croyons que la situation dans les autres pays est comparable), les frais administratifs de l'opération du *tort system of compensation* équivalent à presque 85% des sommes payés aux victimes![52]

Nous ne sommes pas dans une situation qui nous permette d'exprimer une opinion sur ce problème, surtout parceque nous avons vu des chiffres contradictoires. Mais sur un plan plus général, nous croyons, avec Mme Lambert-

---

[48] D. 1982, 449, 451.

[49] "L'arrêt Demares: retour au Néolithique", *J.C.P.* 1982, 3090.

[50] Cass. Req. 13 avril 1934, D. 1934. 1. 41, note Savatier. Pour plus de détails sur l'évolution du droit sur cette matière, v. G. Viney "L'indemnisation des victimes dommages causés par le 'fait d'une chose' après l'arrêt de la Cour de cassation (2e Ch. civ.) du 21 juillet 1982", *D. Chron.* 1982, 201 et s.

[51] A. Tunc, *Pour une loi sur les accidents de la circulation*, Economica (1981), p. 67.

[52] *Pearson Committee Report, supra*, n. 24.

Faivre[53] qu'une rationalisation du système de recours pourrait faire réaliser des économies considérables. Ce qui est encore plus important, en Angleterre ainsi qu'en France, c'est le problème fondamental d'interrelation rationnelle des différents systèmes de compensation. Ainsi, la *Pearson Royal Commission* en Angleterre a très correctement souligné que:

"Les deux systèmes de compensation (responsabilité civile et sécurité sociale) ont pu se développer très longtemps dans un isolement complet, en ignorant le fait que, quelquefois, ils couvrent les mêmes besoins, tandis que, dans d'autres cas ils satisfont peu de tels besoins".[54]

Voilà un autre problème que les juristes traditionnels ont tendance à ignorer ou même déprécier. Et c'est un problème qui présente une importance tout à fait particulière pour le comparatiste soucieux d'introduire dans son pays les idées d'un système étranger. Qu'on pense soit aux accidents de circulation, soit aux dommages causés par des produits défectueux, il est nécessaire, à notre avis, de penser toujours aux systèmes de sécurité sociale prévalant dans le pays dont le droit est examiné.[55] Ainsi, une solution juridique acceptable ans un pays où les décaissements étatiques sont très limités peut être inacceptable dans un système où la sécurité sociale est très développée.

Notre troisième observation concerne l'étendue de l'arrêt *Demares*. Cet aspect du problème n'a évidemment pas échappé à l'attention des commentateurs; mais, pour nous, il présente un intérêt différent. Pouvons-nous limiter la portée de cet arrêt aux cas où l'assurance est obligatoire, y compris évidemment le cas des accidents de circulation? Sur le plan théorique, Geneviève Viney[56] semble croire qu'une réponse affirmative à cette question est dirable en soutenant qu'il serait rationnel de lier la suppression des partages en responsabilité non pas à l'application de l'article 1384, alinéa 1 du Code civil, mais à l'esitence d'une obligation de s'assurer.

Mais si une telle distincion paraît souhaitable en principe, le problème de son application dans un système fondé sur le Code paraît problématique. Il y aura sans doute des juristes qui soutiendront que le système francais est moins beien placé que le système anglais pour faire les distinctions nuancées que les cours anglaises (américaines) font tous les jours.[57] Sans doute, dans ce cas-là, l'étude de la méthodologie de la *common law* pourait faire apparaître des idées intéressantes aux juristes francais. Mais, au fond, une telle constatation nous paraît douteuse. L'édifice jurisprudentiel construit sur les articles

[53] " Aspects juridiques, moraux et économiques de l'indemnisation des victimes fautives", *D. Chron.* 1982, 207, 209.
[54] *Pearson Report*, t. I, § 271. Le livre de Atiyah, *op. cit.* n. 32, *supra*, représente un effort unique et en même temps très intéressant d'étudier le système de compensation dans son ensemble. V. aussi Tunc, *op. cit.*, n. 5 *supra* p. 34.
[55] Dans le même sens, Weir, "Product Liability: some Comparative Remarks on the Law of England and France " dans *Rechtsentwicklung in der Produkthaftung* (éd. W. Posch et B. Shilder) 45, 57–58 (Vienne, 1981).
[56] *Op. cit.*, n. 50, *supra*, p. 207.
[57] V. ainsi, Durry, *Rev, trim. dr. civ.* 1982, 606, 608.

1119–1121 et 1384 du Code civil, pour donner deux exemples qui sont bien connus, nous persuade que le droit francais a la possibilité de se renouveler alors que l'on a pris conscience de la nécessité d'une réforme. Cela ne veut pas dire que la réforme législative ne soit pas préférable dans des cas particuliers. Le domaine des accidents de circulation, avec ses propres problèmes et données, est l'un de ceux-là.[58] Tout ce qu'on suggère—étant toujours conscient du fait que nos réactions peuvent être erronées à cause de notre faible connaissance du droit francais—est que l'arrêt *Demares,* correctement limité aux situations d'assurance obligatoire, représente une étape importante vers une réforme souhaitable.

5. CONCLUSIONS

Peut-on tirer quelques conclusions générales de cette brève analyse d'une série d'arrêts de responsabilité civile tirés de trois systèmes juridiques différentes? Notre analyse est certainement insuffisante pour formuler des conclusions fermes. Mais certaines idées ou tenances semblent émerger et méritent au moins un examen plus approfondi. Nous en mentionnons deux.

La première est que, dans tous ces arrêts, l'assurance, ou d'autres facteurs économiques liés la pratique de l'assurance, ont joué un rôle essentiel dans le résultat, sans avoir toujours été mentionnés dans les textes des arrêts ou correctement appréciés par leurs commentateurs. En revanche, les raisons avancées pour justifier la solution ne sont pas convaincantes; elles sont confuses ou obliques ou restent complètement abstraites et schématiques. Tout cela n'est pas nécessairement un désastre, tant que les praticiens, les enseignants et les juges savent qu'ils; parlent d'une chose mais qu'en même temps, ils sont influencés par une autre. Pour des raisons que nous avons mentionnées, il est probable que les juges préfèrent s'exprimer par des concepts abstraits. Pour la France, c'est même inévitable tant que la motivation et le style des arrêts de votre Coure de cassation restent tellement delphiques, ou en tout cas austères.[59] Mais nous admirons les conclusions des avocats généraux pour leurs opinions franches et souvent courageuses. Et il me semble, en tant que professeur de droit, que je suis obligé d'enseigner ma matière en la liant aux réalités de la vie moderne. Bien sûr, les étudiants ont besoin de notions et de concepts pour exprimer leurs idées et leurs conclusions. Mais ils doivent aussi savoir que ceux-là ne sont rien que des formules qui permettent de rendre une décision, mais presque jamais de l'expliquer.

Nous pensons également que les arrêts que nous avons considérés justifient

---

[58] V. sur ce problème la collection très intéressante des essais sur les propositions, *Pour une loi . . . op. cit.* n. 51, supra.

[59] Critiqué par MM. Touffait et Tunc dans leur célèbre article "Pour une motivation plus explicite des décisions de justice notamment de celles de la Cour de cassation", *Rev. trim. dr. civ.,* 1974, p. 481.

une seconde conclusion. Ne serait-il pas préférable, dans tous ces cas, de reconnaître ouvertement la réalité de l'assurance et discuter alors intelligement ses implications, plutôt que de prétendre appliquer mécaniquement des notions abstraites? L'assurance a radicalement transformé le droit de la responsabilité civile. Nous ne cessons d'admirer le fait que de telles transformations aient pu s'accomoder d'un système de responsabilité civile qui, admettons—le, dans ses lignes essentielles a peu changé depuis des siècles. Mais l'élabortion d'un ensemble de règles extraordinairement subtiles et la confusion, voire même la trahision, des notions traditionnelles en ont été le prix. Il est clair que le droit de la responsabilité civile vit une période de transition. Et c'est bien cette qualité qui, à notre avis, continue de prêter à ce sujet son intérêt théorique et pratique tout à fait particuliers.

17

The Right to be Let Alone Versus Freedom of Speech

1. INTRODUCTION

The protection of human privacy is a modern, difficult, intriguing problem, particularly instructive for the purposes of teaching foreign law and applying the comparative method. It is modern in the sense that increased technological means for collecting, collating and disseminating information are making intrusions into human privacy both effective and (at times unnecessarily) devastating. It is a difficult problem since its solutions must often be sought in different branches of the law (e.g. constitutional law, criminal law, tort law) which then have to be skilfully combined in order to produce an acceptable result. This, in effect, is a process which strives to achieve a balance between equally important social interests: the respect for human personality and the preservation of freedom of expression.[1] The search for the right solution is not only hampered by the difficult issues alluded to in the previous sentence; it also presupposes answers to some difficult technical questions which, arguably, are also used as excuses for continuing inaction. For example: What does privacy mean? Who should define it: the legislator or the courts? What remedies should be available to the aggrieved victim?[2] All these problems, not being particular to any one system,[3] make this an excellent subject for comparative research. Indeed, the more one studies the foreign solutions the more

---

[1] To attribute *equal* value to these interests is, in itself, a potentially controversial statement and one which, we shall see, not all systems adopt in an absolute form. But empirical evidence suggests that concern about the respect of individual privacy can be just as high as the concern for freedom of expression, race and sex equality: see App. E of the *Report of the Committee on Privacy* (the Younger Committee Report), Cmnd. 5012 (1972).

[2] These points are considered by all the major works on the subject. From the immense literature, see the *Younger Report* (*ibid.*); *Justice, Privacy and the Law* (1970); Westin, *Privacy and Freedom* (1970); Marshall, "The Right to Privacy: A Sceptical View" (1975) 21 *McGill L.J.* 242; Seipp, "English Judicial Recognition of a Right to Privacy" (1983) 3 *O.J.L.S.* 325 (with rich references).

[3] For France see, inter alia, Lindon, *Dictionnaire juridique: les droits de la personnalité* (1983); Kayser, *La protection de la vie privée* (1984). For Canada, see Burns, "Law and Privacy: The Canadian Experience" (1976) 54 *Can. B.Rev.* 1; Gibson, "Common Law Protection of Privacy. What to do until the Legislators Arrive" in L. Klar (ed.), *Studies in Canadian Tort Law* (1977); Pedrick, "Publicity and Privacy: Is it any of our Business" (1970) 20 *U.T.L.J.* 391. References to German law are given in the next note; here suffice to mention two works in English: Handford, "Moral Damage in Germany" (1978) 27 *I.C.L.Q.* 849 and Zweigert and Kötz, *An Introduction to Comparative Law*, vol. II, para. 20 (English trans. by T. Weir, 1977).

this intuition becomes a conviction. For the comparison of the different systems reveals here, as elsewhere, similarities which are as noteworthy as the undoubted differences. More intriguingly, however, it also reveals areas where comparative transplants are possible and where the explosion of many commonly held myths is long overdue.

In this article I shall try to substantiate these points by concentrating on two narrow instances of the right to be let alone. Before doing so, however, it is desirable to attempt a brief review of the general state of the law in the three systems under comparison (United States, England and Germany).[4]

2. UNITED STATES, ENGLAND AND GERMANY: AN OVERVIEW

This can be done in two ways. The first is to describe briefly each system separately. The other, which will be adopted here, is to try to bring together the evolution of these systems in the form of some general propositions.

First, the need to protect human privacy was in all three systems first stressed by academics who advanced similar arguments in favour of "honour" and—it could be argued—indirectly the wider right of personality.[5] In all these systems analogous arguments were also advanced to counter these proposals. Notable amongst these were (a) the danger of increased litigation; (b) the impossibility to define privacy without encroaching too much on the interest of free expression; and (c) the need for certainty in the law.[6]

---

[4] For general accounts of German law, see Brandner, "Das allgemeine Persönlichkeitsrecht in der Entwicklung durch die Rechtsprechung", *JZ* 1983, 689; v. Caemmerer, "Der privatrechtliche Persönlichkeitsschutz nach deutschem Recht", *Festschrift* v. *Hippel* (1967), p.27; v. Gamm, "Persönlichkeitsschutz und Massenmedien", *NJW* 1979, 513; Hubmann, *Das Persönlichkeitsrecht*, 2nd edn. (1967); Larenz, "Das allgemeine Persönlichkeitsrecht' im Recht der unerlaubten Handlungen", *NJW* 1955, 521; Mertens, "Persönlichkeitsrecht und Schadensersatz BGHZ 35, 363", *JuS* 1962, 261; Schwerdtner, *Das Persönlichkeitsrecht in der deutschen Zivilrechtsordnung* (1977); *idem.*, "Der Zivilrechtliche Persönlichkeitsschutz", *JuS* 1978, 289. For a comparative discussion in *German*, see Dworkin, Fleming, Hubrecht, Strömholm, Finzgar and Kübler, *Die Haftung der Massenmedien, insbesondere der Presse, bei Eingriffen in persönliche oder gewerbliche Rechtspositionen* (Arbeiten zur Rechtsvergleichung, 1972). More specialised works will be referred to in appropriate parts of the text. (Professor Hassemer's "Vorverurteilung durch die Medien?", *NJW*, 1985, 1921 appeared too late for consideration in this article.)

[5] Germany: O. v. Gierke, *Deutsches Privatrecht*, vol. I (1895), p.707; vol. III (1917), p.887; Kohler, "Das Recht an Briefen", *Archiv für bürgerliches Recht*, vol. VII, p.94 *et seq.*; R. v. Jhering, *Jahrbuch für Dogmatik*, 23, 155. England: Winfield, "Privacy" (1931) 47 *L.Q.R.* 23. United States: Warren and Brandeis, "The Right to Privacy" (1890) 4 *Harv.L.R.* 193. Canada: Falconbridge, "Desirable Changes in the Common Law" (1927) 5 *Can. B.Rev.* 581.

[6] Compare RGZ 28. 12. 1899, RGZ 45, 170 (1899) (where, however, the right of "personality" was upheld and the publications of phtographs taken without the subject's permission was prohibited) with *Robertson* v. *Rochester Folding Box Co.* (1902) 171 N.Y. 538, 64 N.E. 442. See, also, Prot. 11, 641; *Bericht der Reichstagskommission über den Entwurf eines Bürgerlichen Gesetzbuches und Einführungsgesetzes nebst einer Zusammenstellung der Konmissionsbeschlüsse* (1896), p.98.

Secondly, the reaction to protect human privacy came in the form of statutory interventions[7] and wide-ranging judicial pronouncements.[8] In Germany and the United States these first moves coincide chronologically, though a generalised right of privacy was created earlier in the United States than it was in Germany.[9] A general right of privacy has yet to be accepted by English law, though judicial pronouncements in this direction are growing both in number and strength of conviction.[10]

Thirdly, before the generalised position was reached, all systems chose to protect aspects of human privacy by invoking various parts of their law, notably the law of torts, the law of crime, the law of copyright and the law of restitution.[11]

Fourthly, the present protection of privacy in all these systems is quite extensive. Moreover, Prosser's well-known subdivisions (appropriation of likeness; unreasonable intrusion; false light cases; and the public disclosure of private facts on a matter which would be "highly offensive and objectionable to a reasonable person of ordinary sensibilities") can be used fairly successfully to categorise the law of all these systems.[12] Of these headings, the last is the most troublesome and the one which forms the main subject of this paper.

Fifthly, despite the previous assertion, the protection afforded to privacy by English law can be patchy. For different reasons, the protection afforded by American law can also be seriously diminished and appear deficient when compared to German law and, at times, even English law.

Sixthly, the preceding statement becomes meaningful if one appreciates the impact that the differing constitutional background has had on the development of the private law of these three different systems. This influence has been both positive and negative. An instance of the former can be found in the development of the general right of personality as it has evolved in Germany under the influence of the Constitution of Bonn of 1949.[13] One sus-

---

[7] Paras. 22, 23 of the Gesetz betreffend das Urheberrecht an Werken der bildenden Künste und der Photographie of January 9, 1907 (RGBI s.7)—which is still in force and is usually quoted under the shortened title of *Kunsturhebergesetz*. N.Y. Sess. Laws 1903, ch. 132, §§ 1–2. Now, as amended in 1921, N.Y.—McKinney's Civil Rights Law, paras. 50–1.

[8] *Pavesich* v. *New England Ins. Co.*, 122 Ga. 190, 50 S.E. 68 (1905); *Flake* v. *Greensboro News Co.* (1938) 212 N.C. 780, 195 S.E. 55.

[9] BGHZ 13, 334 (Schacht), reproduced in translated form in Lawson and Markesinis, *Tortious Liability for Unintentional Harm in the Common Law and the Civil Law*, Vol. II (1982), pp.105–10.

[10] To be found collected in Seipp's article quoted above n. 2.

[11] For a summary of the development of German law, see Zweigert and Kötz and Handford, *op. cit.*, above n. 3. For the fragmented approach of the common law, see Seipp, *op. cit.*, above n. 2. For the United States, see Prosser and Keeton, *Torts*, 5th edn., Ch. 20.

[12] "Privacy", (1960) 48 *Cal.L.R.* 383. Thus, *Tolley* v. *Fry* [1930] 1 KB 467 can be compared with BGHZ 26, 349 (appropriation of plaintiff's picture, image); *Peay* v. *Curtis Publishing Co.*, D.D.C. 1948, 78 F.Supp. 305 can be compared with BGHZ 35, 363 (false light cases); *Briscoe* v. *Reader's Digest*, 4 Cal. 3d 529, 93 Cal.Reptr. 866, 483 P. 2d 34 (1971) can be compared with BVerfGE 35, 202 (highly offensive disclosures of public (or private) facts).

[13] BGHZ 13, 334. Also noteworthy is the large number of decisions of the Federal Constitutional Court on this matter. Among the many important decisions, one could cite the following: BVerfGE 30, 173; 34, 269; 35, 202; 54, 129; 54, 148= NJW 1980, 2070; 54, 208.

pects the same would occur in England if, say, a Bill of Rights were introduced or, at least, the European Convention of Human Rights were made part of municipal law.[14] A "negative" repercussion of the constitution can be found in the United States where freedom of speech has seriously (some might say disastrously) obscured if not actually stunted the development of this type of protection of human privacy (and the related tort of defamation).

Finally, the protection of privacy can vary at the "level of available remedies". In general, all systems opt for a combination of criminal sanctions and civil remedies (damages, injunctions, etc.). But, again, the constitutional background may help make one of these more prevalent than the others.

3. PEOPLE WHO DO NOT SEEK PUBLICITY AND THEIR "RIGHT" TO BE LET ALONE

Some are born with publicity; others seek it, or achieve it involuntarily as a result of their acts; yet others have publicity thrust upon them. A legal system that cannot differentiate between these categories and, for example, treats a publicity-seeking politician in the same way as a traumatised victim of rape, would appear to be defective. Yet it would seem that the common law has, on the whole, refused to make such a distinction. Thus Prosser and Keeton remark that "Caught up and entangled in [the] web of news and public interest [are] a great many people who [have] not sought publicity, but indeed, as in the case of any accused criminal, [have] tried assiduously to avoid it. They [have] nevertheless lost some part of their right of privacy. The misfortunes of the frantic victim of sexual assault, the woman whose husband was murdered before her eyes, or the innocent bystander who was caught in a raid on a cigar store and mistaken by the police for the perpetrator, could be broadcast to the world, and they [have] no remedy".[15] German law on the other hand, being much more anxious to strike a balance between free speech and privacy, is more *nuancé*, and in the case of persons accused of criminal offences a distinction is made between persons who are in the public eye (politicians, actors, etc.) and persons who have attracted public attention as a result of a single occurrence which brings them into the limelight.[16] The

[14] Article 8(1) of which provides that "Everyone has the right to respect for his private and family life, his house and his correspondence". See, also, Art. 12 of the Universal Declaration of Human Rights (1948) and Art. 17 of the International Covenant on Civil and Political Rights (1966).
[15] *Torts*, 5th edn., p.861 and references in nn. 39–41. See also Restatement Second of Torts, section 625D, comment f; *Sipple* v. *The Chronicle Publishing Co.*, 201 Cal.Reptr. 665 (1984). On the other hand, some California courts seem to pay some attention to the fact that some plaintiffs in privacy actions have "voluntarily acceded to a position of public notoriety": *Forsher* v. *Bugliosi*, 608 P. 2d 716, 726 (1980).
[16] Lampe, "Der Straftäter als 'Person der Zeitgeschichte'", *NJW* 1973, 217; Bornkamm, *Pressefreiheit und Fairness des Strafverfahrens. Die Grenzen der Berichterstattung über schwebende Strafverfahren im englischen, amerikanischen und deutschen Recht* (1980), Part 3, Ch. 3, p.249.

dividing line is not always easy to draw; nor is this the sole criterion when deciding when an actionable publication has taken place. But it is taken into account by the court, with the result that the former category of persons have a more restricted right of anonymity than the latter.

In this article, I shall take a closer look at the protection (if any) received in these three systems by (a) victims of sexual offences notably rape, and (b) ex-criminals and their close relatives, e.g. their children.

A. *Victims of Sexual Offences, Notably Rape*

Some systems, e.g. the German, provide no specific statutory protection of the anonymity of such victims. Indeed, this aspect of anonymity seems to have received little attention from the legal literature. There is no doubt, however, that in some cases the general right of personality—one of the new protected rights of section 823 I BGB—could be used. But it must be remembered that its applicability depends on the violation of privacy being grave, blameworthy and, it is often said, not compensated satisfactorily by different means.[17] In deciding whether the interference is grave and unacceptable, the courts have often been forced to attempt a very fine balance of the competing interests.[18] Thus, in one important decision[19]—not involving a victim of a sexual crime—the Federal Court suggested that the following criteria might be of particular relevance: (i) the wide circulation of the publication that carried the statements; (ii) whether the person involved gave his consent (with or without monetary reward); (iii) the desire to make a profit from the publication and, more generally, the aim the publisher was trying to achieve (scurrilous gossip or information and education); and (iv) the effect that the publication would have on the plaintiff. Parallel to this possible legal protection is the unofficial protection given to such persons through the self-restraining mechanisms that the Press and the television services adopt and thus avoid mentioning such persons by name. It would appear that the latter method of protection has worked quite effectively in practice and has thus taken away the pressure to strengthen the protection of the victims by means of specific legislation.

This latter course was, in fact, adopted in England in 1976 when section 4 of the Sexual Offences (Amendment) Act made it an offence to mention the name of a victim of a "rape offence" (defined in section 7(2) so as to include "attempted rape, aiding, abetting, counselling and procuring rape or attempted rape, and incitement to rape") on radio, television, or in the Press. Clearly, the self-restraining mechanisms which still apply in, say, the unauthorised use of a person's picture for the purposes of advertising products was

---

[17] BGH, *NJW* 1982, 635 (with further references at p.636).
[18] See, e.g. BGHZ 73, 120. As will be noted below, this balancing of competing interests is undertaken with great care when newspapers are reporting the commission of crimes.
[19] BGH, *NJW* 1971, 698.

held to be inadequate.[20] Though the reform is to be welcomed, it provides an excellent illustration of the typically English case-by-case way of filling gaps in the law as and when they are perceived to be unacceptable. Thus, the victims of "lesser" sexual offences (e.g. indecent assault) or, indeed, other sexual offences (such as unlawful sexual intercourse, incest or buggery) who wish to be left to forget their traumatic experiences, will receive no legal protection in the absence of a "general right of privacy". The same may happen when a conviction for rape seems unlikely (and/or the complainant wishes to avoid being put into the witness-box) and the prosecution is thus forced to resort to plea-bargaining, and settles for a "lesser" offence. In such cases the victim loses her right to remain anonymous.

Comparison with the United States can be instructive even though (because of lack of space) it will be limited to one example. Georgia is one of the states that have a special statute which make it a misdemeanour to publish or broadcast the name or identity of a rape victim. In the important judgment of *Cox v. Cohen*,[21] however, the United States Supreme Court held that the statute was unconstitutional being contrary to the First and Fourteenth Amendments. In delivering the opinion of the Court, White J. conceded that whenever a "collision" takes place between "claims of privacy and [the claims] of the free press, the interests of both sides are plainly rooted in the traditions and significant concerns of our society". In the instant case, however, the information concerning the victim's name had been gleaned from a public document (the indictments) and to prohibit its publication by the Press "would invite timidity and self-censorship and very likely lead to the suppression of many items that would otherwise be put into print and that should be made available to the public. At the very least, the First and Fourteenth Amendments will not allow exposing the Press to liability for truthfully publishing information released to the public in official records".

The judgment—to foreign eyes at least—appears remarkable not only because of its belief that self-censorship is necessarily a bad thing but mainly

[20] On this, see Frazer, "Appropriation of Personality—A New Tort?" (1983) 99 *L.Q.R.* 281.

[21] 420 U.S. 469, 95 S. Ct. 1029 (1975). Other states have similar, though not identically-phrased statutes, e.g. South Carolina paras. 16–81, Code of Laws of South Carolina 1962, (applied in *Nappier* v. *Jefferson Standard Life Insurance Co.*, 322 F. 2d 502 but, presumably, now of doubtful authority because of *Cox* v. *Cohen*); Wisconsin (Statutes of 1945, §348.412); Florida (Statutes, §794.03). Similarly, statutes making it possible for a court to prohibit the publication of the names of victims or persons accused of certain criminal sexual conduct have been declared unconstitutional as being contrary to the First Amendment: see, e.g., *WXYZ Inc.* v. *J. Hand*, 658 F. 2d 420 (1981). Even more dubious—to the eyes of a foreign observer—are decisions which declare unconstitutional statutes which seek to punish newspapers identifying juvenile offenders by name. From the voluminous case law, see *Smith, Judge et al.* v. *Daily Mail Publishing Co.*, 443 U.S. 97 (1979). The interest of the State to preserve the anonymity of the juvenile was laconically brushed aside by Berger C.J. as "not sufficient" to overcome the traditional dislike for any form of "prior restraint". See, also *Globe Newspaper Co.* v. *Superior Court*, 102 S.Ct. 2613 (1982). The *Smith* case is strongly criticised (on grounds analogous to those put forward in this article) by P. Marcus, "The Media in the Courtroom; Attending, Reporting, Televising Criminal Cases", (1982) 57 *Indiana L.J.* 235, 273 *et seq.*

because of the narrow basis of the ruling that appears at the end of the quotation. Certainly in the area of the topic under consideration the idea that it is in the public interest that everything that is contained in an official record may be given even wider publicity appears questionable.[22] As Dean Keeton has observed[23] "the prospects of a privacy recovery, even within the limits of the *Sidis* principle[24] of outrageous publicity, have been sharply curtailed in consequence [of this decision]".[25] Disclosure of facts not a matter of public record (public or private) might, on the other hand, entail liability. This possible exception, however, would be inapplicable in the case of a rape victim whose name would always appear in some official document. For present purposes therefore the decision must be considered as unsatisfactory and, indeed, it has provoked some notable criticisms even in the United States.[26] It is submitted that the weaknesses of this decision—even allowing for the different constitutional backgrounds—become more obvious once this judgment is compared with the *Lebach*[27] decision of the German Federal Constitutional Court which will be discussed in the next section.

B. Ex-Criminals and their Close Relatives (e.g. Children)

"The Moving Finger writes; and, having writ,
Moves on: nor all thy Piety nor Wit
Shall lure it back to cancel half a Line,
Nor all thy Tears wash out a Word of it."
Omar Khayyám

The idea that even a criminal has a right to have his past forgotten—at least in some cases and for some purposes—was slow to gain any acceptance in England. Thus, the idea that compassion and understanding (not to say anything of forgiveness) can be just as important values as truth in any civilised society was not reflected in the law until the passing of the Rehabilitation of Offenders Act 1974. This complicated and stylistically unfortunate enactment provides that after a set rehabilitation period (depending on the type of sentence imposed and its duration) convictions must be treated in law as "spent".

---

[22] *Virgil* v. *Time Inc.* 527 F. 2d 1122, 1129 contains analogous *dicta* though in practice the picture appears to be quite different, with courts invariably opting for freedom of expression at the expense of privacy.

[23] *Torts*, 5th edn., p.863.

[24] *Sidis* v. *F.R. Publishing Corp.* (2d Cir. 1940), 113 F. 2d. 806, *cert. denied* 311 U.S. 711, 61 S.Ct. 393.

[25] In *Cox*, the Supreme Court took the view that "The First and Fourteenth Amendments command nothing less than that States may not impose sanctions for the publication of truthful information contained in official records open to public inspection": *ibid.* at p.495. In the earlier decision of *Time, Inc.* v. *Hill*, 385 U.S. 374, 87 S.Ct. 534 (1967), the Court had accepted the possibility of liability in tort for an unwarranted publicity of the truth.

[26] See, e.g. Hill, "Defamation and Privacy Under the First Amendment" (1976) 76 *Colum.L.R.* 1205; Linder, "When Names are not News, They're Negligence: Media Liability for Personal Injuries Resulting from the Publication of Accurate Information" (1984) 52 *UMKL L. R.* 421.

[27] BVerfGE 35, 202.

Thus, the unauthorised disclosure of official criminal records is, in certain circumstances, an offence (s.9); and evidence of spent convictions is rendered inadmissible in (certain) judicial proceedings (s.4). These provisions go some way towards preserving the anonymity of those ex-criminals covered by the Act (ss.1 and 5). But it does not protect all ex-criminals (which is in many instances quite understandable); nor even those criminals whose names appear in the Press since section 8 of the Act preserves three important defences from the law of defamation namely those of justification, fair comment and privilege (absolute and qualified). The only concession made here to ex-criminals *covered by the Act* is that malice will destroy the defence of justification (s.8(5)).[28] Thus the possibility of a past crime being thrown in the ex-criminal's face, shattering his (and his family's) newly-found respectability remains a distinct possibility. This result does not appear to bother many lawyers and only in exceptional circumstances has it been regarded as so incongruous as to merit some sanction. Where this has been the case, the intervention has been typically English: case-by-case in technique, patchy in its result. The following recent wardship case[29] provides an excellent illustration.

In 1968, Mary Bell, a juvenile, was convicted of manslaughter and sentenced to detention for life. In 1984, she was released on licence and, some time later, gave birth to a daughter who was made a ward of court at the initiative of the local authority. Somehow this became known to the Press and an application was made by her mother and the local authority to the High Court for an injunction prohibiting the disclosure of the identity and present whereabouts of *both* child and parents. The application, made on the ground that any such disclosure would be detrimental to the family's newly-found peace and stability, was accepted by Balcombe J. and an order prohibiting publication of the said information (but not of the fact of the birth) was duly granted.

In an earlier wardship case,[30] the first attempt ever was made to use the wardship jurisdiction in this type of situation in order to prohibit the publication of a book concerning the ward's deceased father and containing material which, as the defendants conceded, was likely to cause her serious psychological damage if it ever came to her notice. A unanimous Court of Appeal took the view that freedom of speech should prevail. In the event, therefore, the carefully balanced judgment of the trial judge was reversed, Lord Denning M.R. declaring that "it would be extending the wardship jurisdiction too far and infringing too much upon the freedom of the Press for us to grant an injunction in this case".[31] Roskill L.J. echoed similar views, though he felt that in appropriate circumstances a balancing of the competing

[28] For a recent case where malice was not proved and the plaintiff's action thus failed, see *Herbage v. Pressdram* [1984] 2 All ER 769.
[29] *Re X* [1984] 1 WLR 1422.
[30] *Re X* [1975] Fam. 47.
[31] *Ibid.* at p.59.

interests might have to be attempted. Sir John Pennycuick was also anxious to preserve, at least "in exceptional circumstances",[32] the right to make such an order in favour of the ward. In his view, it was the courts' clear duty to attempt to balance the competing interests, even though in this instance freedom of speech prevailed.

One could of course try to reconcile these decisions by reference to their particular facts, even though to the reader of the law reports a clear distinction is not all that obvious. (The preference for free speech in the earlier *Re X* case is even more remarkable considering that the offending parts of the book—a mere eight pages—could have been removed at a very small cost which the parents of the ward were more than willing to meet.) Could one then look at the second *Re X* decision, delivered almost ten years after the earlier one, as reflecting a greater sensitivity to human privacy, especially in the light of adverse reactions—national and international—to the telephone tapping case of *Malone* v. *Metropolitan Police Comissioner*?[33] Linking these two cases may strike some people as odd; but, it is submitted, one can legitimately treat *Re X* as a privacy case or, more precisely, as a case dealing with that type of privacy which Judge Cooley described as "the right to be let alone".[34]

Seen in this light, *Re X* is a remarkable decision since it protects the anonymity of the (innocent) child and, at the same time, the anonymity of the mother/ex-criminal. Remarkable and yet typical of the way that protection is afforded by pushing into existing tort pigeon-holes certain fact situations; and where tort law cannot afford a remedy, by extending an inherent jurisdiction which was meant for many things but was hardly devised as a substitute for a non-existent tort of violation of privacy.

Re X, however, also makes the patchy nature of the protections most obvious. Thus, the mother's anonymity is only incidentally protected. And once the wardship ends (through the death of the child or its reaching the age of 18), the protection will disappear. The Rehabilitation of Offenders Act, mentioned above, will in this case afford no protection (s.5); and mother and child will run the risk of having their lives destroyed because some popular tabloid feels that the revelation of their new identity may interest its gossip-thirsty readership. The limited nature of the protection is also obvious when one considers that the nature of the infringement of the judge's order would render liable for contempt proceedings only those who were aware of it in the first place. To put it differently, a publication of the identity of Mary Bell by another newspaper which independently made the same discovery and published it before the delivery of the judgment would go unpunished. Are these really acceptable results? Should a young girl of 17 be entitled to protection against her mother's distant past but lose it once she has become 18? Should

---

[32] *Re X* [1975] Fam. at p.61.
[33] [1979] Ch. 344. *Tort*, 2nd edn. (1889), p.29.
[34] *Tort*, 2nd edn. (1889), p.29.

an ex-criminal *par excellence* of the Mary Bell type—who committed the crime just barely after attaining the age of criminal capacity (ten), be haunted by it for the rest of her life?

In *Briscoe* v. *Reader's Digest Association Inc.*,[35] the plaintiff complained that the defendant wrote an article discussing the hijacking of lorries and referred to him by name in connection with an eleven-year-old incident of that nature in which he had been involved. The plaintiff also alleged that after the incident he had become fully rehabilitated and had led a perfectly respectable life until the publication of the article shattered this newly found peace and caused even his daughter and closest friends to shun and avoid him. The trial judge took the view that there was no legal cause of action. Reversing, the Supreme Court of California said of the plaintiff:

> "Ideally, his neighbours should recognise his present worth and forget his past life of shame. But men are not so divine as to forgive the past trespasses of others, and plaintiff therefore endeavoured to reveal as little as possible of his past life. Yet, as if in some bizarre canyon of echoes, [the plaintiff's] past life pursues him through the pages of *Reader's Digest*, now published in 13 languages and distributed in 100 nations, with a circulation in California alone of almost 2,000,000 copies.
>
> In a nation built upon the free dissemination of ideas, it is always difficult to declare that something may not be published. But the great general interest in an unfettered press may at times be outweighed by other great societal interests. As a people we have come to recognise that one of these societal interests is that of protecting an individual's right of privacy. The right to know and the right to have others not know are, simplistically considered, irreconcilable. But the right guaranteed by the First Amendment does not require total abrogation of the right of privacy. The goals sought by each may be achieved with a minimum of intrusion upon the other.
>
> We do not hold today that plaintiff must prevail in his action. It is for the trier of fact to determine (1) whether plaintiff had become a rehabilitated member of society, (2) whether identifying him as a former criminal would be highly offensive and injurious to a reasonable man, (3) whether defendant published this information with a reckless disregard for its offensiveness, and (4) whether any independent justification for printing plaintiff's identity existed."

The *Lebach* decision was based on similar though not identical facts. A not insignificant difference is the fact that the plaintiff (*Lebach*), a former accessory to a gang which carried out an armed robbery on an American military installation in Germany, was hardly a rehabilitated person—certainly not a rehabilitated offender in the sense of the English Act. In fact the television film made about the robbery and identifying *Lebach* in person (and also referring to his homosexual tendencies) was about to be shown more or less at the time when he was to be released from prison having received remission of part of his sentence for good behaviour. Other interesting differences between these two judgments are the following. First, the court openly had to consider at

---

[35] 4 Cal. 3d 529, 483 P. 2d. 34 (1971).

some length the incompatible values of privacy *versus* freedom of expression. The point has, of course, been made in American decisions. But the length and thoroughness of the German discussions must, in part at least, be attributable to the fact that the German Constitution protects both interests expressly, whereas in the American Constitution freedom of expression receives a more explicit protection. (This is further evidence of the impact that constitutional law can have on the development of private law.) Secondly, as in *Briscoe* so in *Lebach* the court set out some factors that have to be weighed carefully before the final decision is taken. But in *Lebach*, factors in favour of the plaintiff were stressed in a way that was not done in *Briscoe*. The Constitutional Court for example noted the wider interest of "reintegrating the criminal into society".[36] The time and purpose of the publication is another factor[37] (which, arguably, is included in the fourth factor given by *Briscoe*) and this, too, must be taken very carefully into account.[38] A sensational, one-sided or inaccurate account (echoes here of *Time* v. *Hill*) is likely

---

[36] BVerfGE 35, 202. in *Forsher* v. *Bugliosi*, 608 P. 2d 761 (1980), the Supreme Court of California suggested that the "most important" consideration in *Briscoe* was "the fact that the State has a compelling interest in the rehabilitative process and that a continuing threat of media disclosure of the identity of past criminals is counterproductive in this process" (*ibid.* at p.726). Though reference was made in this case to *Cox* v. *Cohen*, the court did not appear to recognise its incompatibility with the *Briscoe* ruling and the anonymity of ex-criminals. *Contra Rawlins* v. *The Hutchinson Publishing Co.*, 543 P. 2d 988, 995 where the Supreme Court of Kansas held that *Cox* would now dictate a different result in both *Melvin* v. *Reid* 112 Cal. App. 285, 297 p. 91 (1931) and *Briscoe. Readers Rigest Ass'n Inc.* 93 Cal. Rptr. 866, 483 P. 2d 34 (1971).

[37] It must be noted that in German law the balancing of the competing interests of freedom of information and anonymity depends on the stage of the proceedings. Thus, greater anonymity is guaranteed during the preliminary investigations (unless the identification of the accused is necessary for his arrest or the prevention of further crimes). Anonymity is respected even during the trial, with the accused's name and image not being published at this stage either. The publication of the judgment of the trial is a turning point in the sense that from that stage onwards the accused's right to remain anonymous takes second place. Once the interest in current information has been satisfied, the right of the convicted person to be left alone regains the ascendancy and eventually this means that in principle he must no longer be associated with the crime. The concluding sections of the *Lebach* decision make this clear. For further discussions, with rich references, see the works of Lampe and Bornkamm cited above n. 16. See also v. Becker, *Straftäter und Tatverdächtige in den Massenmedien: Die Frage der Rechtmässigkeit identifizierender Kriminalberichte* (1979), pp.20 *et seq.*; "Richtlinien für die redaktionelle Arbeit nach den Empfehlungen des Deutschen Presserates Stand 31.12.1981", in *Das gesamte Recht der Publizistik*.

[38] This was stressed most forcefully in *Virgil* v. *Time, Inc.*, 527 F. 2d 1122 (1975) where the court said: "In determining what is a matter of legitimate interest, account must be taken of the customs and conventions of the community; and in the last analysis what is proper becomes a matter of the community mores. *The line is to be drawn when the possibility ceases to be the giving of information to which the public is entitled, and becomes a morbid and sensational prying into private lives for its own sake*, with which a reasonable member of the public, with decent standards, would say that he had no concern" (emphasis added). Did the complete identification of the ex-criminal in the *Briscoe* case satisfy such a legitimate purpose? If the answer is 'no', could the same result be reached and the *Virgil* and *Briscoe* tests applied when the identity of the ex-criminal has been gleaned from a public record? *Cox* v. *Cohen* would suggest the opposite, though there are some interesting cases where courts, taking, advantage of *dicta* in *Cox*, have successfully limited its ambit. See, e.g. *Ayers* v. *Lee Enterprises Incorporated*, 277 Or. 527, 561 P. 2d 998, especially at p.1003 (Oregon statute exempting from public disclosure certain official records, including records naming rape victims, held to be constitutional).

to receive less protection than one which is clearly aimed at satisfying the *legitimate* desire of the public to be informed and educated. Clearly, any attempt to summarise this seminal judgment is bound to be crude and do it injustice. But both in terms of style and substance, it indisputably deserves the closest possible study. Finally, it is noteworthy that, whereas the German court was prepared to prohibit the showing of the film, the American courts are disposed to award damages (simple or punitive) *ex post facto*. (That is on the assumption that they do decide to act at all. In view of *Cox* v. *Cohen*, however, this must be a matter of some doubt.) This point, however, is best discussed in the next paragraph.

4. THE AVAILABLE REMEDIES

It is not enough to make certain violations of human privacy actionable. The successful plaintiff must also be given the appropriate remedy. In theory four solutions are possible: criminal sanctions, damages, injunctions, or any combination of them. In the instances examined in this article (for example, section 4(5) of the Sexual Offences (Amendment) Act 1976), English law has shown an inclination in favour of criminal sanctions (though where a privacy case can be brought under an existing tort, damages are also possible). American law, largely because of the doctrine of prior restraint, is very reluctant to grant injunctions. As one judge puts it:[39]

"A free society prefers to punish the few who abuse rights of speech *after* they break the law than to throttle them and all others beforehand. It is always difficult to know in advance what an individual will say, and the line between legitimate and illegitimate speech is often so finely drawn that the risks of free-wheeling censorship are formidable."

Constitutionally permissible prior restraints can be found in exceptional cases. In *Near* v. *Minnesota*,[40] Hughes C.J. gave three illustrations of such exceptional cases: (1) restraints during wartime to prevent the disclosure of military deployments or obstruction of the military effort; (2) enforcement of obscenity law, and (3) enforcement of laws against incitement to acts of violence or revolution. How narrowly these exceptions are construed is seen from the important decision in *New York Times Co.* v. *U.S.*[41] where the Government failed to prevent the publication of classified Pentagon Papers dealing with United States activities in the Vietnam War prior to 1968. Not surprisingly in the context we are dealing with, the number of cases where a claim for injunction has succeeded appear to be very few. One of the most

---

[39] *Southeastern Promotions Ltd.* v. *Conrad*, 420 U.S. 546, 559 (1975).
[40] 283 U.S. 696, 716 (1931).
[41] 403 U.S. 713 (1971). See also *Nebraska Press Association* v. *Stuart*, 427 U.S. 539 (1976).

notable exceptions can be found in *Commonwealth* v. *Wiseman*[42] where the court prohibited the showing of a film which became known as the *Titicut Follies* containing scenes from a mental institution depicting some of the inmates in inhuman and degrading positions. The importance of the ruling is, unfortunately, somewhat diminished by the fact that the court had to consider the validity of the "consents" given by the mentally-ill persons. It is also further reduced by the fact that a subsequent New York court, dealing with the same facts, refused to grant an injunction.[43] But in this case, the prohibition of the showing of the film was not absolute. Showing to the general public on a commercial basis was prohibited; but showing to "legislators, judges, lawyers, sociologists, social workers, doctors, psychiatrists, students in these related fields . . ." was permitted. In the opinion of the Massachusetts court: "the public interest in having such persons informed about [life in the mental institutions] . . . outweighs any countervailing interests of the inmates and of the Commonwealth (as *parens patriae*) in anonymity and privacy".

To sum up, one cannot help but be impressed by the reverence American lawyers have for freedom of expression.[44] As Prosser and Keeton suggest, "if the Press thinks there is enough justification for publishing the truth as news, then it is *always* [*sic*] in the public interest not to subject it to harassing lawsuits about the appropriateness of a publication." The corollary of this is American distaste for all forms of censorship which, in Professor Tribe's words,[45] "tends to develop its own institutional momentum and also lacks the procedural safeguards characteristic of the judicial process". As one American author (who has written extensively on defamation, free speech and the First Amendment) recently observed,[46] American "decisions [seem] to embody a strategy of granting too much protection to speech as the only alternative to granting too little". Yet it is submitted no interest, even that in life itself, has an absolute value. Competing interests must be weighed and the publisher is not always the best person to do this.[47] Nor should the difficulty of this

---

[42] 356 Mass. 251, 249 N.E. 2d. 610 (1969), discussed in "The 'Titicut Follies' Case: Limiting the Public Interest Privilege" (1970) 70 *Colum. L. R.* 359. Another instance can be found in the prolonged litigation of Doe v. Row, summarised in Franklin and Rabin, *Tort Law and Alternatives*, 3rd edn. (1983), pp.982–3. I am grateful to Professor David Anderson for drawing this to my attention.

[43] *Cullen* v. *Grove Press Inc.*, 276 F. Supp. 727 (S.D.N.Y. 1967).

[44] *Torts*, 5th edn., p.862.

[45] *American Constitutional Law* (1978), p.732.

[46] Schauer, "Public Figures" (1984) 25 *William and Mary L.R.* 905, 909.

[47] In most cases that I have seen, only lip service seems to have been paid to the need to balance the competing interests with the consequence that freedom of expression prevails almost invariably over the rights of victims of sexual crimes, ex-criminals and even juvenile offenders to have their anonymity protected. An unusual and welcome exception can be found in the judgment of Rehnquist J. in *Smith, Judge et al.* v. *Daily Mail Publishing Co.*, 443 U.S. 97, 106 *et seq.* (1979), though regrettably in his final conclusion he sided with the majority. (The issue in this case was the constitutionality of a West Virginia statute which made it a crime for *newspapers* (but not radio or TV) to publish without court permission the name of juvenile offenders. The statute was held to be unconstitutional, with the consequence that the juvenile offender's identity could be revealed with impunity by the media.)

balancing task deter us from undertaking it. The post-Second World War German legal experience is in this respect particularly useful. For the German State, during the unfortunate period of National Socialism, disregarded both interests; and the disregard, indeed the contempt, in which human dignity was held (at least for some human beings) was just as lamentable as that regime's dislike of truth. The antithesis to that thesis was the Constitution of Bonn which decided to treat both values as essential parts of the liberal democratic order. The *Lebach* decision shows how courageously a compromise synthesis can be reached and how even an injunction will be granted in appropriate circumstances. Indeed, from the plaintiff's point of view, injunctions are in most cases the preferable remedy. But the plaintiff's interests are not the only ones that seem to be taken into account by the German judges when deciding the quantum of the award. For, at times, the defendant's opprobrious conduct is such that in Lord Devlin's words the court must show the defendant "that tort does not pay."[48] In the common law, this has led to the acceptance of punitive damages. Modern civil lawyers on the other hand almost invariably assert that this is a peculiarity not known to their systems. However, the German judicial practice in the context of defamation and actionable violations of privacy would seem to suggest that the difference between the systems is—in this area of the law at least—one of semantics. For in a number of cases where the successful claimants declared in advance that if the court granted them damages they would be given to charity, the courts have in fact occasionally made some substantial awards.[49] This can only be explained on the grounds that a small award would have no impact on large media defendants. If this is a correct interpretation, the resemblance to the *Cassell* v. *Broome*[50] type of situation is quite striking.

5. CONCLUSION

This is far too important a subject to be dealt with satisfactorily in the confines of a short article, but what we said about the two specific instances of violations of privacy may justify some more general thoughts. Thus, we cannot help but notice that in practice the laws of the different countries tend towards similar results. However there are also important differences which should make us pause and reflect on our own system. The main question probably is the following: is the English approach better than the German?

[48] *Rookes* v. *Barnard* [1964] AC 1129, 1227.
[49] See Christian v. Bar, "Schmerzensgeld und gesellschaftliche Stellung des Opfers bei Verletzungen des allgemeinen Persönlichkeitsrechtes", *NJW* 1980, 1724. The size of penal awards, compared to the American equivalents (e.g. *Diaz* v. *Oakland Tribune*, 188 Cal.Reptr. 762 (1983)), is much smaller; but the German practice is ingenious in so far as it manages to "punish" the unmeritorious defendant without unjustly enriching the plaintiff (since, as stated in the text, the money goes to charity).
[50] [1982] AC 1027.

We are all, of course, aware of the difficulties of providing a workable definition of privacy; but could we not operate a rule which, in principle, made it a tort to reveal a person's intimate life or his past record if it served no serious legitimate purpose and the revelation outraged the community's notions of decency? Surely, the common law courts could then work out the parameters of such liability on a case-to-case method as the German ones have done with, it is submitted, considerable success.[51] This would appear to be particularly appropriate for the case of victims of sexual offences and, perhaps more controversially, certain types of ex-offenders whose plight or past record is often publicised for no better reason than to satisfy the public's insatiable thirst for gossip and sensational journalism. Another question to be answered is the following: is the victim's anonymity best protected by a small fine (£500 according to section 4(5) of the Sexual Offences (Amendment) Act 1976) or are damages or an injunction (or some combination of the two) the most appropriate remedies? And then, of course, there is the question of free speech and the extreme to which the American courts (and, it is submitted, the English Court of Appeal in the first *Re X* case) have taken this interest in this type of privacy. A glance at the American solutions must, if anything, reinforce this belief that even free speech must be given certain limits. Free speech to criticise the Government is one thing; free speech that fattens the publishers' purses while hurting weaker individuals is another matter. Surely much can be learnt from the fine art of balancing competing interests undertaken by the superior German courts. Finally, one can enquire whether the transplantation of ideas and remedies is appropriate and technically feasible.[52] These issues have been approached in different ways. My own inclination in favour of the German position has been made clear. But what is more interesting to note is how the study of this subject can help explode two well-established myths: *first*, that the Germans work through statutes and that the common (especially English) lawyers work through cases and, *secondly*, that our judges are bold and make law whereas their judges are cautious and simply apply the Codes. In this area at least, German judges, remaining impervious to the pressures of the media—which have stunted all legislative intervention both in

[51] The Federal Constitutional Court in the decision of 3 June 1980, BVerfGE 54, 148, 153–4= NJW 1980, 2070–1 admitted that "Having regard to the special character of the general right to personality, the practice of the [courts] has been not to define the content of the protected right conclusively but to develop its features from case to case".

[52] In the English context, the existence of the two narrow enactments discussed in this text would pose a difficult technical problem: should they be widened by amending legislation or should the courts somehow develop the common law in order to fill those gaps in the statutory law that one deemed to be unacceptable? Other problems remain to be solved. For example, it is intriguing to speculate why the First Amendment has been used to curtail the right to anonymity of juveniles, rape victims and ex-criminals but has receded into the background in such recent cases as *Carson* v. *Here's Johnny Portable Toilets Inc.*, 698 F. 2d 831 (1983) where the court gave an extended and, arguably, excessive protection to the new and ill-defined "right of publicity". For criticism and further references, see Goldstein, "Comment" (1985) *Hastings J. of Communications and Entertainment Law* 319.

England and Germany—have displayed the characteristics usually attributed to their common law brothers. Thus, despite a number of important limitations in their Code, they have managed to transform the original framework and develop a set of rules which are sophisticated, humane and, I believe, just.

18

Subtle Ways of Legal Borrowing: Some Comparative Reflections on the Report of the Calcutt *Committee "On Privacy and Related Matters"*

1. HONOURING WERNER LORENZ

I was never, alas, a pupil of Professor Lorenz except in the wide sense of belonging to the large number of jurists who have learnt much from his varied and erudite work. At different times both of us, however, came under the spell of that great Oxford comparatist—the late Professor F. H. Lawson—and, I believe, it was largely because of this fact that Professor Lorenz kindly agreed to contribute a complimentary foreword to the first edition of my *German Law of Torts*.[1] It is thus with special pleasure that I am able to repay in a small way my many debts to him and his work by contributing a short piece to this *Festschrift*. The pleasure, however, has been accompanied by much agonising as to the selection of the right topic. Should one, for example, write about products liability, which the colleague that is being honoured helped put on the legal map in Germany?[2] Certainly it would have been interesting to inform European lawyers, busy expanding this area of liability, how the Americans, who once inspired them, appear to be trying to curtail some

---

[1] Which was published in 1986. The second edition, with a foreword by Lord Goff of Chieveley, appeared in 1990.

[2] With his "Rechtsvergleichendes zur Haftung des Warenherstellers und Lieferanten gegenüber Dritten", *Festschrift H. Nottarp* (1961), 58–89. Professor Lorenz has returned to this constantly evolving topic several times since. See, for example, "Warenabsatz und Vertrauensschutz", *Karlsruher Forum* (1963), 8–16; "Beweisprobleme bei der Produzentenhaftung", *AcP* 170 (1970), 367–91; "Einige rechtsvergleichende Bemerkungen zum gegenwärtigen Stand der Produktenhaftpflicht im deutschen Recht. Zur Entscheidung des Bundesgerichtshofs im 'Hühnerpest-Fall'", *RabelsZ* 34 (1970), 14–55; "Das internationale Privatrecht der Produktenhaftpflicht", *Festschrift E. Wahl* (1973), 185–206; "Some Comparative Aspects of the European Unification of the Law of Products Liability", (1975) 60 *Cornell Law Review* 1005–26; "Die Haftung des Produzenten für 'Design Defects' in den USA. Überlegungen zum 'Uniform Product Liability Act 1979'", *RIW/AWD* 1980, 609–16; "Die Beendigung von Vertriebsverträgen europäischer Produzenten mit Vertragshändlern in den Vereinigten Staaten von Amerika", *Festschrift K. Lipstein* (1980), 157–86; "The Duty of the Manufacturer Regarding 'Later Defects' ", (1989 9 *Tel Aviv Univ. Studies in Law*, 79–92).

of their worst abuses.[3] Or should one say something about the liability of accountants for pure economic loss caused by their negligent certifications?[4] In England the recent decision of the House of Lords in the *Caparo*[5] case not only shows the scope that modern comparatists may have to influence municipal law by highlighting foreign law; it also shows, especially when compared with the Court of Appeal decision,[6] that our supreme court (like so many others) is infallible because it is final and is not final because it is infallible. No doubt German lawyers must experience from time to time similar frustrations with their supreme court!

After such initial hesitation, I decided to add a few personal thoughts to the illuminating lecture that Professor Lorenz recently gave in London on the German law of privacy.[7] My choice of this subject was determined by the fact that it has lately attracted much attention in Great Britain. In this context, it is significant that both the Calcutt Committee,[8] which has recently made some very interesting recommendations on this subject, and our Court of Appeal[9] have shown their willingness to look at German law in their attempt to find an acceptable solution to this intractable problem. Finally, this subject gave Professor Lorenz the chance to demonstrate in his London Lecture one of the two greatest gifts that a comparative lawyer can possess. Quite simply this is to make foreign law intelligible to a jurist accustomed to operating in a different environment using different concepts and techniques. Perhaps, then, here one could emphasise the second and, in a sense, reverse gift that the comparatist must possess, namely the ability to transform an attractive foreign idea into a form or shape that becomes acceptable to his own system. The Calcutt Committee "On Privacy and Related Matters" may have shown itself very adept at understanding the significance of this point.

---

[3] On this see the seminal article by J. A. Henderson and Th. Eisenberg, "The Quiet Revolution in Products Liability: An Empirical Study of Legal Change", (1990) 37 *UCLA Law Review* 479.

[4] On which topic the honoree has made a learned contribution. Thus, see: "Das Problem der Haftung für primäre Vermögensschäden bei der Erteilung einer unrichtigen Auskunft", *Festschrift K. Larenz* (1973), 575–620. *See* also his contribution to the *Essays in Memory of the late Professor F. H. Lawson* (1986), 86–100, under the title "Some Thoughts about Contract and Tort".

[5] *Caparo Industries Plc* v. *Dickman* [1990] 2 WLR 358.

[6] [1989] 2 WLR 316. Lord Justice Bingham's careful judgment repays close study.

[7] "Privacy and the Press—a German Experience", *Butterworth Lectures 1989/90* (1990), 79–119.

[8] *Report of the Committee on Privacy and Related Matters*, henceforth referred to by the name of its Chairman, David Calcutt Q.C., Cmnd. 1102 (1990).

[9] In its decision of 23 February 1990 in *Gordon Kaye* v. *Andrew Robertson and Sport Newspapers Ltd*. The text of the judgment has not been officially reported despite the impact it had on the deliberations of the Calcutt Committee—a sad reflection on the selection criteria that determine which decisions are made available to the wider public! Fortunately, the Committee itself has reproduced the decision as Appendix 1 of its Report.

2. THE CASE LAW PROTECTION IN ENGLISH LAW

In my *Tort Law*[10] I devoted, somewhat unusually, eleven pages to the protection of privacy. I say unusually, for English law does not recognise a tort of unlawful invasion of human privacy; nor has the subject as a result of this received anything but a passing reference in English tort classes. The contrast with Germany is thus striking, not least since the privacy actions under §823I BGB seem, if anything, almost to have displaced the traditional defamation action (§187 StGB in conjunction with §823II BGB) and other, narrow, criminal provisions from the pride of place they held before the 1950s.

To say that English law does not have a tort of privacy is not, however, the same as to say that English law does not protect human privacy.[11] Rather one is stressing the patchy and case-by-case protection that various aspects of human privacy received more or less as they did in German law prior to the *Schacht* decision. The deficiencies of English law were made particularly obvious in the very recent *Kaye* decision concerning a well-known British television actor and this can help illustrate to a continental jurist the tortuous path an English litigant has to pursue in order to achieve the kind of protection that French and German courts have nowadays little difficulty in granting to their litigants.[12]

In *Gordon Kaye (by Peter Frogatt his next friend)* v. *Andrew Robertson and Sport Newspapers Ltd.* the Court of Appeal condemned an offensive intrusion into Mr Gordon Kaye's privacy and made what are, so far, the strongest appeals to Parliament to reform our patchy law on the important issue of privacy.[13]

Mr Kaye's sufferings started with the 1990 winter storms. He was severely injured by a broken section that fell from an advertisement boarding. It smashed through the windscreen of his car and severely injured his head. For three days after the incident (5 January) he was on a life-support machine; another seven days followed in intensive care. His condition remained critical throughout this period. Visits were severely restricted, not least in order to limit the risk of infection. As is usual, complete calm and peace were ordered to facilitate recovery; and so as to ensure that those medical decisions were observed, a special notice was pinned on the door of the room to this effect.

The two defendants were the editor and owning company of the *Sunday Sport*. This is a weekly publication which the judge at first instance described as having a "lurid and sensational style". Lord Justice Glidwell who, along

---

[10] Written with R.W.M. Dias, 2nd edn. (1989).

[11] As D. Seipp has shown in his "English Judicial Recognition of a Right of Privacy", (1983) *Oxford J.L. Studies* 324 *et seq.*

[12] See above n. 9. For a comparative discussion of American, English, and German law see my *The German Law of Torts—A Comparative Introduction*, 2nd edn. (1990), 270–328.

[13] Thus Lord Justice Glidewell said in the *Kaye* dispute: "The facts of the present case are a graphic illustration of the desirability of Parliament . . . to protect the privacy of individuals" (p. 100 of the Calcutt Report).

with his brother judges inspected some recent copies of this publication, thought it had a strong bias to pornography. The 4 March issue, which eventually published the Kaye story, leaves little doubt of this, since over a photo of Mr Kaye lying asleep (or, probably, unconscious) in bed is printed a photo of a scantily-clad woman with the title "red-hot Donna had four men in the snow".

Disregarding these notices the defendants' agent entered Mr Kaye's room where they photographed him with a flashlight and took an interview of sorts. At the trial the editor admitted—proudly one suspects—that his staff had achieved a "great old-fashioned scoop". He also accepted that other publications might well be willing to "pay large sums of money for the privilege" of talking to and photographing Mr Kaye. Though the defendants claimed Mr Kaye had consented to all this, the available medical evidence suggested that he was, at best, only in very limited control of his faculties. Indeed, a quarter of an hour after the alleged "voluntary" interview had taken place, Mr Kaye had no recollection of the event. Though in the subsequent publication the defendants claimed to have been motivated by a desire to inform Mr Kaye's fans of the state of his health, the facts described above (and given more fully in the judgment) point in another direction. For the average reader this lurid and sensational journalism must have had much baser motives.[14]

Mr Justice Potter issued a series of orders, in effect banning the publication of the story (in its original form). The defendants appealed and *Glidwell, Bingham* and Legatt LJJ's essentially upheld the plaintiff's claim but, as a result of their careful review of our patchy law, had to issue a more restricted order. Basically, this allowed the defendants to publish some photos and their story, provided they made it clear that neither had been obtained with Mr Kaye's consent and this they did. The reasoning of the learned justices as well as the reduced protection which, to their obvious regret, they were able to give to Mr Kaye, reveal (a) the legal contortions that have to be made in order to protect deserving victims and (b) the need to establish some wider principle of privacy. Indirectly, the case and judgments also show how inadequate the Press's current attempts are to demonstrate that they can police themselves on this matter.

The leading judgment was delivered by Lord Justice Glidwell; but the other two Justices delivered concurring opinions which present particular interest not least because of their comparative content. In these judgments four causes of action were considered. In inverse order of likely success they were: passing off, trespass to the person, libel and malicious falsehood.

Passing off was dealt with briefly. It was rejected since the case was not considered to be covered by the House of Lords' decision in *Warninck* v.

---

[14] *The Sunday Times* of 8 April 1990 carried a long story about the paper's publisher whom it described as the "soft-porn king" whose activities have earned him a place in the list of Britain's 200 richest people.

Townend and Sons.[15] The plaintiff's claim seemed to have foundered mainly on the grounds that he was "not in the position of a *trader* (italics supplied) in relation of his interest in his story about his accident". True, but an extension of the tort could have been made, indeed was almost made, in the case of *Sim* v. *Heinz*[16] where Heinz, the food manufacturers, apparently used the actor Ron Moody to simulate the voice of another well-known actor, Alastair Sim, in advertising their products. Mr Sim's attempt to obtain an interlocutory injunction on the grounds of defamation failed, though the alternative argument that an actor has an interest in his voice similar to the one that a trader has in his wares, held out some appeal both to McNair J. who heard the application at first instance,[17] and to Hodson L.J.[18] who decided the case on appeal. *Sim* v. *Heinz* which was not, apparently, cited to or by the court in either *Warninck* or *Kaye* shows that an extension of this very "commercial" tort could be attempted in order to avoid the "grave defect in the law [of allowing one] party, for the purpose of commercial gain, to make use of the voice of another party without his consent".[19] And if that could be done for the voice of an actor, why not for his image, especially when the appropriation of the likeness is used to enrich another person?

The attempt to use trespass to protect Mr Kaye did not fare much better. Two reasons were given, the first more convincing than the second.

First, because no case could be found to support the view that the taking of the flashlight photograph amounted to battery; and secondly that there was no causal evidence to show that, as a result of their act, Mr Kaye had suffered distress and a set-back in recovery. In Lord Justice Glidwell's words there was "no evidence that the taking of the photographs did in fact cause him [Mr Kaye] any damage". The second point is, it is submitted, not very telling since battery is a tort action *per se* and will succeed without proof of any damage. But the first point presented a greater obstacle given that, apparently "there can be no battery unless there is *contact* with the plaintiff".[20] Now, flashlight contact might be treated as sufficiently close to physical contact to justify, as Glidwell L.J. was willing to entertain, an extension of the tort of battery. It must be noted, however, that in novel situations the current tendency is to resort to the tort of negligence rather than expand the older tort of battery and even to bypass the latter tort by having resort to criminal law. Why not then try negligence? This ever-growing tort, unlike battery, requires proving the existence of a duty of care—something which would have caused no problem in the instant case; but it also required proof of damage which, as stated, was not forthcoming. It may thus be that the two elements of the two torts

[15] [1979] AC 731.
[16] [1959] 1 WLR 313.
[17] *Ibid*. at p. 317.
[18] *Ibid*. at p. 319.
[19] *Sim* v. *Heinz* [1959] 1 WLR 313, 317.
[20] Street, *On Torts*, 8th edn. (1988), 23.

were inadvertently telescoped into one. Clearly, the learned judge regarded this part of his judgment as secondary to the main thrust of his arguments which came in the remaining two causes of action: libel and malicious falsehood.

Libel was, according to Glidwell and Bingham LJJ's, strongly arguable. *Tolley* v. *J. S. Fry and Sons Ltd.*[21] was the authority that persuaded the judge who heard the application at first instance; and it also appealed to the learned justices. If it was not used in the end it was because of the rule in *Williams Coulson & Sons* v. *James Coulson and Co.*[22] which held that interim injunctions are to be used sparingly in libel actions—a rule confirmed in *Herbage* v. *Times Newspapers Limited and others* (unreported), despite the decision of the House of Lords in *American Cynamid* v. *Ethicon*.[23] So, though the justices felt that the publication was libellous, they also felt that a jury might well not take the same view and, in the circumstances, a general injunction should not be and was not granted.

But was the publication libellous on the authority of *Tolley* v. *Fry*? *Tolley* succeeded because an *innuendo* was discovered. It was in 1931—but would it still be now?—defamatory for an amateur golfer to give the impression that he had "prostituted his amateur status for gain". But the *ratio* of the case would not have covered a professional golfer even though he, too, needs (perhaps even more strongly than the amateur) to prevent the unauthorised use of his image. So where is the *innuendo* here? Given the nature of the publication in question, one could argue that any respectable member of society who appears to be associated with the *Sunday Sport* is automatically defamed. But the learned justice, hinting, perhaps, at this possibility, was right in suggesting that such "a conclusion is [not] inevitable". And if a jury were to decide that there was no defamation, that would be the end of Mr Kaye's interest to be left in peace in his hospital bed. Yet, as Lord Justice Bingham said, "If ever a person has a right to be left alone by strangers with no public interest to pursue, it must surely be when he lies in hospital recovering from brain surgery and in no more than partial command of his faculties". And yet this right, *de lege lata*, depends on the quaint facts of *Tolley* v. *Fry*; and the result, judging from the Court of Appeal judgment in *Tolley*[24] was not so obvious

---

[21] [1931] AC 333.

[22] (1887) 3 TLR 46. The impression that this writer has is that the defences of justification or fair comment that are often advanced at the interlocutory stage, become unconvincing at the trial stage. They have, however, succeeded in stopping the issuing of an injunction and this, in cases which cry out for a quick correction, can be disastrous for the plaintiff. This consequence, coupled with the unavailability of legal aid, and in defamation cases, the total inability to compel an apology, tilts the scales of justice heavily in favour of media defendants who, I believe, retain the upper hand until the case comes to full trial. From that moment onwards the scales may tip in favour of the persevering plaintiff as juries express their growing dislike for the tabloid press through the medium of extravagant awards.

[23] [1957] AC 395.

[24] [1930] 1 KB 467.

even in those halcyon days of the 1930s when sportsmen played for their sport and not for money!

In the end Mr Kaye succeeded by the skin of his teeth because the justices were able to rely on the tort of malicious falsehood. This is not an easy tort, as any reading of a textbook will reveal; nor is it frequently used either. But, at least, it avoided the injunction problems of *Coulson* v. *Coulson* since in malicious falsehood the test of that case[25] applies only to the requirement that the plaintiff must show that the words are false; and the (original) statement by the *Sunday Sport* that the photos and interview were taken with Mr Kaye's consent were, clearly, false.

So Mr Kaye won; but won only a limited protection in that the publication of the photos and story could only go ahead if the paper made it clear that they were taken without his consent. Moreover he won, but only just, because judges anxious to do justice were willing "to be persuaded" that something, somehow, should be done. In this, they were following other distinguished courts which had tried to put old torts on the procrustean bed in order to protect privacy[26] or resort to old procedures (wardship)[27] in order to rectify the patchy way in which English law has faced a new problem: our increased ability to collect, collate and disseminate information about other persons under the pretence of *public* interest but, often, for no better reason than *private* gain.

3. THE REPORT OF THE CALCUTT COMMITTEE

The late Sir Otto Kahn Freund, who like most of the distinguished British and American comparatists was of Germanic origins, once wrote that use of the comparative method can make national lawyers feel both "humble and proud" about their own law.[28] The ingenuity of English lawyers in stretching and twisting existing torts to cope with the modern dimensions of the problem of invading human privacy must provide illuminating material to German or, come to that, French lawyers in the art of using case law both in the classroom and the court. But it must also make them feel proud at the richness and effectiveness of their own law. The *Gordon Kaye* case, for example, would cause little difficulty in these two systems. Thus, in Germany, §823 I BGB and the *ratio decidendi* in the *Paul Dahlke* decision[29] would, I suspect,

---

[25] *Ibid.* In the *Kaye* case the *Sunday Sport* had originally stated that Mr Kaye's photographs were taken *with* his consent. After the Court of Appeal ruling the photographs were reproduced but, in accordance with the Court's decisions, the statement was added that they were taken *without* his consent.

[26] *Bernstein* v. *Skyviews and General Ltd.* [1978] QB 479.

[27] *Re X* [1984] 1 WLR 1422, discussed in Markesinis, *The German Law of Torts—A Comparative Introduction*, 2nd edn. (1990).

[28] "Comparative Law as an Academic Subject" (1966) 82 LQR 40, 60.

[29] BHGZ 20, 345, 354–5. In his Butterworths Lecture, *op. cit.* above n. 7, p. 119, Professor Lorenz has suggested that the *Soraya* case (BGH NJW 1965, 685; BVerfGE 34, 269)—which dealt

provide a satisfactory remedy for the plaintiff; but a remedy under the general right of personality would not be the only one. The violation of the right to one's portrait under §22 of the Law of Artistic Creations could be combined with paragraph 823 I BGB and give relief under this key provision of the Civil Code. (The exception of §23 II No. 1 of that same Act would be inapplicable in this case.[30]) The use of extremely bright flashlight might, at a stretch, amount to *Körperverletzung*, though the German courts would, probably, experience here difficulties similar to those encountered by the court in the *Kaye* case when considering the suitability of the action of trespass. The owner/occupier of the building (as, perhaps, the English hospital in the *Kaye* case) might, in certain circumstances, also be able to obtain a criminal sanction under paragraph 123 StGB (*Hausfriedensbruch*), though this would probably not give a civil remedy to the patient/plaintiff under §823 II BGB since he would not be deemed to be covered by the ambit (*Schutzbereich*) of the norm in question.

In France, too, a plaintiff in Mr Kaye's position would find himself equipped with an impressive array of criminal and civil remedies. Thus, article 184.2 of the Criminal Code (criminal trespass in a dwelling) might be applicable since the word dwelling (*domicile*) has been interpreted very widely to include hotel clients using a hotel room, even for one night only.[31] Articles 368–71 of the Criminal Code deal with what are known as *atteintes à l'intimité personnelle*, and were enacted in 1970 contemporaneously with the introduction of the new article 9 of the Civil Code which protects *l'intimité de la vie privée*. These criminal provisions punish the listening to, recording or transmission (always by mechanical means) of words spoken in a private place (note: *dans un lieu privé* and not *en privé*) by a person without his permission, or the recording or transmission of his image, again without his permission. (In both cases the punishment can be a fine of between 2–60,000 FF and a term of imprisonment of up to two years.) The violation of article 9 of the Civil Code can lead to an award of damages, the ordering of the publication of an appropriate apology and, even, the confiscation of the offending publication. That is quite a collection of remedies; and, on the whole, they have

with a fictitious interview with the divorced wife of the former Shah of Iran—most resembles the *Kaye* case "for there is no substantial difference between an interview which has never taken place and an interview obtained from a person who was in a state of subconsciousness". Incidentally, the *Soraya* case has a French counterpart involving Marlene Dietrich—*see* Paris 16.3.1955, D. 1955, 295. The sums awarded by German courts are, by Anglo-American standards, small—usually in the order of 4–5,000 DM. But there have been a handful of larger awards—the protracted litigation involving the Nobel Laureat Heinrich Böll offering, perhaps, the most interesting example. He was finally awarded 40,000 DM: BGH, NJW 1982, 635.

[30] See BGHZ 24, 200, 210.

[31] Crim. 31 janv. 1914, D.P. 1918.1.76; R. Merle and A. Vitu, *Traité de droit criminel. Droit pénal spécial*, vol. I (1982) nos. 296 *et seq.*; vol. II (1982) nos. 2020 *et seq.* This provision is thus, apparently, given a wider scope than §123 StGB.

proved very effective. Thus, the photographing of Brigitte Bardot,[32] Catherine Deneuve[33] and Romy Schneider[34] has, on different occasions, been condemned, despite the public profile of the plaintiffs, and been accompanied by the imposition of all or some of the above-mentioned sanctions. Also severely reprimanded was the photographing in his sick-bed in hospital of the young son of the actor Gérard Philippe;[35] and even President Pompidou, suing in a private capacity, succeeded in stopping the use of his image in a commercial advertisement.[36] Finally, in addition to the above provisions, French litigants are always free to invoke article 8 of the European Convention on Human Rights and article 17 of the International Covenant of Civil and Political Rights, both of which form part of French municipal law. Overall, however, one observes a marked tendency to invoke the provisions of the Civil Code.[37]

Compared with the above, the Kaye case, British academic writings, and the Calcutt Report all show how varied, rich, and yet woefully patchy the English remedies are, especially when compared with those found in such systems as the German, French and Dutch. Why?

Mono-causal explanations can never be satisfactory to such complex questions. The case-by-case approach of the English common law may be one reason for this difference in approach. Deeply-ingrained techniques do not change overnight, though the study of the American law often shows how one must be careful not to treat those two systems as the same, both in general and on the topic under discussion. The absence of a written constitution and/or the lack of incorporation into municipal law of international conventions such as the European Convention on Human Rights may also explain the lack of an incentive, lying outside the realm of what European lawyers would call the civil (private) law, to bring the latter into line with ethical and legal values contained in a "superior" document. Yet if one reason above others were to be chosen I think it would probably be found in the British

---

[32] 24 nov. 1965, J.C.P. 1966. II.14521. The action was directed against the *Daily Express* for publishing a photograph (taken with tele-lens) of the actress with her young son at her home. The defendants were condemned on the basis of art. 1382 CC to (a) pay nominal damages; (b) publish the judgment condemning their activity in the same prominent place that they had published the photographs; (c) meet the cost of a similar publication in those papers of Miss Bardot's choice and (d) carry the costs of the trial. Mr. Lindon's note to the case provides interesting information from the pleadings. See also 23 fév. 1967, D.1967, 450.

[33] 14 mai 1975, D. 1976, 291. 10,000 FF were awarded in this case to Miss Deneuve for a nude photograph taken by her husband but published by *Lui* without her permission.

[34] 5 juin 1979, J.C.P. 1980.II.19 343. 20,000 FF were awarded to Miss Schneider for nude photos taken by tele-lens on her yacht which was moored out at sea. The defendant/journal was also ordered to publish an apology.

[35] J.C.P. 1965.II.14 223; D. 1967, 181. The issue that carried the pictures of young Philippe was confiscated by order of the court. The fact that some of these pictures had appeared elsewhere carried no weight with the court which thought that the taking of the photographs amounted to *"une immixtion intolérable dans la vie privée de la famille Philippe"*.

[36] 4 avril 1970, J.C.P. 1970.II.16 328.

[37] For a full discussion of French law see P. Kayzer, *La Protection de la vie privée* (1984); R. Lindon, *Dictionnaire juridique—Les droits de la personalité* (1983)—both replete with references to the interesting case law.

Press, its varied membership, and its insistence on being effectively the main if not the sole arbiter of its activities even though its track record on this matter has been less than satisfactory.

In frustrating repeated attempts to legislate on these matters the Press and a fair number of commentators have advanced three broad arguments. *First*, privacy cannot be defined in a legally satisfactory manner and, in any event, most of the necessary protection could be achieved through the law of defamation or breach of confidence. *Secondly*, any attempts to legislate on the matter would impair investigative journalism and dilute the proper and worthy function that a free Press must perform in a democratic society. *Thirdly*, policing the inevitable digressions from accepted norms of behaviour should be done by those who understand the industry and this means the Press itself, Press Ombudsmen, the Press Council, but not lawyers and judges. That all these arguments—crudely enumerated here[38]—have some merit cannot, really, be doubted. And yet it is submitted they cannot be determinative if one is to judge by the fact that many other societies, in most respects similar to ours, have managed to find answers to these objections and achieve a more delicate balance between competing interests. Let us, therefore, look at these objections briefly, leaving the first of them—the more legalistic—for the end.

The British Press prides itself on its investigative journalism; it also believes that it is in this respect more rigorous in this role than, say, the French or German Press. It is not for a foreign, non-expert, observer to contradict this statement though his general impression from reading foreign publications would cast doubts on the English claims. Certainly *Le Canard Enchaîné* or *Der Spiegel*, to mention two foreign publications, have had their share of rows with authorities and important personalities who felt that they were pursuing their investigative functions rather too seriously. But the point, surely, lies elsewhere. Political investigative journalism is one thing; photographing, taping, harassing private citizens, often for the purpose of pure sensationalism and gain must be another. The *Lebach*[39] criteria of balancing the competing interests of free speech and privacy strike this observer not only as admirable

---

[38] Another argument against legislation was that there was no evidence of serious infringement of privacy. Though the Calcutt Committee "found no reliable evidence to show whether unwarranted intrusion into individual privacy has or has not risen over the last 20 years" (paras. 4–8), I am inclined to agree with Lord Alexander of Weedon's publicly expressed view that "few would think today that the problem was not serious. We have only to think of recent intrusions into the private lives of members of the Royal Family, of the publication of stories revealing details of the lives of hitherto unknown individuals, or of the way in which victims of tragedies or disasters are sometimes pursued, to realise that there is clearly scope for securing protection for individuals": *The Daily Telegraph*, 21 January 1989. The 36th Annual Report of the Press Council (published after the Calcutt Committee had published its report) states that overall there were 1484 new complaints in 1989 compared with 1421 in 1988 (p. 11). Despite the adoption of a new code of conduct, newspaper ombudsmen and the general perception that recourse to such bodies will hardly help victims, the number of complaints during the first seven months of 1990 have, apparently, increased from 803 to 995.

[39] BVerfGE 35, 202, translated in my *German Law of Torts—A Comparative Introduction*, 2nd edn. (1990), 308–15.

but also as totally compatible with the common law desire to handle each case on its facts. The harassment by the Press of the victims of, say, the *Zeebrugge* disaster,[40] and the *Kaye* case itself, show that in cases such as these the media's desire to report the news (occasionally exaggerating it or even distorting it in order to make it even more newsworthy) may well have to take second place to the victims' need for peace and privacy.

The argument that a greater protection of privacy might impede investigative journalism was in various forms advanced before the Calcutt Committee. *The Times* has, on several occasions, advanced this view forcefully and an important extract from one of its leading articles deserves to be quoted more fully:[41]

> "It is none the less the sincere conviction of responsible journalists, from *every type of newspaper* that *any* law to enforce ethical conduct—by attempting, for instance, to prohibit the invasion of privacy—would seriously harm the public interest. In the name of protecting the innocent, it would shelter the guilty. *Many a crooked alderman would sleep easier in his bed, knowing the press was barred from making the enquiries that might bring the disgrace he deserved* . . . The right of journalists—to ask questions, state facts, express opinions—are in essence no different from the rights of the citizenry at large. They rest on an identical perception of what it means to be free. Held inalienably by journalists and non-journalists alike, they constitute the right to freedom of speech itself. If that is curtailed, it is curtailed for everyone, and that would be to the detriment of democracy." (*italics supplied.*)

Read in the lively and deliberately controversial ambience of a classroom these words—especially if considered against the background of the *Gordon Kaye* type of case considered here—might well prompt the cynical comment that the respectable newspaper of a publishing empire was invoking high moral principles so that the lurid activities of some of its less respectable sister papers could continue to prosper. In the more reflective setting of a legal essay the word hyperbole springs to mind. Misleading hyperbole in fact, since it deliberately merges into one category cases which, as stated, should be kept

---

[40] Dr. W. Yule, Professor of Applied Child Psychology in the University of London, has treated many of the survivors and relatives of victims of such major disasters as the *Zeebrugge* tragedy, the *City of Poros* terrorist attack and the sinking of the *Jupiter*. In his submission to the Calcutt Committee, which he has kindly allowed me to see, he describes how photographers "blocked victims' access to ambulances", "screamed at one girl asking her to show more tears" so that they could photograph her and, apparently, "tripped another girl so that she could be separated from the party" and thereby interviewed. He concludes that "there is a need for better education of reporters . . . about the impact of trauma on victims so that the reporters fully appreciate that for hours or days after a major event people are too numb to be able to give informed consent to interviews. Clearly, most will agree that reporters should never impede any aspect of rescue, including the need for survivors to telephone home. Any help that reporters give should never be contingent on 'exclusive' stories [as happened in one case] as that is an abuse of power". It is doubtful whether such modestly-couched suggestions will, in the absence of effective legal sanctions, ever be heeded by the news-thirsty staff of the gutter press.

[41] 28 November 1989.

separate in two. The critics of the Calcutt Report do not seem to have given much thought to the need to make this distinction.[42]

So we come to the second excuse. Adjudication on misbehaviour should be undertaken by other bodies—actually or apparently independent of the Press—but not the judges who cannot be trusted to perform such a task. This view, which if it had been put forward to a trade union leader in the context of a trade dispute would have attracted the full wrath of this paper, was, in this context, espoused by *The Times* itself in the following grandiloquent passage contained in its editorial of 25 January 1989:

> "In the history of freedom won by the Press, restrictions have a general tendency to become wider in their compass, not narrower. Lord Alexander[43] enjoins us to put our faith in judges. *We would betray our duty to a free press to be so trusting of those who are themselves so fallible and inconsistent*" (italics supplied).

Self-control is thus better according to this school of thought; and the major newspaper owners still seem to prefer it as they have—reluctantly one assumes—accepted the Calcutt Committee suggestion to set up a Press Complaints Commission in order to avoid further statutory regulation.[44] Outside the newspaper industry this view seems to have the support of at least one of our most learned judges, the Vice-Chancellor Sir Nicolas Browne Wilkinson who, in his address to the International Press Institute assembly in Istanbul in 1988 said:[45]

> "I think it is extremely difficult for a legal system to apply a general concept of privacy, because it is hard to distinguish what is meant by it. On the other hand, it seems to me impossible to draw a comprehensive list of those things which, in any one society, are to be treated as private. *As a legal technician, I would be unhappy dealing with the law of privacy. It seems to me that the legal difficulty of defining what is privacy and what are the proper defences are too elaborate. The courts I would have to say, are quite good at some things, but they are not famed for their delicacy of touch, and when you have matters which are a very complicated balancing of imponderables, where the essence of the matter is flexibility, not certainty, I believe the courts may not be the ideal body to administer it*" (italics supplied).

This statement will, no doubt, surprise continental European lawyers who have a very different perception of common law judges. The Continental case law, however, might surprise our Vice Chancellor even more since it shows how what he regards as difficult (if not impossible) can be and has been achieved. Are our judges less imaginative or creative than their Continental brethren? Has our law of confidence not been developed by them? Indeed, is not the better part of our administrative law the product of their minds? Personally, I find such judicial timidity unconvincing, when we consider how

---

[42] Thus, see the attack by Hugo Young published in *The Guardian* of 26 June 1990.
[43] Article mentioned above n. 38.
[44] See *The Times*, 6 August 1990.
[45] Quoted by the Calcutt Report at p. 47.

our judges have over the centuries responded to social pressures and filled some of the most glaring gaps in our law. In any event, at the end of the day the crucial question is not how good our judges *might turn out to be* in fleshing out the statutory provision some of them think is necessary, but how effective the Press Council *has been* since its inception in 1953.

The Press Council is currently comprised of thirty-six members, eighteen Press representatives and eighteen laymen and, according to its current constitution, has as its objectives, *inter alia*, the preservation of the established freedom of the British Press and the investigation of complaints about the conduct of the press. Its history, functions and record is briefly given in Chapter 14 of the Calcutt Committee Report. Two features stand out from their very readable summary. First that the newspaper industry has, all along, been fighting a rear-guard action. Opposition, delay, or hurriedly-prepared proposals for self-reform have all been tried as three Royal Commissions and the Younger Committee investigated the possibilities of Press self-regulation and, over the years, tinkered with various proposals for improvements. Yet, overall, the work of the Press Council has, at best, received very mixed reactions, its impartiality has been doubted, its effectiveness as an adjudicating body increasingly questioned. This last and most serious condemnation has been prompted partly by the Council's inability and unwillingness to offer any remedies to complainants other than publication of its adjudication in the complaint, and partly by its insistence that complainants waive any legal right they may have against the paper in question before the Council investigates the complaint. The Press Council was, in short, a watchdog without teeth and, indeed, with the expressed desire never to acquire any teeth! No wonder that the Calcutt Committee stated that[46] "We do not consider that the Press Council, even if reformed as proposed in its internal review, should be kept as part of the system". The Committee thus "recommended that the Press Council should be disbanded and replaced by a new body, specifically charged with adjudicating on complaints of press malpractice". "This body" the Committee went on, "must be seem to be authoritative, independent and impartial. It must also have jurisdiction over the press as a whole, must be adequately funded and must provide a means of seeking to prevent publication of intrusive material". The Committee concluded: "We consider it particularly important to emphasise the break with the past. The new body should, therefore, be called the Press Complaints Commission".

Finally, let us briefly consider the last, and in some respects, major objection that the newspaper industry has advanced against the right of privacy. This is the notion's inherent vagueness coupled with the claim that other parts of the law can fill the gap that may currently exist.

The Calcutt Committee deals with this, the core issue, in the twelfth chapter of its Report. For a variety of reasons, which may be taken to suggest that

---

[46] Para. 14.38.

the Committee may have found this a difficult issue to agree upon in its private deliberations, the Committee stresses that "an *overwhelming* case for introducing a statutory tort of infringement of privacy has *not so far* been made out" (*italics supplied*). The possibility of doing so in the future is expressly not foreclosed; and in a key passage (para. 12.12) the Committee clearly states that "our grounds for recommending against a new tort do *not* . . . include difficulties of definition". The point is, further on, put in affirmative terms (paras. 12.17 and 12.18): "We are satisfied that it would be possible to define a statutory tort of infringement of privacy". And how could it be otherwise? In the United States, definitional difficulties have been overcome by the common law aided, in some instances, by statute; in Germany, by imaginative courts following a very common law and case-by-case method; in France first (and mainly) by relying on a very general tort provision (article 1382 of the Civil Code) and later by adding a general clause of privacy in the Civil Code and a number of specific provisions in the Criminal Code;[47] in Switzerland through a skilful combination of statutory provisions which in the words of two eminent German comparatists,[48] "are as specific as is possible and as general as is necessary"; finally, in various Canadian Provinces (such as British Columbia and Saskatchewan) by means of specific statutes.[49] The Committee rightly refused to be defeated by definitional difficulties (real or imagined) and expressed its thoughts on this in a way[50] which is as convincing in its substance as it is English in its tone:

"We accept that it would be impracticable to create a general wrong of infringement of privacy, since this would give rise to an unacceptable degree of uncertainty. However, this would not necessarily rule out the formulation of a tort directed towards the publication of personal information to the world at large. The absence of a precise or exhaustive definition has not presented insuperable problems in the areas of negligence and defamation. Concepts such as the 'reasonable man' and 'right thinking member of society' are to be found in daily use. We consider, therefore, that it would be possible to define a satisfactory tort of infringement of privacy (and we show in paragraph 12.17–12.18 how this might be done)".

What, then, of the related argument that privacy, even if definable, need not be the subject of a new statutory regime since defamation and breach of confidence can provide adequate protection from existing gaps? The recent

---

[47] See text and above nn. 31–6. Still further provisions protect particular types of violations of privacy. Thus, to the list given above, add: article 378 of the Criminal Code (protection of professional secrecy); article 187 Criminal Code (protection of the inviolability of the mail); article 35 of the Law of the Press of 1881 (private life of plaintiff in defamation actions); article 6 of the law of 17 July 1978 dealing with the right to have access to administrative documents (this right may be curtailed when disclosure might harm *le secret de la vie privée*); article 4 and 31 of the law of 6 January 1978 dealing with Data Protection etc.

[48] Zweigert and Kötz, *An Introduction to Comparative Law*, 2nd edn., translated by T. Weir (1987), 399.

[49] Reproduced in Appendices D and E in the Calcutt Report, pp. 88 and 90 respectively.

[50] Para. 12.12.

Chairman of the Press Council, Mr Louis Blom-Cooper Q.C., argued the former point when he said:[51]

> "The demand for legislation needs to be assessed in the broader context of the relevant law relating to defamation and confidentiality. The injury inflicted by an invasion of privacy bears a *striking resemblance [sic]* to the wrong for which a remedy is provided in the law of defamation. Both appear to touch on wounded feelings, beyond *amour propre* . . ."

With respect, the point is unconvincing (as Mr Blom-Cooper admits further down in his article) since defamation in English law is narrower than privacy but also because the privacy we are dealing with in these cases is connected with true *facts*, the revelation of which can be more hurtful than *lies* with which defamation is concerned.[52] Nor is the present law of confidence able to cover the existing gaps since the law of confidence is not designed to protect individual privacy where there is no confidential relationship between the confider and the confidant (whether contractual or otherwise). At best the developing law of confidence could cover some types of infringements—but the *Kaye* case among others clearly shows its limitations.

4. CONCLUDING OBSERVATIONS

The Committee's refusal to recommend (at this stage) the introduction of a statutory tort of infringement of privacy has cheered some members of the Press. Simon Jenkins, a member of the Committee and now the (Senior) Editor of *The Times* was thus able to claim[53] that "the Calcutt's conclusion was, in essence, no different from that of the Younger Committee of 1972" in taking a view against the tort of privacy. The statement, factually accurate in a narrow sense, is disingenuous since the Calcutt Committee (Mr Jenkins concurring): (a) not only rejected, as we saw, the definition difficulties of the concept as a determinant argument (and this differed from the Younger Report), but it also (b) recommended a series of new criminal offences (leading to civil remedies as well) that would, for example, provide plaintiffs in cases like Mr Kaye's with effective remedies,[54] (c) increased the anonymity for victims of sexual offences for reasons which this author has been advocating for over five years now[55] and (d) envisaged a new body (or bodies) to take over the

---

[51] *The Times*, 25 January 1989.

[52] Compare Professor J. Fleming's observation in his excellent *The American Tort Process* (1988), 100: "in competition with freedom of information, privacy has higher credentials than reputation, precisely because it concerns matters of private interest whereas reputation duplicates a public concern."

[53] *The Times*, 22 June 1990.

[54] See text of the Report at the end of this contribution.

[55] See my letter to *The Times* of 26 March 1986 quoted with approval in the House of Lords Debates, Hansard (H.L.) 1987, pp. 962, 1319; my article in *The Times* of 18 November 1987 (written jointly with John Spencer who was subsequently a member of the Calcutt Committee); and

ineffective work of the Press Council. The Committee's Report will require careful reading. Lack of space makes it impossible to elaborate here its proposals so it is best to reproduce at the end of this contribution the Committee's own summary recommendations. A few words, however, may be desirable as to the technique adopted by the recommendations.

The recommendations as well as the Report are first and foremost notable for their pragmatic nature. A comparative lawyer can also see in them a subtle comparative influence—sometimes explicit but often implicit. It is the combination of these two ideas that makes this document so fascinating to a comparatist.

In my published work[56] as a comparative lawyer I have always advocated that one should concentrate one's efforts on relatively narrow areas of the law, study them in some depth (by looking, among other things, at cases, the socio-ecoomic background and actual court practice), and then show how one's own law can benefit from such a study. As Lord Goff put it recently in an extra-judicial context: "To be influential in a more practical way, comparative law material has to be far more closely focused: and, not only that, it has to be readily comprehensible, practically orientated, and thoroughly reliable, by which I mean both accurate and up to date".[57] In its efforts to avoid the straight-jacket of individual torts the Court of Appeal in the *Kaye* case did not conceal its preference for a wider definition of privacy which two of the justices were able to find in American and German law. The willingness to look abroad for ideas (as to what to do and what to avoid) is also manifested in the Calcutt Committee, the Report of which bears many references to, inter alia, Dutch, French, German and Scottish law.

The comparative lawyer, however, must not only describe foreign law in a way that is comprehensible to his own nationals; if the foreign solution contains an interesting idea he must also find ways to make it transplantable into his own system. The time for a statutory tort of privacy was not, apparently, ripe; and a general clause formulation would, it seems, have been alien to the English drafting techniques. Personally I regret that the Committee did not recognise a tort of infringement of privacy. Yet I also admire the pragmatism that runs throughout the Report. For Mr Calcutt must have rightly sensed that a unanimous report would have a far greater chance of being accepted by the Government and its recommendations somehow being enacted. He and his Committee must have also realised that a series of criminal offences, coupled with some hitherto unnoticed civil sanctions, could significantly enlarge the protection of deserving victims without requiring a privacy bill to be placed

---

my comparative article in [1986] *Public Law* pp. 67–82 entitled "The Right to be Let Alone v. Freedom of Speech". The author's views were subsequently espoused by, among others, Professor J. Temkin, *Rape and the Legal Process* (1987), 197.

[56] Most recently see "Comparative Law—A Subject in Search of an Audience' (1990) 53, M.L.R. 1–21.

[57] Foreword to my *German Law of Torts—A Comparative Introduction*, 2nd edn. (1990).

before Parliament. Instead, its various proposals can and might well be included in various Administration of Justice Bills or Criminal Justice Bills; and, if not slipped unnoticed through Parliament, they will certainly pass with lesser opposition that one otherwise could expect from a major privacy bill.

How much of all this new thinking will become law? This is difficult to predict at this stage even though the Home Secretary has accepted the recommendations of the Report. Also difficult to predict is the nature of the amendments that will, no doubt, be proposed as the bill or bills go through the two houses of Parliament. The Press, for example, may object that the defence proposed in recommendation 2(a), namely that the intrusion into private property was done for the purpose of detecting or exposing any "seriously anti-social conduct" is too vague. Such a point would merit careful consideration, though one should also note that the vagueness occurs in a defence to criminal liability and not the definition of the offence. Looking at the Report from a different perspective one might complain that the Calcutt Committee was too timid when it limited the new offences it proposed in its first recommendation to the taking of photographs or recording voices "with a view to publication". This formulation may adequately cover the media; and since the Committee was appointed "to consider what measures . . . are needed to give further protection to individual privacy from the activities *of the Press [sic]*. . ." one can understand why the Committee did not criminalise mere snooping.[58] On the other hand, if the unauthorised collecting of data from private property was not made an offence whenever it was done solely for the purposes of providing information to the intruder, then private information would be protected as against a prying press but not, say, an industrial spy. In the absence of American-type punitive damages such an intruder would, at best, be subjected to nominal (or very low) tort damages for trespass[59]—a state of affairs which, clearly, requires a closer investigation before it is allowed to be enshrined into a statute.

Equally difficult is to say how the Press Complaints Commission will turn out in practice. Past history suggests that the chances of success for the Commission must be low even though the major Press barons now appear anxious to support it in order to avoid the setting up of the Press Complaints Tribunal envisaged by the Calcutt Report. The reason why one expresses this doubt is because, unlike other professions, journalists do not have to belong to the club that may censure their misbehaviour. *Maverick* newspapers—as the Calcutt Committee Report called them—will always exist that will work outside the framework that the major newspapers owners will set up. Indeed,

---

[58] There is a hint of this in para. 6.32 of the Report.

[59] Unless violence was used to secure entry, in which case it would be an offence under section 6 of the Criminal Law Act 1977. In Chapter 6 of the Report the *Calcutt* Committee gives various reasons why it refused to consider the possibility of an offence of criminal trespass on private property. Though this may be understandable given the Committee's terms of reference, I remain unconvinced that the proposed new offences should be tied to the intention to publish and thus be limited to the media.

the more the established Press barons reform their ways, the more will others be tempted to move in to satisfy the appetite for gossip and curiosity that human beings develop for the misfortunes or difficulties of their fellow men and women. Since the public's appetite for gossip is insatiable there will always be journalists who will say that their activities, however lurid, unpleasant or unnecessarily hurtful to some are in the interest of others. It is for lawyers to argue, however, that not everything that interests the public must be published in the public interest. The quest for balancing competing interests is thus bound to continue. The Calcutt preference for new, narrow, criminal sanctions may thus not remove the need for a wider statutory tort of wrongful invasion of privacy. Such a move from individual crimes to wider torts is noticeable in the civil systems; and it may well be found one day in the English common law as well. If sections of the Press continue to misbehave themselves the arguments for an even wider protection of privacy will be found in the chapter of the Calcutt Report which, on its face, rejected the establishment of a broader tort.

Calcutt Committee Report: Summary of the Recommendations

Physical Intrusion

1. The following acts should be criminal offences in England and Wales:

(a) entering private property, without the consent of the lawful occupant, with an intent to obtain personal information with a view to its publication;

(b) placing a surveillance device on private property, without the consent of the lawful occupant, with intent to obtain personal information with a view to its publication; and

(c) taking a photograph, or recording the voice, of an individual who is on private property, without his consent, with a view to its publication and with intent that the individual shall be identifiable.[60]

2. It should be a defence to any of these proposed offences that the act was done:

(a) for the purpose of preventing, detecting or exposing the commission of any crime, or other seriously anti-social conduct; or

---

[60] For the purpose of these offences we would define private property as any private residence, together with its immediate curtilage (garden and outbuildings), but excluding any adjacent fields or parkland. In addition, it should cover hotel bedrooms (but not other areas in a hotel) and those parts of a hospital or nursing home where patients are treated or accommodated. (In such cases the lawful occupant should be regarded as the relevant Health Authority or proprietor.) For the offence [described in 1 (c), above] to be committed it would not be necessary for the offender himself to enter on to private property. To these offences the ordinary principles of criminal responsibility would apply, and it would therefore be necessary to show that the defendant knew or was reckless as to the fact that private property was involved before he could be guilty of an offence (paragraph 6.34).

(b)   for the protection of public health or safety; or

(c)   under any lawful authority.

3.   An individual having a sufficient interest should be able to apply for an injunction against the publication of any material obtained by means of any of these criminal offences or, if the material has already been published, for damages or an account of profits.

4.   Further consideration should be given to the extent to which the law in Scotland needs to be extended to cover the proposed offences and civil remedy and how this might best be done.

Legal restrictions on press reporting

5.   Consideration should be given to amending the legislation on the non-identification of minors in England and Wales to eliminate any inconsistencies or uncertainties.

6.   The statutory prohibition on identifying rape victims in England and Wales should be extended to cover the victims of the sexual assaults listed at Appendix H.[61]

7.   In any criminal proceedings in England and Wales, the court should have the power to make an order prohibiting the publication of the name and address of any person against whom the offence is alleged to have been committed, or of any other matters likely to lead to his or her identification. This should only be exercised if the court believes that it is necessary to protect the mental or physical health, personal security or security of the home of the victim.

8.   After consulting the press and broadcasting authorities, the Press Complaints Commission (see 11 below) should issue early guidance on jigsaw identification.

---

[61] The list includes:

(a)   procurement of intercourse with a woman by threats (Sexual Offences Act 1956, s.2);

(b)   procurement of intercourse with a woman by false pretences (Sexual Offences Act 1956, s. 3);

(c)   administering drugs to obtain intercourse with a woman (Sexual Offences Act 1956 s. 4)

(d)   intercourse with a girl under 13 (Sexual Offences Act 1956, s. 5);

(e)   intercourse with a girl under 16 (Sexual Offences Act 1956, s. 6);

(f)   intercourse with a mental defective etc. (Sexual Offences Act 1956 ss. 7 and 8; Mental Health Act 1959, s. 128);

(g)   incest (Sexual Offences Act 1956, ss. 10 and 11; Criminal Law Act, s. 54);

(h)   buggery with a woman (Sexual Offences Act 1956, s. 12);

(i)   buggery with a male person (Sexual Offences Act 1956, s. 12 as qualified by the Sexual Offences Act, 1967);

(j)   indecent assault on a female (Sexual Offences Act 1956 s. 14);

(k)   indecent assault on a male (Sexual Offences Act 1956, s. 15);

(l)   assault with intent to commit buggery (Sexual Offences Act 1956, s. 16);

(m)   burglary with intent to rape (Theft Act 1968, s. 10).

Right of reply

9.   A statutory right of reply should not be introduced.

Tort of infringement of privacy

10.   A tort of infringement of privacy should not presently be introduced.

Press complaints commission

11.   The press should be given one final chance to prove that voluntary self-regulation can be made to work.

12.   The Press Council should be disbanded and replaced by a Press Complaints Commission.

13.   The Press Complaints Commission should concentrate on providing an effective means of redress for complaints against the press.

14.   The Press Complaints Commission should be given specific duties to consider complaints both of unjust or unfair treatment by newspapers or periodicals and of unwarranted infringements of privacy through published material or in connection with the obtaining of such material.

15.   The Press Complaints Commission should publish, monitor and implement a comprehensive code of practice for the guidance of both press and the public.

16.   The Press Complaints Commission should operate a hot line for complainants on a 24–hour basis.

17.   Press Complaints Commission adjudications should, in certain cases, include a recommendation that an apology be given to the complainant. The precise form of the apology, including whether it should be given publicly or privately, could also be prescribed. Where a complaint concerns a newspaper's refusal to give an opportunity to reply to an attack made on a complainant or to correct an inaccuracy, the Press Complaints Commission should be able to recommend the nature and the form of reply or correction including, in appropriate cases, where in the paper it should be published.

18.   The Press Complaints Commission should have an independent chairman and no more than 12 members, with smaller sub-committees adjudicating on complaints under delegated powers.

19.   Appointments to the Press Complaints Commission should be made by an Appointments Commission with explicit freedom to appoint whoever it considers best qualified. The Appointments Commission itself should be independently appointed, possibly by the Lord Chancellor.

20.   The Press Complaints Commission should have clear conciliation and adjudication procedures designed to ensure that complaints are handled with

the minimum of delay. Whenever practical it should first seek conciliation. There should also be a fast track procedure for the correction of significant factual errors. The Commission should also have a specific responsibility and procedure for initiating inquiries whenever it thinks it necessary.

21.   Complaints committees should have delegated power to release adjudications, subject to a right of appeal for either party to the full Press Complaints Commission before publication.

22.   The Press Complaints Commission should not operate a waiver of legal rights.

23.   If the industry wishes to maintain a system of non-statutory self-regulation, it must demonstrate its commitment, in particular by providing the necessary money for setting up and maintaining the Press Complaints Commission.

Statutory complaints procedures

24.   If the press fails to demonstrate that non-statutory self-regulation can be made to work effectively, a statutory system for handling complaints should be introduced.

25.   If maverick publications persistently decline to respect the authority of the Press Complaints Commission, the Commission should be placed on a statutory footing. It should be given sufficient statutory powers to enable it to require any newspaper, periodical or magazine to respond to its enquiries about complaints and to publish its adjudications as directed. It should be able to recommend the payment of compensation.

26.   The Government should set the budget for any statutory Press Complaints Commission and provide the money which it should then reclaim from the industry. The industry should set up a funding body which would apportion the cost between, and collect the money from, various industry bodies or individual publications.

Press complaints tribunal

27.   Should the press fail to set up and support the Press Complaints Commission, or should it at any time become clear that the reformed non-statutory mechanism is failing to perform adequately, this should be replaced by a statutory tribunal with statutory powers and implementing a statutory code of practice.

28.   There should be two separate triggers for the replacement of the Press Complaints Commission by a Press Complaints Tribunal.

29.   A Press Complaints Tribunal should perform two distinct functions. First, it should attempt conciliation and investigate complaints. Secondly,

where necessary, it should resolve disputes by ruling whether there had been a breach of the code of practice. This should be reflected in its structure and procedures.

30.   The Press Complaints Tribunal should be able to award compensation. Unless the complainant can show financial loss, the amount of compensation should be limited by statute. This limit should be periodically reviewed.

31.   In privacy cases, the Press Complaints Tribunal should be able to restrain publication of material in breach of the code of practice by means of injunctions. No injunction should be granted if the publisher could show that he had a good arguable defence.

32.   The Tribunal chairman should be a judge or senior lawyer appointed by the Lord Chancellor. He should sit with two assessors drawn from a panel appointed by the Home Secretary.

19

Some Comparative Reflections on the Right of Privacy of Public Figures in Public Places

English judges are becoming more comparatively minded than they might be willing to admit; and current developments suggest that this trend is bound to increase, not decrease, with the passage of time. For instance, the gradual divergence of common law jurisdictions on such important matters as liability for pure economic loss[1] will increase the pressure on our judiciary to reconsider their views on this perennial problem and, more importantly, towards the principle of incrementalism which they imported from Australia with such enthusiasm.[2] A change of attitude here will put tort law into forward gear, something which the judges of the 1980s have feared but which seemed to have left their predecessors in the 1970s relatively undaunted.

Commonwealth law will not be the only source of inspiration. There are signs that references to the law in the United States are also increasing in some areas of the law, encouraged perhaps by the looming presence of the European Convention on Human Rights.[3] On the other hand, interest in the laws of continental Europe remains the predilection of only a few of our more academically-inclined senior judges;[4] though even those who choose not to cite

---

[1] Contrast *Murphy* v. *Brentwood District Council* [1991] AC 378 with *Winnipeg Condominium Corp. No 36* v. *Bird Construction Co. Ltd.* (1995) 121 DLR (4th) 193 (Canada); *Invercargill City Council* v. *Hamlin* [1994] 3 NZLR 513 (New Zealand); *Bryan* v. *Maloney* (1995) 128 ALR 163 (Australia). Note that the divergence is appearing in other areas of the law of tort as well. Thus contrast *Cambridge Water Co. Eastern Counties Leather Plc* [1994] 2 WLR 53 with *Burnie Port Authority* v. *General Jones Pty* (1994) 68 ALJR 331. The Privy Council has now sanctioned this divergence but not without regret. See *Invercargill City Council* v. *Hamlin* [1996] 2 WLR 367.

[2] *Sutherland Shire Council* v. *Heyman* (1985) 157 CLR 424. The contrasting views over the meaning and significance of incrementalism can best be seen in Lord Mustill's judgment in *White* v. *Jones* [1995] 2 WLR 187, 214 *et seq.* and *Canadian National Ry* v. *Norsk Pacific Steamship Co.* [1992] 91 DLR (4th) 289 and *Bryan* v. *Maloney*, above n. 1.

[3] See, for instance, *Derbyshire County Council* v. *Times Newspapers Ltd.* [1993] AC 534, 547 ff; *Rantzen* v. *Mirror Group Newspapers* (1986) Ltd. [1994] QB 670, 690.

[4] Lord Goff has thus referred to German law in a number of his judicial opinions. See, for instance, *Woolwich Equitable Building Society* v. *IRC* [1993] AC 70, at 174; *Henderson* v. *Merett Syndicates Ltd.* [1994] 3 WLR 781; *White* v. *Jones* [1994] 2 WLR 187 at 194–5 and 201–3. But other illustrations do exist. For instance see the Master of the Rolls' judgment in *Kaye* v. *Robertson* [1991] FSR 62 (reproduced in the *Report of the Committee on Privacy and Related Matters*, Cmnd. 1102, 1990 at p. 103). Commonwealth courts on the other hand, are much more willing to go into continental European material. The *Norsk* case, above n. 2, offers an excellent illustration; *London Drugs Ltd.* v. *Kuehne & Nagel International Ltd.* [1992] 3 SCR 299, another

Continental law in their opinions have, clearly, been prompted by its solutions to rethink (if not alter) their own.[5]

Finding and addressing the reason for this judicial introspection may help make our courts less parochial—an accusation levied against them by one of the most distinguished tort lawyers of our times.[6] This piece on privacy is thus mainly addressed to our judges since it is now clear that the present Government, terrorised by the Press, will never do anything about our patchy and defective law of privacy.

One explanation for this judicial timidity towards continental European law must be dismissed straight away—at any rate in an academic environment. It takes the form of "yes we are interested, but we are short of time". Is that argument really convincing? As it is, counsel waste enough time talking at excessive length in court; would it really make a great difference if they also passed on to our judges some information as to how the problem before them has been handled by other systems? Our judges, too, are not always obvious economisers of time. For one thing, they use too much space in their opinions recycling citations and, indirectly, increasing their volume through unnecessarily long opinions[7] instead of considering novel arguments or looking at traditional case law in the light of new socio-economic developments. One of them—Lord Steyn—was bold enough to admit to some of these failings;[8] and a famous predecessor of his—Lord Devlin—gave the boredom which resulted from such waste of judicial time, as one of the reasons for his early retirement.[9]

Can we substantiate these complaints further? Take the recent spate of important defamation cases to which we have already alluded. The treatment which the issues they raised had received in the practitioners' books took no account of the impact of the European Convention on Human Rights, perhaps on the ground that though the United Kingdom is a signatory to the Convention it has never incorporated it into its municipal law. From this it seemed to follow that any speculation about it was best left to academic lawyers only.[10] American law, too, has only been used as a kind of "make

one. *Ellis* v. *Wallsend District Hospital* (1989) 17 NSWLR 553 at 564 offers an excellent example from New Zealand.

  [5] Lord Mustill's learned dissent in *White* v. *Jones*, above n. 2, offers an excellent example. He has also considered extra-judicially the Continental alternatives in "Negligence in the World of Finance" (1992) 5 *The Supreme Court Journal* 1.

  [6] John Fleming, in (1993) 1 *Tort Law Review* 68, 74.

  [7] For illustrations see Markesinis and Deakin "The Random Element of their Lordships' Infallible Judgment: An Economic and Comparative Analysis of the Tort of Negligence from *Anns* to *Murphy*", (1992) 55 *MLR* 619 at 642.

  [8] In *White* v. *Jones* [1993] 3 WLR 730, 750–1.

  [9] See R.F.V. Heuston "Patrick Arthur Devlin" (1994) 84 *Proceedings of the British Academy* 247, 256.

  [10] Thus see the discussion of *Bognor Regis UDC* v. *Campion* [1972] 2 QB 169 in Carter Ruck, *Libel and Slander*, 4th edn. (1992), 73; Gatley, *Libel and Slander*, 8th edn. (1981), paras. 958–9; Clerk and Lindsell, *Torts*, 16th edn. (1989) paras. 2–43, 21–18, 21–25. None considered the effect of the Convention; and two out of three of these practitioners' books thought that the ruling in *Bognor* was unlikely to be disturbed.

weight" factor, one suspects after the decision has been taken on some other grounds. Indeed, in some instances, its use may have been prompted by the sub-conscious feeling that it is better to be tempted by the devil one knows (United States) than to flirt with the devil one suspects (Europe).

Yet time can always be found for novel and interesting views if a court is willing to listen to them with an open mind; and when such novel views creep into a judgment, their effects can be truly monumental. We believe this to be true of the recent defamation cases since no one can say with confidence what their long term effect will be on the entire law of defamation. We are, in short, experiencing only the beginning of a new era.

So, if time is not a convincing factor, why have our judges closed their minds to Continental ideas and thus enabled our practitioners to feel that they need not address this angle of their case? The erudite work of academics such as Professor Zimmermann has shown that this introverted attitude was not always *en vogue* with our judiciary; and Lord Roger of Earlsferry has demonstrated the qualitatively important role that contacts with Germany had on the Scottish legal profession during the last century.[11]

The reluctance to look at modern civil law may thus lie not in the lack of time but in the belief that it belongs to a different legal family and that its solutions (and reasoning) are thus alien to our legal environment. Many a judge has said this to the first of the authors of this piece in the informal setting of a Gray's Inn lunch or dinner; and there is no reason to doubt that it is one of the psychological blocks which, subconsciously perhaps, operates against the opening of minds. The "lack of time" factor is then used to reinforce this frame of mind and culminates in the parochial approach criticised by Professor Fleming.

Once again, this explanation provides only part of the answer. Grouping systems into families does not mean that legal borrowing from within one family entails no dangers. English judges may, somehow, feel that because they can read the original American text they can also borrow its ideas more easily. Sometimes this is, indeed, true. Yet taking one's cue from American constitutional cases, for instances on freedom of expression, is as fraught with dangers[12] as is any similar attempt to be inspired by comparable ideas found in the German Constitution. The language factor can thus lull English lawyers into underestimating the dangers of legal borrowing. For American constitutional case law is deeply influenced by that country's different history, its federal structure, and the presence of a written and entrenched constitution or

---

[11] "Scottish Advocates in the Nineteenth Century: the German Connection" (1994) 110 *LQR* 563.

[12] Lord Keith seemed to have accepted this in his judgment in the *Derbyshire* case (above n. 2) since, after citing from a number of American cases he added (at p. 457): "These propositions were endorsed by the Supreme Court of the United States in *New York Times Co.* v. *Sullivan* (1964) 376 US 254,277. *While these decisions were related most directly to the provisions of the American constitution concerned with securing freedom of speech*, the public interest considerations which underlaid them are no less valid in this country" (emphasis added.)

its continued use of the jury system.[13] One ignores these *structural* differences at one's peril, as the House of Lords found out in a different setting—*Murphy*—when it (erroneously) treated a decision of the United States Supreme Court in an admiralty dispute[14] as depicting the state of the tort law in the United States, and was severely criticised by an eminent New Zealand judge who has now joined its ranks.[15] One thus over-simplifies matters to the nth degree if one pretends that fundamental differences do not exist simply because, for other purposes, English and American law have been bracketed together in the same legal family, or because they use the same language.

In the matter under consideration the above observations can be translated into the following statement: the German preference for balancing the competing interests of free expression and personality rights (in the broadest sense of the words) lies much closer to the English way of thinking than the American which has, especially since the 1960s, accorded vastly preferential treatment to free speech. Widening our observations for a minute, one could add that one can think of other areas of the law where the underlying assumptions in England are closer to those found in France or Germany than they are to those accepted in the United States; but this assertion goes so much against the accepted way of thinking that the idea has thus far received inadequate consideration let alone support. This, clearly, is no place to launch the assault on such a widely-held belief.

Be that as it may, the above thoughts lead one to the conclusion that the *major* reason the Continental legal systems are ignored is not because they belong to a different family[16] but because of the language differences which make their material inaccessible to our judges.[17] If this obstacle can be overcome, and suitable linguistic and conceptual adjustments are made to the foreign material in order to downplay some of its more frightening differences *in appearance*, its relevance would soon begin to be noticed.

In this short paper we wish to demonstrate how this can be done; and we have attempted this task by sharpening our focus by narrowing it to a particular factual situation—in our case one of great practical significance: the rights (if any) of public figures who find their privacy interfered with in public places. We have tried to do this by eschewing theories and dogmas and concentrating instead on case law and court practice. A recent German

---

[13] Professor Fleming's *The American Tort Process* (1988) contains an excellent account of the impact which these peculiarly American background factors have had on the development of American tort law.

[14] *East River Steamship Corporation* v. *Transamerica Deleval Inc.* 476 US 858, 106 S.Ct 2295 (1986).

[15] Sir Robin (now Lord) Cooke in "An Impossible Distinction" (1991) 107 *LQR* 46 *et seq*.

[16] The existing classification in legal families is, in any event, very superficial and misleading and has often been attempted on the basis of the private law of the systems.

[17] For a similar view that language is a real barrier see Tony Weir "Die Sprachen des europäischen Rechts: Eine skeptische Betrachtung", (1995) 3 *Zeitschrift für Europäisches Privatrecht*, 368. His arguments are refuted by Professor Zimmermann in "Savigny's Legacy. Legal History, Comparative Law, and the Emergence of a European Legal Science", (1996) 112 *LQR* 576, 595.

decision shows how one can be "sucked" into the study of foreign law, first by looking at it at a rather high level of specificity and then gradually by moving towards the consideration of some of its wider features. In *controlled doses*, use of continental law could thus help persuade our judges of its richness and utility and thus encourage them to consult it whenever their own law strikes them as being either unclear or unsatisfactory. Other collaborative papers, produced by colleagues associated with the Oxford Centre for the Advanced Study of European and Comparative law, will, in the fullness of time, attempt the same exercise in other contexts so that over a number of years we can demonstrate more clearly to our English colleagues the richness of Continental law and the utility of the comparative method.

Although part of the German law of privacy can be found in statutory form,[18] the bulk of it has been developed by the courts in a pragmatic manner, adopting a case-by-case approach which in many respects greatly resembles ours. In the ultimate analysis, therefore, neither the German source material nor the methodology used to develop the law should cause too much concern to the common lawyer. Here, at any rate, there is none of the Pandectist structuralism which has so frightened generations of common lawyers.[19] Thus, since the 1954 decision of the Federal Supreme Court[20] a general personality right, covering privacy, has been recognised; and this despite the fact that the draftsman of the Code had considered including such a right in the Code but had, ultimately, rejected this idea.[21] This decision took account of the value system of the Constitution of Bonn of 1949 (which came into force in 1950), where after the dark years of the Nazi period, human dignity (Art. 1) and free development of personality (Art. 2) took centre stage in the new constitutional order and thus took precedence over the (hierarchically inferior and, in any event, older) Civil Code (BGB). An excellent example here of how the constitutional background can affect (and is affecting in every modern legal system) the development of private law. As has already been noted, this trend is particularly obvious in our law of defamation, even though the "Constitution"

---

[18] The Constitution of 1949, articles 1 and 2; para 823 I BGB and a number of specific statutes such as the Law of Artistic Creations of 1907 which will be referred to in the text above.

[19] How this has affected our understanding and use of German contract law is explained by Dannemann and Markesinis, "The Legacy of History on German Contract Law" in *Festschrift for Professor Roy Goode* (forthcoming)

[20] By the so-called Schacht decision, BGHZ 13, 334, translated in Markesinis, *The German Law of Torts*, 3rd edn. (1994), 376.

[21] Among the reasons given for this one finds the following remarkable statement: "It is repugnant to the dominant opinion of the people to place non-material values on a level with property interests and to make good non-material damage with money. The Code should not ignore this view especially prevailing in the better circles of society [sic] Only the worse elements would try to gain advantages therefrom. Pursuit of profit, selfishness and covetousness would be promoted and wrongful proceedings started from ulterior motives would be encouraged." See *Protokolle der Kommission für die zweite Lesung des Entwurfs des Bürgerlichen Gesetzbuchs*, vol. I (1897), 622–3.

which is making us "discover" that the common law has always protected human rights effectively is not our own.

Schacht was a seminal case in declaring the existence of a new right (or, rather, creating an interest) protected by § 823 I BGB; but it did not go further than the facts of that case dictated. The affected lawyer was allowed to claim a correction by the offending newspaper. No damages were either sought or awarded; no general principles proclaimed beyond the one mentioned above and, again, that was done in a way which made it clear that its precise content would have to be fixed by subsequent case law. The German law thus developed pragmatically and case by case; and it has ended up by providing efficient protection for individuals, without making the German Press less free than ours. Nor, as we shall see, has the price of all this been a flooding of the courts by frivolous or vexatious claims.

The most recent decision of the German Federal Court illustrates the current status of the case law.[22] It was handed down on the 19 December 1995 and involved the publication of photographs of Princess Caroline of Monaco having dinner with her boyfriend in a secluded part[23] of a garden restaurant in France. Our Princess of Wales would almost certainly have failed if similar facts had occurred in this country and she had wished to assert her right to be let alone by the Press. Alternatively, her lawyers would have been forced to resort to some strained construction of some other remedy—perhaps, breach of confidence—to come up with some kind of protection. Yet this lack of protection, apparently, enjoys the support of Lord Wakeham, the Chairman of the Press Council, the very body which is there to protect aggrieved citizens. For Lord Wakeham was recently reported to have told *The Times*[24]: "that Diana [*sic*] had sacrificed her right to privacy by going on television, so I think she is fair game to be publicly analysed". Well, that is one view of things; but German law shows that it is not the only one. Arguably, it is not even the best one; and the fact that the screening of the offending programme on English television was, in the end, cancelled by the television company which had commissioned it,[25] suggests that the English and German senses of dignity and propriety may not be that different after all. Another reason why legal borrowing may thus be less difficult than is believed.

In the German case the Princess's claim for an injunction against further publication in Germany was denied by the Court of First Instance, and this decision was upheld by the Court of Appeal. This latter Court expressly relied

---

[22] BGH 19. 12. 1995 , NJW 1996,1128. The recent case law is reviewed by the attorney who won the case for the Princess in Prinz, "Geldentschädigung bei Persönlichkeitsrechtsverletzungen durch Medien" *NJW* 1996,953. See, also, Frömming and Peters, "Die Einwilligung im Medienrecht" *NJW* 1996,958.

[23] Where, however, a number of other patrons of the restaurant were also seated.

[24] 2 May 1996, p. 16.

[25] Michael Grade, chief executive of Channel 4, described the programme as "an exercise in exploitation": *The Times*, 3 May 1996.

on § 23 I *Kunst-und Urhebergesetz*[26] which allows the non-consensual *publication*[27] of pictures of "figures of contemporary history". But the Court of Appeal also accepted that even figures of contemporary history are, in certain circumstances, entitled to have their privacy respected. If their own legitimate interests concerning their intimate and private sphere are endangered, these figures can invoke § 23 II KUG and thus exclude public interest and prohibit publication. Despite this admission, however, the Court of Appeal finally came down in favour of the view that the photographs in question did not violate Princess Caroline's private sphere, because she was in a restaurant, i.e. a public place, when the photographs were taken and not at home. The thrust of its argument was thus that public figures, by virtue of their position in society, have to accept a greater interference with their private lives, especially when this occurred in a public place.

This judgment was reversed by the Federal Court which focused strongly on the idea that even public figures are entitled to have their privacy respected under certain circumstances. This *basic* point has, of course, a long pedigree in German law, starting with the *Spätheimkehrer* case in 1957.[28] The case is interesting for a variety of reasons, including its wider definition of the term "public figures" (*Person der Zeitgeschichte*) to include even ordinary individuals who, at a certain moment in their life, happen to attract unusual public attention.[29]

In the *Spätheimkehrer* case a POW, long lost in Russia, returned to Germany in 1953. When he tried to move into his wife's apartment, her landlady unaware, like others, of his existence, caused a great fuss. The incident attracted much local attention, so a reporter secretly photographed the landlady in her shop and subsequently published her photograph along with a story about the affair. This led to her being harassed and her shop boycotted; as a consequence she decided to sue the defendant newspaper for damages resulting from the boycott. Her action was successful on the grounds that the photographs were taken without her consent while she was in her "private sphere". The court went on to say:

---

[26] Henceforth KUG = Law of Artistic Creations of 1907.

[27] The protection given by the KUG applies only to the *publication* of pictures taken of the plaintiff but there is no doubt that the filming of the plaintiff in public may also be tortious even in the absence of an intention to publish. Thus, in BGH NJW 1995, 1955 it was held that the permanent surveillance (by means of a video camera fixed on the defendant's land) of a public footpath separating his land from the plaintiff's, amounted to an intolerable interference with the latter's right (and that of his visitors) to come and go un-observed. Once again, however, the court was quick to stress that every case turns on its facts so that, for instance, video surveillance in a bank or a post office would not be actionable.

[28] BGHZ 24, 200.

[29] The so-called "relative" public figures to distinguish them from the "absolute" public figures (e.g. monarchs, prime ministers, actors, etc. who are public figures by virtue of their prominent office or position). See the seminal piece by Professor Neumann-Duesberg, "Bildberichterstattung über absolute und relative Personen der Zeitgeschichte" *JZ* 1960, 114.

"Even figures of public interest [as defined above] within the meaning of § 23 I KUG do not have to tolerate being photographed with a view to publication in their private sphere without their knowledge and consent. This follows from the general right of personality which protects everyone against all violations of their private sphere which are not justified by a higher value".[30]

This basic position has been confirmed many times since, notably in an important decision of the Federal Court of 1978.[31] This case involved the illegal taping of a telephone conversation between two leading political figures (Dr. Helmut Kohl and Dr. Kurt Biedenkopf) of the CDU (then in opposition) by an individual who subsequently sold the story to the defendant newspaper. The plaintiffs' action for an injunction restraining further publication of the story met with success.

The Federal Court's starting point was, once again, the same. "Everyone" reasoned the court,[32] "even politicians who are in the limelight, are entitled to have their privacy respected. This stems from articles 1 and 2 of the Constitution. . . and it is reinforced by § 201 of the Criminal Code which makes it illegal to record private telephone conversations without the consent of the persons involved". The court was thus happy to repeat that "in his private sphere [even a public person] must be shielded from public sight otherwise the basis for maintaining and developing his personality would be endangered". But, as is typical of German case law, the Court was also quick to stress that:

"It must not be forgotten that the constitutional guarantee of a free Press would be alarmingly curtailed if the Press were denied the right to publish information which resulted from an infringement of confidentiality so long as it [the Press] had played no part in its illegal procurement. The Press must be allowed to report incidents of public interest, even if the persons affected do not consent to the publication of information that came from their private sphere. That means that on the one hand the Press is not limited to generally accessible sources, and may even use information obtained through a breach of confidence or in an otherwise illegal manner. On the other hand, however, the Press is obliged to show due consideration and respect towards the person whose private sphere has been invaded".

In the circumstances, the Federal Court came to the conclusion that the injunction should be granted since the conversation was clearly private and its subject-matter not one of legitimate public interest.

In the light of the above it can now be treated as axiomatic that in German law neither private nor public figures are obliged to tolerate the publication of photographs taken in their main *private sphere* (e.g. their home) without their consent. But the recent "Caroline" decision took matters further by incrementally extending the spatial zone of legal protection of privacy of

[30] *Ibid.*, at p. 208. This is a free and somewhat abridged translation of the relevant passage of the decision of the court.
[31] BGHZ 73, 120.
[32] *Ibid.* at p. 122–3.

public figures to public places or, as the court put it, the plaintiffs "have transferred their private sphere of life to a place outside their home".

The *Bundesgerichtshof* was conscious of the novelty of the extension but
had no hesitation in holding that there was nothing in the *travaux prépara-
toires* of the relevant legislation to prevent it from such an interpretation—
quite the contrary. Moreover, this extended protection was not being granted
without any qualifications. Chief among them was that the public figure must
be in a place secluded from the general public (e.g. a secluded room of a hotel
or restaurant, a sports centre,[33] a telephone box, in certain circumstances,
even out in the open: examples given by the court itself). The court expressed
this idea thus:[34]

> "Like all humans, persons of contemporary history have the right to retreat to places
> outside their home where they may wish to be let alone, protected [as it were] from
> the public gaze. This may occur even in places which are open to the general pub-
> lic, though this presupposes that in the place in question the person [of contempo-
> rary history] somehow 'shuts himself off' from the public at large. This 'seclusion'
> must be ascertainable in an objective manner".

And the court continued:

> "This will be the case where the person, relying on the 'seclusion' of the place, will
> behave in a manner which he would not do if he felt he was in full view of the pub-
> lic, for instance by expressing emotions which are clearly not intended for the eyes
> of third parties".

Thus, if this condition of "seclusion" is met, then the public figure will be
on the way to winning his case provided, however, that he can also show that
he had clearly manifested a desire to be left alone and was behaving in a manner appropriate to a private moment. Princess Caroline was able to satisfy the
court on both of these requirements because she was, as stated, (a) having dinner with her boyfriend in a secluded part of the restaurant and (b) she was,
as could have been objectively ascertained, having a private encounter with
him. Thus, according to the Federal Court, the Press violated the Princess' private sphere since the photographs, having been taken stealthily, had been
given wide publicity.

This is no place to discuss this judgment in detail nor can one deny that it
will have to be refined by subsequent case law. Suffice it to say, however, that
the court considered in some detail the crucial three factors which influenced
its decision—seclusion, private character of the situation, and the informational value of the material concerned—in order to provide guidelines for the

---

[33] The express reference to a sport centre makes one wonder whether the German judges had
Princess Diana in mind who, as is well known, was secretly photographed while exercising in a
private sport centre. The incident took place in London in November 1993 and received great
publicity in Germany. The case law discussed in this paper would have made such an incident
clearly actionable under German law.

[34] BGH NJW 1996, 1128, 1129.

future. The judgment shows great awareness of the fact that guidelines must be laid down for the future but also realises that its *dicta* must be interpreted in the light of the facts of each subsequent case.

As regards the last-mentioned of the court's relevant factors—the informational value of the disclosed material—it can generally be stated that the smaller its value the more extended is the protection of privacy. In the instant case, the court had this to say on the matter:

> "When balancing the competing interests, the informational value of the events depicted will be of crucial significance. The greater the need for the public to know, the more limited will be the rights of the person of contemporary history. By contrast, the need to protect this person's privacy will become greater as the information gained by the public becomes less valuable. In this case the photos which show the plaintiff with VL in a garden restaurant contain little or no valuable information".

An *ad hoc* evaluation of the merits of the publication is thus often undertaken; and as the *Lebach* decision shows, it is done in a manner which is both thorough and, more interestingly, finds equivalents even in some American decisions.[35] The relevant part of the *Lebach* ruling is so important that it deserves an extended quotation.

> "In solving this conflict [between protection of personality and free expression] it must be remembered that according to the intention of the Constitution both constitutional concerns are essential aspects of the liberal democratic order . . . with the result that neither can claim precedence in principle over the other.[36] The view of humanity taken by the Constitution and the corresponding structure of the community within the State, require both the respect for the independence of individual personality and the guarantee of a liberal social atmosphere; the latter cannot be realised at the present time unless communications are unimpeded. In case of conflict, both concerns of the Constitution must be adjusted, if possible. If this cannot be achieved, it must be determined which interest must be postponed having regard to the nature of the case and to any special circumstances. For this purpose, both concerns of the Constitution, centred as they are on human dignity, must be regarded as the nucleus of the system of constitutional values. Accordingly, the freedom to broadcast may have the effect of restricting any claims based on the right of personality; however, the damage to "personality" resulting from a public representation must not be out of proportion to the importance of the publication

---

[35] BVerfGE 35, 202. Cf. *Briscoe* v. *Reader's Digest Association Inc.* 483 P. 2d 34 (1971). Though the authority of this decision of the Supreme Court of California may have been seriously weakened as a result of the decisions in *Cox Broadcasting Corp.* v. *Cohen* 420 US 469 (1975) and *The Florida Star* v. *B.J.F.* 491 US 524 (1989), the case is, methodologically speaking, very close to its German equivalent. At best, this shows that the German reasoning is transplantable into a common law setting—even one as committed to free speech as the American—and, at the very least, the Californian decision provides an excellent medium for a study of the two systems in parallel.

[36] This position is not unique to German law. Thus Canadian Courts also seem to have rejected the idea of a hierarchy of constitutional rights. See *Hill* v. *Church of Scientology* [1995] 2 S.C.R. 1130 at p. 1179. We are grateful to Mr John Craig for drawing our attention to this point.

upholding the freedom of communication . . . Furthermore it follows from these guiding principles that the required weighting of interests must, on the one hand, take into account the intensity of the infringement of the personal sphere by the broadcast; on the other hand, the specific interest which is being served by the broadcast . . . , must be assessed and examined so as to discover whether and to what extent it can be satisfied without interference—or a less far-reaching interference—with the protection of personality".

Thus, to return to the Caroline type of setting, if the photographs were demonstrably taken to satisfy the insatiable curiosity of readers, or the public's usual craving for sensation, gossip, and superficial entertainment, then these interests will not prevail over the plaintiff's interest to privacy.[37] Establishing a profit motive for the defendant will also not help his cause.

The limited or non-existent informational value of a publication has thus enabled German courts to accord some privacy protection even to ex-criminals whose criminal past was unnecessarily exposed just as their rehabilitation into society was about to begin.[38] The protection accorded in such cases can, once again, profitably be compared to the very limited protection given by our Rehabilitation of Offenders Act 1974. As the first of us said in a letter to *The Times*[39] over ten years ago "not everything which interests the public should be published in the public interest". German law accepts the validity of this statement.

The court's conclusion in the Princess Caroline case was that an injunction against further publication should be granted. Additionally, the court held that any breach of this order would entail a fine of up to 500,000 DM (£200,000) or up to six months imprisonment.

In the aforementioned Princess Caroline case[40] the question of civil damages was not raised by the plaintiff. In principle, however, German courts are prepared to award civil damages where (a) the interference with the plaintiff's personality is, "objectively" speaking, grave and (b) the interference cannot reasonably be rectified in another way. Whether there is a grave violation or not depends on the significance of the interference, the motives of the person of the "tortfeasor", the extent of the dissemination (*Verbreitungsgrad*), and the degree of fault.[41] These additional requirements, which become relevant only when the court has accepted that the tort has been committed, further reduce the potential "chilling effect" which the court's decision might have on the Press because of the extension of the spatial zone of privacy.

Despite these limiting or controlling factors, the German Press has taken the judgment seriously; and a number of newspapers have already indicated

---

[37] BGHZ 24, 200, 208; BGH NJW 1996,1128, 1130; BVerfGE 34, 269, 283; BGH NJW 1965, 2148, 2149; OLG Hamburg AfP 1992, 376, 377.
[38] BVerfGE 35, 202 (Lebach) translated in Markesinis, *op. cit.* above n. 20, p. 390 *et seq.*
[39] 18 November 1987.
[40] BGH 19. 12. 1995, NJW 1996, 1128.
[41] BGHZ 128, 1, 13.

that they would respect its spirit and stop pestering the Princess. This promise reflects the educational impact of the decision, and though these are early days to judge the overall effect of the judgment, it does appear to have had a promising impact.

The compliant reaction of the German newspapers may also have been influenced by the fact that the Federal Court has in recent times begun to take into account factors such as deterrence[42] and the economic value of the publication to the defendant when awarding damages to plaintiffs who have satisfied the conditions described above. Thus, up to now, in cases when an injury to a personality right is objectively significant, the only aspect which was considered when calculating damages was the need to "satisfy" the victim's offended human dignity and honour.[43] Consequently, the level of immaterial damages has so far tended to be low—on average somewhere in the order of 10,000 DM (£4,000).[44] This trend peaked in 1968 when the LG Hamburg[45] granted Prince Bernhard of the Netherlands 50,000 DM.

For a long time this was as far as the German courts were, apparently, prepared to go. But in the recent case concerning the publication of the *fictitious* interview with Princess Caroline,[46] the Federal Court observed that the newspaper deliberately exploited her personality to promote its own commercial interests. The Court thus felt that the paper's economic gain was a legitimate factor in the determination of damages, though it did not go as far as suggesting that their amount should take the form of an account of profits. Thus, the amount originally fixed by the Court of Appeal for non-pecuniary damages (*Schmerzensgeld*)—30,000 DM was, following the aforementioned observation of the Federal Court, increased by the Court of Appeal of Hamburg (to which the matter was referred for final determination) to a record 180,000 DM (plus interest).[47] Though an appeal against this ruling is possible by either party—Princess Caroline's lawyers had asked for 400,000 DM and, thus, expressed their dissatisfaction with this award—and the odds are that if launched the total awarded sum would be reduced, the real significance of this

---

[42] The idea was advanced by Professor von Bar as early as 1980. See NJW 1980, 1724; and, more recently, it has also found favour with another leading comparatist—Professor Kötz. See his "Ziele des Haftungsrechts" in *Festschrift für Ernst Steindorff zum 70. Geburtstag*, (1990) 643 *et seq*. In Germany, however, the traditional view that "compensation is the first and most important aim of the law of torts" (Deutsch, *Haftungsrecht I, Allgemeine Lehren* (1976), 73) retains its wide appeal.

[43] BGHZ 35,363, translated in Markesinis, *op. cit.* above n. 20, 386 *et seq*. See, also, BGHZ 39, 124.

[44] BGHZ 26,349; OLG Köln NJW 1987, 2682; OLG Hamburg NJW-RR 1988, 737, translated in Markesinis, *op. cit.* above n. 20, 376, 398, 407.

[45] OLG Hamburg of 19. 2. 1970, *UFITA (Archiv für Urheber-, Film,- Funk- und Theaterrecht)* 1971, 322.

[46] BGHZ 128, 1.

[47] *Frankfurter Allgemeine Zeitung*, 26.7.1996, 12. This is combined damages for the Caroline cases which, for this purpose, were consolidated in one hearing. The estimates which we have been given for the combined costs suggest an *additional* 200–300,000 DM bringing the total cost of the losing defendant to approximately 500,000 DM.

judgment lies in the fact that it forms part of a strong new trend to teach the sensational Press a lesson. To that extent, it may be heralding a move away from the excessive restraint of the past.

Another important factor in the calculation of the damages is the "intensity" of the violation of privacy. This is considered to be especially grave in the case of publication of *fictitious* interviews as shown by the recent developments on this aspect of the problem.[48] When this is contrasted with the treatment recently accorded to the television programme which involved a *fictitious* psychoanalysis session with the Princess of Wales (and Lord Wakeham's reactions quoted above) it reveals, once again, German law as commendably more unsympathetic to such base forms of journalism. By granting damages, the amount of which must be so calculated as to deter future similar cases, the Federal Court may thus be demonstrating its sympathy to victims of such unnecessarily hurtful intrusions but also its contempt for fictitious interviews and sensationalist journalistic practices. In this context, therefore, it is interesting to note a report published in the *Frankfurter Allgemeine Zeitung*[49] which stated that this recent, very large award had been welcomed by the Association of German Journalists (*Deutscher Journalisten-Verband*).

There are some signs that this particular aspect of the decision of the Federal Court[50] may now be followed by lower courts.[51] For example in an another decision of the Court of Appeal of Hamburg both issues of satisfaction for the victim and deterrence of future tortfeasors played a role in the judgment which concerned the broadcasting by the TV station RTL of false allegations of money-laundering by the owner of a Formula 1 team.[52] The Court of Appeal raised the amount of immaterial damages from 15,000 DM to 50,000 DM, because of the seriousness of the allegations. If the latest of the Caroline cases withstands a possible appeal, these larger figures may thus become the new "norm".

This case law may thus signal a move away from the rather small sums awarded in the past. Yet it also demonstrates that the German courts have shown themselves able to react flexibly to the seriousness of publications by balancing the aspects of privacy, press freedom, and potential wider benefit of the publication. These figures also show that the excessive damages awarded in some English defamation cases have also so far been avoided; and if a change is about to take place, it is largely the result of understandable reaction to low forms of journalism. Again, one is thus tempted to say that the results reached in German law are more "balanced" than those reached in England where we witness the whole range of variations from no protection

---

[48] BGHZ 128, 1. See, also, BVerfGE 34, 269 (*Soraya* decision).
[49] Of 26.7.1996, p. 12.
[50] BGHZ 128, 1 (fictitious interview ruling) of 15. 11. 1994.
[51] See, for instance, OLG Hamburg NJW-RR 1996, 90.
[52] OLG Hamburg, NJW RR 1996, 90.

(on the grounds that no tort can be found to peg on a decision) to crushing levels of damages whenever the law of defamation can successfully be invoked, damages which can be even disproportionate to levels of awards made in serious personal injury cases.

The figures which have hitherto prevailed in Germany may, at first sight, strike the English reader as excessively modest; yet a comparison with the figures which the Lord Chancellor's proposals on privacy[53] thought might be appropriate in our country as well reveals, once again, an interesting trend: the current German practice *moving up* its awards to the kind of levels English courts would like to see their awards *come down to*.

To this sketch, one must add a postscript. When comparing these sums one must also remember that the German figures given above refer to the *non-pecuniary* part of the award; if German plaintiffs can also prove (additional) economic loss resulting from the invasion of privacy—for instance, a photograph of the plaintiff sunbathing in the nude in the English Gardens of Munich is subsequently published in a newspaper with the consequence that he loses his promotion[54]—then that loss may be claimable on top of whatever damages may be awarded to the plaintiff for his non-pecuniary loss.

The Caroline litigation reveals further interesting features of German law. In the case of the fictitious interview, the Princess succeeded against several German newspapers in another respect, as well: she sued for and was granted corrections and a disclaimer.

In general the publication of a counter statement, disclaimer, or a correction, are also available in German law and, indeed, form the most typical consequence of such litigation. The counter statement is an explanation by the person concerned, (i.e. the person affected by the publication), which contradicts the published article. Its legal base is to be found in the law of each state (*Land*) but which in content is virtually identical. The claim must be limited to facts, does not need to be proven by the plaintiff, and can be enforced by a preliminary injunction which can be obtained fairly expeditiously. This leads finally to a publication of the counter statement *in the same part of the publication and with the same lay-out as the offending article*. The editor, however, may add a clarification saying that he was obliged to publish the counter statement regardless of its truth.

---

[53] Infringement of Privacy, Consultation Paper, July 1993, 44.5.

[54] OLG München NJW 1988, 915. In that case the plaintiff was able to convince the court that he lost his promotion due to the publication of the photograph and was thus allowed the difference of pay between his present and expected post. (Sum not specified in the judgment.) The paper's defence that the plaintiff was photographed as part of a crowd failed since the picture which was eventually published focused on him only. The defence that by sunbathing in the nude in a public place he had, implicitly, consented to the publication of his photo in a newspaper was also rejected. To English eyes, the case differs from the Caroline case on one or two points the most important of which is, arguably, the fact that the sunbather was not a public figure. Indicative of how German courts use earlier case law is the fact that the "sunbather" case was not cited in the Caroline case.

The second instrument is the disclaimer, an explanation by the editor that the published statement about facts was wrong. The legal base is an analogy of §§ 823, 1004 BGB (*actio negatoria*) to stop an unlawful violation.[55] But it must be kept in mind that the plaintiff has to prove in the proceedings that the facts in the article were wrong. The rules on the disclaimer also cover the claim for a correction which concerns ambivalent, incomplete, or misleading statements of facts.[56] With regard to disclaimer and corrections the courts are cautious to grant what in their view is suitable and appropriate to stop the violation, and not more, since the defendant is being legally forced to make a statement.

In the incident of the fictitious interview with Princess Caroline the court forced the newspaper to print a disclaimer on the same page where the alleged exclusive interview had been published earlier i.e. on the front page. The Federal Court held thereby that the lay-out of the disclaimer must be able to attract the same degree of attention as the disputed statement itself. Even if the disputed article was published two years earlier, this period of time was not enough to neutralise the permanently damaging impression of the untrue statements in a newspaper with a wide circulation. The publication of a counter statement by the plaintiff was held not to be able to balance the violation, because of the limited protective function of a counter statement which is solely aimed at giving the alleged victim the right to make his points regardless of the truth. The two other complaints, dealt with in the same judgment[57] involved the publication of an alleged photograph from Caroline's photo-album and alleged plans to marry her boy-friend. The Court decided that corrections have to be printed on the grounds of §§ 823, 1004 BGB because of the infringement of Caroline's personality right.

It is also interesting to consider the length of these proceedings. Because of the growing number of TV stations and newspapers, the competition for market shares is sometimes tempting publishers to a reckless and sensational style of journalism. The number of cases in the Court of First Instance of Hamburg (which includes inter alia newspapers like *Spiegel*, *Stern*, and *Bildzeitung* within its exclusive jurisdiction and is thus, in practice, the most important court for such proceedings) may run to 700 a year, most of which lead to the publication of a correction. But the number of cases going to appeal and, more importantly to the Federal Court, remains very small. Thus between 1985 and 1995 there have been only 26 published decisions of the Federal Court.[58] Even allowing for the fact that there may exist other, unpublished

---

[55] BGHZ 34, 99; BGHZ 128,1.

[56] BGHZ 31, 308.

[57] BGHZ 128,1.

[58] BGH 22.1.1985, NJW 1985, 1617 (damages granted, case sent back to lower court because 3,000 DM deemed to be too low); BGH 9.7.1985, BGHZ 95, 212 (no final decision on damages; case sent back for evaluation); BGH 20.5.1986, NJW 1987, 1398 (injunction denied); BGH 3.6.1986, BGHZ 98, 94 (injunction and damages denied); BGH 10.3.1987, NJW 1987, 2667 (injunction granted); BGH 24.11.1987, NJW 1988, 1984 (damages denied; but lower court asked

decisions, the overall figure is very small indeed, especially when one considers that the Federal Court hands down over eight hundred "motivated" decisions per year.[59]

Yet even these figures should not frighten the English readers who are accustomed to lower levels of litigation. After all, the German law of privacy is, despite the limitations described above, quite liberal—certainly if it is compared with the proposals recently put forward (but then unexpectedly abandoned) by the Lord Chancellor, Lord Mackay of Clashfern.[60] One must further not forget that the cost of litigation in Germany is much lower than it is in England and thus one should be entitled to assume that in this country costs would act as a further brake on litigation. Thus, though there is no way of estimating what the likely number of cases would be if privacy was ever recognised as an independent cause of action in English law, the Lord Chancellor's estimates might well be correct, or even on the high side.[61]

Finally, also noteworthy is the fact that German civil procedure is sufficiently flexible to allow these cases to be decided fairly quickly. Thus the restaurant case involving Princess Caroline was heard at First Instance in February 1994 (the writ having been issued in August 1993), on appeal in December 1994, and by December 1995 the written judgment of the Federal Court was made public. The case involving the fictitious interview with Princess Caroline was decided by the Court of First Instance in December 1992, by the Court of Appeal in December 1993, and a mere one year later we had the judgment of the Federal Supreme Court. Here, again, therefore,

---

to evaluate the chances of future damage: if high, damages would be assessed on that basis); BGH 15.12.1987, NJW-RR 1988, 733 (damages and disclaimer granted, case sent back for evaluation); BGH 13.10.1988, NJW 1989, 384 (*droit moral*); BGH 11.4.1989, NJW 1989, 2941 (no final decision on damages, case sent back for evaluation); BGH 8.6.1989, NJW 1990, 1986 (claim to remove a faked signature from a painting was, in principle, successful); BGH 11.7.1989, NJW-RR 1990, 1058 (no final decision on injunction and damages, case sent back for evaluation); BGH 20.2.1990, JZ 1990, 754 (no final decision on injunction; case sent back for evaluation); BGH 13.11.1990, NJW 1991, 1532 (injunction denied); BGH 4.12.1990, NJW 1991, 1180 (case concerned overhearing of a private talk to obtain evidence for a trial); BGH 10.12.1991, NJW 1992, 1312 (injunction denied); BGH 17.11. 1992, NJW 1993, 930 (no final decision on injunction, case sent back for evaluation); BGH 12.10.1993, NJW 1994, 124 (injunction denied); BGH 8.2.1994, NJW 1994, 1281 (damages denied; injunction granted); BGH 9.6.1994, BGHZ 126, 208 (injunction denied); BGH 12.7.1994, DtZ 1994, 343 (injunction granted); BGH 10.11.1994, WRP 1995, 186 (injunction and damages denied); BGH 15.11.1994, BGHZ 128, 1 (disclaimer granted by lower court; Federal Court did not rule on plainitff's claim that the disclaimer should be in larger print. On the damages issue, the case was sent back for re-consideration because 30,000 DM were deemed to be too low); BGH 25.4.1995, NJW 1995,1955 (injunction against being filmed from neighbouring premises granted); BGH 5.12.1995, NJW 1996, 984 (damages granted, but case sent back because 15,000 DM deemed to be too low); BGH 12.12.1995, NJW 1996, 985 (damages granted, but case sent back for evaluation); BGH 19.12.1995, NJW 1996, 1128 (injunction granted).

[59] For further details see Markesinis, "Litigation Mania in England, Germany and the USA: Are We So Very Different?" (1990) 49 *CLJ*, 233 *et seq.*

[60] *Op. cit.* above n. 53, pp. 20 *et seq.*

[61] *Op. cit.* above n. 53 p. 52.

there may be hidden lessons for English law since it, too, is troubled by the delay of dispute settlement as Lord Woolf's recent proposals clearly show.

These facts indicate that there is no reason to fear that a flood of long lasting cases will hit the courts. Because of the flexible German civil procedure judges can deal quite briefly with the cases; and only decisions involving large amounts, or raising important issues of law, can be appealed against in the Federal Court. The given examples show that it is possible for the courts to grant remedies against blatant infringements of privacy, keep truly offending publishers under reasonable control and yet not stifle free speech where it matters most i.e the political arena. In this context it is interesting to note that the possible extra-marital affairs of German politicians and businessmen hold little or no appeal for most readers of German newspapers and have thus figured much less prominently in the German press and the law reports than has been the case in England. Thus one can summarise the position in Germany in the following way.

First, the availability of counter statements, based on the states' Press Laws, disclaimers, and corrections have proven effective for most cases and the issue of a counter statement can be disposed of without necessarily going to full trial.

Secondly, the courts can grant an injunction against further publication. In some cases, of course, this may be of little practical value to the people concerned, since the damage has already been done. The only sanction against the publisher is, in these cases, the costs of the trial. But in other instances, the plaintiff may have a legitimate need to restrain further publications and, in such cases, the order, coupled with what we would call a heavy penalty for "contempt of court", can act as an effective deterrent. We noted that this happened in the latest of the Princess Caroline cases.

Thirdly, the German courts seem to be moving towards the view that, when fixing the level of damages to be given to the successful plaintiff, proper account should be taken of the economic value which the publication had for the defendant. The purpose of this is, clearly, to deter the exploitation of the personality of the victims. Some authors, however, have gone further and would argue that these awards contain a punitive element[62] and this even though German law does not, in theory, recognise such a role for tort law.

Fourthly, the zone of privacy enjoyed by public figures in public places has been enlarged under the above mentioned conditions. The exact limits of this new development will, however, emerge only with the passage of time.

This summary shows that German substantive and procedural law may not be ideal. For every one of the points made in this short article there is, clearly, a countervailing argument; and the reader will not be surprised to be told that it has also been advanced in Germany. But, overall, German law has worked well; and there does not seem to have been any ground-swell reaction against

---

[62] Thus Stoll in *International Encyclopedia of Comparative Law*, vol 11.

this judge-made regime. On the contrary, had it not been for the judges, the law might never have been changed since Parliament's only two attempts to legislate on this subject came to grief under heavy pressure from organised Press interests. The corpus of law which has thus emerged is, therefore, both rich and case-based. On closer examination, it should not appear to be too alien to English eyes and, for that reason as well, it deserves to be examined more closely rather than be rejected simply because it is German or European.

Finally, one can conclude in the vein in which one started namely, by making a general observation about comparative methodology.

Those of us who believe that English law needs a new start, also believe that we are not likely to make it by having more reports from official or semi-official bodies. The wider, definitional and philosophical points about privacy have been aired sufficiently (in this country and elsewhere) during the last twenty-five years or so and re-opening them at some stage in the future will only be a way to delay reform further. If a change is to come, it is more likely to come through the medium of judicial intervention as, indeed, happened in Germany; and judicial intervention is more likely to be forthcoming once our judges are given details as to how privacy has worked in other systems and how it could be integrated into ours.

Some fifteen years ago the late Sir Otto Kahn-Freund argued that "what is taught [in law schools] are the general doctrinal foundations to which in after life the lawyer will cling as he may cling to the religious beliefs he learned at his mother's knee. *Practical details are negotiable. Fortunately, for the future of Europe what matters are the practical details; and the diverse doctrinal foundations can look after themselves*".[63] He was, it is submitted, right. The debate about a possible future of a tort of privacy will best be advanced through a careful study of how other systems which recognise the tort have fared in practice. This paper offers a first attempt.

---

[63] "Common Law and Civil Law—Imaginary and Real Obstacles to Assimilation" in M. Cappelletti (ed.), *New Perspectives For A Common Law Of Europe* (1978), 137, 146–7, emphasis added.

20

Litigation-Mania in England, Germany and the United States: are We so Very Different?

This paper was prompted by the *feeling* that the differences between the systems under comparison are not as great as they are commonly believed to be and by the *knowledge* that lawyers in each of these countries tend to have a vague if not distorted picture of each other's laws. The way I have tried to approach my subject has been through the use of statistics so, before I say anything about the differences between the systems, real or apparent, let me make some cautionary remarks.

1. SOME PRELIMINARY OBSERVATIONS

The dangers entailed in the use of statistics have been emphasised by many well-known statements including Disraeli's famous aphorism about there being three types of lies: lies, damned lies and statistics. These dangers are greatly multiplied when statistics from different systems are compared. Here are some of the difficulties that one encounters; and they do not include the major one which is that as one moves from West to East the lack of legal statistics affects the researcher almost as much as the underlying suspicion that where they do exist they may either be unreliable or difficult to convert into statements meaningful to a different legal order.

A. Courts/Judges

There is a vast number of different courts to be found in the various legal systems. When comparing these courts with those of other countries considerable difficulties may arise. For example, names are different and where they are the same they can, in fact, conceal different functions. Moreover, some courts are difficult to classify, e.g. the English magistrate courts which are mainly staffed by lay, unpaid, part-time and, until recently, rather secretly selected men and women. Their inclusion in any statistics would seriously alter the number of judges in England and Wales. Yet, though they handle over 90 per cent of all criminal cases, they are usually not included in the kind of calculations I shall be attempting. For my purposes this may be right since their jurisdiction in tort matters is non-existent and my main focus in this paper will be on tort law. Overall, however, their exclusion tends to falsify comparisons with other systems since they do legal work which, in other systems, professional judges have to do. Court Masters and Registrars also tended to be excluded from official calculations but, as we shall see, their omission is, for comparative purposes, even less defensible since they perform important judicial functions (including quantification of damages in personal injuries litigation) typically carried out by German or French judges. The County Court Registrars in fact hear more cases than the "proper" judges so their exclusion from statistics is really quite unjustifiable. In 1987, for example, the number of judgments given by judges at hearings was 18,871. The corresponding number for Registrars was 142,528![1]

More difficult to count are Recorders (of whom there were 609 in 1987) and Assistant Recorders (of whom there were 417 in 1987). These are part-time judges and statistics show that whereas High Court judges sat for 14,152 days in 1987, Recorders and Assistant Recorders sat for a total of 22,458 days.[2] As Table 1 thus shows, the total figures of judges in England comes to about 842. Subject to what was said previously, this must be one of the lowest figures in the world. But a relatively small alteration in the statistics to include magistrates, Court Masters and Registrars can place this country at the top of this league. And the figure of 28,000 or so still does not include those who hear disputes in Tribunals. (There are other differences between our systems and those of major European countries. For example, the average age of our judiciary, though coming down, is higher than that of France and Germany; and the number of women judges is, in the higher echelons of our system, pitifully low compared with some of our closest neighbours, though this last point can be partly explained by the fact that the pool from which judges are drawn is very small and contains very few women. These, however, are matters that fall outside the scope of this paper.)

The American courts are also equally difficult to classify and available statistics vary from state to state.[3] Most statistics refer to courts of *general jurisdiction* (and in this article I use the term loosely to include state trial courts of general jurisdiction as well as federal courts exercising diversity jurisdiction) but a large number of courts of *limited jurisdiction*, each subject to

---

[1] *Judicial Statistics* (Cmnd. 428) 1987, pp. 35–6. The figures are for "money" plaints: if one includes plaints for the recovery of land, they become, respectively, 22,616 and 155,239. *Ibid.* at p. 41.

[2] *Ibid.*, p. 79.

[3] The estimates given in Table 1 are taken from Professor Abrahams, *The Judicial Process* (1986) p. 23. The number of federal judges includes 9 Supreme Court Justices, 158 judges of the US Circuit Courts and 576 judges of the District Courts. To this total of 753 one should add other federal judges such as: the bankruptcy judges (232), the federal judges of the US Tax Court (19), the Court of Military Appeals (3), the Claims Court (16), the Court of Appeals for the Federal Circuit (12) and the US Court of International Trade (9). One should, perhaps also include all "senior" (i.e. retired) appeals judges and district judges voluntarily serving on a full or part time basis as well as US Magistrates.

Table 1: *Number of Judges in England, Germany and the United States in the mid-1980s*

	England (and Wales)*	Germany			United States†
Civil & Criminal					
Appellate Judges	34	Amtsgerichte	6,100	State Courts	8,000
High Court Judges	79	Landgerichte	4,685	Fed. Courts	1,500‡
Circuit Judges	393	Oberlandes-			
Recorders**	72	gerichte	1,640		
Assistant	52	Bundes-			
Recorders**		gerichtshof	128		
Registrars	212				
Total	842		12,556		9,500
Other Courts					
Magistrates (approximately)	28,000		4,240		
Grand Total					
	29,000 (?) (approx.)		16,796		28,000‡

* This list does not include Deputy High Court Judges, Deputy Circuit Judges, Deputy County Court Registrars, High Court Masters or members of Tribunals, all of whom discharge duties carried out by judges in other systems.

** During 1987 the 79 High Court Judges sat a total of 14,152 days. 609 Recorders sat for 12,976 days and 417 Assistant Recorders sat for 9,482 days. Converting this part-time work to full-time work makes approximately 72 full-time Recorders and 52 Assistant Recorders.

† Judges of general jurisdiction only.

‡ See n. 3 of text.

different rules, also handle tort litigation. Indeed, estimates suggest[4] that of civil suits 54.5 per cent may go to courts of general jurisdiction and 45.5 per cent may end up in the (inferior) courts of limited jurisdiction. Thus, the figures given by most statistics concentrating on courts of general jurisdiction may often be well below total figures. (Note, however, that whereas tort litigation in courts of general jurisdiction represents about 10 per cent of the total, in courts of limited jurisdiction the percentage of tort disputes is about 4.9 per cent of the total.)[5] On the whole, one could say that we have good statistics for federal courts, statistics of variable quality for state courts of general jurisdiction and meagre statistical evidence for courts of limited jurisdiction.

The German courts included in this survey pose another difficulty. This is caused by the high degree of specialisation which is evident from Figure 1.[6]

[4] Kakalik and Pace, *Costs and Compensation Paid in Tort Litigation* (1986), p. 9. This and other statistical studies quoted in this paper were published by the Rand Corporation.

[5] Kakalik and Pace, *op. cit.* above n. 4, p. 9 n. 19.

[6] Reproduced from Markesinis, *The German Law of Torts*, 2nd edn. (1990).

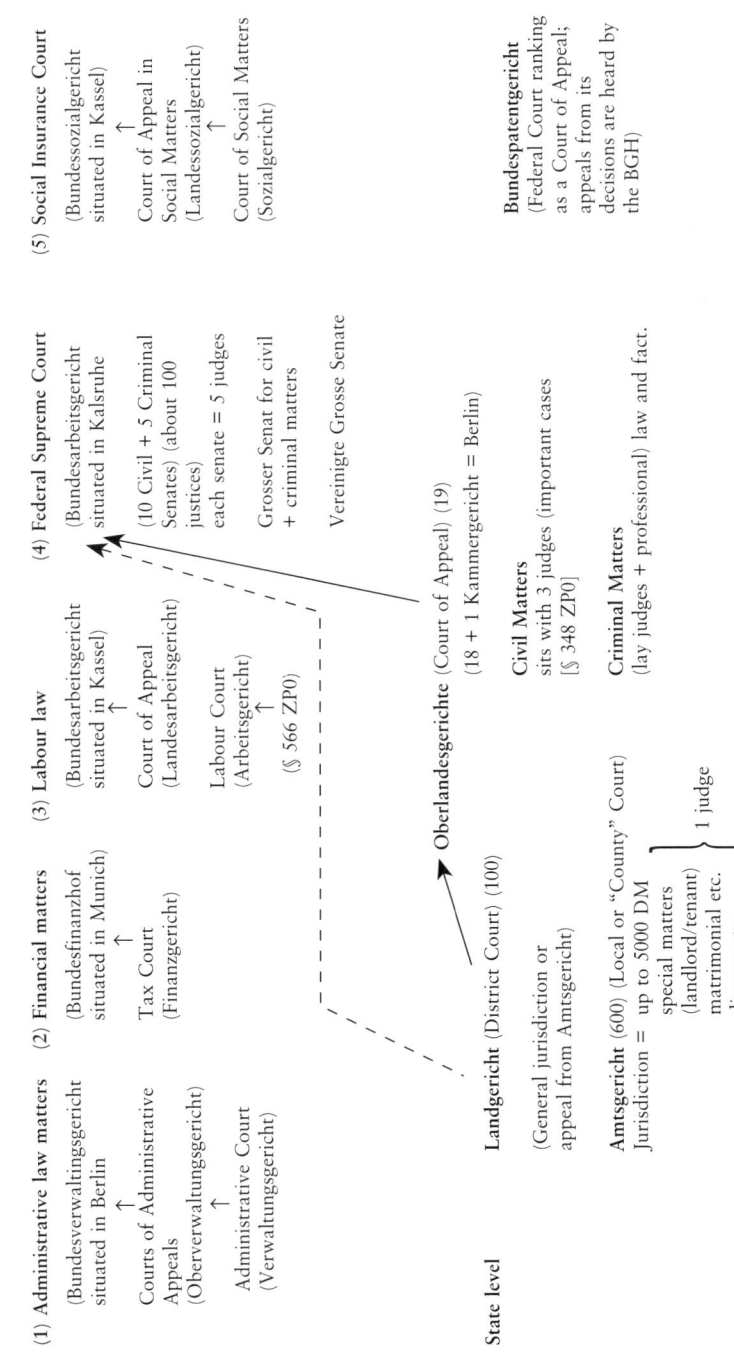

Figure 1: *The Structure of the German Courts*

There are thus six Supreme Courts and 11 Senates in the Bundesgerichtshof (Supreme Federal Court) alone. A vicarious liability dispute, for example, could thus go to the Labour Court, the Federal Court and, within the latter, to its tort or contract section. Because of the system of cumulation of actions (*Anspruchskonkurrenz*) many tort cases are *also* pleaded in contract. Moreover, certain types of claims, which in systems such as ours are tortious in nature, would be handled under the contractual doctrine of *culpa in contrahendo*.[7] Thus, it is not always obvious exactly how these cases are classified and counted for the purposes of statistics. Table 2 provides some idea of the kind of work done by the various Senates (or Divisions) of the Federal (Supreme) Court and, incidentally, also provides some data about the number of final judgments given on merit (not merely on procedural grounds), the average time of hearing in the Bundesgerichtshof as well as the average monetary value of litigation. Since the average time taken to dispose of a case varies from Senate to Senate[8] the allocation of a case to a particular Senate may also be a matter of importance. Similar considerations may also influence American litigants who have a choice between going to a federal or a state court.

B. *Writs/Claims/Filings*

These terms are often used interchangeably but they mean different things. In this country, for example, the medical defence societies constantly talk of an "increase in claims" but we are not told how many of these claims actually turn into writs. Some knowledgeable colleagues have suggested to me that some of these claims may consist of nothing more than a letter from a solicitor which is then not followed up by any further action. Yet they are still recorded as claims, thus possibly distorting the overall impact that this information can have. The secrecy with which the medical defence societies shroud this part of their operations makes any comment on such views impossible. Difficulties are also compounded by the fact that court filings are defined in different ways in the United States. In some states, for example New York and New Jersey, civil filings are included in judicial statistics only when the

---

[7] Thus, the equivalent of our tort case of *Ward* v. *Tesco* [1976] 1 WLR 810 is BGHZ 66, 51 and it was heard by the eighth civil division of the Federal Court which, normally, deals with sales of goods and leases. Since the plaintiff also won on tort grounds, the sixth civil division could also have heard the case. Finally, since *culpa in contrahendo* is a contractual doctrine the case could, in theory, also have been claimed by the seventh division which handles contractual disputes. Other divisions could handle and have handled such claims which we classify as tortious. For examples see Markesinis, *The German Law of Torts*, 2nd edn. (1990), Ch. 3, section B.2. This problem of proper or, rather, consistent classification also exists at the state level in the United States where, apparently, "not all state courts distinguish tort litigation from other civil cases such as commercial and contract writs". Hensler, Vaiana, Kakalik, Peterson, *Trends in Tort Litigation. The Story Behind the Statistics* (1987), p. 6.

[8] The average time of a disposal of a case by means of a judgment on merits in the BGH is 15.8 months. For more precise details depending on the nature of the disputes see Table 2. The *average* time from issue of writ to judgment by the BGH seems to be 34.2 months.

Table 2: *Bundesgerichtshof Senates, Specialisation/Number of Final Judgments/ Average Awards 1986*

Senate	Type of case considered	Nos of judgments	Average time in BGH (months)	Average value of claims (ex. costs) DM
I	Competition, trademark	101	25.4	188,200
II	Companies, Stock Exchange Disputes	95	10.4	473,400
III	Building and planning, Bankruptcy, § 839 BGB	82	16.3	279,500
IVa	Insurance contracts	94	20.3	165,500
IVb	Family Law	63	13.7	63,600
V	Land Law	56	17.3	328,000
VI	Tort	80	13.2	122,600
VII	Contracts	51	13.3	179,500
VIII	Commercial law, landlord/tenant	70	12.0	232,700
IX	Execution of judgments	49	9.3	211,000
X	Patents, copyrights	12	14.1	229,500
	Kartellsenat	12	16.4	426,800
	Dienstgericht (staff disputes)	5	7.2	14,000

case has been "placed on the calendar" or has reached "issue" or "readiness". Thus, in those two large states, a case that settles early in the process is never recorded for statistical purposes.[9]

C. Damage Awards

There are three major dangers here. First, the terms *average* (sometimes more accurately referred to as *mean*) and *median* are not always used precisely or consistently while the equally interesting statistical indicator of the typical award—the *mode* (i.e. the value that occurs most frequently)—seems to be rarely used. Secondly, there are enormous variations on the basis of (a) regions within federal states such as the United States (e.g. California and Chicago

[9] Kakalik and Pace, *op. cit.* above n. 4, p. 7.

compared to Louisiana[10]) or even with some unitary states (e.g. France[11]) and (b) type of tort litigation, e.g. products liability and medical malpractice, compared to other tort cases (about which further on). Thirdly, the average figures given are, more often than not, stated without reference to out-of-court settlements—which account for approximately 90 per cent of all payments; and they do not include defendants' verdicts or subsequent adjustments by means of settlements, remittiturs or appeals. In practice this can make an enormous difference. For example, in the notorious *Ford Pinto* case a jury award of US$ 125 million was subsequently reduced to US$ 3.5 million.[12] Finally, figures given are often not properly adjusted to take into account factors such as inflation. Thus, though it is generally accepted that recorded claims have exceeded the rate of inflation since the 1970s, the exact amount is not beyond dispute.[13] In my experience the only entities which have figures are the insurance companies and, once again, they tend to guard them jealously.

2. WHY THE DIFFERENCES?

Despite the caveats expressed concerning the dangers inherent in statistics, comparisons can be and have been made between various legal systems. Making use of such figures, England and the United States have, in particular, often been compared and such exercises have prompted various conclusions among which the central one is that American society is much more lawyer-oriented and litigious than the English. For example, Professor Atiyah, paraphrasing Bernard Shaw, has referred to England and America as two

---

[10] California and Illinois (Cook County in particular) seem to have received enormous attention whereas other states are hardly ever mentioned. Even between these two states the differences can be impressive. For example, punitive damages were awarded in business/contract cases three times more often in major urban Californian jurisdictions than they were in Cook County. *Punitive Damages. Empirical Findings* (Rand Corporation, 1987), p. 34. Punitive damages are not as easily available in Louisiana—a state with a civil law background.

[11] On this see Viney and Markesinis, *La Reparation du Dommage Corporel—Essai de Comparison des Droits Anglais et Française* (1985), para. 30.

[12] *Grimshaw* v. *Ford Motor Co.* 119 Cal.App. 3rd 757. Punitive damages in product liability cases have caused much discussion yet the Rand Corporation study quoted above (p. v) states that "our analyses indicate that punitive damages were awarded in only four product liability cases in San Francisco and two in Cook County from 1960 through 1984". Apparently, before 1980, 60% of all punitive awards occurred in intentional torts. After 1980 the percentage dropped to 22 and business/contract cases generated 67% of all punitive awards. *Ibid.*, p. 19. About 2% of trials involving personal injury resulted in punitive awards (*ibid.*, p. 11). In another study by a Rand Corporation team—Hensler, Vaiana, Kakalik and Peterson, *op. cit.* above n. 7, above, at pp. 22–3 it is said "that awards most likely to be viewed as 'excessive' . . . are most likely to be cut substantially".

[13] On this, see Galanter, "Reading the Landscape of Disputes: What we know and don't know (and think we know) about our allegedly contentious and litigious society", (1983) 31 *UCLA Law Rev.* 4 and, especially, Galanter, "The Day after the Litigation Explosion", (1986) 46 *Maryland L. Rev.* 3. For a more *nuancé* description see Hensler, Vaiana, Kakalik and Peterson, *op. cit.* above n. 7, at pp. 14–24.

countries separated by a common legal culture.[14] Figures 2 and 3 tend, at first sight at least, to support the view that even allowing for the population differences, there exist important differences between the systems. However, as we shall see further on, the real differences are not to be found in overall figures but in particular types of litigation. The reasons for these differences are many and some of them may have been overstressed or, conversely, understressed in importance. The use of German figures tends to support this scepticism and can introduce an altogether different dimension to the enquiry since it is obvious that the Federal Republic in some respects shows greater affinity with the American scene than it does with England. How, then, can we explain some of these differences between the various systems? Here, first, are some possible explanations covering the Anglo-American differences.

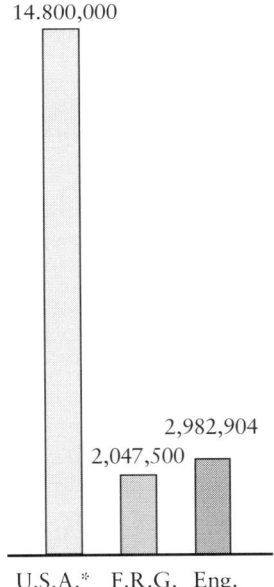

Figure 2: *Total Number* of Civil Actions*

* Figures refer to filings in courts of general *and* limited jurisdictions. 54.2% of this total—i.e. 8.02 million—are *estimated* to be general jurisdiction filings.

A number of reasons have been advanced to explain the differences between England and the United States suggested by the figures. One can go through them quickly since a number of authors have already examined them in a number of works.[15]

[14] "Tort Law and the Alternatives: Some Anglo-American Comparisons", (1987) *Duke L. Journ.* 1002, p. 1005.

[15] John Fleming's *The American Tort Process* (1988) is one of the most recent and it provides rich references to further related literature.

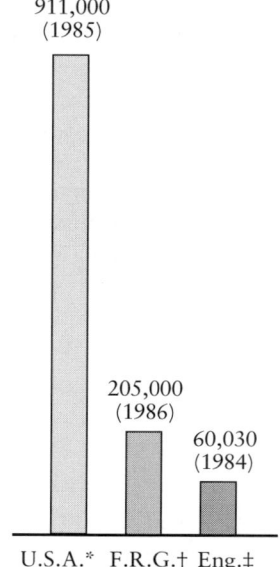

911,000
(1985)

205,000
(1986)

60,030
(1984)

U.S.A.* F.R.G.† Eng.‡

Figure 3: *Number of Tort Suits*

* American figures refer to filings in courts of *general* jurisdiction (see Table 1). Of the 911,000, 869,000 were filings in state courts and 42,000 in federal courts.

† This is an estimate based on (a) the percentage of tort actions fought to the end in the Bundesgerichtshof (BGH) which, over the years, has been somewhere in the order of 8% of that court's total number of decisions and (b) the opinions expressed to me that for various reasons the BGH figure is likely to be higher than the overall percentage.

‡ Judicial Statistics Annual Report 1987 (Cmnd. 428) 1988: 31,470 writs issued in High Court for pers. injuries; 24,060 owrits issued in County Courts for pers. injuries. In addition: 550 non-personal injury tort suits in High Court; 4,920 non-personal injury tort suits in County Court.

A. Political Judges with Definite Ideas for Social Reform

The paralysis of legislatures, provoked by competing lobby pressures, is a notorious phenomenon in the United States and is one reason for the fact that much of American tort reform was achieved after the Second World War by means of judicial initiatives at state level and *not*, as in England through legislative action. Another and related reason is the optimistic belief that change always entails progress. This, in turn, induces a sense of mission to improve the existing legal order that many of my American colleagues, students and legal friends display at times with endearing if somewhat naïve fervour. Judicial innovation thus fits in with the mood of a society which is physically and intellectually constantly "on the move". By contrast static or traditionalist societies like ours seek refuge in notions like *stare decisis* and opt for incremental changes and—what is worse—phased corrections of admitted errors. What, however, is most striking to a foreign observer is the American judge's *open* commitment to social reform which is often connected with the fact that many judges (a) are elected by popular vote and (b) may have run for judicial office only after they failed in their bid to capture high political office. Robert Neely, an elected member of the Supreme Court of West Virginia, unusually outspoken even by American standards, is a good example since in his many writings he has clearly expressed the attitude that I have just mentioned.[16]

B. *The Pro-Plaintiff Bar*

The pro-plaintiff bar effectively represented by its own organisation—the Association of Trial Lawyers of America (ATLA)—is also a well-documented phenomenon as is its influence as a pressure group both in local politics and judicial appointments. ATLA has, with evangelical fervour, been particularly active in fending off moves to undo by legislative action (promoted with equal fervour by the insurance industry) judicial decisions that were favourable to plaintiffs. The introduction of no-fault automobile plans—avoiding jury involvement—and the attempts to limit the extent of medical liability were thus strenuously opposed. Even more questionable—at any rate to non-American lawyers—is the extensive political mobilisation, often furthered by substantial financial donations, to secure the appointment of demonstrably pro-plaintiff lawyers to the highest judicial offices; or, as happened with California's Chief Justice Rose Bird, to secure her re-election as Chief Justice in the face of growing opposition towards her judicial activism, especially but not solely in criminal matters. (In my opinion the recent defeats of pro-plaintiff justices in the Supreme Courts of some states—such as Texas and California—indicate in part that the electorate may be slowly becoming aware of some of the excesses of the pro-plaintiff lobby but non-American lawyers should be slow in formulating definite opinions on such complicated issues.) The pro-plaintiff bar, however, has also had influential academic defenders who saw nineteenth century American tort law as deliberately subsidising nascent industrialisation at the expense of the working classes[17] and thus welcomed the pro-plaintiff decisions as an inevitable attempt by the courts to fill the gap left by a non-existent welfare state. These pro-plaintiff views may, in many respects, be closely linked to the next factor.

C. *The Absence of a Strong Welfare State System*

This results in many victims of accidents being left with little or no coverage for their medical treatment and, therefore, being forced to seek redress

---

[16] See, for example: *How Courts Govern America* (1981) and *The Product Liability Mess* (1988). For a more restrained account see Atiyah and Summers, *Form and Substance in Anglo-American Law* (1987), Ch.s 10 and 12.

[17] e.g. Horwitz, *The Transformation of American Law 1780–1860* (1977), severely criticised by among others, Schwartz, "Tort Law and the Economy in Nineteenth Century America: A Reinterpretation" (1981) 90 *Yale L.J.* 1717; *idem.*, "The Character of Early American Tort Law" (1989) 36 *UCLA L. Rev.* 641.

through generous tort awards. The importance of this factor is mentioned here partly because it explains the generosity (real or apparent[18]) of American tort awards—something which has often been forgotten by potential imitators on the other side of the Atlantic (for example when, in the 1970s, they became excited about American products liability law)—and partly because in some (European) systems the existence of a generous welfare system has resulted in the reduction or even total absence of a certain type of litigation which, by contrast, has been very popular in another. Thus, Professor Lorenz wrote to me that "The German social security system has the effect that many cases are not litigated. A typical example seems to be *Asbestos*. Certainly, the number of illnesses and even deaths due to asbestos is alarming.[19] However, thus far no asbestos case has been reported from the BGH. I have discussed the matter with my colleague Dieter Medicus [an eminent Professor of Civil Law at the University of Munich] . . . and he, too, knows of no relevant litigation". As we shall see, in this matter the United Kingdom is somewhere in between these two extremes with a tiny number of cases—apparently only twenty-nine—*tried* by courts in England, Scotland and Northern Ireland between 1970 and 1987 and rather more writs issued but settled without a final judgment. Why exactly the German social security system has discouraged this type of litigation, whereas the English has not done so, is not entirely clear. The comparative generosity of German and English social security awards is thus another topic that warrants further investigation.

D. *The Presence of a Large Number of Lawyers and the Availability of the Contingency Fee System*

These are also crucial factors as far as "easy access to justice" is concerned. The American figures in Table 3 would, again, *appear* to support this conclusion. Critics of the contingency fee system also blame this method of payment of the legal fees for much of the litigation. Defenders of the system have not only drawn attention to the shortcomings of our own legal aid scheme but have also stressed, with some measure of accuracy, that attorneys can be quite sophisticated in calculating their chances of success and will refuse to take on a case if it looks hopeless or even weak. In this context, an interesting feature of the American system is the use of in-house doctors to advise a firm whether to take on a medical malpractice case—a course of action which, apparently, leads to something in the order of 85 per cent of potential plaintiffs being turned down by legal firms. Still, one also hears of a number of quite frivolous tort claims brought before American courts, a fact which suggests that

---

[18] I shall return to this point below.

[19] Thus, for example, the *Süddeutsche Zeitung* reported in its issue of 26 June 1989 that the *Deutscher Gewerkschaftsbund* (German Trade Union Association) had recorded 292 instances of asbestos-related complaints—46 of them being fatal. It would be interesting to see a comparative study of social security payments in comparable situations in England and Germany in order to explain the apparently total lack of litigation in Germany.

not all lawyers are as selective; these claims also reveal something of the litigious nature of the Americans to which I shall return later in this lecture.[20]

Table 3: *Number of Practising Lawyers**

	England (and Wales)		Germany	United States
Barristers	5,369	Attorneys	41,724	674,000
Solicitors	50,337	Attorneys/ Notaries	7,250	
		Notaries	1,003	
Total	55,706	Total	50,347	674,000

Judges and Lawyers per 1 million of population[†]

Judges	16.8**	278	116
Lawyers	1,120	810	2,808

* Source: *Whitaker's Almanac* 1989.
** Counting only the 842 (see Table 1). The figure is thus suspect.
† Population of *United Kingdom*: 56,972,700 from England: 47,254,000; Wales: 2,821,000; Scotland: 5,121,000; N. Ireland: 1,575,200. Population of *Federal Republic of Germany*: 61,149,000; United States: 239,283,000.

E. Juries

Here, I think, lies one of the crucial differences. According to Professor John Fleming of the University of California at Berkeley it would not be an exaggeration to say that the transformation of American tort law owes much to the surrender of most legal concepts to civil juries.[21] As a result, the ambit of many tort rules has been widened beyond the limits accepted by English law. Thus, the combined effect of lax attitudes by judges (especially trial judges) and juries had led to tort liability moving even further away from fault than

[20] A number of amusing/outrageous examples are given in *U.S. News and World Report*, 4 December 1978. For those who collect these stories the *California Lawyer*, July 1989, vol. 9, no. 7, p. 34, contained the latest outrageous example: a fifteen-year-old girl and her mother filed a claim against the girl's boy friend claiming $49.53 for "the cost of the shoes, flowers and hairdo (that the girl) never got to wear" because the boy "stood her up for the date. Filing the claim cost $31.75". This type of situation has, apparently, led to court filings in the past. See *U.S. News and World Report* 1978, p. 50. Stories like these, and the one with which Mr Bernard Levin entertained his readers (*The Times*, 29 June 1989) are amusing, but they are dangerously misleading if they provide, as they often do, the only conception that ordinary people have about the American system and how it works in practice.
[21] Fleming, *op. cit.* above n.15, p. 131.

it has in English law (e.g. product liability law); and many non-liability enclaves of English law have vanished in the United States (e.g. liability for certain types of omission).

The effect that juries have had on the development of American substantive tort law was recently examined by Professor John Fleming and little need be added here. For present purposes, however, three things are worth stressing—and they emerge clearly, from various statistical surveys. The *first*, clearly supported by the various Rand Corporation studies, is the juries' propensity to vary and adjust the amounts awarded depending on the circumstances of the accident. Thus, if the loss of two legs in a car accident will result in an average $250,000 in compensation, *the same loss to the same kind of plaintiff*, resulting from an accident in the workplace (probably as the result of a defective product) can produce, on average, three times as much compensation. The *second* thing that juries do is to relate damages to the defendant's degree of fault and his financial resources. That juries, once again, treat identical injuries differently depending on *who* is being sued does not seem to be in doubt. What does remain unsettled is the extent that jury damage awards deny equal justice. Thus, one Rand Corporation study[22] has claimed that government defendants pay three times more than private defendants and corporate defendants pay four and a half times more. The result, according to the same study, is that "where a government defendant might pay $75,000 and an individual defendant $50,000 to a severely injured plaintiff, a corporate defendant would pay $220,000." Other studies, however, suggest that the differences may be much less pronounced,[23] while yet a third study, which has focused on median awards made by Cook County juries in cases involving damage to property, distinguished between "moderate" and "serious" cases. In the first category median awards against individuals were $27,000, against corporations were $35,000 and against government entities were $41,000. In the second category the figures were $37,000 against individuals, $98,000

---

[22] Chin and Peterson, *Deep Pockets. Empty Pockets. Who Wins in Cook County Jury Trials* (1985), p. vii. Interestingly enough post-verdict reduction of awards is also smaller where deeppocket defendants are involved. See Hensler, Vaiana, Kakalik and Peterson, *op. cit.* above n. 7, p. 22. The tendency to punish corporate defendants is even greater in cases involving punitive awards. These results have been replicated by two other researchers using a mock juror experiment. As MacCoun, who reports the work in *Getting Inside the Black Box: Toward a Better Understanding of Civil Jury Behaviour* (1987), p. 34, puts it: "Hans and Ermann created a brief trial summary in which several workers received permanent lung damage following exposure to a toxic substance during a landscaping job. Students read one of two versions of the case in which the defendant was described as either 'Mr. Jones' or 'the Jones Corporation'. This simple manipulation influenced *both* liability and damage judgments. The corporation was held liable for *significantly* more claims than the individual, and awards against the corporation were *significantly* larger than awards against the individual in each category of damages: *hospital bills*, and especially '*pain and suffering*' " (italics supplied).

[23] See, for example, *Claim File Data Analysis: Technical Analysis of Study Results*, Insurance Services Office (ISO) Data. Inc. (1988) pp. 39, 45. Where average loss for single defendant claims (involving $25,000 or more) are stated to be $91,466 for government defendants, $90,320 for business defendants and $758,821 for individual defendants.

against government entities and $161,000 against corporations. As the study concludes "this 165 to 335 per cent difference is staggering".[24] There is no detailed study showing to what extent, if any, judges—consciously or unconsciously—do the same thing in those systems where juries are ignored. In Germany, however, judges tend to increase the size of awards in privacy and defamation case where media defendants were involved. And there is also anecdotal evidence to suggest that the same happens in French contract and tort law. Since, however, the open linking of damages to the degree of the defendant's fault and his status would, automatically, justify a *pourvoi* to the Court of cassation, there is little evidence of such practice in the reports. *Finally,* the lack of even a relative degree of consistency in some cases of jury awards must make it more difficult for extra-judicial settlements to be reached. Thus in the mid-1980s an ABA conference was told that "the same injury might lead to a tort award ranging from $10,000 to $2 million".[25] At about the same time Judge Klein (a Philadelphia Common Pleas judge) said in *Blue* v. *Johns-Manville Corp.*:[26]

> "In two cases before this judge, two men had similar physical problems. They each had pleural thickening and some shortness of breath. In the case involving the man who most counsel believed to be the sicker of the two, the jury awarded $15,000. For the other plaintiff, the jury awarded $1,200,000. These results make this litigation more like a roulette than jurisprudence".

3. WHAT DOES THE COMPARISON WITH GERMANY SUGGEST?

If we look again at Figures 2 and 3 and Table 1 (and allow for population differences given in Table 3) we see that the Germans bring approximately 55 per cent of the total number of suits brought by the Americans but have (again allowing for population differences) almost 100 per cent more judges (though fewer attorneys)[27] to handle their judicial load. The English, on the other hand, seem to have the *same* overall number of actions as the Americans, though when it comes to judges they tend to underplay their numbers.

If we shift to the tort scene the picture changes. If the German estimate of tort suits is correct—a big assumption as one sees from the second note to Figure 3—the rate of tort litigation in that country is about the same as it is

---

[24] Kelly and Beyley, "Large Damage Awards and the Insurance Crisis: Cause, Effects and Cures", (1986) 130 *Illinois Bar Journal* 140, 153.

[25] *Towards a Jurisprudence of Injury: A Summary of the Report of the A.B.A.'s Special Committee on the Tort Liability System* (1986), pp. 2–26.

[26] 10 Phila. 23 (1983). This statement was quoted as one illustration of the kind of difficulties encountered in asbestos litigation by Judge Weis in the important *In Re School Asbestos Litigation* 789 F 2d. (1986). A Rand Corporation Study by Hensler, Felstiner, Selvin and Ebener entitled *Asbestos in the Courts* (1985) states at p. 42 that those problems may in part be due to the difficulties experienced by juries when "dealing with probabilistic [*sic*] evidence".

[27] The word is used in a neutral way to avoid distinctions between barristers, solicitors, Rechtsanwalt, notaries, etc.

in the United States. In terms of tort suits per 1 million of population that means some 3,750 suits in America as against 3,278 suits in Germany—a roughly comparable figure. England, on the other hand, reveals a different picture. Tort suits are, apparently, about three times less numerous than they are in the United States and Germany or about 1,200 tort actions per 1 million of population. In view of the above, are we right to compare ourselves with the Americans and claim that they are afflicted by a tort crisis and we are not? If so, what are the reasons that have provoked the American crisis and can they affect us as well? Should we bracket Germany with the United States and claim—as they, themselves, do not—that there is a tort crisis in Germany? Could it be that we in England have been spoilt by low rates of litigation[28] and, if so, why do we sue less in tort than other nations but, in other contexts, we are apparently willing to chance litigation as much as they do? The introduction of the German figures—despite the uncertainty that surrounds them—thus forces one to re-examine the validity of the reasons given to explain the differences between England and the United States.

The German scene makes a number of things clear. You do not need a politically-minded judiciary in order to encourage frequent recourse to the courts. Nor does the absence of the contingency fee system necessarily avoid it. (The Scottish version of the contingency fee system seems to be different.) The absence of a pro-plaintiff bar in the American style has also not discouraged Germans from going to court. Finally, a stronger social security system may make tort awards *appear* to be smaller than they actually are in terms of total compensation; and it does not always stop aggrieved citizens from having recourse to tort law. What about the legal rules: are they more or less generous to plaintiffs than the American ones?

Conventional wisdom has it that American tort rules are more generous towards plaintiffs than the English ones. But when you compare American and German tort rules the verdict does not appear to me to be uniformly in favour of one or the other system. Thus, German law blazed the trail in actions for pre-natal injuries; it is still more generous than Anglo-American law to victims of nervous shock; and it has never taken a completely hostile view towards liability for harmful omissions in the way that English (and less so American) law have done. On the other hand, it took longer to reach the levels of strict liability attained by American product liability law; and in the context of fatal accidents actions, it has drawn the list of dependants who can claim damages in a more restricted way, preferring, perhaps, certainty to flexible justice (as the French do in this matter). In matters of causation it has also treated the adequate cause test in an expansive manner, not dissimilar to our foreseeability test—so much so that for some time now the trend has been

---

[28] It is clear, for example, that there have been fewer asbestos-related suits in this country than there have been in the United States even though, as we shall note below, where legal action was taken it produced remarkably similar awards in both systems. Felstiner and Dingwall, *Asbestos Litigation in the United Kingdom* (1988), especially pp. 17 *et seq.* and Table 12.

to rely more on normative tests of causation, such as the scope of the rule theory.[29]

Yet, paradoxically perhaps, one cannot find in its generous legal rules the reason for greater litigiousness since nervous shock cases, omission cases and the like never seem to have produced a formidable body of case law. On the contrary, the great generators of litigation have been such well-known causes as traffic accidents (despite the strict liability Road Traffic Act which by avoiding fault liability was meant to facilitate the compensation of victims of traffic accidents) and the related difficulties of evaluating damages for personal injury. According to the *Statistisches Jahrbuch* for 1988, a total of 160,975 such actions were instigated in 1986 of which the vast majority— 123,237—were commenced in the *Amtsgerichte* (which suggest that they involved claims below 5,000 DM). The other highly litigated subjects are sales of goods (often raising tort problems as well, a total of 277,440 actions), the law concerning builders and architects (27,188), and the law of landlord and tenant (270,510 actions),[30] all well known both in England and the United States. Matrimonial disputes also account for a substantial proportion of litigation. One cannot, therefore, find here, either, a special explanation for the greater volume of litigation. Indeed, as already stated, in terms of law suits *commenced*—proportionate to their populations—the difference between the three countries compared in this paper is not as great as commonly believed. Figure 2 suggests as much. Certain types of product liability and medical malpractice disputes may, as we shall see, provide the greatest differences with the United States in terms of number of suits brought and, above all, in the potential to lead to "mega-awards".

But if the reasons for the greater volume of litigation have not yet been identified, and all that we seem to have managed to do so far is to weaken the value of the explanations of the American phenomenon, the reasons for

---

[29] For more details on all these topics see my *German Law of Tort: A Comparative Introduction*, 2nd edn. (1990). In his study "Das Problem des Kausalzusammenhangs im Privatrecht" reprinted in his *Gesammelte Schriften*, I, p. 395 *et seq.*, Professor Ernst von Caemmerer reached the conclusion that the plaintiff's claim will rarely if ever fail if adequate causation is the only "corrective" device in the hands of the judge. Our foreseeability test can reach similarly outrageous results. See *Meah* v. *McCreamer (No. 1)* [1985] 1 All ER 367 and *(No. 2)* [1986] 1 All ER 943.

[30] *Statistisches Jahrbuch* 1988, p. 331. The statistics give no details about particular types of negligence litigation under para. 823 I BGB such as for example the number of medical malpractice claims that reach the courts. Thus I have only been able to find *estimates* that put the figure of claims satisfied (by Arbitration Board *and* courts) at about 3,000. Deutsch, Schreiber and Lilie, *Medizinische Verantwortlichkeit und Verfahren* in *Medical Responsibility in Western Europe* (1985), pp. 226 *et seq.* esp. 230. Most commentators, including the aforementioned authors, draw statistical information from Professor Hans-Leo Weyers's empirical work published in *Gutachten A für den 52. Deutschen Juristentag. Empfiehlt es sich, im Interesse der Patienten und Artze ergänzende Regelungen für das ärztliche Vertrags- (Standes-) und Haftungrecht einzuführen?* (Verhandlungen des 52. Deutschen Juristentages, München, 1978) Bd. 1, p. 37 *et seq.* This survey, however, though replete with interesting information, invariably refers to claims met by Arbitration Boards and courts. Moreover, it seems to me to suffer from the fact that its information is: (a) about fifteen years old and (b) its estimates derived from inadequate sources.

Table 4: *Civil Proceedings Before the German Courts*

Number of writs issued		
1.	*Amtsgerichte* (general civil jurisdiction)	1,306,628
2.	*Amtsgerichte* (family division)	368,406
3.	*Landgerichte* (as court of first instance)	353,292
	Total:	2,028,326
Number of actions decided in 1986		
1.	*Amtsgerichte*	
	settled out of court	576,122
	undefended (resolved by court)	353,907
	fought to the end	376,599
	Total:	1,306,628
2.	*Landgerichte*	
	settled out of court	175,963
	undefended (resolved by court)	72,987
	fought to end	104,542
	Total:	353,292
3.	Family Division (only matrimonial) (divorce cases reported only)	
	undefended	29,597
	fought to end	124,630
4.	*Landgerichte* (sitting as court of first instance)	
	Total:	87,981
	number fought to end	48,007
5.	Courts of Appeal	
	Total:	53,633
	fought to end	25,668

the greater number of judges are less difficult to discern. Obviously, a greater volume of litigation needs more professionals to handle it properly. Overall at the writ stage there are, as Figure 2 demonstrates, some differences in the volume of litigation. What is important, however, is not the number of law actions *commenced*—England, for example, as Figure 2 shows, has a higher number than Germany despite the fact that it has a smaller population—but how many of them actually run *their full course* and end by means of a judgment of the court pronouncing on the merits of the case. Here, if we compare figures in Tables 4, 5 and 6, we see that in England a remarkably low num-

Table 5: *Summary Analysis of Queen's Bench Division in 1986*

Total proceedings commenced	234,782
Matters involved —debt	183,199
—breach of contract	9,150
—personal injury & death	24,183
—recovery of land	5,190
—other	13,060
Judgments given without trial (by default; Order 14 etc.)	100,967
Contested cases ending with judgment	
—personal injury and death	2,670
—other	1,010
Total:	3,680

ber actually reaches the very end. Moreover, if one takes the County Court figure (Table 6), one notices that over half of these cases are resolved through arbitration with the intervention of one official—the Registrar—whom as I said we do not (yet) dignify with the title of "judge". Here then, we have a very significant difference between the English and German scenes.

A second reason for the need for more judges in Germany is, of course, the fact that in that system (as in all civil law systems) the judge has to do so much more in a case than his common law counterparts. So, while in the procedure of civil law courts the advocate plays, on the whole, a more passive role, the judge, in the context of the prevailing inquisitorial system, has the direction of the entire proceedings, including the examination of the witnesses and the finding of the appropriate law, assigned almost entirely to his charge. *Iura novit curia* is an expensive compliment to pay to a judge! Thus, overall,

Table 6: *The Workload of the County Courts in 1987**

All nature of plaints	2,375,431
Judgments enforced by default or with consent	1,184,264
Cases decided by formal trial	**23,248
Cases decided by arbitration of Registrar	†47,841

  * Source: *Judicial Statistics* 1987, p. 35.
  ** 14,675 decided by a judge; 8,573 decided by a Registrar.
  † 45,612 after arbitration by a Registrar; 229 after arbitration by a judge.

the civilian judge tends to be overworked whereas the civilian advocates tends to be underworked—at any rate in the context of litigation.[31]

Here is no place to consider the merits of the inquisitorial versus the accusatorial system; but the large number of cases that in Germany may be allowed to drag on to the end must be noted. In this context I think our system is preferable; and, I believe, a factor that contributes to this German phenomenon is the way lawyers are paid the more or less low, predetermined sums (almost invariably determined by the sums in dispute) they are entitled to claim for each case they handle. For payment is, on the whole, "front loaded" and with costs being low, compared to English and American law, the litigant seems to have little or no incentive to withdraw or compromise his action. (Note, however, that a court-approved compromise (*Vergleich*) entitles the attorney to a (usually small) additional sum (*Vergleichsgebühr*).)

4. WHAT REALLY MAKES PEOPLE GO TO COURT?

A number of reasons have, at times, been advanced to explain the differences between the scenes in the United States and England. The fact, however, that one finds analogous trends in the Continent of Europe would suggest that the reasons that we have examined briefly are, at most, local factors that strengthen other forces at work. I focus on three in particular.

The *first* is the relative cheapness of having access to the courts. Comparatively speaking, from the litigant's point of view, this is true if one compares, on the one hand, the United States and Germany and, on the other hand, England. The contingency fee system in the United States, coupled with the class action mechanism (in practice rarely used because of its complexities), punitive damages and psychological effect that "mega-awards" can have on potential litigants, all combine to encourage more persons to chance their luck in court. The German pattern is, on the other hand, different, though it leads to the same results. Tables set the fees that can be charged and these, as already stated, are modest and are mainly related to the disputed amount. The way the remuneration is computed is difficult but it is interesting to note that the figures given in these official tables represent minimum amounts. I am told, however, that these are observed in practice—at least at the two low levels. Thus, half a million pounds in legal expenses for a defamation case (Jeffrey Archer) or a tax-evasion prosecution (Ken Dodd) are, I am told,

---

[31] "To the common law lawyer . . . the German judge will seem to be highly vocal and dominant whereas counsel will appear to act with somewhat subdued zeal": Kötz, "The role of the judge in the court-room: the common law and civil law compared" (1987) *Tydskrif vir die Suid-Afrikaanse Reg* 35. The idea of increased judicial control over the conduct of the action is increasingly appealing to some American and British proceduralists. See Langbein, "The German Advantage in Civil Procedure", (1985) *U. Chicago L. Rev.* 823, 858–862; Jolowicz, "Some Twentieth Century Developments in Anglo-American Civil Procedure", *Studi in onore de Enrico Tullio Liebeman* (1979), p. 217.

unimaginable figures in civil law countries such as Germany or France. In any event, the fee levels seem low and, coupled with the wide availability of litigation insurance, make it relatively easy for a German citizen to sue and then think, if at all, of a possible compromise. So the Americans, by shifting the risk of litigation costs to the attorney, and the Germans, by keeping them low, tend to achieve the same objective which is easy access to the courts.

The cheapness of litigation in Germany is also reflected in their court-appointed system of experts—usually just one. These experts are paid an hourly rate of 70 DM (just over £20) a figure that may "in extreme cases" rise to 105 DM. Because the proceedings are different, and the time that an expert has to spend "in court" is also considerably less than that of his English or American counterpart, the final bill is invariably much lower. By contrast, in our system each party engages its own experts—often two or more on each side—and in many instances—including medical cases—these experts can spend many hours in court, adding significantly to the total cost of the trial. Whether they improve the chances of discovering what went wrong is, I think, a matter of some doubt. What appears to be less in doubt is the falsity of the old myth that one cannot find doctors to testify against doctors.

This cheapness must be, at the very least, an important contributory factor in the important difference that exists between England and Germany when it comes to the number of cases that are actually fought to the end. For even the system of court-approved amicable settlement of proceedings (*Prozessvergleich*), encouraged by section 279 *Zivilprozessordnung* and achieved in about 15 per cent of cases,[32] still leaves a large number of actions to be fought to the very end, and the pre-trial phase in civil (but not criminal) cases does not cut down significantly the number of cases that reach what we would call "open court". The possibility of pre-trial discovery and the narrowing of the issue in dispute is, also, on the whole weaker than it is in English law. In one word, the legal background is in tune with the Continental mentality which regards access to the courts to be free to all and not restricted to the few who can afford to litigate, let alone fight to the end. This attitude is also reflected in the appeals system, my civilian colleagues always being shocked (and, if they are judges, not a little envious) of the minuscule number of cases heard annually by the House of Lords.

The second reason is, I think, the greater awareness that victims have in the United States and Europe of their *rights* to go to court. Freer advertising by lawyers—compared to England—insurance to cover litigation costs (in Germany) and a growing number of semi-official bodies and consumer organisations informing citizens of their rights as victims also help reinforce the feeling that recourse to the courts is, as it were, a natural right and not a privilege to be availed of rarely. An interesting illustration of this can be found in

---

[32] On the whole matter see Stein-Jonas, *Kommentar zur Zivilprozessordnung* 20th edn. by Grunsky, Leipold, Münzberg, Schlosser and Schumann (1984) § 279. The percentage is, apparently, higher in medical malpractice cases.

the comparison of what, for brevity's sake, I shall call the Unfair Contract Terms Acts of England and Germany, for in the latter we find that consumer organisations, as well as the contracting parties, have the right to challenge the validity of potentially unfair clauses in standard form contracts.[33]

The role of consumer-orientated bodies that inform plaintiffs of their potential rights is one that deserves much closer empirical study, so that it can be both encouraged and controlled. Here suffice it to say that in English medical cases bodies like the AVMA (Association of Victims of Medical Accidents) have contributed to making patients more alert to possible legal redress of their grievances; and there is some evidence to support the view that in the United Kingdom asbestos-related claims have been pursued more vigorously by victims who have belonged to those trade unions which have taken a more active interest in this matter than other unions.[34] To put it differently: here, as elsewhere in tort litigation, easy access to qualified para-legal counselling services may be a major determinant of the victim's decision to have recourse to the courts.

The third factor, not unrelated to the previous two but even more difficult to measure, is national temperament. How different, for example, is the American mentality on this matter? As already stated, in the United States, recourse to courts—especially in personal injury cases—can be seen as a way of coping with the financial adversities of accidents in the absence of a caring state. In many cases this is a perfectly legitimate reaction. (German litigation could, in part, be explained by the plaintiff's wish to top up social security payments or, in the case of strict liability statutes, the wish to claim additional damages for pain and suffering which are not recoverable under the statutes. Furthermore, insurers' ability to invoke the defence of contributory negligence often pushes into court claims which could or should have been settled without litigation.) In other instances, however, recourse to the courts by American plaintiffs also demonstrates a low threshold of coping with the vicissitudes of life. I have more sympathy with the former explanation than with the latter. But there are other reasons. A mobile population, accustomed on the whole to a comfortable standard of living, declining family ties, looser doctor/patient relationships and the kind of loneliness that leads so many to seek psychiatric help (for companionship rather than treatment which they often do not need), also encourages, I suspect, many to go to court when faced with the slightest adversity. This may sound a harsh assessment by a foreign observer, but the former Chief Justice of the United States Supreme, Court Warren E. Berger, expressed similar thoughts when in 1982 he addressed the American Bar Association and said:

---

[33] The *Gesetz zur Regelung des Rechts der Allgemeinen Geschäftsbedingungen* of 9 December 1976, para. 13.

[34] Felstiner and Dingwall, *Asbestos Litigation in U.K. An Interim Report* (1988), p. 17.

"One reason our courts have become overburdened is that Americans are increasingly turning to the courts for relief from a range of personal distresses and anxieties. Remedies for personal wrongs that once were considered the responsibility of institutions other than the courts are now boldly asserted as 'entitlements'. The courts have been expected to fill the void created by the decline of church, family, and neighbourhood unity".[35]

Well-publicised high awards may aid and abet this attitude and often result—for example in cases of foetal injuries, loss of companionship and other such claims—in what one suspects are often gold-digging actions. Pro-plaintiff judges and juries appear to be more sympathetic towards them; and, in this instance, the contingency fee system provides a further inducement to "have a go" at litigation, since many claims, because of their nuisance value, result in some payment being made to the plaintiffs. Certainly, the number of frivolous if not outrageous actions reported from time to time is not easily explained by reference to rational considerations.

Are all these factors totally absent from England? British writers have often been quick to stress that recourse to courts is seen here as an exceptional and costly move not to be undertaken lightly. Tony Weir, for example, recently suggested that in England "resort to the law is reluctant, infrequent and deplored"; and, as is often the case with the writings of this brilliant colleague, he has backed his assertion with a humorous quotation from Henry James's *An International Episode*.[36] Yet the duller world of statistics that I have described does not fully support this assertion. For even if recourse to the courts is "reluctant", it is not, overall, infrequent, as Figure 2 demonstrates. Indeed, it is extraordinarily high given the absence of the contingency fee system and the unavailability of legal aid for victims with middle-range earnings and above.

But the systems do show a marked difference when we look at tort litigation. Could "temperament" (not in the sense of deploring litigation but in the sense of treating litigation as a step of last resort) explain this difference? The reputed tendency of Americans to file a suit (in order to demonstrate to their opponent that they "mean business") and then to compromise may contrast with the Englishman's attitude somehow to seek a resolution to the dispute without resorting to the courts if at all possible. Yet even this point cannot provide a complete explanation of the differences between the systems for there is in the American medico-legal field intriguing statistical evidence to suggest that only a tiny percentage of injury-producing errors leads to claims being made against insurance companies and of these an even smaller percentage develops into suits that end with a jury verdict.[37] In one sense, there-

---

[35] "Isn't there a Better Way" (1982) 68 *American Bar Association Journal*, 274, p. 275.

[36] Weir, "A Strike Against the Law", (1986) 46 *Maryland Law Rev*. 133.

[37] Daniels, "Jury Verdicts in Medical Malpractice Cases", paper delivered to the Annual Meeting of the Law and Society Association on 11 August 1989; *idem*, "The Shadow of the Law: Jury Decisions in Obstetrics and Gynaecology Cases", ABF Working paper No. 8806 (1988) both kindly sent to me by their author.

fore, what we should be investigating is not only the number of filings in the systems under comparison but also the reasons which prevent disputes from developing into full-blown legal suits, the "barriers", as one of my American colleagues put it, that stop the potential disputes entering the legal stream. My own inclination is to attribute the differences in filing primarily to ignorance of one's rights and financial fears associated with litigation rather than to temperament although I suspect that in this increasingly urbanised, industrialised and cosmopolitan world, differences in national mentality are being steadily eroded. But even temperament or mentality, these most unquantifiable of factors invoked by so eminent a jurist as Professor Atiyah[38] as the *differentia specifica* between English and American law, may be changing. The medico-legal scene may, through careful analysis of the available statistics, provide a positive indication that this type of change is slowly taking place aided by greater information and specialised services being made available to victims of iatrogenic injuries and this may even not be a bad thing.

Table 7A: *Annual Numbers of Tort Claims for Personal Injury or Death by Type of Claim, UK**

	Claims		Payments	
	000s	%	000s	%
Employers' Liability	114.7	46.0	90.5	42.0
Motor Vehicle	102.2	40.9	98.3	45.7
Products & Services (excluding medical)	2.2	0.9	1.7	0.8
Occupiers' Liability	12.2	4.9	10.8	5.0
Medical Services (doctors, dentists, pharmacists)	0.7	0.2	0.3	0.1

* Estimates in round numbers for 1973. Source: Pearson Commission, Cmnd. 7054-II. 19 (1978).

Table 7B: *Complaints Lodged with the Medical Arbitration Boards of the Federal Republic of Germany 1982–83**

Total number of complaints received	16,434	
Closed on procedural grounds	8,392	(51% of total)
Cases decided on merit	7,969	(100%)
Decided in favour of plaintiff	2,152	(27%)
Decided in favour of defendant	5,817	(63%) [or 13% of total]

* Source: Giesen, *International Medical Law* 91988), p. 510.

[38] In his article in the *Duke Law Journal* (1987) 1002, 1043.

Though there is much talk these days of a medico-legal crisis, the reality is that in England medical malpractice cases form, as Table 7 shows, a tiny minority of tort claims. The 700 or so claims made (and, be it noted, that these are not necessarily writs) in 1973 had, apparently, increased to 2,000 by 1983/4 and to above 4,000 by 1987. The figure of 2,000 must be compared to the figure of about 40,000 claims made in the late 1970s, early 1980s in the United States[39] and about 8,000 claims considered in the 1980s by the voluntary arbitration boards to which German victims of iatrogenic injuries are encouraged (but not obliged) to have resort, if possible in lieu of litigation.[40] The German figure and the apparent success rate of about 27 per cent call for three comments. First, the overall number of German *claims* considered by the Arbitration Boards *and* the courts is, allowing for population differences, close to that of the United States but double or even treble the English figure. Secondly, how many of these claims actually turn into court actions we do not know, or at least I have not been able to discover (see however note 30 above and note 42 below). Nor do we know how many cases go *directly* to the courts totally by-passing the voluntary arbitration boards. We do know, however, that the German Federal Court[41] has drawn attention to the increasing number of malpractice suits. Such an increase, however, can be seen across the board of tort litigation; medical malpractice cases still form a small percentage of the overall volume of tort litigation; and none of my German correspondents felt that the existing levels could be described as "alarming". Finally, it is worth noting that the success rate of 27 per cent of *all claims* which results in some payment to the plaintiff, whether by agreement or as a result of a court award, is close to the figure given for England though, as stated, in this last case one is talking of a much lower number of total claims.[42] Since it is fair to assume that the level of medicine practised in

---

[39] American Medical Association, Special Task Force on Professional Liability, (1984) 1 *Professional Liability in the '80s*, 10.

[40] The Boards are comprised of four members—two coming from the doctors' professional body (*Arztekammer*) and one representative (usually a lawyer) for the potential plaintiff and defendant. Their majority opinion, on liability but not, apparently, on *quantum* of damages, if accepted by the parties, will be honoured by the insurance company. Though recourse to court is always possible, the Winterthur A.G. Versicherung of Munich (one of Germany's leading doctors' insurance companies) informed me (through Professor Lorenz) that "the number of cases resolved by this sort of arbitration is considerable". These boards seem to take anything between 4–9 months to reach a decision. See Eberhardt, "Zur Praxis der Schlichtung in Arzthaftpflichtfällen", *Neue Juristiche Wochenschrift* 1986, 747–8. Judicial resolution of medical disputes takes significantly longer—mainly because of the difficulties associated with scientific evidence.

[41] Press Release to the *Frankfurter Allgemeine Zeitung*, 4 Feb. 1986, p. 14. Significantly, this prestigious newspaper attributes the increased volume of claims to, inter alia, a change in mentality.

[42] Bowle and Jones, "A Health Authority's Experience", *New Law Journal*, 27 January 1989, p. 119. For Germany, see Deutsch, Schreiber and Lilie, *op. cit.* n. 30. According to the same authors, only 10% of claims resolved by judicial decision go in favour of plaintiffs. *Ibid*. at p. 230. Reichenbach, in "Arzthaftpflicht aus der Sicht des Versicherungsmediziners", *VersR* 1981, 807, p. 809 gives a similar figure for cases resolved by the courts. The success rate is higher—about 34%—for claims resolved through the intervention of the conciliation boards.

Table 8: *Claims Made on Medical Defence Societies*

1973*	
Total	500
Abandoned	305 (60%)
Settled out of court	170 (34%)
Ended in Court	25 (5%)
Won by defendant	20 (4%)
Won by plaintiff	1 (1%)
Success rate (claims partially satisfied through settlement or more generously compensated through court payment)	35.4%

1984**	
Total	100
abandoned	73
Settled out of court	12
Pending (3 years later)	14***
Lost by plaintiff in court	1
Success rate	12–28 %

1987†	
Total	4,000
abandoned	2,920 (74%)
Settled out of Court	480 (12%)
Pending††	760 (14%)

Summary Conclusion 1973–1987 (approximate figures)

—Frequency of claims	—*up* by 700%
—Total cost of settlements	—*up* (no exact figure available)
—Abandonment rate	—*up* from 60% of claims to about 75% of claims made
	—Proportion of claims which succeed *down* from 30–40% to around 25%

* Source: Pearson Commission Report

** Source: Hawkins and Patterson: study based on 100 files randomly selected out of a total of 324 of the West Misland region which is the largest in the NHS.

*** Of which 9 likely to go to court.

† Total number of claims reported (unofficially) by the medical defence societies. How do they fare? The last three sets of figures are *estimates* based on Hawkins and Paterson data.

†† On the Hawkins/Paterson figures about 360 might end up in court. This would be 9% of the total—instead of 5% in the Pearson era. Estimates based on figures from studies of individual regions suggest a success rate for plaintiffs of 2–4% of total claims, i.e. 80–160 actions most of which probably being settled by the parties.

Table 9: *Defence Society Subscription Rates*

Year	Rate £	Annual Increase %
1978	40	—
1979	70	75
1980	95	36
1981	120	26
1982	135	13
1983	195	44
1984	264	35
1985	288	17
1986	336	17
1987	576	71
1988	1,080	87

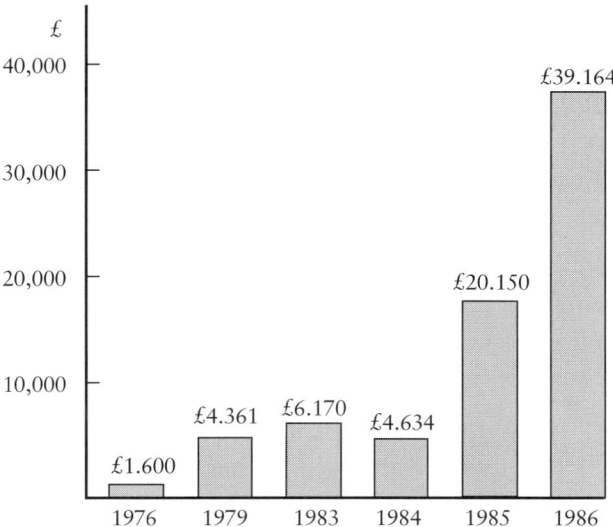

Figure 4: *Maximum Awards Paid by the Medical Protection Society for Failed Sterilisation**

* Source: Hamm, Dingwall, Fenn and Harris, *Compensation and Accountability* (1988), 11.

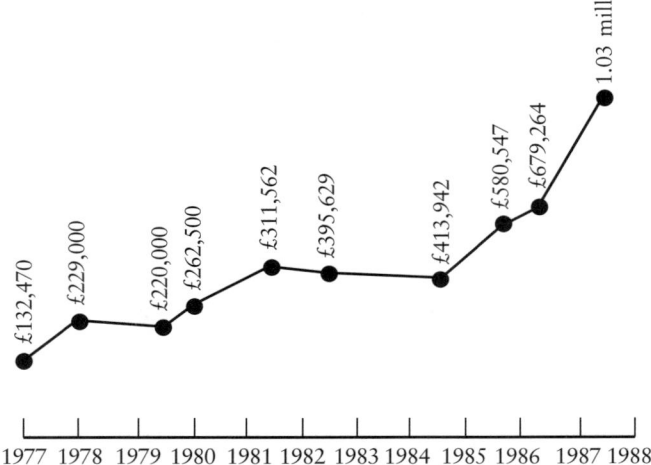

Figure 5: *Highest Sum Awarded in Medical Negligence Cases 1977–1987**

* Source: M.D.U./Hamm, Dingwall, Fenn and Harris, *Compensation and Accountability* (1988), 11.

England and West Germany must be similar, it would not appear to be unreasonable to hypothesise that for various reasons, in England, a number of injury-producing medical errors do not reach the legal system and do not result in legal redress.

Table 8 also suggests that in England, despite alarmist cries, the proportion of claims that are successful through *litigation* does not appear to have increased significantly since Pearson: indeed it may be decreasing. The rate of abandonment of claims has also gone up: from 60 to about 75 per cent of all claims made. What have also gone up, however are (a) the number of total claims initiated; (b) arguably the number of claims that reach court; and (c) the size of payments made in the last 15 years (though, again, the figures— provided by the medical defence societies—are ambiguous in many respects and must be treated with considerable caution). Insurance rates have also gone up (Table 9), but this, I think, is mainly due to (a) defending more— often useless—cases; (b) the higher size of some exceptional awards; and (c) the profitability of insurers' investment policies which, admittedly, is a hazardous operation because of the time lag between injury, claim and payment. In England this last factor has been conspicuously ignored by all who talk of an insurance crisis and explicitly or implicitly blame the lawyers for it. As for the United States, there is growing awareness that profit-oriented insurance companies may have been too eager to underwrite doubtful risks when interest rates were high. Bad insurance practices were thus concealed while returns from investments of premium money remained high.[43]

Comparison with Germany is interesting but again patchy, mainly because of the lack of meaningful statistics. Professor Weyers' figures are the most detailed that I have seen but I must remind the reader of the caveats expressed in note 30 above. Professor Weyers gives the average as 35,000 DM. At about £12,000 this is about two-thirds the average English medical *settlement* though, of course, one must stress that Weyers's figures come mainly from the early 1970s. Weyer's study found that 25–30 per cent of the claims were for 3,000 DM or less; 65–70 per cent related to 3–50,000 DM; 2 per cent were for 50,000 DM; and about 3 per cent concerned 100,000 DM or more. Deutsch, Schreiber and Lilie, writing in 1985, suggest that 100,000 DM awards are "nowadays" much more common, while Reichenbach, writing in 1981, has noted that even at that time there were cases where the 500,000 DM compulsory insurance maximum coverage proved inadequate. Precise figures, however, are not given. Weyers also found that the greater complexity of medical cases tended to make them more costly to litigate than the usual tort case (the cost of litigation incurred by the loser tended to be in the order of 20 per cent of the total amount claimed). One must remember, however, that the bulk of medical-legal disputes are nowadays resolved by the voluntary arbitration boards, referred to earlier in this paper, and the cost of presenting a claim before such boards tends to be very low. The unavailability (to me at least) of more precise figures makes further comparisons difficult. What one can say, however, is that the near-panic reaction of the British medico-insurance profession has not been reflected in Germany even though the total number of claims is greater than it is in England and the average awards similar if not higher. But then German industry in general and the insurance industry in particular here satisfactorily weathered changes in the other areas of the law which, when mooted in this country, send shivers down the spines of British industrialists. The abolition in Germany in 1972 of the state of art defence for pharmaceutical products is an example akin to our subject.

Do these figures, then, suggest that a crisis has reached our shores? An increase in willingness to litigate, yes, but a crisis, no—not yet, at any rate. But just as doctors (or rather insurers, since nowadays most doctors no longer fully pay their insurance premiums) are concerned by the increase, I am interested in its causes. Figure 6 shows that there are considerable variations among regions. Local factors seem to be at work but urbanisation is not, apparently, one of them. American studies, on the other hand, suggest that urbanisation is a factor, though it is also said that the greater litigiousness in urban areas cannot be linked to a greater concentration of lawyers, but it can be linked to a greater awareness of one's rights.

---

[43] Remarkably, this was openly admitted by R. J. Haaven, Chairman and Chief Executive Officer of the Allstate Insurance Company in a public speech given in Pennsylvania entitled "Balancing Risk and Reward" published by the Insurance Information Institute in 1987 at p. 6.

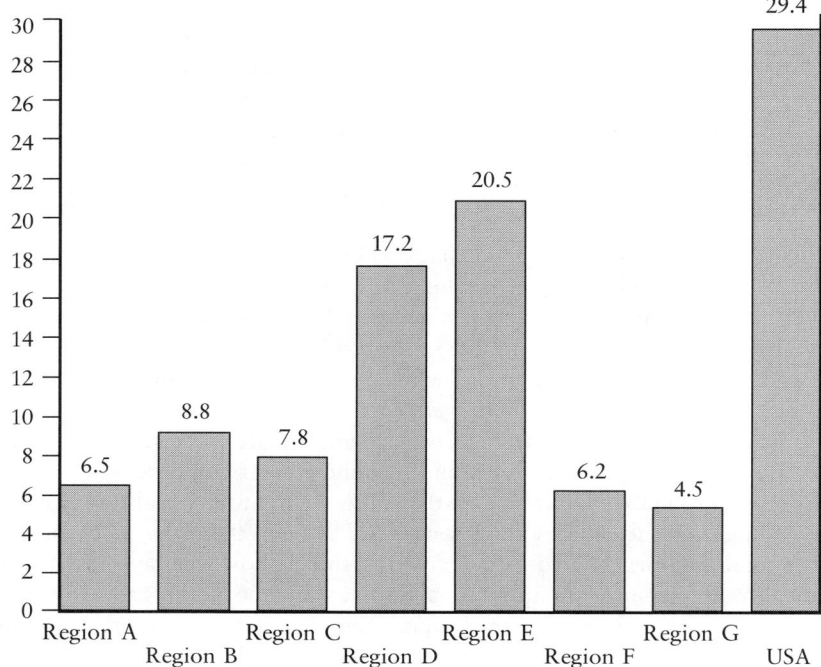

Figure 6: *Annual Claims per 100,000 Population**

* Source: R. Dingwall, forthcoming in *Health Care UK* (1989).

Remarkably, these figures also suggest that the average number of claims in the United States is about three to four times higher than in England and only about one-third higher than the number of claims made in some (relatively few) regions. Once again, however, note the apparent similarity of German and American figures on the total number of claims made and the calmer level of debate that prevails in the former of these two countries, which is almost certainly due to the absence of the American-style "mega-awards".

But let us return to the British scene. In my opinion, the major reason for the change we are witnessing must be greater publicity of awards and, above all, a greater effectiveness of pressure groups like the AVMA which was founded in 1982 and the resulting willingness to chance marginal claims. On the whole, I would regard this as a healthy development. But there is another reason that may contribute to more claims and this is less easy to justify. The lack of any medical screening of the merits of the case at the legal aid stage of the process enables many unmeritorious claims to generate considerable defence costs by potential defendants. Clearly, more information is needed to draw firm conclusions, information which is available to the medical defence societies but which they are unwilling to release. But there is already some evidence to suggest that the national reluctance to sue, to the extent that it really exists, may be weakening where there is greater activity by pro-consumer groups and easy access to legal aid. Or, to put it more bluntly, an aggrieved Englishman will sue if given half the chance by the legal system! My overall conclusion, therefore, is that medical malpractice presents our tort system with a challenge: the challenge is not how to suppress deserving cases for the sake of a streamlined legal system, but how to separate the unmeritorious from the meritorious claim in a fair and efficient way. And once again, the study of the German system can help us decide whether the American system is "dangerous" by being outrageously pro-plaintiff or whether ours is aberrant by being excessively pro-defendant.

5. PUTTING MATTERS INTO PERSPECTIVE

The danger inherent in the use of figures and the difficulties of comparing (inadequate) judicial statistics from different countries were mentioned at the outset and, perhaps, should be stressed again. Yet these dangers do not, I believe, outweigh the advantages that may follow such empirical studies. Lawyers, and I am now thinking not only of British lawyers but also of continental European lawyers, should not frown upon such additional tools, especially since, if properly used, they could have an impact on the kind of policy arguments that lie concealed behind the more formal judicial reasoning. Let me give one or two examples of what I have in mind, drawing again, for convenience's sake, from the medico-legal scene.

Some lawyers and most doctors nowadays tend to talk of a real or impending medico-legal crisis; some may refer to the American scene as the apocalypse that may be about to descend on us. The latter point can, for present purposes, be disposed of briefly. The situation in America is, as I indicated, a complex phenomenon produced by many factors, institutional, political and demographic, that cannot be duplicated in this country. Imitation tendencies may, to some extent, change the medico-legal scene, but let us face it, this was a non-subject until a few years ago and any change will be seen by many— wrongly—as one for the worse. Any increase in legal activity can be interpreted as opening uncontrollable floodgates. After all, ten cases being resolved by judicial means instead of five represents a one hundred per cent increase! Few, however, will stress (or have stressed) that greater accountability may make doctors more careful in (a) the way they conduct their profession (b) in the way they handle their patients, and (c) in the way they keep their records. If the Germans can cope, why can't we?

This is not to deny that changes are taking place and that if they are *abrupt* in manner and *substantial* in proportion, they could put the NHS under stress. But the use of statistics can help put the problems into proper perspective. For example, a different doctrine of informed consent has not, apparently, caused unbearable stresses to either the American or German systems. And the so-called phenomenon of defensive medicine may not, as some have claimed, be attributable (or substantially attributable) to changing patterns of litigation. It may, for example, be linked to the fee-for-services system which gives doctors a financial incentive to order as many tests and procedures as are technically justifiable. Is this too harsh a comment to make? I do not think it is for American doctors; nor, apparently, is it for German doctors. And in Germany, too, we have witnessed recently an increase in tests carried out *even though* there has been no outrageous rise in medical malpractice litigation. The increase must be partly linked to the overall method of remuneration.

The position in England, as far as defensive medicine is concerned, may be even less clear. Though a recent study has claimed that "defensive procedures are fairly widespread",[44] its conclusions admit that the questions did not address the problem of the respondents' perception of what is meant by defensive medicine. A knowledgeable commentator has also warned me that:

> "the reasons people give for their actions in a survey may be very different from those that motivated the actions in the first place. We think, for instance, that it may be used as a justification for clinical interventions which are controversial between doctors and midwives: legal responsibility is a trump card for the doctor in an argument".

Thus, not only is it arguable that in some—perhaps many—cases one doctor's defensive medicine may be another's good practice; it is also possible that unnecessary procedures may often be authorised because the doctor is unsure of what responsible medical practice, as judged by his peers, requires him to do.[45] In any event, one thing is reasonably clear: a doctor is mistaken if he adopts unnecessary defensive procedures because he thinks the law requires him to do so in order to protect himself. The law makes no such demands of any doctor.

Statistical works on the English medico-legal scene reveals other things. The Hawkins/Paterson study,[46] for example, vividly illustrates how time-consuming and costly is the process from complaint to writ to judgment by the court. Worse still, the "avalanche of correspondence" that this process entails often turns out to be totally wasteful since, as I have indicated, in 39 per cent of the total number of cases investigated, the condition complained of is due to natural causes and unavoidable risks and not to doctors' errors. Could not the use of doctors on the legal aid panel prevent these cases from even getting off the ground? Moreover, what can we learn from the German arbitration

---

[44] Jones and Morris, "Defensive Medicine: Myths and Facts" (1989) *Journal of the Medical Defence Union* (Summer part) 40, p. 42.

[45] *Ibid.*, pp. 41, 42.

[46] "Medicolegal audit in the West Midlands region: analysis of 100 cases" (1987) 295 *British Medical Journal*, 1533.

boards and the way they manage to suppress the gladiatorial nature of our procedure?

Many cases also show that voluminous correspondence is produced for immensely trivial injuries (12 per cent) that in the end are not worth pursuing, while in another 6 per cent of claims the dispute has been caused by various forms of breakdown in the doctor/patient relationship or, even, created by irresponsible speculation by other doctors or nurses not immediately involved in the case in point. It does not take radical law reform to cut down some of these instances and concentrate efforts either on compensating cases where negligence is undeniable (12 per cent settled out of court on these grounds) or expediting the resolution of the truly disputed cases which, according to this study are about 9 per cent. Of course, one could, and one day must, envisage more radical methods of solving these disputes, which could include a no-fault non-adversarial process of compensation rather than litigation, but that is another matter.

Another point that can emerge from studying these statistical variations is the complexity of factors that lie behind them. This is a crucial point for we are apt, whenever we see an increase in litigation figures or premiums, to talk of the American crisis reaching our shores. This would, as I have indicated, tend to underestimate the many local and institutional differences that exist in the United States which are not duplicated in the United Kingdom. On the other hand, if the crucial factor is one of mentality, capacity to endure the adversities of life, access to justice and the like, then there may be some subtle changes taking place in this country which will move it closer to the pattern we find elsewhere. One thing, however, must be made clear. While increased litigation-consciousness may place great strains on the NHS and the courts, it cannot be totally condemned in all its aspects.

Moving away from the specific instances of medico-legal disputes to more general issues, does my brief and tentative survey reveal any great differences between the three different systems we have looked at? The glass of water provided for me for tonight's lecture is, at this moment, 50 per cent full of water. I could, with equal accuracy, describe it as half full or half empty. The material that I have given you could, with a minimum of ingenuity, support a conclusion that there exist great differences or great similarities. After all, one only has to select a few "mega-awards" from the United States and the current picture of outrageous differences between the systems remains intact. Despite this, I prefer to look at things from the second angle, not least because so many of us, instinctively it would seem, opt for the first. With this as my starting point, I think one must be cautious when talking of a litigation explosion. Though there is a steady increase in litigation, the words "explosion" or "crisis" have not been used by my German colleagues. I think they are inappropriate in our case, as well; and to the extent that they can be used to describe the legal scene in the United States, I think they should be limited to certain areas, some courts and, possibly, some types of case—for example products cases (particularly latent toxic torts) and medical malpractice. Indeed, one research officer of the Institute for Civil Justice of the Rand Corporation, when giving evidence before a special sub-committee of the US House of Representatives in 1986, stated:

> "Increasingly, the civil justice systems seems to be two different systems. One is a stable system that provides modest compensation for plaintiffs who claimed slight or moderate injuries in automobile and other accidents that have been the major source of litigation for 50 years. The second is an unstable system that provides continually increasing awards for claims for serious injuries in any type of lawsuit, and for all injuries, serious or not, in product liability, malpractice, street hazards and workplace accidents".[47]

The figures given in Table 10 tend to support this assertion. They show in a summary way the increase in the volume of litigation in the federal courts between 1975 and 1984. One can, of course, immediately object that they must be treated with great caution since some 97 per cent of claims are litigated in state not federal courts. Notwithstanding this legitimate caveat, focusing on the activity in the federal courts is advisable since: (a) the most reliable information available, on the whole, refers to the federal courts; (b) the increase in federal litigation is the one most commonly used as an example of runaway litigiousness and (c) the recent growth of filings has, apparently, been far greater in federal courts than it has been in state courts.[48] Now, if you look at these figures carefully you will see that the two major increases have taken place in categories 2 and 4 and they represent a deliberate official policy "to recover over-payments of veteran's benefits by litigation and to curtail disability benefits by summarily removing beneficiaries from the rolls". As Professor Galanter continues:

> "Is the 413 per cent increase in social security cases to be understood as an outbreak of litigiousness among Social Security claimants? Does it make sense to take the 6,683 per cent increase in recovery cases as evidence of an outbreak of litigiousness among federal officials?"

The tort increase by contrast is interesting in that it reveals two things: (a) an overall increase more or less in tune with the increase in population during the same period and (b) the bulk of the overall increase is taken up by one type of tort litigation—products liability—which, indeed, was itself dominated by two major incidents: the asbestos litigation and the Dalcon Shield

---

[47] M. A. Peterson, *A Summary of Research Results: Trends and Patterns in Civil Jury Verdicts*, testimony presented to the Sub-Committee on Oversight, Committee on Ways and Means, US House of Representatives on 13 March 1986 (Rand Corporation, 1986), p. 4.

[48] Galanter, "The Day After the Litigation Explosion", (1986) 46 *Maryland L. Rev.* 3, 15 n. 44 on which this section and Table 10 are based. The National Centre for State Courts, in a *Preliminary Examination of Available Civil and Criminal Trend Data in State Courts for 1978, 1981 and 1984* (1986), based on statistics supplied by twenty states has concluded that "During 1981–4, tort filings increased 7% while population increased 4%. For the entire period 1978–84, total tort filings increased 9%, but the population also increased by 8%".

Table 10: *Federal District Court: Filings in Selected Categories 1975 and 1984**

Category	1975	1984	Per cent change	Increase	Fraction of absolute increase 1975/1984
Total filings	117,320	261,485	122.9	144,165	100%
1. Prisoner Petitions	19,307	31,107	61	45,509	8.2%
2. Recovery of Overpayment and Enforcement of judgments	681	46,190	6,682.7	45.509	31.6%
3. Civil Rights	10,392	21,219	104.2	10,827	7.5%
4. Social Security	5,846	29,985	412.9	24,139	16.7%
5. Torts					
General	25,691	37,522	46	11,831	8.2%
Products Liability	2,886	10,745	272.3	7,859	5.4%

* Adapted from Prof. Galanter's "The Day After the Litigation Explosioin", 46 *Maryland L. Rev.* 3, 16 which, in turn, is based on Director of the Administration Office of the United States Courts, *Annual Reports* 1975 and 1984.

disputes.[49] The recent Special Report of the Institute for Civil Justice, *Trends in Tort Litigation. The Story behind the Statistics*,[50] thus appears to be right when it claims that in the United States the

> "answer to the question of how much tort litigation there really is depends on which world of litigation the data describe. (i) Auto accident [and other routine personal injuries] are a steady or declining percentage of court action. (ii) Non-auto personal injury cases such as malpractice and product liability are growing moderately in state courts and more dramatically in federal courts. (iii) Mass latent injury cases have the potential for explosive growth as new evidence of harms is developed".

[49] In 1981 there were some 16,000 asbestos claims which, by 1986, had grown to more than 30,000 in state and federal courts. 7,500 Dalcon Shield-related suits in 1981 had grown to more than 325,000 in the Bankruptcy court after A. H. Robbins had sought the protection of Chapter 11.

[50] By Hensler, Vaiana, Kakalik and Peterson, *op. cit.* above n. 7, at p. 11. The figures in California are similar. Thus, for the period 1980–4 there were 46 punitive damages awards in personal injuries cases—6 in San Francisco, 15 in Los Angeles, and a further 15 in other metropolitan jurisdictions. Hensler, *Trends in California Tort Liability Litigation* (Rand Publications, 1987), p. 11.

So, despite the difficulty of keeping these three categories rigidly separated, I believe that here, perhaps, lies the main difference from the European scene. Otherwise it seems that the Europeans go to court as often as the Americans or, at any rate, if they can help it, do not avoid it as the prevailing opinion would like us to believe.

This brings me to the second and, I think, really major difference. Going to court is one thing, staying there to the end is another. A system that encourages settlements must be good: a system that forces settlements through complexity and high costs may be less defensible. I have neither the time nor the expertise to attempt comparisons in procedural law; but the impression I have is that English law belongs to this second category; and this, coupled with the cost of tort litigation, may explain the lower level of tort suits in England. This is a fertile area for comparisons as the growing number of articles suggests, though one must also add that in the area of procedural law, national lawyers seem to be even more protective of their own "turf" than they are in substantive law (and we all know how unwilling they are even here to be influenced by foreign ideas).

What about the size of awards? In this paper I have skimmed the surface of this subject, yet I should like to make five tentative observations. First, do not focus on the mega-awards but look at the median or, better still, at mode awards in order to avoid distortions by a few mega-awards that can grossly affect average awards. Take, for example, the figure of $1.1 million which was in 1984 the average product liability award made by juries in San Francisco. The median award for the same period was $200,000 which was (and is still) a lot of money, but only a fifth of the average figure inflated by a tiny percentage of mega-awards. The Cook County, Illinois, median figure was lower—$187,000: and there is every reason to believe that the nationwide median figure would be even lower.[51] Similarly, the medical average of $1 million in San Francisco for the same period becomes a median of $156,000.[52] Or look at the punitive awards made in Cook County during 1980–84 for personal injury cases. The *average* award was $1,934 million. This makes the headlines. But this average was produced by *less than a handful* of very substantial punitive awards (including a 1980 medical malpractice award which, in 1984 dollars, was worth $9.3 million).[53] The median award, on the other

---

[51] The Administrative Office of the US Courts, *Guide to Judiciary, Policies and Procedures Transmital* 64, vol. XI, 1 March 1985 showed median awards in non-asbestos product cases of $70,000 (1980), $100,000 (1981) and $135,000 (1982).

[52] Hensler, *Trends in California Tort Liability Litigation* (1987), p. 5; Hensler, *Summary of Research Results on Product Liability* (1986), p. 4. Professor Stephen Daniels, in his "Verdicts in Medical Malpractice Cases", *Trial*, May 1989 reviews the collected data on all cases that went to jury in 46 counties in 11 states between 1981–5. Daniels observed that "Generally speaking, median awards in successful money damages cases [other than medical malpractice] in most places were below $40,000. Only four sites [out of the 46] had medians for the total verdicts over $100,000, one in California and the other three in New York City".

[53] In *Djon Pjetri and Zoja Petri v. N. Y. City Health and Hospitals Corporation* ((1989) 20 *Trial Lawyers Quarterly* 37 et seq.) the Supreme Court of the State of New York followed suit by

hand, was worth $82,000. If to that you add the fact that there were in Cook County between 1980 and 1984 only 14 punitive awards in personal injury cases, the whole picture changes and, with the change, much of the news-worthiness value disappears.[54] These median figures are still high—I strongly suspect quite a lot higher than the European equivalents—but remember that they are found in some types of tort litigation only and if one looks at tort litigation across the board the levels drop even further. (The *average* tort award *nationwide* in the United States in 1985 was a mere US$29,000.)

Secondly, never forget the significant, at times outstanding, regional varia-tions in *median* (and, of course, *mean*) awards. Table 11 provides some idea of this phenomenon and is based on a study of 24,625 civil verdicts from state trial courts of general jurisdiction in 46 counties in 11 states covering the years 1981–85. Some medians are affected by the low number of successful mal-practice suits; others, however, present variations that call for explanation. What accounts for such variations (e.g. between New York and Dallas)? Are they the product of different political environments (liberal/democratic versus republican/conservatives)? Could they be the result of conscious jury tenden-cies to award more to poor victims (assuming this is so)? Could the level of services be of inferior quality in the poorer areas, inevitably leading to more malpractice? Could all these factors be combined? American researchers have offered some explanations.[55] From the point of view of a foreign observer what matters is that these variations are probably to be found in other areas of civil litigation such as product cases and business/tort situations. The local variations may, therefore, if taken with appropriate jurisdiction and *forum*

awarding to the plaintiff who was brain-damaged as a result of an anesthesia error a total of $35,517,578 which was reduced by the Appellate Division on 1 June 1989 to $9.2 million. More precisely the injured plaintiff received $20 million for pain and suffering; $142,000 for past med-ical expenses: $3 million for future medical care; $1.3 million for future loss of earnings (even though he was 32 years of age and, at the time of the accident, was earning as handyman-porter $320 per week). His wife—who, incidentally, left him three years after the accident—was also awarded $3 million (reduced on appeal to $1.5 million) for "loss of services". Additionally, the jury awarded $6 million (completely set aside on appeal) to Pjetri's mother and sons who were not plaintiffs in the action! The reader can decide how much of the blame (or praise?) for this result can be attributed to the jury and how much to the trial judge.

[54] *Punitive Damages. Empirical Findings* (Rand Corporation, 1987), pp. 21–2. Peterson, in the study quoted above n. 47, states (p. 2) that throughout the 1960s and 1970s jury awards did not change in the "bulk of lawsuits". (After adjusting for inflation, the median jury award remained almost constant in both Cook County and San Francisco—less than $20,000 during the decades. The "mega-awards", on the other hand, seriously distorted averages. Thus "In San Francisco dur-ing the 1960s, only five cases had a value of $1 million (in 1979 dollars)—0.3% of all cases in which plaintiffs received an award. The total amount of money awarded in these million dollars verdicts represented eight per cent of all money awarded to plaintiffs. During the 1970s, 26 cases (2.3 per cent of all cases in which plaintiffs received an award) produced awards exceeding $1 million. These cases accounted for 30 per cent of all money awarded in the first half of the decade and nearly half of all money awarded in the second half of 1970s. [Preliminary results for 1980–1985 indicate that] although million dollar awards occurred in less than four per cent of all cases won by plaintiffs during this period, they now account for roughly two-thirds of all money awarded to plaintiffs" (*ibid.* at p. 3).

[55] Daniels, *op. cit.* above n. 37.

Table 11: *Median Medical Malpractice Awards 1981–85 (in 1985 dollars)**

Location	Number of cases	Success rate	Median award	Expected award
Maricopa, AZ	50	28.0	124,180	34,770
Alameda, CA	32	31.1	141,802	44,384
Los Angeles, CA	305	30.8	156,520	48,208
Sacramento, CA	27	22.2	260,818	57,902
San Diego, CA	39	41.0	136,210	55,809
San Francisco, CA	38	39.5	187,200	73,944
Denver, CO	29	20.7	70,000	14,490
Fulton, GA	37	48.6	40,815	19,836
Cook, IL	134	33.6	194,326	65,294
DuPage, IL	28	17.9	17,280	3,093
Lake, IL	22	40.9	66,600	27,239
Johnson, KS	17	41.2	280,000	115,360
Wyandotte, KS	10	50.0	810,000	405,000
Jackson, MO	38	28.9	69,500	20,086
Bronx, NY	43	55.8	602,195	336,025
Kings, NY	150	46.7	370,100	172,837
Nassan, NY	121	29.7	220,316	65,434
New York, NY	224	43.3	255,300	110,545
Queens, NY	85	48.2	166,500	80,253
Suffolk, NY	36	41.7	351,166	136,645
Westchester, NY	46	21.7	276,750	60,055
Dallas, TX	42	21.4	58,240	12,463
Harris, TX	117	10.3	597,000	61,491
King, WA	33	27.3	130,000	35,490

* Source: S. Daniels, "Verdicts in Medical Malpractice Cases", *Trial*, May 1989 (adapted from tables 1 and 2).

non conveniens rules, greatly influence the decision to chance litigation in the United States.

This last point deserves a small excursus; and it is well-illustrated by the Piper-Alpha disaster and the ensuing mid-Atlantic settlement. For briefly in that case the Scottish victims, desirous of obtaining higher compensation than that likely to be available locally, had a choice between three *fora*: California, de facto excluded by its *forum non conveniens* doctrine; Louisiana, riddled by technical obstacles (short limitation period; rules excluding certain dependants if others were alive) and, in any event, because of the absence of punitive damages likely to produce lower compensation than other American states; and Texas, apparently open to foreign litigants after the Court of Appeals of

Texas, overruling a trial court judgment, had in *Alfaro v. Dow Chemical*[56] held that there was an absolute right to bring a fatal accident action in Texas without being subject to *forum non conveniens* dismissal. Largely on the basis of this judgment the plaintiffs pressed their case threatening Texas actions and the defendants offered a settlement in October 1988. The plaintiffs were lucky. Barely a month later the Texas Supreme Court, distinctly more conservative as a result of recent elections, granted a writ of error indicating its willingness to adopt or fashion a *forum non conveniens* doctrine. Had this event taken place a month earlier the defendants would have almost certainly pitched their offers at a significantly lower level reflecting the fact that Louisiana (with all its drawbacks) would be the only realistic American *forum* left to the plaintiffs. This sequence of events, little noticed by the otherwise watchful press,[57] thus illustrates (a) the importance of regional variations in the United States; (b) the vacillation of legal doctrine as changing political fashions shape and reshape the composition of state courts; and (c) the dangers of asserting unequivocally that litigation in the United States is always and indisputably in the interests of British (or European) victims. Here, as elsewhere, a more nuancé approach must be adopted; and contact with the United States made, if at all, through the intervention or with the assistance of British legal help. Otherwise the American judicial process could adopt the words that Thomas Mann put into the mouth of Goethe as he bid his final farewell to Charlotte Kestner: "I am the flame, and into me the poor moth flings itself . . . once I burned you . . .".[58]

Thirdly, try to compare totals, including where possible medical bills, which in the European scene tend to be concealed because they are borne by the State. These can represent a substantial part of a tort award and thus make an American award seem much larger than it really is.

Fourthly, remember that American awards—especially mega-compensatory and mega-punitive awards—are frequently and substantially reduced as a result of settlements, remittiturs and appellate court decisions.

Fifthly, bear in mind that awards are bound to be higher where salaries, stipends and standard of living are higher and when, as in the United States, they include a substantial percentage that will go not to the victorious victims but his legal advisor. Remarkably, perhaps, one can even find court decisions openly admitting that a particular tort rule, generous to the plaintiff, is adopted precisely because it can lead to a larger award and thereby, indirectly,

[56] 751 SW 2d 208. Writ of error granted in November 1988.

[57] I have derived much information and assistance in this matter from Mr. Graeme F. Garrett of the Edinburgh firm of solicitors of Allan McDougall and who also successfully represented a number of victims in this case.

[58] *Lotte in Weimar* (Penguin edition) p. 330. This metaphor was also used by Lord Denning in *Smith Kline, Ltd.* v. *Bloch (No. 1)* [1983] 1 WLR 730, 733. Jurisdictional aspects of the points discussed in the text, above, are considered by Baade, "Foreign Oil Disaster Litigation Prospects in the U.S. and the Mid-Atlantic Settlement Formula", (1989) 7 *Journal of Energy and Natural Resources Law* 125.

finance litigation. The American version of the collateral source rule has been justified on such grounds;[59] and another court came up with the same reason in order to deny subrogation rights to an insurer of medical costs.[60]

Finally, do not only be struck by the differences but also be impressed by some uncanny similarities. Note, for example, how German and English law have arrived at about £100,000 as the right figure for compensation for loss of amenities of a severely injured but conscious plaintiff.[61] Note, also, that the proportion of all claims which result in some payment in medical malpractice cases is approximately the same in both England and Germany. Finally, note the similarity in the size of average awards in asbestos claims in England and the United States—at any rate during the first phase (up to 1982) of this massive tort litigation. Let me pursue this last point further.

Recent studies on awards made in the asbestos litigation seem to support the view that there exist greater similarities between the English and American systems than has hitherto been believed. Indeed, Table 12 reveals an uncanny similarity of awards which makes one wish that there existed more comparative data on other types of tort litigation to test the validity of my supposition about relative equivalence of awards. More remarkable still, however, are the preliminary conclusions of a study conducted by the American Bar Association and the Oxford Centre for Socio-Legal Studies which has suggested that in extra-judicial *settlements*, British asbestos victims may have done significantly better than their American counterparts.[62] Overall, therefore, if you adopt a critical approach, I suspect you will find that, though some differences persist between our systems, they seem to cease to be spectacular. My hunch is that if one attempted the same kind of study in other areas of tort litigation one would also find that the differences that exist between the systems are much less spectacular than they are commonly believed to be once allowance has been made for differences in cost of medical care, standard of living and the cost and method of funding litigation. Indeed, I should not be surprised to be told that variations in the size of awards are often greater within one and the same country than they are between the median, perhaps even, average awards of some of the leading countries of the western world. Certainly France has produced some quite astounding awards which have, however, passed unnoticed by the English who choose rather to be mesmerised by American headlines. More studies of

---

[59] See *Helfend v. Southern California Rapid Transit District* 465 P. 2d. 61 (1970).

[60] *Frost v. Porter Leasing Corp.*, 436 NE 2d. 387, 391.

[61] e.g. 300–400,000 DM (approximately £100,000) awarded to a severely disabled, conscious, twenty-six-year-old plaintiff for loss of amenity and pain and suffering: OLG Nürnberg 13.7 1984, VersR 86, 173 quoted by Hacks, Ring, Böhm, *Schmerzensgeld Beträge*, 13th edn. (1987). Cf. *Brightman v. Johnson, The Times*, 16 December 1985 (also reported in Kemp and Kemp, *The Quantum of Damages*, 4th edn. (1975), Vol. 2, 1-010): £95,000 for loss of amenity to a conscious plaintiff and *Lim Poh Choo v. Camden and Islington Area Health Authority* [1980] AC 174 (£20,000 for loss of amenity to an unconscious plaintiff. In 1988 values this should be about £40,000).

[62] *Asbestos Litigation in the U.K.*—an Interim Report (1988), p. 16.

Table 12: *Asbestos Cases: Tried Claims*

British Average Award*	US Average Award
£-55,130	$-220,000**
	$-116,600***
$-88,208††	$-100,700†

* British awards between 1970–1987.

** $220,000 *includes* 47 per cent. plaintiffs' litigation expenses, i.e. $103,400, so amount received by plaintiff must be reduced to approximately $116,600. British costs assessed separately and added to the above figure, i.e. *not* included in figure of £55,130.

*** This amount *includes* 53 per cent. of $30,000 punitive damages, i.e. $14,900. Most asbestos trials, however, did *not* result in punitive damages. The $30,000 figure is the sum of all punitive damages averaged over all trials. Rand Corporation, *Costs of Asbestos Litigation* (1983), 20 n. 10. Note, however, that the first punitive awards were not made until early in 1981. In the fifteen months or so that elapsed between that date and August 1982 (when the Manville Corporation filed a petition for reorganisation and protection under Chapter 11 of the Federal Bankruptcy Code) punitive damages against Manville alone averaged at $616,000. See P. Brodeur, *Outrageous Misconduct, The Asbestos Industry on Trial* (1985), p. 283. The cut-off rate of the Rand research may have thus affected its figures downwards.

† Sum excluding punitive element of $15,900. See previous note.

†† Converted at $1.60 to £1.00.

N.B. Comparing the $88,208 to the $100,700 one must further bear in mind two things: (a) the American award includes elements of medical expenses covered by the NHS; (b) the difference of real wage levels between Britain and the USA.

this type might well surprise us all by making the differences between the systems less pronounced.

6. CONCLUSIONS

The inadequacy of the available statistical information inevitably means that this can only be described as a preliminary study. Nevertheless, some broad patterns have emerged from this study which make the following tentative conclusions fairly plausible.

First, American tort law is not, as I have tried to explain in this paper, one system but many with different figures, patterns and even rules applying to each sub-category. Secondly, *overall* volumes of litigation do not appear to be significantly different in the three systems that have been compared. What is significantly different, however, is the volume of tort litigation in Germany and the United States on the one hand and England on the other. When we look at the number of cases that are fought to the end, England and the United States fall (in percentage terms) into one group and Germany into another. This may be linked to costs, procedural rules, national mentality or all three. Thirdly, the common law systems considered in this paper manage with significantly fewer judges than exist in Germany. This may be largely because they are not accustomed (or not yet accustomed) to the advantages of "managerial judging", especially in smaller cases. Fourthly, juries account for some intriguing differences between the United States on the one hand and England and Germany on the other. A closer examination of the juries' contribution to the state—crisis some would say—of modern tort law will, I think, be found to be not in their typical awards but, primarily, (a) in their capricious inconsistencies and, (b) in a small number of cases, in their outrageous generosity (especially under the non-pecuniary heading of damage currently "capped" by widely differing American statutes). For these inconsistencies trial judges may also share in the blame. These variations and geographical inconsistencies must, overall, impede the smooth conclusion of settlement. Fifthly, notwithstanding the above, I strongly suspect that the difference in median and mode awards between these three nations, though significant, are less spectacular than is often believed. American awards must, in particular, be discounted for legal fees, medical expenses and higher average earnings. Though there is inadequate comparative statistical evidence to support detailed comparisons, I think there is enough evidence to suggest that potential plaintiffs should not be too quick to allow themselves to be enticed to sue in American courts. The nature of their action, the location of the potential American court and the character of the defendant may be very important factors in reaching the final decision. Sixthly, while doctrinal analysis of our systems is highly developed, our knowledge of how exactly they work in practice may be less complete and thorough. The absence or neglect of empirical data may be one cause; another may be the misuse of existing data by partisan groups. The first explanation is appropriate for the European scene, the second may be relevant in the United States.

All of the above must, of course, be read with the caveat that I am neither a statistician nor a knowledgeable practitioner but a law teacher trained first as a civil lawyer and then as a common lawyer. It is, therefore, primarily as a teacher that I have spoken tonight. Like Saint Paul I have come to believe that one should be prepared to look at everything and retain what is good wherever this may come from. As a civil lawyer I have to combat the ingrained instinct to become too abstract and too conceptual; as a common law lawyer I must guard against the danger of reducing everything to the level of analytical distinctions. Both approaches have their merits. In their different ways they can produce good doctrinal analysis and provide a good picture of a particular legal system. Nevertheless, though the picture it gives is good, it is not complete so long as it underplays or ignores the impact that the institutional, political and social backgrounds can have on the operation of the legal rules. These backgrounds have, on the whole, been ignored by traditional lawyers who have been slow to avail themselves of the kind of quantitative data and institutional facts that are necessary for the wider analysis. This data, which social scientists are good at selecting, has been excluded from the traditional law schools which seem to regard it as a threatening instead of an enriching source of ideas. This point has, I believe, been well made by, among others, Judge Richard Posner,[63] and it need not be further laboured here except in order to stress that in my opinion this wider approach is particularly valid in the context of comparative studies and comparative law. That is why I have tried to adopt it tonight in an attempt to repeat the *leitmotif* of much of my work, namely that common lawyers and civil lawyers though different are *not as different* as common mythology considers them to be. My belief thus is that many if not most English and American lawyers have a very foggy image of how each other's systems works in practice—an image often shaped by anecdotal evidence, media accounts or partisan literature. Despite my many caveats, I think my statistical analysis reveals a more balanced as well as a more complex situation. But I remain to the very end conscious of the dangers involved in the use of statistics; so let me end with a warning for those of you who may be showing signs of being convinced by my figures! The warning, in Lord Beveridge's words, reads as follows: "No one believes a theory except the one who formulates it; everyone believes a figure except the one who calculates it!"

[63] *The Federal Courts. Crisis and Reform* (1985), Ch. 11.

Index

mentality 173-4, 192 (handwritten)

Plays down Abigah

Sees G, Rh as very dated

poor index

translation: 20-1

much detail 173-4, 192

Gray 25